D0938727

Sexual Desire Disorders

Sexual Desire Disorders

Edited by
Sandra R. Leiblum, Ph.D.
and
Raymond C. Rosen, Ph.D.

Foreword by Harold I. Lief, M.D.

THE GUILFORD PRESS
New York   London

© 1988 The Guilford Press
A Division of Guilford Publications, Inc.
72 Spring Street, New York, NY 10012

All rights reserved

No part of this book may be reproduced, stored in a retrieval system, or transmitted, in any
form or by any means, electronic, mechanical, photocopying, microfilming, recording, or
otherwise, without written permission from the Publisher

Printed in the United States of America

Last digit is print number: 9 8 7 6 5 4 3 2 1

Library of Congress Cataloging in Publication Data

Sexual desire disorders.

    Includes bibliographies and index.
    1. Psychosexual disorders. 2. Desire.
I. Leiblum, Sandra Risa. II. Rosen, Raymond,
1946–   . [DNLM: 1. Psychosexual Disorders.
WM 611 S5125]
RC556.S476   1988   616.85'83   87-21192
ISBN 0-89862-714-1

Contributors

BERNARD APFELBAUM, PH.D., Director, Berkeley Sex Therapy Group and the BSTG Seminars, Berkeley, California

DAVID G. BULLARD, PH.D., Departments of Medicine and Psychiatry, University of California School of Medicine at San Francisco, San Francisco, California; Mental Research Institute, Palo Alto, California

ELI COLEMAN, PH.D., Associate Director, Program in Human Sexuality, and Department of Family Practice and Community Health, University of Minnesota Medical School, Minneapolis, Minnesota

JERRY M. FRIEDMAN, PH.D., Private Practice, Stony Brook, New York

D. CORYDON HAMMOND, PH.D., Department of Physical Medicine and Rehabilitation, and Codirector, Sex and Marital Therapy Clinic, University of Utah School of Medicine, Salt Lake City, Utah

JULIA R. HEIMAN, PH.D., Department of Psychiatry and Behavioral Sciences and Director, Interpersonal Psychotherapy Clinic and Reproductive and Sexual Medicine Clinic, University of Washington School of Medicine, Seattle, Washington

ARNOLD A. LAZARUS, PH.D., Graduate School of Applied and Professional Psychology, Rutgers University, New Brunswick, New Jersey

SANDRA R. LEIBLUM, PH.D., Department of Psychiatry and Codirector, Sexual Counseling Service, University of Medicine and Dentistry of New Jersey–Robert Wood Johnson Medical School, Piscataway, New Jersey

STEPHEN B. LEVINE, M.D., Department of Psychiatry, Case Western Reserve University School of Medicine, Cleveland, Ohio; Medical Director, Center for Human Sexuality, University Hospitals of Cleveland, Cleveland, Ohio

JOSEPH LoPICCOLO, PH.D., Department of Psychology, University of Missouri, Columbia, Missouri

WILLIAM H. MASTERS, M.D., Cochair, Board of Directors, Masters and Johnson Institute, St. Louis, Missouri

MARGARET NICHOLS, PH.D., Director, Institute for Personal Growth, Highland Park, New Jersey

REX REECE, PH.D., Private Practice, West Hollywood, California

RAYMOND C. ROSEN, PH.D., Department of Psychiatry and Codirector, Sexual Counseling Service, University of Medicine and Dentistry of New Jersey–Robert Wood Johnson Medical School, Piscataway, New Jersey

DAVID E. SCHARFF, M.D., Director, Washington School of Psychiatry, Washington, D.C.; Department of Family Practice, Uniformed Services University of the Health Sciences, Bethesda, Maryland; Georgetown University Medical School, Washington, D.C.

MARK F. SCHWARTZ, SC.D., Consultant, Masters and Johnson Institute, St. Louis, Missouri; Department of Psychiatry, Tulane University, New Orleans, Louisiana; Director, Clinics for Marital and Sex Therapy, New Orleans, Louisiana

R. TAYLOR SEGRAVES, M.D., PH.D., Associate Director, Department of Psychiatry, Cleveland Metropolitan General Hospital, Cleveland, Ohio; Department of Psychiatry, Case Western Reserve University Medical School, Cleveland, Ohio

JOHAN VERHULST, M.D., Department of Psychiatry and Behavioral Sciences, University of Washington School of Medicine, Seattle, Washington; Residency Training Director and Clinical Director of Psychiatric Services, University Hospital, Seattle, Washington

BERNIE ZILBERGELD, PH.D., Private Practice, Oakland, California

Foreword

I am pleased and honored to be asked to write the foreword to this state of the art collection of papers on disorders of sexual desire, pleased because this is a topic which I have been studying for many years, and honored presumably because I was the first person, at least in recent times, to suggest that inhibited sexual desire should be identified and labeled as a sexual dysfunction on a par with inhibitions of sexual excitement and orgasm (Lief, 1977). However, the major credit for describing the dysfunction itself, as well as for the ways in which it can be treated, must go to Helen Kaplan (1977, 1979, 1985), who credits me with calling this extraordinarily frequent clinical problem to the attention of our colleagues. Until now, she has had the major voice in the delineation of the causes and treatment of problems of sexual desire. The editors of this volume, however, rightly felt that it was necessary to broaden the scope of inquiry and so have brought together widely recognized experts in the field of sexology to discuss the many ramifications and dimensions of sexual desire.

Sexual desire is an extraordinarily complicated aspect of human life, and it requires a multifaceted approach to its understanding. Even its definition lacks precision. One cannot simply count sexual outlets, as Kinsey did. A person could conceivably masturbate 20 or more times a week, but lack desire to have sex with a partner, or a person could have sex 20 times a month with a partner, yet never once truly desire it. If the dysfunction cannot be based on counting the number of sexual encounters or orgasms and essentially requires subjective labeling, are we completely dependent on a person's self-report? If the answer is yes, how valid is it? People are not equally capable of recognizing sexual feelings or bodily sensations that are indicative of sexual appetite ("horniness"). Some people even seem to be capable of keeping sensations of orgasm from conscious awareness. Graduate students given the task of pressing a wrist counter every time they have a sexual thought, fantasy, or feeling may count over 300 a day, while other people report that they rarely, if ever, have a sexual thought or fantasy. One can see the enormous range in subjective identification of sexual desire.

Even the name of the dysfunction causes trouble. In DSM-III, it was labeled Inhibited Sexual Desire (for which Dr. Kaplan and I bear joint responsibility, along with Dr. Robert Spitzer). However, the Task Force recommending diagnostic categories for DSM-IIIR thought that the word *inhibited* suggested psychodynamic causality and did not fit the more acceptable phenomenological perspective. Hence *inhibited* was dropped in favor of the rather awkward term *hypoactive*.

The term *libido* is often used interchangeably with sexual desire, adding to the confusion. As used by Freud, libido means the love of pleasure. Because Freud developed an overarching theory of psychosexual development in which oral pleasure or *oral libido* (even *narcissistic libido*) became organized into a general theory of psychosexual development, libido took on an indiscriminate sexual meaning in which no distinction was drawn between pleasure in all its diverse forms and sex itself. This confusion continues to this day. (The word libido appears in this volume as a synonym for sexual desire.) At times, Freud used the term in a nonspecific fashion to mean love of pleasure; at other times, he used it more specifically in its sexual context. In an example of the latter usage, he states, "The execution of the sex act presupposes a very complicated sequence of events, any one of which may be the locus of disturbance. The principal loci of inhibition in men are the following: the turning aside of the libido at the initiation of the act (psychic unpleasure [unlust]); absence of physical preparedness (nonerectibility); abbreviation of the act (ejaculatio praecox), which may equally well be described as a positive symptom; suspension of the act before its natural culmination (absence of ejaculation); the nonoccurrence of the psychic effect (of the pleasure sensation of orgasm)" (Freud, 1926/1936, p. 12). The sequence of events he first described in 1926 involves the triphasic stages of sexual response, namely desire, excitement and orgasm, and predates Masters and Johnson and Kaplan by half a century. The quotation also indicates that neither Helen Kaplan nor I can justifiably claim to be the originators of the identification of sexual desire disorders, although I guess we deserve some recognition for bringing it to the attention of our colleagues.

Sandor Rado was another psychoanalyst who identified and studied this phase of sexual adaptation. He posits a sequence of events that clearly indicates the importance of an internal readiness for sexual arousal, which he labeled "the sexual motive state" (See Figure 1). Rado described the factors affecting this state as follows: "It is generally assumed that the direct impact of humoral factors upon the brain is the physiologic basis of sexual arousal. The problem is complicated by the fact that, in order to become effective, such internal stimulation must be psychologically 'received' and built up to a sexual motive state. Obviously, the strength of stimulation from within varies widely in different individuals, and in the same individual, from time to time; and so does the degree of attention paid by the individual to the arriving internal stimuli. He may foster his sexual desire almost to the exclusion of other pursuits. Or, by subduing this desire, he may save for other purposes the vital resources which would have been absorbed by this desire" (Rado, 1949, p. 165). Thus both Freud and Rado were well aware of a psychic state which had to be present in order to receive and respond to internal and external stimuli. Another way of saying this is that there has to be a cognitive script or blueprint ready to be put to use in order to experience sexual arousal. Rosen and Leiblum, the editors of this volume, discuss this at length in Chapter 7.

While perhaps all facets of human behavior deserve a biopsychosocial approach, this one most certainly does. One cannot examine sexual desire without being aware of its biological underpinnings. Almost forty years ago, long before the terms "neurotransmitter," "neuromodulator," or "neuromessenger" were coined, Rado talked about the "direct impact of humoral factors upon the brain as the physiologic basis of sexual arousal."

The two original neurotransmitters identified were acetylcholine and norepinephrine. Now approximately 100 chemical substances influencing central nervous system activity have been identified, but many of these seem to be grouped into neurotransmitter "systems" (Persky, 1987). The three of greatest interest to us are the dopamine, serotonin, and norepinephrine systems. In general, the dopamine agonists seem to facilitate sexual behavior, and the serotonin agonists to suppress sexual activity. Cloninger (1987), in attempting to develop a neurobiology of learning, describes three genetically independent dimensions of personality that are mediated by the three main neuromodulator systems in the brain. The first is "novelty-seeking" ("frequent exploratory activity and intense exhilaration in response to novel or appetitive stimuli", p. 413), which he links with the dopamine system ("leading to behavioral activation"), and thus with alcohol-seeking behavior. But since we know that dopamine facilitates sexual behavior as well, it is possible that the dopamine system is also

---

Submanifest excitation from internal stimulation establishes receptivity to psychologic stimulation.

Automatic mechanisms of arousal incite sensory and intellectual stimulation.

Sexual motive state mobilizes and organizes the resources of the organism toward attainment of orgastic pleasure.

Figure 1. The sexual motive state (desire). Adapted from S. Rado (1949). An adaptational view of sexual behavior. In *Psychosexual development in health and disease* (p. 164). New York: Grune and Stratton.

connected with sex-seeking behavior and hence with desire. Cloninger describes a second personality dimension as "harm avoidance" (p. 414), an intense response to aversive stimuli leading to an inhibition of behavior in order to avoid punishment, frustration or harm. This system seems to reduce anxiety and is dependent on the second major neuromodulator system, namely serotonin. Perhaps stimulation of the serotonin system is required not only to control drinking behavior, but also to control high-risk sexual behavior. We know that serotonin agonists depress sexual functioning. Cloninger's third dimension of personality, "reward dependence" (p. 414), is linked to maintenance behavior and is mediated by the third neuromodulator system, norepinephrine. Since this system is linked with activities of the locus ceruleus in the pons (a structure important in anxiety, panic reactions, and phobias) one can speculate that overactivity of this system may be involved with sexual phobias and aversion, and underactivity with sexual addictions.

The relationship of these systems to specific dimensions of personality is highly speculative; nonetheless, we are forced to recognize that there is nonreporting brain activity (outside awareness) which must play a role in the readiness to engage in sexual behavior. Steve Levine refers to this as a "motor" or "generator" that has to be running in order for a person to be able to respond to sexual stimuli (Chapter 2). It is not too farfetched to think of this nonreporting cerebral generator as being mediated by the dopamine system, for it certainly involves "novelty seeking" and "intense exhilaration" in response to the appetitive stimuli of sexual approach behavior. Indeed Frank Beach (1976) and John Money (1980) have called this *proception* ("the phase of invitation, of solicitation and seduction, and of attraction"). We know that dopamine agonists, such as certain antidepressants, alcohol itself, amphetamines, cocaine, and other opiates facilitate sexual-seeking behaviors.

When one thinks of the biology of sexual desire, one cannot omit consideration of testosterone, for it seems to be the hormone most responsible for sexual desire in both men and women (Persky, 1987). Its positive effect has been demonstrated with hypogonadal men and with postmenopausal and oophorectomized women (Sherwin, Gelfand, & Brender, 1985), and its use with premenopausal women with hypoactive sexual desire is currently being explored. The relationship between menopause and decreased sexual desire is puzzling. Why does a minority of women lose interest in sex following the menopause, even when none of the usual psychological reasons is present?

It is clear that the subject of sexual desire lends itself to neurological and endocrine reductionism, but it would be a serious error to examine the subject at this level alone. Just think of the psychological consequences of injecting testosterone, or giving any medication, for that matter, to a human being in the treatment of hypoactive desire. Placebo responses can occur for a variety of reasons, not restricted to a patient's suggestibility. The patient may think that he or she now has permission to engage in sex, or that he or she can avoid taking responsibility for a change in his or her sexual behavior ("It's not me, it's the drug that's causing the increase in sexual desire"). For example, if the patient has had a fear of submitting to a partner, he or she now might have a convenient reason for engaging in sexual behavior which no longer has the previous interpersonal implications. On the other hand, negative placebo responses to the drug also occur. The patient who has been avoiding sexual activity by a decrease in sexual desire may react with anxiety to an increased physiological response to sexual stimuli since his or her new bodily sensations may threaten a previous well-established equilibrium. Judging the effects of new medications like bupropion on the basis of desire risks failing to take these psychological contaminants into account.

As clinicians, we often think of psychological conflict when we think of intrapsychic phenomena which may influence sexual desire. A drive toward pleasure in conflict with guilty fear inhibits the seeking of pleasure or makes a modification of behavior necessary to avoid the feared consequences. The man who grows up with guilty feelings about sexual activity or with a misconception about sex in which there is a fear of hurting or being hurt in sexual activity (especially penetration) may develop an aesthetic aversion to the vagina. In this case anxiety has been succeeded by a protective disgust which hides the original emotion as well as its remote causes. It is easy to see how this aversion could lead to a gradual decrease in sexual desire. But what of other (ego) psychological factors, such as attention and memory? What of the people who seemingly cannot "take in" their sensory experiences? What of the women who regularly have an orgasm during sex and yet have no desire for it? Why is it that the memory of a pleasurable event in these people is so unstimulating that it fails to lead them to desire such pleasure again?

At a psychological level, where does depression fit? We know that depression characteristically reduces sexual desire. Is this primarily a consequence of the psychological parameters of depression, such as low self-esteem, guilt, helplessness, and hopelessness? Or does a reduction in sexual desire occur because one of the biological dimensions of depression, the workings of the neurotransmitter systems suggested above, might affect "nonreporting brain activity"? Or is lowered desire a nonspecific effect of the reduced energy level typical of the depressed state?

One cannot easily separate intrapsychic from interpersonal events, even if a person enters a relationship with a well-defined neurotic conflict, like the madonna-prostitute complex (Lief, 1985). Transference to the partner changes the relationship, and the response to and from the partner may modify the original neurotic conflict so that interpersonal behavior is changed. The schema one partner develops about the other not only influences perception through a process of selective attention and inattention, but also augments and perpetuates itself by modifying behavior. In his chapter David Scharff develops the whole notion of object relations as applied to couples by illustrating the ways this model can be used to understand the sometimes puzzling behavior of people enmeshed in their mutual transferences (Chapter 3). A connected way of looking at this is through the systems perspective developed by Verhulst and Heiman (Chapter 10). Their use of Elkaim's theoretical framework, in which a person's overt "official program" differs from the covert "map of the world," often finds its root in the "splitting" in the object relations model. Verhulst and Heiman demonstrate some of the psychological dimensions I am referring to when they describe three levels: sensation, affect, and cognition. These are dimensions, of course, also embedded in Lazarus's BASIC I.D. (Chapter 6).

Clinicians are pretty much in agreement that the major cause of hypoactive sexual desire is marital conflict. In addition to studying patients who come to sex therapists and sex clinics, we have the experience of screening patients for new medications used in treating hypoactive sexual desire. More than half the applicants for these research programs have to be eliminated because of apparent marital conflict. When marital conflict is the source of the problem, in most instances the patient continues to have fantasies of other partners: The decrease in sexual desire is situational, not global. There are exceptions since some people seem to "give up" interest in sex when they have lost the desire for their primary partner. Although anger is the most frequent emotion in these instances of marital disharmony, some complain of boredom. One must be careful to look for hidden anger in such cases, but in others the lovemaking has become too mechanical, too routine and unimaginative. Since novelty seems to be such an important aphrodisiac, it is an important consideration for the clinician in dealing with these cases. It is fascinating to me that habituation and novelty are associated with different central nervous system chemicals, and that novelty introduced into the life of a habituated animal produces chemical changes (Reiser, 1984).

The clinician is often faced with the problem of attempting to weight differentially the intrapsychic and the interpersonal, as has been suggested earlier. This has important ramifications because the choice of individual therapy versus marital therapy, or as a third alternative, some combination of the two, has practical significance.

In studying the history of these cases, one is struck by how often a marked decrease in sexual desire occurs after the birth of a child. This need not be the first child. Sometimes it doesn't occur until the third child has been born. Strenuous efforts to demonstrate the usual psychological causes of this decrease in desire (the burdens of parenting, the concentration on the offspring, the neglect of the spouse, the connection of procreation with sexuality, the fulfillment of the parental role regarding sex only as a means of having a child, new equilibrium in the family situation) sometimes draw a blank. One cannot find a satisfactory psychological explanation for this phenonemon. Are there indeed biological changes that occur of which we are completely unaware?

Another set of interesting questions has to do with the people who have a lifelong history of low sexual desire. Obviously some, or perhaps many, of these people have had traumatic events in their lives, such as rape, incest, unwanted pregnancies, etc., but this is not true of all. Sometimes one cannot find an adequate explanation based on faulty learning experiences or psychological conflict for the decreased interest in sex. Are there indeed unknown genetic or constitutional factors that leave some people at the low end of the spectrum of sexual desire? Is it a dimension similar to other dimensions in life, such as height, weight, intelligence, etc., or can we always find, with sufficient probing, reasons within the family of origin for this seeming lack of interest in sex? Many fascinating questions like these are taken up in this volume, but not all questions are answered. Much still remains to be done, but this volume does represent what is known about the subject at this time and, in itself, will serve as a stimulus for much additional research. While we are still in the dark about significant aspects of sexual desire, we have taken a major step forward in the last decade by labeling this an important area for basic and clinical research and treatment.

Harold I. Lief, M.D.
University of Pennsylvania School of Medicine

References

Beach, F. A. (1976). Sexual attractivity, proceptivity, and receptivity in female mammals. *Hormones and Behavior, 7,* 105–138.

Cloninger, C. R. (1987). Neurogenetic adaptive mechanisms in alcoholism. *Science, 236,* 410.

Freud, S. (1936). *The problem of anxiety.* New York: W. W. Norton. (Original work published 1926)

Kaplan, H. S. (1977). Hypoactive sexual desire. *Journal of Sex and Marital Therapy, 3,* 3–9.

Kaplan, H. S. (1979). *Disorders of sexual desire.* New York: Brunner/Mazel.

Kaplan, H. S. (Ed.) (1985). *Comprehensive evaluation of disorders of sexual desire.* Washington, DC: American Psychiatric Press.

Lief, H. I. (1977). Inhibited sexual desire. *Medical aspects of human sexuality, 7,* 94–95.

Lief, H. I. (1985). Evaluation of inhibited sexual desire: Relationship aspects. In H. S. Kaplan (Ed.), *Comprehensive evaluation of disorders of sexual desire* (pp. 59–76). Washington, DC: American Psychiatric Press.

Money, J. (1980). *Love and lovesickness: Science of sex, gender difference and pair bonding.* Baltimore: Johns Hopkins University Press.

Persky, H. (1987). *Psychoendocrinology of human sexual behavior.* New York: Praeger.

Rado, S. (1949). An adaptational view of sexual behavior. In *Psychosexual development in health and disease* (159–189). New York: Grune and Stratton.

Reiser, M. F. (1984). *Mind, brain, body.* New York: Basic Books.

Sherwin, B. B., Gelfand, M. M., & Brender, W. (1985). Androgen enhances sexual motivation in females: a prospective, crossover study of sex steroid administration in the surgical menopause. *Psychosomatic Medicine, 47,* 339–351.

Preface

The decision to edit a book dealing with current theories on the etiology and treatment of desire disorders was not made post-haste. Rather, although we both considered ourselves skilled and experienced clinicians, we frequently encountered uncertainty, frustration, and bewilderment in understanding and resolving cases involving problems of desire. We engaged in lengthy discussions—sometimes even heated ones—concerning the nature of desire. Is it a constitutional, biological given, doled out equitably to each of us at birth, or do individuals vary in the neuroendocrinological underpinnings of sexual motivation? Is it a fixed or variable entity across the life cycle? Do males and females differ in their experience of sexual desire? In their expression of sexual interest? Can one identify individuals who display hypersexuality, who are not psychologically impaired in other respects? In couples where one partner complains that he or she rarely experiences desire for a mate, is it possible to create passion? Are such couples better advised to settle for companionable, albeit infrequent, sexual relations, or to seek another relationship in which the "chemistry" is better, or the sexual appetites more comparable? These and other questions intrigued us.

Our interest in these issues led us to interview a group of sexually functional individuals about the waxing and waning of sexual interest across the life cycle. We would question each of our respondents about the first emergence of sexual interest in childhood or adolescence and about subsequent variations in sexual desire across the years for them. We inquired about when sexual interest was likely to peak, and when it was the least insistent. We asked about the factors that seemed to enhance it and those that seemed to discourage it. After lengthy discussions with several groups of individuals—married and single, young and old—we came away with a somewhat improved understanding of the enormous variation in the manifestation and expression of sexual desire, but unfortunately, without significantly greater understanding of how to intervene in cases involving desire difficulties.

In August 1986, we invited a panel of experts in the field to discuss their conceptualizations of sexual desire at the annual meeting of the International Academy of Sex Research in Seattle, Washington. Although the panel was successful in raising a number of key issues, it was clear that little consensus existed among these sexual authorities. Each presented a unique conceptualization of sexual desire, including quite different notions about how to assess and treat desire disorders. It was clear that no unanimity was to be found among the experts!

It was shortly after that meeting when we decided to edit a book embracing a variety of clinical perspectives on problems of sexual desire. It was relatively easy to generate a list of superb clinicians who had written about and treated large numbers of cases. We were gratified by their enthusiastic willingness to contribute chapters to our volume. Many of our authors expressed the same curiosity about, and bafflement by, the questions we had posed about desire and welcomed the opportunity to express their ideas in writing. This book is the product of that effort.

We are pleased with the finished product and believe it reflects the range and diversity of current viewpoints concerning the etiology and treatment of desire disorders. While it is clear that no final answer or consensus has emerged from these chapters, we believe that they represent an accurate reflection of the current thinking about sexual desire. Given the diversity and multiplicity of patients presenting with desire difficulties, it seems reasonable to incorporate a variety of different viewpoints concerning assessment and treatment.

In any such undertaking, a number of acknowledgments must be made. Helen Singer Kaplan and Harold Lief must be credited with their perspicacity in drawing our attention to the critical importance of desire in the sexual response cycle. At around the same time, they identified desire as pivotal for the initiation of sexual behavior and discussed the factors they believed to contribute to the experience of desire. Joe LoPiccolo and Bernie Apfelbaum were among the first clinicians to systematically address problems of low desire in their clinical work, and we are delighted with their contributions to the present volume. At a more theoretical level, we are indebted to the work of John Bancroft, Julian Davidson, John Gagnon, and Steve Levine for drawing our attention to the many facets of sexual desire in both clinical and non-clinical populations.

Finally, we must acknowledge those individuals who were significant in the production of this book. We thank our secretary, Agnes Bertelsen, who has been a devoted secretary and friend to both of us for many years, and who attended to the voluminous correspondence and innumerable manuscript drafts involved in the execution of this volume. We also wish to thank our editor, Maxine Berzok, and publisher, Seymour Weingarten, for their wise and helpful advice throughout the lengthy process of editing such a book. Most of all, we wish to thank our contributors for giving so much of themselves in these chapters. They were willing to consider the questions and dilemmas we posed about desire disorders, and to thoughtfully and honestly share their clinical experiences with us—and with you. They were willing to admit ignorance when cases turned out less successfully than they had hoped. Finally, they were willing to tolerate our lengthy and often obsessive editorial suggestions for rewriting their chapters! We are indeed grateful for their good humor and valued friendship.

Sandra R. Leiblum
Raymond C. Rosen
Piscataway, New Jersey
January, 1988

Contents

PART II. COGNITIVE AND BEHAVIORAL PERSPECTIVES

PART III. SYSTEMS AND INTERACTIONAL PERSPECTIVES

PART IV. BIOLOGICAL AND MEDICAL PERSPECTIVES

PART V. HOMOSEXUALITY AND SEXUAL DESIRE

Introduction: Changing Perspectives on Sexual Desire

SANDRA R. LEIBLUM AND RAYMOND C. ROSEN

Throughout history, sexual desire has rarely been viewed from a neutral or disinterested stance. Rather, attempts have been made—often from one generation to the next—either to stimulate or to stifle libido. Cultures, too, differ dramatically in the climate and customs surrounding sexual expressiveness. Commenting on the role of culture as not only reflecting but also determining attitudes towards sexual desire, Stone (1985) has aptly observed that "libido has always been subjected to conflicting influences of ascetic repression and erotic stimulation" (p. 26).

Perhaps the most striking example of the relativity of cultural influences on sexual interest may be seen in the evolving "love–hate" attitude toward sexuality in Western culture over the past two decades. The start of the 1970s witnessed a burgeoning of enthusiasm for all things sexual—from "masturbation training groups" to sexual attitude reassessment (SAR) seminars, from "sex shoppes" and California hot tubs to "swinging clubs", from "open marriage" to the flourishing of casual and anonymous sex. Clearly, the societal message was "Sex is good for you, and the more the better!" Sexual enthusiasts were championed by the media, and those individuals for whom sex was a source of neither great interest nor great pleasure felt alienated and abandoned in this new sexual climate.

It is, therefore, not surprising that complaints involving insufficient sexual desire (but rarely the reverse!) first became recognized as a discrete clinical entity in the mid-1970s. Specifically, Lief (1977) recommended that the diagnosis of "inhibited sexual desire" (ISD) be applied to those patients who chronically failed to initiate or respond to sexual stimuli. Furthermore, Lief suggested that ISD had become the most common presenting complaint among patients in sex therapy clinics at that time. Writing in the same year,

Kaplan (1977) criticized the conventional Masters and Johnson approach to sex therapy for failing to address problems of desire. Kaplan further recommended the introduction of a triphasic model of sexual arousal, positing desire as the first and most fundamental component of the sexual response cycle. With little ado, problems of inhibited desire became universally recognized as worthy of discrete diagnosis and treatment.

In contrast, as we approach the end of the 1980s, uninhibited expressions of sexuality are increasingly viewed with suspicion, concern, and even hostility. Since the recent epidemic increase in sexually transmitted diseases (e.g., chlamydia, herpes, and of course acquired immune deficiency syndrome [AIDS]), continuing escalation in the frequency of unplanned pregnancies, the growing prevalence of sexual abuse and victimization among both children and adults, and the increasing uneasiness about the effects of violent pornography, it is not surprising that we are experiencing a dramatic retreat from sexual permissiveness and the pursuit of pleasure. As the present decade draws to a close, the topics of hypersexuality and sexual addiction are becoming important foci of attention. It is ironic, indeed, that following a decade in which the philosophy of "more is better" was enthusiastically embraced, we should now be questioning today whether "more" is not "too much."

Given the ever-changing attitudes toward sexual expression from one historical time or place to another, our views about what constitute "normal" levels of sexual desire are in a constant state of flux. Clearly, what is deemed acceptable and appropriate levels of sexual interest today may not have been similarly viewed in the recent past or may not be so viewed in the foreseeable future. With this perspective in mind, one of the recurrent themes of the present volume is the lack of consensus regarding definitions of "normal" or deficient sexual desire, and, conversely, the difficulty in diagnosing disorders of desire.

What Is Sexual Desire?

For most people, the concept of sexual desire conjures up visions of an energizing force that motivates the individual to seek out or initiate genital sexual relief. Like hunger or thirst, the so-called "sexual drive" is thought to be an instinctive, spontaneous, and insistent source of motivation. Linked to this idea is the popular notion that if the sexual drive is not permitted free expression, it will seek an outlet through other means. This, in essence, is the "drive reduction" model of sexual desire, which reached its acme with Freud's (1905/1962) libido theory. This view asserts that the primary goal of sexual expression is to relieve libidinal tension and to restore emotional equilibrium. It suggests that sexual desire is endogenous and inevitable. From a Freudian perspective, a lack of desire results from the active repression or inhibition of the spontaneous urge for sexual contact as a result of intrapsychic conflict.

Several important assumptions of this model may be identified. First is the idea that sexual drive is an innately determined, biologically mediated entity. In recent years, particular attention has been paid to the likely role of brain mechanisms and endocrine factors as the neural and chemical catalysts of libido. As Kaplan (1983) suggests,

> Sexual desire depends on the activation of a specific system of circuits and nuclei in the brain. Lust is experienced when the "sex circuits" are activated. . . . Although all levels of the central nervous system are involved, the main regulatory mechanism is believed to be located in the most ancient part of the brain. . . . Adequate levels of testosterone and a proper balance of the neurotransmitters serotonin and dopamine and the catecholamines are necessary for the normal functioning of the brain sex circuits, both in males and females. (p. 242)

At present, there is considerable controversy regarding both the existence and relative importance of the biological basis of libido. The androgens, in particular, testosterone, are widely credited in both the professional and popular press as being the "libido" hormone and, in fact, there are some studies supporting this assertion. For example, in a recent large-scale study of both men and women with problems of global low desire, Schiavi and Schreiner-Engel (1988) found that ISD men had significantly lower levels of testosterone (measured over a 10-hour nocturnal period) than the matched controls (although there were no significant hormonal differences between ISD women and controls).

Furthermore, in cases of marked androgen deficiency, such as the hypogonadal syndrome, administration of exogenous hormones is undoubtedly the treatment of choice. Studies by Davidson, Camargo, and Smith (1979) and by Bancroft and Wu (1983) have clearly demonstrated a restoration of normal levels of libido and sexual functioning (e.g., erections and ejaculation) in hypogonadal men receiving androgen replacement therapy.

For men who have normal to high baseline levels of testosterone, there seems to be a complex and variable association between androgens and sexual desire/activity. For instance, while some studies have suggested a positive, albeit modest, relationship between serum testosterone levels and sexual frequency or interest, there is a major difficulty in determining the direction of causality: For example, does a high frequency of sexual behavior result in elevated testosterone levels, or vice versa? It is also conceivable that some third factor, such as mood state, may mediate both sexual interest and testosterone levels. For example, Knussmann, Christiansen & Couwenbergs (1986), in a study involving young male subjects, reported a significant positive correlation between serum testosterone and the frequency of orgasm. Also noted, however, was a positive correlation between the amount of preceding sexual stimulation and subsequent levels of serum testosterone.

Regarding hormonal influences on desire in women, several authors have emphasized the difficulties in establishing hormone–behavior relationships. The baseline levels of circulating androgen are substantially lower in women than in men, and are subject to wider fluctuations because of the menstrual cycle, pregnancy and lactation, menopause, and other life cycle changes. Nevertheless, two independent studies have reported evidence suggesting an association between frequency of intercourse and women's midcycle levels of testosterone Morris, Udry, Khan-Dawood, & Dawood, 1987; (Persky, Lief, Strauss, Miller, & O'Brien, 1978). Morris *et al.* found that the midcycle values of both total testosterone and free testosterone—but not the baseline or average testosterone levels—predicted average frequency of intercourse in a sample of young married women. These authors admit that "no theoretical mechanism is self-evident to explain these results." Certainly, the manner in which androgen may exert its effect is uncertain, although Davidson, Kwan, and Greenleaf (1982) have hypothesized that androgen may act to "facilitate sensitivity to or pleasurable awareness of both sexual thoughts and activity."

Additional evidence for an association between testosterone and sexual motivation in women comes from the work of Sherwin and Gelfand (1987) and Sherwin, Gelfand, & Brender (1985) on surgically menopausal women. Specifically, these authors reported enhanced arousal, desire, and fantasy in women receiving androgen replacement, either alone or in combination with estrogen. In evaluating these findings, however, it has been pointed out that libido-enhancing effects may only be obtained with administration of relatively high doses of testosterone (Davidson & Myers, in press).

It is clear that, at present, the validity of a biologically based model of sexual drive is equivocal. On the positive side, such a model is helpful in understanding those patients who present with a chronic, lifelong lack of sexual interest. Often we are unable to identify evidence of psychic inhibition of libido in such individuals, but rather seem to be dealing with a permanent state of "asexuality." Sexual stirrings or urges seem *not to occur,* instead of being blocked or repressed. Those who subscribe to the biological drive model might regard such individuals as constitutionally hyposexual. In addition, there are certain cases, as indicated earlier, in which hormonal deficiencies are clearly linked to a lack of sexual interest, such as hypogonadism, and hormone replacement therapy quickly and effectively restores libido (see Segraves, Chapter 11, this volume).

On the other hand, several contributors to this book (e.g., Apfelbaum, Chapter 4; Zilbergeld and Hammond, Chapter 8; Nichols, Chapter 14) downplay the clinical importance of constitutional/biological factors to sexual interest on either empirical or theoretical grounds. Other authors, such as Levine (1984), have proposed a multidimensional model of sexual desire, in which biological drive is viewed as one of three core components, the other two being psychological motivation and cognitive aspiration (see Chapter 2). Similarly, the chapters by Lazarus (Chapter 6), LoPiccolo and Friedman (Chapter 5), and Schwartz and Masters (Chapter 9) all acknowledge the contributions of biological and psychological factors in shaping sexual desire.

Despite the inherent difficulties in definition, we would like to offer our own conceptualization of "sexual desire." We view desire as a *subjective feeling state* that may be triggered by both internal and external cues, and that may or may not result in overt sexual behavior. Adequate baseline levels of neuroendocrine functioning are clearly essential for this feeling state to occur, as well as exposure to sufficiently intense sexual cues, arising from sources either within the individual (e.g., fantasy, genital vasocongestion) or from the environment (e.g., a candlelight dinner with an interested partner). Given the obvious link between sexual interest and reproductive survival, we do not discount the possible genetic underpinnings of sexual motivation. Nevertheless, the heretofore invariant association between procreation and sexual activity is less inevitable today, with the widespread use of contraceptives and the present mushrooming of reproductive technologies that permit conception without intercourse.

In the presence of intact neuroendocrine functioning and adequate opportunities for expression, we view sexual desire as primarily determined by sexually salient intrapsychic and interpersonal processes. From this vantage point, sexual desire is as much a consequence as a cause of sexual interaction. Furthermore, sexual desire needs to be acknowledged as readily conditioned or "scripted" to socially sanctioned as well as socially proscribed cues. An extreme example of this is the fetishistic patient who is repetitively driven to seek out unusual objects or situations for sexual gratification. The notion of sexual desire as contextually determined is elaborated further in Chapter 10 by Verhulst and Heiman and in Chapter 7 by us.

Can Sexual Desire Be Measured?

Past efforts to quantify desire have focused on frequency measures of sexual behavior, such as intercourse frequency, incidence of sexual thoughts or fantasies, and number of sexual contacts leading to orgasm. For example, Kinsey and his colleagues (Kinsey, Pomeroy, & Martin, 1948; Kinsey, Pomeroy, Martin, & Gebhard, 1953) used the total number of orgasmic outlets as the primary index of sexual drive, based upon the assumption that sexual activity levels reflect desire. Kinsey's group also proposed that the frequency of orgasmic outlets in *masturbation* was a particularly sensitive measure of sexual interest in women, given that heterosexual contacts were more likely to be influenced by male initiation. More recently, this approach continues to predominate in self-report measures of sexual behavior, such as the Derogatis Sexual Functioning Inventory (Derogatis & Melisaratos, 1979). In this particular instrument, an index of sexual desire is derived from the summation of all sexual behaviors, including intercourse, petting, masturbation, and fantasy.

The limitations of this approach are several. First, one may engage in sexual behavior for a variety of motives, which may or may not include the subjective experience of desire. For instance, an individual may initiate or accept sexual overtures from a myriad of motives (e.g., guilt, obligation, financial recompense, need to please, etc.) without intrinsic sexual motivation. Conversely, one may experience high libidinal levels, as manifested by such nonobservable phenomena as sexual urges, fantasies, thoughts, and feelings, yet may not initiate or engage in overt sexual activity because of a lack of opportunity, a fear of negative consequences or sexually transmitted disease, or a history of sexual dysfunction.

In addition, an "outlet" measure of desire may not reflect degree of either the intensity or urgency with which one experiences sexual desire. This is particularly striking in cases of sexual compulsivity. For example, exhibitionists often report an irrepressible urge to expose themselves, which may vary in frequency, but which is so intense as to be impossible to ignore. On the other hand, the high-desire spouse in a happily married couple may have frequent urges for sexual contact, but may find it easy to delay or postpone sexual encounters because of the relative lack of intensity of these feelings. An outlet measure in either instance would fail to reflect adequately the relative intensity or urgency of the sexual drive.

Presently, researchers tend to use both objective and subjective criteria in determining sexual desire. For example, Schreiner-Engel and Schiavi (1986) defines sexual desire in terms of both (1) the frequency of all sexual activities engaged in and (2) the individual's subjective interest in participating in each activity. From this perspective, the absence of *either* internal motivation or overt behavior constitutes a desire disorder. Garde and Lunde (1980) differentiate between *spontaneous* desire for sexual activity from desire elicited via some form of external sexual stimulation (e.g., partner caresses).

At times, we have also included the patient's self-rating of "ideal" versus current sexual frequency on a variety of sexual behaviors, including masturbation and intercourse, as an additional measure of sexual desire (Leiblum, Bachman, Kemmann, Colburn, & Swartzman, 1983). This is particularly relevant in assessing levels of desire in special populations, such as widowed or elderly women or disabled men, where access to functional partners is often limited.

In the absence of norms for various populations and age groups, it is difficult to specify with any reliability criteria for libidinal deficiency or excess. Furthermore, in cases of situational desire disorders or desire discrepancy problems, genuine problems exist in deciding who or whether to diagnose. These issues are frequently alluded to in the chapters that follow, and are readdressed in our concluding chapter.

Diagnostic Issues

The rapid evolution in diagnostic practices with regard to desire disorders is strikingly illustrated by the changing nomenclature of sexual disorders used in the *Diagnostic and Statistical Manual of Mental Disorders* (DSM) of the American Psychiatric Association over the last 20 years. In the second edition (DSM-II; American Psychiatric Association, 1968), all psychosexual dysfunctions were lumped together into one category, termed "Psychophysiologic Genito-Urinary Disorder." No mention whatever of desire disorders was included in this diagnostic category, and the only examples given of psychosexual dysfunctions were dyspareunia and impotence. Furthermore, Masters and Johnson (1970) failed to include desire as a component of the sexual response cycle, and did not identify desire disorders as having diagnostic significance.

In fact, it was not until 1977, when Lief and Kaplan independently identified desire disorders as among the most pervasive and intractable of sexual difficulties, that sex therapists began to direct attention toward problems of this type. Kaplan (1977) reconceptualized the sexual response cycle as consisting of three major phases (desire, excitement, and orgasm), while Lief divided the cycle into a total of five phases (desire, arousal, vasocongestion, orgasm, and resolution). Both Lief and Kaplan independently recognized the previous neglect of a fundamental aspect of sexual functioning—the motivation and inclination to be sexual. Reflecting this new emphasis, the third edition of the DSM (DSM-III; American Psychiatric Association, 1980) included desire problems as an independent entity, entitled "Inhibited Sexual Desire," which is defined as "Persistent and pervasive inhibition of sexual desire" (p. 278). It is notable that no specific behavioral referents were included in the definition.

DSM-IIIR (American Psychiatric Association, 1987) has elaborated this classification approach even further by dividing desire disorders into two categories: Hypoactive Sexual Desire Disorder (302.71) and Sexual Aversion Disorder (302.79). Specifically, Hypoactive Sexual Desire Disorder is defined as follows: "Persistently or recurrently deficient or absent sexual fantasies and desire for sexual activity. The judgment of deficiency or absence is made by the clinician, taking into account factors that affect sexual functioning, such as age, sex, and the context of the person's life"

(p. 293). The criteria thus include reference to both objective and subjective dimensions of sexual motivation. Sexual Aversion Disorder, by contrast, is defined dependently in the following manner: "Persistent or recurrent extreme aversion to, and avoidance of, all or almost all, genital sexual contact with a sexual partner" (p. 293).

Several aspects of these definitions should be highlighted. First, the diagnosis of Sexual Aversion Disorder implies a highly negative response to interpersonal and genital sexual contact, as distinct from solitary sexual behaviors, such as fantasy or masturbation. Second, although not explicitly noted in the definition of Sexual Aversion Disorder, this diagnosis tends to be applied with greater frequency to women than men. Finally, where individuals displaying hypoactive desire are often neutral or indifferent toward sexual engagement, sexual aversion implies disgust, anxiety, or even panic responses to genital contact. While none of our authors in the present volume specifically discusses sexual aversion, it is clear that the treatment implications for these two disorders are quite different. With sexual aversion, treatment would be directed toward the elimination of the specific phobic or aversive response pattern, typically through behavioral interventions or tricylic drugs (Kaplan, 1979; Kaplan & Kline, 1987). With ISD, on the other hand, therapeutic interventions are more diverse and varied, as becomes apparent from the array of clinical approaches illustrated in this book.

An important diagnostic issue not addressed by the current classification system is the frequent clinical complaint of a *desire discrepancy* between partners. Here, neither individual is clearly excessive or deficient in sexual interest, but there is sufficient discrepancy to cause significant marital or sexual conflict. Most frequently, it is the partner with less sexual interest who is identified as having "the problem," with treatment interventions all too often devoted to activating and instilling "libido" in this individual. Rarely is the higher-desire partner acknowledged as being overly interested in sex, despite the glaring lack of interest of his or her partner. This important issue is discussed at some length in Chapter 4 by Apfelbaum.

The fact remains that the diagnosis of low desire or ISD is highly controversial. Although most contributors to the present volume regard desire disorders as a legitimate clinical diagnosis, there is no consensus regarding operational criteria for patient classification. This state of affairs has generated two predominant reactions among sexologists. One position, which is articulated by LoPiccolo and Friedman (Chapter 5), states that despite the need for better definition, practitioners can readily assess and treat such cases when they present clinically. This viewpoint can be paraphrased as "You know it when you see it."

In contrast, Clearing-Sky and Thornton (1987) have recently reviewed diagnostic dilemmas in this area and have come to this conclusion:

> Non-organic ISD may not be a disorder but a symptom or solution to an interactional problem in the relationship. In attempting to sort through the myriad causes and manifestations of ISD suggested by various writers, it appears ISD may be the schizophrenia of sex therapy. It may be a popular "catch all" diagnosis with blurred boundaries and symptoms distributed on a normal curve in the "normal" population. (p. 31)

These authors summarize their position by suggesting that ISD may be best viewed as a symptom requiring further assessment, rather than as a separate disorder. Just as high fever may be a signal that something is awry in the body, but does not constitute a discrete diagnosis in itself, Clearing-Sky and Thornton (1987) suggest that low desire should be viewed as a warning signal. There is much to be said for this argument. Specifically, there is a real danger of pathologizing normal variations in sexual interest and of unnecessarily stigmatizing the individuals so labeled.

Finally, the topic of excessive sexual desire, otherwise referred to as "hyperactive desire," "sexual compulsion," or "sexual addiction," has received considerable attention in the past few years (Carnes, 1983; Quadland, 1985). Despite its popular appeal, we have not encountered clinically more than a handful of such cases in the past decade, and then primarily with our paraphilic patients. There are, however, numerous individuals who are on the high end of the desire continuum—who are sexually enthusiastic with little provocation, who never seem to become satiated, and who engage in high frequencies of both self- and partner stimulation. These individuals tend to be admired or envied rather than diagnosed! It is noteworthy that none of our contributors presents a case in which the high-desire individual is the focus of treatment. In Chapter 4, Apfelbaum does raise the question as to why the higher-drive person continues to "demand sex" from an uninterested partner. Nevertheless, at the present time, libidinal excess is regarded considerably more favorably than lack of libidinal interest.

Desire Disorders in Clinical Practice

Regardless of the difficulties in diagnosing desire disorders in the general population, it is apparent that complaints involving lack of desire are increasingly prevalent in sex therapy practice. In addition to coining the term "ISD," Lief (1977) was among the first to note the high frequency of desire complaints as either a primary or a secondary diagnosis in sexual dysfunction. For instance, in two field trials conducted at the Marriage Council of Philadelphia in the late 1970s, ISD was diagnosed in 20% of male patients and 37% of females in one trial and in 14% of male patients and 31% of women in the second (Lief, 1985).

Even higher prevalence rates were reported by L. LoPiccolo (1980) in an informal review of 37 cases treated at the Stony Brook Sex Therapy Center. Of this sample, 63% of the men and 37% of the women identified low sexual desire as a couple problem. In a subsequent outcome study at Stony Brook involving a larger sample (152 couples), Schover and J. LoPiccolo (1982) reported that 38% of the husbands and 49% of the wives were given a diagnosis of low desire. In addition, 18% of the desire disorders in women involved problems of sexual aversion. The most recent prevalence figures from J. LoPiccolo's research are even higher, as discussed in Chapter 5. Clearly, these incidence figures support Lief's contention that problems of desire have become highly prevalent—at least on the East Coast of the United States!

Findings from our own sex therapy service (Rosen, Leiblum, and Hall, 1987) indicate that about twice as many women as men present with desire complaints, although many men with the primary diagnosis of erectile dysfunction also evidence desire problems. Furthermore, male ISD patients tend to be older, to report more marital difficulties, and to require a greater number of treatment sessions than women with this diagnosis.

In a study of a British sex therapy population, Hawton, Catalan, Martin, and Fagg (1986b) have recently reported a similar incidence of desire problems (37%) among female patients, but a markedly lower rate (1%) among male patients. This finding can be interpreted as indicating that British men are generally less susceptible to problems of desire, or, more likely, that they are less inclined to admit to such difficulties. It is noteworthy that in a large sample of 262 German couples seen for sex therapy, desire disorders were not presented as a distinct diagnostic group, although about one-third of the women in the sample "suffered from general sexual unresponsiveness" (Arentewicz & Schmidt, 1983, p. 94). In contrast, none of the male patients were given this diagnosis.

Finally, in a recent survey of 289 sex therapists, Kilmann, Boland, Norton, Davidson, and Caid (1986) reported that desire discrepancy between partners was the most common presenting complaint (31%) seen in treatment, followed by individual desire problems (28%). Although these incidence figures are not dissimilar to those reported by Lief (1985) or those in our own survey, the failure to report separate prevalence rates for men and women limits the usefulness of the findings.

In general, it seems that the incidence of complaints indicates that individuals feel they have gained the right to voice their frustrations and unhappiness concerning their mates' sexual apathy. Alternatively, it may be that in the process of applying a diagnostic label to the problem, we have inadvertently created new sexual performance standards. Currently, individuals in our culture have come to expect not only technical competence in bed, but sexual enthusiasm and lusty appetite as well. Stated boldly, the controversy is between those who believe that sex therapy has advanced to the point of recognizing and treating the most fundamental of sexual problems, to those who maintain that current diagnostic practices are responsible for creating or maintaining a major iatrogenic disorder.

Gender Differences in Desire

According to common sexual mythology, men are sexually ever-ready and ever-able (Zilbergeld, 1978), whereas women need to be stroked, stimulated, and ignited into action (Tevlin & Leiblum, 1983). The implication behind these beliefs is that men are under the influence of a highly charged and constant libido, which may be activated with little or no external stimulation, while women are basically asexual or neutral with respect to spontaneous libido. Age-old ploys to overcome the presumed sexual apathy of the "fairer sex" have been to seduce women into receptivity via drugs, alcohol, or "sweet talk," as Ogden Nash advised in his well-known humorous verse: "Candy is dandy, but liquor is quicker." In contrast, little attention is usually directed at the need for stimulating sexual appetite in men.

The issue of gender differences in desire has created a lively dialogue among past and present sex researchers. While the overall trend in the last two decades has been to minimize male–female differences in all aspects of sexual response, earlier authors tended to view desire as fundamentally dissimilar to men and women. Kinsey *et al.* (1953), for instance, asserted that females experience sexual interest on an essentially intermittent, "discontinuous" basis:

> Between periods of activity there may be weeks or months and sometimes years in which there is no activity of any sort. This is true of masturbation in the female, of nocturnal dreams to the point of orgasm, of pre-marital petting, of pre-marital coitus, of extra-marital coitus, and of homosexual experience.
> . . . Some females who at times have high rates of outlet, or none at all. But then after a period of inactivity the high rates of outlet may go for week's or months or even years with very little outlet, may develop again. Discontinuities in total outlet are practically unknown in the histories of males. (1953, pp. 681–682)

Kinsey and colleagues believed that males experience an incessant and invariant sexual appetite, possibly due to constitutional factors, whereas for women, libido fluctuates widely, and waxes and wanes according to a host of biological and psychosocial circumstances. Although little systematic attention has been paid to the notion of constant versus variable desire levels in men and women, we have accumulated case history support for this distinction. In a series of in-depth sexual histories collected from a nonclinical population, we have been impressed by how easily some women seem to adapt to the absence of sexual opportunity and lengthy periods of involuntary abstinence. As one female respondent commented, "When I don't have a partner I don't think about sex. And to tell you the truth, I don't miss it that much. As soon as I'm in a new relationship, though, and sexually active again, I think about it all the time!"

Some sociological data support the notion of women's sexual drive as being less insistent than males. For example, a recent large-scale study of 40-year-old Danish women revealed that about one-third of the respondents never experienced "spontaneous libido" (Garde & Lunde, 1980). Furthermore, 42% reported themselves to have little motivation for intercourse, even though they were likely to be receptive if approached by their partners. It should be emphasized that these data were obtained from a nonclinical population, none of whom were specifically seeking sexual therapy and none of whom perceived this state of affairs to be problematic.

Along these lines, it is noteworthy that sexual interest levels tend to be lower in lesbian couples than in all other forms of pair-bonded relationships (e.g., heterosexual couples, gay males). For example, Blumstein and Schwartz (1983) found that 47% of lesbian couples in their sample had genital sexual contact less than once monthly. As discussed by Nichols in Chapter 14, lesbian sexual relationships can perhaps be viewed as epitomizing the purest expression of intrinsic female sexual interest and preference, apart from the demands of male expectations and initiatives.

Even though women may experience a less insistent and constant sexual appetite than men overall, several studies suggest that heterosexual women do view the the absence of sexual interest in a relationship as an issue. For example, Frank, Anderson, and Rubinstein (1978), in a survey of 100 nonclinical American couples, found that 35% of the women reported problems of lack of sexual interest. By contrast, only 16% of the men in this study had similar complaints. Similarly, Osborn, Hawton, and Gath (1987) found in their study of a random community sample of 436 British women aged 35–59 that 17% were identified as having impaired sexual interest. Among British men, however, self-reported lack of sexual interest tends to be very low, and neither men nor their partners tend to seek sex therapy for desire problems (Hawton, Catalan, Martin, & Fagg, 1986a).

In some countries, desire problems are reported infrequently by both women and men. For example, findings from a Dutch study of 250 married or cohabiting couples (Frenken, & van Tol, 1985) indicated that only 2% of the men and 6% of the women complained of experiencing problems with sexual desire. When this study was replicated 8 years later with a larger sample of 548 Dutch respondents (Vennix, 1985), similar results were obtained.

Despite marked inconsistencies in the research findings to date, our own observations suggest that there are some important differences in the *experience* of sexual desire between men and women. Overall, it does appear that men have a more insistent and constant sexual appetite, which is readily accessed through a large variety of internal and environmental prompts. Women, on the other hand, have less intense and more sporadic sexual desires, which they are more likely either to suppress or to ignore if a host of conditions are not met. The pathway between desire and execution seems to be longer—with more byways, detours, and obstacles—for women than for men!

In accounting for these apparent behavioral differences, a number of factors need to be considered. First, women are socialized into a gender role which actively discourages sexual curiosity and exploration. Instead, women are all-too-well aware of the negative consequences of unrestrained sexual expression. Additionally, many women are not attuned to the physiological concomitants of arousal, such as vaginal lubrication (Tevlin & Leiblum, 1983). Thus, they may fail to recognize a salient cue for "w(h)etting" their own sexual appetite. Furthermore, female sexual initiation remains problematic, despite the current rhetoric of sexual equality. Many women are unlikely to initiate or seek sexual encounters even when they are keenly cognizant of sexual stirrings. From this viewpoint, socialization and sexual script factors, rather than constitutional or biological variables, may account for the apparent difference in sexual interest levels between men and women.

Another possible source of male–female differences in desire is the possible mediating role of sexual fantasy in sexual desire. According to Kinsey *et al.* (1953), women are far less responsive to all forms of "psychosexual stimulation," including fantasy, imagery, and all forms of visual erotica. More recent studies have shown that women are capable of responding with sexual arousal to visual stimuli (e.g., Heiman, 1977; Schmidt & Sigusch, 1970), and in fact are quite similar to men in genital hemodynamic and groin temperature measures of arousal to erotic films (Rubinsky, Eckerman, Rubinsky, & Hoover, 1987). Nevertheless, it appears probable that most women are less likely to conjure up or focus on erotic imagery between sexual encounters. To the extent that sexual desire is fueled or maintained by ready access to sexual fantasy and ideation, women appear to be less sexually alert or desirous. Along similar lines, it is interesting to note that when antiandrogenic therapy is used in the treatment of paraphilic or sexually compulsive behavior in men (Berlin & Meinecke, 1981), sexual ideation declines rapidly, and with it the urge to engage in deviant behavior.

On the other hand, both anatomical and hormonal factors, as well as neurophysiological and constitutional differences, may influence male–female differences in desire. To the extent that erections function as a clearly visible and impelling stimulus, men are "prompted" to think and feel sexually more frequently than women. Female sexual anatomy discourages visual feedback and ready evidence of sexual arousal, and hence may contribute to somewhat reduced levels of sexual awareness.

Treatment Approaches to Desire Disorders

Kaplan (1977) was among the first to note that desire difficulties are often refractory to conventional sex therapy approaches. Performance anxiety did not appear to be the prime etiological factor in most cases of ISD, so that treating desire problems by reducing performance anxiety (e.g., sensate focus) was often found to be ineffective. According to Kaplan (1977), disorders of desire are an indication of deeper levels of sexual conflict or anxiety and require a more intensive, psychodynamic treatment approach. J. LoPiccolo and his colleagues subsequently observed a high relapse rate following treatment for sexual dysfunction, and attributed the poor outcome to undiagnosed and untreated desire problems. In contrast to Kaplan, however, LoPiccolo has reported successful outcome for desire problems using a directive, broad-spectrum approach (see Chapter 5).

Over the past decade, sex therapists have increasingly acknowledged the diversity of etiological factors responsible for desire difficulties. Consequently, current treatment approaches are quite varied, ranging from long-term, individual psychotherapy to short-term, problem-focused couples therapy. While some therapists have explored the efficacy of exogenous hormone administration to stimulate sexual appetite, others eschew any form of biological intervention. While some therapists continue to recommend structured sex therapy assignments, others have found that such exercises have little value, and may in fact exacerbate the very problem that they are designed to overcome. Some therapists favor the adoption of a broad array of eclectic interventions, including hypnosis, transactional analysis, and Gestalt therapy techniques.

In part because of theoretical inclination and in part because of therapeutic frustration, desire problems are currently managed by means of a wide variety of clinical approaches. Having evaluated and treated hundreds of these cases in our own sex therapy clinic, we are struck with the importance of approaching desire problems with a versatile and diverse treatment armamentarium. In fact, this awareness sparked our initial interest in editing this book. We felt that a forum in which outstanding clinicians could elaborate their conceptual and clinical approaches to desire disorders would realize a significant clinical need. Contributors were selected to represent each of the major theoretical orientations (i.e., psychodynamic, systems, or broad-spectrum behavioral) or to illustrate their unique expertise with particular populations or treatment modalities.

We felt that the breadth and heterogeneity of treatment interventions currently available would be best represented by requesting authors to present their theoretical conceptualization regarding desire problems, as well as to illustrate treatment approaches with extensive case examples of both successful and unsuccessful treatments. Authors were invited to comment on factors contributing to favorable or unfavorable treatment outcomes. The case presentations and subsequent discussions constitute the clinical "heart" of this book. Not only do they illustrate the translation of theory into clinical practice, but they highlight the heterogeneity of individuals and couples complaining of desire disorders. We believe that the following chapters serve to reflect both the broad compendium of treatment approaches and the diversity of individuals currently grappling with this prevalent and challenging "20th-century problem."

References

American Psychiatric Association. (1968). *Diagnostic and statistical manual of mental disorders*. (2nd ed.) Washington, D.C.: Author.

American Psychiatric Association. (1980). *Diagnostic and statistical manual of mental disorders*. (3rd ed.) Washington, D.C.: Author.

American Psychiatric Association. (1987). *Diagnostic and statistical manual of mental disorders*. (3rd ed., rev.) Washington, D.C.: Author.

Arentewicz, G., & Schmidt, G. (Eds.). (1983). *The treatment of sexual disorders: Concepts and techniques of couple therapy*. New York: Basic Books.

Bancroft, J., & Wu, F. (1983). Changes in erectile responsiveness during androgen replacement therapy. *Archives of Sexual Behavior, 12,* 59–66.

Berlin, F. S., & Meinecke, C. F. (1981). Treatment of sex offenders with anti-androgenic medication: Conceptualization, review of treatment modalities, and preliminary findings. *American Journal of Psychiatry, 138,* 601–607.

Blumstein, P., & Schwartz, P. (1983). *American couples: Money, work, and sex*. New York: Morrow.

Carnes, P. (1983). *Out of the shadows: Understanding sexual addiction*. Minneapolis: CompCare.

Clearing-Sky, M., & Thornton, D. (1987). *Inhibited sexual desire: A diagnostic dilemma*. Unpublished manuscript.

Davidson, J., Camargo, C., & Smith, E. (1979). Effects of androgens on sexual behavior in hypogonadal men. *Journal of Clinical Endocrinology and Metabolism, 48,* 955-958.

Davidson, J. M., Kwan, M., & Greenleaf, W. (1982). Hormonal replacement and sexuality in men. In J. Bancroft (Ed.), *Clinics in Endocrinology and Metabolism, 2,* 599-624.

Davidson, J. M., & Myers, L. B. (in press). Endocrine factors in sexual psychophysiology. In R. C. Rosen and J. G. Beck, *Patterns of sexual arousal*. New York: Guilford Press.

Derogatis, L. R., & Melisaratos, N. (1979). The DSFI: A multidimensional measure of sexual functioning. *Journal of Sex and Marital Therapy, 5,* 244–281.

Frank, E., Anderson, C., & Rubinstein, D. (1978). Frequency of sexual dysfunction in "normal" couples. *New England Journal of Medicine, 299,* 111–115.

Frenken, J., & Van Tol, P. (1985). *Sexual problems in gynaecological practice: Prevalence and treatment*. Leiden, The Netherlands: Leiden Psychological Reports.

Freud, S. (1962). *Three essays on the theory of sexuality*. New York: Avon Books. (Original work published 1905)

Garde, K., & Lunde, I. (1980). Female sexual behavior: A study in a random sample of 40-year old women. *Maturitas, 2,* 255-240.

Hawton, K., Catalan, J., Martin, P., & Fagg, J. (1986a). Long-term outcome of sex therapy. *Behaviour Research and Therapy, 24,* 665–675.

Hawton, K., Catalan, J., Martin, P., & Fagg, J. (1986b). Prognostic factors in sex therapy. *Behaviour Research and Therapy, 24,* 377–385.

Heiman, J. R. (1977). A psychophysiological exploration of sexual arousal patterns in females and males. *Psychophysiology, 14,* 266–274.

Kaplan, H. S. (1977). Hypoactive sexual desire. *Journal of Sex and Marital Therapy, 3,* 3–9.

Kaplan, H. S. (1979). *Disorders of sexual desire.* New York: Brunner/Mazel.

Kaplan, H. S. (1983). *The evaluation of sexual disorders.* New York: Brunner/Mazel.

Kaplan, H. S. & Kline, D. (1987). *Sexual phobias and aversion.* New York: Brunner/Mazel.

Kilmann, P. R., Boland, J. P., Norton, S. P., Davidson, E., & Caid, C. (1986). Perspectives of sex therapy outcome: A survey of AASECT providers. Journal of Sex and Marital Therapy, 12, 116–138.

Kinsey, A. C., Pomeroy, W. B., & Martin, C. E. (1948). *Sexual behavior in the human male.* Philadelphia: W. B. Saunders.

Kinsey, A. C., Pomeroy, W. B., Martin, C. E., & Gebhard, P. H. (1953). *Sexual behavior in the human female.* Philadelphia: W. B. Saunders.

Knussmann, R., Christiansen, K., & Couwenbergs, C. (1986). Relations between sex hormone levels and sexual behavior in men. *Archives of Sexual Behavior, 15,* 429–445.

Leiblum, S. R., Bachman, G., Kemmann, E., Colburn, D., & Swartzman, L. (1983). Vaginal atrophy in the postmenopausal woman: The importance of sexual activity and hormones. *Journal of the American Medical Association, 249,* 2195–2198.

Levine, S. (1984). An essay on the nature of sexual desire. *Journal of Sex and Marital Therapy, 10,* 83–96.

Lief, H. I. (1977). Inhibited sexual desire. *Medical Aspects of Human Sexuality, 7,* 94–95.

Lief, H. I. (1985). Evaluation of inhibited sexual desire: Relationship aspects. In H. S. Kaplan (Ed.), *Comprehensive evaluation of disorders of sexual desire.* Washington, DC: American Psychiatric Press.

LoPiccolo, L. (1980). Low sexual desire. In S. R. Leiblum & L. A. Pervin (Eds.) *Principles and practice of sex therapy.* New York: Guilford Press.

Masters, W. H., & Johnson, V. E. (1970). *Human sexual inadequacy.* Boston: Little, Brown.

Morris, N. M., Udry, R., Khan-Dawood, F., & Dawood, M. Y. (1987). Marital sex frequency and midcycle female testosterone. *Archives of Sexual Behavior, 16,* 27–37.

Osborn, M., Hawton, K., & Gath, D. (1987). *Sexual disorders in a community sample of women with partners.* Unpublished manuscript.

Persky, H., Lief, H., Strauss, D., Miller, W., & O'Brien, C. (1978). Plasma testosterone levels and sexual behavior of couples. *Archives of Sexual Behavior. 7,* 157–173.

Quadland, M. (1985). Compulsive sexual behavior: Definition of a problem and an approach to treatment. *Journal of Sex and Marital Therapy, 11,* 121–130.

Rosen, R. C., Leiblum, S. R., & Hall, K. (1987). *Etiological and predictive factors in sex therapy.* Paper presented at the annual meeting of the Society for Sex Therapy and Research, New Orleans.

Rubinsky, H., Eckerman, D., Rubinsky, E., & Hoover, C. (1987). Early-phase physiological response patterns to psychosexual stimuli: Comparison of male and female patterns. *Archives of sexual behavior, 16,* 45–56.

Schiavi, R., & Schreiner-Engel, P. (1988). *Inhibited sexual desire in men.* Manuscript submitted for publication.

Schmidt, G., & Sigusch, V. (1970). Sex differences in response to psychosexual stimulation by films and slides. *Journal of Sex Research, 6,* 268–283.

Schover, L., & LoPiccolo, J. (1982). Effectiveness of treatment for dysfunctions of sexual desire. *Journal of Sex and Marital Therapy, 8,* 179–197.

Schreiner-Engel, P., & Schiavi, R. (1986). Life-time psychopathology in individuals with low sexual desire. *Journal of Nervous and Mental Disease, 174,* 646–651.

Sherwin, B., & Gelfand, M. (1987). The role of androgen in the maintenance of sexual functioning in oopharectomized women. *Psychosematic Medicine, 49,* 397–409.

Sherwin, B., Gelfand, M., & Brender, W. (1985). Androgen enhances sexual motivation in females: A prospective, cross-over study of sex steroid administration in the surgical menopause. *Psychosomatic Medicine, 46,* 339–351.

Stone, L. (1985, July) Sex in the west. *The New Republic,* pp. 25–37.

Tevlin, H., & Leiblum, S. R. (1983). Sex role stereotypes and female sexual dysfunction. In V. Franks & E. Rothbaum (Eds.). *The stereotyping of women: Its effects on mental health.* New York: Springer.

Vennix, P. (1985). *Ontwikkelingen in heteroseksuele relaties; een vergelijkende analyse.* Zeist, The Netherlands: NISSO Studies.

Zilbergeld, B. (1978). *Male sexuality.* Boston: Little, Brown.

Psychodynamic and Interpersonal Perspectives

I

2

Intrapsychic and Individual Aspects of Sexual Desire

Stephen B. Levine

One of the major stumbling blocks in understanding sexual desire problems is the lack of a comprehensive theory on the nature of libido and its role in the intrapsychic and interpersonal life of the individual. Clearly, what is needed is a conceptual framework that is broad enough to include the interactive effects of biological, psychodynamic, and interpersonal determinants of desire. In addition, such a model should be clinically useful in focusing the practitioner's attention on key issues for assessment and treatment. We have chosen to begin this section with Levine's chapter, both because it exemplifies the value of an integrated model of desire, and because he raises a series of fundamental questions concerning sexual desire.

Levine begins with a straightforward discussion of current theories of desire. In addition to offering his own definition, he draws our attention to two essential characteristics of desire—its tendency to fluctuate markedly and to be "personally baffling." While we are likely to be reasonably well aware of the sources of our sexual arousal, Levine argues, the sources of desire can be most elusive! Several essential elements of desire are also identified, such as biological drive, cognitive aspiration ("wish"), and psychological motivation. In fact, the elaboration and integration of these separate dimensions constitute the heart of Levine's model. In his characteristically clear and lucid fashion, he highlights key issues and provides a conceptual framework that is broader and more encompassing than anything that has preceded it.

Among the many impressive features of this model is its focus on the subtlety and variety of psychological motivations that may be expressed via sexual desire. Levine discusses, for example, the importance of "self-regulation" and "partner regulation" as sources of sexual motivation. Sexual desire can also be influenced by past transferential relationships, as well as by present relationship conflicts and issues. The depth and variety of these psychological determinants contribute largely to the sense of desire as "personally baffling." While acknowledging the potential importance of biological factors in cases involving clear-cut organic etiology, Levine sets the stage for much of the current thinking in the field with his assertion that "Motive seems to be the most important element of desire under ordinary circumstances."

Each of the three contributors in this section share a basic psychodynamic orientation to problems of desire, although they differ markedly in their theoretical and clinical perspectives. Despite the focus on psychodynamic factors, these chapters all emphasize the importance of interpersonal determinants in desire disorders as well.

Stephen B. Levine, M.D., is Professor of Psychiatry at Case Western Reserve University School of Medicine and Medical Director of the Center for Human Sexuality at the University Hospitals of Cleveland. He is a major contributor to the field of sex therapy.

The young field of sexuality is in a healthy state of conceptual flux. During the less than 20 years of renewed interest in sex research and therapy, its nomenclature has undergone a series of revisions. Labels for psychogenic sexual problems have evolved from the traditional triad of impotence, frigidity, and perversion to the *Diagnostic and Statistical Manual of Mental Disorders,* third edition (DSM-III) categories: Inhibited Sexual Desire, Inhibited Sexual Arousal, and Inhibited Orgasm; Ego-Dystonic Homosexuality; Gender Identity Disorders; and Paraphilias. These shifts reflect emerging notions about the physiology and psychology of sexual response, as well as a political commitment to base diagnoses on description rather than ideology.

Refinements in understanding both normal and dysfunctional sexual experience are likely to continue and will eventually find their way into official nomenclature. Nomenclature change can be a slow process. This chapter suggests a modification of the classification of sexual desire problems. Nosological change is not a major focus of this chapter, however; understanding normal and dysfunctional sexual desire is.

"Sexual desire" is a key concept because it is relevant to all human beings, not just those with sexual function or sexual identity problems. A productive resonance exists between the understanding of sexual desire and its disorders. When clinicians consider one of these topics, the other is invariably nearby. The study of desire disorders has the potential to illuminate some of the mysterious comings and goings of sexual desire in all people. The appreciation of normal fluctuations in sexual desire may clarify some desire disorders. Until separate and distinct forces are shown to govern sexual desire in health and in illness, it seems reasonable to assume that progress in one area may illuminate the other.

This chapter's title notwithstanding, any thorough discussion of sexual desire must include its interpersonal aspects. Interpersonal factors play a vital role in the psychological organization of desire in the developing person, as well as in the generation of sexual behavior in adults. The intrapsychic and interpersonal aspects exist in interactive dynamic equilibrium. The study of this equilibrium during therapy occasionally suggests how an individual's sexual desire was organized and how, once it was mentally programmed, it has determined subsequent experience.

Defining Sexual Desire

I have been trying to answer the question "What is sexual desire?" for several years. Although the answer is relevant to the large percentage of patients who experience their desire as deficient and the smaller percentage for whom it appears hyperactive, my interest has been more fundamental. I have been trying to understand the nature of "normal" sexual desire. To accomplish this I have eavesdropped, originally in befuddlement, on how patients, colleagues, and the culture have used terms such as "sexual desire," "libido," "urge," "passion," "horniness," "impulse," "need," and "instinct." Three incomplete answers to the question "What is sexual desire?" have emerged:

- Sexual desire is that which precedes and accompanies arousal.
- Sexual desire is the psychobiological propensity to engage in sexual behavior.
- Sexual desire is the energy brought to sexual behavior.

When combined, these answers suggest a more substantial definition. Sexual desire is the psychobiological energy that precedes and accompanies arousal and tends to produce sexual behavior. It has two essential characteristics:

1. Its energy fluctuates.
2. Its sources are often personally baffling.

The understanding of the determinants of these two characteristics suggests that the definition of sexual desire is, in fact, deceptively simple. Something complicated produces both the fluctuating energy of desire and its capacity to be baffling.

The Basic Elements of Sexual Desire

Sexual desire is the product of the mind's capacity to integrate three reasonably separate elements: drive, wish, and motive (Levine, 1984). For the sake of clarity, each of these elements is discussed separately here, even though it is the interaction of these elements that accounts for sexual desire. The term "sexual desire" is henceforth used only when the product of the interaction of these elements is being discussed. Otherwise, either "drive," "wish," or "motive" is the term used.

Sexual Drive

What Is Sexual Drive?

Sexual drive is the product of a neuroendocrine generator of sexual impulses. The activity of this testosterone-dependent brain system tends to have a frequency or rhythm pattern over the life cycle. This is usually clinically stated as "high," "moderate," "low," or "absent" drive. Drive per se, especially in males, diminishes gradually from young to middle to older adulthood (Martin, 1981). Sexual drive—what Freud sometimes meant by "libido" or "the sexual instinct" (Compton, 1981)—insures the perpetuation of the species and therefore must be genetically organized (MacLean, 1975).

Sexual drive is evidenced by endogenous or spontaneous manifestations of genital excitement. These typically include (1) genital tingling, tumescence, or lubrication; (2) a perceptual shift whereby physical attributes of others achieve a dominant place in the hierarchy of stimuli impinging upon consciousness; (3) erotic fantasies; (4) erotic dreams; and (5) partner-seeking behavior or masturbation. These five manifestations may be summarized as spontaneous endogenous arousal and heightened sexual excitability.

Endogenously stimulated changes occur in most, but not all, adolescents and young adults. Sexual drive is most dramatically manifested in adolescence because either its intensity is strongest or the teenagers' capacities to mask it are weakest. Adolescents are often temporarily overwhelmed by their drive manifestations and as a result periodically do not feel in control of themselves.

Drive manifestations are commonly referred to as "horniness," but the term is imprecise for our purposes because laypeople also use it to indicate genital excitement stimulated by interactions with another person. This is unfortunate, because "horniness" is intuitively understood to refer to drive phenomena much better than the phrase "sexual drive" itself. "Horniness" or "drive" refers both to obvious spontaneous arousal experiences and to the excitability that enables previously ignored stimuli to become pre-occupying. While drive manifestations are not the sole prerogatives of adolescents and young adults, spontaneous arousal and susceptibility to excitement are most clearly seen at this time of life.

Drive manifestations force adolescents to come to grips with their sexual selves. How they do this may set the pattern for their subsequent adult sexual comfort. The process whereby drive is integrated into personality may be considered a line of development that probably reaches its mature form after adolescence. As in other developmental lines, what comes earlier influences how adolescents come to accept their sexual selves. Tracing this developmental line for any individual is always a speculative matter.

Although the notion of a genetically organized hypothalamic generator that tends to produce a certain level of sexual energy over long periods of the life cycle is useful in explaining the patterns of our subjective selves, it is not the whole story of sexual drive. Sexual drive is easily overridden by personal psychological adversity in persons with low to moderate sex drive. In people, with higher drive adversity seems to have relatively little impact on the frequency and intensity of drive manifestations. It is of great interest that men with the highest frequencies of sexual expression through midlife have the lowest incidence of sexual dysfunction as they grow older (Martin, 1981).

How Does the Clinician Recognize Drive Activity?

It is a considerable clinical challenge to appraise the drive component of sexual desire correctly. The periodicity of spontaneous excitement is one indication: "Approximately how often do you feel in your body like having sexual experience?" One can also ask, "How much time passes after an orgasm before you feel a physical need for another one?" Erotic dreams, nocturnal orgasms, nocturnal and morning erections, and spontaneous erotic changes in perception may indicate the activity of this brain system. Women, in addition, should be asked whether they recognize a portion of their menstrual cycle when they are typically interested in sex. Masturbation may be a means of regulating sexual tensions resulting from drive, and so its frequency should be ascertained; however, caution is needed, because factors other than drive lead to it (e.g., excitement arising from interaction with others, habit, anxiety reduction).

Drive is a clinical assessment problem because it is more subjective than behavioral. When it is carefully evaluated, however, many individuals with "inhibited desire" are recognized as having drive manifestations. Of the three elements comprising sexual desire, drive is the most likely to be scientifically measurable; for example, effects of pregnancy, lactation, menopause, grief, or age manifestations can be studied. Most of the allegations regarding the impact of medications on sexual desire are based upon the effect of these medications on the hypothalamic drive mechanism (Segraves, Madsen, Carter, & Davis, 1985).

The natural history of sexual drive through the life cycle for either sex is not well studied. It is possible that the frequency and intensity of drive manifestations decline by early middle life, even though the frequency of sexual behavior does not. Many men in their 30s who are in psychotherapy for other problems report that their sexual feelings are less insistent. This pattern seems even more apparent clinically in men in their 40s. The clinical assessment of drive among the elderly is especially problematic, because some older people lose their drive entirely or evidence it only rarely. The neuroendocrine mechanisms for such changes have not been elucidated, but may involve a lessening limbic sensitivity to testosterone.

There is no reason to assume that drive decline follows the same time course in both sexes. There is significant individual variability within each sex in every age group. While males are often glibly assumed to have more sex drive than females, skepticism is in order. Drive is subjective and must be reported or deduced. The rules governing sexual expression seem to be different for females and males and are changing to some extent.

Sexual Wish

Many older men and women whose sexual drive manifestations are infrequent and weak have a decided wish to behave sexually. This strong wish has a great deal to do with their sexual behavior. The reasons for the wish have usually been established over their earlier years of adulthood:

- It makes them feel good physically.
- It makes them feel loved, valued, and important.
- It makes them feel vital or energetic.
- It makes them feel masculine or feminine.
- It makes them feel connected to another and less alone.
- It makes them feel they are pleasing their partners.

By contrast, young people with frequent spontaneous arousal and high levels of excitability may simultaneously wish not to have sex. This wish causes them not to express sexual feelings or to express them with discomfort. Young people have many reasons for wishing not to have sex:

- They feel emotionally unready.
- They do not know exactly how to do it.
- They do not like anyone enough yet.

- They are still frightened of feeling a high degree of sexual arousal.
- They fear pregnancy.
- They fear sexually transmitted diseases.
- They have a conviction that it is morally wrong.
- They do not wish to disgrace or displease their parents.

For these and similar reasons, the wish to engage with a partner in sexual behavior can be conflicted. Although the person's drives are pushing in one direction, moral, social, and danger factors push in the opposite direction. Although wishes often involve matters of conscience, they also include developmental sense of readiness and the sense of appropriateness. In a larger sense, the wish aspect of sexual desire reflects self-governance.

In young and middle adulthood, the wish to have sex may involve the sense that it is normal, expected, and valuable. Besides being a rite of passage and a privilege of adulthood, it seems that "everyone else is having sex." Ideas about how often one's peers have sex can be powerful influences on behavior and personal satisfaction. Schein *et al.* (1988) have shown that most adults overestimate the frequency of sexual behavior of their peers.

The wish component of sexual desire is a cognitive aspiration. This designation emphasizes the purely ideational aspect of sexual desire. The complex role of the thinking process in the production of sexual desire is related to the fact that the mind represents itself both to others and to itself. These representations are often contradictory. Wishes to engage in and to avoid sexual behavior may simultaneously coexist or fluctuate from moment to moment. The representation of the self to others is often influenced by the person's sense of what is expected and what is at stake.

The clinical discussion of sexual wishes often involves deceit or illusion on the part of the patient. Clinicians must beware of equating the aspiration to be sexual with sexual desire. As patients represent themselves to a therapist, the truth told about sexual wishes is often only a partial truth.

Sexual desire is not simply an interaction between wishes regarding sex and biological drives. The most important element, especially in adulthood, is the willingness to have sex. This behavior, willingness, is a product of psychological motivation.

Sexual Motive

General Factors Inducing Sexual Motivation

The clinical understanding of sexual motivation requires an immersion in the individual's and couple's psychodynamics. This process is analogous to studying the cellular structure of tissue under a microscope. Scrutiny of a tissue begins with the naked eye, not with the microscope. Similarly, the consideration of motivation to be sexual begins with a simpler, more superficial overview of what is known to facilitate sexual willingness. Six general factors induce sexual motivation:

1. Drive
2. Decision
3. Interpersonal behavior
4. Voyeuristic experience
5. Attraction
6. Drugs acting on the central nervous system (CNS)

The first inducer, sexual drive, is the biological antecedent of sexual motive. It is much easier for many people to engage in sexual behavior when they are experiencing spontaneous endogenous arousal. Couples rarely experience their sexual drive manifestations simultaneously, however. The sexual drive of one person may induce the partner's cooperation in sexual behavior, but this receptivity is not the same as sexual drive. Other factors account for the response to the partner's sexual interest.

An intact sexual drive center may be more important for enabling response to an aroused partner than for provoking the sexual behavior in the first place. This surprising notion is based on two observations: The frequency and intensity of drive slowly declines with increasing age, and partner receptivity is not explained by simultaneous drive. For much of adulthood, therefore, "horniness" is probably not the most frequent inducer of personal sexual willingness.

Individuals may decide for one reason or another to behave sexually. This decision per se is another inducer of sexual willingness. Sexual willingness typically requires personal consent. Consent is sufficient to enable arousal to orgasm with a partner, even though immediately before it no drive manifestations may have been evident. Similarly, masturbation to orgasm does not require prior spontaneous endogenous arousal. The presence of drive may enhance the intensity of any sexual experience, but it is consent that allows the arousal to persist. The freely made decision to participate in sexual behavior is a subtle, though vital, inducer of willingness.

Interpersonal behavior is the most important inducer of sexual willingness. This behavior typically involves combinations of nonverbal, verbal, and tactile contacts. The relative proportions of these interpersonal contacts vary with the stage of the relationship and the individuals involved. Lingering eye contact plays an important role in signaling sexual interest between strangers as well as within established couples. Holding and caressing during foreplay are requirements for sexual willingness and subsequent arousal in many women and men.

Empathic verbal exchange, generally described as intimacy, should not be underestimated as a powerful interpersonal inducer of sexual willingness. Indeed, the establishment and maintenance of psychological intimacy may be the most crucial ingredients of a lifelong motive to behave sexually.

Voyeuristic experience involves hearing of, reading about, or seeing the sexual excitement of others. Voyeuristic stimulation has a ubiquitous power to generate arousal, which in turn increases willingness to behave sexually. Voyeuristic stimulation works best to increase willingness in couples when it is used occasionally.

Attraction to another person often leads to temporary willingness to behave sexually, or at least to a fantasy of behaving sexually. Attraction often involves a perception of another that meets some need in the attracted. The other has something that the observer wants—for example, beauty, power, money, intelligence, organization, or emotional control. Attraction does not require any actual interchange between two people.

CNS agents such as alcohol and other commonly abused drugs may induce sexual willingness. To the extent that this is considered a pharmacological effect on the drive center, however, these drugs are drive inducers, not inducers of willingness. The possibility that such agents are also useful because they diminish the experience of anxiety generated by anticipating and participating in sexual behavior makes them a candidate for the list of inducers of sexual willingness.

Each of the six inducers of sexual motivation may involve a transient fantasy. Fantasy, conscious or inapparent, may be part of the intrapsychic mechanism for generating the earliest peripheral manifestations of arousal. Bancroft and Wu's (1983) demonstration that testoterone deficiency limits arousal using fantasy, but not erection formation, is instructive. Testosterone deficiency or the inability of the brain to respond to this hormone may subvert this sequence. An inducer leads to fantasy, which leads to motivation, which leads to arousal.

The motivational element of desire can be thought of as subserving the need for attachment. This places the subject of motivation in the realm of object relations (Scharff, 1982).

The three elements of desire are only conceptually separate. Clinically and experientially, they blend into one another and into sexual arousal. Ideally, the elements work in concert, but clinically it is apparent that they often do not. It is crucial to keep the concept of motive separate from drive and wish, in order to make astute clinical decisions.

The Major Determinants of Sexual Motivation

Four intrapsychic–interpersonal contexts contribute to sexual motivation:

1. Sexual identity
2. Quality of the nonsexual relationship

3. Self- and partner regulation
4. Transference from past attachments

Sexual Identity. Sexual identity consists of several closely related dimensions: gender identity, sexual orientations, and sexual intention. Sexual motivation never achieves any psychological independence from the dimensions of sexual identity.

"Gender identity" is the sense of oneself as masculine, feminine, ambiguous, or neuter. Depending upon the current form of gender identity, the experience of arousal either inconspicuously reinforces the gender sense or conflicts with and confuses it. For example, a male who feels more like a female may feel anxious and uncertain in response to his drive manifestations.

Sexual orientation has two subtly different aspects. In its most important subjective aspects, "sexual orientation" refers to the specific sex and gender characteristics of those images that elicit arousal through daytime or masturbatory fantasy and dreams. Based upon erotic attraction, an adult orientation can be thought of as heteroerotic, homoerotic, bierotic, or anerotic. In its more widely understood objective aspect, however, "sexual orientation" refers simply to the biological sex of one's partners. Based upon the sex of actual partners, an adult can be thought of as heterosexual, homosexual, bisexual, or asexual. Erotic imagery and the sex of a partner are not invariably consistent. Conflict over homoerotic images or experience may diminish sexual desire.

"Sexual intention" refers to the behaviors that adults wish to engage in with their partners. Conventional intentions involve a variety of sexual practices predicated upon a peaceable mutuality of pleasure. Unconventional intentions often involve a hostile relationship between an aggressor and a victim (Stoller, 1975). Paraphilias (e.g., sadism, exhibitionism, masochism) involve hostility rather than affection and represent unconventional intentions.

For every adult, the subjective erotic response and its translation into arousing partner behavior involve an integration of preconditions based upon the person's gender identity, sexual orientation, and sexual intention. Many desire problems, of both the "inhibited" and "hyperactive" varieties involve unconventional aspects of sexual identity that are either hidden from the partner or incompletely recognized by the patient. This intrapsychic context, programmed to a great extent during child development, can be a major determinant of willingness or unwillingness to behave sexually. Two case examples follow.

A young adult woman with conventional gender identity and orientation recalled masturbating to orgasm almost every day of her life to themes of anal, urethral, vaginal, oral, and breast penetration with medical instruments. She kept these "sick" fantasies and her uncontrollable need to masturbate intensely private. She experienced minimal and unsustainable arousal with her husband. She had no motivation to make love with him and avoided his advances until her guilt over his deprivation was great. Her husband had no idea about the masochism. She had no idea about the origins of erotic response to pain and humiliation. She was entirely unwilling to confront her masochistic self during behavior with her partner, and felt trapped by her inability to enjoy sexual behavior without pain.

A man who adopted three children and eventually underwent sex reassignment surgery because he could not bear his male social role refused to have sex with his wife after the first several months of marriage. During this behavior he invariably imagined that his penis was her penis and her vagina and breasts were his. The painful reminder that this was only fantasy kept him motivated to avoid sexual contact for 20 years until his quest for gender and sex reassignment began in earnest (Levine & Shumaker, 1983).

The presence of sexual desire indicates a willingness to recognize one's gender sense, sexual orientation, and sexual intention.

Quality of the Nonsexual Relationship. An unacceptable nonsexual relationship can render two sexually normal individuals asexual when just one partner can no longer tolerate the relationship. This may rest upon one partner's perception that the other has been self-centered and emotionally unavailable. Clinicians must learn to recognize and respect "inhibited sexual desire" as simply motivation not to engage in sex. These motivations often arise before their source is recognized by the individuals involved. This interpersonal context (Talmadge & Talmadge, 1986), which may have little to do with childhood, is perhaps the most common cause of motivation not to behave sexually.

The presence of sexual desire implies an acknowledgment that, all things considered, the relationship outside the bedroom is acceptable.

Self- and Partner Regulation. Sexual drive manifestations and excitements arising from interactions with others may leave a person preoccupied with sexual fantasies and behavior and sexually aroused. The preoccupation and arousal disrupts the usual internal psychological milieu and (as is so frequent in teenagers) makes concentration on other things difficult. There are four obvious choices: The person can (1) wait until it dissipates; (2) force an interest in something else; (3) masturbate; (4) behave sexually with a partner. The latter two are means of regulating the self through sexual behavior.

Many individuals discover that sexual behavior, especially orgasm, can be useful in dealing with nonsexual disruptions of their internal milieu. Orgasm can distract a person from mild sadness or anger; it can induce sleep in someone worried about insomnia; it can temporarily calm anxiety or relieve premenstrual tension. A person's motives for sexual behavior may include dissipation of unpleasant nonsexual feelings, the relief of sexual tensions produced outside of the couple's relationship, or an erotic response to the partner.

During the years in which a person is single, he or she may learn to regulate various feeling states through masturbation. When two individuals become a couple, each person has a more complex opportunity. Each may learn to regulate the self through the other and may learn to cooperate with the partner for his or her self-regulation. Some people always feel obligated to indulge their partner's interest in sex—no questions asked. Others only have sex when their own personal requirements have been met (e.g., after spending a pleasant evening together, when they are sexually excited, or after a bath).

Couples tacitly or explicitly agree to behave sexually together for a host of individual reasons. A husband and wife may readily agree to make love, but their individual reasons for doing so may be quite different. In addition, each may poorly understand the other's motives. Although sexual behavior may occur regularly, the motives and their intensity vary considerably. Here are a few of many possible examples of individual transient motivations for sex that may be disguised within a regular sexual relationship:

Self-regulation
- To ease the private pain of an upcoming 2-day business trip.
- To rid oneself of the excitation stimulated at the office.
- To preclude the need to use words to express pleasure over being reunited.

Partner regulation
- To please the partner when he or she wants to have sex.
- To comfort the partner after he or she has been insulted or disappointed.
- To convey the feeling that the partner is still valued in spite of a mastectomy or stroke.

Mutual regulation
- To gratify the wish to have sex in as many cities that the partners visit as possible.
- To express simultaneously feelings of affection and love.

Manipulation
- To minimize any suspicion of an ongoing affair.

Very quickly in a new relationship, the fortunate couple realizes that sexual behavior is fun. Sexual behavior becomes valuable to each of them. They intuitively know that the creation of physical pleasure is associated with an emotional pleasure. They make certain that regular opportunities for sex exist. At least some of the deep pleasure in sex stems from the renewal of the couple's emotional bond that derives from turning their bodies over to each other (Scharff, 1982).

The presence of sexual desire implies an agreement to behave sexually for any specific reason, such as self- or partner regulation of affection, sadness, or anxiety.

Transference from Past Attachments. Transferential determinants of motivation have an explanatory power that is difficult to ignore. Sexual expression may mobilize positive or negative attitudes toward the partner that are actually derived from previous experience with the love objects. Good sexual relationships presume a positive transference of trust and safety from the residue of childhood experience. Problems of desire may relate to unconscious expectations of harm or deprivation—that is, negative transferences.

One common form of a transferentially based motivational problem is exemplified by a person with drive manifestations who wishes (aspires) to behave sexually with his or her valued partner, but who is only motivated to have sex with another person. This motivation begins after engagement or marriage when a deep emotional attachment to the partner is experienced. Freud (1912/1957) considered this a product of Oedipal dynamics in which the adult has failed to unite the sensual and affectionate trends of his or her sexual instinct. Originally combined and focused on the opposite-sex parent, these trends are normally separated for a long period of post-Oedipal development only to recombine when normal adult love occurs. Thus, such patterns represent a form of immaturity—specifically, the developmental failure to direct love and lust toward the same love object. Another explanation is that the motivation not to make love stems from the sense of vulnerability that arises from the transference to the partner of the painful experiences with parents.

In order to provide a loving attachment, the partner usually offers protection from pain, rejection, abuse, disrespect, torture, or harm. In many troubled couples the partner is, indeed, trustworthy. The archaic image of the parent is not; it is the childhood residue that is unconsciously bestowed upon the partner. The one who is motivated not to have sex acts as though sex will lead to the repetition of the painful aspects of past attachments. There are many unsolved childhood dilemmas that can be transferred to the current partner.

The presence of sexual desire implies that the person is able to transfer positive internalized images of past important attachment figures to the partner.

Sexual Desire: An Interim Summary

Sexual desire is the psychobiological energy that precedes and accompanies sexual arousal and tends to produce sexual behavior. It is the product of the interaction of the neuroendocrine system that produces drive, the cognitive processes that generate wish, and the motivational processes that result in willingness to behave sexually. Drive manifestations show many differences from person to person, yet slowly decline over the life cycle; wishes, too, demonstrate individual differences and a somewhat predictable time course during the life cycle; and motivation depends heavily upon the quality of present and past interpersonal relationships. As a result of all these factors, sexual desire fluctuates in intensity and is baffling in the reasons for its appearances and departures. Because drive and wish tend to increase motive for sexual expression, these three elements do not appear in pure form. Under ideal interpersonal circumstances, the elements of desire blend well together and enable a person to experience desire as a unitary phenomenon. But under even mild biological, social, or psychological adversity, an individual or a clinician may readily sense the relative separateness of drive, wish, and motive. Motive seems to be the most important element of desire under ordinary circumstances.

The Treatment of Desire Disorders

The Role of the Clinician

Patients seek treatment that relieves, enables, or cures. Experienced clinicians have the reputation for skillful, efficient conduct of such treatment, but actually spend a great deal of their time just trying to understand what is wrong. While something is known about how to generate sexual desire—for example, creation of a new intimacy in a conflicted relationship, education in how to sexually stimulate one another, and provision of permission to engage in sensuous activity—the therapist knows far less than the patient thinks about how to catalyze the appearance of the crucial psychobiological energy. A sexual desire problem begins as a mystery to both patient and doctor. Clinicians should be mindful that the first crucial question is "What is wrong that this person is unable to feel and use the fluctuating energy of desire?" It is not "How do I treat this patient?"

Although bringing about improvement in some desire deficiencies requires only a medication adjustment or a brief educative discussion, such simple cases are often handled by the physician who initially hears the complaint. By the time a specialist in sexual disorders meets a patient or couple, the problems are usually not amenable to simple interventions. The complexity of most cases seen by specialists requires thoughtfulness concerning the quality of the alliance between therapist and patient. The quality of the alliance ultimately determines what will be initially revealed to the therapist, who then, on the basis of this information, formulates a causal hypothesis and a treatment plan.

The alliance is even more central to sustaining the treatment process. Treatment usually is a matter of identifying, appreciating, and overcoming the resistance to behaving sexually. How the therapist deals with the resistance may determine persistence in or abandonment of the treatment process. The higher dropout rate for patients of beginning sex therapists in our clinic may reflect increases in understanding of and ability to deal with resistance as the therapists gain more experience. The therapist is well positioned to help if his or her interest in understanding the intrapsychic and interpersonal situation is paramount. If the therapist acts as though the technology to cure the problem exists, the patient may realize the therapist's naiveté before the therapist becomes disillusioned about the treatment's capacity to help.

Clinical research on sexual dysfunction in recent years has centered on the problems of sexual desire. These problems may occur both in the absence and in the presence of arousal and orgasmic difficulties. Since desire is a psychobiological energy that precedes and accompanies arousal, the problems of desire seem more fundamental than the psychophysiological difficulties of arousal and orgasm. Moreover, resistance to treatment of arousal and orgasmic disorders often is manifested by a sudden motivation not to behave sexually. Thus, even if a problem is not primarily one of sexual desire, it can quickly become one (Arentewicz & Schmidt, 1983).

Treatment as Evaluation

The evaluation may proceed along the lines of the elements of desire:

1. Does the patient possess sexual drive? How frequent? How intense? How has it changed recently? In response to what? Are street drugs or medications playing a role? Are diagnosed or unrecognized physical or emotional disorders involved? Are they being adequately treated?

2. What are the patient's wishes about sexual behavior? Does the patient recognize any reason for not behaving sexually at this point in time? What are the dangers of behaving? What are the advantages of avoiding sexual activity? What moral constraints exist concerning sexual activity with this partner?

3. What are the patient's gender identity, sexual orientation, and sexual intention, in terms of both fantasy and behavior? How do any unconventional sexual identity characteristics relate to the willingness to be aroused? Is masturbation more comfortable than partner behavior? Why?

4. How does the patient describe the "goodness of fit" with the partner, both sexually and otherwise? What are the struggles between them? How do they regard each other? What are their plans for their relationship? What will they do if this therapy is not helpful?

5. Under what conditions have the partners had sexual experiences together? What have been the circumstances that generated sexual behavior? Why have they behaved as they have when they have?

6. What has been the history of previous love relationships? What is the remembered quality of past parental and sibling relationships? Was psycho-

logical, physical, or sexual abuse involved? Were parental divorce, serious loss of parental health and function, prolonged separation, and or death part of the developmental experience?

In the process of answering such questions, much about the patient's life and personality becomes apparent. The manner of dealing with this information is instrumental in establishing the therapeutic alliance—that is, the doctor–patient (or doctor–couple) bond that will enable a more thorough consideration of the factors identified in the earliest phases of treatment.

Sexual desire involves the integration of intrapsychic biological and psychological forces. It involves meanings and interpretation of present and past experience. It involves compromises between the longing for and fear of intimacy and attachment. It involves self-acceptance of emotions and conflicts that are not always initially pleasant or complimentary. If a sexual desire problem is ultimately diagnosed as psychogenic, the therapist ought to be able to explain what good the symptom is doing for the individual patient and/or the couple.

The therapist must be skilled at supporting patients while they learn about themselves. The therapist's perspective about the universality of intrapsychic struggle is often reassuring. The therapist needs patience and the capacity to tolerate those who can understand but who cannot change the way they feel and behave.

The Differential Diagnosis of Sexual Desire Problems

The schema presented below for differential diagnosis of sexual desire problems is an outline summary of factors thought to contribute to clinical inhibitions and excesses of desire. Such a listing should be used with care, for several reasons: The mechanism whereby these factors produce the problem are not well understood; the reasons why similar factors exist in those without desire problems are not known; and it is easy to err by assuming that the problem is explained once one of these factors is demonstrated.

In any particular patient or couple, more than one factor may be implicated. The psychological generation of desire symptoms adheres to the general principle of multiple determination of symptoms. Moreover, diseases or medications that organically lead to drive deficiencies may have psychological effects in both the person and the spouse that lead to motivation to avoid a sexual experience. The cause of a desire problem is usually a complicated matter, even though it is efficient to refer to successfully treated cases as having been due to a drug, an unresolved argument, or a deteriorated marriage. Despite what we occasionally say, clinicians need to guard against thinking that a particular case was due to just one factor.

The evaluation process begins with the search for a predominant casual factor. But as treatment ensures, both the therapist and the patient may appreciate that the cause may lie closer to the interactions between or among factors than to the factors alone. For example, a 70-year-old man who is thought during initial evaluation to be experiencing an effect of aging on his drive mechanism may on continued scrutiny be found also to have a growing resentment of his wife and a new medication for ulcers. The interaction of these factors may be what has eradicated his desire.

A schema for differential diagnosis of sexual desire disorders is as follows:

    I. Diminished or absent drive manifestations
       A. Depressive disorder
       B. Medication side effect
       C. Unrecognized or inadequately treated physical illness
       D. Aging
       E. Constitutional or lifelong pattern
          1. Klinefelter syndrome
          2. No apparent disease
       F. Psychotic disorder—not medication-induced
       G. Response to other sexual dysfunction
       H. Impact of being raised in a vastly different culture
   II. High drive manifestations
       A. Psychotic disorder
          1. Mania or hypomania
          2. Schizophrenia
          3. Borderline personality disorder
       B. Substance abuse
       C. Sexual abuse as a child
       D. Perversion
       E. Low desire in partner
       F. Constitutional, no apparent problem
  III. Diminished or low motivation for partner sexual behavior
       A. Nonsexual relationship deterioration
          1. "Secret" extramarital affair or plan for divorce
          2. Same as above, but not secret
       B. Variation in sexual identity
          1. Fully known by the person but not the partner
          2. Not well understood by the person
       C. Confusion of partner with parent
          1. Traumatic past relationship with parent
          2. Inability to love and have sex with same person
       D. Sexual relationship problems
          1. Significant other dysfunction in person or partner

2. Difficulty with means and timing of initiating sex
3. Deficiency in knowledge of sexual technique
4. Incompatible levels of sexual desire

This particular differential diagnostic schema avoids the term "inhibited sexual desire" (Kaplan, 1979) by attempting to clarify the element that appears to be fundamentally amiss. The terms "sexual aversion" and "sexual phobia" are also avoided, because they primarily describe the intensity of the motivation not to behave sexually and the style of coping with the intrapsychic–interpersonal dilemma.

A Case with a Positive Outcome

A Brief Overview of the Process

Alice, although mentally and physically well, portrayed herself during 6 months of weekly treatment as having no sexual drive manifestations. She consistently maintained that this pattern was lifelong. "I think I am different. I could not comprehend what everyone was talking about concerning sexuality when I was a young woman." She failed to develop the capacity for sexual pleasure and high levels of arousal during her long marriage.

Alice came to therapy with a hollow-sounding intellectual wish for sex. Conjoint therapy enabled her to organize a new motivation to engage in sexual behavior—the use of her body for her pleasure. The therapist thought this was gradually accomplished by overcoming a number of resistances in her and her husband. The couple frequently commented on how the therapist was helpful. They repeatedly stressed five factors: the therapist's understanding of Alice's feelings; his protection of her against her husband's impatience and misconceptions about her sexual responses; the therapist's willingness to be a sex educator; his active encouragement when she failed to concentrate fully on sensation and to stay with the sensuous experience; and the clarification that some of the husband's "high sex drive" was only an attempt to dissipate nonsexual feelings of boredom and anxiety. The couple and the therapist were respectful of the differing views of the process. The couple emphasized the education they were getting; the therapist emphasized their unacknowledged anger and its impact on each of them.

The Case

Alice, a strikingly attractive 50-year-old woman, and Bob, her 52-year-old husband (a recently retired consultant), sought help to improve their rarely occurring sexual relationship. They had three grown but still problematic children. Over 30 years, their sexual experience had consisted of Alice's providing sex for Bob when he returned from his frequent travels. In both their good and their problematic times, she had obtained no pleasure from sexual activity. Secretly angry at his turning over all responsibility for their children to her, she had felt generally abandoned.

Bob was a cheerful, energetic man who loved sex and had endlessly "pestered" Alice upon his returns from travel. He would minimize what she reported was happening in the children's lives with statements such as "All kids have troubles," "You are a good mother," or "You can handle it!"

Alice could not recall ever having sexual desire, masturbating, being aroused, having a sexual fantasy, or achieving orgasm. She never thought about sex and could not comprehend her husband's interest in the physical experience. Now that he no longer traveled without her, their children were out of the house, and the anger over her abandonment was dissipating, she was interested in seeing whether she could discover what her husband insisted she was missing.

Alice had become a competitive ballroom dancer in the last 5 years. Her pleasure in dancing was enormous; it included grace in movement, admiration of others, and skill in sewing the costumes. Her husband encouraged her, even though he was not skilled enough to be her partner. He was reassured that her partners were gay.

At least half of the therapy was spent discussing dilemmas, past and present, with their children. The remaining time was devoted to "sex." Using masturbatory and sensate focus exercises, Alice was able to concentrate on sensation and learn to pursue pleasure for herself. Bob was delighted with his wife's new interest and did all he could to stimulate her. Within 2 months, she began to be regularly orgasmic. She now seemed to want to have sex and was willing to both please her husband and herself.

She did not evidence any spontaneous drive manifestations. "Why?" Alice asked. The therapist answered, "Why?" not so much to encourage further self-reflection as to acknowledge that she was formulating one of the great questions about sexual desire. "How is it possible to increase wish and motivation for sexual behavior and pleasure without affecting sexual drive?"

A Case with a Negative Outcome

A Brief Overview of the Process

In this sad situation, a family of four was buffeted by the husband and wife's inability to love each other more fully. Much more was learned about the couple than in the previous case, because the resistances to behavioral change were so entrenched. Sexual education and sensate focus played an unimportant role. Most of the work involved clarifying feelings and trying to understand one another. The therapist often had to be supportive of the despairing husband, who persisted despite his enormous frustration.

The Case

Richard, a very bright, highly achieving man who favored reason and mathematical precision over emotion and nuance, was felt by his other therapist to possess dogged obsessive–compulsive character. He was a man dominated by his obsessive father, whom he recalled as having paid him attention only when he made good grades. He had grown up with a sense of alienation from his peers. His high intelligence and athletic skill had led him to outward success. His first marriage, which was childless, had ended when he discovered his wife's prolonged infidelity.

Several years later he had married a young immigrant, vowing not to do anything to destroy this relationship. Sonia had immediately grasped his inability to know how things worked in an emotional sense. She was very good at this and eagerly helped him with business and social strategy. Now, 6 years later, her superiority seemed to be backfiring: He was frightened to describe his feelings about anything personal to her. He routinely read in the evenings rather than talking, and he remained anxious when making love. He was able to freely demonstrate love for his children, but he could not demonstrate affection for his wife.

After 4 years of marriage, Sonia had refused to have sex because Richard was "insensitive." She complained that his preoccupation with work, inability to grasp the importance of feelings in life, unfriendliness to her friends, and self-centered rapid ejaculation made her feel alone in her marriage. He was terrified by her stinging comments, because his first wife had also complained how unfeeling he was. He sought individual therapy when his boss informed him that his perfectionism was causing problems.

After 6 months of individual psychotherapy, and after several months of marital therapy, Richard began to be more expressive at home. Although now pleased with her husband, Sonia remained sexually unreceptive. He realized that her lack of motivation was not simply tied to his "lack of feelings." She seized opportunities to criticize him. The fact that the behavior to which she vociferously objected had greatly improved did not stop the criticism.

The therapist had thought that Sonia's ne'er-do-well father—who had committed suicide when she was 5, leaving the family in financial ruin—explained some of her negative perceptions of her husband. She was unable to grasp the possibility of this. When Richard continued to press for an understanding of the sexual avoidance, she engineered an individual session.

During this session, Sonia steadfastly introduced her intent to divorce

Richard, even though she valued the close relationship between her children and her husband and felt her husband might kill himself. At the end of the session, she suddenly cried saying she was not the strong person she had imagined herself to be. Before the next session, she had a flood of memories, and said to the therapist in the session that she was going to tell "her secret." She described herself as a much-loved child who was aware from an early age that her sister was unwanted, less loved, and always very difficult. Unlike the patient, who always was highly regarded, the sister was forever in trouble. Richard (a very successful man) reminded her of her sister. Sonia emphasized her pity and guilt about her sister's misery. She cried over her helplessness to relieve her suffering. Over the next few sessons she was able to acknowledge her subtle pleasure in her sister's misfortune. She described her guilt over the comfortable economic circumstances she had achieved through marriage, while her sister barely survived. The therapist wondered how much her willingness to destroy the family's structure had to do with her own family's misfortune when she was her daughter's age. She thought it was coincidence.

At the sixth and final session, Sonia revealed that her sexual standard was based upon a 1-year relationship she had had prior to her marriage with a man who was a friend of her mother. She then decided there was nothing more to talk about and went away. The therapist saw Richard briefly. He was grateful when she was able to resume sexual relationships briefly, but remained wary of her capriciousness.

A year later, Sonia returned in great crisis. They had decided to divorce after Richard discovered she had been having an affair for the past 18 months. Sonia became panicky, lost 20 pounds in 2 weeks, and could not sleep. The legal process had started. She paid a lawyer a large retainer, and quickly got into a dispute with him. When the lawyer refused her request for a refund, she and her husband joined forces to sue the lawyer. Thus united against a common enemy, they came back from the brink, and sex between them resumed.

A Synthesis

Sonia never lacked sexual drive; she lacked motivation. She felt that if she tolerated the passionless experience without complaint, she would never be happy with Richard. When she made love, the subjective experience was a fraction of what she had known with a former lover. When she did not, he was miserable and more "pathetic than before." But she could not or would not stop herself.

She seemed unreasonable throughout therapy. The "secret" she confessed during an individual session may have been important in understanding her development, but it was not the secret that needed to be told. The many accusations of her husband's cowardice came to mind. It did not occur to the therapist at this point that she was projecting. When she was "caught" she felt like "a naughty child." In reality, the stakes were higher than in childhood: She had no independent source of income, she was about to separate her children from their valued father, and her lover was uninterested in leaving his family.

Honesty is required for full utilization of any psychotherapeutic endeavor. Even if Sonia had been more honest, she would have been confronted with Richard's limitations as a man and her dilemma of choosing a man for the very reasons for which she soon came to despise him. As long as Sonia could only see Richard's defects and remained resistant to considering her contributions to the difficulty, little progress would have occurred. Sonia would have had to consider that her motives for not making love were more complicated than she presented. She would have had to stop dismissing the possibility that her father's criminality and suicide, her mother's turning her over to an aunt to raise, and the family's derision of males had had subtle influences upon her development. The uncivilized intrapsychic meanings of falling in love with her weak, helpless, but financially well-situated husband would have had to be considered, at least until a better understanding of her withdrawal from sexual behavior was forthcoming.

Sonia, Richard, and their children went through considerable agony. Her lack of sexual desire—her motive to avoid sexual contact with her husband—disappeared quickly when she brought their lives to the brink of separation. Her eager lovemaking while fighting the "evil' lawyer suggests that some problems do not need to be "fixed" as much as understood; they "fix" themselves under the right circumstances. The therapeutic challenge is to create those circumstances in the office without having the lives of the patients and their children thrown into more chaos, which only keeps the cycles of wariness about trusting loved ones alive from one generation to another.

Hyperactive Sexual Desire

Hyperactive sexual desire is much more of a mystery than are the deficiencies of desire. One cannot be sure whether there is a basic brain abnormality generating so much drive that personality development is grossly disrupted, or whether excessive eroticization is a relatively unusual psychological response to unmasterable life circumstances. A compelling argument can be made for each viewpoint. The resolution of the issue awaits further information about the physiology of drive.

The revision of DSM-III (DSM-IIIR) does not recognize the problem of hyperactive desire as sufficiently separate from paraphilia, mania, and character disorder to warrant a separate category. But several of the promising treatments for hyperactive sexual desire depend upon the recognition that it is the quantity of incessant and disruptive drive manifestations, and not the paraphilic images per se, that require treatment. The use of Depo-Provera to suppress the brain generator of drive (Bradford, 1983); the restructuring of erotic imagery through behavioral techniques such as masturbation satiation (Abel & Blanchard, 1974); and individual and group psychotherapy to learn ways of handling negative affect states other than acting out sexuality are specifically directed to the problem of insistent drive rather than to paraphilia, mania, or character disorder.

Concluding Remarks

It was only a short time ago that sexual life was conceptualized as consisting of two phases—arousal and orgasm. Now a third phase, desire, has been added to the understanding of sexual psychophysiology. With this conceptual advance, three other realizations that center on diversity have come into clearer focus:

1. Biology, culture, and personality interact to shape highly individualistic adult patterns of sexual desire.
2. There are many forms of sexual desire problems.
3. Clinicians can be useful to people with desire problems in a number of ways.

The clinical field of sexuality has made genuine progress, in large part because these diversities have been appreciated.

To be sure, much remains to be learned about the nature of sexual desire and how to help those with too little or too much of it. Progress may come from many fields, because sexual desire is at one and the same time a neuroendocrine physiological event, a product of personality development, a subjective barometer of an interpersonal relationship, a cognitive reflector of the social and moral self, and more. The challenge to the therapist is to be able to learn from those who speak of sexual desire in different technical languages and from different perspectives. This is not just a matter of psychoanalysts and behavior therapists learning from one another. It is a question of how to facilitate the mental health profession's grasp of emerging work in sources as diverse as philosophy (Scruton, 1986) and neuropharmacology (Foreman & Moss, 1979).

Finally, in some ultimate sense, understanding sexual desire requires coming to grips with a more basic question: "What is the nature of any kind of desire?" This philosophical issue is so fundamental that I have been avoiding it for fear that some of the seemingly useful notions about sexual desire will evaporate in uncertainty and confusion.

References

Abel, G., & Blanchard, E. (1974). Role of fantasy in the treatment of sexual deviation. *Archives of General Psychiatry, 30*(4), 467–475.

Arentewicz, G., & Schmidt, G. (1983). *The treatment of sexual disorders: Concepts and techniques of couple therapy.* New York: Basic Books.

Bradford, J. (1983). Research on sex offenders: Recent trends. *Clinics of North America, 6*(4), 715–731.

Bancroft, J., & Wu, F. (1983). Changes in erectile responsiveness during androgen replacement therapy. *Archives of Sexual Behavior, 12,* 59–66.

Compton, A. (1981). On the psychoanalytic theory of instinctual drives: The beginnings of Freud's drive theory. *Psychoanalytic Quarterly, 50,* 190–218.

Foreman, M., & Moss, R. (1979). Role of hypothalamic dopaminergic receptors in the control of lordosis behavior in the femle rat. *Physiology and Behavior, 22,* 283–289.

Freud, S. (1957). On the universal tendency to debasement in the sphere of love. In J. Strachey (Ed. and Trans.), *Standard edition of the complete psychological works of Sigmund Freud* (Vol. 11). London: Hogarth Press. (Original work published 1912)

Kaplan, H. (1979). *Disorders of sexual desire.* New York: Brunner/Mazel.

Levine, S. (1984). An essay on the nature of sexual desire. *Journal of Sex and Marital Therapy, 10,* 83–96.

Levine, S., & Shumaker, R. E. (1983). Increasingly Ruth: Towards understanding sex reassignment. *Archives of Sexual Behavior, 12,* 247–261.

MacLean, P. (1975). Brain mechanisms of primal sexual function and related behavior. In M. Sandler & G. L. Gessa (Eds.), *Sexual behavior, pharmacology and biochemistry.* New York: Raven Press.

Martin, C. (1981). Factors affecting sexual functioning in 60–79-year-old married males. *Archives of Sexual Behavior. 10,* 399–420.

Scharff, D. (1982). *The sexual relationship: An object relations view of sex and the family.* London: Routledge & Kegan Paul.

Schein, M., Zyzanski, S., Levine, S., Medalie, J., Dickman, R., & Alemagno, S. (1988). The frequency of sexual problems among family practice patients. *Journal of Research in Family Medicine, 7,* 122–134.

Scruton, R. (1986). *Sexual desire: A philosophical investigation.* London: Weidenfeld & Nicolson.

Segraves, R. T., Madsen, R., Carter, C. S., & Davis, J. M. (1985). Erectile dysfunction associated with pharmacological agents in diagnosis. In R. T. Segraves & H. W. Schoenberg (Eds.), *Diagnosis and treatment of erectile disturbances.* New York: Plenum Press.

Stoller, R. (1975). *Preversion: The erotic form of hatred.* New York: Pantheon Books.

Talmadge, L. D., & Talmadge, W. C. (1986). Relational sexuality: An understanding of low sexual desire. *Journal of Sex and Marital Therapy, 12,* 3–21.

3

An Object Relations Approach to Inhibited Sexual Desire

David E. Scharff

David Scharff is an unusually gifted clinical psychiatrist who has been able to integrate traditional sex therapy with an object relations approach to individual and couple treatment. Scharff believes that object-related difficulties play a far greater role in sexual problems than has been heretofore acknowledged. In the case of problems of desire, Scharff believes that an understanding of the object relations of the patient is essential to successful treatment outcome.

Scharff acknowledges the contributions of Fairbairn in his conceptualization of the individual ego as containing a system of internal objects and parts of the self that are in dynamic interaction. He suggests that we decode the world and approach sexuality as a function of our internalizations of past exciting and rejecting objects and current conscious central ego assessments. Desire is defined as the emotion that characterizes the libidinal ego's longing for its object. However, the rejecting object system (the antilibidinal system) may interfere with the experience of desire if the object is viewed as rejecting, persecuting, angry, frustrating, or negligent. In this case, the individual will probably complain of inhibited or absent sexual interest. On the other hand, in instances of exaggerated sexual desire, the ego acts in such a way as to repress the rejecting object and behaves in an overly sweet or sexually stimulating manner; that is, sex is used to control the object.

In understanding a couple's relationship, Scharff suggests that we must understand each individual's projective and introjective identifications of significant objects, for the nature of these will help predict whether partners will behave in an empathic or hostile manner to each other. Scharff indicates that all relationships contain conscious and unconscious aspects—current interactions and projective identifications based on the partners' individual histories. Assessment involves understanding the role of internal objects in the inhibition or exaggeration of sexual desire.

Scharff moves readily between object relations therapy and traditional sex therapy in his work with individuals and couples. He explores the systemic nature of the relationship as well as the contributions of each of the partners. At the heart of his object relations approach to treatment is the analysis of the transference and countertransference relationship. Here Scharff suggests that it is important to understand both the focused transference which derives from internal objects and the contextual transference, which expresses the patients' experience of difficulties in feeling held and cared for, because if the latter is negative, it is unlikely that treatment will proceed successfully.

As Scharff's chapter indicates, he is an extremely talented clinician who feels as comfortable with individual psychoanalysis as with family therapy, and hence is able to switch therapeutic formats as the situation dictates. His elucidation of object relations theory is particularly helpful for the clinician unfamiliar with this approach, because it can help clarify why we may fail with patients who present with desire problems but are refractory to more directive sex therapy approaches.

David E. Scharff, M.D., is Director of the Washington School of Psychiatry, Washington, D.C., and Associate Clinical Professor of Psychiatry at the Uniformed Services University of the Health Sciences, Bethesda, Maryland and at Georgetown University Medical School, Washington, D.C. He is the author of three books: Between Two Worlds: Aspects of the Transition from School to Work *(with J. M. M. Hill);* The Sexual Relationship: An Object Relations View of Sex and the Family, *and* Object Relations Family Therapy *(with Jill Scharff, M.D.).*

In her description of "inhibited sexual desire" (ISD) in 1977, Kaplan identified a large group of patients who exhibit a limited response to the sex therapy treatment format introduced by Masters and Johnson (1970) and modified by her (Kaplan, 1974). It was only after the development of sex therapy that patients who had a physical sexual dysfunction could be differentiated from those whose difficulty stemmed more clearly from deeper anxiety, and who therefore were closer to the kinds of patients psychodynamic therapists had for years thought they should be able to treat with intensive, insight-oriented psychotherapy or psychoanalysis.

Kaplan's 1979 book, *Disorders of Sexual Desire*, described desire disorders as a spectrum of difficulties stemming from varying kinds of anxiety and occurring at different phases of the subjective experience of desire. As she then noted, the syndrome of a congenitally low level of sexual desire is rare, since most cases that present clinically ultimately represent an inhibition of desire rather than its congenital absense. However, there are some cases in which desire is impaired because of toxic or organic disease— for instance, as a result of ccrtain medications, a number of endocrine diseases, some chronic diseases, and chronic pain (Horwith & Imperato-McGinley, 1983; Kaplan, 1983).

Kaplan noted, "Clinical experience suggests that for the desire phase dysfunctions the relationship between immediate and remote pathogenic factors is closer than it is for many genital phase dysfunctions" (1979, p. 154). In approaching these disorders, the therapist needs most to understand the effect of underlying factors; of the more distant causes of anxiety; and, finally, of the patient's history of internal objects. This is true both because the causes of disorders of desire will often be located in these more distant causes of anxiety, and because of the relatively greater role of insight in initial treatment and in the stabilization of results. If it is true, as Kaplan states (1979), that the cases coming for help with sexual disorders represent more difficult cases than when the field was young, then we need to investigate the complexities underlying the whole spectrum of cases that now come to sex therapists and psychotherapists.

Object relations theory gives us a way of understanding the complexity of the development of the individual, and it does so in a language that readily translates into the realm of sexual and emotional relationships. In *The Sexual Relationship* (Scharff, 1982), I described the way in which sexual and psychological development is rooted in family experience. This point of view allows us to take findings from the assessment of each partner's intrapsychic life and apply them to marital and sexual interaction. It also allows us to examine a couple's interpersonal emotional and physical relationship for the impact of current events on their intrapsychic functioning. To help us move easily between these areas in this chapter, I outline the basis (1) for an object relations view of individual development and psychological organization; (2) for an object relations view of sexual functioning; and (3) for an object relations view of marriage and the family. Finally, I turn to (4) an object relations approach to assessment and treatment that follows from these.

An Object Relations Theory of the Individual

Ronald Fairbairn (1952) revised Freud's notion of individual development by positing that what organizes the baby in the beginning is not the unfolding of a sequence of innate drives, but the baby's innate need for a relationship. The vicissitudes of the relationship to the mother (or other primary caretaker) in the beginning, and the subsequent relationships with the few primary members of the child's closest family, determine psychological development. The child progressively internalizes experience with the mother and family, but it is a version of experience that reflects the developing child's limited capacity to understand.

Fairbairn held that the child begins with a pristine, undifferentiated ego, but internalizes those aspects of experience that are too unpleasant to be tolerated and splits them off from relatively conscious internal experience, repressing them precisely because they are intolerably unpleasant. In this way the child, having an original unitary ego, modifies its experience of an original unsplit, "preambivalent object"; in sorting out experience in this way, it modifies its own psyche at the same time. The child also takes in aspects of good experiences with the object and organizes mental structure around them. Although Fairbairn thought that the child only internalizes the good experiences with the object to compensate for the bad experiences already internalized, the fact that every child also internalizes good experiences makes it likely that both good and bad experience are internalized from the beginning on an equal footing (Scharff & Scharff, 1987). The difference is that because they are so painful, the "bad" object experiences are subject to repression or "defensive exclusion," to use Bowlby's (1980) term.

What is repressed in each case is (1) *an image of the object,* along with (2) *a part of the self in interaction with that object,* and (3) *the affect that characterizes the painful interaction* (Sutherland, 1963). This constellation can be termed "an internal object system." There are three principal internal object systems, identified by Fairbairn (1963) and shown diagramatically in Figure 1.

1. *The central ego and its ideal object.* The central ego and its object constitute the relatively conscious and relatively reasonable set of rela-

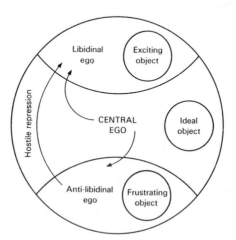

Figure 1. Fairbairn's model of psychic organization. (From *The Sexual Relationship: An Object Relations View of Sex and the Family* by D. E. Scharff, 1982, London: Routledge & Kegan Paul. Reprinted by permission.)

tionships which each of us has internalized. The ideal object is characterized as neither excessively rejecting nor excessively exciting.

The other two systems are both "bad object" systems, in that they are associated with painful affect.

2. *The libidinal ego and object.* The libidinal object is felt to be excessively exciting of need, or, as Ogden (1983) has noted, is felt to be "tantalizing." Part of the self or ego is attached to this object by an affect of painful and unsatisfied longing.

3. *The antilibidinal ego and object.* This term, which seems difficult to many people, was introduced by Fairbairn for the sake of consistency. It refers to the kind of "bad" object that is felt to be rejecting, negligent, or persecuting. A part of the self adheres to a relationship, so that while the relationship is characterized by anger, frustration, and hate, it is sticky nevertheless.

It is not possible to do justice to this rather dense theoretical construct here, or to the internal dynamics that follow from Fairbairn's formulation. The reader who is unfamiliar with them should still be able to take away the notion of a system of internal objects and parts of the self that make up the organization of the individual's psyche, and that have a dynamic relationship to each other. At a clinical level, we can say that relatively unmetabolized aspects of the mother, the father, and a few other central figures, and of the self in relationship to each of these, constitute the unconscious world. The more conscious and more reasonable aspect of psychic functioning, the central ego, manages relatively reasonable relationships in the day-to-day world. The degree to which the central ego's functioning is invaded by the repressed aspects of relationships varies with the amount of splitting the individual does. This is determined by the individual's experience with his or her family during the entire period of development.

However, an internal object does not represent a simple internalization of a concrete experience. Rather, it represents the imprint of experience as the individual understood it at the time. Thus a child whose actual mother (i.e., external object) is sympathetic to its needs but is temporarily too busy or too ill to attend to them, still partly takes her in as an internal "bad mother," even if the child also consciously understands the reasons for her temporary rejection. Or a mother who is teasing and exciting at a moment of play is introjected as an exciting object when she cannot be available in this way. Thus every child, no matter how well parented, internalizes experiences of painfully exciting and rejecting objects.

The Object Relations of Sexual Development

We can now say that sexual desire bears an immediate relationship to exciting and rejecting objects. Desire is the emotion that characterizes the libidinal ego's longing for its object. Fairbairn's exciting or libidinal object includes sexuality as a major source of excitement. Sexual relatedness is a model of the excited attraction between two people. In the beginning, the infant longs for a relationship. Because the infant relates primarily through physical processes in the beginning, the earliest relationship is mediated through the way the mother holds and handles the baby, through the baby's excitement as she responds to its physical needs, and through the way the baby signals and responds to her. In turn, the mother experiences a rise and fall of excitement in response to the baby. The relationship is not sexual in these beginnings, but sexual development is born out of this partnership, which Winnicott called "the psycho-somatic partnership" because psyche and soma are closely intertwined during this period (Winnicott, 1960).

Later sexual development grows out of this original psycho-somatic partnership. At certain points, sexual issues take the leading edge of development—for instance, during the period when the 1-year-old learns about his or her genitals through self-stimulation, which becomes a focused masturbation during the second year. The only precondition for a child's learning masturbation is adequate holding and handling by a mother who has an adequate emotional relationship to the baby (Kleeman, 1966, 1977). So there is a way in which infantile masturbation is a marker for the internalization of such a relationship.

Later periods in which sexual development takes the lead in overall emotional growth include the phallic and Oedipal periods, in which the child sexualizes relationships and the parents respond to this sexualization with their own reactions, which reflect the quality of their internalized objects. There is again a pressure toward sexualization within the family in the early adolescence of a child; at this point, it is clustered around the child's uncertainty whether to keep the excited sexual interests inside the family circle or whether to venture outside to the peer group. Most older adolescents have managed to focus their sexual interest well away from the family.

We can now see that Fairbairn's model of the need-exciting object and the part of the self that longs for it is a model of *desire for a relationship,* and that when this is connected developmentally with the part of the psycho-somatic partnership that becomes sexualized, we have a developmental model for sexual desire. What can we now say about factors that interfere with sexual desire?

It is to the rejecting object system—or the antilibidinal system, as Fairbairn called it—that we now look for interferences with sexual desire. In this part of the individual's psyche, the object is felt to be rejecting, persecuting, angry, frustrating, or negligent. Although part of the self is tied to this object, it is a wedding of anger, frustration, and hate. These are obviously not emotions of ordinary sexual interest. Fairbairn made an interesting clinical note that is crucial for our purposes. He said that the rejecting object system takes an attitude of uncompromising harshness toward the need-exciting object, acting to repress it further (see Figure 1). In clinical terms, we can say that it is far less painful to be angry at someone than it is to retain the painful longing of unrequited love. It is this dynamic relationship between internal objects that forms the basis for the repression of ordinary sexual desire. But this mechanism has other interesting features. To begin with, I have been using these terms partly as though they apply to unconscious internal aspects of psychological functioning, and partly as though they apply to conscious functioning. The fact is that in the clinical situation, both are true. What I have said so far applies to the internal organization of the individual spouse, but it also is a guide to the way two people treat each other. Thus, partners who have failed to find love or sexual satisfaction will often turn to angry and bitter ways of relating, which serve to cover the painful longing that each partner has in feeling unloved.

The opposite defensive arrangement also occurs in the case of exaggerated sexual desire. The libidinal ego and object act to repress the rejecting object, and in this case the individual or couple act in syrupy-sweet or sexually overexcited ways in order to keep from recognizing the pain of underlying rejection, loneliness, or anger. In this picture we may see an oversexualized couple or individual, in whom we can sense an underlying anger and frustration. We also see the hypersexual individual whose entire personality is organized to exaggerate sexual longing as a defensive arrangement to repress the pain of the rejecting object, and who uses sex to control the object.

The Object Relations of Couples and Marriage

These emotional arrangements may be partly conscious and partly unconscious. A paradoxical situation exists, in that many unconscious aspects of an individual are observable in interactions with sexual or marital partners, or in the situation of transference to a therapist. This happens because of "projective identification" and "introjective identification." These terms, coined by Melanie Klein (1946/1975), describe the process by which one person projects an unwanted part of self outside into another, and the process by which a person takes in an identification with another, respectively. These are described succinctly by Segal: Introjective identification "is the result when the object is introjected into the ego which then identifies with some or all of its characteristics." Projective identification "is the result of the projection of parts of the self into an object. It may result in the object being perceived as having acquired the characteristics of the projected part of the self but it can also result in the self becoming identified with the object of its projection" (Segal, 1973, p. 126). There are many motives for projective identification: to get rid of a hated part of the self or to get it into a "better" object to control the source of danger. But valued parts of the self are also projected in this way in order to keep them safe from internal harm (Segal, 1973, p. 27).

Klein saw projective identification as primarily operating within the single individual. It can be observed during treatment as a transference phenomenon. Dicks (1967), Main (1966), and Zinner (1976) have developed this notion as a phenomenon that exists mutually between marital partners, or "mutual projective identification." This means that the relationship between marital partners is by definition characterized by the mutuality of projective identifications, which on the one hand form the normal basis for empathy and in-depth understanding between two people, and which on the other hand give rise to fundamental misunderstanding by the action of projected unwanted parts of the self onto each other. When this occurs, the other person is treated and is *actually felt to be* the hated, tantalizing, or frustrating object that has been projected. The essence of projective identification is that it is an *unconscious process,* and that therefore the other person (spouse, partner, or therapist) actually feels and behaves as if he or she is that part of the projector—in other words, is taken over by the projection without knowing it. Box and her colleagues at the Tavistock Clinic in London (Box, 1984; Box, Copley, Magagna, & Mousta-ki, 1981; Williams, 1981), and Jill Scharff and I, working with colleagues of the Washington School of Psychiatry's Psychoanalytic Family Therapy Program (Scharff & Scharff, 1987), have elaborated on the use of projective identification in the transference–countertransference exchange as the basis of an object relations treatment approach to families and couples. In this approach, the therapist is willing to accept the projections, knowing that this involves unconsciously absorbing them at first, and then to work to use this countertransference experience to understand the couple's failed relationship and the way it skews their transference to the therapist. This use of the transference–countertransference interaction is the hallmark of the object relations contribution to psychosexual therapy.

The Psycho-Somatic Partnership and the Sexual Relationship

What I have said so far establishes the basis for an object relations approach to individual and marital therapy. When we think of the treatment of sexual difficulties, it is helpful to recall the earliest physical relationship—the psycho-somatic partnership between mother and infant. The adult sexual relationship is the most intensely physical relationship since that first psycho-somatic exchange. Echoes of the relationship between mother and child intertwine with the vicissitudes of the adult sexual relationship. But as with any psychosomatic route, internal psychological factors of enormous complexity have to be modified to fit the relatively simple pathways of response the sexual organs can give. Thus, fear of engulfment by the object may result in premature ejaculation, or fear of intimacy with an object that is felt to threaten danger or rejection may result in ISD. Which symptom will result is a complex, multidetermined matter, but symptoms should make sense if we can get a good object relations history of the individual and couple. The complications of human development make it unlikely that we will be able to predict that a given developmental situation will lead to a certain syndrome.

In describing the interactive elements of the couple, I mean to make it clear that the couple has a relationship that involves the following elements:

1. A current relationship, which is at least partly conscious and susceptible of reasonable understanding.
2. A shared history of interaction, which is also at least partly conscious.
3. An unconscious aspect of the relationship, which is characterized by mutual projective identification that is both normal and pathological, and that unconsciously is partly reassuring and partly disruptive.

Therefore, the relationship is based partly on current interactions, partly on the couple's shared history, and partly on projections of the partners' individual histories.

Finally, we can note that those internal object patterns that are laid down early in life have a tenacious quality, tending to influence everything that comes later. It is a fundamental tenet of treatment and of development that internal objects can be modified and new ones added throughout life. It is this possibility that gives hope not only to treatment, but to marriage, to the growing of one's children, and to all new relationships.

Assessment

History Taking

Evaluation from the object relations point of view involves an assessment of the role of internal objects in the inhibition or accentuation of sexual desire. This is not to underestimate the role of the current relationship, nor of the specific aspects of sexual functioning that may be involved—all the aspects of specific sex therapy that we began to learn from Masters and Johnson (1966, 1970). But it is to say that object-related difficulties play a role in many more sexual difficulties than was at first thought. In the case of problems of desire, object relations play a decisive role for most of our patients. This is not to say that the difficulty is profound in all cases. We still need to differentiate among (1) situational or transient difficulty in sexual desire; (2) the kind of difficulty that has become chronic and indigenous to a relationship; and (3) those inhibitions of sexual desire that belong to one individual and are not a function of the current relationship. Consequently, the assessment phase should consider the following areas specifically pertinent to the object relations of the couple:

1. The current status and history of the individual's and/or couple's sexual relationship.
2. The current status and history of the individual's and/or couple's overall intimate relationships.
3. An estimate of the degree of congruence or disparity between sex and the overall capacity for intimacy.
4. An in-depth family history, which includes as much information as is available about the relationship of each individual to parents, siblings, and other important figures. Such a history should include not only the quality of the bond of the person to the parents of the same and opposite sex, but also the feeling about the bond between the parents themselves at different stages, the adequacy of the parents' functioning as parents, and the quality of peer relationships as the individual moved away from the family.

More important than information per se is the *feel* the therapist gets during the history-taking process. Some of the "feel" comes directly from the patient through open and conscious communication, while other aspects will be more apparent from other clues (e.g., vagueness in the description of the parents, a whitewashing of relationships, or a furious tirade against one or both parents).

The Spectrum of Desire Disorders

The gathering of this kind of history allows us to estimate where the individual or couple falls in the spectrum of desire disorders. By this, I mean that we try to place the difficulty in relation to a number of areas representing both internal and external object relations:

1. *The couple's marital relationship.* At the strong end is the committed, caring, and trusting relationship; at the weak end is the angry, mutually frustrating, and distrusting one. In the middle are the needy but workable ones: loving and longing, but hurt and in retreat.

2. *The object relations history of each individual as it impinges on sexual functioning and capacity for intimacy.* Here the spectrum is large and complex. At one end is the person with a capacity for intimacy, but not for

physical intimacy. At the other is the person with no qualms about sex, but little capacity for emotional intimacy. In the middle there is the person with ambivalence about both. We also have the situational elements: the person who can combine physical and emotional intimacy when relaxed or on vacation, or with someone who has no permanent claim on a relationship, or with a spouse who is subservient but not one who is strident or dominating. The list of these conditions is long, but we must assess how much the situational issues can be resolved with brief therapy or with couples work, and how much the internal psychological life of the individual will need to be addressed. Often, at the beginning, we can only guess.

In addition, we must make some estimate as to the depth of the individual intrapsychic issues. Although it is not possible to be entirely accurate about this at the beginning, our assessment does determine our recommendation. Once we begin treatment, we need to monitor the early treatment to see whether a modification in the plan should be considered.

3. *The current family constellation: the impact of the desire disorder on the current family, and the impact of the family on the couple and individual.* Here I include the presence of children, living arrangements, and the developmental state of the family. Often it is the birth of a child that causes a change in sexual patterns for a couple, or that triggers loss of sexual desire in one of the parents. Other developmental family steps, such as the last child leaving home, can have similar repercussions. But the couple's sexual difficulty also often has an effect on the children, and the kinds of changes that are set in motion may tend to begin a cycle of difficulty.

Transference During Assessment

A final aspect of information—one that is crucial to the course of treatment—comes from the early transference reaction that the assessment process often triggers. This is illustrated in the following case example.

Tamara's husband, Roy, insisted on an evaluation about their sexual life "when her excuses finally ran out." Both were aged 38, and they had been married 4½ years. During the marriage Tamara had never liked sex, although it had been fully gratifying to her before their marriage. It was at the moment that she had first felt fully committed to Roy that the sex had become vulnerable, and soon after that it had become an unpleasant chore. Despite this, she was capable of arousal and orgasm on the few occasions when they made love.

In the initial couples interview with me and a woman colleague, Tamara was guarded and anxious. She said it was all her problem. As she valued her marriage, she owed it to Roy to get help. In an individual interview with my cotherapist she said she was relieved to be able to talk; she remained vague, however, especially about her parents, whom she idealized in an uninformative manner. When the therapist made a tentative comment that she might have more mixed feelings about her mother than she had so far acknowledged, Tamara erupted into a rage, screaming, "I won't stand to be treated like that! Are you just going to criticize me?" She quickly recovered, and apologetically said that this kind of outburst was the kind she increasingly directed at Roy and her children. She could not understand these eruptions, which seemed to come from nowhere. Why did she only rage at those she loved most? The interview concluded amicably, and in a subsequent interview with me, Tamara was both more reasonable and more insightful.

On the basis of this event, we guessed that Tamara felt misunderstood and criticized by her mother, but had repressed a great deal of the persecuting and rejecting object. From the differential transference reactions to me and to the female cotherapist, we hypothesized that she used an excited idealization of her father in support of the repression of the "bad object" aspects of her mother. In this early assessment, it appeared that it was the "bad" image of the mother that was projected onto her children and husband when she raged at them. Why this was expressed almost purely by Tamara's ISD could not yet be said.

Other aspects of the assessment were of interest here, some of them typical of this kind of difficulty with sexual desire. So far, there had been no significant deterioration of the marital relationship, nor did Tamara complain of a difficult relationship. Roy echoed her contention that their intimacy was generally good and that they had a loving relationship. He said he would support whatever was recommended for them together or for her individually. Our overall evaluation led us to believe that their relationship was good, but that it was maintained by Tamara's internal splitting of painful object relations into the sexual arena, and by her repression of sexual desire. Unconsciously, she held sex to be a situation fraught with danger because it threatened to release aspects of her repressed bad objects, which for many years had been inextricably intertwined with sexuality. No more could be said at this point about how this had come about. On the basis of this assessment, and of Tamara and Roy's agreement that her problem had a life of its own independent from their relationship, we recommended psychoanalysis to Tamara, and she agreed.

The Onset of ISD

In addition to illustrating the workings of transference in the assessment, Tamara's story highlights features of the kind of ISD that appears at a certain moment in a relationship. Often it appears at the point of marriage, although for Tamara it hit before marriage, at the moment when she first felt committed to Roy. Later, in analysis, she remembered that this had also happened before marriage in a previous long-term relationship. There also, it had happened at the point she had made a commitment to the man.

Object relations gives us an interesting way of understanding why these shifts are so common. In courtship, couples are drawn together by the resonance between their libidinal or need-exciting object systems. They project into each other aspects of their internal objects that hold out the promise of exciting and fully satisfying sexual and emotional needs. This mutually idealized projective identification has a vigor that represses the rejecting objects, allowing the couple to share the feeling that all bad objects are now safely outside the universe they are constructing together. This must be so, for if the rejecting object aspect of the relationship is too prominent, the couple will be wary of each other and unable to make a commitment.

However, whenever the relationship finally achieves the kind of commitment that makes it a new primary relationship, then the repressed aspects of each of the partners seek expression within the relationship. They do so because each of us seeks to be loved for our whole selves in our primary relationships. With this "return of the repressed bad objects," the bad part of the self also has to be dealt with (Fairbairn, 1952). Our patients with ISD have managed a kind of psychosomatic splitting and repression, in which the relationship with their bad objects is tied up with sexual functioning, and the renewed efforts to maintain repression of the bad objects requires the continued repression of their sexual interest. Why this should be so is specific for each patient. The reasons may be clarified during the evaluation, but they may not emerge until treatment has gone on for some time.

Psychoanalysis for Inhibited Sexual Desire

Tamara's partially successful treatment offers illustration of the kind of understanding that may eventually be achieved in treatment.

She had four psychoanalytic sessions a week for $2\frac{1}{2}$ years. During psychoanalysis, she discovered that she had idealized a largely absent father and had a great deal of bitterness about her mother, which she had previously denied. For instance, after some months of analysis, she reported a dream:

> I was at home, pushing furniture against the walls of my living room to make more space, trying to arrange a table like our neighbors have done in a way I like. Mother was there. She said, "That looks terrible. You should put it back the way it was." I remember being really angry she said that. When I woke, it occurred to me my mother is always there in my house telling me how to rearrange it. If the house signified my mind, then she's there, too.

We can see that this dream was a metaphor for Tamara's attempt to make more space in her body for sexual interests, now inhibited by her internal image of a harsh mother. This dream led to material about how mother had also criticized Tamara's childhood masturbation, and led to Tamara's realization that she could not admire her own genitals (my "living room"). The rejecting internal mother continued to forbid sex. With this realization, Tamara began to masturbate after years of abstinence, and tenuously initiated sex with her husband a few days later.

As the analysis progressed, I was treated in the transference as a marginally good father, more available than her own idealized but largely absent father. But I constantly felt in danger that she would suddenly brand me as the critical and disapproving mother. If I tried to link her dreams to her sexual difficulty, I immediately became the probing mother. When I once questioned Tamara's practice of allowing her children in her bed, since I considered that to be one of the ways she fended off sexual demands, she said I was just like her critical mother. Then she had another dream:

> I was in my childhood bedroom. I heard a noise, so I went into my parents' room, where I took a stick off Mother's night table. I got frightened and ran back to my room.

This dream was a memory of finding a thermometer by her mother's side of the bed—certain proof to the preadolescent Tamara that her mother had sex with her father and that the Catholic couple was using the thermometer as an aid in birth control. It also represented stealing her father's penis from her mother. This session was followed by another dream:

> I was in my family's Victorian house, under the old grand entrance for coaches. My brother and I were playing King and Queen. My sister pushed me and I fell down the stairs.

This dream of her wishing to take her mother's place and being injured for wanting to do so came near the end of the analytic work. Tamara had become more openly critical of her mother, and was just realizing her longing to take her mother's place. Along with these feelings came memories of how she missed her father during his many extended absences while she was growing up. Tamara also connected her mother's reputed antisexual Catholic attitude to Tamara's own guilt over an abortion she had had before her marriage. Despite two subsequent successful pregnancies, the abortion confirmed her own badness for Tamara, thus tempering her right to be angry at her mother or to allow herself to recognize her sexual feeling for her father. In her current life, sexual feeling for her husband had to be inhibited lest it harm her, as she had presumably previously wished to harm her mother and feared harm from her in return.

As this material began to emerge, Tamara grew wary of me in the transference. She resumed the practice of taking her daughter into bed with her, and when I wondered if she was doing so because she felt a renewed sexual threat from inside herself, she felt I was again criticizing her. While I could link this wariness of me with the emerging sexual and competitive themes, I could not keep Tamara from acting on the building fright she experienced from the relentlessly emerging sexual feeling. Not long after this, she decided to stop analysis. She did so at a time that her husband changed jobs and lost the good insurance they had for analysis. When she did stop, she was having periods of passionate sexual feeling for her husband, alternating with periods of no sexual feeling. She had stopped raging at her children and husband, and achieved a new energy in her work.

In this case, analysis was moderately successful in the treatment of ISD, although it was more thoroughly successful in treating the patient's other family relationships and work. Although the improvement in sexual functioning was intermittent, a trial of sex therapy would probably not have added to the result, since the patient was already completely aware of her own sense of inner blockade. She was so terrified of the emergence of sexual feeling that more direct pressure would likely have driven her from therapy even sooner.

Treatment

The methods of treatment available are those that are familiar to practitioners schooled in the treatment of sexual disorders. They include the following:

1. Sex therapy
2. Couples therapy
3. Intensive individual therapy, including psychoanalysis
4. The phasing and combining of treatment modalities, including family therapy

I want to make two preliminary comments about treatment before giving additional case illustrations.

Treatment of the Individual with a Desire Disorder Who Has No Partner

The individual patient with a desire disorder is often more difficult to treat, partly because our options are more limited. We can offer psychoanalysis, individual psychotherapy, or group psychotherapy. The therapy may include a behavioral component, the use of fantasy enhancement, or other modifications. Part of the difficulty is that the individual patient with ISD or a hypersexual response will often also have difficulty in making relationships; this may well be the case because the person defensively seeks isolation for fear of threatening aspects of the internal world projected into external objects. When this is true, our job is more difficult because this fear of relationships becomes a theme in the transference, inhibiting the treatment relationship in the same way it inhibits sexual desire.

Transference and Countertransference in the Treatment of Disorders of Desire

Several of the treatment vignettes given below include references to the transference and countertransference, which are at the heart of an object relations approach to treatment (Scharff & Scharff, 1987). There has been debate about their relevance to the treatment of sexual disorders, so that there are few references to the constructive use of transference in the treatment of sexual disorders (Kaplan, 1979; Levay, Kagle, & Weissberg, 1979).

I differentiate between two types of transference. The intense "focused transference" is that transference in which the therapist becomes a screen for the playing out of the internal object relations of the individual. This type of transference characterizes the unconscious aspects of the couple's relationship, and it is seen in intensive treatments that go on over many months or years.

But each individual and each couple bring a more immediate transference to therapy—a transference to the therapist's capacity to provide the holding and manage the psychological space for treatment. I have called this transference the "contextual transference" (Scharff & Scharff, 1987). Attention to the couple's contextual transference—that is, to their confidence in the therapist to provide safety and help—and the therapist's countertransference to this aspect of the relationship will provide immediate and crucial clues as to trouble in the couple's relationship and their shared attitude toward the potential of the therapist to provide help for their problems. Thus a couple with a determinedly positive contextual transference is easier to treat than one in which the partners share a view of the world as a dangerous or rejecting place and bring this shared attitude with them when they meet the therapist. The ramifications of this use of transference are too great to explore in this chapter, but they are crucial to the practice of an object relations therapy. In the case already discussed, Tamara's early difficulty in the contextual transference could eventually be understood as a series of focused, object-related issues. But it was her continued difficulty with contextual transference that limited her success and eventually led to her discontinuing treatment.

Illustrations of Treatment

Treatment begins in the evaluation phase. The following two cases illustrate opposite outcomes: In the first, the case stopped because there was no basis for the marriage to continue; in the second, growth during evaluation ushered in the next stage of treatment.

Loss of Desire and Marital Failure

Mr. H brought his wife because she had lost all interest in sex with him. He had already taken her to a gynecologist, who had given her testosterone injections. After each injection she had become hypersexual, and they had had intercourse several times in impulsive ways (e.g., she would grab him on the stairs of their house). Without injections, she had no interest in him. Could I help?

Mrs. H was uncommunicative in the joint interview, but when I saw her alone, she said that her husband was a confirmed alcoholic, insensitive to her, and self-centered. She felt she had catered to him for years, but she was currently earning a college degree in order to become independent and to leave him. She was glad he traveled a great deal; she disliked having him home. She felt intense sexual desires for men in her classes and masturbated with fantasies of intercourse with them, but she had avoided actual sexual interaction with them for fear it would compromise her legal marital rights. She could not explain why she had agreed to the testosterone injections, which I thought were indicative of the same passive compliance that had kept her in the marriage for years.

Mr. H was incapable of understanding his wife's point of view. He denied alcoholism, although his own description of his drinking established the diagnosis. He was incapable of opening issues that might lie between him and his wife, and remained fixed on the idea that the problem was confined to her loss of sexual interest in him. When I finally said that there was no more I could do, he left—indignant at my incompetence—and immediately sought remedy from another therapist.

The Use of Revelation of Affairs During the Evaluation as a Temporary Boost to Sexual Desire

This patient experienced a temporary loosening of sexual inhibition when her husband's one brief affair was revealed during the evaluation. This was used to ease her entrance into further treatment.

Mr. and Mrs. J came after 11 years of marriage and two children, because she had never been interested in sex. She had enjoyed the cuddling and holding of courtship, but during the honeymoon she had had so much vaginal pain and spasm that they had not been able to achieve penetration. A hymenectomy and advice that "Things will be all right" left them on their own to work out a sexual life. Eventually, Mrs. J accommodated to her husband's wishes. For the next 10 years they had intercourse two or three times a week, but she never felt desire or had orgasms. The rhythm was set by his pressure and her reluctance. If she dragged her feet for more than 3 or 4 days, he began to get angry; as she said, "I knew I had better give him the sex he wanted." Although sometimes their sex was bitter, she usually managed to hold her breath and get it over with.

Mr. J had had one affair, a one-night stand on a business trip. He was reluctant to tell his wife for fear of her "psychological fragility." In the transference struggle with me, I could see his struggle to control his wife, and the way she must feel controlled by him. I worked on this issue with him, urging him to use the opportunity to let her see part of the consequences that the sexual problem engendered, but also to "clear the decks" for a more honest and balanced attempt at rebuilding their sexual and marital relationship (Scharff, 1978, 1982; Scharff & Scharff, 1987). Mr. J did tell his wife, and the result was an instantaneous burst of sexual interest—an almost hypersexual response. They made love amidst the tears with an energy and passion Mrs. J had never been able to allow. In the midst of this, she was now also able to say that her parents had been proponents of an exaggerated sexuality, flaunting their own sexual relationship in a way that had always threatened her. It had all spelled catastrophe when they divorced when she was 12. She was then a preadolescent with budding breasts and sexual interests. The blow had been too much for her developing sexual feeling.

Over a period of several weeks, the intense sexuality began to decline. Mrs. J understood that she still did not know how to have orgasms, and she could feel the sexual inhibition return. But the intense period of sexual interest served to convince her that she had been repressing an interest all these years out of fear that it would lead to the same marital disaster that had befallen her mother—abandonment by her idealized and highly sexual father. Mrs. J was now able to ask for a more intense period of sex therapy and to use the newly recovered memories as an aid to understanding her lifelong ISD.

*Successful Psychoanalytic Treatment Followed by a
Transient Loss of Desire in the Spouse*

Following evaluation, the major treatment options are individual therapy and sex therapy. Couples therapy also offers resolution for those cases in which ISD turns out to be marital difficulty. The next example illustrates the use of psychoanalysis to treat a man's profound ISD. It was later followed by brief family work, which treated a reactive loss of desire in his wife and the sexualization of their young daughter's development.

Ron, aged 31, and Sally, aged 30, came to see me after a year of marriage. He had been sexually active before meeting Sally and remained so throughout their courtship. Once they were married, he lost all sexual interest. Typically, he would avoid Sally at night, going to bed hours after she did. The couple had had a brief trial of sex therapy before he saw me, and it had left Ron cold. Sally was desperate. She still loved him, but she wondered if he could ever love her. She had endometriosis, which put her under pressure to get pregnant as soon as possible. She wanted a child and she had been told that pregnancy often cures endometriosis.

During the evaluation, Ron had two dreams. The first was the following:

> I was being crucified by a woman at work. I woke thinking of her as Judas, with the phrase in my head, "You will betray me before the cock crows."

He told me that his mother had been cold and distant and his father had been quite unavailable to him, preferring Ron's more athletic older brother. His mother was in the process of dying during the evaluation. Ron's second dream was as follows:

> The night before Mother died, I dreamt that I was in a hotel room which was furnished like a hospital. My landlady came to me dressed as a whore. I tried to make love to her, grabbing for her breasts and trying to kiss her.

In the office, he said that the landlady looked like his mother. He agreed when Sally said that he was trying one last time to get his mother to love him.

This young man had a clear internalization of a rejecting mother, although his dreams led me to believe that there had been an experience of combined sexualization and rejection with his mother, which led to Ron's withdrawal from the sexual aspect of the relationship in order to desperately preserve a loving aspect of the relationship. In the contextual transference, I felt in his yearning an urgency that looked as though it would support treatment. I recommended psychoanalysis to Ron, and he pursued a difficult analysis over several years to a successful conclusion. The couple was subsequently able to conceive.

I saw them again when their daughter was $2\frac{1}{2}$ years old. She was an anxious girl who masturbated compulsively. Ron's wife, Sally, was now uninterested in sex. Ron told me that when he held his daughter, he felt a rush of feeling that was in part sexual. It was evident that he had an excited

relationship with his daughter, which had begun to sexualize her development (as signified by the excited masturbation), and which also threatened
to exclude his wife. Over a period of a few family sessions, we were able to
discuss his wish to compensate for the lack of love he had felt, and the
resulting sexualization of the relationship to his daughter and resentment in
his wife. As they discussed this, the girl put a father doll and a girl doll in
bed together, sending the mother doll away. When I called this play to their
attention, Ron and Sally understood that there had been an unconscious
shift in their marriage. Sally described her resentment when Ron turned to
their daughter, and her own fear of being pushed out. Ron was able to
adjust his relationship to his wife, calming his penchant for an excited
relationship with his daughter. With this confrontation Sally's anger abated,
and her sexual interest returned promptly. Their daughter also stopped the
pressured masturbation and related to the two of them in less excited ways.

Sex Therapy for Treatment or Extended Evaluation

In the last 10 years sex therapy has offered a major addition to our capacity
to treat ISD. Previously, these problems had always been considered to be in
the province of more deeply seated intrapsychic problems, to be treated with
intensive psychodynamic therapy (Kaplan, 1979). With the application of
sex therapy to these disorders, a number of issues have become clarified.

First, for a significant group of patients, the loss of desire occurs with a
growing disaffection in the marriage. That is to say, the loss of sexual desire
is a reliable indicator of loss of overall marital satisfaction, but the couple
has not yet been able to face this directly. Here the work with the couple
initially entails clarification that the difficulty centers around the marital
dissatisfaction, not with a primary sexual problem. The case of Mr. and
Mrs. H illustrates such a situation, in which the wife's loss of desire
accompanied her wish to leave the marriage.

Second, some of the problems that were formerly thought to be firmly
rooted in more profound psychopathology can now be treated by a combination of sex therapy and psychodynamic interpretive work. Kaplan
(1979) has called this brand of therapy "psychosexual therapy," to make
the point that its efficacy comes from combining the behavioral and educational techniques of sex therapy with the interpretive work of dynamic
psychotherapy.

Third, there is a large group of patients who do indeed have the
profound underlying causes that psychodynamic therapists have long been
familiar with. Here a sex therapy format may still make a significant
contribution, because such patients may not understand the need for an
extended intensive therapy until it can be demonstrated convincingly to
them that the more direct and short-term methods are not enough. In these

cases, sex therapy is used for an extended evaluation; the places in the sex therapy format at which the couple gets stuck offer opportunities for demonstrating where the issues lie within the couple or within one individual, and why the behavioral approach can go no further. Many of these patients are then able to move into intensive psychotherapy or psychoanalysis, knowing now why it is worthwhile to do so. But some patients will opt to stop at this point and to live with the ISD and with their current individual and marital adjustment.

Treatment with Sex Therapy, Individual Therapy, a Women's Group, and Repeat Sex Therapy

In the following case, sex therapy led to an impasse that required intensive individual therapy. Women's group treatment and a few additional sessions of sex therapy were also useful for this couple.

Ginger came reluctantly at her husband Max's insistence. She was 28; he was 37. They came because of her lack of sexual desire, but Max also admitted that he had lifelong premature ejaculation. Ginger acknowledged that she was completely uninterested in sex, and had no wish to change except that it threatened her marriage. Through a stormy evaluation, the cotherapists experienced a battle of control and withholding in the transference, which also characterized the spouses' relationship to each other. Their shared difficulty in trusting spoke for the internal distrust that they handled together partly through sexual symptons. We discovered that Max was having multiple affairs, which had begun during Ginger's pregnancy. She became nauseaed at learning of this, but after a period of couples therapy, she acknowledged that she must have known about their existence. In fact, she had met Max by having an affair with him during his first marriage. She thought his affairs were to some extent the result of her sexual intransigence. He agreed to end the affairs. She agreed to try sex therapy.

Ginger threw herself into sex therapy, but during the period when the sensate focus exercise involved genital arousal, she experienced a dissociative episode. They were in a 12th-floor hotel room when she found herself in the bathtub imagining herself floating to the window and throwing herself out of it. Although terrified, she was able to explore the pressure she felt from the sex therapy. We stopped the sex therapy, and Ginger began individual psychotherapy. Over the next several months, she discovered that she had had an intense rivalry with her mother, who had been depressed and self-effacing. When she was an adolescent, her father had supported the feeling that she would have been a better wife to him than her mother was. So when, as a young woman, she had liked the physical contact and cuddling of the affair and courtship with Max, genital sex had never been what she valued. What she loved was the renewal of the feelings she had felt for her father. Her dread and sexual inhibition had set in after the birth of her daughter, when she felt she would certainly be pushed aside by the new couple (Max and their daughter), just as she and her father had pushed aside her mother.

For a long time, these realizations did not increase Ginger's interest in sex. Then after a year of individual therapy, she and Max were on a trip when she discovered he had torn a page on massage parlors out of the Yellow Pages. This time she confronted him about his return to this behavior. He said that he could no longer stay married without sex. Now, even though she was furious, she suddenly became arousable and interested. She enrolled in a group for nonorgasmic women, learned to masturbate to orgasm, and transferred this into their shared setting. However, she also said that Max must get help for his wanderlust. As she became sexually arousable, he agreed to begin individual psychotherapy himself. His history of a dominating and terrifying mother who idealized him while controlling his father now made sense of his effort to splinter Ginger's control over him by multiple affairs. He was eventually able to settle into a commitment to her. Finally, after her sexual interest was established and his fidelity to a relationship was improved, we used a brief period of sex therapy to treat his remaining premature ejaculation successfully.

This case briefly illustrates the use of several treatment modalities to enhance each other. A crisis during the use of one treatment modality may lead to the highlighting of issues that can be successfully treated with another format. Of particular interest here is that sex therapy was used to highlight the need for individual therapy. In turn, the individual work seemed unsuccessful until a crisis allowed the patient to capitalize on the work she had been doing over the preceding year. The external situation prompted an internal crisis of integration by propelling the patient to a moment of reckoning. It is only then that the psychotherapy was suddenly integrated.

Sex Therapy for ISD Mixed with Sexual Avoidance: A Negative Therapeutic Result

The case just described was one in which the failure of sex therapy convinced the patient to undertake more intensive work. The next case documents that sex therapy can also simply fail as a treatment. Here treatment stopped when the patient decided she did not wish to allow desire to return.

Jessie B was a 48-year-old mother of three who said she was uninterested in sex. She was having a relationship with an older man, Bob, whom she admired and to whom she said she was committed. She had been divorced 10 years earlier after her husband had left her for a younger woman. She had raised her children, who were now young adults, and she valued her privacy. She felt that sexual arousal would bring her back to dependency on a man. So although she loved and admired Bob, with whom she had an exclusive relationship for the last 7 years, she had been fearful of a passionate sexual relationship.

Bob said that he was in love with Jessie, but found it frustrating and hurtful that she avoided sex and rarely got aroused or had orgasms. He felt something crucial was missing from their relationship. Eventually we agreed to a trial of sex therapy for this couple, with a working diagnosis of ISD. Jessie said she wanted to overcome the fears that interfered with her sexual desire.

As they got to the sensate focus exercises with sustained genital massage, Jessie grew more restless and irritable, both with Bob and with me for attempting to explore issues. She now could masturbate to orgasm without Bob present; she did not mind that. But she found it excruciating to do so with him there, or to allow him to "manipulate my genitals." In the same way, attempts in treatment to explore her reluctance brought to mind an aspect of her relationship with her parents: When she had fallen or hurt herself, they had said "Don't cry!" Indeed, their restrained manner, which reflected their British origins, had made the expression of pain or joy difficult. As a child, she had learned not to express any emotion around them for fear of being rejected and diminished. She felt that when she expressed pain, they denied it, and when she expressed joy, they "popped her balloon." She had felt able to have a marginally more expressive relationship in her marriage, but when her husband left—perhaps partly because of her emotional reserve—she shriveled inside and vowed never to become close to anyone again. It had been different with Bob, but only if she managed not to become aroused. Any beginning of arousal now in the exercises frightened her into a more general withdrawal. And in the treatment she found my inquiries intrusive and threatening. Now she felt her only choice was to withdraw from Bob and from the therapy. Despite attempts to support her and to deal with her transference reaction, she did not want to pursue any other therapy, either. She said she preferred to "lick her wounds and regroup." If this relationship could not survive her lack of sexual interest, she would see whether she could again venture another relationship at a later date.

This case presented with a mixed picture. The patient's avoidance of arousal was built on a foundation of a general inhibition of desire—one that had not been so clear during her marriage. While it may have contributed to the marital failure, it surfaced clearly after the hurt of the divorce. Often the mixture of pictures makes it hard to tell which aspect is primary, because the avoidant, almost phobic, picture is built on a foundation of a deeper unconscious resolve to inhibit desire because of the fear of punishment, disapproval, or abandonment by a rejecting object. Once we began sex therapy, it became clearer that Jessie's lack of desire built to a more avoidant posture under the pressure of sex therapy. This represented the combined rejections of her childhood experiences and of her adult marital failure.

In retrospect, I would have preferred to have begun with individual psychotherapy to explore the history and impact of these rejections more gradually, and to have clarified Jessie's fear of meeting a rejecting object in any intimate experience, including the treatment. This might have allowed the transference to illustrate the more gradual emergence of this fear, and to have absorbed and processed it at a distance from the dreaded sexual arena. In sex therapy, her defenses were attacked too frontally by the threatened emergence of the exciting object relationship. This was far too painful for her to bear, and it happened too quickly to allow for realignment. If I had offered a period of individual psychotherapy, this patient might well have then been more tolerant of sex therapy.

A Mixed Case of ISD and Impotence: Successful Treatment with Sex Therapy

The last case to be presented here was treated successfully by sex therapy alone, despite a mixed diagnostic picture in which many years of low desire had been complicated by an increasing problem with impotence. Although I was suspicious that the ISD might be part of a profound neurotic problem with identity and with fear of a dominating exciting object, the sex therapy proved sufficient. I have also used this case to illustrate more fully some aspects of an object relations approach to sexual treatment, including the transference and countertransference.

Dr. and Mrs. T were both 35 when they were referred by an adoption agency a month after they had adopted an infant girl, Tammy. Dr. T had experienced impotence occasionally during the infertility evaluation and attempts to conceive. But he had never been very driven about sex, and after that time 2 years before, he had withdrawn from sex and had little interest in it. Mrs. T had hardly noticed at first, being busy with her own career as a sports executive, but gradually she realized that she felt neglected. It had taken the perspicacity of the adoption social worker for the couple to admit that their sexual difficulty was a source of concern in a relationship they otherwise both viewed with continuing joy and mutual love.

During the evaluation, Dr. T admitted freely that he had become distracted from sex by his interest in professional and community matters. He was consciously aware that he withdrew from sexual encounters because of his fear of impotence, but he underscored his feeling that he had not felt very motivated about sex since his marriage. The only time this was not true was during vacations, when the couple relaxed and enjoyed sex easily. The case sounded partly like one of impotence and performance anxiety, and partly like one of ISD. Dr. T's history supported both pictures. His interest in sex had always been rather low, and during his years in boarding school he had had several homosexual encounters, which had made it difficult for him to establish an adolescent sexual identity. He said that his relationship to his parents had been good, as was the parents' relationship itself until his mother got more sedentary with age while his father's energy continued unabated. Then, 7 years ago, the father had suddenly left the mother for another woman. Dr. T had felt sympathetic to his mother, although he still got on well with his father.

Mrs. T told me that she came from a loving family. She was the baby, and the only girl after five boys. Pushed to be as athletic and competitive as the boys, she had never had much confidence as a woman. This difficulty left her on shaky grounds in asking Dr. T to be more interested in her sexually.

When I saw the couple for the interpretive round table, they brought their child, and I was therefore able to see an enactment of their physical awkwardness. Mrs. T held Tammy straight out from her body, balanced on the edge of her own knees with the child's feet nestled in her genitals. She supported Tammy's head with one hand and offered the bottle like a syringe with the other. The whole scene seemed awkward and stilted—not a cozy, cuddling experience. While she was tender and obviously loving, Mrs. T tended to handle the child at an unusual distance from her body, and I felt I could imagine a similar awkwardness with her own body and her husband's. When Dr. T took the baby, he seemed a bit lost and overwhelmed, yet he was clearly overjoyed to hold her. The whole situation was not the slightest bit unloving or pathological—just physically restrained and awkward.

I told the couple I thought they shared in the avoidance of sexuality because of a shared shakiness about themselves as sexual people. I had already encouraged Dr. T to tell his wife about his anxiety about impotence and the shame he had been feeling about it. He had done so, to their shared relief. I said now that underneath the performance anxiety leading to the impotence seemed to be a difficulty with desire, which they shared, but which Dr. T expressed for both of them. I suggested that we begin with sex therapy, with the option of turning to marital or individual work, though I wondered silently whether Dr. T would eventually need intensive psychotherapy or psychoanalysis. But as the couple was open, friendly, articulate, and trusting, my feeling about them was both fond and optimistic. I felt that this countertransference should bode well prognostically. They readily agreed to my suggestions for treatment.

The first crucial intervenion involved the question of whether Dr. T would stay in town to begin therapy. He was scheduled to spend several weeks in a postgraduate training program during the summer, and my own

schedule dictated that I begin treatment then or else refer them to a colleague. When I told them this, Dr. T became obviously anxious. The choice
this required of him hit close to the defensive way he put his marriage
second to professional interests. Mrs. T colluded. At first she encouraged
him to go on his trip, and with my probing was able to say that she could
hardly bear to ask him to stay in town and put their relationship first. She
related this to her guilt about asking for anything for herself, just as her
mother would never have offended her father by asking for consideration. It
was a blow to my fondness for them that it was such a struggle to decide on
treatment, but I felt I was now warned about the depth of their reluctance. I
now felt that it might be difficult to hold them in treatment and felt on my
guard. After considerable distress, Dr. T finally decided to stay for therapy.
Within hours of doing so, he felt he had passed a crisis of commitment. He
said he felt like a renewed man, almost as if he had made a decision not to
leave his wife. He said the decision seemed to make him different from his
father.

The early exercises went well. The couple relaxed with the protection
from anxiety, and felt the loving "vacation" feelings they had been missing.
But when genital stimulation was assigned, Dr. T reported that he could feel
no arousal. When I asked whether he had any dreams, he obliged promptly
by reporting one from two nights before.

> I dreamt that a teacher I hardly knew at medical school came over and sat
> down to talk to me. He never would have then, all the more so because he was
> arrogant about students. That was the dream. I had read the day before that
> he had killed himself because he was depressed. That reminded me of my
> wife's brother, who had been depressed but who did not kill himself. He got
> through it. We used to worry that her brother had an organic condition, just
> as I worry that my impotence is organic.

I said that since we knew from the evaluation he had no organic basis
for his sexual difficulty, we could look to the dream for help with causes.
Mrs. T joined in, "I worry that he is uninterested because I'm just not
sexually attractive." And she continued to elaborate on her feeling that she
had a boyish figure and her fear that she had been such an athlete as a young
woman that she could not be sexually attractive. She had not had a menstrual period until the age of 23, presumably because of physiological
inhibition from the strenuous exercise of college athletics. "I never feel I can
be sexy like a real woman. I never got there; I got stuck at 16."

I said to them, "You both have a sense of having deficient bodies. This
contributes to your sexual fear and lack of interest, Dr. T, and to your
feeling, Mrs. T, that you cannot expect any better." They were then able to
reassure each other about their mutual attraction to each other's bodies and
other attributes. I said that they both felt as if they were stuck in mid-
adolescence, in a period whose focus was their shared shaky sense of
themselves as attractive and sexual. I also said that we should not un-

derestimate Dr. T's fear about the depth of the problems—the life-and-death quality expressed in the dream. In addition, I pointed out to them the anxiety in their relationship to me, the "medical school teacher" of the dream. They shared a fear that I might be disdainful of them, and also that their condition would kill me off, making me unavailable to them.

The next two sessions produced the same reports of mutual enjoyment. Mrs. T became easily aroused, while Dr. T enjoyed the massage without arousal or erection. Even during the individual sessions of self-pleasuring that I assigned each of them, he did not feel arousal. In the countertransference, I began to feel the anxiety they shared—that perhaps they would not get far, and that they were less easily treatable than I thought. This is to say that in the countertransference, I began to absorb their doubts that I would be able to help them—that they would "kill off" my efforts to help them—and so I experienced them as disappointing exciting objects. I momentarily had the fantasy that they might leave treatment without improvement, and that I would be relieved. To use their language, I felt "sick of treating them" and, in a way, lost my "desire" to do so. They had now recruited me, through projective identification, to join in their shared unconscious view that sexual desire would bring them to a hopeless and potentially lethal impasse. So in this transference–countertransference replay of their internal problem, I now felt seduced by them, as exciting objects, into hopefulness, and let down by the failure that they also feared.

Then Dr. T brought in a second dream, which he assured me was completely unrelated to the therapy.

> I was standing with 10 or 15 people in a large room with our backs to the wall. It occurred to me that we were going to be executed one by one. Whoever had organized it was huddling at the head of the room. My first reaction was to be defeatist. I took off my jacket and rolled up my sleeves, just as I did a few minutes ago in here, and I thought, "If they are going to do it, I hope they'll hurry. Waiting is agony." Then I realized they hadn't started, and it was a long time. I thought, "I don't want to die, so why not fight?" They were demonstrating how people died by carbon monoxide poisoning, the same way as that teacher of mine in medical school died recently. They showed that you went to a bed covered with garbage baggies and you have a gas mask with oxygen until it is changed to carbon monoxide. I thought it was awful, so I asked to use the telephone. They let me, and I called my mother. But there was no answer. My fight juices were finally going by now, so I just walked out the front door of the office. I took off my shirt because somehow it was a telltale sign, and I started to run. It felt terribly slow. After 2 or 3 minutes, I realized a motorcycle policeman was following me. I still ran for my life. I was running through a territory like the strip places on a highway, gas stations which were closed because it was 2 A.M. The policeman caught up with me. I thought he was going to catch me, but just at that moment, a bad guy came out of a trailer and took a shot at the cop, who took off after him, and I got away.

Dr. T's associations left him in no doubt that the execution he feared was the sexual exposure of the exercises. The odd method of execution was the assigned sexual exercises on a bed which felt threateningly smothering. In the dream, he had called his mother, as he had done in his youth when he felt helpless. He said, "Hers is the one number that hasn't changed all these years. I was counting on her. She should have been home in the middle of the night, but she wasn't there. So I ran for my life." When I said that I was the cop he feared, he replied, "No doubt about that!" He talked about fearing being controlled by me, and by sex. The building the dream had occurred in reminded him of his junior high school. He had left there to attend boarding school at a time he felt he had to escape from his mother, but when he left home he missed her terribly. I said I thought it might have related to his fearful recognition of his parents' sexual life before he left. He said, "Well, they did have a last child just after I left. In fact, we named Tammy after that sister."

I felt the fear of the persecuting object was now out in the open—in the dream, in his acknowledged fear of sex, and in his agreeing that he feared me. I summed up my speculations about this dream by saying that Dr. T had felt threatened with annihilation by me and by the sex—by the smothering engulfment of his wife, who now stood for the seductive and threatening part of his mother. And he was expressing a fear of sex for both of them. He had been on the run ever since. "You can't get aroused when you're on the run!" I said to him. Although I was the cop and executioner in the treatment, it was his wife who had been in that role up to now. And she had accepted it because she felt no one would willingly have her.

In the exercise following this session, Dr. T was easily aroused, and the treatment followed a rapid course to successful completion. Dr. T found that he was able to relax through any periods of anxiety he felt, and progressively his anxiety and fear receded. Mrs. T also found it progressively easier to avoid backing off, lest she be seen as the cop. The couple continued on to a new level of integration of their sexual and emotional intimacy. When I last saw them with Tammy, she had made the perch at the end of her mother's knee a throne from which to command parental attention and joy—a giggling 3-month-old and her loving parents. I have not seen the Ts again, but 18 months later, I received an unexpected announcement of the birth of their son. Mrs. T wrote, "We never could have predicted this would happen. Thanks for your help."

This case illustrates the marriage of sex therapy with psychodynamic, object-related understanding. I was able to bring an interpretive approach to bear on dream material in which the husband's transference to his wife and to me, and their shared contextual transference, could be suddenly understood in a way that was convincing to him. The improvement was uncharacteristically prompt and thorough. Although we cannot expect all patients to respond so promptly or so profoundly, some of them do. Most, however, gain new insights that grow over time or that lead them to accept longer-term exploratory therapy.

The other feature of this case is the way in which impotence and superficial anxiety were built on a foundation of ISD. Ordinarily, we would expect that intensive individual treatment would ultimately be required. But often, as in this case, even though the causes of the inhibition originated in developmental and object-related difficulties, the positive shared contextual transference, the couple's loving relationship, and their motivation allowed them to work through their shared problem and their individual parts of it quickly but thoroughly. They illustrate that while ISD is often part of a complex picture, this does not mean that such patients are untreatable.

Conclusion

There is a spectrum of difficulties that constitute inhibitions of sexual desire. The object relations approach contributes to our efficacy by encouraging us to consider the internal object relations of an individual or couple before arriving at a treatment plan. Almost inevitably, when we can understand the object relations history of our patients, we can make sense of their in- hibitions. But to do so we must know not only something of the literal history of each person, but what was made of that story as experience was taken inside. Much of this evidence is enshrined in the transferences that spouses have for each other, and that they bring for us to see. Other information about their capacity to trust a therapist is provided in the treatment via the shared transference they form to us. The early stages of treatment often offer additional crucial information, part of it through the transference. Attention to our own responses often leads to the formulation of helpful interpretations and interventions. It is also useful to consider offering different types of treatment when one modality has run aground.

The treatment for the disorders of ISD is more variable in outcome and less reliably successful than that for other forms of sexual dysfunction. Nevertheless, attention to our patients' internal object relations increases our capacity to understand them—and to help them feel that they, too, can be loved for themselves.

References

Bowlby, J. (1980). *Attachment and loss: Vol. 3. Loss: Sadness and depression.* New York: Basic Books

Box, S. (1984, April). *Containment and countertransference.* Paper presented at the Washing- ton School of Psychiatry's Fifth Annual Symposium on Psychoanalytic Family Therapy, Bethesda, MD.

Box, S., Copley, B., Magagna, J., & Moustaki, E. (Eds.). (1981). *Psychotherapy with families: An analytic approach.* London: Routledge & Kegan Paul.

Dicks, H. V. (1967). *Marital tensions: Clinical studies towards a psychoanalytic theory of interaction.* London: Routledge & Kegan Paul.

Fairbairn, W. R. D. (1952). *Psychoanalytic studies of the personality.* London: Routledge & Kegan Paul.

Fairbairn, W. R. D. (1963). Synopsis of an object-relations theory of the personality. *International Journal of Psycho-Analysis, 44,* 224–225.

Horwith, M., & Imperato-McGinley, J. (1983). The medical evaluation of disorders of sexual desire in males and females. In H.S. Kaplan, *The evaluation of sexual disorders: Psychological and medical aspects.* New York: Brunner/Mazel.

Kaplan, H. S. (1974). *The new sex therapy: Active treatment of sexual dysfunctions.* New York: Brunner/Mazel.

Kaplan, H. S. (1977). Hypoactive sexual desire. *Journal of Sex and Marital Therapy, 3,* 3–9.

Kaplan, H. S. (1979). *Disorders of sexual desire and other new concepts and techniques in sex therapy.* New York: Brunner/Mazel.

Kaplan, H. S. (1983). *The evaluation of sexual disorders: Psychological and medical aspects.* New York: Brunner/Mazel.

Kleeman, J. (1966). Genital self-discovery during a boy's second year. *Psychoanalytic Study of the Child, 21,* 358–392.

Kleeman, J. (1977). Genital self-stimulation in infant and toddler girls. In I. Marcus & J. Francis (Eds.), *Masturbation: From infancy to senescence.* New York: International Universities Press.

Klein, M. (1975). Notes on some schizoid mechanisms. In M. Klein, *Envy and gratitude and other works, 1946–1963.* London: Hogarth Press and the Institute of Psycho-Analysis. (Original work published 1946)

Levay, A. N., Kagle, A., & Weissberg, J. (1979). Issues of transference in sex therapy. *Journal of Sex and Marital Therapy, 5,* 15–21.

Main, T. F. (1966). Mutual projection in a marriage. *Comprehensive Psychiatry, 7,* 432–449.

Masters, W. H., & Johnson, V. E. (1966). *Human sexual response.* Boston: Little, Brown.

Masters, W. H., & Johnson, V. E. (1970). *Human sexual inadequacy.* Boston: Little, Brown.

Ogden, T. (1983). The concept of internal object relations. *International Journal of Psycho-Analysis, 64,* 227–241.

Scharff, D. E. (1978). Truth and consequences in sex and marital therapy: The revelation of secrets in the therapeutic setting. *Journal of Sex and Marital Therapy, 4,* 35–49.

Scharff, D. E. (1982). *The sexual relationship: An object relations view of sex and the family.* London: Routledge & Kegan Paul.

Scharff, D. E., & Scharff, J. S. (1987). *Object relations family therapy.* New York: Jason Aronson.

Segal, H. (1973). *Introduction to the work of Melanie Klein* (new, enlarged ed.). London: Hogarth Press.

Sutherland, J. (1963). Object relations theory and the conceptual model of psychoanalysis. *British Journal of Medical Psychology, 36,* 109–124.

Williams, A. H. (1981). The micro-environment. In S. Box, B. Copley, J. Magagna, & E. Moustaki (Eds.), *Psychotherapy with families: An analytic approach.* London: Routledge & Kegan Paul.

Winnicott, D. W. (1960). The theory of the parent–infant relationship. *International Journal of Psycho-Analysis, 41,* 585–595.

Zinner, J. (1976). The implications of projective identification for marital interaction In H. Grunebaum & J. Christ (Eds.), *Contemporary marriage: Structure, dynamics, and therapy.* Boston: Little, Brown.

4

An Ego-Analytic Perspective on Desire Disorders

BERNARD APFELBAUM

Bernard Apfelbaum is one of the most original and creative theoreticians in the field of sex therapy. He brings a fresh approach to the understanding of desire disorders by reminding us that our historically recent enthusiasm for sexual expressiveness has created oppression rather than liberation for many individuals. The insistence that one ought to experience sex as positive and pleasurable can become a psychological burden. Nevertheless, most sex therapists and their clients have come to believe that a state of sexual receptivity is both natural and necessary, and we tend to ignore or minimize the fact that sex may not always be valued or desired. To admit to such feelings has become, in fact, socially unacceptable; hence, individuals who fail to enjoy or desire sex often feel humiliated and inadequate. While therapists acknowledge the widespread existence of performance anxiety and its deleterious consequences, there is no such term to describe the fear of not being aroused, which is quite different from pleasure anxiety or anxiety about experiencing sexual pleasure. Consequently, Apfelbaum coins a new term, "response anxiety," to refer to the anxiety associated with not feeling aroused, and he suggests that this may be the basis for most (if not all) cases of inhibited desire.

Reviewing the historical evidence, Apfelbaum reminds us that from the 17th century onward, sex has been viewed as a drive requiring "control." For several centuries, sexual discharge was believed to result in a debilitated physical and mental state, and thus sexual caution was advised by both medical and moral authorities. It was not until the turn of the century and with the publication of Van de Velde's Ideal Marriage *that lack of sexual release was regarded as problematic. The "sexual revolution" of the 1960s and 1970s further endorsed sexual release, but, as Apfelbaum notes, only provided the freedom to say "yes" to sex.*

The core of Apfelbaum's theoretical view of desire disorders is his insistence on the recognition of the causal role of response anxiety in the genesis and maintenance of desire problems. In Apfelbaum's view, successful treatment of desire cases involves endorsement of the legitimacy of the sexually apathetic person's negative or neutral response to sexual stimulation. He contends that giving individuals permission to feel sexual "pleasure" when they are, in reality, sexually turned off may not only be ineffective, but may actually intensify response anxiety. Paradoxically, clients must first be relieved of their pressure to respond positively to sex, if they are ever to feel sexual pleasure. To conceptualize all cases of desire disorders as reflecting conflicts about sexual pleasure, intimacy, or partner hostility is misguided. Rather, therapists must assist their clients in becoming aware of the disastrous consequences of both societal and individual pressures to be sexual when they simply do not feel sexual. Once therapists can affirm clients' reality (the fact of their not feeling aroused), and can support them in not feeling guilty because they are not aroused, the path is cleared for the resolution of desire difficulties.

Apfelbaum's approach is a uniquely valuable one from several respects. It affirms the sexually apathetic individual's personal reality; it reduces the pressure of being or feeling sexual when one is not; and it permits the therapist to direct attention to the high-drive partner as perhaps overly "driven" to engage in sex, despite the other partner's lack of interest.

Bernard Apfelbaum, Ph.D., is Director of the Berkeley Sex Therapy Group and the BSTG Seminars in Berkeley, California, and the author of numerous articles and chapters on an ego-analytic approach to sex therapy.

People who have always experienced a low level of sexual desire typically appear neither apprehensive toward sex nor in conflict about it. For this reason, this state can look like a simple absence of desire, which should be treated by sexual enhancement techniques such as exposure to sexually explicit materials and fantasy training. Since this appearance is deceptive and enhancement techniques are therefore likely to fail, the succeeding explanation is likely to be that the absence of desire represents an unconcious resistance to sexual arousal (Kaplan, 1979) or possibly a hormonal imbalance.

I propose that, in these cases, what looks either like simple apathy or like a case of unconscious resistance is in actuality a state of *withdrawal* from negative reactions. This withdrawal is a consequence of the pressure that everyone is under in sex to respond positively (of course, excluding those whose culture prohibits sexual response). This pressure is created by the expectation that in all relationships one should respond positively and not cause friction—a pressure that is intensified in sex by the belief that sexual response should be automatic, since it represents a biological drive. The obvious manifestations of this performance pressure in sex are the profound humiliation and sense of inadequacy felt by those who cannot respond automatically, and the pride felt by those who can. These reactions are so ubiquitous that the self-help books in this field are full of exhortations not to think of sex as a performance or a contest, but instead just to think of it as an opportunity for pleasure and intimacy.

Because rapidity of sexual response is expected, those who succeed in meeting this expectation typically are dependent on a highly accommodating partner, or (as is more often the case) are adroit at calling up fantasies of such a partner. This may be one reason why men respond more rapidly than women: They can more easily expect and imagine an accommodating partner, whereas women need to spin out elaborate scenarios in order to construct a believably accommodating partner. Those whose automatic response to sex is not to expect or imagine an accommodating partner, but who expect to be forced to *be* accommodating, have no opportunity to live out their reactions. Those who expect to be sexually exploited have no way to bring their reactions into their sexual encounters. They and their partners typically disqualify such expectations. This is especially true of marital partners.

This disqualification of sexual oppression can be seen in the maxims that "sex is beautiful," or "sex is natural," or "sex is communication." Everyone is aware of rape and of sexual abuse and harassment, but these are dismissed as aberrant—in effect, as distortions of what sex really is. Thus, the woman who feels used by her husband may decide that this simply is her role and/or that she is frigid; she then complies in sex but feels apathetic. She has no awareness of performance pressure, and there is no way it could be detected by the casual observer. However, as I attempt to demonstrate in this chapter, if her withdrawn state is closely examined, evidence can be found that she feels alone and left out in sex and also that she disqualifies these reactions; as a result, she feels inadequate and guilty. In other words, she believes that she is having the wrong reactions to sex. Instead of experiencing sex as beautiful, she experiences it as a failure area. Sex is beautiful, but she is not. She is under pressure to respond positively, but this is so taken for granted that she has no way to be aware of it.

If it were not for this pressure, the woman would no longer be withdrawn, but would be actively responding to sex by expressing to her husband her anticipation of exploitation and the way that this turns her off. I am sure that the reader's reaction to the prospect of her doing that is that it is impossible to imagine. No one can express such reactions in sex. That is my point. The pressure not to have such reactions is so universal and so taken for granted that it is essentially invisible.

In fact, as should be familiar to everyone, all the sex books recommend being extremely tactful when expressing any kind of dissatisfaction in sex. For example, Hartman and Fithian (1972), under the heading "Accentuating the Positive—Always Saying Yes" (which states the rule in a nutshell), advise: "A negative response often seriously inhibits further lovemaking efforts and, therefore, should be avoided wherever possible." If you don't like something that your partner is doing, they recommend that you move your partner on to something that you would like. Hartman and Fithian have no advice for the person who cannot think of *anything* that he or she would like. This is also true of the authors of the other sex books, who are willing to consider negative reactions only of the most minor sort, and even these require masterpieces of tact that the guilty and self-blaming partner has no way to summon up.

Consequently, it is far too much to expect that oppressed sex partners will have any way to include their reactions in sex; therefore, in such cases, some degree of withdrawal is inevitable. For the same reason, it would be a mistake to think that the solution is for them to express their reactions somehow. This would be of little value even if it could be done, since the problem is that they and their partners disqualify their reactions, whether expressed or unexpressed. However, it should also be clear that to attempt to get them to respond positively (as through the use of sexual enhancement techniques such as exposure to sexually explicit materials and fantasy training) requires an arduous therapy at best, because it intensifies performance pressure. As I shall be arguing here, this was Masters and Johnson's basic insight, revolutionizing a field that had until their work been dominated by the sexual enhancement approach.

The solution for those who are sexually apathetic is to become aware of the pressure we all are under to "always say yes," as Hartman and Fithian approvingly put it. This universalizes the dilemma and also relieves the self-blame that is at the heart of the problem. They can then begin to think, often for the first time, about what is turning them off. This is where all the more obvious causes of sexual apathy are relevant. My point is that these other causes do not create the impasse that sexual apathy represents unless they are locked in by performance pressure.

An example from work with erection problems can best illustrate this point. It is widespread belief that impotence can be caused by depression, job worries, fatigue, or the like. This is a seemingly empirical finding. All sex therapists will report that many of the men who come to them with erection problems are suffering from depression, and it is easy to conclude that depression is a cause of impotence. As an informal check on this inference, I did a quick survey of five analytic therapists (none of whom were sex therapists), asking them to list the men they could recall who had symptoms of depression, and then to check which of these also experienced erectile dysfunction. Of the 40–50 men they had seen, none had this complaint. Since this suggests that depression does not necessarily *cause* impotence, how can we account for the association between the two in men who seek sex therapy?

Many men who are depressed and preoccupied get *relief* from sex. They need it more and get more out of it. But the object of sex for them is reassurance and support, not performance. To the extent that a man is susceptible to male sex-role expectations, the object of sex is performance, and he will try to avoid sex when he is depressed or preoccupied or just does not feel up to it. In other words, he will avoid sex when he needs reassurance and support. If and when he cannot find a way to avoid it, he will be "unable to perform."

One way to put this is to say that with regard to erectile dysfunction, performance anxiety potentiates depression. Most often the man is not aware of his anxiety about performance. He just tells himself, "I'm not up to it," without conceiving of the possibility that it is possible to begin a sexual encounter without being "up to it" and to look forward to it as a way to have that readiness stimulated.

It may be that the most formidable obstacle to recognition of the role of performance anxiety is the widespread belief among the sex professionals that it is a conscious anxiety. It can be entirely conscious, but more often than not people believe so totally that they should be able to perform that they have no way to isolate this influence. To the extent that the therapist shares this belief, treatment intensifies the pressure.

Performance anxiety may be least apparent in those who are sexually apathetic, and this may be why sex therapists such as Kaplan (1979) consider this condition to be among the most difficult to treat of the sexual disorders. Also, Kaplan's "behavioral-analytic model" is likely to miss covert performance anxiety because the therapist is looking too far down the causal chain—practicing "id analysis" as compared with the "ego-analytic" approach, in which the therapist looks not for the deepest causes, but for those that are most superficial (Apfelbaum, 1977a; Apfelbaum & Gill, 1987; Fenichel, 1941).

To clarify these assertions, I shall first attempt to show the universality of performance pressure in sex and the ways in which it is reinforced by the biological-drive fallacy and by the concept of frigidity. I shall then try to put this in historical and cultural perspective. Following this, I shall review Masters and Johnson's nondemand paradigm and the way it represented a radical breakthrough in relation to what had preceded it: the emphasis on sexual technique (i.e., on sexual performance) presented in the marriage manuals. Finally, I shall explain how rapid sexual response is possible in view of the universality of performance pressure. Many people experience a rapid sexual responsiveness that looks like simply "letting go," like the action of a reflex. The standard explanatory model takes this rapid responsiveness for granted as the basic reference state; therefore, from the perspective of that model, it requires no explanation.

Performance Anxiety

What primarily gives us something to worry about when we find ourselves to be unaroused is the "drive" metaphor: the idea that sex is a biological drive that pushes for expression. This idea generates the belief that the only genuine response in sex is to feel aroused. Here is a statement of this belief, if one is needed, from McCary's *Human Sexuality* (1973). McCary was a recognized authority in the field, and this was until recently one of the best-selling undergraduate texts:

> The more reckless and uninhibited the response, short of causing severe physical pain, that a woman makes at the peak of sexual excitement, the more pleased most men are. This is not to say that a man expects his partner to be physically violent and uncontrolled, or verbally loud and offensive. Most men want a woman to express her excitement and involvement in somewhat more subtle ways, but nevertheless to leave little doubt that she has let herself go completely and has responded—authentically—exactly as she felt. This sort of open communication is not as difficult to achieve as it might sound. It can be assisted by actions such as smooth, silky, rhythmical body movements accompanied by low moans and gasps, all building to an expressive crescendo at the moment of orgasm. But whatever form the communication takes, freedom of response and expression is the key. (pp. 146–147)

Notice that McCary's permission to be "open," "uninhibited," and "authentic" refers only to the "freedom" to be encouraging and supportive of your partner—to authentically echo Molly Bloom's "yes, yes, oh yes, yes." This is reminiscent of the idea that the sexual revolution has only freed women to say "yes." It is like the expectation we all feel to smile when smiled at, although that expectation is, if anything, even more invisible, since we just automatically smile back. Similarly, faking orgasm is the same as laughing at the boss's joke; however, the pressure to have an orgasm is greater because, unlike our laughter, it is expected to be authentic, just as McCary tells us.

The example of faking orgasm has several implications for my line of argument. I think it is the most dramatic and most pointed example of performance anxiety, in that the woman who fakes orgasms usually is responding to the pressure to be responsive in order to support the male ego, as well as to her own need to affirm her womanliness (it is of course also true that women will fake orgasms just to get sex over with, and this is a different motivation). Interestingly enough, even though faking orgasms may be the best example of performance anxiety, I have never seen it mentioned in this connection. The answer to why this should be so is especially revealing: It lies directly in the term "performance anxiety." It is evident from the term itself that this anxiety is more easily recognized when it is a concern about performance (i.e., about erections and orgasms) than when it is a concern about subjective arousal. The most extreme example of this way of thinking is in the familiar idea that women do not experience performance anxiety, because it is only men who have to perform.

When we look for a corresponding term that refers not to performance but to subjectively felt arousal, we encounter the familiar term "pleasure anxiety." This confronts us with a striking contrast. Performance anxiety refers to the fear of *not* being able to perform, but pleasure anxiety refers to the fear of being *able* to feel pleasure. Sex therapists are so much more concerned with the fear of *being* aroused that there is no term for the fear of *not* being aroused. Sex therapists are much more concerned with the fear of not being able to perform. Performance anxiety refers to the *absence* of performance. Pleasure anxiety refers to the *presence* of pleasure. As a result, we have no way to refer to anxiety about not feeling aroused. Theoretically, "performance anxiety" should do the trick, since becoming aroused can be seen as "performing," but this term has only served to interfere with the recognition of the fear of becoming aroused.

Can it be that sex therapists have not felt the need for a term to refer to the fear of lack of erotic arousal because this fear is not as pronounced as the fear of lack of performance? Helen Kaplan (1979) has asserted that the opposite is the case:

> The existence of [inhibited sexual desire] is not always apparent during the evaluation because patients do not tend to complain of this directly. They are more likely to cite erection and orgasm problems as the chief complaint. It is often much easier and less threatening for the symptomatic patient, as well as for the spouse, to define their problem as a genital dysfunction than to admit that "I feel no desire" or, even more threatening, that "I feel no desire for you." (p. 67)

If, as Kaplan suggests, performance anxiety about desire is greater than performance anxiety about performing, then why haven't sex therapists felt the need to name it? ("Performance anxiety about desire" obviously will not do, so I use "response anxiety" instead.) Part of the answer is present in Helen Kaplan's statement. Desire problems in general may not come to the clinician's attention as much as they should, because patients may feel even more deficient about not responding than about not performing, and hence the former may not be mentioned. For example, we frequently hear of cases in which the problem is defined as a dysfunction and the couple becomes functional but then continues to avoid sex. The therapist concludes that the couple must have an investment in keeping sex a problem, without considering the possibility that there is an underlying desire disorder that has never been treated.

Of course, another possible reason for the neglect of response anxiety may be that even if it is more intense than performance anxiety, it may be less widespread. Perhaps the most pithy observation on this point has been made by Zilbergeld (1981), who remarked that although 70% of women have at some time faked an orgasm, 100% of people fake feelings. This refreshing recognition of the universality of response anxiety stands out as the only reference to it that I have come across.

To explain this blind spot in the field, we have to consider the fact that lack of desire has been a female disorder, whereas lack of performance has been a male disorder. Historically, everyone has been male-identified, and it has been the man's job to perform and the woman's job to appreciate it (with, in McCary's terms, "low moans and gasps"). A woman could not be impotent, because she had no need for power, and a man could not be frigid, because it didn't matter how warm he felt.

From the male-identified point of view, the failure to perform is relatively understandable. People are usually relatively indulgent about it, telling the dysfunctional young man that he will soon get over it and telling the experienced man who has had some trouble with performance that it may have been the drinks he had and that he just needs to get "back in the saddle" before he loses his nerve. In both instances, people typically respond with amusement; they are usually even more amused at the man who is chronically dysfunctional. But people are not amused when a woman cannot fulfill her role. Here the reaction is grim. This is the male point of view. If anyone doubts that "frigidity" is a more accusatory term than "impotence," consider the fact that even though the two terms are equally benighted, "impotence" as a diagnostic term still has currency, whereas "frigidity" has largely been dropped.

Frigidity

The notion of frigidity is a good example of the invalidation of a "no" response to sex, although even the frigid woman with her proverbial headache has to plead a headache, or simply to be passive in sex, rather than being able to say "no" directly (itself testimony to the pressure to say "yes"). Feelings about frigidity run high, and it has not been easy to eliminate them or even to be aware of their continuing influence. Masters and Johnson deserve the credit for being the first authorities to drop the term, and as a result of their influence it now is rarely used (in the sex field; it still is used in the psychoanalytic literature).

Here may lie the answer to the question of why Masters and Johnson (1966, 1970) did not mention desire disorders—what they later (Kolodny,

Masters, & Johnson, 1979) have called the "nondysfunctions." No one has offered an answer to this question (or even has asked it); however, the answer is of some importance, because their exclusive focus on the dysfunctions was what kept sex therapists from attending to desire disorders until recently, and even led some to believe that sex therapy was indicated only for performance symptoms.

The plot thickens when we learn (R. S. Kolodny, personal communication, 1985) that "A review of dozens of cases done in the early 1970s, using MJI [Masters and Johnson Institute] tapes and case notes, identified many cases which would be diagnosed today as 'low sexual desire' but were then called impotence, since this was the presenting symptom." My guess is that Masters and Johnson discussed only the dysfunctions because they could think of no other way to remove the stigma from frigidity and thereby to relieve response anxiety (performance anxiety about responding on the feeling level). Their logic would have been that if they defined all sexual disorders in behavioral terms, this would take the pressure off the feeling level, and erotic feeling might then return spontaneously. Thus, in effect, "frigidity" was redefined as "female orgasmic dysfunction."

This solution (if this is indeed what it was) only led many therapists to believe that Masters and Johnson must not have treated frigidity. The recent solution, the category of "Inhibited Sexual Desire" (ISD) in the *Diagnostic and Statistical Manual of Mental Disorders,* third edition (DSM-III), indicates that it is difficult to find a nonblaming way to refer to the lack of erotic arousal: The "inhibition" implies that the conditions for desire are present but that it is being withheld, and one of the accusations packed into "frigidity" is that the woman who does not experience erotic arousal is a withholding person. The work group on psychosexual disorders for the revision of DSM-III (DSM-IIIR) (Seagraves, 1986) has recognized this and recently recommended that ISD be renamed Hypoactive Sexual Desire Disorder, arguing that this more awkward term is necessary because it "reflects greater neutrality as to etiology" (p. 3).

Although cleaning up our nomenclature hardly begins to solve the problem, the fact that it is still necessary illustrates how difficult it can be to liberate ourselves from common-sense prejudices. And it is my impression that low sexual desire—or sexual apathy, as I prefer to call it—is the sexual disorder that brings out our most basic sexual prejudices. Although much of what I have already said bears on this point, an additional way to illuminate these prejudices is to set them in a historical and cultural context.

Sexual Apathy in Historical and Cultural Perspective

The prejudices that I hope to illuminate historically are themselves embedded in the historiography of the sex field. This is to say that the received version of the history of our sexual prejudices does not so much reveal them as exemplify them. According to this version, sexual apathy is a historical accident—one that need not have happened, and that in fact has not happened in other cultures. Sexual apathy is explained as a Victorian holdover and a result of the continuing influence of the early Church. In contrast, I believe that that some form of sexual apathy has always been the rule rather than the exception, and that this reflects the reality of our sexual relationships. The way in which this sexual reality is dismissed reflects how we typically deal with reality in general.

Freud provides a striking example of the way in which we have dismissed sexual reality. It is well known that he thought of civilization as a threat to the sex drive—so much so, in fact, that he came to the staggering conclusion that we may lose sexual desire so totally and so universally as to imperil the continuation of the human race, at least in the remote future: "It is quite impossible to adjust the claims of the sexual instinct to the demands of civilization . . .[and therfore] renunciation and suffering, as well as the danger of extinction in the remotest future, cannot be avoided by the human race" (1912/1957, p. 190).

Subsequent discussions of Freud's position have invariably overlooked the observations on which he based this conclusion that the sex drive is so imperative it cannot be adapted to the requirements of civilization and therefore may be repressed out of existence. He observed the *weakness* of the sex drive, not its strength. What he observed was the prevalence of sexual apathy in clinical practice; he inferred from this, not that the sex drive was weak, but that it had been strongly repressed. Thus, in the same paper in which the statement quoted above appears, he also said:

> If the concept of psychical impotence is broadened and is not restricted to failure to perform the act of coitus . . . we may in the first place add all those men who are described as psycho-anaesthetic: men who never fail in the act but who carry it out without getting any particular pleasure from it—a state of affairs that is more common than one would think. . . . An easily justifiable analogy takes one from these anaesthetic men to the immense number of frigid women. . . .
>
> If . . .[in addition] we turn our attention not to an extension of the concept of psychical impotence, but to the gradations in its symptomatology, we cannot escape the conclusion that the behavior in love of men in the civilized world bears the stamp altogether of psychical impotence. (1912/1957, pp. 184–185)

This was the sexual reality that Freud observed, only to reject it as aberrant. There was no way in which his belief in the strength of the sex drive could be invalidated. The weaker he observed it to be, the stronger (and the more repressed) he thought it was. However, where Freud, along with many others, concluded that civilization is a threat to the sex drive, I think a better case can be made for the proposition that it is only through cultural elaboration that the sex "drive" can develop.

For example, reflexes are supposed to drop out in the course of evolutionary development, whereas female orgasm is one that only *appears* in humans. Masters and Johnson point out that although a lower spinal center for reflex erections has been identified in men, "no similar response center has been described for the human female" (1966, p. 62). Therefore, they note, it may be that the entire orgasm reflex arc involves both the spinal cord and higher cortical centers; this means that psychogenic stimulation is critical.

Although no explanation has yet been advanced for this unusual development, it appears to be intrinsic to the change of function sex has undergone as it moves away from its original tie to procreation toward facilitating pair bonding. The drive mystique that still surrounds sex is more appropriate to infrahuman mammalian species, in which sexual arousal is still restricted to estrus, with the role of the female largely confined to the emission of pheromones. This is, of course, sufficient for the purpose of procreation. With pair bonding as the evolutionary objective, year 'round desire appears, and with it the introduction of higher cortical centers into the pathways of desire. This has connected sex with self-esteem, much to the frustration of sexual self-help authors, some sex therapists, and most sex patients, all of whom believe that we should be able to decorticate sex—to unbite the apple and return to our mammalian heritage.

Even if men somehow could turn back the evolutionary clock, women would have little to go back to, at least orgasmically. But as it is now, desire is mediated by the cultural context: in authoritarian cultures, by the way status and attractiveness are defined; and in less role-dependent, more individual-oriented cultures, by more potent and more complex regulators of desire (e.g., romantic love and the possibility of emotional intimacy). Thus, the sex "drive" is dependent on civilization rather than in some way opposed to it.

Of course, when Freud said "civilization," he meant Vienna, and he was still seduced by cultural Darwinism and its assumption that more primitive societies are closer to nature. Because, like the drive metaphor, this is another idea that dies hard, a summary of the cross-cultural data can help anchor the model I am proposing:

> In most of the societies for which there are data, it is reported that men take the initiative and, without extended foreplay, proceed vigorously toward climax without much regard for achieving synchrony with the woman's orgasm. Again and again, there are reports that coitus is primarily completed in terms of the man's passions and pleasures, with scant attention paid to the woman's response. If women do experience orgasm, they do so passively. In the Ojibwa, a North American Indian group, it is reported that women are passive during intercourse and orgasm; however, they may take the lead in initiating coitus. In the Guinea survey of young single adults from several African ethnic groups, the women overwhelmingly reported passivity during coitus, embarrassment at expressing satisfaction during intercourse, [and]

distaste for caressing[,] and many admitted an inability to achieve orgasm. (Davenport, 1977, p. 149)

Most cultures are sexually restrictive and hence can be thought of as suppressing the sex drive; prominent examples are China, India, Russia, Latin America, and the Islamic cultures. Even the two cultures thought of as being sexually permissive—premissionary Polynesia and pre-Confucian (Taoist) China—can also be seen on closer examination to have been highly restrictive, although in a different way; performance demands were severe (Marshall & Suggs, 1971; Tannahill, 1980).

Certainly the early Church Fathers were restrictive (although St. Augustine of Hippo, in *The City of God,* Book XIV, Chapter 18, said that he concluded that sex is shameful because everyone seemed to ashamed of it). However, as in other cultures, this was simply part of the restrictions on behavior in general found in authoritarian societies. (Victorianism can be seen as a regressive phase in the development of some Western cultures toward recognizing the authority of personal experience.)

Thus, there is a way in which human societies appear to be opposed to spontaneous sexuality. However, this restrictiveness can be seen simply as part of a larger picture that includes arranged marriage and, in general, arranged relationships. This ritualization is an early stage in human ego development, in which the struggle is to avoid interpersonal anxiety by rigidly channeling behavior. The history of sex counseling and therapy should be seen in the light of this struggle.

The Nondemand Paradigm

Performance anxiety is often obvious, and there were some early mentions of it in the literature. It was also represented in the work of behavior therapists, but Masters and Johnson were the first to make it the key explanatory principle: *"Fear of inadequacy is the greatest known deterrent to effective sexual functioning"* (Masters & Johnson, 1970, p. 12, their italics). Masters and Johnson have often been represented merely as popularizers of the behavioral approach to sex (Apfelbaum, 1985). However, behavior therapists have no point of view regarding sex, in contrast to Masters and Johnson, whose philosophy of sex represented a revolutionary departure from the sexual philosophy that preceded them.

Before Masters and Johnson, the sex experts were the authors of the marriage manuals, one of the earliest and most prominent of whom was Van de Velde (1926/1930). Van de Velde and his followers emphasized sexual performance and the necessity to work at sex: for example, "Foreplay should never last less than fifteen minutes even though a woman may be aroused in five" (Butterfield, 1964, p. 168). Masters and Johnson saw this emphasis as conducive to performance pressure and insisted that "sex is natural," meaning that working at sex causes rather than solves sexual problems.

Masters and Johnson were the first sex experts explicitly to decry the technique approach to sex. What made this position especially revolutionary was that it was proposed in an era in which the technique approach to sex had suddenly become popular, and it was largely as a result of their work that this era came to a close. Its demise was dramatic. We no longer hear about the "erogeneous zones," the key concern of the marriage manuals. And even more dramatic, where reaching orgasm was almost what sex was all about for Van de Velde ("ejaculation is the aim, the summit and the end of the sexual act" [p. 103]), Masters and Johnson proposed that the pursuit of orgasm and the associated concept of foreplay is a primary cause of sexual problems. Their term "goal-directedness" is now so familiar that it is hard to imagine that before Masters and Johnson it would have made no sense.

The era that preceded Masters and Johnson's work was reviewed in "Sex as Work," a well-known critique of the marriage manuals by two sociologists, Lewis and Brissett (1967), who concluded that "the play of marital sex is presented by the counselors quite definitely as work" (p. 16). These authors clearly had no inkling of the impending revolution in sex counseling and therapy that would identify such recommendations as part of the problem rather than part of the solution. They were so convinced of the permanency of this approach and its hold on us that they saw it as a symptom of American industrialization and the work ethic: We had turned play into work. Interestingly enough, Lewis and Brissett were not interested in sex as such. As Marxist sociologists, they wanted an example of the way in which our personal relationships merely reflect the character of our political and economic institutions, and the recommendations of the marriage manuals looked like a perfect example. We were putting our bodies on the assembly line.

Although as late as 1967 Lewis and Brissett believed that the philosophy of the marriage manuals was unlikely to change without a change in our political and economic institutions, the effect of the Masters and Johnson revolution has been so profound that it is difficult to recall the preoccupations of the sex counseling that preceded it. In the years since *Human Sexual Inadequacy* (1970) appeared, what had been widespread gospel at the time of its publication now sounds strangely antiquated as a result of its impact.

What Lewis and Brissett did not take into account is that the marriage manual approach was itself an enlightened response to attitudes of the previous era. In this earlier era, sex had been neither work *nor* play, being too brisk to be either. Sex was treated phobically; it was put in a tight compartment and kept brief. At least from the 17th century onward, this approach to sex was the one given authoritative endorsement, both morally and medically (Comfort, 1967). Sex was thought of as a drive that required control; this idea had evolved out of the earlier animistic paradigm of possession by spirits. What the later centuries added, in addition to various toxins and vapors, was the metaphor of the erosion of the will—a literal degeneration of the nerves responsible for self-control (hence "de-generates").

With the tendency to make anxieties concrete that characterized pre-scientific thinking, the fear of allowing sexual discharge was made literal by imagining that it created a debilitating state (this notion may be a con-cretization of the postcoital blues, as in the belief found in most cultures that sexual discharge saps one's strength). This concretization has persisted into the modern era; even such an eminent psychoanalytic authority as Ernest Jones (1918, cited in Comfort, 1967) asserted that "true neurasthenia . . . will be found to depend on excessive onanism and seminal emissions" (p. 111). As a consequence of this ideology, at least in part, people suffered from pleasure anxiety. Sexual pleasure was morally and medically risky.

In the effort to relieve pleasure anxiety, Van de Velde and those who followed him aggressively attacked this phobic system. Where Jones and others had warned that too much sexual pleasure could cause neurasthenia, Van de Velde countered with the opposite threat—that too little sexual pleasure could cause neurasthenia. Even the lack of *peak* sexual pleasure could still cause neurasthenia. Thus, Van de Velde warned that the practice of *coitus interruptus* with orgasm could still cause neurasthenia, because when the man ejaculates outside the vagina, "the intensity and *abandon* [italicized in the original] of his pleasure is diminished and impaired" (Van de Velde, 1926/1930, p. 190). (For a more recent version of this idea, compare Reich's [1942] contention that lack of full-body orgasms causes neural shrinkage, gangrene, and ultimately cancer.)

The earlier concern that the pursuit of sexual pleasure may be immoral as well as unhealthful was directly countered by the insistence in the marriage manuals that *not* arousing one's partner to the point of orgasm is immoral and unhealthful. Van de Velde was a moralist and a propagandist. Where before him it had been selfish and immature to study manuals of sexual technique, he made such study one of the moral obligations of a responsible sex partner. Even Van de Velde's use of the word "marriage" instead of "sex" was a master stroke. No one appeared to notice that it made the title of his book nonsensical: *Ideal Marriage: Its Physiology and Technique*. This new morality brought the sex manuals out of the closet (they could now be given to newly married couples by their ministers), with the result that the decades before Masters and Johnson saw a flowering of the technique approach to sex.

Thus, the stern insistence on not being casual about sex that now appears comic was part of a vigorous campaign to break down a phobic resistance to sex. But the marriage manuals did not free us to become more aroused; they only made us work at it. To the extent that they succeeded, it is as if they transformed what had been a phobia into a compulsion.

Masters and Johnson were the first sex therapists to make no direct attempt to intensify erotic feelings—a far cry from the popular vision of the sex therapist that had been promoted by the marriage manuals. This made their successes appear to be "miracle cures," since they even went out of their way *not* to promote an erotic or romantic atmosphere. A few simple reorienting assignments that block the compulsion to work at sex can in some couples quickly restore sexual pleasure and relieve symptoms, even those of long standing. The systematic implications of this strategy are such that its having worked at all has been been of far-reaching significance. It raised the possibility that sexual enhancement techniques are unnecessary and perhaps antitherapeutic, their effect being to intensify performance anxiety in the effort to reduce pleasure anxiety.

If Masters and Johnson's contribution was so revolutionary, how can we explain the widespread belief, noted earlier, that their work was merely derivative? I have already suggested that the effect of the Masters and Johnson revolution has been so profound that it is difficult to recall the preoccupations of the sex counseling that preceded it. In the history of ideas, it can be surprisingly difficult to detect a new idea. The new idea can be so immediately convincing and can so completely obliterate the old idea that the old one vanishes, and people are left with the impression that the new idea was the one they had had all along. Also, the new idea often coexists with the old on a level of generality that makes contradictions easy to ignore. What makes this issue of more than academic interest is the fact that the view of Masters and Johnson's contribution as merely derivative is an obstacle to the appreciation of the Masters and Johnson paradigm—and hence, I am suggesting, to the understanding of desire disorders.

Since the penetration of Masters and Johnson's insights has been limited, many sexologists and sex therapists are still fighting the good fight against the belief that it is medically and morally risky not to control the sex drive. Their work is entirely in the tradition of the marriage manuals, with the same sense of spreading the gospel of sexual freedom. However, just as it was for McCary, and for Van de Velde, and as has been said of the sexual revolution, they have only promoted the freedom to say "yes." Thus, we have *The Yes Books of Sex* (National Sex Forum, 1973 *et seq.*). Those who work from this model label people as either "sex-positive" or "sex-negative." People who are still sexually apathetic after having been given permission to enjoy sex are simply poor dupes who need more extensive deprogramming. In the name of sexual liberation, we have new rules about how to think.

Many contemporary sex therapists find the technique approach to be just as inevitable as did Van de Velde. They rely on sexual enhancement techniques, professional sex films (for a critique, see Apfelbaum, 1984b), pornography, fantasy assignments, vibrators, and instruction in techniques of stroking and massage (especially self-stroking and self-massage). Sex therapists who use these techniques will also use Masters and Johnson assignments without regard to the incompatibility between the demand quality of direct efforts to manipulate level of arousal and the nondemand Masters and Johnson assignments (Apfelbaum, 1985). Masters and Johnson's comparatively abstinent approach is typically seen by these sex therapists as an expression of a personal preference rather than as an inevitable consequence of Masters and Johnson's theoretical and therapeutic model.

As suggested above, the sexual permission-givers think of those who do not respond as hopeless dupes. Psychodynamic sex therapists either see nonresponders as having an investment in their apathy or simply think that this means the problem is deep-seated and therefore requires more extensive exploratory or relationship therapy. Missing is the Masters and Johnson insight that the "sex-positive" reaction against what we can call the "sexual drive phobia" represents a new tyranny. Just as the fear of being dysfunctional can create a dysfunction, so the fear of lacking a "yes" response to sex can create a desire disorder. As Kaplan (1979) has suggested, people can feel even more humiliated, inadequate, and abnormal about an arousal problem than about a performance problem. This should not be surprising, considering the male-identified climate of opinion regarding frigidity that I have reviewed.

Recognition of the causal role of response anxiety is blocked by the focus on pleasure anxiety. This jeopardizes brief treatment, because in working to dispel guilt and fear about pleasure by permission giving, authoritative exhortation, and other forms of endorsement, the sex therapist can intensify the patient's anxiety about *not* feeling pleasure. Reassurances that sexual pleasure is normal and natural can liberate the patient who does experience it, but it can make the patient who does not experience if feel all the more abnormal and unnatural.

Before Van de Velde, keeping sexual contact brief and compartmentalized not only protected people against becoming too turned on; it also protected them from experiencing the fear of not being turned on. If becoming sexually aroused is medically and morally risky, then it is clearly okay to not feel aroused. Certainly, if coitus is to be endured while thinking of England, a woman need feel no pressure to enjoy it. To the extent that coitus is just a matter of reaching orgasm quickly, and to the extent that both partners believe it is the man's privilege, then the man has no one to perform for and the woman is not required to respond.

The need to be adequate in our socially assigned roles—a need that typically is considered superficial by psychodynamic therapists—is, I would argue, the "deepest" of all motives. Although postindustrial Western cultures are substantially liberated from the total duty-boundness of anthill-like tribal societies, we are still dominated by role definitions. Thus, when presented with new personal goals, we instantly experience them as new duties. Even self-actualization, as in the form of sexual fulfillment, becomes just another duty; as such, we feel the pressure to accomplish it.

The effect has been that in the present period these goals themselves have been discredited because people ape self-actualization and authenticity as a consequence of the pressure to be self-actualized and authentic already. Therapists who are sensitive to this new tyranny, as I have just characterized it, try to reassure people that it is okay not to be self-actualized or authentic, and also that it is okay not to be sexually free and not to enjoy sex fully. We are told that sex is not always exciting, that we should not expect fireworks, and that maybe even a return to older values is appropriate. (Just what is meant by "older values" is unclear; we may hope that this does not mean a return to the concern with "excessive onanism" or with demoniacal possession by incubi and succubi, who stole beneath the bedclothes while we slept, causing us to have wet dreams.)

My impression is that these well-meaning exhortations are ineffective denials that only intensify what I (Apfelbaum, 1984a) have called "performance-anxiety anxiety"—the anxiety about still feeling performance anxiety after being told that it is not only unnecessary to feel it but perhaps foolish as well.

The Neo-Van de Veldian Approach

Since many people experience a rapid sexual responsiveness that looks like simply "letting go," it can easily appear that those who have difficulty responding are *resisting* letting go, whether out of fear or guilt or hostility. This logic has generated a neo-Van de Veldian approach, best exemplified by Kaplan (1974, 1979), in which the patient is exhorted to work at overcoming this resistance.

What makes the rapid sexual response style of special significance is the fact that it seems to represent "sexual freedom," meaning the freedom to allow the expression of the sex drive. This seeming independence of sexual responsiveness from its context is, after all, the most convincing evidence for the drive metaphor. People who are rapidly sexually responsive are often that way in all their sexual relationships, and often that way under conditions that would be expected to turn them off (e.g., an apathetic, dysfunctional, or uncongenial partner; fatigue; illness; or uncomfortable circumstances) (Apfelbaum, 1977b, 1977c).

An explanation for this sexual facility that does not rely on the drive metaphor is not hard to find. It does not immediately come to mind, partly because the drive metaphor is so taken for granted that alternative models are never considered, and partly because it conflicts with our idealizations of sex (see below). Consider Helen Kaplan's (1979) sketch of the person who is "conflict-free about sex":

> The person who is conflict-free about sex mentally does the opposite of the inhibited one, in the sense that he does *not allow* [italicized in the original] negative feelings or thoughts to intrude upon his sexual pleasure. He arranges the weekend to be free of business intrusions; he avoids arguments with his partner—in fact, he acts so as to bring out the best in her. In order to put her in a receptive mood, he focuses only on her positive attributes—makes her feel special—all in the service of his pleasure. When he is in a sexual situation, he does not criticize his partner's taste in bedroom furniture, or see figure flaws, or comment on less than brilliant conversation. His behavior instinctively maximizes his erotic experience. (pp. 84–85)

Addressing herself to women's hesitancy to block out the partner, Kaplan (1974) advises that "a woman must learn to 'shut out' the nuances of her partner's behavior, at least to the extent that it [sic] will not inhibit her sexual response; she must learn, in short, to develop a more autonomous pattern of sexual functioning" (p. 358). Thus, Kaplan (1974) speaks approvingly of a woman who was "easily multiorgastic in almost any situation" (p. 169) and who even "was perfectly orgastic even when feeling rejected!" (p. 172), citing this as evidence that "she had no sexual difficulties." To develop this sexual style, Kaplan, as is well known, strongly recommends working at summoning up fantasies and trains partners not to interfere with each other's efforts to concentrate.

In these few incisive formulations, Kaplan reminds us that erotic arousal does not fit the metaphor of a drive that pushes for discharge, but rather is a response based on autonomy from the partner and on a narrowing of one's mental set—a mental set that may require careful cultivation. Accordingly, what can make sexual arousal independent of even the most adverse conditions is the motivation to accomplish exactly that objective. This has nothing to do with degree of maturity, the capacity for intimacy, or being in touch with one's body, much less with good nutrition and getting lots of rest.

This is not obvious, partly because of the continuing influence of older modes of thought, but also because this vision of sex conflicts with our idealizations. For example, sexually apathetic or anorgasmic women are often treated by having them practice focusing on bodily sensations (e.g., stroking their forearms, brushing themselves with a feather, taking a bubble bath) and by masturbation training, in which they develop a routine that can be brought into sex with a partner. Although this training is entirely in accordance with Kaplan's recommendation to develop sexual autonomy by practicing focusing on sensation and on fantasy to block out the partner, this objective is never mentioned.

Instead, training of this type is surrounded with the rhetoric of sensory awareness. The idea presented is that women need to reclaim their bodies (presumably from men). There also is a rhetoric of entitlement: Women have the *right* to possess their own bodies. No one mentions that the objective is to learn to block out the partner. The reason for this is that we do not like to think of sex as a solo pursuit, as is attested to by masturbation guilt. However, this clarification can be quite relieving to women who resist such assignments or who find them unhelpful or unpleasant. When sex therapists think about or talk to people who are sexually apathetic, they compare them with an idealization—someone who is sexually in tune with his or her surroundings or even who is willing to be vulnerable—despite the fact that the person who is sexually free is, as Kaplan suggests, someone who is able to tune out the context and who hardly need worry about being vulnerable.

When we offer a clarification of this type, some people who are sexually apathetic discover that they do not want to be sexually free, or they realize that their sexual apathy is a consequence, at least in part, of their scruples about blocking out the partner. They may just realize that they are not that kind of person—that they really want to stay in touch with the partner and to feel contact, even if this means a loss of the arousal that a fantasy can bring. In other words, this explanation does much to de-pathologize so-called "desire disorders," as on the theoretical level it does much to demystify the drive metaphor.

On the therapeutic level, under the influence of the drive metaphor, most sex therapists have followed the lead of those who are good at blocking out the partner (and the relationship), taking this sexual style as their reference model for normal sexuality. This has resulted not only in recommending to patients that they try to keep their relationship issues out of the bedroom; it has also resulted in sex therapists' paying little attention to the particular ways in which sex partners affect each other. This means that little attention has been paid to the conditions for erotic arousal. In effect, arousal is assumed, and if it is not present, then the therapist wants to know the reason why. In contrast, my assumption is that the conditions for arousal are not necessarily present, and so if arousal *is* present, I want to know the reason why.

Up to this point, I have largely limited my argument to the ideological battlefield. These points can be clarified by appealing to a clinical case. After this, it will be easier to specify the therapeutic interventions that differentiate the strategy assuming that desire disorders are created by response anxiety from the strategy assuming that they are created by pleasure anxiety. My objective is to show that the two strategies are both ideologically and therapeutically incompatible.

A Case of Low Sexual Desire

Background

Nan and Len were a couple in their 30s married 11 years, with two children. The presenting complaint was Nan's lack of sexual interest. From the beginning of their relationship, Nan had never initiated sex, and Len felt that if he did not she never would. Nan had no difficulty reaching orgasm in oral sex, but was slow to become aroused and, in general, did not get much out of sex. Nan initiated the therapeutic contact, saying that she had begun to feel more discouraged about the problem, although nothing new had happened recently. Nan and Len said that they got along well and that there were no other serious problems in the relationship. The cotherapists (myself and another therapist) concurred in this assessment.

At the end of the first visit (each visit was 2 hours long), they were given a sensate focus assignment to do three times and were told to write reports on each time. My colleagues and I at the Berkeley Sex Therapy Group always require written reports; this is stressed in the written instructions for the assignments that we give to the couple. Both the use of written instructions for the assignments and the requirement of written reports are, as far as I know, unique to our center, reflecting our interest in discovering what the patients actually are responding to. Nan and Len took 3 weeks to do this (the usual time period) before returning for a second visit, in which they read their reports (after being asked about reactions to the tape of the previous session—they were given a copy—and anything else of interest that had happened since). They were then given the second sensate focus assignment.

What follows is an excerpt from the tape of their third visit. It is of Nan beginning to give her report on the first time they did this second assignment, and is followed by a brief excerpt from Len's remarks.

In the excerpt, Nan mentions writing about "the passive front." In the instructions for the assignments, the client is told to report on the four phases: passive and active, front and back. Note that Nan begins by talking and then goes to reading from her notes, which she interrupts at one point to add a comment. (This transcript appeared in its entirety in a previous publication [Apfelbaum & Apfelbaum, 1985], in which it was subjected to a detailed analysis. In that discussion, there was no additional presentation of the case itself.)

Excerpt from the Couple's Sex Therapy Transcript

NAN: *(Discussing her notes on the second sensate focus assignment)*
Up 'til now, if you asked me how I felt when Len touched me, I'd

say "Blank." I'd say that I had no feelings at all. Then the first time we did the assignment I noticed that it wasn't so much a blank feeling as that I was turning it off—that I didn't want to think about it or feel about it.

I realized that when Len is touching me I don't want to be aware of anything, especially my feelings, my emotions. I seem to focus all my thoughts on how I should be reacting to what he's doing, and nothing of what I'm feeling.

As I started to write about the passive front [meaning the sequence in which she was supine and Len did the touching] and I thought about it—I didn't really think about it when he was doing it, but when I started writing about it—*(She begins reading from her notes:)* "I started to feel really angry at having to be touched, and I didn't know if it was at him or men in general. I couldn't define it in myself. I was downright mad at having to be touched.

"Then what confused me even further is that I knew I wanted to be touched and I wanted to be loved—but the two don't seem to coincide—and with this normal-type life that I want to have it wouldn't work.

"I sat and I thought about it a long time and I couldn't get at what was causing it, or the root of it. I think the argument we had earlier in the day might have something to do with it." *(She pauses to comment:)* But I would say there is a sense of—I would say most of the time—*(She resumes reading:)* "When Len first starts to touch me I feel angry or irritated or hostile at the touch. I guess that's why I would rather touch *him*.

"Then a lot of questions started going through my mind, like: 'Why can't I just enjoy making love?' 'Why can't I just accept it for what it's supposed to be: an expression of love and closeness, a fulfillment of needs and desires?' I got very frustrated at that point.". . .

LEN: *(Stating his position later in the session)* She's always been real slow to get into it, and I knew from the beginning—I've had to be real patient, real careful. At first [in high school, at the beginning of the relationship] she would just freeze up. The other guys, they would back off, but I knew what I wanted. So I just took plenty of time and all, and she would gradually come around.

She really enjoys it when we get started, but there's this resistance she's got. Once she gets over it there's no problem and she's the best in bed I've ever had. I know she really wants it. She's just afraid of being a bad girl. *(Laughs.)* I don't need to tell *you* about all that.

I just wish by now it wasn't still always so much work to get her into it, but I know she really wants it.

The Course of Treatment

As I see it, Nan's report is a snapshot of her response anxiety. However, what makes her report of value for my argument is the way it can easily be interpreted as a snapshot of pleasure anxiety. In fact, when this transcript was presented to therapists attending our human sexuality courses, most of whom had recently completed their training (very few had had training in sex therapy), almost all of them saw Nan either as suffering from pleasure anxiety or as having an investment in being withholding. Of 426 therapists, only 11 saw Nan as suffering from response anxiety; this was despite the fact that they had just listened to a lecture on response anxiety, and also despite the fact that many felt that Len was clearly part of the problem.

After Nan read her notes, my cotherapist and I commented, "It sounds like you think you should just enjoy being touched." We thought that, in a nutshell, this was her problem. What made it so impossible for the therapists who responded to the transcript in our courses to see it this way was that they themselves also thought that she should enjoy being touched. That was the assumption behind their interpretations that she was afraid of pleasure or that she was withholding. Had they made these interpretations to her, this would have reinforced her belief that she should just enjoy being touched.

We told Nan (still in response to her report) that we thought she was feeling a lot of pressure to respond positively, but that she took this pressure for granted; we added that it was very perceptive of her to see how hard she was trying to have the "right" reaction. We noted that it looked as if this was having the effect of making her "blank"—that is, of blanking out the reactions she actually was having—and that recognizing this was a start.

We said that we needed a better X-ray of her reactions, and that to begin with we would give her the 50-item Script Lines Checklist (Apfelbaum & Apfelbaum, 1985, pp. 479–481) to complete in relation to the third assignment, which was genital sensate focus. When they returned for the fourth session, Nan had checked the following 18 lines:

> I feel I'm supposed to like everything you are doing.
> I'm worried about what you're thinking.
> That doesn't feel good but I don't know what would.
> It feels like you're being too careful.
> It feels like you're trying too hard.
> Right now my mind is a blank.
> I wish I could enjoy your stroking.
> This is a chore for me.
> I feel turned off.
> I'm afraid you're going to feel rejected if I don't enjoy this more.
> I feel like you need me to be more involved.

> I want something, but I don't know what it is.
> I'm afraid you're going to be disappointed.
> I'm afraid you're getting bored.
> I'm feeling that there's too much I don't like.
> I'm afraid of discouraging you.
> I'm feeling too finicky.
> I wish this wasn't so important.

We also got her to talk about how guilty it made her feel to have these reactions and how worried she was about their effect on Len. However, Len insisted that this was okay; it didn't bother him.

Then we had the couple repeat the third assignment, (something we typically do) and did our version of assertion training with Nan, getting her to assert, not her wishes or rights, but her guilt and her fears. We worked on ways she could say, when Len was touching her, that she felt pressured to enjoy it and uptight if she did not. In other words, having identified and specified Nan's response anxiety, we then worked on helping her to express it.

In the fifth session Nan said that she got a lot of relief out of doing just a little of this, bur Len said that he was beginning to get discouraged, and that it was hard to keep doing the assignment with her "complaining" like that. In view of Len's reaction, we decided to interrupt having Nan express her reactions and instead asked them to write up one of their spontaneous sexual encounters.

When they returned for the sixth session, it became clear from their reports that Nan was still suppressing all her reactions, despite her disclosures during the assignments. We then suggested that in their spontaneous sexual encounters they practice taking breaks; our purpose was to have Nan use these as a vehicle for talking about her reactions more fully and for Len to have a chance to respond. For this purpose, we gave them what we call the "stop" exercise, a formal method for taking breaks and talking.

In reaction to our proposing this, Len suddenly got upset for the first time. He said that doing this might just make it impossible to "finish the act." When we interviewed him we discovered that he had found it almost unbearable not to go on to intercourse and orgasm when doing the assignments, and that he resented this restriction from the beginning.

We told him that in our experience this typically means that that the person has not been able to relax fully. He reacted defensively, countering that there was no way he could relax if he could not count on "really having sex." We then told him how the compulsion to reach orgasm often limits arousal, and described to him how Masters and Johnson came to the concept of goal-directedness. We also said that with greater relaxation he could expect to have better ejaculatory control. Nan at this point said that

Len actually seemed a lot more relaxed in the assignments than he did in sex, and that in fact he never seemed relaxed in sex.

Len tried to dispute this, but further elaboration by Nan helped bring him around. We then developed the picture of Len as a driven sex partner who, from the beginning of their relationship, always had to "complete the act." Based on their reports in the seventh session, we could identify signs of tension in Len, such as involuntary pelvic movements.

By the eighth session, Nan was feeling significantly less responsible for her lack of sexual interest and consequently was free to call breaks both when Len seemed tense and when she did. At this point their positions had significantly shifted. Len was now the identified patient, and Nan was looking forward to the assignments. She even got to the point of being able to call off a sexual encounter in the middle because she felt they were both too tense.

By the ninth session Nan reported no longer feeling blank and no longer feeling the flashes of hostility at Len's touches that she had reported earlier (see the transcript). She also was at times looking forward to sex and even initiating it. She was now less compulsively active and more in control of what was going on. (Her compulsive activity had been her defense, enabling her to avoid response anxiety by touching Len. As they are designed to do, the sensate focus instructions blocked this defense by forcing Nan to lie there and not touch Len.) They both reported that Len was more relaxed and was now able to enjoy long periods of genital stimulation, half an hour or so, without experiencing urgency.

We saw them for the 10th and last session about 2 months later, and found that there had been no return of Nan's apathy. This also appeared to be true on a 1-year follow-up questionnaire.

Discussion

Another woman might also have had negative reactions to Len's pressured way of acting and might also have felt some some corresponding response anxiety. But she might have had the motivation and the ability to concentrate on what she could respond to, blocking out what turned her off about Len. This is the kind of person for whom sex is thought of as purely physical, although it would be more accurate to think of it as purely mental. As Kaplan (1979) put it in one of the passages cited above, such a person "mentally does *not allow* negative feelings or thoughts to intrude upon his sexual pleasure." This is what "sexual freedom" ultimately means; it has more to do with industriousness than with freedom, as I have proposed earlier.

This sexual response style is widely taken to represent the simple freedom to let go and to abandon oneself to sensation. However, it always turns out that when people with this style do appear to let go and abandon themselves, they experience only "positive feelings and thoughts," to use Kaplan's phrase. The simple fact in Nan's case is that if she had had this freedom to let go and abandon herself, what she would have felt would have been the experience of oppression: She would have abandoned herself to feeling turned off by a compulsively driven partner and to feeling threatened by the possibility that his "patience" would eventually run out, as well as feeling pressured to respond positively nevertheless.

The standard model makes no provision for getting in touch with such experiences. The reason for this is that such experiences are interpreted as resistances to experiencing pleasure. As I have indicated, almost all the therapists who examined Nan's report thought that she was suffering from pleasure anxiety. They did not consider the possibility that there was little pleasure available for her to feel anxious about, because, as I have suggested, the typical assumption is that sex is a drive and so a person will be aroused unless he or she has some resistance to it.

The Rejection of Reality

These therapists speculated that Nan must have had a restrictive sexual upbringing and that she may have been an incest survivor. They were right about the former, but there was no evidence for the latter. However, as I see it, her restrictive sexual upbringing (and, if she had experienced it, an incest trauma) would have been among the influences that contributed to Nan's dependency on reality. In other words, these experiences would have made her more sensitive to sexual oppression and hence less able to block it out.

These therapists also speculated, in time-honored fashion, that Nan was withholding (the frigid woman, by tradition, is ungiving and cold). They thought that she might be angry at men and/or that her lack of sexual interest was a weapon she used in a power struggle with Len. They also thought that she should take responsibility for her lack of assertiveness and learn to ask for what she wanted.

Notice how, in all these interpretations, reality evaporated. Nan was thought of as creating her reality, or, if not, she was expected to change it. In no instance was her experience of it likely to be brought out. Indeed, the feminist therapists who did insist that Len's contribution to the problem had to be recognized had no way to cope with it therapeutically other than to recommend that Len seek treatment on his own, even though they realized that this was a highly unlikely possibility.

The rejection of reality was especially apparent in the recommendation that Nan learn to ask for what she wanted. This is, of course, a familiar intervention, the idea being that your partner is not a mind reader and therefore cannot know how and where you want to be touched unless you

communicate it. Although this is a logical, if somewhat risky, recommendation (telling your partner what you want often results in him or her either
being unable to remember it or else doing it relentlessly, and this is the up
side; the down side is that you may be attacked for being too demanding), it
often is applied mindlessly on the implicit assumption that you can indeed
specify how you want to be touched.

Consider what this might mean in Nan's case. Suppose that what
turned her off about Len's touch was that it was too insistent because he
was trying too hard, or perhaps that it was absent-minded and mechanical
because he was discouraged. Or his touch may have been too hesitant
because he was worried about how she would respond. Or, if he was simply
committed to doing his part no matter how Nan felt, his touch may have
been too determined and conscientious. Another possibility is that his touch
may have been too possessive, conveying his sense of having conquered Nan
where lesser men had given up (apropos of his report). Given these quite
ordinary and likely possibilities, it is a rash assumption, first, to think that
Nan could be aware of what she did not like about how she was being
touched; and second, to think that even if she could have been aware of it,
Len would have been able to adjust accordingly.

If we try to infer the rock-bottom assumption underlying these therapists' interpretations, it is that you make your own reality, and if you refuse
to, you must have an investment in keeping it as it is. Consequently, there
was surprisingly little empathy for Nan's dilemma. Those who did identify
with her found themselves without a way of helping her, as if the standard
therapy model requires an adversarial relation to patients and therefore a
rejection of their reality.

Resistance to Pleasure

The one interpretation that best identifies the climate of opinion regarding
desire disorders is that the person so afflicted is resisting sexual pleasure.
This is what ties together all the interpretations of Nan's case that I elicited
from the therapists who reviewed it. These interpretations can be divided
into two subgroups of types of resistance to pleasure.

The first subgroup concerns pleasure anxiety as such. Here the idea of
some therapists was that Nan may have been resisting pleasure—that is,
resisting letting go or losing control—because she believed that nice girls
should be restrained or because she had been taught that sex is bad or dirty.
(Needless to say, the implicit assumption here was that sex is not bad or
dirty; this is one of the standard denials of sexual reality that is becoming
harder to maintain as we are increasingly confronted with the realities of
sexual harassment, abuse, and the varieties of rape.)

In this same subgroup is the interpretation that Nan was resisting erotic arousal because of a fear of intimacy (such an interpretation flies in the face of the reality that in most sexual encounters there is very little intimacy to be afraid of). Another interpretation based on the assumption of resistance to pleasure was that Nan might not feel that she deserved pleasure.

The second subgroup concerns resistance to arousal based on a need to thwart or defeat the partner. Here the motive might be simple hostility, as to men in general (as if this were somehow inappropriate), or it might be the product of power struggle, as in a need to punish or get even with the partner. This would be the idea that Nan withheld arousal because she felt ripped off in other areas of the relationship.

This is a very popular interpretation of desire disorders (and undoubtedly will be well represented by my colleagues between these covers), but I have yet to see anyone remark on the more pertinent issue that underlies it—the fact that if you use the withholding of sexual response for the purpose of barter or retaliation you must not feel that sex is really for you. Imagine Kaplan's woman who was "orgastic" even when feeling rejected: She would have not have given up sexual satisfaction even if she felt ripped off in every other respect. Indeed, I think if that were the case, she would have demanded sex all the more. Sex was something she took, not something she gave.

Also, people will brood on past injustices as a way to *justify* feeling turned off, getting themselves genuinely to believe that they could be turned on if these wrongs were righted. To the therapist, this can look like convincing evidence that such patients wish to be turned off. However, my impression is that they are defending against the self-blame they would feel if they realized that, even if the slate were wiped clean, they would still not be turned on.

Of course, the issue really turns on the question of what it is that is being resisted. The standard interpretation that pleasure is what is being resisted is almost routinely and therefore uncritically applied. In Nan's case, at least, it seems clear that she was resisting the expression and the awareness of her own dissatisfactions. In effect, she was resisting being resistive. To put it less paradoxically, her problem was compliance rather than resistance.

From the ego-analytic perspective, Nan's problem was not that she was resistant, but that she was unable to resist and that she needed to be able to do so. I would even argue that the way in which standard interpretations disqualify resistance makes people more vulnerable to sexual abuse, since what causes the victim to be abused is the inability to resist.

This is not to deny the truth of many of the standard interpretations, even if, as I have tried to indicate, some of them are quite capricious. Nan might have experienced a degree of sexual shyness; she might indeed have felt that she did not deserve pleasure; she might well have felt at least ambivalent toward Len; and she might also have been passive–aggressive.

However, to think of these as primary causes of her lack of sexual interest is to indulge in what I would call "id analysis" as contrasted with "ego analysis." These causes all proved to be secondary to Nan's inability to feel entitled to her lack of erotic arousal, and also secondary to the self-attribution of responsibility for her lack of arousal that created her response anxiety.

To relieve Nan's response anxiety required us to demonstrate to her the ways in which she was not responsible for it, which in turn required a careful investigation of her sexual reality. Therapists who assume that the patient's reality is of secondary importance—either on the grounds that you make your own reality ("where there's a will there's a way") or on the belief that the sex drive is prepotent—would be likely to take Nan's initial report at face value: "Up 'til now, if you asked me how I felt when Len touched me, I'd say 'Blank.' I'd say that I had no feelings at all." Nan's apparent lack of feelings would then be accepted by these therapists and taken as a point of departure for the interpretations I have listed: That is, she would be seen as having "no response" because she was afraid to have it or was withholding it. Nan would have been quite likely to cooperate in such interpretations, since she disowned all her feelings and hence was convinced that she was blank (i.e., had no response), and that this represented a personal failing.

Recall that it was only during the second assignment that Nan had any clue that she felt anything besides blankness, and even then she said that it was only when she began writing her report that she became aware of her feelings. Add to this the possibility that Nan might even yet have escaped confronting her blankness if assignments had been used in which she was free to reciprocate Len's touch. Such assignments would have lacked the set-breaking effect made possible by the strict division into active and passive roles intrinsic to Masters and Johnson's version of sensate focus.

Failure Cases

We find cases of low sexual desire among the easiest to treat, and have not had a failure case of this type in which treatment was pursued to its conclusion. This fact is deceptive, however, since we have had a sizeable number of dropouts—perhaps 15% of the total. Since such cases are often quite brief, it is difficult to find one that has sufficient systematic signifi-cance. Hence, an impressionistic summary may be of greater value.

We have had a number of cases like Nan and Len's, in which the man is much more threatened than Len was by our calling his sexuality into question. He feels much more strongly than Len did that his partner is determined to resist arousal and to thwart him, and that our approach will only undermine his position and thus allow her to go on depriving him.

We also have had a sizeable number of dropouts among cases of patients who are in concurrent individual therapy with other therapists or who are themselves therapists. They are so convinced that the problem represents hostility or fears of intimacy, and game playing generated by these issues, that they are impatient with detailed explorations of their sexual encounters; they believe that our approach is too superficial and that we overlook unconscious motivations.

We also find cases more difficult when the woman is the sexually demanding partner. If Nan's and Len's positions had been reversed, we would not have been able to solve the problem so expeditiously. A woman is more likely to feel rejected by her partner's lack of a positive response, and this makes it harder to expose the way she intensifies the performance pressure experienced by her partner. Also, when a man is the oppressed partner, he typically feels less entitled than a woman does to feeling left out or used.

Conclusion

Kaplan's contention that response anxiety is even more intense than performance anxiety leads to the conclusion that the ultimate working through of Masters and Johnson's insight into performance–response anxiety has to do with being able to tolerate lack of erotic arousal. Of all the abilities that sex requires, this is perhaps the most difficult one to develop.

My impression is that few people do not experience response anxiety. In our own practice, we have only been able to help people to approximate the goal of eliminating it. To test yourself, just consider whether if sex goes well for you you feel proud, and whether if it goes poorly you feel humiliated or inadequate. As a check on whether in addition you experience response-anxiety anxiety, consider whether you feel that you should not have responses to sex such as pride or shame, since you think that sex is not a test of skill.

What ultimately will help us to progress in this area of ego development is the consciousness raising that has been steadily forcing us to recognize disowned realities regarding sexual oppression: sexual exploitation, sex-role demands, and the effects of male dominance. The more we recognize legitimate reasons for lack of arousal, the less responsible for it we will feel, and hence the less response anxiety we will experience, with the result that we will be less likely to become locked into experiences of lack of arousal.

References

Apfelbaum, B. (1977a). A contribution to the development of the behavioral-analytic sex therapy model. *Journal of Sex and Marital Therapy, 3,* 128–138.

Apfelbaum, B. (1977b). On the etiology of sexual dysfunction. *Journal of Sex and Marital Therapy, 3,* 50–62.

Apfelbaum, B. (1977c). Sexual functioning reconsidered. In R. Gemme & C. C. Wheeler (Eds.), *Progress in sexology*. New York: Plenum Press.

Apfelbaum, B. (1984a). Ego-analytic sex therapy: The problem of performance-anxiety anxiety. In R. Segraves & E. J. Haeberle (Eds.), *Emerging dimensions of sexology*. New York: Praeger.

Apfelbaum, B. (1984b). Professional sex films versus sexual reality. In R. Segraves & E. J. Haeberle (Eds.), *Emerging dimensions of sexology*. New York: Praeger.

Apfelbaum, B. (1985). Masters and Johnson's contribution. *Journal of Sex Education and Therapy, 11*, 5–11.

Apfelbaum, B., & Apfelbaum, C. (1985). The ego-analytic approach to sexual apathy. In D. C. Goldberg (Ed.), *Contemporary marriage: Special issues in couples therapy*. Homewood, IL: Dorsey Press.

Apfelbaum, B., & Gill, M. M. (1987). *Ego analysis, interpretive neutrality, and the relativity of defense: The technical implications of the structural approach*. Manuscript in preparation.

Davenport, W. H. (1977). Sex in cross-cultural perspective. In F. A. Beach (Ed.), *Human sexuality in four perspectives*. Baltimore: Johns Hopkins University Press.

Butterfield, O. M. (1964). *Sexual harmony in marriage*. New York: Emerson Books.

Comfort, A. (1967). *The anxiety makers*. London: Books and Broadcasts.

Fenichel, O. (1941). *Problems of psychoanalytic technique*. New York: The Psychoanalytic Quarterly.

Freud, S. (1957). On the universal tendency to debasement in the sphere of love. In J. Strachey (Ed. and Trans.), *Standard edition of the complete psychological works of Sigmund Freud* (Vol. 11). London: Hogarth Press. (Original work published 1912)

Hartman, W. E., & Fithian, M. A. (1972). *The treatment of sexual dysfunction*. Long Beach, CA: Center for Marital and Sexual Studies.

Kaplan, H. S. (1974). *The new sex therapy*. New York: Brunner/Mazel.

Kaplan, H. S. (1979). *Disorders of sexual desire*. New York: Brunner/Mazel.

Kolodny, R. S., Masters, W. H., & Johnson, V. E. (1979). *Textbook of sexual medicine*. Boston: Little, Brown.

Lewis, L. S., & Brissett, D. (1967). Sex as work: A study of avocational counseling. *Social Problems, 15*, 8–18.

Marshall, D. C., & Suggs, R. C. (1971). *Human sexual behavior: Variations in the ethnographic spectrum*. New York: Basic Books.

Masters, W. H., & Johnson, V. E. (1966). *Human sexual response*. Boston: Little, Brown.

Masters, W. H., & Johnson, V. E. (1970). *Human sexual inadequacy*. Boston: Little, Brown.

McCary, J. L. (1973). *Human sexuality* (2nd ed.). New York: Van Nostrand Reinhold.

National Sex Forum. (1972 et seq.) *The yes books of sex*. San Francisco: Author.

Reich, W. (1942). The carcinomatous shrinking biopathy. *International Journal of Sex-Economy and Orgone-Research, 1*, 11–54.

Seagraves, R. T. (1986, May). Report of the workgroup on DSM-IIIR. *Society for Sex Therapy and Research Newsletter*.

Tannahill, R. (1980). *Sex in history*. New York: Stein & Day.

Van de Velde, T. H. (1930). *Ideal marriage: Its physiology and technique* (rev. ed., S. Browne, Trans.). New York: Random House. (Original work published 1926)

Zilbergeld, B. (1981). Contribution to panel. *Some nonstandard deviations from current thinking in the sex profession*. Panel presented at the annual meeting of the American Association of Sex Educators, Counselors, and Therapists, Las Vegas.

Cognitive and Behavioral Perspectives

II

5

Broad-Spectrum Treatment of Low Sexual Desire: Integration of Cognitive, Behavioral, and Systemic Therapy

Joseph LoPiccolo and Jerry M. Friedman

A striking feature of LoPiccolo and Friedman's perspective on problems of sexual desire is the comprehensive manner in which they approach both assessment and treatment. Couples seeking treatment for these problems are seen for several intensive evaluation sessions, during which they are requested to complete standardized questionnaires as well as to respond to diagnostically subtle open-ended questions. Attention is directed to the systemic nature of the presenting problem and the manner in which the desire difficulty may affect the maintenance of homeostatic balance within the couple. LoPiccolo and Friedman suggest that low desire may play an adaptive role in the couple's interpersonal system. An early focus in treatment on the homeostatic issues sets the stage for insight-oriented treatment. Furthermore, therapists are forewarned about the potential resistances to therapy.

LoPiccolo and Freidman postulate that the etiology of sexual desire problems is broad; they cite 12 individual causes, ranging from the role of anhedonic obsessive–compulsive personality types to that of masked sexual deviation, as well as 7 separate relationship factors that influence desire problems. They acknowledge that many factors may operate simultaneously, in a multiplicative fashion, to determine the severity of the desire difficulty. These authors suggest that because of the complexity of these cases, the treatment approach needs to be comprehensive and broad-spectrum.

The treatment model recommended is an innovative, integrated approach. The first phase is devoted to helping individuals develop experiential/sensory awareness, since many low-desire individuals are unable to articulate feelings or even to identify their affective reactions to sexual stimulation. The goal of this phase of treatment is to assist patients in recognizing bodily cues and to begin to label them as anger, anxiety, and so forth. Body awareness exercises, including Gestalt-like experiential interventions, are employed. Couples are encouraged to develop insight regarding their desire problems either concomitantly with their experiential/sensory awareness, or occasionally prior to this first phase. The authors further suggest that individuals require an adequate explanation for their lack of sexual interest, in order to reduce associated anxiety. Insight also helps to set the stage for the cognitive and behavioral interventions that follow, and to provide a rationale for these subsequent interventions. The third phase of therapy typically involves cognitive restructuring, in which the therapist assists the couple in altering irrational thoughts that may inhibit sexual desire. The patients' worst fears are explored, and coping strategies are devised. Finally, behavioral interventions are proposed, ranging from basic sex therapy desensitization procedures to other nonsexual exercises.

LoPiccolo and Friedman indicate that this comprehensive model requires considerable therapeutic skill, as well as an eclectic conceptual approach to treatment. Positive therapeutic outcome is associated with a high motivation for change on the part of both partners, in addition to therapist–couple rapport.

Joseph LoPiccolo, Ph.D., is one of the major innovators in the field of sex therapy and a highly prolific author. He has written and lectured widely about every aspect of treatment, and has conducted a series of large-scale follow-up studies as well. He is Professor and Chairman of the Department of Psychology at the University of Missouri. Previously, he was the founder and Director of the Sex Therapy Center of the Department of Psychiatry, School of Medicine, State University of New York at Stony Brook. Dr. LoPiccolo is the coauthor (with Julia R. Heiman) of Becoming Orgasmic: Personal Growth and Sexual Health for Women *(2nd ed.), and editor (with Leslie LoPiccolo) of the* Handbook of Sex Therapy.

Jerry M. Friedman, Ph.D., is a sex therapist in private practice in Stony Brook, New York. He is the author of numerous publications in the area of sex therapy.

Low sexual desire was not even mentioned as a discreet diagnostic entity in the important early works on sexual dysfunction, such as Masters and

Johnson (1970) or Kaplan (1974). The earlier behavioral approaches to sexual dysfunction, such as Wolpe's 1958 volume and Ellis's 1962 work, also did not consider low sexual desire. It was only in the late 1970s that clinicians working in the area of sexual dysfunction began to write about low sexual desire. Kaplan (1977, 1979), L. LoPiccolo (1980), and Zilbergeld & Ellison (1980) provided among the more comprehensive early presentations of this problem.

Clinicians' interest in low sexual desire was stimulated by a number of factors. In earlier conceptualizations, low sexual desire was simplistically conceptualized as the *result* of a sexual dysfunction. The etiological formulation was that if every sexual experience is a disaster, this repeated stress leads to a decline in sexual desire. However, as clinical experience accumulated, it became clear that in many treatment failures, these ideas of causality were incorrect. For example, in some cases of erectile failure, low sexual desire is the primary problem that is the cause of the erectile failure, not the reverse. In cases in which a sexual performance disorder coexists with low sexual desire, clinical experience now indicates that focusing primarily on the dysfunction tends to result in treatment failure. If the patient does not want to have sex, it is unlikely that he or she will function adequately during lovemaking, but the dysfunction is only a symptom of the underlying low desire.

A second factor leading to increased clinical interest in low sexual desire has been a change in the nature of the cases presenting for sexual therapy. As our culture became more positive in its attitudes about sexual expression in the 1970s, we began to see more and more patient couples presenting with the complaint of lack of sexual desire in one of the partners. As our culture became more accepting of sexuality, the "normal"-drive partner of a patient with low sexual desire seems to have become more comfortable about putting pressure on the spouse to seek treatment. We now see cases in which women coerce their low-drive male partners into therapy with threats of divorce. Until women had adequate cultural support for the legitimacy of a higher drive level, such cases were unlikely to appear for treatment.

A third factor leading to increased clinical interest in low sexual desire concerns the result of a number of long-term follow-up studies (D'Amicis, Goldberg, LoPiccolo, Friedman, & Davies, 1985; J. LoPiccolo, Heiman, Hogan, & Roberts, 1985). These follow-up studies showed that there was a tendency for "relapse" in some cases that had apparently been successfully treated. Much of this relapse seemed to revolve around a decline in the frequency of sexual activity, which was commonly observed at 3-month and 1-year posttreatment follow-ups. When these treatment relapses were investigated, it was found that an undiagnosed and untreated problem of low sexual desire often underlay the relapse.

The study of failed cases indicates that standard behavioral interventions are of limited effectiveness with this disorder, as is psychoanalytic therapy. However, good treatment results can be obtained with a focused, broad-spectrum approach (Schover & LoPiccolo, 1982). In this chapter, we present such a program.

Definitions

In this chapter, we make use of the multiaxial descriptive diagnostic system developed in our clinic (Schover, Friedman, Weiler, Heiman, & LoPiccolo, 1982). Within this system, desire-phase disorders are described as "low sexual desire" or "aversion to sex," with the defining difference between these categories based upon the degree of negative emotions associated with sexual activity. Diagnosis is further refined by describing the problem as "global" or "situational" and as "lifelong" or "not lifelong." These three dimensions allow for shorthand but precise and specific diagnostic labeling.

It is currently fashionable to include in discussions of low sexual desire a disclaimer about how difficult it is to decide just what "low" means. In actual clinical practice, this concern about differentiating normal from low sexual desire is often academic. That is, most clinical cases are so clearly beyond the lower end of the normal curve that definitional issues become moot. With this preliminary caution in mind, some of the issues involved in definitional problems may be mentioned.

One problem in defining "low" desire concerns the lack of an empirical baseline. While a number of studies (e.g., Blumstein & Schwartz, 1983; Hunt, 1974) include relatively recent data on frequency of sex in a large sample of American couples, frequency of sex is not isomorphic with desire for sex. Rate of occurrence of sexual activity may be higher or lower than actual desire, as a function of partner pressure, lack of opportunity, or other factors. In developing norms for our own sexual assessment questionnaires, we have administered these instruments to a sample of 93 normal, nondysfunctional couples with a mean age of 33 years. Table 1 presents desired and actual frequencies of sexual intercourse for males and females in this sample. With the limitations of sample size, volunteer bias, and age, these figures provide only a rough normative framework for evaluation of low desire.

Another problem with defining low sexual desire concerns changing cultural values and norms. For example, one would not expect young, highly educated, nonreligious couples to have the same ideas about what constitutes low sexual desire as would elderly, less well-educated, highly religious couples. Therefore, patients' subjective distress about lack of sexual activity at a "normal" level is not necessarily a valid diagnostic definition.

Some clinicians have suggested that an extreme discrepancy should be

Table 1. Desired versus Actual Frequency of Sexual Intercourse for Males
and Females in a Sample of Nondysfunctional Couples

| | Percentage reporting Frequency as "desired" | | Percentage reporting Frequency as "actual" | |
Frequency	Males	Females	Males	Females
More than once a day	12.2	3.3	2.2	1.1
Once a day	28.9	19.8	2.2	3.3
Three or four times a week	42.2	50.6	35.6	39.6
Twice a week	12.2	16.5	30.0	24.2
Once a week	4.4	9.9	15.6	20.9
Once every 2 weeks	0.0	0.0	8.9	8.8
Once a month	0.0	0.0	2.2	2.2
Less than once a month	0.0	0.0	3.3	0.0
Not at all	0.0	0.0	0.0	0.0

Note. $n = 93$ couples. Demographic characteristics: mean age, 34 for males, 32 for females; mean years married, 9; mean number of children, 2.6; mean family income, \$33,000.

the criterion of low desire, such as one partner wanting sex every day versus the other partner wanting sex only once a week. In this example, however, both once a week and once a day statistically fall within what might be considered the "normal" range of frequency of sex. Furthermore, consider a couple in which both partners feel sexual desire only once a month. On grounds of statistical and clinical judgement, it could be argued that both members of the marriage suffer from low sexual desire. However, they will obviously be very unlikely to seek treatment; indeed, they may be ideal mates.

In diagnosing low sexual desire, then, the clinician's subjective judgment must be included, as well as objective information on the frequency of occurrence of sex with the partner, extrarelationship sexual activity, masturbation, sexual fantasy, and sexual urges.

Incidence

In 1982, following development of the multiaxial diagnostic system by Schover *et al.* (1982), the staff of the Sex Therapy Center at the State University of New York at Stony Brook (with which we were then both affiliated) rediagnosed every case in the files using this system. This center came into existence in 1974, and by 1982, we had approximately 1,000 cases in our files. This rediagnosis was done by two independent clinical staff members. Since this rediagnosis was done retrospectively in 1982, changes in percentages of cases presenting with low desire could not represent a drift in our diagnostic categorizations over the years.

In the years 1974–1976, roughly 32% of our couples presented with a diagnosis of low sexual desire. In the years 1977 and 1978, this figure increased to 46% of presenting couples. In 1981–1982, the incidence of low-desire cases was 55%. Interestingly, the sex ratio of identified patients within couples also changed over these years. In 1974–1976, in cases in which a low-desire diagnosis was assigned, the female was the identified patient about 70% of the time. In 1977 and 1978, this figure had declined to only 60%. In 1982 and 1983, in a noteworthy change, 55% of all low-desire cases involved *male* low desire.

This increased incidence of low sexual desire among males has given rise to much clinical speculation. One such speculation has been that a side effect of the women's movement has been to produce low sexual desire in men. In point of fact, the vast majority of men who present with low sexual desire are in relationships with women who are not notably involved with the women's movement. Many male patients with low sexual desire are married to very traditional women. It is clear that the simplistic notion that the women's movement is scaring men so badly that they lose sexual interest is not clinically accurate.

The women's movement has had the effect of making women feel much more comfortable about their own sexual needs. The women's ideal role has shifted from being attractive, feminine, and flirtatious, but not being actually sexual, to being *highly* sexual (J. LoPiccolo & Heiman, 1977). As the culture has become more accepting of female sexuality, women have felt more comfortable about confronting their partners with their sexual frustration caused by the partners' low sexual drive. Women's greater comfort with their own sexuality allows them to put sufficient pressure on their low-drive husbands to get the couple into sex therapy; this was not true until the woman's movement legitimized female sexuality.

Assessment Strategies

Cases of low sexual desire present an especially difficult challenge during the assessment phase. Simple reports of actual frequency of sexual behavior can be very misleading in regard to assessment of sexual desire level. A low-desire person may engage in sex frequently under an ultimatum from the spouse. In addition, sex may be occurring infrequently, not because of low sexual desire, but because of a sexual dysfunction that has turned sexual interaction into a failure experience for the couple.

Directly asking patients about their level of sexual desire as opposed to their frequency of sex is also problematic. There is a strong social pressure to report that one *does* desire sexual activity. Therefore, many low-desire patients, when questioned about their desire level, will report that they would like to have sex two or three times per week.

One component of our assessment procedure is the use of standardized self-report inventories. Currently, we use the following instruments:

> Sex History Form (Nowinski & LoPiccolo, 1979)
> Locke–Wallace Marriage Inventory (Kimmel & VanderVeen, 1974)
> Sexual Interaction Inventory (J. LoPiccolo & Steger, 1974)
> Brief Symptom Inventory (Derogatis, Lipman, & Covi, 1973)
> Zung Depression Scale (Zung, 1973)

We also ask for a brief health and medication history, and a statement of goals for therapy. Details of the entire questionnaire assessment strategy and further information on the questionnaires are available in Nowinski and LoPiccolo (1979), L. LoPiccolo and Heiman (1978), and J. LoPiccolo and Hogan (1979).

The second phase of our assessment consists of the initial intake interview. Low-desire couples are normally scheduled for a 2-hour initial assessment. For the first 45 minutes of the assessment, the clinician meets with both husband and wife simultaneously. During this conjoint interview, questions are asked regarding the history of the couple's relationship, current nonsexual stresses on the marriage, the histories of the partners' development in their families of origin, and their shared perceptions about the nature of their current sexual relationship. Very commonly, the couple disagrees dramatically on a number of issues regarding sex. While both partners may have some distortion of their perception of the frequency of sex, it is usually the low-drive patient who is more inaccurate in overestimating sexual frequency. For example, in one case of male low sexual desire, the husband reported that sex occurred at variable intervals ranging from once a week to once every 3 weeks. His wife removed a diary from her purse in which she had noted each occasion on which they had had sex in the last 8 months. There were a total of two such occasions.

Following the initial 45-minute joint session, the clinician sees each member of the couple separately for 15 to 20 minutes each. In the couple session, the clinician asks more general, open-ended questions about the sexual relationship, and avoids asking questions that present the patient with the dilemma of either having to disclose new and upsetting information suddenly to the spouse, or telling a lie to the therapist. For example, if the clinician asks, "Do you feel sexual desire for anybody other than your spouse?", this can be a problematic question for the patient. Rather than putting the patient in this dilemma, it is better to ask such questions during the separate session.

In the separate session, the obvious taboo topics are covered. The clinician asks about frequency and content of sexual fantasies, masturbation, desire for sex with other partners, occurrence of sex with other partners, and enjoyment of specific sexual activities (including oral, anal, and manual sexual activities). The clinician also asks whether the patient loves his or her spouse, whether the patient finds the spouse physically and sexually attractive, whether the spouse has adequate personal hygiene habits, whether the spouse is a sexually skilled and rewarding lover, and so forth. The clinician also asks each member of the couple why *he or she* thinks the low-desire problem is occurring, and what the person would do in terms of the continuance of the relationship if the problem cannot be resolved.

The third phase of the initial intake interview occurs in the remainder of the session, which is another conjoint session. In this session, the clinician presents an initial formulation of what might be involved in the low-desire problem, and the issues that therapy might begin to explore. Also, during this session, decisions are made as to whether or not sex therapy is indicated for the couple.

Screening for the appropriateness of sex therapy revolves around several issues. We tend to defer sex therapy and suggest other forms of treatment if assessment indicates any of the following major issues:

Depression
Severe psychopathology
Alcohol or drug dependence
Spouse abuse
Active extramarital affairs
Severe marital distress, with imminent separation/divorce

The third stage of assessment consists of medical evaluation, because there are a variety of medical conditions that inhibit sexual desire; a number of medications that have the side effect of suppressing sexual desire; and a number of hormonal conditions that decrease sexual desire. Further details on physiological evaluation procedures are discussed in other chapters of this volume.

The final phase of our assessment procedure consists of taking a detailed sex history of each person. This is done in a separate 1- to 2-hour interview with each member of the couple. When one is working with sexual desire problems, it is important to obtain a clear picture of the onset and history of the problem, any situational factors that interact with the problem, and the way in which the emotional relationshiop between the couple interacts with their sexual desire problem.

By this time, there should be good rapport between clinician and patient. The clinician can now ask about some of the more taboo or deviant sexual activities, with an expectation that the client will not be offended and may reveal any such deviant activities. In this section of the history, it is often helpful to begin with a "permission statement" indicating that most people at some time in their life try some of the more playful, exotic, or variant types of sexual activity. The clinician asks first about any experience with sexual play, such as tying each other up, spanking, or tickling. He or she then moves on to ask about variant sexual activities, such as pedophilia, sadism, masochism, exhibitionism, voyeurism, transvestism, and so forth. The clinician also asks about any gender identity issues at this point, and about any homosexual behavior or homoerotic wishes, urges, and fantasies. Careful questioning is needed in regard to the issue of sexual trauma. Many women who have been molested as children, either incestuously or by strangers, are very reluctant to report this information. Similarly, many rape victims are quite reluctant to reveal this information, and need to be asked specific questions in a supportive way.

Up to now, our assessment procedure has been focused on the behavioral, emotional, and cognitive aspects of this sexual desire problem in each person. As a final step in the assessment, the clinician begins to present strategic or systemic approaches to sexual desire problems, and to identify the systemic issues involved in the couple's desire problem.

Systemic intervention begins by posing to the couple the notion that a marriage relationship involves maintenance of homeostatic balance on the issues of power, intimacy, control, trust, and vulnerability, among others. The clinician points out that sexual desire problems can have enormous impact on the maintenance of homeostatic balances. Couples very quickly grasp the notion that their sexual desire problem has disrupted their relationship balance in a number of negative ways, often causing problems in the emotionally loaded areas of marriage mentioned above. However, the clinician also suggests the notion that there may be *positive or adaptive homeostasis-maintaining value* in having low sexual desire. Clinicians need to be very careful how this notion is presented to couples. If phrased poorly, this interpretation can sound as if the clinician is accusing one of the partners of having low sexual desire "on purpose," because it gets that partner something in the marriage.

The clinician should carefully explain that both partners are suffering equally from the low sexual desire, and that neither one of them is causing it "on purpose" because it gets the person something. It should be stressed that there are two victims and no villains in the systemic approach being presented. The clinician can suggest to the patients that human beings are very adaptable creatures, and are able to find a silver lining in the darkest cloud. In other words, although the sexual desire problem is 90% negative for both partners, it may indeed have a 10% positive payoff for each of them. Assessment is now focused on finding what that 10% positive payoff may be. Unless the positive value is identified and dealt with, clients may show "resistance" later in therapy, as successful interventions threaten to remove the 10% positive as well as the 90% negative.

To focus the clients' thinking on these "system homeostasis" issues, the clinician asks each patient whether he or she can identify positive effects of the problems, potential dangers of recovering sexual desire, changes in the relationship that might occur if the sexual desire problem were solved, and so forth. Helping the couple to understand systemic issues in the maintenance of low desire sets the stage for insight-oriented treatment, and also offers an understanding of the partners' apparent resistance to change.

Following a complete assessment as described here, the clinician should have a good understanding of the low-desire problem. Hogan and Friedman (1983) have suggested that crucial information the clinician must have includes the following: (1) description of each partner's family of origin and relationship with parents; (2) the client's general self-esteem and approach to life; (3) a complete history of sexual desire over the clients' lifetimes; (4) gender identity, object choice, or sexual deviation/variation issues; and (5) relationship factors, stressing homeostatic balance on the major issues of power sharing, conflict resolution, affection, intimacy, closeness, trust, anger, child rearing, and so forth.

Causes of Low Sexual Desire

Currently, most of our knowledge of the causes of low sexual desire is based on clinical experience, rather than on more empirical and objective research. It has become clear that there is no single cause for low sexual desire. Rather, low desire is a final common pathway, and patients can arrive at this pathway through the operation of a large variety of etiological mechanisms. In what follows, we stress both individual and couple relationship causes of low sexual desire. While some causes fall more into what might be considered a behavioral realm, others involve cognitive factors, and still others are systemic in that low desire has an adaptive value for maintenance of homeostatis in the relationship.

In addition, it should be noted that most cases of low desire do not represent only a single causal element at work. Many cases involve several of the causal factors working simultaneously, in a multiplicative fashion, to produce the severity of the low desire that is noted.

As most of our knowledge about low sexual desire is based on clinical experience, the discussion that follows below must be viewed with some caution. It may well be that many of these causal factors operate in a rather weak fashion, so that many people with the same histories can have intact levels of sexual desire. This phenomenon has already been demonstrated in regard to the etiology of other sexual dysfunctions (Heiman, Gladue, Roberts, & LoPiccolo, 1986). In earlier clinical thinking, there was an assumption that sexual dysfunction are caused by simple social learning in childhood and adolescence. The notion was that if a person has been exposed to a variety of negative familial and cultural attitudes toward sex, that person is likely to become sexually dysfunctional. This viewpoint was based on histories from dysfunctional patients. However, Heiman *et al.* (1986) found that these supposedly pathognomonic histories were also quite common in a control group of normally functioning nonpatients. In other words, such events may be simply high-base-rate events for people raised in our culture. When such supposedly crucial learning experiences result in dysfunction, there may not be a direct causal relationship; rather, the action of some as yet unknown mediator variables may be involved. Some people may be exposed to learning experiences that, through the action of some mediator variables, become very potent for them. The result for them is sexual dysfunction. Other people may have the same experiences, but also may be exposed to some as yet unspecified protective mediators, so that the experience does not traumatize them. A similar situation may occur in regard to our clinical knowledge about low sexual desire. It may well be that although the causal factors described below are necessary for low sexual desire to develop, they are not sufficient in and of themselves. Many people who have similar histories, cognitive schemes, or couple relationships may have intact sexual desire because of the action of mediating protectors.

Individual Causes of Low Sexual Desire

Religious Orthodoxy

Virtually every standard work on sexual dysfunction lists religious orthodoxy as a major cause of sexual dysfunction. Given that many religiously devout people are sexually functional, and that many sexually dysfunctional patients are not religious, this relationship between orthodoxy and dysfunction seems oversimplified at best. However, as the following example indicates, religious orthodoxy can be the cause of low sexual desire (albeit a relatively uncommon one).

Mr. A was a 34-year-old man, married for 2 years. Prior to marriage, Mr. A had no dating or sexual experience of any kind, and he denied ever having masturbated. Mr. A had been raised in a devout Catholic family, and had been in Catholic schools through high school. He had attended a Catholic university, and entered the seminary planning to become a priest. He withdrew from seminary approximately 6 months before he would have been ordained. Mr. A then became a a teacher in a Catholic school. His motivation for becoming married was an admonition from the priest who was principal of the school that, for appearances' sake, all male teachers should be married.

Mr. A denied that his religious beliefs contributed to his low sexual desire with his wife. He could intellectually discuss diversity within modern Catholic thought about sexuality, and bluntly stated that he had completely rejected his church's views on sexuality. He denied that any further working through of this issue would be helpful. Progress was made on this issue only when he admitted that he regretted not having become a priest, and considered that this avenue remained open to him, as his marriage had never been consummated.

Anhedonic or Obsessive–Compulsive Personality

Some patients suffer from low sexual desire because they essentially lack the capacity for play. These patients may be very ambitious, task-directed, high achievers who simply are not oriented toward any sort of nonproductive, frivolous, or self-indulgent activity. These patients often express fears that if they were to develop a sex drive, they would never get their work, child rearing, or house management responsibilities done. In transactional analysis terms, these patients are unable to express their "playful child"; instead, they operate in a combination of a highly achieving "adult" mode and a critical and demanding "parent" mode.

As the anhedonic syndrome shades over into a more obsessive–compulsive personality style, an additional element emerges. Sexual activity involves the overt display of emotion, which is difficult for the obsessive–compulsive personality to manage. Yet another factor is that sexual activity involves close bodily contact, including contact with bodily fluids, such as sweat, saliva, semen, and vaginal lubrication. For patients who are mildly obsessional, this close bodily contact can be sufficiently unpleasant to suppress sex drive. The following example illustrates all of these factors.

Mrs. B, a 29-year-old attorney, presented with her husband for her low sexual desire. In addition to working very hard to build a successful legal practice, Mrs. B had major responsibilities for taking care of their two small children. She was doing extremely well as an attorney, and her practice was expanding beyond her ability to keep up with the increased workload. She expressed fear that if she were to respond to her husband's sexual overtures, they would spend too much time in bed and she would never get her work done. She was also afraid that she might become interested enough in sex herself that she would fail to meet her already very demanding schedule. She was a very neat and fastidious person, and found perspiration, saliva, semen, and her own vaginal lubrication to be "gross and disgusting."

Gender Identity or Object Choice Issues

When a person who is basically homosexually oriented enters a heterosexual marriage, low sexual desire is an unsurprising outcome. These cases can be divided into two types.

In one type, the patient is aware of homoerotic interest, fantasies, and desires, and may have an overt homosexual history. However, adopting a fully homosexual lifestyle is unacceptable to the patient, and he or she often has a history of having received therapy to "convert" to heterosexuality. Marriage to an opposite-sex person often represents a "flight into hetero-sexuality." Sexual functioning in such a marriage is often moderately good at first. The initial sexual interest represents in part a novelty effect and in part the sexual drive induced by feeling new and intense love toward another person. However, with the passage of time, the patient typically loses much of his or her ability to function heterosexually and again begins struggling with homosexual urges, as in this example.

Mrs. C, a 28-year-old woman, presented with her husband for her low sexual desire. On assessment, she revealed that she had struggled with homosexual urges since early adolescence. She masturbated during adolescence with homosexual fantasies, using her brother's *Playboy* centerfolds as stimulus objects. In college, she felt very out of place because of her homosexual interests, and married her husband because he was someone whom she felt close to and could communicate with well. While she initially found sex "interesting" as a new experience, she fairly rapidly came to find it unpleasant. After 6 years of marriage, she had her first sexual experience with another woman and found it to be much more rewarding than hetero-sexual activity. This crisis occasioned their entering therapy.

In the second type of case in which homosexual orientation is an issue, the patient vigorously denies any homosexual orientation, and expends a great deal of energy in keeping such wishes out of active consciousness. Despite the patient's denials, there is often a wealth of information from the partner (and, indeed, from the patient) to support this etiological formulation.

Mr. D and his wife presented after several years of marriage. Mr. D was a small-statured, rather "pretty" man who was notably effeminate in his speech, body posture, gestures, and other mannerisms. When questioned about any homosexual interests, Mr. D exploded and vehemently denied any such urges, interests, or activities. He made a number of extreme statements about homosexuality, including an opinion that all homosexuals should be executed. When questioned by his wife as to how this statement reconciled with the fact that many of his male friends were homosexuals, he replied that as he was interested in the arts, he had no choice but to associate with homosexual men. Mrs. D further revealed that the only times that intercourse was possible for them was when, at her husband's request, she would verbalize the idea that his penis was actually *her* penis and that she was inserting it into his body.

Obviously, in cases where homosexual object choice is so unacceptable as to be successfully kept out of consciousness by the patient, therapy is very challenging.

Specific Sexual Phobias or Aversions

One type of sexual phobia or aversion is almost diagnostic of male low sexual desire: Low-desire men almost uniformly have some degree of aversion to the vagina and female genitals. These men, on initial evaluation, will typically state that they enjoy sex and that nothing about sex is unpleasant for them. However, careful questionning will elicit the information that they find the vagina to be ugly, messy, foul-smelling, and so forth. Sometimes this attitude seems to represent only an exaggeration of our culture's general ambivalence about the aesthetic qualities of the vagina, as evidenced in the multimillion-dollar trade in "feminine hygiene" products. Less commonly, some men have had specific aversive experiences (e.g., discovering menstrual blood on the penis; having intercourse with a woman who had a vaginal infection with an associated odor; or, in one case, a traumatic history of having impaled the glans penis on the protruding tail of his wife's intrauterine device).

Women who have been sexually molested as children, or raped as adults, often have specific aversion reactions. These women often have a very specific aversion to exactly what was done to them during the sexual assault, and will sometimes even have visual flashbacks with associated emotions when they attempt to engage in sex. The disastrous long-term effects of incestuous or other molestation during childhood are just now beginning to be appreciated by psychologists, as are the long-term sequelae of rape. Many women who have experienced such assaults are unable to function sexually for years afterward, if at all. As each sexual experience reactivates the memory of the molestation or rape, it is not surprising that sexual desire is completely disrupted in these women, as in the following case.

Mr. and Mrs. E sought treatment for Mrs. E's low sexual desire following 5 years of marriage. During this time, sex had been infrequent, because each time they engaged in sex she became frightened and nauseated. Mrs. E had a strong aversion to looking at or touching her husband's penis. She had no idea as to the origin of this aversion until she attended her uncle's funeral shortly before beginning therapy. During this funeral, she found herself becoming angry as the eulogy was read. Her uncle had been a famous concert musician, and was a widely respected and admired figure. As Mrs. E became more angry, she suddenly recovered the memory of having been sexually molested by her uncle from the ages of 9 to 12. During this time, Mrs. E was receiving special music tutoring, as a gifted child, from her uncle. This tutoring included her uncle "teaching her rhythm" by having her caress his penis in time with the beating of the metronome. She was repulsed by this activity, but was too frightened to tell her parents about it. She finally refused to continue the lessons at age 12, without ever telling her parents why. At some point during her adolescence, she repressed the memories of the molestation. She only recovered these memories when they were activated during her uncle's funeral. Treatment of this case is discussed in a later section of this chapter.

Fear of Loss of Control over Sexual Urges

Some patients lack the capacity for modulated affective discharge. Such patients basically fear that if they allow themselves to feel any sexual desire at all, they will lose all control over themselves and begin acting out sexually in ways that would have disastrous consequences. Since they fear that they would not be able to modulate and control their sexual urges, they suppress them completely. Often such a patient fears that having sexual desire will give the spouse too much power and control over him or her, because the patient would be subject to manipulation or domination by the spouse as a price for the spouse's sexual favors.

Mrs. F felt virtually no sexual desire for her husband. When she was in her late 20s, she had married a man considerably less physically attractive, less well educated, and less successful than she. At age 18, while a high school senior, Mrs. F had become extremely infatuated with the leader of a local motorcycle gang. This was not a gang of high school youths, but a hard-core criminal and psychopathic motorcycle gang. The leader of the group coerced Mrs. F into having group sex with all the gang members as a condition of his being interested in her. From this encounter, Mrs. F became pregnant and also contracted venereal disease. She had an abortion, which was illegal at the time and which nearly killed her. When her parents came to the hospital (where she had been admitted on an emergency basis) and discovered what had happened, they literally disowned her. As a result of complications from the abortion, she became sterile. Mrs. F reported that after this experience, she decided that she would never let herself be compulsively drawn to another man, as she had been to the leader of this gang. After remaining celibate for many years, she picked out her current husband as someone who would not threaten to activate any of her sexual urges.

Masked Sexual Deviation

Although sexual deviations are not common in patients presenting for low sexual desire, such cases do exist. In our experience, the most typical masked deviation is male transvestism. These are men who would have intact sexual desire if their wives would allow them to engage in sexual activity while cross-dressed. However, as they are fetishistically drawn to cross-dressing, they have low desire for any other form of sexual activity.

Less frequently seen masked sexual deviations include pedophilia, exhibitionism, sadistic or masochistic urges, and virtually any of the other paraphilias. It takes very careful assessment to uncover these masked sexual deviations, because the low-drive patient often extracts a promise from the spouse that the deviation will not be revealed, as a price for agreeing to enter therapy.

Before coming for the first assessment session, Mr. G elicited a promise from his wife that she would not reveal his interest in cross-dressing. However, during the course of the interview, Mrs. G let "slip" the statement that her husband especially liked her pantyhose, even to the point of his wanting to wear it during sexual activity. Upon supportive but probing questioning during individual assessment, Mr. G reported that since early adolescence he had cross-dressed, and masturbated while cross-dressed. He had tried introducing cross-dressing into sexual activity with his wife, but she had been repulsed, horrified, and tearful in response to this. As is not unusual in such cases, Mr. G had periodically purged himself of his feminine attire, but then would gradually accumulate a new set of female clothes. At one point, Mrs. G had agreed to allow him to wear pantyhose during sexual activity, and his sexual desire level had been very high. However, after some time he began to find this partial cross-dressing unsatisfactory, and his wish to dress up more fully occasioned their entry into therapy.

Fear of Pregnancy

Fear of pregnancy is also often a "masked" cause of low sexual desire. In these cases, the patients typically deny that this could be a problem, as both agree that they wish to have children. However, whenever the onset of low sexual desire coincides with discontinuance of contraception, or with the beginning of discussions about starting a family, the clinician should be highly suspicious. What is often involved is that one member of the couple is markedly ambivalent about having children and more or less reluctantly agrees to do so under coercion from the spouse, or simply because he or she cannot logically justify the negative feelings about having children.

"Widower's Syndrome"

The "widower's syndrome" is caused by a combination of population demographics and the male's unwitting acceptance of our cultural stereotype of the male role. Given differential life expectancies and differential remarriage rates after divorce, there is a great disproportion between the numbers of elderly single men and elderly single women. Census data indicate that there are 2.5 single women for every single man over the age of 40, and more than 5 single women for every single man over the age of 60.

Men who become widowed later in life, therefore, often find themselves being vigorously pursued by single women. Often such a woman becomes emotionally important to a man during the illness and death of his wife. At some point, the woman initiates sexual activity, in which the man's erection and orgasm are often problematic. If the couple remain together, the male's sexual desire is often noticeably low.

Mr. H was widowed at age 55 following his wife's death from cancer. His wife's best friend was supportive and helpful during the terminal stages of the illness, the funeral, and the early grief period. Within a month or so of the death of the wife, the friend initiated sexual activity. Mr. H was unable to obtain erection or orgasm in this encounter. Blaming this problem on his feelings about nonmarital sex, he married her. Following the marriage, his sexual functioning improved slightly, but his sexual desire level was extremely low.

When Mr. H was interviewed, it became apparent that he had not completed mourning for his wife, and was still depressed about her loss. He described his relationship with his current wife as one of close friendship. He reported that he had not been feeling sexually needy after his wife's death because of his depression. Mr. H stated that he responded to his current wife's sexual initiation because it would have hurt her feelings had he refused. He also said that he could not conceive of a "real" man declining the opportunity for sexual activity. Interestingly, Mr. H resisted this "widower's syndrome" interpretation as the cause of his low sexual desire. He reported that on her deathbed, his wife had stated that if her husband and her best friend were to have sex together after her death, it would be fine with her. He reported that she had even said, "I'll be in heaven watching you two." Since his wife had given her blessing to their relationship, Mr. H found it difficult to believe that feelings about the death of his first wife could be contributing to his low sexual desire.

Depression

It is basic clinical knowledge that depression suppresses sexual drive, yet it is surprising how often depression is overlooked in the etiology of low sex drive. In many cases, there is a cause–effect question that tends to obscure the issue. That is, there is a tendency for some clinicians to mislabel symptoms of depression as results of low sexual drive, rather than correctly labeling low sexual drive as a symptom of underlying depression.

We have tried treating low sex drive in cases of mild to moderate clinical depression. The results have not been good. An underlying depression may inhibit sexual drive sufficiently to make psychotherapy for the low drive very difficult. A preliminary course of treatment to bring the depression under control is much more appropriate.

It should be noted that the low sexual desire is often the only vegetative or somatic sign of depression. Many of these patients have intact sleeping and eating patterns; their energy levels may be only mildly lowered; and their affect may also be only slightly depressed. In cases where there is a question about the severity of the underlying depression, we recommend assessment with the Zung (1973) depression scale. If clinical scores in even the mild or moderate range of clinical depression are obtained, these patients are better treated for depression before the problems of sexual desire are addressed.

Hormonal Issues

While hormonal issues are a relatively uncommon cause of low sexual desire, some assessment of hormonal parameters is indicated in most cases. A number of hormonal conditions can affect sexual desire. We assess for levels of prolactin, luteinizing hormone, testosterone, and estrogen. Special attention should be directed to hormonal issues in women who are taking oral contraceptives and in women who are postmenopausal. For a more complete discussion of hormonal factors in sexual desire, the reader can consult the reviews by Bancroft, Sanders, Davidson, and Warner (1983) and by Pogach and Vaitukaitus (1983), as well as Chapter 11 of this volume.

Medication Side Effects

A number of different classes of medications can also have the effect of suppressing sex drive. These medications include the neurotransmitters dopamine and serotonin; antipsychotic, antianxiety, and antidepressant drugs; recreational or street drugs; antihypertensive medications; sedatives; and antihistamines.

The whole area of medication and drug effects on sexual drive is open to a great deal of controversy. Much of the information about drug effects is based on clinical experience, rather than on empirical assessment of drug effects in placebo-controlled, double-blind studies. Further information on medication effects is available in Sandler and Gessa (1975), Buffum (1986), and Chapter 12 of this volume.

Aging-Related Concerns

Some men who present with low sexual drive will reveal, in individual assessment, that their low drive is specific to their aging wives. Several of these men have expressed the belief that if they were in a relationship with a young woman, their sex drive would be intact. As one patient put it, "The real trouble is, I have to have sex with an old lady, and who's interested in sex with old ladies?"

Women, too, may be victimized by our culture's double standard about aging and sexual attractiveness. Some women do begin to lose their own sexual drive as they age. These women no longer define themselves as sexual beings and find their sexual interest to be embarrassing once they are in their 40s, 50s, or 60s. Obviously, if an aging woman begins to receive negative messages from her husband about her sexual attractiveness, she becomes additionally vulnerable to developing low self-esteem and low sexual desire.

Of course, not all aging cases involve our culture's double standard. One does see cases in which aging men have lost their sex drive because they are ashamed of the bodily changes that occur in aging. We occasionally see elderly women who have lost sexual interest in their husbands because of the husbands' aging changes.

Relationship Causes of Low Sexual Desire

Many cases of low sexual desire are caused by something in the structure of the relationship that makes sexual desire threatening, risky, or psychologically too costly to be experienced. Some of the more common relationship-centered causes of low sexual desire are briefly reviewed here.

Lack of Attraction to Partner

As psychologists, we often tend to look for complicated psychodynamic or relationship system causes of low sexual desire, and sometimes overlook the obvious. If a person simply does not find his or her spouse physically attractive, low sex drive is hardly a surprising result. Perhaps the most common case of this type involves excessive weight gain by one member of the couple. While some people do not have their sexual interest level suppressed by large weight gain in the partner, for many people such a weight gain effectively suppresses sexual desire. While the weight gain may be a sexual turn-off, the situation may be complicated by the normal-weight partner's finding some systemic rewards in having an obese spouse. For example, this may give the normal-weight spouse considerably more power in the relationship, may make him or her feel more secure about who is the more loved member of the relationship, or may serve as protection against fears of the partner's having an affair. However, in some cases one cannot identify any systemic payoffs for the nonobese spouse, and the partner's weight gain seems to be an unreservedly negative event for the couple.

Poor personal hygiene habits account for another group of cases caused by lack of attraction to the partner. If one's partner is consistently sweaty, dirty, smelly, or unshaven, or has bad breath, it is not too surprising that sexual interest declines. We have also seen cases in which a nonsmoking member of a couple loses sexual desire for the spouse who does smoke, because the nonsmoker finds the smell of cigarette smoke in the partner's hair and on the partner's skin to be revolting.

Poor Sexual Skills in the Partner

One sees cases in which the sexual desire level of one spouse is suppressed by the unrewarding nature of each sexual interaction. These patients complain that their spouses are basically "lousy lovers." Sometimes the complaint is that the spouse is very inhibited and will not engage in much manual or oral foreplay, or will not experiment with different positions and settings for intercourse. In other cases, the complaint may be that the partner does not become particulary aroused, and this lack of responsiveness suppresses the patient's own level of sexual interest. In yet other cases, the complaint is that although the patient's spouse is an aroused and willing participant, he or she is extremely clumsy. Sex then becomes an awkward, fumbling, and often painful experience, as in the following case.

Mrs. I's low sexual drive was almost entirely caused by her husband's extreme clumsiness during sexual activity. She reported that she frequently ended up bruised and battered after sexual experiences, not because of her husband's being deliberately rough with her, but because of his awkwardness. Mrs. I complained that her husband stuck his fingers into her eye; inadvertently pulled her hair; stuck his elbow into her neck, chest, or ribs; gave her bruises in the legs by accidentally banging his knees into her; and so forth. She reported that on occasions when she could induce Mr. I to slow down and be more passive during lovemaking, sex was more rewarding for her. It should be noted that during the assessment sessions, while the therapist on this case was questioning the genuineness of Mr. I's clumsiness, Mr. I dropped a full cup of coffee on a glass table, thereby shattering the table top. When leaving the office, he managed to stumble and fall into a large potted plant. At this point, the therapist gave more credence to Mrs. I's complaints.

Marital Conflict

The issue of marital conflict interfering with sexual desire is so obvious as to require no elaboration. The only real issue here is sorting out the cause–effect relationships. Some clients will claim that marital squabbles and fighting do not suppress *their* sex drive, and therefore do not believe that their partners' low sex drive can be caused by this issue. Sometimes the higher-drive member of a distressed marriage will even attribute causality in the opposite direction, with marital squabbling caused by frustration over low levels of sexual activity. The relationship between marital distress and low sexual desire is often a reciprocal, mutually causal relationship, rather than a simple one-way linear causality.

Fear of Closeness

When one makes love with a spouse, one tends to feel especially close to, involved with, and emotionally dependent upon him or her. For those of us who find such closeness to be rewarding, this is part of the "warm after-glow" of making love. However, if closeness brings with it negative emotions, each sexual experience then becomes a trigger for negative feelings, and sexual drive may be suppressed in a self-protective way.

Fear of closeness often revolves around a fear of vulnerability. These patients, at some level, are afraid of being vulnerable to the pain that losing their partners would cause them. In a sense, these patients have a trust deficit: They do not really believe that their partners love them as much as they love the partners, that they can depend on their partners to be there for them in the future, or that their partners will not hurt them by leaving them. For such patients, making love brings them into contact with their feelings of dependency and need for their partners, and because these feelings are very frightening, they are avoided by refraining from sexual activity. Thus, sexual desire comes to be suppressed.

Often such a patient comes from a family of origin in which he or she saw the same-sex parent badly hurt by the other parent; women who saw their mothers abused by alcholic or emotionally erratic husbands are especially vulnerable to this causal factor. A patient who has been in a previous marriage in which he or she was badly hurt by the spouse's leaving may also suffer from this syndrome. The following case illustrates both of these factors.

Mrs. J had been rescued from a chaotic family of origin by being married at age 18 to a man some 10 years her senior. Her mother had been extremely devoted to her father. However, in adolescence, Mrs. J had come to realize that her father regularly cheated on her mother and had repeated affairs. Both of her parents also had moderately severe drinking problems, so Mrs. J had often been the glue that held the family together and had taken care of her younger siblings when her parents were drinking. After several years of marriage to Mr. J, he suddenly left her for another woman. Following the divorce, Mrs. J did not even date for 2 years. When she eventually married, she picked out a man who was extremely attentive to her and placed her on a pedestal, almost as an object of worship. However, when they made love she would often find herself on the verge of tears, for reasons that she could not put into words. In the course of assessment, it became clear that during lovemaking she was powerfully in touch with her needs for her current husband and her fears of losing him. Consequently, her sex drive diminished in a defensive manner.

Couple Differences Regarding Point of Optimal Closeness

Marital relationships differ in style. Some marriages are very close, with both partners spending virtually all their time together. Other relationships are characterized by a more distant style. There is no difference in the intrinsic happiness or success of closer versus more distant marriages. However, a problem arises when one person who wants a very close relationship marries someone who wants a much more distant relationship. The spouse who needs more distance will tend to feel suffocated and intruded upon by the partner. If one is feeling constantly intruded upon by one's spouse, this does tend to suppress sexual desire. In addition, once the partner who needs more distance develops low sexual desire, the problem comes to have an adaptive value. The higher-drive partner's feelings are likely to be hurt by what he or she perceives as repeated rejections by the spouse. Feeling hurt, the higher-drive partner is likely to withdraw a bit and, without realizing it, may begin to meet some of the more distant partner's need for more space. Thus, the symptom of low sexual desire comes to have an adaptive value for the identified patient, in that a more comfortable homeostatic point on the issue of closeness is reached.

Passive–Aggressive Solution to Power Imbalance

If one member of a couple overtly has all the power and control in a relationship, it is not surprising to see low sexual drive in the other partner. Obviously, a person who feels constantly bullied and controlled by his or her partner will not tend to feel sexual desire for the partner. In addition, once the low sexual desire develops, it comes to have an adaptive value for the powerless patient. That is, although one partner has all the power in the relationship overtly, and can even force the other to have sex, he or she cannot make the patient want to have sex. Thus, sexual desire become the last area of power and control for the low-drive patient. Again, the symptom can come to have an adaptive value: The higher-drive partner may stop being as dominant and overbearing, if he or she discovers that building more equality into the relationship raises the partner's level of sexual desire.

Mr. and Mrs. K presented for treatment of Mrs. K's low sexual desire. Mr. K was a rather loud, overbearing, and very forceful person. He came from a family in which everyone shouted, argued, and sometimes came to blows over any conflictual issues. Mrs. K, on the other hand, came from a family in which voices were never raised, overt disagreements virtually never occurred, and displays of overt emotion were disapproved. When Mr. and Mrs. K married, it very quickly became apparent that they had virtually no conflict resolution skills. Mr. K would express himself forcefully, and Mrs. K would give in. What seemed to her like major blowups were to Mr. K merely trivial incidents that he forgot about virtually as soon as they occurred. Once Mrs. K lost her sexual desire, Mr. K gradually came to realize that, as he put it, she "got the sulks" whenever he raised his voice to her. However, sufficient changes were not made in the balance of power in the relationship for her to recover her sex drive.

Inability to Fuse Feelings of Love and Sexual Desire

Freud (1950/1962) first identified what he called the "Madonna–prostitute" syndrome. In this syndrome, women are divided into two mutually exclusive categories: They are seen as *either* sexual objects *or* loved and respected mother-like figures. While a man who holds this view may wish to have sex with a woman who is highly sexually provocative, obviously he will marry and have children with only the more Madonna-like figure. For such men, seeing a woman as sexual is incompatible with feelings of love and respect for her.

Mr. and Mrs. L presented for treatment after 2 years of marriage. Mr. L reported that he had had sex with over 200 women before becoming married. He estimated that perhaps 90% of these women had been prostitutes. He described his premarital sexual partners as "sluts" or prostitutes exclusively. During the engagement to Mrs. L, he did not initiate any sexual activity, stating that he felt this would be disrespectful to her parents. Although Mrs. L was physically quite an attractive woman, he discouraged her from dressing or wearing makeup in ways that highlighted her attractiveness. He became uncomfortable, embarrassed, or angry if she attempted to sexually provoke him, or even if she simply directly asked whether they could make love. Mr. and Mrs. L had had their first child about a year after being married, at which point his sexual desire had virtually disappeared. On one occasion when she initiated sex, he reminded her that she was a mother and such behavior was unbecoming to her.

This syndrome, of course, does not occur exclusively in men, although it is much more common in men than in women. There are women who also suffer from this syndrome, dividing men into mutually exclusive categories: "respectable but not sexual," or "sexually stimulating but not respectable."

Treating Low Sexual Desire

There are several difficulties with devising a treatment program for low sexual desire. First, the interventions originally suggested by Masters and Johnson (1970), which form the basis for most sex therapy programs, were not designed to deal specifically with low sexual desire. While many of these behavioral exercises may enhance arousal and orgasm, they often fail in increasing sexual desire or motivation. A second problem is that many cases of low sexual desire are not only quite complex, but are diverse in apparent etiology and maintaining factors. Kaplan (1979) notes that the majority of desire-phase dysfunctions are rooted in profound sexual and marital conflicts, as opposed to less complex problems with arousal or orgasm. This makes sense, as the sexual response cycle is interrupted at its earliest point—desire—rather than at a later point, such as orgasm. Zilbergeld and Ellison (1980) point out that each case of low desire must be examined on its own terms, and treatment must be tailored to the specific needs of the individual case. They warn that "cookbook" approaches will probably be ineffective.

Behavior therapy and social learning theory have contributed most of the effective techniques that comprise current sex therapy. However, other therapy approaches have been used as adjunct techniques or proposed alternatives. These include cognitive therapy, strategic therapy, psychodynamic therapy, and Gestalt therapy. All have contributed conceptualizations and techniques that appear to be helpful at the clinical level. However, there has been little attempt to integrate interventions from these theoretical orientations into a single, comprehensive treatment program. Our broad-spectrum approach attempts to provide such an integration, while remaining sensitive to the need to "fine-tune" the program to the individual case. This treatment program is essentially a broadly focused conceptual framework that allows for flexibility and individualization. Our program is based on several key therapeutic assumptions:

1. Many patients with low sexual desire are not aware of their affective responses to sexual stimuli. In fact, many low-desire patients actually have an aversion to sex, but do not recognize this. They frequently state that sex is a neutral experience, yet behave as if engaging in sexual activity is negatively valenced, or as if they derive some positive gains from avoiding sexual activity. One cannot help wondering why, if sex is truly a neutral experience, the low-desire patient does not engage in it simply to satisfy the higher-desire partner and eliminate the relationship distress. Clearly, for such patients, sex is not a neutral experience, but one that is actively avoided. Therefore, one goal of therapy is to help patients become aware of the physical responses associated with their affective experience, under the assumption that these responses can provide important informational feedback.

2. It is clinically useful for patients to have some idea of *why* they have low desire. Being able to attribute their low-desire difficulties to something concrete and understandable allows them to adopt a solution-oriented cognitive set. While insight may not be sufficient to produce therapeutic change for low sexual desire, we believe it is necessary. Many low-desire patients are unaware of any possible explanation for their problem, and state something such as "That's just the way I am."

3. It is extremely rare for an individual to present for therapy for low sexual desire, since this is almost always only a problem within the context of a relationship. Therefore, it is important for the *couple* to be involved in the therapy, although some therapy time may be spent with each partner alone. This is based on the clinical observation that the higher-desire partner is often contributing to the maintenance, if not the original cause, of the problem.

4. The use of a graded series of sexual tasks beginning with mutual sensual pleasuring and leading eventually to intercourse, as proposed by Masters and Johnson (1970), remains an integral part of this treatment program. In the current program, these tasks serve two functions: to elicit emotional responses during the course of therapy, and to provide a set of behaviors for the patients to use in practicing some of the self-help skills gained during therapy.

Four major overlapping elements provide the conceptual framework for treating couples with low sexual desire or aversion to sex in one or both partners. These elements are drawn from four different theoretical orientations, integrated into a brief therapy framework of 15–25 sessions. Special emphasis is placed on maintenance and generalization of the therapeutic gains. The four elements are experiential/sensory awareness, insight, cognitive restructuring, and behavior therapy.

Step 1: Experiential/Sensory Awareness

Many patients presenting with low sexual desire are unable to verbalize their feelings and are often unaware of their affective responses to situations involving sexual stimulation. Such feelings may include anxiety, anger, resentment, or disgust, but are only vaguely accessible to the patient. Sensory awareness exercises are used in this stage of the program to help these patients become aware of their unacknowledged feelings. Those who experience aversion to sex and who acknowledge this aversion need less work in this stage of the program.

This program assumes that sexually related anxiety underlies most cases of low sexual desire, even when patients claim neutrality about sex. In some cases, negative affective reactions in addition to anxiety are operative. The goal of the experiential phase of therapy is to help patients recognize, using bodily cues, when they are experiencing feelings of anxiety, pleasure, anger, disgust, and so on. Thus, in this stage of our program, patients are taught to attend to bodily cues, to recognize the early stages of their affective response, and to identify and label these feelings. Anger is a good example of an "umbrella" emotion, which often covers other feelings, such as fear of rejection, fear of intimacy, frustration, or hurt. This phase of therapy can help patients to make these differentiations. Body awareness exercises and other experiential interventions derived from the Gestalt tradition (Fagan & Shepherd, 1970; Zinker, 1977) are used extensively in this phase of therapy.

Patients are asked to focus on and describe their feelings both in the therapy session and at home. The therapist frequently asks questions such as "How do you feel about . . . ?" and helps the patient to distinguish cognitions from emotions. When a feeling is stated, questions are asked such as "How do you know that you are feeling happy [sad, etc.]? Describe the sensations in your body at the time of the feeling." Homework and in-session assignments include sensate focus exercises, body awareness exercises, and fantasy training. After patients have learned to fantasize, a typical assignment might be to spend several minutes fantasizing a pleasurable scene and identifying the associated bodily responses. This procedure is repeated with an unpleasant scene, fantasizing the associated bodily responses. Frequently, it may be necessary to elicit emotional responses in the session from patients who deny their feelings. The elicitation of emotional responses can be done through encouragement, by provocation, and by giving permission. The use of such Gestalt techniques as the "empty chair," with imaginal recreations of earlier traumatic experiences, are often a part of this phase of therapy. Another technique is for the therapist to lead the patient in a guided fantasy involving visualization of intense sexual activity, noting the patient's emotional and physical reactions. If the patient shows slight muscle tension, for example, the therapist may ask the patient to tense up even more and examine the emotions that accompany this tenseness. Work on sensate awareness will continue throughout the therapy process, although the primary focus will move on to other phases of the therapy.

Step 2: Insight

The insight phase of therapy sometimes begins concurrently with the sensory/awareness phase. If the patient demonstrates strong resistance to the experimental exercises or is unable to engage in these exercises, the insight phase may be implemented first. In the insight phase of therapy patients, with the help of the therapist, attempt to learn and understand what is causing and maintaining their low desire. Frequently, patients with low sexual desire have misconceptions and self-defeating attributions as to the cause of the problem. We have often seen, in clinical practice, men who are stressed at work, and impatient, irritated, or angry with their sexual partners, but who attribute their lack of sexual desire to increasing age or a physiological disorder. In the insight phase of therapy, patients are helped to reformulate attributions about the cause of the problem in a way that is conducive to therapeutic change. For example, if a patient attributes low sexual desire to the fact that "That's just the way I am," this implies that "I can't change." If the same individual is helped to see that anxiety about sex is lowering his or her desire, the person can understand that this is a factor that can be changed. Insight enables patients to understand and take responsibility for their own behavior, and to recognize that change is possible.

When individuals have an explanation for why they behave in a particular way, their anxiety tends to decrease. Insight sets the stage for the cognitive and behavioral interventions to follow, and provides a rationale for proceeding with these interventions. The insight phase of therapy can vary in time and focus, based on the particular factors involved. For example, it is easier to help a patient to recognize that the problem may be due to severe marital distress than it is to help a patient to deal with issues such as displacement of anger and fear created by the opposite-sex parent. Techniques during this phase of therapy include having patients conceptualize family-of-origin issues within a learning framework ("Where did you learn that it is uncomfortable to allow yourself to get too close to someone you love?"), empathic reflections, reframing, interpretation, and response prompting ("Give me three reasons, even if you have to make them up, why getting too close to someone may be frightening to you?"). During this phase of therapy, the higher-desire partner is helped to gain insight into how he or she is helping to maintain the problem.

If the patient remains resistant to recognizing and "owning" a causal explanation for the low desire, a dialogue involving role reversal is often used. In this procedure, the therapist expresses puzzlement over why the patient cannot accept what appears to be an obviously valid explanation for the cause of low desire. The therapist then offers to take the patient's role, and argue that the insight is *not* correct. This procedure is explained as a mechanism by which the therapist may gain an empathic understanding of the patient's point of view. Almost as an afterthought, the patient is asked to argue that the insight is valid, merely to give the therapist someone with whom to have a dialogue. In this procedure, by playing the therapist's role, the patient is acting "as if" he or she believes the insight. As the patient argues that the insight is correct, he or she may become aware of the validity of the new formulation of the cause of the problem.

Step 3: Cognitive Restructuring

The cognitive phase of therapy is designed to alter irrational thoughts that inhibit sexual desire. Patients are helped to identify self-statements that interfere with sexual desire. Our procedure involves identification of self-statements that mediate emotional arousal. Patients are helped to accept the general assumption that their emotional reactions can be directly influenced by their expectations, labels, and self-statements. They are taught that unrealistic or irrational beliefs may be the main cause of their emotional reactions, and that they can change these unrealistic self-statements. With change, patients can re-evaluate specific situations more realistically, and can reduce negative emotional reactions that cause low desire.

With the help of the therapist, the patient generates individualized statements to help him or her to cope with, rather than avoid, emotional reactions to particular sexual situations. The effective implementation of these strategies usually has an impact beyond the sexual area as well. This phase of therapy can begin once the patient has accepted the explanation or explanations for the low sexual desire, and is making good progress toward recognizing bodily cues and identifying feelings. Coping statements thus are used to compensate for dysfunctional feelings that may be keeping the patient from engaging in sexual activity. These feelings, in turn, are cued by bodily responses that the patient has learned to focus on through the sensory awareness exercises. Typical coping statements might include "Just because I engage in sex doesn't mean I'm a bad person," or " I know that when I was younger I learned to feel guilty about engaging in sex, and I don't want to and don't have to feel that way anymore," or "If I allow myself to enjoy sex, it does not mean that I will lose all control."

Another useful cognitive intervention is to help patients identify and re-evaluate their worst fears. For example, they are asked to imagine the worst thing that can happen if they become sexually aroused. They are taught that their behavior, for the most part, is under their own control and that they can take responsibility for what they currently do, and that it is within their own power to change their own behavior. For patients whose low drive is related to family-of-origin issues, coping statements differentiating the sexual partner from the opposite-sex parent are useful. For example, for a low-drive woman whose father was an alcoholic, a useful coping statement is "My husband is not like my father. I deliberately picked a man whom I can trust, who is dependable, and who is not an alcoholic." We often have our patients write 15–20 such coping statements on cards, and ask them to spend some time every day reading and elaborating on the coping statements.

We have found that a useful clinical tool to help patients bridge the gap between feelings and cognition is a modified transactional analysis framework (Berne, 1964; Steiner, 1974). Patients are asked to imagine that they have two tapes in their heads (figuratively, of course) on which they have been storing all kinds of information since early childhood. One tape, the "Child" tape, contains all of their emotional memories. One side of this tape is the "frightened child," on which all fear and emotional withdrawal responses have been stored. The flip side of this tape is the "playful child," on which all the happy, uninhibited, and playful emotional memories have been stored. The other tape, known as the "parent" tape, also has two sides. One, the "judgmental parent," contains all the dos and don'ts, shoulds and should nots, and other self-critical attitudes that have been accumulated since early childhood. The flip side of this tape is the "nurturing parent"; to the extent that there is information stored on this tape, one is able to provide nurturing not only for others, but for oneself. Thus, emotional responses come from the "child" tape, while attitudes and opinions come from the "parent" tape.

It is also explained that there is a third element, known as the "adult," which processes input from the environment and from the "parent" and "child" tapes to produce rational decisions. Helping the patient to label feelings, thoughts, and behaviors as coming from the "frightened child" or the "judgmental parent" may make him or her more aware of negative responses. For the low-desire patient, it is often the case that the "frightened child" and "judgmental parent" tapes are operating overtime. When the "frightened child" is in charge of the personality, there is no room for playfulness, and when the "judgmental parent" is in charge of the personality, there is little room for nurturing. It is explained that the work in therapy is to replace some "judgmental parent" statements with "nurturing parent" statements, so that the "frightened child" can feel safe and thus leave room for the "playful child" to come out to play. It is explained that in order to have good sex, one must have an active "playful child." Giving patients permission to let their "playful child" out to play often has a direct result in changing sexual behavior.

Step 4: Behavioral Interventions

The final element of this treatment program consists of behavioral interventions. Behavioral assignments are used throughout the therapy process and include basic sex therapy *in vivo* desensitization procedures (Masters & Johnson, 1970), as well as other sexual and nonsexual behavioral procedures. Specific behavioral assignments are chosen to complement and potentiate the other three components. First, behavioral assignments are used early in therapy to evoke feelings in patients during the experiential/ sensory awareness exercises. Thus, patients who have actively been avoiding sexual contact can focus on an label feelings that occur during sensate focus exercises. Second, behavioral interventions are used to help patients change nonsexual behaviors that may be helping to cause or maintain the sexual difficulty. Assertion training, communication training, and skill training in negotiation are examples of such behavioral interventions. Third, behavioral assignments are used for skill training. If patients are successful in therapy, they may find themselves in sexual (and other) situations that they have been avoiding in the past, and thus are ill prepared for. They often need to develop new behavioral repertoires to function effectively and comfortably in these situations.

For those with a particularly strong reaction to sexual activity, hand or body massage is sometimes a less threatening first step in sensate focus. Behavior rehearsal, role-playing other characters (e.g., very sexy women), and role reversal are useful interventions that often elicit affective responses. Depending upon the particular etiological factors, contact with sympathetic clergy, stress reduction interventions, and problem-solving skills all may be used as part of the behavioral intervention. Bibliotherapy, education on human sexuality and sexual techniques, and training in sexual initiation and refusal are additional interventions that may help patients function more effectively, once initial therapeutic gains allow for this skill training.

A particularly useful behavioral intervention for low sexual desire is drive induction or "priming the pump." This intervention makes sex more salient to the low-drive patient, who typically avoids all sexual stimuli. This can be done with the help of a desire checklist or a desire diary, in which the patient records all sexual stimuli, thoughts, and emotions. Another such intervention is the assignment of fantasy "breaks" during the day, in which the patient is asked to spend several minutes consciously having a sexual fantasy. Patients are also assigned to go to films with sexual content, read books with sexual content, rent erotic videos, look at erotic magazines, read collections of sexual fantasies, and so forth.

As part of drive induction, patients are also assigned to engage in casual, low-intensity physical affection. In most low-drive cases, there is very little kissing, hugging, and patting. This affection deficit develops because of the low drive, as the low-drive partner learns not to be affectionate for fear that the spouse will misinterpret casual affection as sexual initiation.

Summary

In summary, this program first focuses attention on bodily cues associated with feelings that result in lack of interest in or avoidance of sex. Second, insight-oriented therapy helps patients to understand the causes of these negative feelings. Cognitive coping statements are then generated to lead to alternative responses. Finally, behavioral interventions provide practice in alternative responses and in learning to be sexual. In its most general form, the sequence of internal dialogue we hope to develop in low-desire patients is as follows: "I am feeling . . . [awareness], which must be because . . . [insight]. Now what can I say to myself that will allow me to respond in a different way in spite of these feelings, or to accept these feelings and behave differently anyway [cognitive restructuring]?" Behaviorally, the patient now can try alternative responses and learn ways to make sex more salient. Once patients have become aware of bodily cues and emotions, and can automatically link a coping response/cognition with these feelings, it is difficult for these individuals to return to the previous avoidant and denying way of responding. In addition, affective responses to other nonsexual situations often trigger a broader cognitive re-evaluation of the patient's life as well. Thus, maintenance and generalization are important parts of this therapy program.

Two factors can impede the implementation of this model in certain clinical settings. First, it does require a high level of skill, knowledge, and sophistication on the part of the therapist. Second, the model requires an eclectic approach to therapy. Therefore, a clinical setting in which only one theoretical approach is rigidly adhered to would be inappropriate for this treatment model. Patient variables that seem to be associated with successful outcome include a strong commitment to the relationship by both partners, motivation for change on the part of both partners (rather than just the higher-desire partner), lack of defensiveness, and a positive working relationship between the patient couple and the therapist.

Case 1: Carol and Dan M

Carol and Dan M were in their late 30s at the time of intake and had been married for 16 years. They were both from a low-socioeconomic-status background and seemed quite naive about sex. Dan presented with global low sexual desire, and Carol complained of a total lack of affection in the relationship. The problem had been present from the onset of marriage but had steadily worsened. Dan had a lifelong history of difficulty in controlling his ejaculation and tended to ejaculate before or immediately after penetration. More recently, he found it impossible to obtain a full, rigid erection, and at the time of intake, the couple had not had intercourse for over 18 months. The low sexual desire predated the erectile problems by some years. Dan had been diagnosed as a juvenile-onset diabetic 20 years earlier, and it appeared that his erectile difficulties might be due to this medical problem. Although Carol and Dan claimed to love each other, the marriage was clearly very distressed, and the couple spent a good deal of therapy time arguing intensively with each other.

Dan was the youngest of four children and the only boy. He attended Catholic parochial school for the first 8 years of his schooling, and was fairly religious until after high school. Dan's father was an alcoholic who was abusive to his wife and occasionally to Dan. There was not much affection in the family, and Dan had a very distant relationship with his father. Sex was never discussed at home, and Dan learned what little he knew "on the street." He began to masturbate at age 13 but did so quite infrequently, less than once a month. Dating began at age 15, and he would occasionally have an orgasm during petting. His first intercourse was at 16, resulting in premature ejaculation. He had three or four sexual partners over the next several years, until he met Carol. He ejaculated prematurely in all these contacts.

Carol had little contact with her parents while she was growing up. Her father spent years in prison for armed robbery, and her mother worked outside the home. Carol received confusing messages about sex. While her mother told her that sex should be a wonderful, beautiful experience, in adolescence she realized that sex was what was keeping her parents connected in a destructive relationship. She had never experimented with masturbation and had had no sexual contact with a partner before meeting Dan. The couple did not engage in premarital intercourse. They argued a great deal, and parted and came together again many times. Following their marriage, sexual experiences were unsatisfying, primarily because of Dan's premature ejaculation. Once he would have his orgasm, the couple would end their lovemaking. Carol frequently found intercourse painful.

Carol was quite naive about her own body and about sexuality in general. Carol described orgasms in a way that left some doubt regarding whether she did, in fact, experience orgasm. At the time of intake, Dan still continued to suffer from severe premature ejaculation, and was ejaculating with a flaccid penis during the few times the couple did attempt to have sex. Approximately 5 years prior to therapy, Carol had become more responsive sexually; however, she had refused sexual contact for several months prior to therapy because intercourse was not possible. Dan and Carol seemed to interact with constant hostility and argument, with Carol being the more overtly hostile of the two.

The initial interview, history sessions, and assessment yielded several hypotheses regarding the etiology and maintenance of Dan's low sexual desire. First, he had a markedly deficient sexual learning history. Sex had never become a salient focus for Dan, because of his severe premature ejaculation and a lack of mutually satisfying sexual experiences in a relaxed setting. Carol, too, had never learned to be a sexually functional individual, and therefore was not able to aid in facilitating Dan's response. It was also hypothesized that Dan's premature ejaculation kept him from any sustained sexual pleasure with high arousal levels. The recent erectile difficulties helped maintain the low desire. The severe marital distress and lack of communication may also have been contributing to Dan's low sexual desire. His low drive was one additional passive–aggressive way to ignore Carol, without responding directly to her hostility.

In the early experiential phase of the therapy, Dan was trained to start noticing his physical reactions to sexual stimuli and to focus on sexual sensations. Sensate focus was introduced, excluding stimulation of breasts and genitals. At first, Dan claimed to be embarrassed by these exercises, since he and Carol had never done anything in the nude, in the light, and without being under the covers. However, he rapidly came to enjoy the exercises, and in fact became sexually aroused (without an erection). Carol enjoyed these sessions also, and the first week the couple broke the orgasm ban after mutual genital caressing. Dan was also given fantasy training and assigned a daily "fantasy break," taking 10–30 minutes per day to generate a sexual fantasy. Carol was asked to spend some time touching her own body and to learn more about how she liked to be touched, particularly in her genital area. A recurring theme presented by the therapist during the first five sessions was that Dan and Carol's early learning history had discouraged both from becoming sexually focused. It was stressed that learning to focus on and become aware of small sexual responses could help increase Dan's desire and Carol's pleasure.

Dan's premature ejaculation was lifelong and global. It was hypothesized that if Dan could increase his ejaculatory latency, then good feelings associated with high levels of arousal would increase his desire level. Consequently, a treatment program for premature ejaculation was introduced early in therapy. Dan and Carol were also helped to restructure their thoughts about the importance of erection in sexual functioning.

Carol and Dan were helped to understand that Dan's low desire might respond to improving their communication in general and their sexual communication in particular, and to facilitating good feelings toward each other. They learned to notice the early stages of feelings of anger and anxiety by focusing on their bodily sensations. They were then able to make coping statements that kept these negative feelings from growing in intensity and that allowed them to react in a more positive manner. An example of such statements was to replace the words "should" and "would" with "would like it to be," which would help to replace outrage with disappointment if they did not get what they wanted. Time was also spent on communication training, problem solving, and learning to negotiate differences. Carol was concrete in her thinking and did not seem to have much capacity for introspection and insight. However, she was able to focus on her feelings of anger and to stop herself before she lashed out at Dan. Because this change produced more positive responses from him, Carol found that negotiating was much more successful in getting what she wanted than her previous demanding and reprimanding had been.

Therapy was terminated after 10 sessions by mutual agreement. Dan and Carol's communication skills had improved greatly, and they were interacting in a much more positive manner. Dan indicated that he thought about sex much more than he had previously, and was very content with their stable frequency of once or twice per week. Carol agreed with this and wrote on her last homework form, "Sexual feelings have greatly improved. It is much easier to talk. We are showing more caring. Dan seems to be more interested. Dan is lasting longer [in intercourse] than I ever thought possible. We are getting more out of our sex life."

It is interesting to note that along with the increases in desire and the alleviation of the premature ejaculation, Dan was obtaining more frequent and rigid erections and the couple was able to engage in sexual intercourse, with Carol experiencing orgasm. Although some of his erectile difficulty may have been secondary to his diabetes, a large psychogenic component was obviously present as well.

By becoming more aware of their physical responses and by being able to have longer-lasting, more relaxed sex in a more pleasant, supportive environment, Carol and Dan were able to experience the positive aspect of good sex. This made it an activity worth looking forward to. By raising the arousal "threshold," Dan was able to have better erections as well, and Carol more intense orgasms.

Case 2: Gary and Norma E

This case has already been described to some extent in the section on etiology. Gary and Norma E presented for the problem of Norma's low desire and aversion to sex. They had been married for just over 5 years and had no children. At intake, their level of sexual functioning was poor. Gary and Norma were having sex approximately once every 1–2 months, at Gary's insistence. Their sexual activity consisted primarily of Gary stimulating Norma to orgasm by manually caressing her genitals while he masturbated himself to orgasm. Norma had a strong aversion to the male genitals and refused to touch his penis. The couple had discontinued attempts at penile–vaginal intercourse in the recent past, because Norma often had vaginismic spasms. Entry of the penis was painful and difficult if not impossible, due to her vaginismus. Marital adjustment was also poor. Gary spent much of his time when not at work visiting his widowed mother and doing errands or household chores for her. He also had a compulsive gambling problem, and went to the racetrack three or four times per week. As the household was only marginally solvent, the additional strain imposed by his gambling losses was rather severe.

Gary's familial and sexual history was a troubled one. His father had been an alcoholic, and the relationship between his mother and father was chaotic. His mother was greatly overinvested in him and had fostered an inappropriately close, almost symbiotic relationship with him. He was very emotionally dependent on her as a child and adolescent, and this dependence had continued in his adulthood. Gary had always been considered socially awkward and isolated through school, and he had not dated any women other than Norma. They met in a junior college class, had a few dates, and were married relatively soon thereafter.

Norma's history provided some rather obvious etiological factors in the development of her low desire and aversion to sex. Of primary importance was her history of having been sexually molested from the ages of 9 to 12 by an uncle. The experience of having been forced to caress her uncle's penis had been traumatic for her, leading to repression of her memories of the entire 3 years of "lessons." It was her recovery of the memories during the uncle's funeral, as described earlier, that motivated the couple to seek therapy.

Because the incest history led to a specific sexual aversion, Norma was seen for several sessions of individual psychotherapy, coinciding with the couple's work in conjoint therapy. In these individual sessions, the female cotherapist devoted considerable effort to working through the aftermath of the incestuous molestation. A combination of catharsis and abreaction for the memories of the event; cognitive mastery and coping statements to help her separate her "adult woman" persona from her "frightened, molested child" persona; and Gestalt "empty chair" dialogues to deal with unresolved feelings toward her uncle and her parents were employed. These sessions were highly emotionally charged for the patient at first, but did have a positive outcome.

In the couple work, training in communication, negotiation, and conflict resolution techniques was used to help the couple deal with Norma's anger about Gary's investment in his mother and about his gambling. With a relatively slow rate of progress and great difficulty, some gains were made in these areas.

In sexual therapy, Norma was exposed to comprehensive sex education material, and was encouraged to develop coping statements (1) to deal with the fear and resentment she felt as a result of her experience of having been molested as a child and (2) to learn to deal more assertively with her husband's current pattern of behavior. Gary was asked not to masturbate in Norma's presence; instead, the two of them were put on a standard program of sensate focus massage, with breast and genital contact forbidden. Norma was also placed on a modified *in vivo* desensitization program to reduce her aversion to the male penis. This program involved her first simply looking at Gary's penis from across the room, and gradually came to include her touching his penis, using her favorite body lotion, during their sensual massage sessions. Some progress, although at a very slow rate, was also made in this component of the therapy.

Because of Norma's vaginismic spasms, she was placed on a program of relaxation training and home use of a graduated set of vaginal dilators. Norma was not successful in using the dilators; she used them infrequently and briefly. She became quite negativistic at this point and began to express a desire to leave therapy. However, in conjoint therapy session with her husband and the male cotherapist present, she would not elaborate on the reasons for her wish to terminate therapy at this time.

Accordingly, the female cotherapist, who had established good rapport with Norma during the individual work on her molestation history, had a separate session with Norma. In this session, Norma revealed two important pieces of information that she had previously withheld. First, she reported that she had come to realize that she did not love her husband, and that she was staying married to him merely for his financial support while she returned to college. When pressed by the therapist, she reported that the only positive value her husband had for her was "noise in the house." She explained that when her dog was asleep, the house was too quiet and was frightening unless she heard somebody else moving about in it. Furthermore, Normal revealed that throughout her adolescence and young adulthood, she had struggled with strong homosexual urges and feelings. She reported that throughout adolescence she had masturbated using her brother's *Playboy* magazines as stimulus objects. In the past month, she had begun a homosexual relationship with a close woman friend. Norma reported that she had just now come to realize that she was a lesbian, and that she was going to accept herself as she was. Norma had denied any homosexual history or homosexual fantasies and wishes during evaluation and history taking, and was feeling somewhat guilty about having deceived the therapists.

The co-therapist offered Norma several options. These included restructuring therapy to focus on making her marriage more gratifying to her, helping her to clarify her own thinking as to whether she wished to leave the marriage, helping her explore the issue of her homosexual feelings, and so forth. She steadfastly declined all these opportunities. Instead, she reported that she wished to discontinue therapy, remain with her husband for his financial support during her remaining year of college, and then divorce him. When the therapist suggested that this was perhaps a bit exploitive, Norma replied that since Gary basically was more interested in his mother and in gambling anyway, she did not feel guilty.

The therapist suggested that Norma consider telling her husband about her newfound lesbian identity. This was not acceptable to her. As she had been promised confidentiality in the private session with the female cotherapist, the therapist did not have the option of raising these issues with the husband. Norma took the initiative in the next conjoint session to terminate therapy, explaining to her husband that she did not feel this therapy was helping them in any way. Her husband, somewhat to the therapists' surprise, agreed with this assessment. He reported that he was having increasing difficulty with carrying out his part of the marital restructuring, which involved controlling his gambling and his interactions with his mother. Gary reported that he had only been cooperating with these therapeutic changes because of the therapists' coercion, rather than out of any genuine desire to change on his part. He also reported that once he accepted his wife's sexual difficulties as being caused by her incestuous molestation, rather than being a reflection on his skills as a lover, he was no longer invested in her increasing her sexual desire and functioning. As a matter of fact, Gary reported that masturbation was quite satisfying to him, and he felt no strong need for sex with his wife.

Despite therapeutic efforts to the contrary, then, this case was terminated after 17 sessions of therapy. The case was a failure in the sense that the wife's level of desire for her husband did not increase. Obviously, there were major systemic rewards for both of them in the maintenance of the low sexual desire. Despite the therapists' feeling of frustration, the patients left therapy feeling pleased with the outcome. If there is a lesson to be learned here, it is that continued and careful assessment is the keystone for treating cases of low sexual desire.

Conclusion

This treatment program does produce good results (Schover & LoPiccolo, 1982). However, as the case of Gary and Norma E indicates, there are treatment failures. Even in successful treatment, the therapy is not a simple, brief, symptom-focused process, but is a complex and multifaceted procedure. A great deal of therapeutic eclecticism is required, because techniques adapted from several theoretical orientations are included in the program. The therapist needs to be a skilled diagnostician, and to be able to elicit much material in assessment that is emotionally charged and often heavily defended. During therapy, the therapist needs to be familiar with the techniques of Gestalt, systemic, psychodynamic, cognitive, and behavioral therapy. Obviously, treatment of low sexual desire cases presents many interesting challenges to the therapist, and working with these cases can lead to a rewarding growth in the therapist's skills.

References

Bancroft, J., Sanders, D., Davidson, D., & Warner, P. (1983). Mood, sexuality, hormones, and the role of the menstrual cycle. *Psychosomatic Medicine, 45*(6), 509–518.

Berne, E. New York: Grove Press. (1964). *Games people play.*

Blumstein, P., & Schwartz, P. (1983). *American couples: Money, work, and sex.* New York: Morrow.

Buffum, J. (1986). Pharmacology update: Prescription drugs and sexual function. *Journal of Psychoactive Drugs, 18*(2), 97–106.

D'Amicis, L., Goldberg, D., LoPiccolo, J., Friedman, J., & Davies, L. (1985). Clinical follow-up of couples treated for sexual dysfunction. *Archives of Sexual Behavior, 14*(6), 461–483.

Derogatis, L., Lipman, R. & Covi, L. (1973). SCL-90: An outpatient psychiatric rating scale. *Psychopharmacology Bulletin, 9*(1), 13–28.

Ellis, A. (1962). *Reason and emotion in psychotherapy.* New York: Lyle Stuart.

Fagan, J., & Shepherd, I. (1970). *Gestalt therapy now.* New York: Harper & Row.

Freud, S. (1962). *Three essays on the theory of female sexuality.* New York: Avon Books. (Original work published 1905)

Heiman, J., Gladue, B. Roberts, C., & LoPiccolo, J. (1986). Historical and current factors discriminating sexually functional from sexually dysfunctional married couples. *Journal of Marital and Family Therapy, 12*(2), 163–174.

Hogan, D., & Freidman, J. (1983). Treatment of low sexual desire. In D. Barlow (Ed.), *Behavioral treatment of adult disorders.* New York: Guilford Press.

Hunt, M. (1974). *Sexual behavior in the 1970's.* Chicago: Playboy Press.

Kaplan, H. (1974). *The new sex therapy.* New York: Brunner/Mazel.

Kaplan, H. (1977). Hypoactive sexual desire. *Journal of Sex and Marital Therapy, 3,* 3–9.

Kaplan, H. (1979). *Disorders of sexual desire.* New York: Brunner/Mazel.

Kimmel, D., & VanderVeen, F. (1974). Factors of marital adjustment in Locke's Marital Adjustment Test. *Journal of Marriage and the Family, 29,* 57–63.

LoPiccolo, J., & Heiman, J. (1977). Cultural values and the therapeutic definition of sexual function and dysfunction. *Journal of Social Issues, 33*(2), 166–183.

LoPiccolo, J., Heiman, J., Hogan, D., & Roberts, C. (1985). Effectiveness of single therapists verses co-therapy teams in sex therapy. *Journal of Consulting and Clinical Psychology, 53*(3), 287–294.

LoPiccolo, J., & Hogan, D. (1979). Multidimensional behavioral treatment of sexual dysfunction. In O. Pomerleau & J. Brady (Eds.), *Behavioral medicine.* Baltimore: Williams & Wilkins.

LoPiccolo, J., & Steger, J. (1974). The sexual interaction inventory: a new instrument for assessment of sexual dysfunction. *Archives of Sexual Behavior, 3*(6), 585–595.

LoPiccolo, L. (1980). Low sexual desire. In S. Leiblum & L. Pervin (Eds.), *Principles and practice of sex therapy.* New York: Guilford Press.

LoPiccolo, L., & Heiman, J. (1978). Sexual assessment and history interview. In L. LoPiccolo, & J. LoPiccolo (Eds.), *Handbook of sex therapy.* New York: Plenum Press.

Masters, W. H., & Johnson, V. E. (1970). *Human sexual inadequacy.* Boston: Little, Brown.

Nowinski, J., & LoPiccolo, J. (1979). Assessing sexual behavior in couples. *Journal of Sex and Marital Therapy, 5*(3), 225–243.

Pogach, L., & Vaitukaitus, J. (1983). Endocrine disorder associated with erectile dysfunction. In R. Krane, M. Siroky, & I. Goldstein (Eds.), *Male sexual dysfunction.* Boston: Little, Brown.

Sandler, M., & Gessa, G. (Eds.). (1975). *Sexual behavior: Pharmacology and biochemistry.* New York: Raven Press.

Schover, L., Friedman, J., Weiler, S., Heiman, J., & LoPiccolo, J. (1982). Multiaxial problem-oriented system for sexual dysfunctions: An alternative to DSM-III. *Archives of General Psychiatry, 39,* 614–619.

Schover, L., & LoPiccolo, J. (1982). Treatment effectiveness for dysfunctions of sexual desire. *Journal of Sex and Marital Therapy, 8*(3), 179–197.

Steiner, C. (1974). *Scripts people live.* New York: Grove Press.

Wolpe, J. (1958). *Psychotherapy by reciprocal inhibition.* Stanford, CA: Stanford University Press.

Zilbergeld, B., & Ellison, C. (1980). Desire discrepancies and arousal problems in sex therapy. In S. Leiblum & L. Pervin (Eds.), *Principles and practice of sex therapy.* New York: Guilford Press.

Zinker, J. (1977). *Creative process in Gestalt therapy.* New York: Vintage Books.

Zung, W. (1973). From art to science: The diagnosis and treatment of depression. *Archives of General Psychiatry, 29,* 328–337.

6

A Multimodal Perspective on Problems of Sexual Desire

ARNOLD A. LAZARUS

Arnold Lazarus, the originator of multimodal therapy and a pioneer in the directive treatment of sexual dysfunctions from a cognitive–behavioral perspective, views most instances of desire disorders as involving issues of desire discrepancy. His therapy goal is to arrive at a satisfactory compromise between the higher and lower sexual interest levels of partners in a relationship.

The cognitive–behavioral approach Lazarus follows initially involves a comprehensive and thorough assessment of both deficits and strengths in the realms of Behavior, Affect, Sensation, Imagery, Cognition, Interpersonal relationships, and biological variables (such as Drugs—emphasized here for the sake of the mnemonic device—or illness). This "BASIC I.D." evaluation of both partners in a relationship permits accurate identification of the obstacles that may be blocking sexual interest and facilitates the targeting of areas for intervention (e.g., the modification of faulty beliefs regarding sexuality, or the elimination of specific affective reactions, such as fear or anxiety). The clients are made active partners in the therapeutic enterprise, both in constructing the BASIC I.D. profile and in determining which modalities require intervention.

Lazarus is an extremely original and effective clinician. In his chapter, he makes several observations that may prove helpful for the treatment of individuals with desire difficulties. For instance, he suggests that clients become aware of the similarity between the appetites of sex and hunger. Both vary considerably across individuals, and both differ greatly at any single moment in time. Individuals who are receptive both to epicurean gourmet dinners (e.g., long, sensual passionate encounters) and to pizza parlor fare (e.g., "quickies") may find the greatest sexual satisfaction.

Lazarus also distinguishes between sexual arousal that relies primarily on central nervous system (CNS) input, and is therefore voluntary (e.g., manual or oral stimulation) versus that requiring autonomic nervous system (ANS) functioning (e.g., erection, which is primarily involuntary). He suggests that partners with differing levels of sexual interest be urged to consider "CNS sex" as both a palatable and pleasurable alternative to an exclusive diet of "ANS sex"—that is, full-blown penile–vaginal intercourse.

Arnold A. Lazarus, Ph.D., is Distinguished Professor in the Graduate School of Applied and Professional Psychology, Rutgers University. He is a prolific and engaging writer and the author of many books in clinical psychology, including Marital Myths *(1985) and (with Bernie Zilbergeld)* Mind Power *(1987).*

Overview: The Kaleidoscopic Heterogeneity of Desire Dysfunctions

Theoretically, problems of sexual desire may be placed on a continuum ranging from hypoactive to hyperactive degrees of intensity. The "normal" degree of libidinal desire would lie somewhere in the middle of the distribution. Attempts to narrow this global description into clinically precise definitions, diagnoses, and descriptions all suffer from the fact that, despite data from statistical surveys and diverse observations, the normal parameters of human sexual behavior have yet to be established. As with height, weight, intelligence, and so on, individual differences regarding the intensity of the sexual drive show wide variations, thus rendering it difficult in many instances to distinguish between "normal" and "abnormal" tendencies. Nonetheless, for practical purposes, there is sufficient professional consensus to identify extreme and clearly pathological patterns of sexuality. For example, a person who appears to be preoccupied with sex and masturbates to orgasm 15 times a day would generally be viewed as sexually hyperactive. An individual who never masturbates, very rarely has sexual thoughts or fantasies, and is attracted to members of neither sex would be regarded as sexually blocked or hypoactive.

Hyperactive sexual desire remains one of the most controversial clinical entities. Kaplan (1979) has stated, "In my experience, excessive sexual desire is so rare as to constitute a clinical curiosity when it is a primary symptom" (p. 76). She separates "primary hyperactive sexual desire" from those instances where high levels of sexual activity are due to manic and hypomanic states, extreme anxiety and tension, and obsessions centered on fears of inadequate sexual performance. Basically, very few individuals experience an excessive or constant desire for sex per se; most who are viewed as sexually hyperactive tend to rely on sexual outlets to relieve discomfort (be it tension, insecurity, anxiety, or any other negative state of mind).

It would seem that hyperactive sexual desire is very rarely a monistic or discrete clinical entity. Thus, the *Longman Dictionary of Psychology and Psychiatry* (Goldenson, 1984) defines "nymphomania" as "a female disorder consisting of an excessive or insatiable desire for sexual stimulation and gratification, due to such factors as denial of homosexual tendencies, attempts to combat or disprove frigidity, a reaction to seduction in childhood, or a response to emotional tension" (pp. 502–503). The same dictionary points out that "satyriasis" (a male psychosexual disorder consisting of an excessive or insatiable desire for sexual gratification) "is not due to being 'oversexed' in the physiological sense but arises from unconscious emotional needs, such as (a) the need for reassurance of potency, (b) a compensation for failures, frustrations, or a poor self-image, (c) a means of warding off anxiety stemming from emotional conflicts, or (d) an attempt to deny homosexual tendencies" (p. 652). It is a matter for debate whether or not some of the paraphilias are special instances of hyperactive sexual desire. The entire area of "deviant arousal" is often typified by case histories in which excessive desire figures prominently, and wherein unusual or aggressive sexual appetites predominate (e.g., Barlow & Wincze, 1980).

Practitioners will be consulted by patients complaining about hypoactive sexual desire far more frequently than by those who seek treatment for hypersexuality. Diminished libido, however, is anything but unitary or easily defined. As Friedman and Hogan (1985) have emphasized, "Although low sexual desire is a topic of current concern for sex therapists, there seems to be little agreement as to what this 'syndrome' is, and particularly, how to operationally define it" (p. 422). Patterns of asexual behavior vary widely. Some people may avoid sexual outlets despite feelings of desire; others simply have minimal or virtually no wish for sex. In rare instances, people have been devoid of sexual interest for their entire lives. Such primary sexual apathy carries a negative prognosis. Some patients with primary hypoactive sexual desire whose asexuality is global (rather than person- or situation-specific) may be constitutionally unable to experience endogenous desire. Kinsey, Pomeroy, and Martin (1948, p. 209) claimed that some persons "never were equipped to respond erotically."

It is more usual to encounter patients who report a loss of sexual drive or interest after a history of moderate to considerable desire and activity. Zilbergeld and Ellison (1980) distinguish between "desire" and "arousal": "Whereas desire refers to how often one wants sex, arousal denotes how high (excited, turned on) one gets during sex" (p. 68). There are those who, despite a lack of sexual desire, can nevertheless perform reflexively if genitally stimulated; others respond to all sexual overtures with nothing but irritation, anger, anxiety, or disgust. A low sexual desire can be total or situational (e.g., the person who has no desire for his or her spouse but is highly active with a lover). Regardless, when consulted by a patient whose sexual frequency is low, a crucial consideration is whether the low sexual activity is basically a function of diminished desire, or fear of sex, or of aversion to sex. There is an important difference between "apathy" and "inhibition." Indeed, what Lief (1977) has called "inhibited sexual desire" (ISD) may be a product of numerous etiological factors.

Prior to the middle to late 1970s, low sexual desire, especially in males, had not been clearly delineated as a discrete problem. Many writers applied the label "frigidity" to women with virtually any sexual dysfunction, ranging from partial or total impairment of desire, to sexual interest and pleasure without orgasm. Among male disorders, the term "impotence" included "premature ejaculation, limited interest in sex, orgasm without experiencing pleasure, coitus without ejaculation, and sexual ability only with prostitutes" (Goldenson, 1984, p. 370). "Gradually, it was recognized that the sexual response is *not* an indivisible entity, vulnerable to a single pathogen, subject to only one disorder, and amenable to a single treatment regimen" (Kaplan, 1979, p. 4). While Masters and Johnson (1966) proposed a sequential continuum of human responses to effective sexual stimulation—excitement, plateau, orgasm, and resolution—desire was not mentioned. Kaplan (1979) has proposed a triphasic concept of human sexuality—desire, excitement, and orgasm. I have found it clinically advantageous to think in terms of desire, arousal, stimulation, orgasm, resolution, and satisfaction. Each of these phases may present discrete problems:

1. *Desire:* Disorders of desire, as already mentioned, are many and varied, but the most common clinical entity is ISD, which is characterized by no or low interest in any form of sexual activity.
2. *Arousal:* Arousal deficits refer to the absolute or relative absence of penile tumescence (erection) or of the vaginal lubrication and distension necessary for coitus.
3. *Stimulation:* Typical problems that may arise during the stimulation phase include loss of erection, premature ejaculation, cessation of vaginal lubrication, and loss of interest or desire prior to orgasm.
4. *Orgasm:* Orgasmic difficulties include anorgasmia, pain, diminished sensation, and ejaculation without sensation.
5. *Resolution:* Resolution difficulties include such phenomena as extreme postorgasmic lassitude or fatigue, depression, headache, or genital pain or discomfort.
6. *Satisfaction:* Difficulties with satisfaction refer to a negative subjective evaluation of the sexual experience, or deficits in the overall

level of gratification or fulfillment that flows from the sexual experience.

A wide range of medical illnesses, especially those of a urological or gynecological nature, may result in loss of sexual interest and/or sexual avoidance. Hormonal deficiency, particularly of testosterone, may produce a diminution of sexual interest in men and women. Drugs may attenuate sexual desire, especially certain antihypertensive agents, high doses of alcohol, sedatives, narcotics, and some neuroleptics. Depression tends to compromise the sexual appetite. On the psychological front, the range of factors interfering with sexual desire is wide: Among the most common are various conflicts; anger and hostility; guilt (often associated with a Puritan antisex ethic and other religious prohibitions); or fears about intimacy, vulnerability, responsibility, rejection, pleasure, and commitment. Severe stress and situational anxiety are also associated with truncated desire.

When called upon to treat disorders of sexual desire, the practitioner will find that problems are usually defined by a dyadic unit: "The person with low desire is often perfectly content with his or her own level of desire, and comes to therapy because of pressure from his or her partner" (Friedman & Hogan, 1985, p. 422). It is for the foregoing reasons that the term "desire discrepancies," proposed by Zilbergeld and Ellison (1980), seems preferable to positing some arbitrary standard of high or low sexual interest. As these authors note, "It is not that one person has too much desire and another too little on some absolute scale; it is rather a discrepancy in two people's styles or interest" (1980, p. 68). The paradoxes of adopting some putative criterion of high or low sexual desire are readily demonstrated. If a couple has intercourse twice a year, but both partners are entirely content with their sex life, should we intervene, attempt to raise their sexual consciousness, and thus perhaps elevate their coital frequency? Is an unattached person who desires and obtains sex once every 3 or 4 months, and who has no complaints about this frequency, in need of help? If we are treating Mr. and Mrs. X because he desires sex once every 2 weeks and she craves it at least three times a week, would we regard him as suffering from low desire? Then if Mr. and Mrs. X get divorced and he marries a woman who wants sex only every couple of months, would we now alter our diagnosis?

Most therapists have tended to focus on the partner who displays the less interest of the two, with a view to increasing the sexual appetite of that individual. The implication seems to be that "more is better" and that a lower level of desire is dysfunctional. Zilbergeld and Ellison (1980) challenge this view and emphasize the necessity to "attend to both partners, trying to increase the desire of the one while at the same time trying to decrease that of the other" (p. 68). In treating desire discrepancies, the goal is to achieve a satisfactory compromise.

The Multimodal Approach

Multimodal therapy (Lazarus, 1976, 1981, 1985a, 1986, 1987) emphasizes the need for a thorough and comprehensive assessment of *Behavior, Affect, Sensation, Imagery, Cognition, Interpersonal* relationships, and *Biological* factors. The convenient mnemonic device "BASIC I.D." is an acronym derived from the first letters of these discrete yet interactive modalities by changing "B" (*Biological*) to "D" (*Drugs*), since most interventions in this area call for neuroleptics, antidepressants, and anxiolytic agents. However, it must be remembered that the "D" modality adresses *all* issues of physical well-being, such as diet, sleep habits, exercise, central nervous system (CNS) pathology, endocrine disorders, and metabolic disorders, in addition to the effects of prescribed medications and recreational drugs.

Multimodal therapy recommends a level of systematic attention devoted to each area of a client's BASIC I.D. that exceeds the thoroughness and diagnostic scrutiny of most other multifactorial, multidimensional, multifaceted, and eclectic orientations. When the assessment template of multimodal therapy is applied to disorders of sexual desire, some salient questions in each modality are immediately apparent:

- *Behavior:* Is the problem that of hyperactivity or hypoactivity? Can specific response deficits or excesses be identified? Are there issues related to sexual skills and performance (e.g., kissing, caressing, massaging, and other forms of stimulation)? What are the details concerning oral–genital contact, masturbation, and the impact of situational variables?
- *Affect:* Is there evidence of anxiety, and/or guilt, and/or depression, and/or anger? Are there *aversions* to any body parts or functions? Is there love, affection, or caring? Are there signs of displaced affect being deflected from a parent onto a partner or spouse? Do there appear to be any specific fears of intimacy?
- *Sensation:* Primarily, are we dealing with pain (e.g., dyspareunia, or postcoital discomfort) or the absence of pleasure (e.g., anorgasmia, or ejaculation without sensation)? Is self-stimulation unpleasant, neutral, pleasant, or nonexistent? Is there arousal, but limited or no pleasure?
- *Imagery:* Does the thought of sexual encounters conjure up negative or intrusive images? Are there reports of any spontaneous seductive or erotic mental images? Can specific fantasies increase or decrease sexual desire? What are the frequency and content of erotic dreams (if any)? Do books, pictures, or erotic films stimulate any arousal or desire?
- *Cognition:* What connection is there between the client's ethics, morals, and religious beliefs, and his or her own sexuality? What

are the client's basic sexual outlook and attitudes? Are there definite sex-role expectations? Which "shoulds," "oughts," and "musts" are self-imposed, and which are placed on the partner? Does the person lack sexual information and/or have misinformation?

- *Interpersonal relationships:* How assertive and communicative is the client? Is there a specific relational problem (e.g., lack of attraction to the partner), and/or is there evidence of generalized interpersonal difficulties? What role does power play? Who have served as sexual role models? What are the details *vis-à-vis* initiation and refusal of sexual activity? Is there any evidence of sexual trauma—rape, coercive incest, parental punishment?
- *Drugs (biological factors):* What medications or drugs does the client ingest? Are there any urological or gynecological dysfunctions? Have other organic factors been ruled out? Do endocrinological tests seem warranted?

The foregoing questions and issues are by no means complete or exhaustive; they provide the basis for more detailed explorations into the specific areas that may call for elaboration and clarification. The point is that even this preliminary BASIC I.D. inquiry provides an impressive degree of precision and comprehensiveness. It differs from most other multidimensional approaches. For example, Friedman and Hogan (1985) have described "a multidimensional behavioral treatment model for inhibited sexual desire" (p. 419) that integrates four therapeutic components: (1) experiential/sensory awareness exercises; (2) insight; (3) cognitive restructuring; and (4) behavioral interventions. In multimodal vernacular, they cover a *trimodal* sequence (sensation, cognition, and behavior).

While broad-based eclectic therapists tend to traverse most aspects of the BASIC I.D., they nevertheless leave much to chance and to the individual clinician's perspicacity. There is a difference between an assessment schema that calls deliberate and specific attention to behavior, affect, sensation, imagery, cognition, interpersonal relationships, and biological factors, and those diagnostic protocols that gloss over one or more of these modalities or condense them into fewer categories. Thus, in their "experiential/sensory awareness" component, Friedman and Hogan (1985) include "fantasy training" as well as "imaginal recreation of an earlier traumatic experience" (p. 437). It is especially easy for novice therapists and trainees to downplay certain elements unless they are explicitly built into the assessment–therapy sequence, and even experienced clinicians tend to require guideposts or reminders to ensure that they do not bypass or overlook less obvious components. In multimodal therapy, the imagery modality (no less than the other six) is explicitly identified and thoroughly assessed (see Lazarus, 1984).

It is important to underscore the way in which treatment interventions are selected within the multimodal approach. Specifically, when there are deficits or problems in several dimensions of the BASIC I.D., how does the clinician decide when and how to intervene? Usually, the areas to be addressed are decided upon in concert with input from the client. The therapist might say, "Perhaps we could begin by dealing with your reluctance to be explicit with your wife about your sexual preferences, and also maybe we can explore some of your attitudes about male–female differences. Or are there other issues that you would prefer to include?" If the client proposes different priorities or additional objectives, the therapist might agree to follow the client's script, unless the therapist has explicit reasons for not doing so. (It would be myopic always to follow the client's predilections. Those with passive–aggressive, manipulative, and sabotaging tendencies usually require firm direction.) In this event, a discussion ensues until a mutually agreeable treatment sequence is reached. The therapist then provides a description of the different pathways toward the specified goal. While eschewing push-button panaceas, the aim is to select those methods most likely to prove beneficial: Tense people are taught relaxation; dysfunctional beliefs call for the "correction of misconceptions"; interpersonal skills training is offered to those who are socially inept or unduly reticent. Some individuals prefer to deal with only one problem at a time. Others respond better when working on two or more issues simultaneously. Regardless, the final goal is to insure that no significant problems throughout the BASIC I.D. are bypassed or glossed over.

It is perhaps necessary to underscore the fact that the BASIC I.D. is *not* a "flat," static, linear representation of human temperament and personality. While it is clinically convenient to divide the reciprocal interactive flux that typifies actual life events into the seemingly separate dimensions of the BASIC I.D., in actuality we are always confronted by a continuous, recursive, multileveled living process. The multimodal approach essentially asks: (1) What are the specific and interrelated problems? (2) Who or what appears to be maintaining these problems? (3) What appears to be the best way in each individual instance of remedying these problems? The BASIC I.D. offers a systematic structure that insures thoroughness and also provides specific methods for identifying idiosyncratic reactions.

A General "Formula" for Resolving Desire Discrepancies

Before I describe some typical multimodal treatment sequences, it may be useful to place the issue of "desire discrepancies" and its potential resolution into some overall perspective. Within any dyad, desire discrepancies are inevitable; perfect sexual harmony and synchrony exist only in romantic novels. It is obvious that times will arise when one partner desires sex and the other is not in the mood for it, or when one person is aroused and the other is uninterested. Usually, these differences pose no problem and constitute no threat, and couples adjust to them as they see fit. Problems arise when the discrepant pattern becomes frequent and unpredictable, or when a significant difference in respective sexual "appetites" seems evident.

The most common complaint within the foregoing context translates into the following: "I desire sexual relations far more frequently than my spouse [partner], and there is therefore something wrong with him [her]." In my experience, the complainant is usually, but not always, the one who wants more sex; the defendant is often the one who requires less. I have stated the problem legalistically because it is frequently presented in this manner. A major overriding difficulty stems from the fact that the person wanting more sex usually insists on "complete intercourse" (foreplay that culminates in penile–vaginal stimulation followed by mutual, if not simultaneous, orgasms). Many such individuals subscribe to unfortunate myths: "If he really loved me, he would want to have sex with me as often as I wish to have it with him"; "If she was truly turned on to me, she would become aroused as soon as I started kissing and caressing her." A first step is to challenge the faulty "if–then" assumptions that many people bring to their sexual encounters. It is also important that the therapist search for implicit or explicit *demands* that undermine sexual activity: "Before I let my husband make love to me, I must be sure that he wants *me* and not just my body"; "My wife wanted me to have intercourse with her last night. How could I, when only 3 days ago she accused me of being stingy?" Of course, the astute clinician will be on the alert for possible hidden agendas that lead some people to latch onto virtually any event as an excuse for sexual distance.

It is often especially helpful in resolving desire discrepancies to underscore the similarities between the "sexual drive" and the "hunger drive." The therapist can point out that these "appetites" show wide individual differences, and that a continuum extends in both areas from compulsive gluttony to total anorexia. The person who always insists on nothing less than a gourmet's epicurean preparation and elegant presentation of delicious cuisine—who will not eat in any place less sumptuous than a four-star restaurant, replete with the best china and crystal, soft music, and subdued lights—might go hungry most of the time, become seriously undernourished, and feel chronically deprived. Similarly, in matters pertaining to sex, those who insist on delicate intimacy, or passionate intensity, under ideal conditions will find their sexual frequency and enjoyment decidedly curtailed. It is more sensible to enjoy a wide range of options—to have the capacity to appreciate and enjoy sumptuous dining on meticulously prepared victuals, while also remaining open to the delights and pleasures (and nourishment) of a pizza or a quick sandwich. Sexually, the couple who develops the ability to enjoy "four-star gourmet lovemaking" on some occasions, and "local pizza parlor fare" on others, will not miss out on those delightful and spontaneous "quickies" from time to time that tend to promote intimacy, caring, and physical relief.

The foregoing analogies translate into the following therapeutic tactics:

When it is the woman who desires more sex than the man, I point out that no man is capable of willing an erection, and I often provide a brief explanation of the psychophysiology of sexuality, emphasizing that much of it is under the control of the autonomic nervous system (ANS). I also stress that activities such as manual, digital, and oral stimulation fall under the domain of the CNS. Therefore, if the woman desires sexual stimulation and relief four times a week to the man's two, I would recommend two "CNS + ANS" sexual unions (foreplay that culminates in coitus) and two purely "CNS" encounters (wherein he engages in loving and erotic foreplay, culminating in oral and/or manual stimulation to bring her to orgasm— repeatedly if she so desires). During "CNS" lovemaking, there is no penile– vaginal stimulation, and the man seeks no sexual gratification for himself unless he becomes erect and sexually excited. I emphasize very strongly that no anticipations and hidden expectations must enter the situation; it is perfectly acceptable for the male to stimulate the female without becoming aroused, and this signals neither the absence of love nor the existence of a sexual problem. (CNS sex is tantamount to a hamburger or a sandwich; ANS sex is at least a three-course meal!)

When the man desires more sex than the woman, I deliver my psychophysiology lecture by explaining that sexual arousal is autonomically mediated, and that the female cannot control vaginal lubrication and distension any more than the male can will an erection. Nevertheless, "CNS" lovemaking may include anything from back rubs to fellatio. The primary objective is for the woman to stimulate the man so that he has an orgasm. One difference in the case of a woman engaging in "CNS sex" is that penile–vaginal stimulation is usually possible; that is, the man (perhaps with the aid of a lubricating cream) is able to enter the vagina and achieve orgasm. One of my clients stated her position very clearly: "Hal wants sex virtually every night, whereas I am in the mood two or perhaps three times a week. So when he wants it and I don't, I have no problem with him masturbating inside of me." In this situation, the problem was that Hal felt insulted and became angry when his wife failed to respond erotically every time he stimulated her, particularly when he entered her. It was necessary to persuade Hal to separate ANS from CNS sexual intercourse and never to confuse the two. I have treated other couples wherein the male had no difficulties receiving CNS sex, but the female objected because she felt "used." Here again, considerable "cognitive restructuring" was required to effect a satisfactory solution.

We have all been successful with couples wherein low sexual desire is due to situational factors: The overly competitive corporate husband or wife is so burned out, or so preoccupied with work, that fun, leisure, sex, and other pleasures have been tabled. Certainly, in my experience, it is not difficult, when at least a modicum of attraction and desire is still present within the dyad, to fan the fire so that it crackles away to a heart-warming degree. Another situational factor that usually responds rapidly to professional intervention is the "desire disorder" that stems from one partner's neglect of basic hygiene. I have had to urge many a spouse to take a bath or a shower before even considering making sexual overtures. Compliance in such cases has usually led to an immediate increase in the formerly reluctant partner's sexual desire.

Recently, a couple consulted me because the wife, who had been sexually responsive for the first 5 years of marriage, had become almost totally unresponsive for the past 3 months. The problem was simply that her mother had come to live with them and the wife was afraid that "sexual sounds" would carry through the "flimsy walls." The solution? The installation of soundproofing tiles in the main bedroom restored a sense of privacy that enabled the wife to return to her uninhibited former self. (I am often astonished how these obvious solutions sometimes prove so elusive!)

Another situationally specific "low-desire" problem involved a 55-year-old physician and his second wife. He stated that the frequency of sex throughout the 26 years of his first marriage (which ended in divorce) had averaged once or twice a month. For the past 2 years, he had been married to a 36-year-old woman who desired sex at least once a week. "At first, this was no problem," the doctor explained, "as I was very stimulated and excited by her. . . . But now I no longer feel so aroused by her." We discussed the natural evolution of most relationships and the impact of "habituation"—the fact that most people, after a while, find that the initial thrills tend to subside if not to disappear altogether. I inquired whether he ever masturbated. "Occasionally," he said. I asked, "Do you use any fantasies while so doing?" He answered, "Yes. I have quite a vivid imagination." I inquired, "Then why not use this 'vivid imagination' to good effect while in bed with your wife?" The doctor had two objections to this idea: (1) He viewed it as "cheating," and (2) he thought it might be considered "abnormal." I was able to persuade him that both of these notions were unfounded, whereupon he accepted my "permission" to season his sex life with the intrinsic powers of erotic imagery. Thereafter, his apparent "low desire" was no longer an impediment.

It should be re-emphasized that medical/biological factors may play a crucial role in desire disorders. The "D" modality is particularly relevant when definite endocrinopathy has been established. Nevertheless, as Reckless and Geiger (1975) pointed out, hormone treatment can increase desire without improving performance, and thus can worsen the patient's plight. (At the very least, a bimodal treatment approach—behavioral–biological—

would seem indicated even where clear-cut medical interventions are necessary.) It is also interesting that certain patients have demonstrated significant improvement when treated with a placebo (Miller, 1968; Sobotka, 1969).

Having discussed some routine and situationally determined problems, I now focus attention on more complex issues calling for the full spectrum of multimodal methods. The first therapy illustration is a description of a successfully completed case, and the second is a description of a treatment failure.

Case Presentations

A Successful Case

Description

Lisa, aged 35, and Al, aged 37, had been married 8 years at the time of intake. Lisa stated (and Al agreed) that during their premarital period (approximately 8 months), sex had been frequent and passionate. As soon as they were married Lisa noticed an attenuation in Al's interest, but the frequency and quality of their sexual interactions nevertheless remained satisfactory for about 2 years. At that juncture, Al evidenced erectile difficulties, and he consulted a psychiatrist who attributed the problem to undue work pressures. (Al's responsibilities on the job had intensified, and he felt harassed much of the time.) Soon thereafter, he accepted a new position that removed many of the previous work demands, and his potency was restored—but never to its former level. Over the next 4 years, intermittent problems (erectile difficulties, rapid ejaculation, nonspecific prostatitis) progressively undermined Al's sexual interest and desire. For the past year, he reported having no spontaneous sexual desires, and Lisa stated that during this time they had had sex "less than three or four times at most."

Al held a master's degree in electrical engineering and had a managerial-cum-technical position with a large company. Lisa had a master's degree in library science, but worked as an advertising representative and free-lance copywriter. They had no children, although for the past 2 years Lisa had felt that a final decision had to be reached, since her "biological clock" was running out. Al seemed highly ambivalent in this regard.

Al's Background

Al had a sister 3 years his junior with whom he had fought "like cats and dogs" and from whom he felt "disconnected." He described his father as "passive," and called his mother "a battle-ax." He said, "She was often on the warpath, and at an early age I learned how to keep out of her way."

When asked whether he had felt loved as a child and whether he had been shown affection and warmth, he stated that despite his father's passivity and his mother's aggressiveness, he had received adequate love and attention from both parents. He regarded them as sexually inhibited—the subject was never discussed in the home. He had learned the facts of life from peers when he was about 11, at which time he started masturbating. At age 16 he started dating, and although he engaged in heavy petting on dates, his first intercourse was at age 20 with a prostitute. Over the next 8 years he had several "serious relationships," but it was only when he met Lisa, when he was almost 29, that he considered marriage for the first time. "I had never seemed to see eye-to-eye so closely with anyone. . . . We laughed at the same things and agreed about everything from agnosticism to our taste in art."

Lisa's Background

Lisa had a sister 9 years her senior, to whom she had always felt very close. Lisa excelled academically and was favored by her father. Her parents tolerated each other, and the home atmosphere was one of "serenity but no real joy." Her mother often voiced the view that wives have to "second-guess" their husbands and see to it that they (the wives) remain in control. When Lisa was about 14, her mother received a small inheritance, which "through cunning and some luck, she managed to turn into a large sum of money." Her mother's financial independence seemed to drive a wedge between her parents. When she was 19, Lisa's mother confided in her that the father was having a clandestine love affair—a fact that her mother seemed to find amusing rather than threatening or annoying. "During my junior year at college, my parents got divorced, and during my senior year, they each remarried."

She was popular in college and dated frequently, "but I hung onto my virginity until the end of my senior year." Soon after graduating, at age 21, she married a man 10 years her senior. "He was super-brilliant, and I was attracted to his intellect." Nevertheless, they had few common interests; Lisa never found him physically attractive; and within 2 years they had grown so far apart that they "simply drifted into a divorce." Thereafter, while she dated several men, it was not until meeting Al that she "fell in love." She described him as "brilliant like my first husband, but infinitely more attractive and sexy."

The Multimodal Assessment

The foregoing information is a summary of the more salient points that emerged from two intake interviews with the couple. At the end of the initial interview, Lisa and Al were each asked to fill out a Multimodal Life History Questionnaire[1] and to return it at the second meeting. This instrument covers the BASIC I.D. in some detail and usually enables the therapist to determine in which particular areas the chief problems reside.

It seemed that Al's background had rendered him especially sensitive to aggression (real or imagined) from women. He reacted to Lisa, who thought of herself as "assertive," as a person who was extremely "controlling and aggressive." In describing Lisa on the Multimodal Life History Questionnaire, Al had written: "She treats me like a moron. One would assume that I lacked the intelligence to compose a business letter or remember simple everyday things." Lisa, in turn, had written: "Al is just too laid back at times, and I think he views any affectionate nudging as a critical attack." During the fourth conjoint session, Lisa stated, "Look here, you two, I want answers and I want them now. I think I've been patient far too long!" I asked Lisa whether this was an example of her "affectionate nudging." I also inquired whether or not it represented her usual style when frustrated. At the end of the session, the following points of agreement had been reached: (1) In general, Lisa was inclined to "come on strong." (2) Al tended to overreact and was needlessly hypersensitive to real or imagined slights from most people, especially from women, and most of all from Lisa. (3) When feeling under attack, Al, instead of asserting himself, almost always withdrew (thereby adhering to tactics that had functional validity as a child, but no longer served him as an adult).

Al alleged that Lisa had been openly derisive and hypercritical of his sexual inadequacies. "When I first had that problem with impotence about 6 years ago, you should have heard the things she said to me!" Lisa retorted, "That was over 6 years ago! Have I said anything since then?" Al replied, "You don't have to. It's more than evident by your actions." Lisa turned to me and said, "That's his main problem; he's so damn negative. Al's forever reading aspersions and contempt into just about everything I say or do." Al responded by saying, "Lisa, I may be way too sensitive, but I'm by no means alone in regarding you as very pushy and too damn controlling. Your own sister remarked that even as a kid you liked to take charge, to be in command, to dish out orders. And didn't Sue, and Phyllis, and your whole tennis group call you the Great Dictator? And how many times has Gordon [her boss] been on the verge of firing you for insubordination? It's not all in my head. Sure, I may be too touchy, but you're one hell of a tough cookie." I interjected, "Just like your mother?" to which Al responded, "Yeah, but at least I could get away from her." I said, "Al, I think you and I should meet alone a few times, man to man, so that we can more closely examine your withdrawal tendencies, your wish to get away from tough situations instead of facing them and beating them. And Lisa, I would like to meet with you

---

1. The Multimodal Life History Questionnaire is obtainable from Research Press, Box 3177, Champaign, IL 61821.

individually for a while to see if you might benefit by acquiring a different interpersonal style. Al, Lisa, how does this one-on-one idea grab you?" They both replied, "Fine."

Before embarking on individual sessions with me, the couple was asked to employ sensate focus twice a week. I strongly impressed upon them that these encounters were to be relaxed, affectionate, unhurried sensual massages that excluded the involvement of breasts and genitals, and explicitly did not include any coitus or orgasms. I ascertained that Lisa particularly enjoyed receiving foot massages, whereas Al enjoyed back rubs, and I obtained a firm agreement that they would pleasure each other in this manner twice weekly. Separate individual sessions with Al and Lisa were scheduled for the following week.

Individual Sessions with Al

Prior to seeing Al individually, I had drawn up the following Modality Profile:

Behavior:	Withdrawal tendencies
Affect:	Anxiety (over attaining an erection)
	Anger (mostly unexpressed)
Sensation:	Tension (mainly in jaws, shoulders, and neck)
	Discomfort in scrotum (during bouts of prostatitis)
Imagery:	Pictures (vivid memories) of negative sexual experiences
Cognition:	Perfectionistic tendencies
	"I can't stand criticism"
	Performance concerns and expectations
	Conflicted about becoming a father
Interpersonal relationships:	Communication dysfunction (does not state sexual preferences explicitly)
	Unassertive (especially in expressing anger)
	Overreacts to aggression, expecially from women
Drugs/biological factors:	Recurrent bouts of nonspecific prostatitis

Al read through the profile and agreed that it pinpointed his main areas of difficulty. After discussing a logical starting point, we agreed on the following: (1) Al would read, most thoroughly, the first chapter of Zilbergeld's (1978) *Male Sexuality* (which deals with significant myths about sexuality and helps men modify unrealistic expectations). (2) We would address his withdrawal tendencies and his basic lack of assertiveness. (3) He would be taught specific relaxation procedures and given cassettes for home use.

Assertiveness training commenced with the usual behavior rehearsal and role-playing procedures, but soon uncovered a host of subjective dangers that characterized Al's perceptions about adopting an assertive stance in life. To Al's way of thinking, it was safer to withdraw, to remain silent, and (if necessary) to retaliate in a passive–aggressive manner when criticized or when placed in any compromising position. The basis of this pattern appeared to be a consequence of contending with his aggressive mother while at the same time identifying with his passive father.

Accordingly, "time-tripping imagery" (Lazarus, 1984) was employed as follows: While reclining on a comfortable chair, Al was given standard relaxation instructions and then asked to close his eyes and imagine a scene in which he, as an adult, stepped into a "time machine" and went back in time to significant encounters with his mother. The following dialogue (taken from a slightly edited transcript of the session) ensued:

THERAPIST: You can stop the time machine and enter your life at any time in the past. Can you imagine that clearly?

CLIENT: Yes. *(Pause)* I remember a time, oh, I was about 5 or 6, and I had done something to enrage my mother, I forget what, but I was playing with some toys in the den and she came in, kicked the toys all over the room, and yelled at me.

THERAPIST: OK, now you enter the picture at age 37. You step out of the time machine and into the den. See and hear your mother yelling. *(Pause)* Look at 5- or 6-year-old Al. *(Pause)* What's happening?

CLIENT: My mother and little Al don't seem to be aware of me, they don't notice me.

THERAPIST: Well, can you make your presence felt? How would you like to gain their attention?

CLIENT: By strangling my mother! *(Chuckles)*

THERAPIST: Can you picture yourself handling the situation *assertively?* You are 37. Little Al is 5 or 6. How old is your mother?

CLIENT: She's about 28 or 29.

THERAPIST: Fine. Now there's no point in telling her who you are, that you are 37-year-old Al on a visit back from the future. Instead, how about simply telling her that she is mistreating 5-year-old Al?

CLIENT: *(A 30- or 40-second pause)* Yes, I can put her in her place.

THERAPIST: Good. In a few moments, let's discuss what transpired. But before you leave that scene, can you say something to little Al?

CLIENT: *(Pause)* I really don't know what to say to him.

THERAPIST: Why not reassure him? Tell him that he's a good kid, and explain to him that his mother's a bit unstable, but that he shouldn't take it to heart when she flies off the handle.

CLIENT: *(Pause)* Okay. In retrospect, I can tell little Al, "The battle-ax means no harm."

THERAPIST: Excellent. Now are you ready to step into the time machine and return back here?

The foregoing imagery excursion was then discussed, and Al was asked to practice similar scenes at his leisure several times a day, wherein he went back in time to comfort his young alter ego and upbraid his mother (assertively, not aggressively). In subsequent sessions, time tripping was employed to encourage his (passive) father to stand up to his mother. Instead, the client preferred not to try to modify his father's behavior, but to inform him that from now on he (Al) was going to be a very different (more assertive) individual. (It seemed that he was seeking permission to stop identifying with his father, and to become his own person.) In my experience, when clients employ these imagery exercises conscientiously, salubrious effects usually accrue. Al was one of those clients who found these imagery exercises "ego-syntonic" and whose treatment gains coincided with their application.

In tandem with the imagery exercises, each item on Al's Modality Profile was addressed. Thus, a nonperformance outlook on sex was underscored; approach responses rather than avoidance behaviors were encouraged; his anger, instead of being suppressed, was to be appropriately vented; relaxation skills were provided to offset his tensions; images of positive and erotic sexual fantasies were to be practiced in place of his negative imagery; a strong antiperfectionistic philosophy of life was advocated; role playing was employed to enhance communication (e.g., stating sexual preferences explicitly); and behavior rehearsal was used to contend with criticism and aggression. The foregoing required eight weekly sessions, at the end of which time significant changes had accrued. (By the fifth session, Al mentioned that during the preceding week, the sensate focus assignments had turned into "passionate lovemaking" on two occasions. Sensate focus procedures thus became their "new version of foreplay," and sexual intercourse occurred twice or three times a week thereafter.) Because Al still espoused certain sexual and marital myths, he was encouraged to reread Zilbergeld (1978), paying particular attention to the myths outlined therein; I also gave him a copy of my book *Marital Myths* (Lazarus, 1985b) suggesting that we might profitably discuss his reactions at the next session. One area that had not been specifically addressed was his ambivalence about parenthood, and it was recommended that we might focus on this issue during some further conjoint sessions.

Individual Sessions with Lisa

One of the significant features of the multimodal approach is its flexibility. Lisa was negatively disposed to any systematic BASIC I.D. exploration, but preferred to address the issues of self-blame and low self-esteem. (A Modality Profile was constructed from her Multimodal Life History Questionnaire for my own enlightenment.) Lisa's penchant for self-abnegation seemed to stimulate acutely defensive and overcompensatory (aggressive, hypercritical) responses. The origin of her self-blame remained a mystery (she did not have the usual condemnatory, overcritical parents so often found in cases of this kind). Attempts through imagery, to determine whether there were more subtle cues that had rendered her so vulnerable, met with no success. Unlike Al, Lisa was unresponsive to mental imagery excursions. Consequently, the mainstay of therapy was focused on "cognitive restructuring," which endeavored to modify her dysfunctional beliefs (Beck, 1976; Ellis & Bernard, 1985).

Lisa was seen six times over a 9-week interval. In addition to cognitive therapy, her interpersonal style was a major focus for discussion in each of the meetings. It was impressed upon her that Al would always remain hypersensitive to actual or implied criticism, which he would tend to construe as an assault. I said, "I am trying to attenuate this sensitive zone, but I know of no method that will eliminate it." Role playing was employed to teach Lisa an essentially supportive, nonpejorative, noncritical way of talking, disagreeing, questioning, and making requests. The virtues of positive reinforcement were underscored; when in doubt, she was counseled to fall back on a principle of positive connotation (i.e., to search for the potentially caring, unselfish, and prosocial motives behind others' actions). "If you ever want to sabotage your marriage, just go ahead and criticize Al strongly, put him down as a man, and cast aspersions on his sexuality."

The sexual area per se required very little attention. Lisa stated that she was easily brought to orgasm, described herself as "sensual and uninhibited," and reported "no hang-ups in this area." She was cautioned again to beware of "coming on strong," of being critical, and of making demands instead of stating her preferences. I inquired, "Is this unfair? Are you being asked to do things or avoid things that are simply impossible in the long run?" "Not if I want this marriage to succeed," she answered.

Conjoint Sessions

Three additional meetings with the couple consolidated their gains and also addressed the question of whether they sould consider having a child. Al summarized it as follows: "I am still uncertain, but I think that's because I want guarantees. But I'm willing for us to stop using contraceptives for the next few months and see what happens."

Follow-Up

At the time of writing (11 months after terminating therapy), Al and Lisa have maintained their gains, and Lisa is in her final weeks of pregnancy.

Amniocentesis showed that they can look forward to having a girl. Al described his feelings as "terrified and thrilled."

Commentary

It is always a pleasure to work with intelligent, motivated individuals who are not extremely disturbed. While the treatment of Al and Lisa called for no heroic, extremely innovative, or intriguing tactics, it nevertheless illustrates the *technically eclectic* multimodal approach quite well. Let us now turn to a case in which my most ardent efforts and ministrations proved utterly futile.

An Unsuccessful Case

Description and Background

Ed, aged 39, the president of a very successful manufacturing company, and Pam, aged 32, a former teacher but full-time homemaker, had been married 4 years and had a 1-year-old son. This was Ed's second marriage. His first marriage, which had lasted almost 5 years, had ended when he discovered that his wife had been having extramarital relations with one of his associates. Ed contended that premarital sex with his first wife had been "fiery and passionate," but that soon after the wedding, his sexual interests had waned: "I shut down sexually, not only to my wife, but to everyone." Ed added, "It's as if when I married, I took on the cloak of righteousness and ultrarespectability." He described his sexual activity as confined to nocturnal emissions and very occasional masturbation (to images of lascivious women). "The day my divorce was finally granted, I came to life sexually again and almost made up for lost time." Ed claimed that during the course of the next 3 years, he dated many different women and was very active sexually. After he met Pam, they dated for 2 years and enjoyed "passionate sex." (According to Pam, while sex with Ed was "just fine," it was never what she would term "really passionate." She explained, "I always felt that Ed was holding back to some degree.") Immediately after Ed and Pam married, the same pattern that had occurred with his first wife re-emerged— Ed's sexual desire rapidly disappeared.

Ed had been raised as a Roman Catholic and had thought of becoming a priest. Instead, he joined the Air Force, obtained a college degree, and opened his own company. He was an energetic, tall, commanding individual; it was not surprising that within 5 years his company had grown into a successful enterprise. An only child, he described himself as having been "close" to his mother and "distant" from his father. When leaving home for the first time at age 18 to join the Air Force, he realized that he had experienced his mother as "cloying and suffocating." He added, "Actually, time and distance led me to realize how much I hated her, what a totally self-centered, neurotic woman she always was, and how she had used me for her own ends and played me against my father." Discussions concerning his hostility to his mother were unproductive. My attempts to mitigate his antipathy (cf. Bloomfield & Felder, 1983) also proved futile. Ed insisted that while he was antagonistic toward his mother, he did not feel this way toward Pam or about women in general.

Pam, highly active in various fund-raising groups and extramural activities for women, was extremely successful in her own right. Most people regarded her as beautiful, elegant, refined, cultivated, sensitive, and sexy. She claimed to be deeply in love with Ed, but stated that her patience was beginning to wear thin. She said that there had been no sexual contact whatsoever since she had become pregnant (a period of approximately 21 months). "I don't know if I am doing something wrong, or if there is a deep-seated problem in Ed, or both." Certainly, during two individual sessions with Pam followed by two conjoint meetings, I was unable to discern any untoward attitudes or behaviors emanating from Pam—except perhaps for (what I viewed as) her unusual tolerance and forbearance.

Treatment

I embarked on a course of systematic desensitization with Ed and soon reached the point in the hierarchy where he could envision having intercourse with Pam while feeling comfortable. I then recommended a series of sensate focus exercises. "The drive's just not there, Doc!" I suggested that the couple rent an X-rated videotape and watch it together. Ed refused. "I just wouldn't feel right watching something like that with Pam." Perhaps he would view it alone and then, if sexually stimulated, have sex with Pam. He agreed, but instead of having sex with Pam, he masturbated. At this juncture, Ed was scheduled to attend a convention at a well-known holiday resort. Pam accompanied him in the hope that the ambience would "turn him on." They did in fact have sex on one occasion, but there was no carry-through.

I again examined to what extent Ed had performance anxiety, and I recommended Janson's (1981) book *Sexual Pleasure Sharing*. In exquisite detail, I discussed with Ed and Pam a variety of tactile practices in which they might engage and how they could do so in a completely relaxed and nondemanding manner. Initially, I thought we were on the verge of a breakthrough. For 3 weeks, they enjoyed several "pleasure-sharing sessions," with Pam achieving orgasm each time orally or manually, and on three occasions they had intercourse. Nevertheless, Ed reverted to his former level—zero contact. "I was pushing myself, Doc. I thought that perhaps if

I bit the bullet I would get back the urge. To tell you the truth, I love Pam but she just doesn't make me the least bit horny."

Ed's Modality Profile contained considerable problematic material in the cognitive and interpersonal areas. Consequently, I decided to switch from behavioral prescriptions and to dwell more heavily on his entire developmental history, to examine the formation of his values and attitudes, and to explore his obvious Madonna–whore complex. I even enlisted the aid of an extremely well-informed and enlightened Catholic priest who met first with Ed, and then with the couple, and endeavored to impart a nonmoralistic outlook on sex. Shortly after the priest's interventions, Pam called to tell me that Ed had approached her two nights in a row and they had had "excellent lovemaking." Thereafter, it was back to base zero! Ed's reasoning? "I really don't know, Doc. There's just something holding me back. I have no turn-off, I just don't have the desire for Pam."

Pam scheduled an appointment with me. "I want you to see Ed more often," she said, whereupon she focused on some of her own problems—the fact that "there's an obedient little girl aspect to me," "I want always to please people," and the realization that "Ed is simply not turned on to me." She mentioned that Ed was talking about having more children, an idea that was for her "out of the question unless we function like a normal couple." Pam underscored that the therapy had rendered Ed "softer, kindlier, and able to apologize and admit when he is wrong." However, there was virtually no improvement on the sexual front after 2 years of therapy. I then referred Ed to a colleague whose orientation is entirely different from my own. He is still in therapy at the time of writing. I referred Pam to a female therapist, who I believe is assisting her in "raising her consciousness." A few days ago I saw Pam in a supermarket. She mentioned, *en passant,* that she is of the opinion that "Ed is delighted that he was able to defeat you so completely."

Commentary

Usually, when one is analyzing unsuccessful cases, the benefits of retrospective wisdom enable one to distill clues pertaining to clinical omissions and commissions that might have made a difference. Second thoughts about the treatment format often lead to speculations about the reasons for failure and point to modifications or interventions that could have changed the outcome. At the very least, one emerges with some sense of specific interactive factors in the therapist–patient relationship or couple relationship that could account for the lack of significant change. With regard to Ed and Pam, considerable analysis and introspection have provided no leads, no clues, no post hoc indications that shed any light on this most frustrating case.

In general, unsuccessfully treated cases of sexual desire disorders display subtle (or blatant) internecine power struggles, encrusted hostility, gross incompatibility, malignant distrust, or extreme demandingness (e.g., individuals who insist on penile–vaginal intercourse and refuse to consider what I have termed "CNS lovemaking"). Successful cases are those in which the partners are willing to negotiate and compromise, and to expend mutual effort in developing an acceptable *modus vivendi*.

Conclusion

The major strength of the BASIC I.D. approach for treating desire disorders is its thorough and systematic format. The multimodal emphasis on problem specification is in keeping with current psychiatric practice, in that it augments cognitive mastery, behavioral regulation, and affective experiencing (Karasu, 1986). This orientation encompasses (1) specification of goals and problems; (2) specification of treatment techniques to achieve these goals and remedy these problems; and (3) systematic measurement of the relative success of these techniques. It is noteworthy that therapists with differing backgrounds and training have reported that multimodal assessment yields significant gains in diagnostic accuracy and enhances clinical creativity (Lazarus, 1985a).

Acknowledgment

In addition to the editors, I thank Allen Fay, M.D., for providing critical comments and constructive suggestions.

References

Barlow, D. H., & Wincze, J. P. (1980). Treatment of sexual deviations. In S. R. Leiblum & L. A. Pervin (Eds.), *Principles and practice of sex therapy*. New York: Guilford Press.

Beck, A. T. (1976). *Cognitive therapy and the emotional disorders*. New York: International Universities Press.

Bloomfield, H. H., & Felder, L. (1983). *Making peace with your parents*. New York: Random House.

Ellis, A., & Bernard, M. E. (Eds.). (1985). *Clinical applications of rational–emotive therapy*. New York: Plenum.

Friedman, J. M., & Hogan, D. R. (1985). Sexual dysfunction: Low sexual desire. In D. H. Barlow (Ed.), *Clinical handbook of psychological disorders*. New York: Guilford Press.

Goldenson, R. M. (Ed.). (1984). *Longman dictionary of psychology and psychiatry*. New York: Longman.

Janson, W. J. (1981). *Sexual pleasure sharing*. Jaffrey, NH: Human Development.

Kaplan, H. S. (1979). *Disorders of sexual desire*. New York: Simon & Schuster.

Karasu, T. B. (1986). The specificity versus nonspecificity dilemma: Toward identifying therapeutic change agents. *American Journal of Psychiatry, 143*, 687–695.

Kinsey, A. C., Pomeroy, W. B., & Martin, C. E. (1948). *Sexual behavior in the human male.* Philadelphia: W. B. Saunders.

Lazarus, A. A. (1976). *Multimodal behavior therapy.* New York: Springer.

Lazarus, A. A. (1981). *The practice of multimodal therapy.* New York: McGraw-Hill.

Lazarus, A. A. (1984). *In the mind's eye.* New York: Guilford Press.

Lazarus, A. A. (Ed.). (1985a). *Casebook of multimodal therapy.* New York: Guilford Press.

Lazarus, A. A. (1985b). *Marital myths.* San Luis Obispo, CA: Impact.

Lazarus, A. A. (1986). Multimodal therapy. In J. C. Norcross (Ed.), *Handbook of eclectic psychotherapy.* New York: Brunner/Mazel.

Lazarus, A. A. (1987). The multimodal approach with adult outpatients. In N. S. Jacobson (Ed.), *Psychotherapists in clinical practice.* New York: Guilford Press.

Lief, H. I. (1977). What's new in sex research? Inhibited sexual desire. *Medical Aspects of Human Sexuality, 2*(7), 94–95.

Masters, W. H., & Johnson, V. E. (1966). *Human sexual response.* Boston: Little, Brown.

Miller, W. W. (1968). Afrodex in the treatment of impotence: A double-blind cross over study. *Current Therapeutic Research, 10,* 354–359.

Reckless, J., & Geiger, N. (1975). Impotence as a practical problem. In H. F. Dowling (Ed.), *Disease-a-month.* Chicago: Year Book Medical.

Sobotka, J. J. (1969). An evaluation of Afrodex in the management of male potency: A double blind cross over study. *Current Therapeutic Research, 11,* 87–94.

Zilbergeld, B. (1978). *Male Sexuality.* New York: Bantam.

Zilbergeld, B., & Ellison, C. R. (1980). Desire discrepancies and arousal problems in sex therapy. In S. R. Leiblum & L. A. Pervin (Eds.), *Principles and practice of sex therapy.* New York: Guilford Press.

7

A Sexual Scripting Approach to Problems of Desire

RAYMOND C. ROSEN AND SANDRA R. LEIBLUM

The concept of sexual scripts as a heuristic device for understanding sexual behavior has received considerably more attention from sociological than from psychological theories. Nevertheless, we have found assessment and treatment of sexual dysfunctions from a scripting perspective to be extremely useful in a variety of instances. This chapter is an attempt to illustrate the application of script theory and assessment to the etiology and treatment of desire disorders.

Scripts both organize behavior and determine the circumstances under which sexual activity occurs. They define the range of sexual behaviors that are acceptable, with whom, under what circumstances, and with what motives. As such, they have considerable implications for the experience of sexual desire and initiative, since most individuals express a limited repertoire of motives and circumstances for endorsing sexual activity. As the chapter suggests, the sexual scripts of partners in a relationship often differ considerably. In some instances, these differences may whet sexual appetite, and a zesty and varied sexual life ensues. In other instances, when sexual script differences between partners are too great or the various dimensions of the script are too narrow, difficulties may arise. Lack of congruence of script parameters between partners frequently paves the way for either the development of a sexual dysfunction or the complaint of lack of desire.

Treatment from a sexual scripting approach requires assessment of each partner's performative (current) and ideal (private) script, with sufficient detail obtained so that script negotiation can occur. Such an approach invites clear communication between partners regarding sexual preferences; it also minimizes the likelihood of blaming or targeting one partner or the other as having "the problem." While not necessarily applicable in all instances of desire difficulties, a scripting perspective is often useful either as an adjunct to treatment, or, at times, the major focus of intervention. It encourages an exploration of factors other than sexual frequency as a salient treatment issue, and it involves an explicit interactional approach to treatment. By bringing to light the complexity of motives underlying sexual behavior in general, and desire in particular, we are able to focus attention on the contextual rather than the biological nature of sexual interest. As such, we have found the scripting perspective to be a particularly helpful one from which to approach the treatment of desire disorders.

Raymond C. Rosen, Ph.D., is Professor of Psychiatry and Codirector of the Sexual Counseling Service, University of Medicine and Dentistry of New Jersey–Robert Wood Johnson Medical School, Piscataway, New Jersey.

Sandra R. Leiblum, Ph.D., is Associate Professor of Clinical Psychiatry and Codirector of the Sexual Counseling Service, University of Medicine and Dentistry of New Jersey–Robert Wood Johnson Medical School, Piscataway, New Jersey.

Sexuality must not be described as a stubborn drive. . . . It is not the most intractible element in power relations, but rather one of those endowed with the greatest instrumentality: useful for the greatest number of maneuvers and capable of serving as a point of support, as a linchpin, for the most varied strategies. (Foucault, 1978, p. 103)

It is just as plausible to examine sexual behavior for its capacity to express and serve nonsexual motives as the reverse. (Gagnon & Simon, 1973, p. 17)

When viewed from an interpersonal perspective, sexual behavior is often seen to be "scripted" to fit the roles, expectations, and themes of everyday social life. In fact, since its introduction into the field by Gagnon and Simon (1973), the term "script" has been increasingly used to refer to the cognitive framework that guides the planning, coordination, and expression of social conduct generally, including sexual behavior. As described by these authors, scripts provide the *cognitive organization* of sexual interactions—defining the situation as sexual, naming the actors, and directing the behavior. In addition to their role in organizing sexual behavior, scripts also determine the circumstances under which sexual activity is to occur (the "when and where"), the range of sexual behaviors to be enacted (the "what"), and the motives expressed in sexual interactions (the "whys"). They function like a "blueprint, or roadmap, or recipe; giving directions, but not specifying everything that must be done" (Gagnon, 1977, p. 6).

Above all, the concept of scripting focuses our attention on the *contextual character* of sexual conduct. In emphasizing this aspect, Simon and Gagnon (1986) have recently theorized that sexual scripts provide a context for at least two essential dimensions of sexual interaction. First, the script invites participation or sets the stage for engaging in various forms of sexual behavior; second, it provides the framework for the emotional experiences that individuals attach to these behaviors. For example, the "falling in love" script is a powerful justification for first intercourse among adolescent girls. The sense of being desired and desirable clearly serves as a strong sexual inducement for many young women, despite the frequent lack of sensual or sexual gratification. In this sense, sexual scripts can be seen to guide and direct sexual motivation or the absence thereof, and to have important implications for the formulation and treatment of desire disorders.

Scripts and the Development of Desire

Script learning can be viewed as a natural corollary or by-product of early social and emotional development. For example, the initial or "primary" scripts include expectations about appropriate gender-role conduct, familiarity and comfort with bodily functions and nudity, tolerance for intimacy and dependency, and attitudes toward sexual morality. During adolescence, these early (childhood) scripts interact with an emerging awareness of erotic and reproductive options to form adult scripts for sexual conduct (Gagnon, 1979). Further script acquisition in adulthood involves identifying appropriate partners and situations for sexual interaction, as well as defining the purposes and motives for engaging in sexual intimacy. Consider, for example, the social scripting of an adolescent girl's sexual behavior, as vividly portrayed in the following passage from Sue Miller's (1986) novel, *The Good Mother*:

> The parties were all the same . . . After the first awkward and tentative approaches by the boys, we paired off and stood in grappling couples. The trick in dancing, I discovered, was to let the boy grind into you without responding, to seem utterly innocent of what was going on. In corners, in the bathrooms at school, the girls would giggle about how hot you could get the boys, about *hard-ons, blue balls, wet dreams*. But with the boys, they maintained an air of stupefying naivete. (p. 50)

When viewed from this perspective, sexual development is consistent with and connected to other forms of social and interpersonal development. In particular, script theory places a strong emphasis on the essential *continuity* between adult and childhood sexual learning. This is in contrast to other developmental models, such as the psychoanalytic and psychobiological, which stress discontinuities and the importance of critical periods and separate stages in sexual development (e.g., Gadpaille, 1975). Moreover, as we have discussed elsewhere (Rosen & Leiblum, 1987), the analytic perspective views libido (desire) and its channeling as the driving force behind personality development, rather than vice versa. In fact, this was the major point of departure for Gagnon and Simon's (1973) original critique of Freudian psychosexual theory.

Male–female differences in sex roles and behavior have also been approached from a script perspective. For example, Laws and Schwartz (1977) consider the powerful sexual scripting for women in traditional heterosexual monogamous relationships, as opposed to the relative absence of agreed-upon scripts for engaging in unconventional scripts, such as lesbian or extramarital encounters. Building upon this assumption, Nichols speculates in Chapter 14 of the present volume that the lack of a recognized script for initiation of sexual exchange between women contributes to the high prevalence of desire problems in lesbian couples, even when both partners are committed to a homosexual lifestyle. Within conventional heterosexual relationships, women's sexual scripts tend to emphasize female passivity and acquiescence to male sexual initiation and direction (Leiblum & Tevlin, 1982). Instead of direct genital gratification, female sexual fulfillment is most often identified with the exchange of gentle affection and verbal intimacy, as would be expected for someone whose eventual roles are those of wife and mother.

Male scripts, on the other hand, have traditionally highlighted the supposed voraciousness and urgency of male sexual appetite, in both heterosexual and homosexual lifestyles. Males are expected to be perennially available for and desirous of sexual encounters of every description. For men, desire is both expected and required. Key elements of the conventional male script have included such beliefs as "The man must take charge of and orchestrate sex," "A man always wants and is always ready to have sex," and "In sex, as elsewhere, it's performance that counts" (Nowinski, 1980; Zilbergeld, 1978). Men also are all too frequently burdened with the responsibility for arousing both themselves and their partners during a sexual encounter. In noting the impact of the male script on sexual dysfunctions, therapists frequently emphasize the etiological role of these gender and script expectations for male sexual performance and desire disorders (Gagnon, Rosen, & Leiblum, 1982).

Clinical Implications

Script modifications are usually required over time as individuals and relationships undergo change. For example, courtship and early marriage are typically the periods of maximal script variation and experimentation, when sexual encounters may occur on almost any day, place, or time. The arrival of children typically diminishes the spontaneity and freedom of sexual encounters. As concerns about privacy, time, and location become paramount, the sexual script must change accordingly. In couples whose sexual communication and flexibility are adequate, these adjustments may be made without noticeable difficulty, and sexual desire remains intact. However, some couples falter in the process of negotiating these script changes in the face of changing life cycle demands, and hence sexual interest suffers. In particular, Blumstein and Schwartz (1983) have reported that sexual script difficulties arise most frequently when there are dependent children in the home, and that husbands are especially sensitive to the lack of undivided attention and affection from their wives at this time. As one husband complained,

> "We don't make love until the kids go to sleep. Then it's 'Be quiet' or 'Don't make so much noise.' She actually put her hand over my mouth once. I was so pissed off. I just lost it." (Blumstein & Schwartz, 1983, p. 204)

With the loss of privacy that accompanies the presence of children in the home, some spouses react with a renewed interest in solitary sexual behavior (fantasy or masturbation), or simply postpone sexual initiation with a mate until the "all's clear [or quiet!]" signal. The loss of a spouse through either death or divorce may similarly create the need for major script modification. Long-married individuals who suddenly find themselves thrust into the "singles scene" may feel at a loss in coping with the new script elements required. The parameters governing sexuality are no longer explicit and mutually agreed upon. When is the right time for making a sexual overture with a new partner? Where? Which sexual acts are acceptable and which are not? Sexual frequency may become more a matter of the accessibility of partners than one of internal desire. Some relationships fail because new partners lack the comfort, awareness, and/or forthrightness that script negotiation entails, and hence feel sexually dissatisfied and discouraged. Regrettably, this entire sequence of events may occur without conscious awareness of the source of the difficulty, and often the partner is identified as the problem, rather than the underlying script deficiencies.

One of the clearest examples in the literature of the clinical application of script assessment is that of the sexual adjustment difficulties commonly associated with physical disability or chronic illness. Thus, Neumann (1978) poignantly describes the particular difficulties faced by spinal-cord-injured persons in dealing with the limitations of the conventional sexual script: "With the scripts and cues for interaction missing, the drama of sexuality and the disabled is reduced to improvisational theater, little more than a set of actors in search of a play" (p. 98). Unfortunately, clinicians frequently mistake such script failures for a lack of sexual desire or interest on the part of the disabled. Research on the sexual adjustment of men with end-stage renal disease (Berkman, Katz, & Weissman, 1982) has similarly emphasized that continued interest in sex, coupled with a lack of script specification, presents especially troublesome conflicts for those patients with higher levels of premorbid sexual drive and satisfaction.

Along similar lines, a common contemporary problem involves redefining and negotiating the script when one partner is found to have a sexually transmitted disease, such as herpes. While previous sexual interactions for such a couple may have emphasized long sessions of nonverbal, spontaneous, and "anything goes" lovemaking, the presence of a venereal disease necessitates explicit discussion of when sex is "safe," what sexual behaviors are acceptable, and which body parts may be "off limits." For single individuals, the critical issue may be when and how to inform prospective partners of their condition. Indeed, many herpes sufferers report greater discomfort with the psychological than with the physical sequelae of the disease—in particular, the uncertainties inherent in conducting sexual relations (Shaw & Rosenfield, 1987). Sexual desire is likely to be negatively affected by these script ambiguities, and the frequency of sexual initiation may diminish significantly (at least initially, in new relationships).

Even more devastating to sexual expressiveness is the fear of acquired immune deficiency syndrome (AIDS) among homosexual and bisexual couples. Cautious rather than casual sex is currently the rule among single adults, with discussion and inquisitiveness about previous relationships preceding passion. Major script changes are becoming evident in the conduct of sexual encounters. The "swept away" script is yielding rapidly to delicate inquiry and sensitive history taking as a sexual prelude. Sexual postponement rather than impetuosity characterizes new relationships. "Safe" sex typically requires a series of explicit negotiations concerning which sexual activities are acceptable, and under what circumstances. The etiquette of proper condom usage remains to be further developed! Determining the rules of conduct in the face of uncertainty and lack of trust in a new partner is especially problematic, because desire must be modulated by reason. Certainly, the cognitive awareness that unsafe sex can have fatal consequences is an effective deterrent to unrestrained sexual ardor. These issues are addressed in greater detail by Coleman and Reece (Chapter 15, this volume).

The process of aging also brings certain inevitable challenges to the sexual script. In particular, the paucity of available repertoires for older couples, as well as the restrictions placed on partner choices, may be particularly problematic. Thus, while the "December–May" relationship may be accepted with some reservations for the older male, it is usually strongly frowned upon for the older woman. Moreover, the process of aging demands script changes along several dimensions, including the purely physical or technical aspects of the script. For instance, research on sexual adjustment in menopausal women (Leiblum & Bachmann, in press) underscores the negative effects on sexual desire and frequency if script modification is not made explicit. Specifically, when reduced vaginal lubrication results in dyspareunia or the necessity for external lubrication, husbands may erroneously interpret such changes as due to a lack of sexual arousal. This may, in turn, result in a reduced frequency of sexual initiation, which further diminishes desire in both partners. In contrast, couples who readily acknowledge and accept the script modifications associated with aging appear to maintain sexual interest.

Sexual Scripts in the Assessment of Desire Disorders

Despite the heuristic appeal of script theory in understanding normal sexual development, this approach has been infrequently applied in the formulation or treatment of desire disorders. Rather, current conceptualizations tend to focus on the biological, intrapsychic, or interpersonal origins of desire, and their etiological roles in desire disorders (e.g., Bancroft, 1984; Levine, 1984). Furthermore, while we have previously discussed the value of sexual script theory in assessing and treating other sexual dysfunctions, such as premature ejaculation and orgasmic difficulties (Gagnon et al., 1982), the purpose of the present chapter is to extend this approach to the evaluation and treatment of desire disoders. In assessing the social and interactional determinants of these problems, we have found that few conceptualizations offer the intuitive and clinical appeal of the sexual scripting approach.

Before preceeding, however, we should emphasize the important link among sexual scripts, sexual performance difficulties, and associated desire problems. In particular, we have observed that the sexual scripts of individuals with desire disorders tend to be either over- or underinclusive, providing too many or too few eliciting cues for engaging in sexual behavior. Thus, the person with low desire may be likened to a stage actor who constantly misses cues, whereas the individual with hyperactive desire can be compared to an overeager performer, inclined to leap onto center stage at every opportunity. In fact, in couples presenting with desire complaints, all too often the problem does not reside with either individual, but rather with a mismatch in sexual appetites or scripts. The problem may be said to lie in the *discrepancy* between the partners' sexual interest levels, rather than in the inherent sexual drive of either person (Zilbergeld & Ellison, 1980). As we discuss here, these discrepancies may occur at either the overt or the covert level, and may involve disagreement concerning one or more of the important elements of the script.

Clinically, our approach to script analysis begins with an assessment and comparison of the "performative" and "cognitive" dimensions of the script. The "performative" script refers to the overt or actual sequence of behaviors typically characterizing a sexual encounter, whereas the "cognitive" script comprises the covert or imaginal aspects, including sexual thoughts, fantasies, beliefs, and attitudes. Particularly important to assess in this regard is the manner in which individuals would script their ideal sexual encounter: That is, if sex could occur in any time, place, and circumstance desired, what would the resulting scenario be like? This question appears on our initial intake questionnaire, and is usually explored further in the initial interview.

Performative and cognitive scripts may be more or less "congruent." An example of incongruity between performative and cognitive scripts is seen in the husband who, while attempting to engage in heterosexual intercourse with his wife, simultaneously fantasizes orgasmic release with an anonymous homosexual partner. Such a discrepancy between the overt and covert aspects of the script can play a major role in either desire or performance difficulties. The following additional script dimensions are also normally assessed:

1. "Script complexity" refers to the extent and variety of script elements, including foreplay options, the repertoire of stimulation techniques employed, and the range of sexual activities, motives, or partners for a given sexual encounter. We have previously noted that sexually dysfunctional relationships tend to be associated with a marked narrowing and restriction of the sexual script (Gagnon et al., 1982).

2. "Script rigidity" refers to the degree of routinization or predictability in the usual sexual encounter. Does the script involve a repetitive sequence of actions, locations, and behaviors? The performative script may be invariant in certain ways (e.g., always involving the same couple), but relatively flexible in regard to the staging or sequence of sexual interactions. Cognitive scripts, on the other hand, may be highly variable, incorporating script elements that are rarely if ever found in the performative script.

3. "Satisfaction" includes comfort with and acceptance of both the overt and the covert scripts. For instance, long-married partners who have established what appears to be a mutually satisfying script may each experience private feelings of boredom and lack of interest, due to the absence of sexual novelty and passion. In such cases, low desire may be a direct consequence of the insufficiency or inadequacy of the script.

4. "Script conventionality" refers to the social acceptability or appropriateness of both the cognitive and the performative dimensions. For instance, for a woman who experiences her most intense levels of sexual arousal only in the presence of rape fantasies or images of sexual submission, the cognitive script may become a significant source of shame and guilt. In turn, this would be likely to lead to a diminution of desire.

Special care needs to be taken in assessing desire discrepancy problems. In particular, when a couple is mismatched in their levels of desire without being individually high or low, each of these script dimensions is evaluated independently for both partners. For example, one partner may experience the overt script as overly limiting and restrictive, and may privately wish for more unconventional and lusty lovemaking. The partner, on the other hand, may be content with the extent and variety of the overt script, but may long for more romance and emotional intimacy. At times, major conflicts may arise from the performative script (i.e., the couple disagree about "who does what to whom"), whereas in other instances the problem is found in the cognitive script (i.e., the partners disagree about the acceptable reasons or motives for sexual intimacy). For example, the man may wish to have sex "just to relax and unwind," while the woman is seeking "closeness, intimacy, and romance" in sexual encounters. Partners may be aware of conflicts at each of these levels, or they may simply report an overall loss of interest.

An example of the *modus operandi* of our approach to script assessment is shown in Table 1. The case history illustrated is that of Mr. and Mrs. B, a professional couple in their mid-30s who had been married for 8 years. Both partners regarded the marital relationship as generally satisfactory, despite their increasing dissatisfaction with the frequency and quality of sexual interactions. While sexual encounters served the limited goal of providing arousal and orgasm for both partners, their enthusiasm and interest in sex had declined markedly over the last year. The frequency of intercourse had decreased to once or less monthly, as compared to about three or four times per week in the earlier years of the marriage. Mrs. B expressed greater dissatisfaction with the current state of affairs than her husband, resulting, after repeated urging, in Mr. B's finally agreeing to undertake counseling.

Over the course of a three-session evaluation with both conjoint and individual sessions, a number of areas of script discrepancy became apparent. Specifically, marked disparities were noted between the performative (actual) script and each of the partners' covert (ideal) scripts, as well as between their respective ideal scripts, Mr. B, unbeknownst to his wife, was an avid collector of pornography, which he used often to fuel and guide his masturbatory fantasies. He was particularly aroused by images of provocatively dressed women acting in a sexually dominating manner—a style of behavior that was completely alien to his wife. In contrast, Mrs. B longed for more extended and sensual caressing, accompanied by greater emotional intimacy and words of endearment during lovemaking. As shown in Table 1, the script discrepancies identified in this case can be categorized according to the four dimensions described above.

Over time, it is likely that major script incompatibilities will lead to sexual performance difficulty, in addition to a loss of desire. Our clinical experience with cases such as this suggests that the first indication of script incompatibility is diminished desire, often followed eventually by erectile

Table 1. Sexual Script Assessment for Desire Discrepancy

Script dimensions	Performative (overt) script	Ideal script (husband)	Ideal script (wife)
Complexity	Highly constricted script with abbreviated foreplay and afterplay; intercourse as sole sexual outlet. No sexual interactions outside intercourse.	Fantasized about a more sexually provocative script, including unconventional elements. *Key themes:* Pornography, dominant women.	Desired more extensive and emotionally intimate script. *Key themes:* Emotional sensitivity, intimate interaction.
Rigidity	Little variety, with relatively invariant sequence of sexual interaction with each encounter.	Rigid ideal script. Invariant script elements.	Strong wish for greater variety and spontaneity in all aspects of script.
Satisfaction	Moderate performance satisfaction experienced by husband. Wife dissatisfied, occasionally anorgasmic.	Mutual satisfaction. Orgasm for both partners.	Mutual satisfaction, but not dependent on orgasm.
Conventionality	Highly conventional overt script. Wife would not view pornography or dress provocatively.	Ideal script involved elements of dominance and submission. Had not disclosed this fully to wife.	Conventional ideal script, with strong emphasis on emotional commitment.

Presenting problem: Couple in mid-30s presenting with complaint of reduced sexual frequency and low desire over the past year. Treatment initiated by Mrs. B. Script evaluation in three sessions with both individual and conjoint interviews. *Sexual script:* Both partners described their sexual interactions as infrequent, dull, and repetitive. Overt script was clearly discrepant from ideal scripts.

177

problems in the male or by arousal problems in one or both partners. Such performance difficulties usually lead, in turn, to still greater constriction and rigidifying of the script, with a corresponding reduction in the extent and variety of sexual activity. The net result is a vicious cycle of script discrepancy, followed by diminished desire, followed by performance difficulties, leading to still further attenuation of the script. In effect, the couple is moving further and further away from their respective images of an ideal sexual encounter. A further prediction from the model is that the partner experiencing the greater discrepancy between his or her covert (ideal) script and the actual (overt) script is at greater risk for the development of lack of sexual interest and/or later performance difficulties.

On the other hand, sexual desire may remain unchanged, despite the existence of clear-cut problems with arousal or orgasm. For example, anorgasmic women often report continuing high levels of sexual interest, despite inadequate orgasmic response. Similarly, we have frequently encountered men with erectile difficulties who nevertheless maintain their enthusiasm for partner sex. In accounting for the persistence of desire in such cases, our approach would argue that the key script dimensions are satisfactorily maintained even though performative problems exist. As one elderly male patient with erectile dysfunction remarked, "I can happily spend all day in bed just caressing and stroking [my partner]. . . . The fact of the matter is that intercourse is simply not my favorite sexual activity." For this patient and other individuals like him, as long as the performative script continues to be experienced as sufficiently varied and satisfying, desire remains intact.

Advantages of the Scripting Approach

Assessment of sexual desire problems utilizing a sexual scripting approach has several clinical and therapeutic advantages, along with certain obvious limitations. The limitations are described later in the chapter; the advantages can be briefly summarized as follows:

1. There is a tendency to regard sexual desire problems as centering on either excessive or diminished *frequency* of sexual encounters. At times it is the frequency of initiation or the partner's response to sexual initiation that forms the basis of the complaint. From a scripting perspective, however, frequency is viewed as only one of several dimensions that contribute to script incompatibility and problems of desire. The degree of variety or spontaneity, in the script, for example, may be equally as important in a given instance.

2. By focusing on script discrepancies between the partners, there is less of a tendency to pathologize or "blame" the partner with low desire. As

Apfelbaum and Apfelbaum (1985) emphasize repeatedly, we should pay as much attention to the question of why the high-desire individual maintains such strong sexual interest in the face of continuing lack of interest expressed by the partner. Overall, we have found little difficulty in combining our scripting approach with a systems–interactional view of desire disorders, as discussed by Verhulst and Heiman in Chapter 10 of this volume.

3. In emphasizing independent assessment of performative and ideal script elements for both partners, we are also clearly highlighting the importance of understanding the *interpersonal context* of sexual choices and conduct generally. In this vein, script modification most often leads us to seek reconciliation or compromise between the ideal and actual scripts of both partners (Gagnon *et al.*, 1982), and reduces the tendency to impose value judgments regarding what is "normal" or expected sexual desire for either individual alone. Similarly, a script modification approach enables the clinician to remain more present-focused and directive in treatment, especially in those instances in which a more depth-oriented or psychotherapeutic approach does not appear to be warranted.

A Case Example of Specific Performance Difficulties

Description

Mr. and Mrs. G, a professional couple in their mid-40s, consulted the Sexual Counseling Service because Mr. G appeared to have "lost his sexual drive." This couple reported that during the first year of their 4 years of marriage (a second marriage for both of them), intercourse had occurred daily, with considerable variety, spontaneity, and mutual satisfaction. However, in the past several years, the frequency of sexual encounters had gradually declined to once weekly, and Mrs. G expressed the concern that her husband had come to prefer solitary masturbation to intercourse or any other form of sexual interaction with her.

According to Mr. G, the problem had originated in his first marriage of 17 years to a woman who displayed little sexual interest. This marriage had ended in divorce after his first wife had been converted to a charismatic religious sect, following which she had abruptly walked out on Mr. G. During the period following his divorce, Mr. G had been sexually active with several women, but had experienced frequent difficulties in obtaining erections or ejaculating during intercourse. He had met his current wife through a dating service, and responded positively to her patience and perseverance in dealing with his erectile difficulties.

Mr. G was an active nudist who enjoyed sunbathing in the nude at home. Although less enthusiastic about nudity than her mate, Mrs. G accompanied her husband to nudist camps. After their marriage, however, Mrs. G's 20-year-old quadriplegic son from her first marriage came to live with them. Because of his severe disability, a full-time nurse was required, restricting the couple's nudist activities in the home. Disagreements occurred frequently between husband and wife over the care of both Mrs. G's son and her 14-year-old daughter. Tension mounted between the partners as they began increasingly to squabble about all areas of their marital life. Mr. G became quite sensitive to what he perceived as his wife's critical comments, and he started to withdraw into solitary TV watching and occasional masturbation. Perhaps partly as a result of her increasing sense of emotional isolation and sexual frustration, Mrs. G had gained approximately 30 pounds during the preceding year.

Prior to initiating sexual therapy, Mr. and Mrs. G had made various attempts to enliven their sexual relationship. In particular, Mr. G had persuaded his wife to engage in "swinging" on two occasions. The first time this occurred, they had "swapped" partners and participated in group sex with another couple. On another occasion, they had participated in sexual play (without intercourse) with a group of nudists. These experiences were less than successful, in part because of Mr. G's erectile difficulties with partners other than his wife. In addition, both Mr. and Mrs. G agreed that they "preferred sex with each other to sex with strangers."

Script Assessment and Treatment

Sexual script assessment in this case revealed that the couple's performative script had evolved into a highly routinized and predictable sequence of initiation, foreplay, and intercourse. Both partners acknowledged the need for greater spontaneity and variety in their lovemaking. Mrs. G. expressed the wish that her husband be more vocal during sex, and even voiced the wish for him to "talk dirty." She complained about Mr. G's frequent use of R-rated movies as the prelude to sexual encounters. Rather, she wanted her spouse to be forceful and passionate in initiating sex. From his vantage point, Mr. G found his wife to be overly passive. He yearned for Mrs. G to be more sexually aggressive in foreplay and intercourse, and, in fact, to "take the lead in stimulating sexual excitement." Both partners acknowledged that greater variety in the type of foreplay and positions of intercourse was sorely needed.

Despite Mr. G's sexual anxiety and performance problems, and the couple's considerable marital conflict, the therapist decided to focus treatment on the immediate problem of declining sexual interest. By formulating the problem as one of script incompatibilities, both partners became actively engaged in treatment. Significant changes in the couple's sexual script were quickly introduced.

Instead of the customary initiation routine of viewing R-rated movies, the couple agreed to incorporate a transitional period prior to sex during which they would relax in each other's company, and attempt intimate and seductive conversation. Instead of using the bedroom exclusively for early-morning or late-evening encounters, the couple began to explore sexual exchange at other times and in other places. With the therapist's support, Mr. G became less defensive in responding to his wife's sexual requests, viewing them not so much as critical assaults on his competence, but as reflecting Mrs. G's private sexual desires.

Gradually Mr. G was encouraged to try more assertive approaches to initiating and directing sexual encounters. Occasionally, he was even able to comply with Mrs. G's request to "talk dirty." In turn, Mrs. G began to display increased arousal and was able to achieve orgasm with greater predictability. This served to heighten her husband's arousal and feelings of sexual competency, which added to his interest and enthusiasm. Finally, in order to reduce the demand for more frequent sexual interactions, the therapist deliberately advised the couple to limit their sexual encounters to no more than once weekly.

Discussion

It is clear that the lack of novelty and script constraints imposed by the presence of Mrs. G's quadriplegic son and his nurse contributed to the problems in sexual desire experienced by Mr. and Mrs. G. Furthermore, Mr. G resisted what he regarded as new performance demands from his wife, particularly in light of his prior history of erectile and ejaculatory problems. It is equally evident, however, that this is not the whole story; other dimensions could certainly have been explored. Nonetheless, as the partners were judged to be uninsightful and disinclined to address deeper issues, the script modification approach seemed appropriate. Certainly their sexual script had become increasingly routinized and attenuated in the past few years.

The successful outcome in this case may be attributed to a number of factors. First, the couple had enjoyed a prior history of mutually rewarding and uninhibited sex. Mr. G's sexual desire difficulty was clearly acute and situational. Second, the couple was highly motivated to comply with therapy. The therapist's formulation of the desire problem as due to script discrepancies was readily accepted by both partners, and helped to diminish Mr. G's sense of guilt and personal responsibility for the problem. Finally, by eliminating the sense of "blame" for either partner, the therapist was able to reduce resistance to the treatment plan and to keep therapeutic motivation high, particularly as the partners began to re-experience their former level of sexual gratification and enthusiasm.

A Case Example of Long-Standing Desire Discrepancy

Script intervention can be effective in resolving desire discrepancies, including situations in which neither of the partners has a specific dysfunction. This is illustrated in the following case example, in which script changes resulted in reversal of a long-standing desire discrepancy problem in a couple who otherwise shared a loving and satisfying marital relationship. In contrast to the previous case, neither partner experienced specific performance difficulties, as both were capable of prompt sexual arousal and reliable orgasm. Nevertheless, the discrepancy in sexual interest levels, especially the wife's relative lack of sexual enthusiasm, was viewed as extremely problematic and potentially threatening to the security of the marriage.

Description

Mr. and Mrs. P, a couple in their late 40s who had been married for 23 years, sought therapy due to mutual disappointment and dissatisfaction with their sexual relationship. Mr. P lamented the fact that his wife did "not show any interest in sex before the act itself." He went on to say that "she does not seem to have any desire to engage in sex. In my opinion, if I didn't initiate it, we would not have any." His wife concurred with this description, noting, "I am experiencing, and have experienced for as long as I can recall, a lack of the physical urge to have sexual intercourse. I chose the words 'physical urge' carefully and purposefully, as opposed to 'desire,' because I do very much desire the intimacy and communication of the act. I enjoy intercourse once I am involved. I believe I respond appropriately, and I usually reach orgasm. However, no matter how pleasant the experience, I do not seem to have the physical need or urge to repeat it, and I feel very inadequate because of this."

Despite the lack of real sexual desire on Mrs. P's part, the couple engaged in frequent sex, three to five times weekly. Mr. P indicated that though he "could have sex at any time if things are right," he would be content with having sex about four or five times a week (which was about the current frequency). Mrs. P indicated that she would be happier with once-weekly sexual relations.

Couple assessment revealed that Mr. and Mrs. P had been lovers since the age of 16 and had been nearly inseparable since they first began dating in high school. They had been married at age 21 and considered their marriage sound. Their home life was comfortable, with sufficient privacy and little marital conflict overall. The one issue that appeared to generate friction in this affectionate and loving couple was the discussion of Mrs. P's work. She had recently accepted responsibility for teaching a sex education course, in which she was greatly invested. Prior to each class, she creatively and enthusiastically organized her materials, and returned each week buoyed up and gratified by her efforts. Mr. P expressed resentment that his wife could display such spontaneous enjoyment in *teaching* about sexuality when she seemed so sadly lacking in enthusiasm for *engaging* in the behavior itself.

Regarding their personal backgrounds, Mrs. P had grown up in a household in which little love was expressed by her parents toward each other or toward her. Moreover, she had been sexually molested by her father, who would devise "games" between his daughter and/or her young playmates and himself, in which the little girls would pull down their underwear and sit on his face. This had occurred between the ages of 6 and 10, until Mrs. P refused to continue "playing." At a later point in her life, she had been sexually coerced by a retarded neighborhood teenager. It is certainly possible that these experiences contributed to Mrs. P's sexual tentativeness and reserve. In understanding Mr. P's strong and persistent desire for sexual encounters, it was noteworthy that he had developed at an early age a poor body image and feelings of masculine inadequacy. As a young child, he felt deprived of affection and attention from his mother. Throughout adolescence and early adulthood, he suffered from severe psoriasis and a form of arthritis that handicapped his movements. These difficulties may have exacerbated his growing feelings of inadequacy, which he sought to overcome through the medium of sexual exchange. That is, he appeared to be using sex as a vehicle for affirming his competence and desirability as a sexual partner.

Script Assessment and Treatment

Script assessment provided further clues as to the origin of the couple's problem. According to their mutual description, Mr. P initiated each and every one of their sexual encounters with the precision of a Swiss clock. After his evening shower and immediately before bedtime, Mr. P would undress and climb into bed, whereupon he would turn to his wife and commence stroking her breasts and genitals in an effective but perfectly predictable fashion. She would usually become lubricated and reach orgasm, and then, with a sigh of relief, fall asleep. The following evening, the script would begin anew. In 23 years of marriage, there had been little deviation from this pattern: Sex always occurred at night, in the bedroom, with little preliminary "sweet talk" and no afterplay. When asked whether he attempted any novel means of initiation, such as seductively undressing his wife, sharing a shower or bath with her, or initiating sex at other times or in places other than the bedroom, Mr. P replied, "No, certainly not in the last several years." Mrs. P indicated that she felt sex between them was "like brushing your teeth, beneficial but not very exciting."

Script modification comprised the major element of treatment with this couple. It was obvious that Mrs. P was being denied the opportunity to become sexually "hungry," because her spouse supplied such a regular and predictable diet of sexual offerings. Moreover, their sexual encounters were like a bountiful meal of meat and potatoes—filling but not terribly exciting. It was suggested to Mr. P that exchanging quantity for quality in sexual encounters might ameliorate their problem.

Mr. P was receptive to the idea of giving his wife more time to become "hungry" for sex, in addition to allowing her to take the sexual initiative by planning their next "feast." She, in turn, expressed enthusiasm about the novelty of being in control over when and how sex would occur. She reported becoming aroused in the car driving home from the session, just thinking about how she would plan the next sexual encounter. The following session, the couple returned in a teasing and playful mood. Apparently, after 5 full days of sexual abstinence, Mrs. P had approached her husband the following weekend in a seductive and provocative way. They shared a long sensual bath together in the afternoon, and then had sex (while the house painters were painting outside their window!). After going out early in the evening for a candlelight dinner, they returned to make love a second time that day. Both were delighted with this escapade, and Mr. P acknowledged that it was a relief to have his wife make the sexual overtures. He acknowledged that it had been something of a burden to be the constant orchestrator and initiator of sex, and that by sharing the responsibility, he enhanced his pleasure.

For the next 3 weeks, Mrs. P continued to accept the major responsibility for scripting sexual encounters, and Mr. P enthusiastically agreed to "act" in her "sexual productions." At this point, he wanted to resume a share of the "directing," and they both acknowledged a wish to assume joint responsibility for sexual initiatives. When seen for a follow-up visit 3 months later, they reported continued satisfaction with this arrangement. Although the frequency of intercourse had in fact diminished to about once or twice weekly, the spontaneity and emotional quality of their interactions were dramatically improved. Mrs. P said, "I have no difficulty being enthusiastic about sex now. I'm no longer satiated. Furthermore, I like the anticipatory planning of the next sexual encounter. I'm aroused before we even get together because I've had the chance to think about it for a couple of days."

Discussion

Although the couple described here appeared to present with a straightforward problem of desire discrepancy, there were clearly a number of issues in each of their backgrounds upon which the therapy might have focused. For example, Mrs. P's relative lack of interest could have been interpreted in light of her past experiences of sexual abuse. Similarly, her husband's relatively high and constant drive for sex might have been viewed in the context of his personal inadequacies and poor self-esteem. While exploring these issues with Mr. and Mrs. P may have proven helpful, it would not have been necessary for resolving the present difficulty. Script analysis and modification, on the other hand, were found to be effective, in addition to providing a parsimonious explanation of the problem. This approach was also intuitively appealing to the couple. It raised little personal or therapeutic resistance, since neither partner was identified as the "patient" and neither was identified as requiring intensive psychotherapy. Rather, the problem was viewed as residing in the "sexual script" they had relied on for too many years.

Like all therapeutic approaches, however, script modification has a number of shortcomings and specific limitations. These can be briefly summarized as follows:

1. A scripting approach appears to be of limited value in treating those individuals who present with chronic, lifelong lack of sexual interest. Such individuals often display markedly impoverished covert sexual scripts—that is, a dearth of sexual fantasy, imagery, or thoughts. Although some clinicians have attempted to increase sexual fantasy and interest by flooding the individual with multiple sources of sexual stimulation, such approaches have met with limited success.

2. At times, script negotiation is successfully transacted, but the lack of sexual interest on the part of the low-desire individual persists. Such cases suggest that the basic problem is not, in fact, script incompatibility, but rather some other factor(s) (e.g., endocrine deficiency, psychological conflict, marital discord, etc.). In some cases desire may not significantly change, but the greater satisfaction experienced (i.e., the improved quality of the sexual interaction and script) compensates for the differing interest levels of partners.

3. Despite the pragmatic advantages to the clinician of the script modification approach, and the intuitive appeal of this approach to many couples, some individuals strongly reject this interpretation of their desire problems. For example, some high-desire partners refuse to acknowledge that their constant and unwanted sexual solicitations may be contributing to the desire conflict. At times, even the low-desire partner, out of a sense of guilt or inadequacy, may defend the "right" of the high-desire partner to persist in sexual demands, despite the lack of reciprocal interest. Such instances of therapeutic impasse may oblige the clinician to explore other therapeutic options.

A Case Example of Unsuccessful Intervention

Description

In an attempt to address their sexual difficulties before "tying the knot," Jack and Alice sought counseling while they were still engaged. They concurred in identifying their problem as one of desire discrepancy: Jack desired sex to a much greater degree than Alice, and his attempt to cast Alice in the role of "sexual siren" often backfired and led to a pattern of sexual avoidance on her part. In fact, she remarked, "From taking the initiative about 50% of the time, I have somehow reached a point of rarely taking it at all. It has only gradually dawned on me that I think of sex in terms of how many days it has been and my subsequent guilt. This frightens me, for I see my disinclination as something that occurs much later in marriage, not where I am—and that forces me to question our relationship, which otherwise is very compatible."

During the assessment sessions, Alice reported several additional sexual concerns. She indicated that she often had difficulty in becoming lubricated, frequently failed to achieve climax, and sometimes experienced dyspareunia. Her pain during intercourse appeared to be related to her lack of sexual arousal and insufficient lubrication, rather than being attributable to any particular organic factor. The couple's emphasis on Alice's "problems in sex" resulted in the therapist's neglecting Jack's role in the couple's sexual incompatibilities. For instance, Jack tended to approach Alice in an insistent and sexually demanding manner. He would beseech her to pose seductively for him or dress provocatively, or would initiate sexual encounters on a near-daily basis. Alice resented his demands and viewed them as an intrusive interruption of her work and legal studies.

History taking revealed that Jack had experienced a series of physical and psychological handicaps as a young child and teenager. His biological father had died when he was 8, and his mother had remarried 2 years later. His stepfather never really accepted him, and, in fact, made Jack's life miserable by goading him to be an avid and accomplished athlete— something Jack had little interest in or inclination for. Having a congenital clubfoot handicapped Jack's few attempts at athletic pursuits and contributed to his poor body image. Further exacerbating his lack of physical self-acceptance was his overweight. Jack indicated that he ate as an escape from the demands he experienced from his overly intrusive mother and demanding stepfather, as well as to avoid dealing with his sense of social inadequacy. Jack had been married once previously, and he had a son by that marriage who was blind following a birth defect.

Alice had been raised in a religiously devout and loving family that tended to avoid any and all discussion of sexual matters. She experienced an overly protective relationship with her mother and grandmother, and tended to be a loner. Her favorite pastimes were solitary hiking through the woods and painting or drawing. She recalled one frightening episode that had occurred when she was 8 years old: A group of young adolescent boys attacked her and attempted to undress her. Fortunately, one of the boys became so frightened and distracted himself that she was able to run away without any further physical violation. Although she indicated that this episode had been quickly "forgotten," she also mentioned that she had not begun to date until age 19, and that she had remained circumspect in her relationships with men for several years thereafter. Alice also admitted that she experienced considerable remorse and spiritual regret about an abortion she had had approximately 4 years prior to meeting Jack.

Script Assessment and Treatment

Script assessment revealed significant script discrepancies between Alice and Jack. From his perspective, Jack indicated that his ideal sexual script would be one in which he would return from work and find Alice lying on the bed wearing sexy undergarments and posed in a seductive fashion. He would approach confidently and begin kissing and caressing, in response to which Alice would avidly return his affections. Following a brief period of foreplay, during which she would be very seductive, he would enter her and have active intercourse for 15 to 30 minutes, at the termination of which they would both experience simultaneous climax.

Alice's ideal script went very differently. Her sexual fantasies contained little explicit "organ grinding," but rather entailed a highly individualistic and unique scenario in which she was in the middle of a pristine, luxuriant forest and came upon a majestic stag in a clearing. He looked elegant and proud, and she became aware of sensual feelings as she gazed at him. The fantasy ended with this rather other-worldly and decidedly sublimated sexual image.

In recent months the couple's performative script had come to include initiation by Jack in most instances, with little emotional interaction and brief foreplay. Jack would penetrate Alice when he believed her to be receptive, although he commented that she never seemed emotionally aroused, nor did she experience significant lubrication. Intercourse, usually in the missionary position, would typically last for 20 minutes or more, culminating in orgasm for Jack but not for Alice. Following Jack's ejaculation, he would light a cigarette and seem self-satisfied. Alice, on the other hand, reported feeling increasingly frustrated and alienated. More recently, Alice complained of pain both during manual stimulation and with deep penetration, which generally persisted following coitus.

Therapeutic intervention included a program of sensate focus exercises in an attempt to make sex more tolerable, if not sensual, for Alice. Interestingly, when a videotape of a sensate focus session was shown to the couple during a therapy session, Jack responded with marked enthusiasm and expressed feelings of sexual arousal. Alice was "turned off" and reported feelings of sexual aversion upon viewing the nude bodies of the screen actors. She told the therapist she felt the need to "avert her eyes" several times during the brief video. Feeling that Alice's discomfort sug-

gested a need for greater desensitization, the therapist continued to prescribe sensate focus exercises for several weeks, despite Alice's clear lack of
interest.

Given the significant discrepancy between Jack's and Alice's covert or
ideal sexual scripts, script negotiation was introduced in an attempt to
develop a more compatible and mutually satisfying sexual repertoire. Unfortunately, this proved difficult to accomplish. Jack insisted on Alice's
adopting a more seductive or active sexual stance, in terms of both her
verbal and her nonverbal behavior. Alice resisted this, saying that she felt
uncomfortable and repelled by Jack's ideals in this respect. She much
preferred a script involving long and intimate conversations, light bodily
caressing with no specific genital focus, and brief intromission that would
readily result in mutual orgasm.

After these issues were discussed at length, a limited agreement was
reached. For his part, Jack offered to wait until Alice would initiate sex, at a
time and in a manner in which she felt comfortable. He also reluctantly
agreed to make use of masturbation in the interim, if he felt the need for
sexual release. Some gains were made, as Alice became more reliably
orgasmic and reported the absence of pain during intercourse. Jack, however, felt resigned to living with a partner who would always be less sexually
desirous than himself. Perhaps prophetically, in an individual therapy session, he wondered aloud whether he might not feel the need to seek out
prostitutes or other sexual partners in the future if Alice did not show a
much greater increase in her level of sexual interest.

In a follow-up session 1 year later, the couple announced that they had
decided to separate. Alice explained that she had fallen in love with a
coworker at her new job, someone who shared similar levels of sexual
interest. She regretted leaving Jack but felt she could no longer tolerate his
sexual demands. In a postsession letter to the therapist, Jack mused on his
sexual behavior during his relationship with Alice. He wrote,

> . . . I knew all about the differences in our levels and thought I was adjusting to
> them. She, on the other hand, was letting sex with me happen whether she was
> in the mood or not, just because it was the weekend and we hadn't been active
> since the previous weekend, and she went along with it as long as she could
> and then popped. . . . I wanted to turn her on like she's never been turned on
> before in her life. I saw lots of XXX-rated movies and tried to do and have
> Alice do what the people in the movies do because it seems to make them so
> happy. Well, I didn't remember the simple fact that I'm not a movie star and
> neither is she.

Commentary

A number of issues are highlighted by this sex therapy "failure." Even
though some success had been achieved in resolving sexual performance

difficulties and in establishing a somewhat more compatible sexual script, these changes did little to resolve the partners' underlying drive differences. Jack continued to feel the need to use sex to bolster his feelings of self-esteem, masculinity, and overall competency. In other words, sex remained his major vehicle for dealing with significant feelings of inadequacy. Despite deriving greater physical satisfaction from their sexual encounters, Alice maintained a general feeling of sexual apathy throughout.

The limited treatment focus, involving mostly sensate focus and script modification, was insufficient in increasing desire for an individual who experienced sex as tolerable at best and aversive at worst. Although the script was altered, the actors and meanings remained the same. Alice had begun to feel increasingly alienated from Jack and found it impossible to regard him with sexual ardor. The final straw was in her meeting a man at work who approximated her ideal lover to a much greater degree than Jack. In fact, her lover displayed similarly low levels of sexual desire, leading her to remark, "We get to sex when we get to it. . . . it just isn't all that important to either of us."

In retrospect, the therapist may have been overly zealous in advocating "compromise" for a couple as disinclined as Jack and Alice were to relinquish their individual interests. Treating sexual desire problems from a script perspective is clearly not equally beneficial in all clinical instances. While we have generally found this approach to have therapeutic and heuristic value, we are all too well aware of the many instances where sexual script changes are either superfluous or unwarranted.

Certainly in situations where the individual reports a chronic, lifelong lack of interest, suggestive of constitutional or early developmental deprivation and/or trauma, working solely from a sexual scripting perspective would be naive. At other times, couples may present with a satisfactory and compatible sexual script, but because of underlying relationship conflicts or hostility, they have little energy or motivation for sexual exchange. Focusing on the script can be used as an adjunct to couples therapy; more commonly, however, marital issues need to be addressed preliminary to script modification.

Conclusion

The emphasis on sexual script factors in assessment and treatment of desire problems offers a number of advantages. First, it leads us to an exploration of factors other than sexual frequency, rather than to a focus on frequency as the major or only therapeutic issue in these cases. Whereas both therapists and patients may otherwise tend to view problems of desire as involving primarily "too much" or "too little" sexual interaction, script analysis highlights the need to consider other key dimensions as well. In this regard, we have found it especially important to consider the degree of complexity, rigidity, conventionality, and satisfaction of both the overt script and the ideal script. In addition, we have emphasized the value of addressing partner discrepancy issues along each of these dimensions. Following a detailed assessment of current and ideal scripts, sex therapy typically entails a process of renegotiation and compromise toward a more mutually accept-able and satisfying repertoire of sexual exchange.

While most clinicians acknowledge the need for detailed understanding of the sexual interaction patterns in these cases, scripts are rarely explored with the systematic and comprehensive focus suggested here. As indicated, the approach described also tends to defuse "blaming" of the low-desire partner, and to focus attention on the role of the high-desire partner in maintaining the problem. We have also found that script interventions may be readily incorporated into a systems–interactional approach to therapy, as described in Chapter 10, or into the broad-spectrum, cognitive–behavioral approaches described in Chapters 5 and 6. In fact, we do not usually recommend a script intervention as the sole treatment intervention. A number of important limitations of the approach have also been identified, as discussed above.

Finally, at a more theoretical level, we believe it is always important to consider the role of contextual determinants and the "multiple meanings" (Gagnon & Simon, 1987) attributable in this society to disorders of desire. Certainly, in the absence of clear-cut or operational diagnostic criteria, and with scant biological data to support the present classification, social expla-nations of the problem retain their plausibility. While remaining open-minded to the possible influence of determinants at many levels, we have found the approach described to be theoretically challenging, as well as therapeutically useful.

References

Apfelbaum, B., & Apfelbaum, C. (1985). The ego-analytic approach to sexual apathy. In D. C. Goldberg (Ed.), *Contemporary marriage: Special issues in couples' therapy*. Homewood, Il: Dorsey Press.

Bancroft, J. H. (1984). Hormones and human sexual behavior. *Journal of Sex and Marital Therapy, 10*, 3–21.

Berkman, A. H., Katz, L. A., & Weissman, R. (1982). Sexuality and the life style of home dialysis patients. *Archives of Physical Medicine and Rehabilitation, 63*, 272–275.

Blumstein, P., & Schwartz, P. (1983). *American couples: Money, work, and sex*. New York: Morrow.

Foucault, M. (1978). *The history of sexuality* Vol. 1. New York: Random House.

Gadpaille, W. J. (1975). *The cycles of sex*. New York: Scribners.

Gagnon, J. H. (1977). *Human sexualities*, Glenview, IL: Scott, Foresman.

Gagnon, J. H. (1979). The interaction of gender roles and sexual conduct. In H. Kachadurian (Ed.), *Human sexuality: A comparative and developmental approach*. Berkeley: University of California Press.

Gagnon, J. H., Rosen, R. C., & Leiblum, S. R. (1982). Cognitive and social aspects of sexual dysfunction: Sexual scripts in sex therapy. *Journal of Sex and Marital Therapy, 8*, 44–56.

Gagnon, J. H., & Simon, W. (1973). *Sexual conduct: The social sources of human sexuality.* Chicago: Aldine.

Laws, J. L., & Schwartz, P. (1977). *Sexual scripts: The social construction of female sexuality,* Hinsdale, IL: Dryden Press.

Leiblum, S. R., & Bachmann, G. (in press). The sexuality of the climacteric woman. In B. Eskin (Ed.). *The menopause: Comprehensive management.* Chicago: Year Book Medical.

Levine, S. B. (1984). An essay on the nature of sexual desire. *Journal of Sex and Marital Therapy, 10*, 83–96.

Miller, S. (1986). *The good mother.* New York: Random House.

Neumann, R. J. (1978). Sexuality and the spinal cord injured: High drama or improvisational theater? *Sexuality and Disability, 1*, 93–99.

Nowinski, J. (1980). *Becoming satisfied: A man's guide to sexual fulfillment.* Englewood Cliffs, NJ: Prentice-Hall.

Rosen, R. C., & Leiblum, S. R. (1987). Current approaches to the evaluation of sexual desire disorders. *Journal of Sex Research, 23*, 141–162.

Shaw, J. A., & Rosenfield, B. L. (1987). Psychological and sexual aspects of genital herpes in women. *Journal of Psychosomatic Obstetrics and Gynecology, 6*, 101–109.

Simon, W., & Gagnon, J. H. (1986). Sexual scripts: Permanence and change. *Archives of Sexual Behavior, 15*, 97–120.

Tevlin, H., Leiblum, S. R. (1983). Sex role stereotypes and female sexual dysfunction. In V. Franks & E. Rothblum (Eds.), *The Stereotyping of Women: Its effects on mental health.* New York: Springer.

Zilbergeld, B. (1978). *Male sexuality.* Boston: Little, Brown.

Zilbergeld, B., & Ellison, C. R. (1980). Desire discrepancies and arousal problems. In S. R. Leiblum & L. Pervin (Eds.), *Principles and practice of sex therapy,* New York: Guilford Press.

8

The Use of Hypnosis in Treating Desire Disorders

BERNIE ZILBERGELD AND D. CORYDON HAMMOND

Like so many contributors to this volume, Zilbergeld and Hammond believe that desire disorders are among the most complicated sexual difficulties to treat, and that these disorders require individualized and often innovative interventions for successful resolution. They note, however, that despite the clinical challenge posed by desire problems, few therapists include hypnotic interventions as part of their treatment armamentarium. Regrettably, therapists and patients alike often regard hypnosis with suspicion, relegating it to the realm of black magic or stage entertainment. Zilbergeld and Hammond argue persuasively that hypnotic interventions provide a veritable gold mine of therapeutic options that may be utilized by therapists of different persuasions with positive outcome.

Zilbergeld and Hammond suggest that individuals are unusually receptive to value-congruent suggestions in a focused hypnotic state. Individuals with a lack of sexual interest may be able to readily imagine themselves behaving in a more sexually receptive fashion, imitating esteemed role models, and experiencing sexual arousal and pleasure. There is a vast array of hypnotic techniques that may be explored, limited only by the therapist's creativity and therapeutic goals. For example, if one is interested in identifying the reasons why a client reacts with fear to a specific sexual behavior, the "affect bridge" may be used. In this technique, the client is invited to re-experience his or her fears under hypnosis and to return to the original situation in which these fears were experienced. Another hypnotic uncovering method is "ego-state therapy," in which the patient is invited to talk to the fearful part of himself or herself.

Other hypnotic interventions include "goal" or "result" imagery, in which the individual imagines having accomplished desired goals; "process" imagery, or mental rehearsal; the use of "inner advisors" to provide encouragement and guidance; posthypnotic suggestions; and positive self-talk. An especially effective intervention for stimulating desire in individuals with low sexual interest is the "master control room" technique. In this intervention, the hypnotized client is asked to imagine entering a control room located in the hypothalamus, in which there is a panel regulating sexual desire. The client then sets the dial on a number ranging from 0 to 10, which reflects typical levels of sexual interest. The therapist then suggests that the dial be set at higher and higher levels, while the patient is simultaneously invited to become aware of the physical experience of arousal. Zilbergeld and Hammond note that patients are often surprised to find themselves feeling sexual arousal. Patients negotiate with the therapist about the number at which their sexual desire should remain fixed for the remainder of the week, and sometimes exhausted spouses later ask the therapist to turn the dial down!

　　Zilbergeld and Hammond suggest that hypnosis is a remarkably useful adjunct to standard sex therapy techniques. While not necessarily indicated in every case, there are few individuals who cannot be readily hypnotized and who will not benefit from the inclusion of carefully selected and individually tailored hypnotic techniques, whether these are employed for the purpose of uncovering repressed sexual traumas, rehearsing sexual behaviors, or experiencing sexual awakening.

　　Bernie Zilbergeld, Ph.D., is an internationally celebrated author and sex therapist in private practice in Oakland, California. He is well known for his creative and original approach to sex therapy, as well as his concern for demonstrating therapeutic efficacy. His latest works are a book, written with Arnold A. Lazarus, Mind Power: Getting What You Want through Mental Training, and an audiotape, produced with Lonnie Barbach, An Ounce of Prevention: How to Talk with a Partner about Smart Sex.

　　D. Corydon Hammond, Ph.D., is Associate Professor of Physical Medicine and Rehabilitation and Codirector of the Sex and Marital Therapy Clinic at the University of Utah School of Medicine, Salt Lake City, and a widely published author on hypnosis as well as sex therapy. He has served for several years as an officer in the American Society of Clinical Hypnosis and is a founding editorial board member of the Ericksonian Monograph series.

––––––––––

Disorders of sexual desire are among the most common problems seen by sex therapists, among the most complex, and perhaps the least effectively treated. There is little agreement on the most effective treatments, or even on the exact nature of what is being treated. Although the diagnosis of inhibited sexual desire (ISD) has enjoyed widespread acceptance since its introduction by Lief (1977), and although there are certainly many patients to whom it is rightfully applied, Zilbergeld and Ellison (1980) caution that many desire cases are more a matter of discrepant sexual appetites in a relationship than of ISD in one partner. If this principle is forgotten, therapists run the risk of always trying to increase the interest of the less desirous partner, even though by most standards it may be adequate. There are also some patients whose sexual interest is so high and so compelling that it might best be conceptualized as hyperactive sexual desire (to contrast it with the other extreme, ISD), or even sexual "addiction" (Carnes, 1983).

We view desire problems, whether lack of desire or desire disparity, to be multicausal and multidimensional (Hammond & Stanfield, 1977), requiring individualized assessment and treatment planning to take into account the broad range of factors that may be involved. Among the many things that can influence sexual desire are the following:

1. Past trauma such as incest or rape.
2. Relationship problems (conflict, resentment, anger, lack of intimacy, lack of physical attraction, power issues).
3. Behavioral deficits (in communication skills, in initiating or responding to sexual invitations, or in other sex-related areas).
4. Cognitive and emotional factors (stereotypes about the nature of men, women, or sex; idealized sexual expectations; fear of pregnancy; anxiety; distrust; depression).
5. Environmental issues (lack of privacy, work stress, extramarital relationships).
6. Perception and understanding of the uses and functions of sex. (As Zilbergeld & Ellison, 1980, have discussed, some people see sex as having very limited uses, while others see it as relevant and useful in many ways.)
7. Organic/medical problems (illness, endocrine abnormalities, pain, fatigue, drug effects).

Therapists need to make very broad assessments and to be aware of a wide variety of variables in working with desire cases, which is what makes these cases complex and difficult. There are simple desire cases—for example, a case in which a wife has no desire but is able to say that this is a result of the way her husband treats her, grabbing her breasts whenever he feels like it and demanding she have sex when he wants to, whether or not she is in the mood. But most cases are far more subtle and complex.

Unlike the situation with, say, premature ejaculation (where fairly similar approaches based on variations of Semans's [1956] pause method work for a large proportion of clients), our experience with desire disorders is that these cases are far more complicated and that no one approach or method is effective for large numbers of clients. Because hypnosis is not a therapeutic school per se, but rather consists of a large number of techniques that can be modified extensively to meet the requirements of particular clients, we have found it to be a helpful adjunct to (and in some cases an effective substitute for) standard sex therapy techniques in the treatment of desire cases. We first explain what hypnosis is, and then discuss why it can be helpful with sexual dysfunctions and desire problems.

Before saying more about hypnosis, however, we want to note that the two groups of therapists claiming great success with sex problems—sex therapists and hypnotherapists—seem remarkably ignorant of each other's work. Sex therapists are often surprised that effective therapy can be done without using any of the standard sex therapy techniques, and hypnotherapists often cannot understand why sex therapists do not use the methods they (the hypnotherapists) find so useful. We think that there is much to be gained from a greater exchange of information between these two groups of therapists. Clients would gain most of all, because their therapists would have at their command a far wider array of methods with which to treat their problems.

The Nature of Hypnosis

The roots of hypnosis as a healing art go back to antiquity, but Franz Mesmer is generally credited with bringing it into the modern world (Buranelli, 1975). Although Mesmer apparently cured large numbers of patients with his methods, his theory of "animal magnetism" was far-fetched even by the standards of 18th-century science, and both he and the methods were discredited. But hypnotism became popular in medical circles during the next century and was in fairly common use when Freud started his career. Freud's use of hypnosis in his early work led to his beliefs about repression and unconscious mental processes (Shor, 1979). But, as is well known, Freud abandoned hypnosis in favor of free association and dream analysis for exploring the unconscious; this development slowed mainstream acceptance of hypnosis as a therapeutic tool. However, hypnosis continued to be used clinically, both in symptom removal and in the exploration of unconscious conflicts.

More recently, hypnosis has enjoyed a renaissance of clinical interest and acceptance—in part because of the creative contributions of Milton Erickson (Rossi, 1980), widely considered to be the greatest hypnotherapist of his time, and in part because researchers have begun to document its therapeutic potential. Crasilneck and Hall (1985) and Gardner and Olness (1981) have reviewed the literature on applications of hypnosis with adults and children, respectively, noting its effectiveness with a variety of disorders. Research has documented the effectiveness of hypnosis in the treatment of pain (Hilgard & Hilgard, 1983), in promoting vascular control in hemophiliacs (LaBaw, 1975), in controlling dermatological allergic reactions (Ikemi & Nakgawa, 1962), and in influencing gastrointestinal function (Sarbin & Slagle, 1979). More and more evidence is accumulating concerning the interaction between mind and body (Ader, 1981), and it is increasingly evident that hypnosis can often powerfully affect both the mind and the body.

Hypnosis is not a therapeutic school or even an approach. It is primarily an atheoretical collection of techniques whose only commonality is their use in a state called "hypnosis" or "trance." The majority of therapists using hypnosis do so in ways influenced by their primary, and usually nonhypnotic, training and framework. In other words, most hypnotherapists are something else—behaviorists, analysts, family therapists—before they are hypnotherapists. The hypnosis used by insight-oriented therapists such as Brenman and Gill (1947) and Wolberg (1948) differs in many ways from the hypnosis used by behavioral and cognitive therapists such as Clarke and Jackson (1983), Kroger and Fezler (1976), and Lazarus (1976, 1984); this in turn differs from the hypnosis used by experiential therapists such as Araoz (1982), transactional analysis therapists such as Barnett (1981), and family therapists such as Ritterman (1983). Hypnosis can be utilized by practitioners of any kind of psychotherapy. The therapist gives up nothing to use it (in the sense that a psychodynamic therapist becoming a behaviorist would have to give up allegiance to the power of insight), yet gains a group of methods that can enhance the results of whatever he or she already does.

"Hypnosis" is a term that elicits divergent and extreme reactions from laypeople and professionals alike. Some think of it as a panacea for all the ills of the world, and probably many more view it as a form of black magic or witchcraft, useful only for entertainment. Neither of these views is correct. Hypnosis, like sex itself, is shrouded in mythology and misconception, largely because of how it has been presented in the media. These myths affect not only clients, but therapists as well.

Although there is some disagreement as to the exact definition of "hypnosis," it is generally defined as a focused state of awareness called "trance" (a term often used synonymously with "hypnosis"), usually but not always induced via relaxation. Contrary to popular belief, the hypnotized person is not asleep, unconscious, or under the control of the therapist. Hypnotized patients can be aware of external sounds such as doors opening and closing, are usually aware of what the therapist tells them, and can usually remember as much of their experience as they choose. And as for being under the control of the therapist, we know hypnotherapists who cannot get their clients to come on time to appointments or pay their bills.

In a focused hypnotic state, the mind is more receptive than usual to suggestions, provided of course that they are value-congruent. Critical faculties seem to be less dominant in hypnosis. Another way of saying this is that hypnosis is perceived by clients as similar to fantasy productions such as dreams. The imagination is given free rein. Clients who ordinarily would think it preposterous that they are or could be potent lovers may be willing, when relaxed, to imagine themselves being just that. If they are willing to imagine this scene often enough, it can help bring about the reality they desire.

Hypnosis is a natural human ability—one that is exercised many times by all of us without training, without formal preparation, and without understanding that the experience constitutes what is called a "trance." Anyone who has been so deeply involved in a book, a movie, an athletic event, or work that he or she has not noticed the passage of time has experienced the state called "trance." Good sex involves a trance. The partners are so focused on their own or each other's sensations and feelings that they do not notice the passing of time or the pain of bites and scratches. Orgasm is perhaps the ultimate trance. The physical sensations are so strong as to rivet one's attention on them. While we have heard many stories from clients about their minds wandering during various sexual acts, we have never had anyone say they were thinking about something else during orgasm. Formal hypnosis is also practiced widely, though it may be called by other names. Many Olympic and other world-class athletes, for example, do forms of imaging called "visualization," "mental training," and "mind scripting." These are all variations of hypnosis.

Hypnotic Techniques

To novices, hypnosis often appears to be a strange array of techniques that have little to do with each other. Zilbergeld and Lazarus (1987) have developed an organization scheme that, though primitive, brings some order to the variety of methods available. At the most basic level, hypnotic methods consist of three categories: induction of the hypnotic state; uncovering techniques; and a group of techniques designed to develop new habits and self-perceptions.

Induction of the Hypnotic State

Evoking the hypnotic state or trance usually involves some kind of relaxation. The client is helped to relax by taking deep breaths, imagining peaceful scenes, focusing on a phrase or word (as in meditation), or engaging in a number of other procedures (Hammond, 1987). Although there are a number of standard hypnotic inductions, anything that helps the client relax and turn inward is acceptable (Zilbergeld, 1986a). The rigmarole of stage hypnotists (swinging pendulums, strident commands to go to sleep, etc.) is unnecessary and often wasteful. For clients who already know how to focus and relax because of experience with meditation or biofeedback, for instance, therapists can increase efficiency by simply asking clients to do what they already know how to do. In addition, clients often go into trance spontaneously—as illustrated below in our first case example—and clinicians can make use of these spontaneous trances to achieve therapeutic goals.

Although some hypnotherapists demonstrate long and involved inductions, sometimes lasting up to an hour, this is not typically necessary. The level of hypnotic depth needed for most therapeutic work takes only 5–20 minutes to attain initially. With a little practice on the part of the patient, typically only a brief induction (about 2–5 minutes) is required.

Hypnotic Uncovering Techniques

Hypnotic uncovering methods attempt to discover the causes of problems—why, for instance, a client reacts fearfully when her breasts are touched. The woman may be asked to re-experience the fear in hypnosis and then allow the feeling to take her back to the first time she felt it. The technical name for this method is the "affect bridge" (Watkins, 1971). Another uncovering method is "ego-state therapy" (Watkins & Watkins, 1981), which is very similar to the technique in Gestalt therapy of talking to different parts of oneself. Using ego-state therapy, the therapist tells the hypnotized patient that he or she wants to talk to the fearful part of the patient (or the part that brings on the fear). The therapist wants to determine why the fear is there and its purpose: For example, is it trying to protect the woman from something, and, if so, what? "Ideomotor signals" (Cheek & LeCron, 1968) constitute yet another rapid uncovering approach. This method is illustrated below in the first case presentation.

Techniques for Developing New Behaviors and Self-Perceptions

Other hypnotic techniques can be grouped into the following categories. Their purpose is to help clients to develop new behaviors and self-perceptions.

Goal or Result Imagery

With "goal" or "result" imagery, also known as "age progression," the patient imagines accomplishing his or her goals or already having accomplished them. A client with erection problems might imagine himself as someone who usually gets erections in the appropriate circumstances and is very confident that he will function. His problem is far behind him, and he has had a number of satisfying, functional experiences. The purpose of this kind of imagery is to effect a change in self-perception. Instead of viewing oneself as a failure who fearfully anticipates each encounter, one practices viewing oneself as a success, eagerly anticipating the next experience. A more detailed discussion of the uses of goal imagery with sex problems is given elsewhere (Zilbergeld, 1986b).

Process Imagery

"Process" imagery is what behavior therapists call "mental rehearsal" and is the kind of imagery commonly used by athletes. The patient imagines himself or herself doing what is necessary to reach his or her goals. A man with erection problems might practice imagining turning down sexual invitations when he is not in the mood. He might also imagine himself directing his partner as she stimulates him and focusing on the resulting sensations and feelings.

One specific technique we have found very helpful with some sex therapy clients involves using a model for one's behavior. Some clients cannot even imagine themselves doing what is necessary (e.g., calmly having a conversation with an attractive stranger). But they usually know someone they have seen do this well, or they can imagine doing it well. These models may range from friends and relatives to celebrities.

One 50-year-old man had spent most of his life avoiding women, but now wanted to marry. However, he could not imagine talking to a woman or asking for a date, to say nothing of getting into bed with her, without a great deal of anxiety. But he could easily imagine his hero, Cary Grant, doing these things. So we had him imagine how Grant would do it, gradually inserting himself into the imagery and taking the place of the actor. In time, he was able to imagine himself calmly and confidently doing everything that was needed, and his behavior followed suit. In this case, the imaginary Cary Grant served both as a model and as an "internal advisor"—another technique commonly employed in hypnosis. Moviegoers may recall Woody Allen using an imaginary Humphrey Bogart in similar fashion in *Play It Again, Sam*.

Changing the Structure of Imagery

Some methods are aimed at altering the *structure* rather than the *content* of a client's internal representations, and have the purpose of giving the client some control over the productions of his or her mind. How a person imagines something determines to a large extent the feeling caused by the imagery.

When we asked a woman we worked with how she saw her most recent positive erotic experience, she replied that she was watching it as if on a movie screen almost 30 feet away. The picture was small, in black and white, and not clearly defined. Her emotional reaction to the imagery was "nothing much, basically neutral." After she moved the image closer, made it larger and clearer, and added color, her feeling was "more positive, even a little turned on." Her perspective, however, was still what Zilbergeld and Lazarus (1987) call "separated." That is, she was observing from outside of her body, watching herself having sex—a perspective that usually decreases intensity of feeling. Since we wanted to increase the strength of her emotion, we asked her to merge with her body in the imagery, to become part of the experience instead of seeing it from the outside. She did so and reported, "Wow! I'd like to go home and seduce Tom [her husband]."

Similar methods have also been helpful with desire cases in which the client is plagued by internal voices that promote unhelpful behavior. The messages these voices convey range from "Sex is dirty and therefore shouldn't be engaged in" to "Sex is proof of love, masculinity, or femininity, and therefore has to be engaged in, no matter what the feeling or cost." Turning down the volume of these voices can limit their power, as can speeding them up or playing inappropriate music (e.g., circus music) in the background.

Posthypnotic Suggestions

"Posthypnotic suggestions" are statements about behavior, thoughts, and feelings that will occur at future times; they are closely related to process imagery. In process imagery, the patient imagines directing the partner in how to stimulate him or her. With posthypnotic suggestion in self-hypnosis, the patient tells himself or herself that he or she will do this. An example might be: "As soon as she starts to touch me, I will tell her exactly how to stimulate me in the most exciting ways, and as she follows my suggestions, I will find myself focusing intently on the sensations and pleasures generated by her touches." As with process imagery, the purpose of posthypnotic suggestions is to help the client prepare a mental blueprint for action, to prime him or her to do what is necessary.

Positive Self-Talk

"Positive self-talk" consists of positive messages used to counteract the influence of the negative messages so many sexually dysfunctional men and women repeatedly give themselves. Instead of words like "You'll never be able to satisfy a woman," "You'll never have an orgasm," "You don't have what it takes to last longer [or keep it up]," and so on, we teach them to give themselves messages such as "I'm doing what's needed to be a wonderful lover," "I'll be orgasmic," "I've succeeded before. Relax and let it happen," and "There's nothing wrong with being selfish. I deserve to have a good time." Positive self-talk is referred to as "self-statement modification" by cognitive-behavior therapists, and a recent review of the relevant literature suggests that it does indeed produce significant therapeutic results (Dush, Hirt, & Schroeder, 1983).

Positive self-talk is closely related to goal imagery. The positive messages say, among other things, that a person will achieve the goals he or she imagines having achieved (in result imagery). The images and thoughts we have of ourselves constitute a large part of our identities. When we continuously tell ourselves that we do not have what it takes and see ourselves being inadequate, our behavior and feelings tend to follow suit. This is what Araoz (1982) has called "negative self-hypnosis." On the other hand, when our images and messages become more positive, we tend to feel and behave differently, and others respond to us accordingly.

We remind clients to congratulate themselves for their efforts and achievements, to substitute positive messages for negative ones, and generally to say nice things to themselves. When they run into negative statements that will not yield to more positive ones, we often teach them how to change the structure of the messages to neutralize or limit their power.

Practicing Hypnotic Techniques

Except for uncovering techniques, which are best done in the office under expert guidance, hypnotic techniques are often practiced at home by patients, using tapes prepared in the office by the therapist. The therapist instructing a client in process imagery, for instance, will record the suggestions on tape and ask the client to use it at home. The tapes are usually 5–15 minutes long, and research indicates that clients believe they are very useful at the beginning of their hypnotic work (Hammond, Bartsch, Grant, & McGhee, in press). With a few weeks of practice, tapes are usually unnecessary.

Benefits of Hypnosis

Hypnosis offers a number of benefits to therapists and clients alike, aside from the fact, mentioned above, that it can be used within the therapist's existing framework. Like sex therapy, hypnosis puts a premium on producing quick and observable results. The uncovering techniques, for instance, can often expose in one to three sessions past traumas or adaptive functions for the problem that were formerly beyond conscious awareness. In contrast, doing the same exploration in analytic therapies can take months or years. Hypnosis can also help uncover trauma that no amount of conscious exploration can discover. For example, several patients have reported in an initial sex history that they had never experienced incest or sexual molestation. However, later, in hypnosis, early childhood sexual abuse was uncovered. (The earlier the abuse occurred, especially before the age of 5, the less the chance that it will be accessible to ordinary waking consciousness.) Hypnotic techniques can help shorten almost any kind of therapy.

Hypnosis as generally done includes training in relaxation, something many sex therapy patients need. It is ironic that despite the emphasis they place on anxiety and on the necessity for greater relaxation, sex therapists rarely instruct clients in how to relax themselves. To be sure, they set up situations (e.g., in which intercourse is prohibited and sensate focus is encouraged) designed to inhibit anxiety, but this is not the same as teaching relaxation skills per se. Hypnosis includes these skills in short forms that are palatable to most patients and give them a sense of self-control. Simply learning to relax with self-hypnosis gives many patients a valuable skill to make the transition from a hectic day at work or with the children to sensual involvement.

The focused attention that characterizes and is taught in hypnosis is also crucial to good sex. When a man or woman is not attending to what is happening, but instead is observing from afar ("spectatoring"), the focus or sexual trance is lost, and dissatisfying or dysfunctional sex is the result. Many of the things sex therapists do (e.g., removing goals such as intercourse and suggesting attending to sensation) constitute attempts to reinstate the sexual trance. Hypnosis is simply a more direct way of doing the same.

Hypnosis lends itself to the treatment of patients without partners. Relatively few treatment options have been available for single patients or those without cooperative partners, except for surrogate therapy. Interestingly, the largest and most extensive outcome reports on the use of hypnosis with sexual dysfunction have been on patients treated individually. Crasilneck (1979, 1982), who used a wide variety of hypnotic techniques, reported follow-ups on a larger number of impotent patients than any other researchers (including Masters and Johnson), with even more impressive results. Unfortunately, his work suffers from many of the same methodological weaknesses as theirs (e.g., lack of independent judgment of success and failure, and lack of clarity about the criteria of outcome) and is therefore as difficult to interpret.

Discouragement is a factor that seems too often overlooked in sex therapy. Many desire patients no longer believe that they, or their partners, will ever be able to experience passion and interest. However, perhaps because of the popularized images of hypnosis as rather mystical, some patients come to therapy with a belief that hypnosis can do for them what they cannot do for themselves: promote change. Hypnosis may also be used more directly to provide hope and confidence that change can occur, and to increase self-efficacy (Bandura, 1977).

"Trance ratification" (Hammond, 1987) is a basic hypnotic principle; it means giving patients experiences that convince them of the power of their own minds and of hypnosis to help them. When patients feel an arm levitate and float up, seemingly involuntarily, they are often convinced that this thing called hypnosis may, in fact, be capable of doing something for them. Similarly, when a glove anesthesia is created in a hand so that a needle may be painlessly put through a fold of skin on the back of the hand, patients are convinced that they have more potential than they realized and that perhaps their minds are powerful enough to stir sexual desire.

Hypnosis also offers the clinician a variety of techniques for altering problematic emotions and increasing desired emotional states. Symbolic imagery techniques often allow a patient to release pent-up feelings such as anger and resentment, without further harming the relationship with the partner. For example, such a patient may experience himself or herself gradually smashing a huge boulder in the mountains while simultaneously venting angry feelings. Other patients may imagine breaking through a barrier, discarding old parental messages that evoke negative emotions, or placing feelings of guilt in the gondola of a hot-air balloon and watching it float away. The chronically fatigued patient may imagine an energy transfusion or withdraw to a serene place in self-hypnosis.

Perhaps because of the phenomenon of "trance logic" (Orne, 1980), which occurs in significant hypnotic states, symbolic imagery that would seem silly or simplistic in a waking state can provide powerful evocative experiences for the patient. For example, the "master control room" technique (Araoz, 1982; Hammond, 1985) has proven surprisingly effective in stimulating feelings of sexual desire, particularly after roadblocks to desire (e.g., relationship problems) have been removed. In this technique, the patient imagines entering a control room in the hypothalamus, where there is a panel regulating sexual desire on which is a dial or lever that may be set from 0 to 10. The patient is told that 0 represents the level of no desire, while 10 is very high sexual interest. The patient tells the therapist what number the dial is set on (most typically 1 or 2). Suggestions are then given to imagine gradually moving the dial upward, one number at a time. Between numbers, suggestions are offered that hormones are being released and that the patient is beginning to feel increasing sexual desire. Many patients are surprised to find themselves feeling arousal during this experience. The therapist then negotiates with the patient the number that the sexual desire should remain set on. Interestingly, several patients have returned a week or two later not only to report daily sexual activity, but also to convey their partners' request that it would be fine if we turned the dial down a couple of numbers!

In the treatment of ISD, hypnotic age regression may be done to revivify memories that may help rekindle and recapture positive sexual and affectional feelings. Through hypnosis, some individuals are able to recall memories of great desire so clearly that they experience the same feelings in the present. Of course, clients may be asked to recall pleasurable experiences without the use of hypnosis, but our experience and that of many other clinicians is that the experience and emotions are more intense with hypnosis.

Another advantage of hypnosis is that there are essentially no contraindications to its use, provided that it is done by a qualified therapist trained in its use. Hypnosis has been used effectively with borderline and psychotic patients (Baker, 1986), as well as with those fitting just about every category in the *Diagnostic and Statistical Manual of Mental Disorders,* third edition (DSM-III). And, contrary to popular belief, negative side effects are infrequent when hypnosis is done by qualified practitioners. The reports of harm that occasionally appear in the popular press are almost invariably due to the antics of night-club performers and others who are not trained therapists.

Limitations of Hypnosis

Despite the many advantages of hypnosis, we wish to emphasize that it is not a therapeutic orientation or a panacea. Our approach to therapy is eclectic, and although we use hypnosis with considerable frequency, we do not rely on or advocate this method alone. As with any single treatment modality, there are also some limitations and cautions in the use of hypnotic techniques.

One is that because hypnosis has historically been primarily associated with the treatment of individuals, therapists may be tempted to overemphasize an individual focus for treatment, neglecting important relationship factors. Individual psychotherapy has been known for many years to have the potential to evoke pathological reactions in the untreated spouse (Kohl, 1962), and deterioration in the marital relationship appears to be a greater risk in individual marital therapy (Gurman & Kniskern, 1978a, 1978b). Furthermore, recent research (Stuart, Hammond, & Pett, 1987) found that couple relationship variables (along with parental attitudes and modeling) were the most important discriminating factors between ISD women and women with normal desire. Individual psychological adjustment and endocrine factors did not differ between the two groups.

In sex therapy, we find that unless individually focused hypnosis is used in a context that involves the partner in assessment and in at least part of the treatment, there is a risk that some patients may feel singled out as the "identified patient," and that relationship factors may be neglected. We recommend, therefore, that the partner be included from the beginning in assessment. When we do individual hypnotic work, the mate is typically involved in behavioral assignments afterward. If the individual work requires more than three or four sessions, we recommend a conjoint session each month to maintain a feeling of involvement in the partner. The temporarily uninvolved partner is also encouraged to call between conjoint sessions if an individual or conjoint session is desired, and/or to send feedback through the spouse.

It should also be noted that spouses may sometimes be present during hypnotic work. Some patients will feel self-conscious, as though they have an audience, and may prefer not to have the spouse in attendance. However, occasionally a patient will feel more secure having the mate present. We suggest inquiring about this matter and respecting the feelings of the patient. When a partner witnesses an age regression to a negative past experience, he or she will generally be more empathic toward and supportive of the mate. Some hypnotic techniques can also focus on both partners simultaneously. Both mates may be age-regressed to a wonderful experience, or projected into the future to share a fantasy of having beautiful sexual experiences together. On the other hand, if the patient is being taught to enter a self-hypnotic state and create sexual fantasies to facilitate sexual desire, and the fantasies are about partners other than the spouse, an individual session will be desirable.

Hypnosis is like other therapeutic technique: It does not work with everyone. Patients vary in their native hypnotic talents. Thus 5%–10% of patients either cannot or will not be hypnotized, and realistically, another 10% of patients may be sufficiently limited in their hypnotic capacity that they will probably receive minimal help from hypnosis. It used to be thought that a large proportion of people could not use hypnosis. But the new view—what Araoz (1985) calls the "new hypnosis"—is that the vast majority of people can make use of hypnosis, provided the therapist takes the time to determine what will help them move into the required state (Barber, 1980). Nonetheless, there are some clients whose abilities are too limited to make hypnosis an appropriate choice for them.

In addition to differences in ability to use hypnosis, there are also a very small number of men and women seeking therapy who, whatever their imagery abilities, refuse to engage in the focused attention required. They say that it is silly, or insist that it reminds them (negatively) of something they saw in a night club (stage hypnosis), or give some other reason. Some of these clients can be persuaded to give hypnosis a chance to help them. With a few others, though, the resistance is strong enough that the best course is to accept it and use other approaches.

A last caution to be mentioned here is that the use of hypnosis with sexual dysfunction is, at this time, only supported by anecdotal and case report data (Brown & Chaves, 1980). We must await more careful research to evaluate more precisely the contribution of this modality to treatment outcome.

A Successful Case: Dot and Gary

Description and Background

Dot and Gary, both college-educated professionals, were each aged 33 and had been married 6 years. The presenting problems were Dot's low desire, low arousal, and lack of orgasm. In the initial interview, Dot explained that she had never had much interest in sex, had never masturbated, only occasionally got highly aroused during lovemaking, and had never had an orgasm. During their courtship, she had been very excited by Gary—thinking she had finally met the man of her dreams—but this excitement transferred only minimally to sex. She found him attractive and sensitive, but she had to fake desire, arousal, and orgasm.

Gary realized from the start that Dot was not as interested in sex as he was and that there was something peculiar about her sexual behavior, but he gave little weight to these matters because they were well matched in so many other ways. He assumed that sex would get better over time and felt hurt when her interest declined over the years; he was especially wounded when she confessed, a few months before they came for therapy, the extent to which she had been faking. He personalized what she said as a reflection of her love for him and of his lack of sexual prowess. His behavior then vacillated between periods of intense desire when he would initiate sex almost every day and periods when he felt little desire himself and made no overtures. Dot's telling him that sex with him was better than with anyone else did not help.

When Dot was asked what she would be feeling if she were not feeling the "neutrality" she experienced during sex, she hesitantly replied, "Fear." She then volunteered that she had been sexually involved with her father from the ages of 5 to 10. He had made her suck his penis regularly and had several times tried to enter her, but was prevented from doing so by involuntary contraction of her pelvic muscles. It was a horrible time for her. She knew there was something wrong but did not know what to do. When she tried to say no to her father, he threatened her and sometimes hit her. She felt she could not confide in her younger siblings and feared her mother would not believe her. The incest ended when she threatened to run away and tell the police.

We were about to seize on the incest as the main area for investigation and treatment,[1] but Dot quickly put an end to this. She said she had seen a therapist about this issue for several years, terminating therapy about a year before she met Gary. The reason for going was that a lover had complained that she was uninvolved and apparently fearful during sex. She and her female therapist had discussed at great length her involvement with her father, and both felt that the issue was resolved. In reality, the main result was that she no longer experienced fear during sex. But her interest and involvement did not increase. Dot made it quite clear during this meeting that she did not want to discuss the incest again.

The couple's goals included more frequent sex; more interest, involvement, and initiations on Dot's part; and orgasms for her. Dot said she felt "totally out of it sexually" and would very much like for sex to be just a regular part of her life with Gary, without the problems it was causing between them.

We felt in a bind. We thought the incest required further work but were confronted with a patient who refused to consider it. We decided to take a more neutral path; if it didn't work, we could then bring up the incest. Accordingly, sensate focus exercises were assigned for several weeks. Dot agreed not to fake feelings and to report her responses honestly.

Progress of the Treatment

Things did not go well. Dot found many reasons to be busy when it was time for the homework. Only one or two sensate focus sessions were done each week. In each case, whether being the receiver or the giver, Dot felt "nothing." Gary's responses had no influence on her. Attempts to explore Dot's feeling of "nothing" got nowhere. "Nothing is nothing, just nothing at all," she replied. When asked whether she didn't find this interesting, she said simply that there was nothing interesting about nothing. When again asked what she would feel if she wasn't feeling "nothing," she said she didn't know.

In an attempt to find something to work on, we focused on their relationship. Dot said she had been frightened by Gary's behavior since her confession of faking; she feared she was losing his love. Gary assured her that this was not the case; his feelings were a response to a situation he couldn't fathom. Although they had an excellent marriage in most areas except sex, Gary was becoming increasingly angry and frustrated. He felt Dot was becoming more guarded and more withdrawn—an impression we shared. Dot became defensive when he said this, and a fight ensued.

The breakthrough (almost literally) came that night. We were

---

1. This case and the following one were each treated by one therapist, but for convenience we use the word "we" in referring to the therapist.

awakened by a call from Gary very early on the morning after the fourth session. Dot had awakened during the night in a panic; she had cried and been incoherent for several hours. Gary comforted her as best he could and called when he realized his efforts were not helping. We agreed to see Dot immediately. Gary drove her over but did not participate in the session, which lasted almost 3 hours. People in shock or panic are essentially in a hypnotic trance (they are very focused, though hardly relaxed), thus providing valuable opportunities for hypnotic work. After calming Dot down a bit, we asked whether she would be willing to play a game that would help her. She agreed and was told about ideomotor signaling. In this method, finger signals are established for "yes," "no," and "I don't want to answer." She was instructed not to try to move the fingers voluntarily, but to "allow your unconscious mind to cause a finger to float up, all by itself."

Because of our impression that Dot was already very focused and very receptive, no formal hypnotic induction was undertaken; we just started asking a series of "yes–no" questions to which she responded. The first question, to which she raised her "yes" finger, was whether something had happened in her past that had caused the present feelings. The second question, to which a "yes" answer was also received, was whether it was acceptable to her to explore that event. Questions were then asked to establish her age at the time of the event. It turned out that the event was really a series of events that spanned several years, starting when she was 5. She was then told to reorient herself in time to just before the first occurrence and to tell us what was happening. She reported being in her "pink jammies" in her bedroom, getting ready for bed and feeling disappointed that she would not be up when her mother came home from work. She was told that something unpleasant was about to happen and that she needed to protect herself from it, perhaps by imagining that she was watching it happen to someone else on a TV screen. She accepted the suggestion and reported seeing her younger self, "Dottie," on the TV—an example of a separated or dissociated perspective, which usually has the effect of reducing the intensity of the feelings.

She was told to let the story unfold, "exactly as it happened but with you now watching it on TV." What happened was her first molestation at the hands of her father. During that session Dot went through a number of these incidents, with the accompanying feelings of fear, rage, and helplessness. There were also other feelings, even harder to acknowledge. She at times experienced physical pleasure during the encounters with her father and at other times a sense of satisfaction at pleasing him. These feelings were shocking and shameful to her then and later. As she became 9 and 10, however, the positive feelings were less frequent and the negative ones stronger and more frequent. She knew she had to stop what was going on, but could not find a way. She gradually developed the feeling of indifference as a way of coping. She dissociated and didn't feel anything, so it wasn't so bad. Not feeling anything was also a way of striking back at her father. He disliked her indifference, but her anger and resistance served only to increase his ardor. Feeling nothing was her way of dealing with an impossible situation; it also became her way of dealing with all men sexually.

The session was cathartic, to say the least. Dot cried, screamed, and trembled through must of it. Perhaps for the first time since the abuse had occurred, Dot dealt with herself directly, without her armor of indifference. With her previous therapist, she had talked about all the incidents and issues, but without much feeling. She had been too fearful that if she let herself go, she would feel exactly as she had as a child. This fear also explained why she resisted going into the subject during the first visit. This time, it was not so much that she chose to deal with her feelings, but that they broke through her defenses and thrust themselves upon her.

Throughout the session, we gave many suggestions, including these two: "Now that you've dealt with this here, it need never again bother you," and, "Now that you've worked it through and worked it out, this part of your past won't trouble you again." She was repeatedly reminded that she was no longer a little girl—that she was not a mature woman with many resources (a number of which were mentioned) who need never again feel helpless.

Dot felt no need to do anything to her father. He had died a painful death from cancer a few years earlier, and she felt he had been justly rewarded for what he did to her. She did, however, feel a great deal of anger at her mother for not knowing what was going on and for not protecting her. But she indicated with her finger signal that she was not ready to do anything about this.

Near the end of the session, Dot had stopped crying and seemed at peace, very much in trance. She responded positively when asked whether she would like to use some of her internal resources to help resolve the problem she was having with Gary and to tie up any loose ends connected to the incest with her father. She was asked to imagine going to a very safe, peaceful place where she would meet her "inner advisor." Once there, we told her to be aware of any signs of life. There soon appeared to her, in a flash of light, a beautiful woman carrying a wand. She learned that this was "my own fairy godmother." They talked at length (in her imagination), and Dot discovered that her godmother was very strong and very wise, very interested in Dot's welfare and willing to help her. After making arrangements to meet again, Dot left her advisor.

Lest some readers conclude that we have gone off the deep end here, we need to say that "inner advisors" are only parts of ourselves that are sometimes best represented as people. Other terms for the "inner advisor" include "the strongest or wisest part of yourself" or "your unconscious mind." However, parts are difficult to conceptualize and deal with, whereas an advisor with a human form and name is easier to talk to.

Later that day, on her own, Dot summoned up her inner advisor in self-hypnosis (which she was taught how to enter near the end of the 3-hour session) and asked what to do next. She was told that Dottie had been lost in time, left by herself in the terrible mess she had been in with her father. Dot had simply gone on without taking Dottie with her. This needed to be rectified; otherwise Dot's problems might return. Dot was frightened, but agreed. Surprisingly, however, her advisor said that this task had to be undertaken with the therapist.

And it was, at an appointment that had already been scheduled for the following day. Dot was given instructions to take her godmother and go back to the still scared and helpless Dottie. Dot was urged to hold and comfort her. Dottie responded by saying how much she loved Dot and wanted to be with her. We gave suggestions that they would always be together, always helping and comforting each other, and that life would be much easier now that they were as one. Dot was encouraged to spend a few minutes a day with Dottie, comforting her and talking to her.

Before the session ended, another topic, inadvertently omitted the day before, was broached. We wanted to help Dot discriminate between her father and other men, especially Gary. We asked her to imagine her father and get a feeling for the person he was, and then to do the same with Gary. A series of questions followed about the differences and similarities between the two men. She agreed there were far more differences. Gary was much more sensitive, was much more concerned about her feelings and needs, and would never coerce her to do anything; therefore there was no need to defend herself against him. Many suggestions were given to the effect that not all men were like her father; that Gary was not at all like him; that she did not need to be indifferent with Gary; and that she would, in her own way and at her own pace, change her feelings and behavior toward men, taking into account her new understandings.

Gary accompanied Dot to the next session the next day. He said that she seemed somehow different and that he was pleased by the change. She had been very affectionate the night before at a movie and in bed, although there was no sex. Dot had felt some sexual desire, but was not quite sure what to do about it. She thought she would have reacted positively had Gary initiated sex. Gary responded that he did not want to be the one who had to initiate it.

Dot indicated that all day yesterday and so far today she had been having sexual feelings. But she pointed out that she had never once made overtures to a man and didn't know how to go about it. Furthermore, she was not sure how to show a man she was interested. A brief hypnotic induction was performed, and she was told to ask her advisor for help. A very strange 10 or 15 minutes followed. As Gary and we watched, she went through a number of facial contortions and body movements. She later reported that her advisor had appeared to her in a different form, as a *femme fatale,* and proceeded to tell and show her how to flirt, how to seduce, and how to respond to invitations. Further lessons would follow. Dot was asked to pick the easiest lesson she had received—to close her eyes and imagine herself doing part or all of what she had seen her advisor do (an example of emulating a model). When this had been accomplished, she was asked to practice it several times a day in self-hypnosis. We made it clear that she was under no pressure to do anything except to continue talking to Dottie, continue the sexual instruction with her godmother, and do the imagery rehearsal just discussed. Gary was told to do whatever he wanted and not to expect too much.

At the next meeting, 4 days later, Gary announced that Dot had twice initiated sex. He was joyful because, as he said, "There was no way she was faking it." She had enjoyed both encounters, experiencing sensations she had never before felt. Gary expressed concern about her not reaching orgasm, but she said she was just getting started and was not yet ready for that. He said he could wait.

In response to our question whether there was anything that needed to be done to help her reach orgasm, she said she just needed more time to integrate all that had happened and to have more sex. She reported that her sessions with Dottie and her advisor were very productive. Another meeting was scheduled in 10 days.

Four days before the session, we spent about 20 minutes with Dot on the phone. She called because she felt "shaky" when she awoke from a dream in which she had been sucking her father's penis. After a brief induction over the phone, she was asked to summon her advisor, who said, "Things are just working themselves out and there's no reason for concern or action." Dot felt relieved.

At our next session, the news was both good and bad. Dot had initiated sex four times and Gary twice. Dot had enjoyed feeling aroused, and they had experimented with a number of positions and practices. Gary had climaxed each time but Dot had not. She now felt frustrated: "I feel ready to come but it's just not happening and I don't know what to do." For once, her advisor also seemed stymied.

We helped Dot to enter a hypnotic state and asked her to imagine the *femme fatale* aspect of her advisor having an orgasm:

> "Just watch her from the outside. See how her body moves and responds as she has a glorious orgasm. Be aware of her feet, her hands, her face, her pelvis, her whole body. Good. Now do it from the inside. Merge with her, imagine being in her body and feeling the sensations of fullness and lushness, the

tension building and growing until it almost hurts, the building and building until it just can't go any higher. And now imagine it breaking and flowing and contracting. Very good. Now let's go through it again, but this time imagine yourself feeling what she felt, just the feelings. Great. Now imagine yourself having an orgasm and your body responding as hers did . . . feet . . . hands, face . . . pelvis."

We went through this rehearsal with her several times, imagining being inside her advisor's body and then imagining herself feeling the same and reacting the same. We requested that she practice this at home several times a day in self-hypnosis.

Dot again reported progress in her private sessions with Dottie and with her advisor. Her anger toward her mother had come up several times. With her advisor's help, she had tried to understand her mother's situation at the time of her molestation. She concluded that her mother had been very unhappy, very tired, and overworked much of the time. Allowing herself to find out about the sexual abuse would have made her life even worse, because she would not have been able to stop her husband without threatening to call the authorities, in which case he might have left. Dot's mother could not have supported herself and the children without his help. Dot said she could love her mother for who she was and what she had done for her, and could also empathize with her wretched life. Dot and her advisor felt that the anger had been released and that nothing more needed to be done about this. There was no point in confronting her mother with the story.

Dot called a few days later to say she had had an orgasm the night before. The therapist congratulated her and asked that she continue her imaging. At the next session she reported more orgasms with and without intercourse. She and Gary felt much better about sex. It was much more frequent and much more enjoyable. Dot was initiating sex more than half the time and was an eager participant. Both said they felt they had achieved their objectives but agreed to the suggestion of another appointment in a month. That session, our last, took only about 25 minutes. Sex continued to be good. Gary was initiating sex more often, and Dot was regularly orgasmic. Their sex was more exciting and fulfilling than either had expected. Dot was no longer talking with Dottie. It wasn't necessary; "she's now here with me all the time, no longer someone separate." But she consulted with her advisor several times a week about many things. Gary had felt envious of her advisor and so found his own, who was proving helpful in both personal and business matters.

This therapy consisted of 11 hours over a period of $8\frac{1}{2}$ weeks, plus a 25-minute follow-up a month later. All parties agreed that it had been highly successful. A phone call 7 months after the last session indicated that although sexual frequency had dropped a bit, everything was well.

Commentary

It is impossible in any given case to say definitively why it was or was not successful and what factors were responsible. We believed that the hypnosis made a major difference, and so did the clients, but that does not constitute proof. In any case, we will proceed on the basis of this belief.

This was one of those rare cases where everything was on one side. The marriage was very good by almost any standards outside of the bedroom. Inside of it, the problems were almost 100% Dot's, and they stemmed primarily from an incestuous relationship with her father many years ago, even though Dot thought this problem had been worked out in prior therapy. As well as we can determine, the reason it was not worked through was that both Dot and her earlier therapist assumed that intellectual discussion alone constituted resolution. Neither Dot nor the therapist realized that her fear was too great to allow anything more than superficial discussion and analysis, even though the earlier therapy had gone on for almost 4 years.

Whether our methods were superior or whether we simply had luck or timing on our side is difficult to say. We admit being taken by surprise. We were not expecting what happened after the fourth session and, in fact, were feeling stuck. We were sure that the incest had to be explored, but were unclear how to facilitate this. Dot's panic opened the way. We were still wondering how to approach the door when it opened in front of us.

Although Dot's resolution of her incest trauma was more rapid than many women's, it should not be thought that most such traumas require months or years of counseling. We have usually found that brief, intensive work is all that is required. In many years of both using and not using hypnosis, we find it an exceptionally useful approach in dealing with these traumas and their aftermath.

Dealing with her incest helped free Dot's sexual interest, but it did not automatically make her the kind of sexual woman she wanted to be. She had behavioral deficits—not knowing how to be seducing and seductive, not knowing how to have orgasm. This point is often overlooked by psychoanalysts and hypnotherapists alike. Just because people are no longer prevented from doing something does not mean they can in fact do it. They may first need to acquire some skills.

In another sense, of course, Dot knew how to do these things at some deeper level, but she did not know that she knew. It is almost impossible to grow up and live in America without picking up a lot of sexual knowledge. Dot had certainly seen women—in movies, on television, and perhaps in reality—being seductive and responding to erotic advances. The fact that she had faked excitement and orgasm for many years, often successfully or at least partially successfully, itself indicates a certain level of knowledge.

The device of learning from her godmother/inner advisor was just a convenient and efficient way for her to get in touch with this knowledge. We took a bigger risk with how we asked her to learn about orgasm. The technique of learning by identifying and emulating her advisor worked for her and others, but it does not work for everyone. Sometimes more traditional scx therapy techniques are required.

We want to emphasize that we do not think there is anything special or magical about our selection of techniques. There are many hypnotic and nonhypnotic methods to choose from, and in many cases it may make little difference which are used. For example, in our first hypnitic session with Dot—the one that lasted 3 hours—we used ideomotor signals to facilitate exploration of her incest. Our guess is that ego-state therapy or the affect bridge would have been just as successful. Similarly, for every use of imagery with Dot, we can think of one or more alternate images or procedures that probably would have produced similar results. The use of methods depends on two factors: what is acceptable to the patient, and what the therapist is skilled and comfortable with. As long as techniques meet these two criteria, our experience is that they tend to work and to produce fairly similar outcomes.

The issue of when to use what procedure can be a vexing one, especially for beginners. Unfortunately, the state of the art in hypnotherapy, sex therapy, and psychotherapy in general is that there is no definitive knowledge about what methods work best for what clients with what problems. Even with a problem like premature ejaculation, for which methods based on Semans's (1956) pause technique have very high success rates, there are clients who will not use these methods or for whom they do not work. The situation is even less clearly defined with other problems. Therapy is still an art, not a science, and our impression is that a great deal of trial and error goes on (and, moreover, must go on). We tend to use the simplest, least complicated methods at first. Then, depending on their acceptance and utility, we decide what to do next. This approach seems similar to Kaplan's (1979) idea of using behavioral techniques at first, then switching to other methods if these do not achieve the desired results. Obviously, a great deal depends on what is acceptable to the client. The most successful method in the world will not work if the patient does not accept it.

We have had many successes with "inner advisors." It is true that some clients find the whole idea ridiculous and will not try it. But most of those to whom we have suggested it respond favorably. They know that it is a metaphor or game, we know that it is a game, and they know that we know, but it works all the same. We have had reports from patients whose therapy ended a decade ago, saying that they still consult their advisors to their benefit.

Anyone who has ever asked, "I wonder how my therapist [coach, teacher, boss, etc.] would handle this?" can have the answer by imagining that person handling the situation. Or they can roll up all the expert wisdom into the person of an inner advisor. Therapists who want to use this technique, however, have to be flexible. Inner advisors are not always what may be expected. We have had clients come up with different-sex advisors, very old ones, very stern and demanding ones, and some that are not even people (e.g., a squirrel named Jupiter and an old cat named Oscar).

Some readers may have been surprised in reading this case to see that, aside from the early and futile use of sensate focus, no standard sex therapy exercises were suggested or employed. This is not a rule. Sometimes we use many standard exercises (Kegel exercises, stop–start, masturbation, etc.), sometimes a few, and sometimes none at all. It all depends on what we think will be acceptable and helpful. In some cases, we have gone straight down the sex therapy path, as if we were following, almost step by step, the procedures in a sex therapy textbook. In other cases—with that of Dot and Gary coming close—we have not used anything most sex therapists would recognize. In still other cases, we use a combination of hypnotic and sex therapy methods. Sometimes they are used almost equally; at other times one is used in the service of the other. We have had some cases where we used mental rehearsal (process imagery) just to get clients to do a sex therapy exercise we thought important but that they at first could not even imagine themselves doing. A few women, for instance, initially resisted role-playing having an orgasm with their partners, but they were willing to do so after having imagined the scene several times. We have also had some cases where we used sex therapy exercises primarily to test whether the hypnotic techniques had worked or to indicate what further hypnotic work was necessary. As we have stated earlier in this chapter, we think that sex therapists and hypnotherapists would both gain if they knew more about each other's work.

But this knowledge still does not tell a therapist when to use what technique, or even when to use hypnosis and when to do something else. Some hypnotherapists use hypnosis in almost every single case. Hypnosis is what they do, and they do it all the time. But many who use hypnosis are more flexible. Even though Milton Erickson considered himself a master hypnotist and was seen as such by colleagues and most of his patients, he reported a number of cases in which he did not use hypnosis. As we have said earlier, a great deal depends on the client's receptivity, and also on the therapist's hunches as to what will be productive.

We also should say something about the length and spacing of our sessions with Dot and Gary, which has more to do with our attitude toward therapy than with any requirement of hypnosis. Ideally, we think the duration and frequency of therapy sessions should be tailored to the client's needs at the moment and to the therapist's idea of what has to be done. Some sessions may last only 5 minutes, while others may last many hours. By the same token, sometimes it is important to see a client every day for a period of time; sometimes a week or longer can go by without an appointment. Although Milton Erickson (Rossi, 1980) came close to following such a pattern, this may have had more to do with his medical training than with his use of hypnosis. Physicians may think that a certain procedure will take 2 hours, but they do not stop in the middle just because the alloted time is up or because the next patient has arrived. And if patients need to be seen daily, as is usually the case when they are hospitalized, daily visits are what they get.

Masters and Johnson (1970) are among a minority of sex therapists who see their patients daily and allow some flexibility as to the duration of these meetings. However, their way is also limited, in that patients who might do better with a once-a-week, twice-a-week, or other schedule cannot be accommodated. We strongly agree with Apfelbaum's (1972) contention that the standard once-a-week, 50-minute hour in psychotherapy has far more to do with convenience for therapists than with producing therapeutic change.

At the same time, however, we need to acknowledge that both therapists and clients need to be able to maintain some kind of predictable schedule. Like most therapists with busy schedules, we often do not have the luxury of following our preferred pattern, but we try to let it guide our practices as much as possible. On the short end, there are no problems. When we think that what needs to be done in a session has been done, we end it—with the client's permission, of course—no matter what the clock shows. On the long end (longer than an hour), there can be difficulties, expecially if other clients are waiting. When we realize we need more time with the patient we are working with, we excuse ourselves and explain the situation to the clients in the waiting room. Only rarely do they object to waiting longer. When we anticipate that a client will take longer than an hour, we make sure not to schedule someone else immediately after. And emergencies, by definition, take precedence. We had other clients scheduled the morning of Dot's panic, but we called to change their appointments as soon as we got Gary's phone call. As for the frequency of sessions, we try to keep our schedules flexible enough that a client who should be seen several days in a row can be accommodated.

One thing that worked in our favor in this case was Dot and Gary's love for and attraction to each other. Once Gary saw that progress was forthcoming, he essentially forgot his hurt about her faking and participated fully. When he became envious of her inner advisor, he did the rational thing—got one of his own—instead of making an issue of it or undermining her progress. In couples whose love is weaker or whose resentment or personal neuroticism is stronger, things do not proceed as quickly or easily. As Zilbergeld and Ellison (1980) and others have noted, it definitely helps to work with loving and committed couples.

An Unsuccessful Case: Stan and Joyce

This is not an easy case to report. It is the kind we would like to forget because of our absolute failure and because of the many unanswered issues that still surround it.

Description and Background

Stan, 41, and Joyce, 36, had been married for 15 years and had one child. Stan's law practice provided a substantial income, and Joyce busied herself spending money and "playing at working" (her phrase) by running a part-time massage practice. The problem was that in all 15 years of the marriage they had had sex fewer than 50 times: Stan was never interested. Joyce had repeatedly complained about this for years. Stan would promise to shape up but he never did, at least not for long.

The marriage was comfortable for both. Stan liked the idea of having a family, liked their home, enjoyed the meals Joyce prepared, and also enjoyed her company. Joyce also liked the idea of having a family, enjoyed Stan's company, and appreciated the lifestyle that Stan's earnings provided. Stan wanted nothing more than he already had—the comforts and amenities of family life without the "burden" of sex. Joyce also liked what she had, except for the lack of sex. She felt unloved and undesired, usually believing that a flaw in her was responsible for her husband's lack of interest. She said she loved sex and had enjoyed it with several men before meeting Stan. Nothing she did turned him on; everything she did seemed to turn him off. She masturbated regularly, but that didn't help. She had several affairs, which, though providing sexual release and temporary reassurance of her desirability, were ultimately unsatisfying. Besides, her rigid Catholic upbringing exacted a heavy toll of guilt for these adventures. Both said they wanted the marriage to work; divorce was unthinkable.

Sex had never been great for the two of them, though there had been more of it when they first met. Stan's explanation was that although the excitement of a new woman had turned him on slightly, the big reason was that he had wanted to make a good impression. Sex was clearly important to Joyce, so sex became more important to him for the 4 months of their courtship. Once he "got her" as his wife, his interest waned. When asked whether he could again feel and act as he did when they were first together, he replied "No," adding that it was far too much work.

Stan had never had much erotic desire. He had never had sexual fantasies, and had masturbated fewer than 20 times in his life. He had not had sex until he was in law school, and it had happened only when a woman seduced him. He would get interested in a woman for a few weeks; he would then come to feel that sex was too much work, and either he or the woman would end the relationship. Sex was not reinforcing—having it did not make him want to have it again. He was in good health and had been examined by several urologists and other physicians. There was nothing wrong with him physically. He found touching "pleasant at best" and did not like kissing. This combination of not liking kissing and touching is, in our experience, almost a sure sign of a deep-seated sexual aversion and/or a difficult course of treatment. Not surprisingly, he would not even consider engaging in oral sex. He described penile stimulation and orgasm as either "OK" or "pleasant," another sure sign of trouble ahead.

Joyce generally accepted sexual deprivation as the price she had to pay for the security of marriage to Stan and her extravagant lifestyle. But at least twice a year she exploded in anger and threatened divorce unless something was done. Stan greatly feared her anger and the possibility that she might leave, so he would shuffle off to yet another doctor for tests and treatment. A number of rounds of testosterone injections had proven fruitless, as had a series of psychotherapies with marriage counselors, psychiatrists, and sex therapists. All the standard and many nonstandard sex therapy exercises and approaches had been tried, with not much to show for them. The only tangible result was their son. One therapist, apparently thinking that having sex would arouse Stan's desire, had somehow exacted a promise from him to have sex three times a week regardless of how he felt. Stan dutifully complied, this being shortly after Joyce had confessed to an affair. They had sex five times in 2 weeks. Joyce got pregnant, and Stan gradually grew to love his son and became a good father.

We were impressed with the difficulty of the case from the outset. Some highly qualified therapists had failed to make a change in Stan, and we were not sure what we could do. Accordingly, we had a meeting with Joyce where we expressed our doubts. She begged us to try. Despite her threats, she said she would never leave Stan and didn't want to discuss the subject. We brought up the possibility of sex with other men, and she said that this might happen, but she couldn't plan a life based on having affairs. For his part, Stan was doubtful that anything would help, but was willing to try. Hypnosis had been tried by two other therapists, but he maintained he had "never gone under."

Course of the Treatment

What happened in the next 28 sessions comes close to being a mystery. Stan proved to be a good hypnotic subject, and we used every technique we knew and some new ones we learned or invented just for him. We explored his childhood, his sexual learning, his concerns about intimacy, his feelings for Joyce, and his feelings about himself. We came up empty or in cul-de-sacs every time. For instance, we had Stan imagine the most erotic situation he could, and it turned out not to be very stimulating. So we wrote a script that we thought might be exciting and read it to him in trance. He found it only mildly stimulating. He practiced it at home and continued to find it only slightly arousing. He had no desire to do anything about it with Joyce or anyone else, not even himself.

We tried to approach things from the point of view of making Joyce happy and saving the marriage, but that didn't work either. We hypnotically revivified the feelings Stan had had at the beginning of the relationship, but he did not want to expend that much effort again. We tried the relabeling techniques discussed by Zilbergeld and Ellison (1980). In retrospect, these were probably doomed from the start, because Stan simply did not find much of anything really exciting. He suffered from chronic low-grade depression, which in the past had responded slightly to cognitive-behavior therapy and antidepressants; these, however, had not increased his sexual appetite.

Perhaps the most valid answer to our uncovering attempts occurred one day when, in ego-state therapy, the part of Stan that controlled his sexual ardor (a part aptly named "Zilch") spoke these words in response to questions from us: "I'm here because no one else is. I have no purpose. I'm not doing anything, and I'm not stopping him from doing anything. I just don't get it and neither does he [Stan]. Sex is a bore and a burden to him. Maybe you should leave him alone." In response to the question, "Would it be OK with you for Stan to be more desirous?" the answer was, "Sure, if you can find a way. By my nature, I can't." In answer to the question, "Is there anyone else in there who can help?", he replied, "Not as far as I know." We had this answer (which was subsequently repeated on two other occasions) in the sixth session, but did not give it much weight until we heard the repetitions.

Most of the sessions were with Stan, but we had several with Joyce and seven with the two of them. Nothing made any difference. Finally, after 30 sessions, we told the two of them there was nothing more we had to try. Stan felt relieved—he had what he wanted, and therapy had not been a joy for him—and Joyce said she would try to live with the status quo. She did feel a little better, because she had come to believe that there was nothing wrong with her—that she had just married a man who by nature was asexual. She wanted to stay with him and would try to control her outbursts, but she wanted him to understand that she might sometimes have sex elsewhere. Stan said this was acceptable as long as he didn't know about it. Both agreed that there was no point in seeking further therapy.

The last time we spoke with them, in a phone call 14 months after termination, they reported that things were pretty much as they had been before they came to us. Joyce had had one weekend-long outburst in the interim; this had come to a halt when, in the midst of berating him, she realized that there was nothing he could do about it. She said she was trying to view him as she would a paraplegic, someone whose disability is beyond his control. Stan felt a bit more comfortable, "knowing I don't have to go to any more doctors." After he got off the line, Joyce said she had recently gotten sexually involved with a college student. "It's not how I thought my life would turn out, but it's safe and better than nothing."

Commentary

This case represents one of the most absolute failures we have ever had with a couple or individual whose treatment lasted more than a few sessions. What is most disquieting about it is that we have very little understanding of what went wrong and what we would do if we had another chance.

Stan apparently belongs to a small group of men and women whose sexual desire is not so much inhibited as it is nonexistent. The various aspects of sex are experienced as "OK," "fine," or "pleasant" at best, rather than as exciting or wonderful. This is not, as far as we can determine, an example of aversion. Sex was not repugnant or frightening to Stan; it just did not seem to be worth the effort it took. Far more to his taste was, as he once put it, "watching a ball game on TV, reading the paper, or playing with my son." Occasionally he felt enough desire—some of it faintly sexual, some of it just to please Joyce—to initiate lovemaking. And he could force himself when necessary (e.g., at the beginning of their relationship and when he made the deal with one of the earlier therapists that resulted in Joyce's pregnancy). But he was always aware of how much energy it took and how little he got in return.

Nothing in sex was reinforcing. When we asked (as several previous therapists had done) that he remain passive and thus preserve his energy while Joyce made love to him, he complied, but concluded that he would still rather watch TV. All of our efforts with hypnotic and traditional sex therapy techniques to stimulate desire and arousal failed, as did our efforts to increase the sensations of orgasm.

We have had successes in helping people with low desire increase their appetites (e.g., Hammond, 1985; Zilbergeld & Ellison, 1980), but in all those cases there was either a barrier to natural desire that could be removed or some desire and arousal to build upon. With Stan, and a very small number of other clients, we felt we had very little to work with.

One issue that logically suggests itself is that of the dynamics between Stan and Joyce. Is it possible that he was trying to get back at her for some real or imagined injury, that he was protecting himself from her, or that some other couple issue was being played out in the bedroom? We cannot definitively say that none of these things was true, but we explored them, in and out of hypnosis, to no avail. Stan seemed to care very much for Joyce and was a good husband in most ways, failing primarily in the romantic/sexual arena. Perhaps this made him only a good roommate, but had Joyce also been uninterested in sex, they probably would have had a great marriage.

We were reminded of this months after we stopped seeing Joyce and Stan. We were consulted on a nonsexual matter by a couple a few years older than they. When this couple noticed all the sex books in our bookcase, they brought up the subject and told us their story, "just so you'll know that people can be happy without sex." Both had realized from adolescence that they differed from their peers because of a lack of sexual interest. They dated and experimented with sex, their experiences confirming their differences. Each decided to try to find an opposite-sex counterpart. The woman found one and married him, but he turned out to be an alcoholic, and they soon divorced. The man kept looking, and one day they found each other. They had been married almost 20 years and had not once had sex. They were physically affectionate and slept in each other's arms, but no one's genitals were touched. We saw this couple for five sessions about their difficulty (the nonsexual one about which they had consulted us), and our impression was that they were indeed well matched in almost all areas, loving, and quite content.

We once suggested to Joyce the possibility of decreasing her sexual interest (though we were aware that there was nothing at all abnormal about it), but she refused. Even though it was causing her great difficulty with Stan, she felt her erotic feelings were an essential part of her. However, this seems a useful option to consider with other couples in this predicament.

We considered the impact of Stan's work on his sex drive, but that also got us nowhere. He and Joyce had been on numerous long and short vacations, including two that we suggested, with no increase in erotic feeling. In fact, trips tended to make things worse, because Joyce hoped something might happen and Stan knew of and feared her expectation.

Although hypnosis did not produce any great results with this couple, it did generate the clearest statement of Stan's position—the answers to our questions from the part named "Zilch." Perhaps we should have taken those answers more seriously and suggested termination at that point. In any case, we hope, despite this evidence that hypnosis cannot cause miracles, that it will not be condemned for our failure.

The only thing we can think of that we did not do was to explore the equilibrium of the marriage: Stan's lack of interest provoking Joyce's outburst, followed by treatment of some sort that always failed, followed by resignation and trying to live with it, followed sooner or later by Joyce's anger and yet another treatment. Was there something in this pattern that might have proved useful? We do not know. Apparently, however, the circle has been broken. There have been no treatments in over a year, and none are planned.

We remain puzzled by this case and a few others like it that we have seen. In each, exhaustive medical testing revealed no abnormalities. And in the two instances where testosterone injections were given, they proved of little value. The speculation closest to hand is simply that there is a small group of individuals, both men and women, who for undetermined reasons have little interest in sex and derive little pleasure from it when they have it. There is really nothing startling about this observation. If we assume that sexual appetite, like so many human characteristics, is distributed in a bell-shaped curve, we should expect at one extreme to have a small number of people whose desires are virtually insatiable. That they exist is attested to by the fact that we have labels for them—"satyrs" and "nymphomaniacs." We should also expect, at the other extreme, a small number of people who have essentially no interest in sex. We believe that Stan is an excellent example of those at this extreme. What we have said about sexual desire is also true of sexual enjoyment. Some people derive great pleasure from their erotic activities, and some derive very little. Obviously, there tends to be a high correlation between enjoyment and desire. Whether the reasons for being at either extreme on these two variables—desire and enjoyment—are primarily constitutional or a result of learning is not a question we can answer.

It is clear, as illustrated by the couple we saw for nonsexual reasons, that those who have no sexual desire can find marital contentment, provided that they attract mates with similar inclinations. The problems come when they marry those who, like Joyce, have discrepant appetites. Exactly how to deal with such couples in therapy is not at all clear. It seems unethical to engage such couples in treatment, especially of long duration, when the probability of success is so low. On the other hand, we have seen so few couples like them that we have been unable to determine when it is fair to conclude that failure is far more likely than success.

Both of the cases presented here were examples of ISD, whereas many of the ones we see represent desire disparities or occasionally sexual aversion. We use hypnosis in about 70%–80% of the desire cases we see, usually with beneficial results, although not all of these cases would be called successes.

Although we used uncovering techniques in both of the presented cases, we do not find them necessary in all cases. Many times, some combination of goal imagery, process imagery, positive suggestion, and posthypnotic suggestion suffices. In some cases, for instance, we use conventional marital (or hypnotic) techniques for working on the anger or other relationship issues that are decreasing or increasing the sexual appetite of one partner; then, if more work is required, we use the previously mentioned "master control room" technique to bring desire to the level the couple wants. In other cases, we may use hypnotic techniques to work on the main issue or conflict, such as spending too much time at work.

Hypnotic techniques are almost infinitely varied. As with other therapeutic methods, their variety and effectiveness depend primarily on the creativity and sensitivity of the therapist. We hope that our presentation will encourage therapists previously unacquainted with hypnosis, as well as those who have used it only occasionally, to consider further training in and use of hypnosis.[2] As we have indicated earlier, there are essentially no contraindications to the use of hypnosis, provided that the therapist is well trained in its application. While not every single client can or will successfully use it, the vast majority of clients can and will do so. Hypnotic techniques work equally well with men and women, whether the therapist is male or female. Although some therapists who do not use hypnosis have raised questions about the possibility of hypnosis complicating transference and countertransference issues, we have not had such difficulties, and neither have the hypnotherapists we know.

The methods of hypnosis have much to recommend them: They are relatively easy to learn and use, permit endless variety and creativity on the part of the therapist, and are very effective with many sexual and nonsexual problems. They are also totally natural, coming down to nothing more than helping clients use the natural abilities of their own minds to best advantage.

References

Ader, R. (Ed.). (1981). *Psychoneuroimmunology.* New York: Academic Press.

Apfelbaum, B. (1972). *On once-a-week therapy.* Unpublished manuscript.

Araoz, D. (1982). *Hypnosis and sex therapy.* New York: Bruuner/Mazel.

Araoz, D. (1985). *The new hypnosis.* New York: Brunner/Mazel.

Baker, E. L. (1986). Hypnosis with psychotic and borderline patients. In B. Zilbergeld, M. G. Edelstien, & D. L. Araoz (Eds.), *Hypnosis: Questions and answers.* New York: Norton.

Bandura, A. (1977). Self-efficacy: Toward a unifying theory of behavior change. *Psychological Review, 84,* 191–215.

Barber, J. (1980). Hypnosis and the unhypnotizable. *American Journal of Clinical Hypnosis, 23,* 4–9.

Barnett, E. A. (1981). *Analytical hypnotherapy.* Kingston, Ontario: Junica.

Brenman, M., & Gill, M. M. (1947). *Hypnotherapy.* New York: International Universities Press.

Brown, J. M., & Chaves, J. F. (1980). Hypnosis in the treatment of sexual dysfunction. *Journal of Sex and Marital Therapy, 6,* 63–74.

Buranelli, V. (1975). *The wizard from Vienna: Franz Anton Mesmer.* New York: Coward, McCann & Geoghegan.

Carnes, P. (1983). *Out of the shadows: Understanding sexual addiction.* Minneapolis: Comp-Care.

2. Monthly training workshops are available through the American Society of Clinical Hypnosis, 2250 East Devon Avenue, Suite 336, Des Plaines, Illinois 60018. Phone (312) 297-3317.

Cheek, D. B., & LeCron, L. M. (1968). *Clinical hypnotherapy*. New York: Grune & Stratton.

Clarke, J. C., & Jackson, J. A. (1983). *Hypnosis and behavior therapy*. New York: Springer.

Crasilneck, H. B. (1979). The use of hypnosis in the control of psychogenic impotency: The second follow-up study of 100 consecutive males. *Australian Journal of Clinical Hypnosis, 7*, 147–153.

Crasilneck, H. B. (1982). The use of hypnotherapy in the treatment of psychogenic impotency: The third follow-up study of 100 consecutive males. *American Journal of Clinical Hypnosis, 25*, 52–61.

Crasilneck, H. B., & Hall, J. (1985). *Clinical hypnosis: Principles and applications* (2nd ed.). New York: Grune & Stratton.

Dush, D. M., Hirt, M. L., & Schroeder, H. (1983). Self-statement modification with adults: A meta-analysis. *Psychological Bulletin, 94*, 408–422.

Gardner, G., & Olness, K. (1981). *Hypnosis and hypnotherapy with children*. New York: Grune & Stratton.

Gurman, A., & Kniskern, D. (1978a). Deterioration in marital and family therapy: Empirical, clinical and conceptual issues. *Family Process, 17*, 3–20.

Gurman, A., & Kniskern, D. (1978b). Research on marital and family therapy: Progress, perspective and prospect. In S. Garfield & A. Bergin (Eds.), *Handbook of psychotherapy and behavior change* (2nd ed.). New York: Wiley.

Hammond, D. C. (1985). Treatment of inhibited sexual desire. In J. Zeig (Ed.), *Ericksonian psychotherapy: Vol. 2. Clinical applications*. New York: Brunner/Mazel.

Hammond, D. C. (1987). Hypnotic induction & deepening techniques. In W. Wester (Ed.), *Clinical hypnosis: A case management approach*. Cincinnati: Behavioral Science Center.

Hammond, D. C., Bartsch, C., Grant, C. W., & McGhee, M. In press. Comparison of self-directed and tape-assisted self-hypnosis. *American Journal of Clinical Hypnosis*.

Hammond, D. C., & Stanfield, K. (1977). *Multidimensional psychotherapy*. Champaign, IL: Institute for Personality and Ability Testing.

Hilgard, E. R., & Hilgard, J. R. (1983). *Hypnosis in the relief of pain*. Los Altos, CA: William Kaufmann.

Ikemi, Y., & Nakagawa, S. A. (1962). Psychosomatic study of contagious dermatitis. *Kyushu Journal of Medical Science, 13*, 335–352.

Kaplan, H. S. (1979). *Disorders of sexual desire*. New York: Brunner/Mazel.

Kohl, R. (1962). Pathological reactions of marital partners to improvement of patients. *American Journal of Psychiatry, 118*, 1036–1041.

Kroger, W., & Fezler, W. (1976). *Hypnosis and behavior modification*. Philadelphia: J. B. Lippincott.

LaBaw, W. L. (1975). Autohypnosis in hemophilia. *Haematologia, 9*, 103–110.

Lazarus, A. A. (1976). *Multimodal behavior therapy*. New York: Springer.

Lazarus, A. A. (1984). *In the mind's eye*. New York: Guilford Press.

Lief, H. (1977). What's new in sex research? Inhibited sexual desire. *Medical Aspects of Human Sexuality, 11*(7), 94–95.

Masters, W. H., & Johnson, V. E. (1970). *Human sexual inadequacy*. Boston: Little, Brown.

Orne, M. T. (1980). On the construct of hypnosis: How its definition affects research and its clinical application. In G. D. Burrows & L. Dennerstein (Eds.), *Handbook of hypnosis and psychosomatic medicine*. Amsterdam: Elsevier/North-Holland.

Ritterman, M. (1983). *Using hypnosis in family therapy*. San Francisco: Jossey-Bass.

Rossi, E. L. (Ed.). (1980). *The collected papers of Milton H. Erickson on hypnosis* (4 vols.). New York: Irvington.

Sarbin, T. R., & Slagle, R. W. (1979). Hypnosis and psychophysiological outcomes. In E. Fromm & R. Shor (Eds.), *Hypnosis: Developments in research and new perspectives*. Chicago: Aldine.

Semans, J. H. (1956). Premature ejaculation: A new approach. *Southern Medical Journal, 49*, 353–357.

Shor, R. E. (1979). The fundamental problem in hypnosis research as viewed from historical perspectives. In E. Fromm & R. Shor (Eds.), *Hypnosis: Developments in research and new perspectives*. Chicago: Aldine.

Stuart, F., Hammond, D. C., & Pett, M. (1986). Psychological characteristics of women with inhibited sexual desire. *Journal of Sex and Marital Therapy, 12*(2), 108–115.

Stuart, F., Hammond, D. C., & Pett, M. (1987). Inhibited sexual desire in women. *Archives of Sexual Behavior, 16,* (91–105).

Watkins, J. G. (1971). The affect bridge: A hypnoanalytic technique. *International Journal of Clinical and Experimental Hypnosis, 19,* 10–12.

Watkins, J. G., & Watkins, H. H. (1981). Ego-state therapy. In R. J. Corsini (Ed.), *Handbook of innovative psychotherapies*. New York: Wiley.

Wolberg, L. (1948). *Medical hypnosis*. New York: Grune & Stratton.

Zilbergeld, B. (1986a). Choosing inductions. In B. Zilbergeld, M. G. Edelstien, & D. L. Araoz (Eds.), *Hypnosis: Questions and answers*. New York: Norton.

Zilbergeld, B. (1986b). Using result imagery with sex problems. In B. Zilbergeld, M. G. Edelstien, and D. L. Araoz (Eds.), *Hypnosis: Questions and answers*. New York: Norton.

Zilbergeld, B., & Ellison, C. R. (1980). Desire discrepancies and arousal problems in sex therapy. In S. R. Leiblum & L. A. Pervin (Eds.), *Principles and practice of sex therapy*. New York: Guilford Press.

Zilbergeld, B., & Lazarus, A. A. (1987). *Mind power: Getting what you want through mental training*. Boston: Little, Brown.

Systems and Interactional Perspectives

III

9

Inhibited Sexual Desire: The Masters and Johnson Institute Treatment Model

MARK F. SCHWARTZ AND WILLIAM H. MASTERS

No discussion of sex therapy would be complete without a presentation of the Masters and Johnson Institute's therapeutic approach. Although their earliest work omitted specific discussion of the desire phase in the sexual response cycle, Masters and his colleagues have more recently affirmed the importance of desire difficulties as a legitimate clinical reality. Moreover, reports from the Institute suggest a major clinical involvement with individuals and couples presenting with these problems.

A number of key issues are raised in this chapter by Schwartz and Masters. First, we find a forceful restatement of their fundamental belief that "sex is a natural function," and that desire, like other components of sexual response, flows naturally in the absence of significant roadblocks. Specifically, these authors assert that desire exists in all individuals, and that it emerges spontaneously in all nonconflictual and loving relationships. Furthermore, they view dysfunctional and destructive relationship dynamics as the most salient factor in inhibiting sexual interest and expression. Not surprisingly, their treatment model is interpersonally based, with their familiar emphasis on the dictum that "there is no uninvolved partner." Moreover, the treatment of desire-phase disorders is quite similar to that of the other sexual dysfunctions, and prognosis is reported to be "no poorer than that for treating [other] sexual dysfunctions."

Schwartz and Masters also take a novel stance in defining and diagnosing desire disorders. In particular, they maintain that sexual frequency is a poor criterion for diagnosing inhibited sexual desire (ISD), as are masturbatory behavior and sexual fantasy. Rather, a desire problem is identified when an individual evidences "low initiatory behavior and/or a persistently negative receptivity to sexual approaches by an established partner." In addition, they differentiate desire problems into those involving sexual dissatisfaction and sexual aversion. Although Schwartz and Masters view desire disorders as fundamentally similar to other sexual dysfunctions, they acknowledge that greater levels of emotional distress may result from these problems.

Only in the case of long-standing intimacy disorders do these authors suggest that long-term psychotherapy is necessary. Rather, they believe that most, if not all, of the intra- and interpersonal contributing factors to ISD can be treated within the traditional 2-week, rapid-treatment format. A number of interesting observations and treatment suggestions are offered, however, including the notion of "whetting the sexual appetite" and scripted playfulness exercises. The overriding emphasis in their treatment approach is on resolving relationship conflicts, which often involves focusing on distancer–pursuer dynamics and other intimacy issues.

Regrettably, Schwartz and Masters have chosen not to illustrate these important clinical issues with case illustrations. While one could easily imagine the kinds of couples for whom this approach would be well suited, specific case examples and commentary would have been helpful in providing a more detailed picture of their approach. We hope that future Institute publications will pick up where the present chapter leaves off.

Mark F. Schwartz, Sc.D., is a consultant to the Masters and Johnson Institute, St. Louis; he is also Assistant Professor of Psychiatry at Tulane University and Director of the Clinics for Marital and Sex Therapy, New Orleans.

William H. Masters, M.D., is the former Director of the Masters and Johnson Institute and is presently Cochair of the Institute's Board of Directors. He is one of the "founding fathers" of contemporary sex therapy.

All humans are born with the natural functions of sexual desire and sexual response. Each culture has a range of appropriate and inappropriate behavior for males and females, out of which sexual responsivity to selected individuals and images unfolds. The presence or absence of adequate parenting and nurturing during childhood and adolescence strongly influences the capacity to master the environment, to engender self-esteem, and to establish and maintain close attachments. Adequate parental role models and caretaking allow a person's gender identity to unfold naturally within established cultural expectations. Genital rehearsals then give an individual physiological feedback and help the individual to integrate his or her unfolding sexuality and developing personality.

As an individual matures, sexual desire manifests itself as an attraction to a person the individual perceives as appealing. This attraction can evolve into a casual or a committed relationship. Once a pair-bond is established, sexual desire is a natural way of expressing the sense of intimacy that develops within the relationship. Therefore, anything that enhances or inhibits relational intimacy may positively or negatively influence an individual's level of sexual desire. Sex is innately pleasurable, unless something mitigates that pleasure. Couples who evidence little intimacy in the living room usually will feel distant from each other inside the bedroom. That is, for some couples, frequency of sexual desire and behavior becomes both a mirror and a manifestation of intimacy in the relationship. Therefore, persons who experience (for intra- or interpersonal reasons) boredom, pressure, fatigue, anger, guilt, fear, anxiety, or suffocation in a relationship are "entitled" to a low level of sexual desire (Apfelbaum, 1983).

If a person with minimal desire continually forces himself or herself or is consistently pressured by a partner into sexual activity, sexual dysfunction or sexual aversion (a phobic reaction to sexual activity) may develop. Alternatively, some husbands and wives may respond with erection or lubrication to sexual opportunity with an attractive mate, and may thus conclude that they are highly aroused sexually. But coexisting relational distresses may result in low or even absent sexual desire, despite obvious genital responsiveness.

The Masters and Johnson Institute model for treatment of desire-phase disorders is similar to the treatment modality for sexual dysfunction. The relationship is the primary focus of treatment, rather than the symptomatology. Intimacy engendered in the relationship is the vehicle of change. When a couple is placed in social isolation and follows specific suggestions to catalyze increasing levels of intimacy between partners (in and out of the bedroom), the roadblocks that have interfered with sexual desire are usually readily activated. Once identified, therapists use techniques of directive psychotherapy to neutralize these roadblocks. When the couple can interact affectionately as a team, with minimal conflict, they tend to evidence their newfound level of intimacy by experiencing a slowly elevating level of sexual desire.

Experience suggests that the prognosis for treating desire-phase disorders is no poorer than that for treating sexual dysfunctions. The prognosis for the treatment of both types of sexual inadequacies obviously depends on specific contributing factors. In cases of individual psychopathology, or cases in which a person is terrified of closeness, or cases in which an individual is extremely dependent or wants to hurt the partner, prognosis depends on the skills of the psychotherapist more than any other single factor.

Definitional Issues

For most people, sexual arousal is a function of situational rather than dispositional factors. From their own biased point of view, many men and women freely label their relational partners as possessed of a low or high level of sexual desire. Frequently, this label serves as a self-fulfilling prophecy or becomes part of the gender role the gratuitously labeled partner assumes. If sexually active partners consistently describe different appetites for sex and are unable to compromise, the problem is labeled as "sexual dissatisfaction" instead of "sexual disorder" and is diagnosed as disparate levels of sexual interest. The diagnosis of "inhibited sexual desire" (ISD) is used only when an individual evidences low initiatory behavior and/or a persistently negative receptivity to sexual approaches by an established partner. Frequency of sexual encounters is avoided as a diagnostic standard, because of extraneous influences such as age or health. Masturbatory behavior and sexual fantasy are not reliable indicators of ISD, except in cases of hypogonadism (Bancroft, 1983).

The diagnosis of "sexual aversion" is employed when a person becomes phobic and reacts to the initiation of sexual activity with panic, disgust, or illness. When seen at the Institute, some ISD cases have appeared to be in a state of retrograde transition in desire-phase disorder: The individuals evidence a minor degree of accompanying sexual aversion.

Psychological Contributing Factors

The Spiral Effect

When sexual interaction is persistently distressing to a couple, one partner tends to withdraw from the sexual experience. This starts a "spiral effect"— a series of deleterious influences on the levels of sexual desire within the relationship. Both partners may label the person more affected as hyposexual. The partner with the greater desire may feel unloved or undesirable, and is likely to increase the frequency of his or her demand for sexual interaction in order to bolster the inevitably deflated ego. In turn, this elevated level of sexual demand creates a sense of performance pressure for the inhibited partner that further lowers his or her level of desire. In self-defense, the inhibited partner may try to respond to this sexual pressure, even though experiencing little desire. In time, such forced sexual performances may result in sexual dysfunction or sexual aversion.

Further spiral effects may include the false belief that the partner with the lower level of sexual desire is no longer in love. In reacting to the low-interest partner's apparent sexual withdrawal, the partner with greater desire may evidence feelings of insecurity about his or her body image and may subsequently develop problems with self-esteem, depression, irritability, or guilt. The final results of the spiral effect are multiple marital problems, usually based on deteriorations in communicative interchange and in problem-solving abilities, which further complicate the relationship.

Sexual Dysfunction as a Secondary Complaint

In the Institute's patient population, ISD is encountered far more frequently as a secondary complaint than as a primary factor in the individual's or couple's concern about sexual inadequacy. Once a state of sexual dysfunction has been established, men and women usually reduce their frequency of sexual encounters or essentially withdraw from sexual interaction. If the impotent man or the anorgasmic woman has experienced a sufficient number of failures to function effectively in sexual interchange, feelings of anxiety or even fear of performance will develop in anticipation of, or during, further sexual encounters.

Once performance anxieties are firmly established and the sexually distressed individuals follow the natural tendency to avoid exposure to sexual encounters as much as possible, the secondary effect of this escape mechanism is a marked reduction in the level of sexual desire. If the sexual dysfunctional individual can console himself or herself with the excuse of little or no sexual interest, there is a greater chance of avoiding sexual encounters and the threat of sexual failure. It is generally true that the longer the individual's history of existent sexual dysfunction is, the more firmly imbedded is the secondary complaint of ISD.

If there is an established relationship, the dysfunctional partner's secondarily acquired ISD usually creates more distress within the relationship than a primary complaint of impotence or anorgasmia. While the functional partner frequently experiences a sense of personal rejection if his or her partner is impotent or anorgasmic, the feelings of rejection are rarely as overwhelming as those occasioned when the ISD partner repeatedly refuses to participate in mutual sexual interaction.

The Institute has long taken the position that the husband of the anorgasmic wife and the wife of the impotent husband usually have problems that require psychotherapeutic support. It is for this reason that the Institute has always insisted on treating existent couples for sexual dysfunction or disorder, rather than individuals. There is no better example in support of this contention than the problems evidenced by the husband or wife of an ISD partner, regardless of whether the desire-phase disorder has been primarily or secondarily acquired.

Attention and Labeling Deficits

Sexual feelings are manifested naturally when children feel permission to explore and discover their own genital sensations. As they mature, they need biofeedback, experimentation, and information to move these sensations into orgasmic responsiveness. When children are taught not to explore and discover, and sexual feelings remain in hibernation or become associated with shame and guilt, genital sexuality may never unfold. When they grow into adult sexual interactions, they may feel uncomfortable with their body image and say they "feel very little." Cognitively, they are not able to attach erotic significance to their genital sensations. Women often will present with orgasmic dysfunction. In some cases, however, women reach orgasm easily, but feel little subjective satisfaction. This behavior pattern eventually may lead to ISD. Men with such backgrounds are susceptible to erectile dysfunction or ISD.

If the person primarily focuses on pleasing the partner, and sex is a manifestation of self-efficacy (Bandura, 1978) as a man or woman, a great deal of performance pressure is created and withdrawal may eventually result. Similarly, if the person makes statements such as "I don't feel anything," "It's numb," "Is that all there is?", or "Why don't I feel more?", he or she has evidenced an all-or-nothing perception. These individuals minimize what they do feel and fail to take the initiative to create more stimulation. They become victims, feeling that there is nothing they can do to increase their arousal levels. Eventually, because of an absence of pleasure and the feeling of too much effort, they stop initiating sex or responding to sexual approaches and are diagnosed as having ISD.

The range of erotic imagery that most people use to become sexually aroused is relatively narrow. This imagery is the doorkeeper of the stimuli that elicit sexual desire. It is common for people to use imagery to enhance their anticipation or involvement in sex, but many have not been given cultural permission to develop this skill with creativity. Sometimes a person's sexual imagery is restricted by fear or anxiety associated with a particular form of sexual behavior. Until such a person can formulate a positive attitude or desensitize himself or herself by trying an activity (with a partner), such as oral sex, the person often cannot find images of the specific activity arousing. A person may be able to imagine sexual desire only with those partners who embody a certain physical appearance, personality, or socioeconomic status. If a partner changes (e.g., gains weight or encounters financial difficulties) and no longer fits comfortably into the required categories, the image user may lose sexual desire.

Relational Transactions

When couples bond, they form explicit and implicit contracts. If these contracts are broken, ISD may result. For instance, a couple may take the implicit contract that he will be the provider, she the homemaker. If either fails in his or her role, sexual desire may be affected. Desire also can be influenced when the contract is contradictory or confusing. If a woman expects her husband to be a busy surgeon, yet also wants him to share housekeeping and parenting duties equally, she may become angry and lose sexual desire when he cannot comply with her theoretically conceived role model. In some double-standard relationships, the husband may experience an obvious reduction in desire level if the wife, working out of the home with mutual agreement, begins to earn more money than he does, or starts making decisions without consulting him.

A common factor in the development of low sexual desire is the inability of a partner to express hurt, frustration, or anger—an inability that keeps these problems from being identified and solved. ISD is most often related to expressed or unexpressed anger and resentment in a relationship, and the reactive distance the partners establish to accommodate such feelings. Both men and women tend to rationalize when they feel irritated or frustrated, rather than allowing themselves to express their dissatisfactions. Men in particular rarely acquire a vocabulary to express feelings effectively. Closely related in frequency of occurrence are relational power struggles in which partner *A* continually tries to make sure that partner *B* thinks, feels, and acts in the "right way," which is, of course, partner *A*'s way. Some couples' only form of intimacy appears to be when they are engaged in the struggle or when they "make up," which is when they are sexual.

Another contributing factor to low desire is the lack of courtship in marriage. A couple may fail to give a high priority to having fun, playing, and being romantic in their marriage. Instead, they fill their time with work-role obligations and childrearing. They forget—or never discover— how to be spontaneous and enjoy non-goal-oriented interactions. Their sexual experience mirrors their serious, hard-working lifestyles and becomes boring. When non-goal-oriented play and sexual interaction are given a low priority in any relationship, a low level of sexual interest on the part of at least one of the partners is almost inevitable.

Finally, when sexual interaction becomes one partner's means of reward and punishment in the relationship, this attitude, especially if it is of long standing, may interfere with the natural manifestations of sexual desire on the part of the targeted partner.

Issues of Intimacy

As with sexual dysfunction, there are also "deeper levels" of contributing factors in desire disorders, which often require intervention. Sexual desire may become the fulcrum of closeness and distance in a relationship. A sexually disordered couple may have systematically established a homeostatic balance of closeness versus distance, independence versus dependence, freedom versus domination, privacy versus self-disclosure—all with minimal mutual sexual involvement. Successful treatment of the couple's sexual disorder usually requires realignment of the entire interactive system. Therefore, treatment of ISD cases typically requires the therapist to identify the factors that have contributed to or reduced the capacity for intimacy in the relationship. At the same time, the therapist must provide support for alterations of the balances in the relational styles that couples have established.

Ambivalent Attachment and Sexual Desire

Many persons have ambivalent feelings about vulnerability and closeness. They frequently have experienced enough abuse, smothering, neglect, or pain as children to make them fear and distrust closeness. They automatically respond as though the relationship is "not safe" (Bowlby, 1969, 1973). These persons may experience passionate sexual feelings during the phase of anxious attachment, when they are attempting to solicit affection and love. But once they have successfully "caught" the partner, they react by reverting to a low level of sexual desire.

A large number of dysfunctional transactions in couples that stem from problems with closeness acquired in childhood could be catalogued. Several are discussed here to show how lack of sexual desire easily becomes embedded within a couple's style of intimacy. Just as demonstrated by Harlow and his colleagues' research into the affectional systems of monkeys, there are interactions between parents and child that influence the child's eventual capacity to form adult pair bonds. Children learn to elicit warmth from unloving parents by taking care of siblings, trying to be perfect, feigning illness, or any other means of emotional manipulation. These patterns may eventually reappear as a repetition compulsion in adult relationships, particularly when there is relational stress. Some people evidence a repetitive compulsion to choose battering, rejecting, or alcoholic partners. It is as if they are still trying to achieve mastery in an earlier struggle with a rejecting parent and end up transferring their unfinished business to their spouses. They have come to expect and accept neglect, abuse, chaos, and hassle, and feel ill at ease and "unloved" without it. They may provide sex to meet their partners' needs, but are unlikely to enjoy it.

Another pattern of repetitive compulsion may occur within a person who, as a youngster, was live ammunition for two fighting parents or who was competitively traded between relatives. In adulthood, such persons often triangulate by bringing a second lover into their relationship and then agonize over which one to choose. Sexual desire seesaws with the lovers.

In a diametrically opposite response pattern, some children cope with difficult family situations by not listening. When such a child grows up, he or she often supports this behavior pattern by choosing a dependent, critical spouse who resembles a parent. Then the person continues the turned-off response pattern, which makes the spouse even more frustrated and critical. When the dependent spouse evidences helplessness in dealing with life's problems, he or she frequently becomes jealous of the nonverbal partner's perceived superiority. This creates a double bind that makes initiating sex difficult, encourages ISD, and prevents the couple from developing significant levels of intimacy.

Another observed behavior pattern occurs when one partner places the other on the proverbial pedestal. This may result when a person marries someone who resembles an aloof, neglecting parent or the parent to whom he or she was overbonded. The relationship frequently moves quickly from high levels of desire to ISD on the part of the worshipful partner as expectations of perfection are not met.

Those who are ambivalent about being close may be more afraid of the idea of being vulnerable than of actually being vulnerable. Sexual desire is often chronically low in such individuals. They fear that if they lower their guard, something terrible will happen. They are also afraid of their reaction to this terrifying possibility. Not being in control at all times during sexual interaction is also frightening for these individuals, and this fear may interfere with sexual pleasure and (particularly in the female) orgasmic release.

Enmeshment and Sexual Desire

Whenever a man and a woman are psychosocially fused or enmeshed in a relationship, levels of codependence usually exist in which one partner seems to be vitally necessary for the other's well-being or even survival. Such closeness may repress sexual desire. It is as though the partners are too filial to arouse each other sexually. These persons may feel they have little intrinsic meaning of their own. With such codependence, boundaries are blurred so that the couple cannot see where one individual's personality ends and the other's begins. Each feels responsible for the other's unhappiness and low sexual desire seems like one of the only functional means of separateness. Sexual initiation sometimes appears normal, although actual sex is frequently devoid of feeling and passion until one partner tries to pull away. The partner looking for greater distance can be described as a "seeker." This causes the other partner, looking for greater closeness, to become a "merger" (Avery-Clark, personal communication, 1982). Under stress, the merger clings to the partner and blames himself or herself, while the seeker tries to isolate himself or herself and blames the partner. The merger's sexual desire increases proportionally as the seeker's sexual desire decreases.

Over time, persons overwhelmed by the psychosocial constructions of an enmeshed relationship may move against their partners by initiating variant behavior, such as compulsive sexual activity outside the relationship, incest, or battering. In these cases, the perpetrator harbors a rarely expressed reservoir of rage that frequently relates to childhood distress. These people are characteristically inept in adult relationships; they experience chronically low levels of self-esteem and sexual desire. They use compulsive sexual activity in an attempt to escape their relational priorities. When their compulsive behavior is neutralized, they need to establish genuine levels of relational intimacy in order to feel sexual desire. ISD is frequently a residual effect when hypersexual compulsive behavior is successfully controlled by effective psychotherapy. Therefore, hypersexual and hyposexual behavior are actually two sides of the same coin, and are indicative of intimacy disorder.

Treatment Issues

The Short-Term, Rapid-Treatment Approach

A prevalent belief in the field of sex therapy is that when reversal of sexual dysfunction or dissatisfaction is impeded by immediate factors such as spectator roles or performance anxieties, brief psychotherapy is useful; however, when more involved issues are identified such as intimacy disorders, it is thought that longer-term psychodynamic psychotherapy is required. The Institute's position is that many of the more involved issues can be treated successfully within the traditional rapid-treatment format. Like sexual dysfunctions, many disorders of sexual desire stem from basic misinformation, lack of experience, or destructive relational transactions. These can be effectively treated with the permission-giving and educational components of sex therapy. Even when deeper issues are involved, brief psychotherapy can produce a reversal of symptoms, which in turn facilitates the resolution of these underlying issues. Our approach is to do as little as necessary to reverse the symptoms of ISD, and to insure that the symptoms do not appear during the 2-year follow-up.

If a couple is placed in social isolation and seen on a daily basis for 14 days, with as few interruptions from work and family as possible, deep-seated roadblocks to the ISD partner's sexual desire usually will manifest themselves or will be catalyzed by therapeutic intervention. Controlled therapeutic situations allow the therapist to increase the couple's skills in intimate interchange. These skills include sending and hearing each other's messages; problem solving; demonstrativeness; responsiveness to each other's needs; creativity in socializing; ways of dealing with long-term hostilities; and ways of handling ambivalence regarding closeness, vulnerability, trust, and bonding. Each day in therapy is both diagnostic and therapeutic because more information about the couple's interactive patterns continually unfolds.

If a couple manifests transactions that are destructive to feelings of intimacy and sexual desire, the therapist actively directs the couple to their mutually stated goals in several ways: (1) by confronting the transaction; (2) by pointing out its potentially destructive consequences; (3) by offering skills to improve the couple's interactions; and (4) by providing specific suggestions on ways and means to practice the new skills. Individuals within the dyad are simultaneously provided support to increase their power in the relationship.

When the therapist sees the couple daily, the partners usually are increasingly motivated by observing rapidly developing changes in their behavior. They feel increased self-efficacy, and they enjoy the newly learned techniques of positive communicative interchange and the resulting affectionate feelings. In turn, this sense of relational well-being increases motivation for further improvement and fuels the process of behavioral alteration.

The goal in short-term, time-limited therapy is to help each individual in a relationship to feel sufficient self-confidence that he or she will not be threatened by the partner's acting and thinking differently or becoming temporarily too close or distant. Whenever an individual in a relationship attempts to coerce, manipulate, or control the other partner, resentment begins to build. The result can be a relational power struggle. Systems of enmeshment and feelings of ambivalent attachment are maintained by such power struggles. The Institute's therapeutic approach is to utilize the relationship as a vehicle for change in the individual. Once the partners feel they are on the same team rather than opponents, and accepted rather than judged, enormous individual change is possible. The partners learn to do small things for each other to show they care. A give-to-get attitude is fostered, reversing the negative spirals. Individuals who have been extremely controlling because of their fear of rejection or abandonment look into the therapist's directive mirror, and acknowledge their destructive behavior and its undesirable consequences. They feel more secure as they minimize the risk that either partner will leave the relationship. These behavioral and attitudinal changes take the pressure off sexual interaction as the couple's only means to express love.

It is common that one partner is threatened by the other's change. In a cotherapy model, the same-sex therapist establishes a degree of rapport with the same-sex client to support him or her in adjusting to change. The single therapist needs to establish rapport with each client, while simultaneously encouraging exchange of affect between the couple, rather than a more traditional transferential relationship between the client and therapist.

The husband and wife also learn how to recognize negative emotional states—boredom, fear, hurt—and then how to use these emotions as signals for creative action to support the relationship. This leads to the learning of self-responsibility and gives the individuals practice at not playing the role of victim or blaming the partner for unhappiness. Husband and wife discover that they do not have to be victims of their negative feelings, as they experience positive feelings created by behavior changes. It is this central concept that eventually provides the couple with the opportunity to enjoy an increased level of sexual desire. One very common misconception is that sexual interest "just happens" when a person loves or cares for his or her partner. In other words, the person remains basically passive and is just "struck" by desire. This belief is closely related to the "love conquers all" and "the male is always ready" myths. The strategy in dispelling myths such as these revolves around teaching the concept of sex as a natural function (Masters & Johnson, 1972).

Sex as a Natural Function

"Sex as a natural function" means that an individual's ability to function as a sexual being is congenitally established. Sexual functioning is in the same category as other natural biological functions, such as respiratory, bowel, or bladder activity. Erection, lubrication, desire develop spontaneously in healthy individuals. What makes sexual functioning appear different from other bodily functions is its exceptional capacity for voluntary control, thus making it more susceptible to taboos and social pressures. Sexual appetite *is* subject to psychosocial trauma, the influence of ill health, and repression by antagonistic marital interaction. Sexual hunger should be resolved when present but never forced if absent, and should always be negotiable, because two people's sexual appetites are frequently not at the same level.

To resolve differences in levels of sexual appetite, individuals can "lend themselves" and begin touching to determine whether they are indeed sexually hungry or whether they can "build" their appetite, instead of reacting with an uncompromising "yes" or "no." Encouraging the couple to enjoy touching, to appreciate a low level of excitement, and to investigate other alternatives to intercourse also allows for more compromise. Touching becomes equated with desire for closeness and may be a signal that one or the other or both partners want "more."

If the sexual appetite of one partner is at a low ebb, too often the emotions of hurt, anger, or rejection are evidenced by the other partner. When these emotions surface, most "low-ebb" men and women force themselves into undesired sexual performance to relieve their partners' frustration. Once a couple accepts the concept of sex as a natural function, the partners are able to comfortably communicate changes in sexual desire as easily as they communicate their demands for food.

The hungers for food, for sex, for affection, and for intimacy are all expressions of natural appetites that vary according to time, place, and circumstance. To attempt to control such natural appetites by rigid, arbitrary standards or by an imaginary concept of "normality" makes sexual interaction a performance. Culturally derived misconceptions, such as the belief that the male should always initiate sex, force an individual to react or perform because of pressure from the partner's needs.

Another analogy to the appetite for food is that sexual appetite can be enhanced. Variety and creativity may be added to a couple's sexual interaction to prevent boredom or erosion of interest. Some individuals may need to have fantasy facilitated or playfulness encouraged in their approach to sexuality. These alternatives are never presented with an emphasis on technique. Rather, they are introduced in the spirit of recreation, enjoyment, and enhancement of intimacy. The couple is encouraged to try new options, understanding that the unfamiliar is uncomfortable and that as familiarity increases, the level of comfort will usually increase as well. As the couple's repertoire of sexual options increases, the initiation of sex is no longer equated with intercourse. Without that implied pressure, sexual feelings tend to unfold naturally.

If needed, specific communicative skills are taught. Couples who have stopped exchanging important information are encouraged to talk about their life experiences before they met, to get to know each other better. This breaks the habit of editing the expressions of feelings. The partners also learn how to ask directly for what they want and how to make requests without eliciting defensiveness or recalcitrance in the other partner. Other skills, taught as needed, are active listening, negotiation, creative problem solving, conflict management, assertiveness, social interaction, courtship techniques, and play and time management.

This comprehensive therapeutic focus on the relationship for 14 days provides a powerful opportunity for alterations in the couple's previously unproductive patterns of interaction and in distressing levels of ISD. Once positive changes occur, couples learn to maintain these changes by monitoring themselves objectively. If old habits manifest themselves, the partners can usually identify their destructive interaction and discuss means of problem solving. If they are unsuccessful, the therapist remains available to intervene as much as needed during the 2 years immediately following the 2-week rapid-treatment phase of the Institute's therapeutic program.

Intervention for Manifestation of Intimacy Disorder

Typically, a patient will resist change in psychotherapy. Resistance brings to the foreground conflictual interaction within the individual or between the dyad, and directs the therapist's intervention. In therapy, the resistance is confronted, allowing the individual or couple to discard their dysfunctional system and build anew. Fears of sexual performance elicit a myriad of destructive responses in cases of sexual dysfunction. For example, one client left his partner while jogging in a dangerous park at night; another was rageful because the partner forgot to get the ice he requested; another invited relatives and "triangulated"; still another decided to reveal an affair from years ago; many clients attempt to engage the therapist in conflict. The therapist utilizes these manifestations to teach a couple how and why the partners are likely to distance themselves. Often individuals fear at some level that if they are not in control at all times things will fall apart, or their partners will hurt them, or they will become enraged, or their partners simply will not like them. They have been made to feel so shameful and unlovable at some point in their lives, and they have been sensitized to collect their negative environmental feedback so effectively, that they become terrified of vulnerability. It is critical that insight be provided as the resistance is manifested. Often the patient is reacting automatically to unresolved childhood traumas which range from an overbearing parent who undermined individuation to a parent who was incapable of loving. The patient is still responding to the re-creation of the childhood situation rather than to the reality of two adults seeking intimacy.

The therapist should slowly invite patients to test their irrational beliefs and eventually to discover that their relationship actually becomes stronger through self-disclosure, rather than the opposite. It may be hoped that the individuals begin to feel more powerful and less shameful as the relationship begins to provide the impetus for growth and change. In this process, sexual desire naturally increases. Differential appetites are no longer manifestations of a power struggle and become unattached to being loved, lovable, masculine, feminine, or generally "OK versus not OK." Without relational pressure, sexual desire is manifested naturally.

References

Apfelbaum, B. (1983). *Expanding the boundaries of sex therapy*. Berkely, CA: Berkeley Sex Therapy Group.

Bancroft, J. (1983). *Human sexuality and its problems*. Edinburgh: Churchill Livingstone.

Bandura, A. (1978). The self system in reciprocal determinism. *American Psychologist, 33*, 344–358.

Bowlby, J. (1969). *Attachment and loss: Vol. 1. Attachment*. New York: Basic Books.

Bowlby, J. (1973). *Attachment and loss: Vol. 2. Separation*. New York: Basic Books.

Masters, W. H., & Johnson, V. E. (1972, June 18). *Sex as a natural function*. Paper presented at the meeting of the American Medical Association, New York.

10

A Systems Perspective
on Sexual Desire

Johan Verhulst and Julia R. Heiman

Among the many challenges presented by desire disorders is the need for a more far-reaching or systemic perspective in evaluating and treating these problems. Beginning with their critique of the traditional disease model of pathogenesis in understanding complex interpersonal phenomena, Verhulst and Heiman propose that a systems perspective is ideally suited for an understanding of sexual difficulties in general, and of problems of desire in particular. From this perspective, low desire is viewed as essentially a problem in synchronization *or* coordination *of the sexual rhythms in a relationship. Verhulst and Heiman further emphasize the subjective nature of the complaint, as well as the interactional context in which the problem typically is manifested.*

While most theorists acknowledge the potential value of a systemic or interactional view of sexual desire and problems of desire, Verhulst and Heiman have taken the bold step of proposing a detailed and specific model of this type. Their approach is important in a number of respects. First, it represents an expansion and elaboration of their earlier statement of the "interactional approach" to sexual disorders (Verhulst & Heiman, 1979), which focused almost exclusively on "affect-regulated interactions," or the emotional responses that each partner brings to the sexual situation. In the present chapter, the authors have broadened their model to include a focus on the sensory/physiological and the cognitive dimensions of partner interactions as well. Each of these dimensions or "subsystems" is described in detail and is viewed as potentially contributing to low desire. Another noteworthy aspect of the model is its emphasis on systemic factors both within *and* between *partners in a relationship. Finally, these authors draw attention to the often overlooked subtleties in a sexual relationship, such as seduction rituals, territoriality conflicts, and the synchronization of sexual rhythms.*

In the cases presented, the authors illustrate graphically the value of treating desire problems from an integrated, systemic approach. For example, the therapist attempts to realign each partner's cognitive aspirations ("map of the world"), while simultaneously instructing the couple in more effective and satisfying means of sensual interaction. This approach can also be of value in understanding the impact of medical interventions (e.g., a surgical implant), as illustrated in the second case. Overall, the authors have presented a highly original and provocative view of systemic factors in assessing and treating problems of sexual desire.

Johan Verhulst, M.D., is Associate Professor of Psychiatry and Behavioral Sciences at the University of Washington School of Medicine; he is also Residency Training Director and Clinical Director of Psychiatric Services at University Hospital, Seattle, Washington.

Julia R. Heiman, Ph.D., is Associate Professor of Psychiatry and Behavioral Sciences, and Director of the Interpersonal Psychotherapy Clinic and the Reproductive and Sexual Medicine Clinic, at the University of Washington School of Medicine.

Medicine has gained most of its victories through the use of a simple and linear concept of disease. From this perspective, disease is viewed as a structural abnormality, which can be localized in the body and which reveals itself by a specific set of symptoms and a characteristic course of illness. The etiology of the disease is a noxious factor, which sets in motion a specific process of pathogenesis. This model of disease contains the conceptual framework that permeates medical thinking about all sorts of health conditions, including sexual dysfunctions. In contrast, general systems theory claims to offer a new paradigm, especially suited for complex, multifactorial phenomena, and scholars have made attempts at reformulating the illness concept from this perspective (Brody, 1973; Engel, 1977, 1980; Glenn, 1984; Sheldon & Baker, 1970). In this chapter, a systemic model is presented that is deemed especially useful in dealing with sexual dysfunction in general, and low sexual desire in particular.

Definition

Low sexual desire is examined from the perspective of synchronization of the sexual rhythms of sexual partners. This approach is essentially defined as follows: First, it is assumed that the frequency of sexual contact between two partners depends upon the ebb and flow of sexual desire in each individual, as well as on the ways in which partners interact to synchronize these rhythms. It is further assumed that the sexual rhythm of each in-

dividual itself reflects cyclical patterns at various levels: At the neurophysiological level, one can consider the cycle of physiological arousal, release,
refractory period, latency, and renewed arousal; at the emotional level, it is
possible to describe a cycle of affective states from increasing desire, satisfaction, and loss of interest to renewed desire; at the cognitive level, one
considers the sexual "scripts" (Gagnon, Rosen, & Leiblum, 1982) of
rhythmicity (i.e., cognitions about men and women's sexual needs, rules for
dealing with perceived sexual tension, frequency norms, and other symbolic
representations).

In the ideal sexual relationship, each individual's sexual rhythm is the
result of synergistic coordination of his or her cyclical patterns, and the
couple's sexual activity is the result of synchronization. *Low sexual desire is
a subjective complaint about the absence of sexual feelings, voiced by one or
both sexual partners and indicating unsatisfactory individual coordination
and/or interpersonal synchronization.* Such a complaint can, for instance, be
voiced by a person whose sexual norms and expectations demand a much
higher frequency of sexual activity than is provided for by his or her
physiological cycle of arousal. Alternatively, the complaint may arise in a
couple that fails to synchronize the partners' markedly different individual
rhythms.

This definition emphasizes the notion that low sexual desire is a *complaint*—in other words, a subjective experience of dissatisfaction—and that
it reflects an imbalance of interactions, rather than a "disease" with a
specific etiological cause and anatomical localization. The dissatisfaction
involved concerns a lack of emotional experience, in contrast to other
dysfunctions, which imply a lack of physiological response. As an emotion,
sexual desire organizes perception: It is a feeling that causes the individual
to "look for sex." Emotions also organize behavior: Patterns of sexual
behavior are thus set in motion and coordinated by sexual desire.

The model presented here assumes two interacting human beings as the
system under scrutiny, and their relationship as the system's context. It is
proposed that the interactions between the two individuals take place at
different yet interdependent levels. Included in these are the level of "symbolic interactions," the level of "affect-regulated interactions," and the level
of "sensate exchanges." In describing the three levels, we introduce the
concept of "interactional fit," and we develop a systemic model of desire
disorders. Finally, we provide clinical examples to indicate the applicability
as well as the limits of the model.

Symbolic Interactions

In talking to one another, people communicate action plans and tell stories.
They reflect upon the world, self-disclose, and express needs and ex-

pectations. The level of symbolic interactions is defined by the formal exchange of words, ideas, symbolic gestures, and other representations.[1]

For effective communication to take place, there needs to be a correspondence or "kinship" between the linguistic structures and processes of the participants. Certainly, two people need to find a common language if they wish to communicate. In addition, both people need to have a similar fundamental understanding of language itself, and of the relationship of symbols to reality. From a clinical perspective, it is important that two people have sufficiently close cultural backgrounds and similar "maps of the world" (Elkaim, 1986) to be able to follow each other's reasoning and presentation. Interpersonal conflicts are often based upon a poor interactional fit between the cognitive scripts and maps of the world of the involved parties. A poor interactional fit, in turn, often leads to mistrust and to the notion that the other is "not quite of our kind," or that he or she is trying to deceive us.

The issue of the (mis)alignment of cognitive constructs by interacting couples is a core feature of several conceptualizations in the field of marital and sex therapy. For instance, Gagnon et al. (1982) have proposed a theoretical framework and clinical methodology for analyzing the sexual "scripts" of patients in sex therapy. Their therapeutic interventions, such as cognitive reframing and homework exercises, can be said to be directed at improving the "interactional fit" between the scripts of the partners. Sager (1976) views the conscious and unconscious expectations and promises that each partner brings to the marriage as unwritten "marital contracts." He demonstrates a practical approach for analyzing these individual contracts and developing a simple joint contract, thus moving toward a closer symbolic interactional fit between the partners. Reiss (1981, 1982) has similarly studied "family paradigms," which he describes as the set of core assumptions, convictions, or beliefs that each family holds about its environment. He suggests that a family's health depends on the conservation of its paradigm (i.e., the interactional fit among the family members), and views disorders as resulting from the collapse of the paradigm.

More recently, Elkaim (1986) has described how a double bind can develop between a couple's symbolic structures. He uses the term "official program" to describe the explicit request of each member of the couple for a change in the behavior of the other. In addition, he refers to the basic blueprint of how the world works, which each partner has drawn up in the course of his or her past, as that partner's "map of the world." For example, the double bind underlying a complaint of low sexual desire in a particular couple might be analyzed as follows: The wife's official program states, "I

1. Speech contains an affective component in addition to a purely symbolic one. However, the model presented here suggests that the affective component is the result of interaction between the symbolic and the affect-regulated levels. The fact that the affective and the symbolic components are located in different brain areas (Ross, 1981) provides some anatomical support for the model.

want my husband to have more sex with me." Yet her map of the world may be in contradiction with the official program, because of a deep-seated belief that sex is dangerous. Thus, messages from her "map of the world" state, "Do not have sex with me." A double bind develops if the husband has a complementary cognitive structure. His official program may read, "I want you to be less demanding in matters of sex"; this may be contradicted by his map of the world, which states, "I need to be pushed and encouraged because I am incapable of joyful sex." The reciprocal double bind in which both partners are locked is based upon a paradoxical interactional fit. If the husband initiates sex, and thus tunes in to his spouse's official program, he threatens her map of the world and "causes" her to push him away with excessive demands and criticism. If, on the other hand, the wife accepts her husband's behavior without making demands, she in turn threatens his map of the world. In a situation such as this, Elkaim favors positive reframing accompanied by a paradoxical commentary as a principal mode of intervention. The therapist might comment on how each partner's behavior "protects" the deep-seated convictions of the other; this comment may facilitate a new interactional fit at a higher level of abstraction. The reframing both encompasses and resolves the contradictions.

To summarize: The quality and the meaningfulness of the symbolic interaction between two people depends upon the interactional fit between their neurolinguistic structures and processes. The more people differ in language skills and abstracting abilities, in cultural heritage and personal memories that shape the meaning of words, and with respect to their cognitive constructs and "maps of the world," the more arduous their interactional fit will be, and the more difficult their communication. At the same time, the interactional fit can be improved by communication—that is, by "tuning in" to each other's maps of the world, by finding common interests and beliefs, and by clarifying and explaining.[2]

Affect-Regulated Interactions

The level of affect-regulated interactions, or "affective level," consists of that part of the total communication that is governed and coordinated by the affective states of the participants. Emotional states are expressed through autonomic responses (e.g., blushing); through posture, movements, facial expression, and spontaneous sounds; through the affective component of speech; and through behavior (e.g., hitting or caressing). Sexual interaction, with its emphasis on nonverbal communication and on desire and arousal as emotional states, offers a special opportunity for studying the level of affect-regulated interactions.

2. Communication that is primarily directed at correcting and improving the interactional fit is called "metacommunication." People spend a great deal of effort in shaping each other's construction of reality, in an attempt to reach consensual validation and interactional fit.

In an earlier paper (Verhulst & Heiman, 1979), we advanced the hypothesis that the complex physiological and behavioral interactions of sexual partners are coordinated by each person's affective state. The expression of sexual arousal and desire by one individual evokes complex sexual emotions in the other, which in turn are expressed and lead to increased arousal in the first, thus creating a self-generating cycle leading to orgasm and resolution. One can say that the partners create a sexual context of meaning by "tuning in" to their own sexual feelings and to the other's sexual expressions.

However, a careful analysis of patients' reports of the interaction during sex therapy exercises clearly reveals that individuals often fail to maintain the sexual context of meaning. Instead, we frequently observe a tendency to become sidetracked in nonsexual interactions, such as the following:

- Attachment interactions, which center around the establishment, the preservation, and the intensity regulation of the affiliative bond between individuals (Bowlby, 1969, 1977).
- Exploratory interactions, which center around the establishment and maintenance of acquaintanceship and familiarity through sensory contact.
- Territorial interactions, which center around the acquisition, management, and defense of ownership rights over space, one's body, food, and other possessions (Bakker & Bakker-Rabdau, 1973; Eibl-Eibesfeldt, 1970).
- Ranking–order interactions which center around the acquisition and defense of social position or status, conferring on the possessor decision-making powers (Rapoport, 1974).

Clinical examples of these interactions are common. For instance, a woman—because of a previous rape trauma—experienced her partner's aggressive expressions of desire as a "territorial invasion" of the integrity of her body and reacted by defending her rights of ownership. Her defensive withdrawal elicited even more determined advances in her partner, who failed to distinguish clearly between feelings of territorial aggression and sexual feelings. Thus, whenever they attempted to engage in sex, the context of meaning of the encounter shifted from sexual communication to a territorial conflict.

Other couples become caught up in issues of dominance, and their sexual communication transforms into a "ranking–order" conflict. Still other individuals, often because of sexual fears, become overly focused on their feelings of tenderness and affection. Such intense attachment interactions can interfere with the cycle of desire. Even exploratory sensual interactions sometimes seem to lead to pleasurable "stroking" rather than to sexual stimulation.

This is not to imply that satisfying sexuality excludes territorial, ranking–order, attachment, exploratory, or other nonsexual interactions. These interactions usually influence and enrich the sexual encounter in satisfactory sexual relationships. Attachment interactions, for instance, build an atmosphere of love and trust and may counteract feelings of guilt, anxiety, territorial fear, or anticipated pain. It is only when the nonsexual interactions become the primary focus of attention that the conditions for sexual dysfunction are established.[3]

Affect-regulated interactions can generally be characterized as follows: The moment of initial contact between two people tends to elicit mixed emotional states in each partner, as it contains complex implicit and explicit information about each person's level of sexual interest in the other, each person's degree of attachment and acquaintanceship, each person's territorial claims, and social rank. Some information is expressed more clearly and may elicit stronger feelings; other information may trigger a special emotional sensitivity in the partner. If there is an interactional fit between the emotional states of the participants, a context of meaning is established and other potential interaction patterns are kept at bay.[4] If, for instance, two people experience and express sexual desire toward each other, the couple proceeds with coordinated sexual activity. However, the focus of interaction can at times shift to alternative patterns. Sexual activity leads quickly to orgasm and resolution when the partners focus exclusively on the sexual context of meaning. On the other hand, sexual intercourse is usually lengthened and enriched by the inclusion of exploratory and attachment interactions, as well as by acknowledgment of territorial rights and ranking–order agreements. Changes of focus are usually more frequent in the early stages of the sexual interaction cycle, followed by a more narrow focusing on sexual activity as erotic tension increases.

3. For a more complete discussion of this level, see Verhulst and Heiman (1979). It may be of interest to note that in the 1979 model, the other levels that are being described here were represented as "intervening variables." This suggested an absolute primacy of the affect-regulated interactions, which is not warranted. The model presented here is based upon the notion of hierarchical levels of organization and upon the idea that each level can be distinguished by its interactional fit.

4. Recently, Stern (1985) has articulated several affective interpersonal processes that evolve in one's first relationship—that of the mother (parent) and child. Late in the infant's first year, a new interactional phenomenon emerges that Stern terms "affect attunement." Affect attunement is characterized by what appears to be the mother's matching some aspect of her behavior (say, her voice) to some aspect of her infant's behavior (say, the infant's rhythmic use of a toy). In fact, what is really being "matched," and therefore shared, is an underlying feeling state. Affect attunement is a way to establish a common feeling context, regardless of the mode of behavior (verbal, gestural, kinesthetic) used to communicate that feeling. Stern's observations suggest that this affect sharing occurs very early, preceding language acquisition. It is likely that attunement in the sexual sphere (being largely nonverbal as an experience) is powerfully yet subtly influenced by a complex array of sensory and perceptual signals being matched cross-modally. Given the complexity, it would seem easy to slip out of a sexual context.

When both partners express emotional states that refer to a different set of interactional patterns, the couple experiences a conflict of meaning. There are different ways of dealing with this conflict. Participants may actively try to coordinate the communication by displaying stronger emotional signals, potentially leading to an escalating conflict of meaning; they may decide to steer the interaction away from the conflictual area and to engage in an alternative type of exchange; both partners may even refuse to engage further in any interactional sequence with definite emotional involvement, preferring to retreat to a superficial, distant, approach–avoidance pattern.

Low sexual desire can often be traced to problems at the affect-regulated level of communication. For instance, raised in an environment where any expression of feelings was ridiculed and manipulated, the husband in a patient couple felt very uncomfortable about intense engagement in affect-regulated interactions. He would focus as much as possible on pure symbolic interactions. His wife referred to him as "Mister Spock," after the totally unemotional Vulcan character in the television series Star Trek. He seemed to be cold, logical, controlled, and controlling. It was not that he wanted to dominate his partner, but rather that he would seek absolute control over the context of meaning in the marital interaction, and in particular over the intensity of affective exchanges. His wife felt that she was not "connecting" with him, and she would try to steer the interaction toward greater emotional clarity and intensity. The couple was caught in a vicious circle: The more he avoided engagement, the more she would steer toward it. In the beginning of their marriage, sex was the only area in which the husband expressed feelings. However, as the above-described vicious circle became more prominent, it became harder for him even to allow expression of sexual feelings, and sex became just another affect-regulated interaction that he avoided and that his wife pursued.

Another couple expressed traditional sex-role expectations: The husband avoided intense affect-regulated interactions of attachment, but not of sex; the wife wanted attachment, but felt less comfortable with sex. The man pursued sexual interactions, while the woman tried to maneuver the interaction toward attachment. The result was a growing polarization. The man increasingly concentrated on establishing sexual interactions and continually observed his partner for the slightest sign of sexual interest. The woman focused on the lack of attachment and became emotionally dependent, angry, and accusatory. The result of the polarization was that sexual initiation by the husband had automatically come to signal "no attachment" to the wife, while the wife's attachment efforts directly signified to the husband "no sex." The wife wanted marital therapy for her husband's "problems with intimacy"; the husband wanted sex therapy for his wife's "low sexual desire."

Lack of attention to *seduction* can also affect the development of a couple's low sexual activity and lack of desire. As we are using the term, "seduction" refers to the maneuvers employed by one partner to evoke feelings of desire in the other. In other words, seduction is an attempt to establish the interactional fit of corresponding sexual desire. In the context of traditional sex roles, seduction rituals have been used to entice a potential lover toward sexual activity. In traditional Western culture until recent times, the male assumed the role of sexual seducer until after marriage. In marriage, a wife was encouraged to seduce her husband, who now could simply demand intercourse as a marital right. Times have changed, and a wife's sexual availability is no longer taken for granted as an inescapable marital duty. Rather, marital rape is increasingly viewed as a legal reality. It is not surprising, therefore, that many couples now feel uncomfortable with the idea of seduction as a useful element in marital sex: For the wife it means a return to a traditional sex-role pattern, while for the husband it feels unnecessary and awkward to seduce his own wife.

Some couples have made an attempt to replace the affect-regulated interaction of seduction with a symbolic interaction pattern: "We are equals. We can simply ask for sex when we experience desire, and refuse when we are not in the mood." Yet the logic of symbolic interaction patterns is not well suited to coordinate an emotional interactional fit. Unless one gender is dominant over the other and can impose its sexual rhythm, a ritual of enticement is often necessary to engage a partner in sex. One can hypothesize that seduction rituals facilitate the coordination of individual sexual rhythms. If this is true, the development of new seduction rituals that are acceptable to both marital partners could be quite important in our culture, and could result in a decreased incidence of low sexual desire. Seduction issues are thus also relevant for treatment.

Sensate Exchanges

The level of sensate exchanges in sexual interaction can be distinguished between humans and other species by focusing on the sensory patterns and the direct neurophysiological responses and motor reflexes that each part-ner elicits in the other.[5] Genital stimulation of appropriate duration and

---

5. Recent research has elucidated the neurophysiological basis of sensory–motor patterns. For olfactory perception, for instance, it has been shown that the individual does not just "pick up" smells via the olfactory receptors. The individual creates—in the olfactory bulb, not in the cerebral cortex—an olfactory "image" that acts as a search image, selecting odors with which it has an "interactional fit." These images incorporate previous experience and learning, and are linked to images of expectant motor activity (Freeman, 1983). Similarly, Kandel (1979, 1983), in a series of elegant experiments on the snail *Aplysia*, has shown how a complex environmen-tal event such as a conditioning situation becomes incorporated and represented in physiolog-ical structures for perception and coordinated motor activity.

intensity (i.e., a stimulation pattern that has an appropriate interactional fit with the sensory structures of the subject) will lead to sexual response in rats, even after transsection of the spinal cord below the brain (Hart, 1969). As for humans, male patients who react with an erection when receiving a bed bath in the hospital usually feel embarrassed. The patient may also wish to explain to the nurse that the sexual response is neither an expression of feelings of desire, nor an attempt to steer the interaction toward a sexual context of meaning.

Investigations of the sexual response cycle at this level have been a major contribution of Masters and Johnson (1966). The treatment of sexual dysfunctions had until then almost exclusively been conducted through psychotherapeutic interventions at the symbolic level. Masters and Johnson focused their therapy instead on coordinating sensory stimulation and on decreasing the inhibitory effects of other interactional levels. The effectiveness of this approach in cases of low sexual desire has been rather disappointing, however, according to some authors (Kaplan, 1979; LoPiccolo & Stock, 1986). Our explanation of this is that low sexual desire is a problem in the integration of all levels and/or in the coordination between the partners.

Low sexual desire can originate at the sensate level in some instances (e.g., inappropriate stimulation due to lack of sexual knowledge and experience, or pain during intercourse). A desire problem can develop when one partner requires a more lengthy period of stimulation than the other in order to reach orgasm. One man, for instance, would readily reach orgasm after a period of intercourse, while his wife always required considerably more stimulation. Because of his "sexual scripts" and her demands, he felt obliged to continue stimulating her manually after his ejaculation. Sometimes this would lead to orgasm, usually after about 20 minutes. Many times, however, the wife would become increasingly tense and "performance-oriented," and would not reach orgasm at all. During this additional period of stimulation the husband would experience a total lack of sexual desire, in part because he found it difficult to maintain emotional desire without physiological arousal, and in part because he also adopted an attitude of performance—of trying to induce orgasm as quickly as possible. It would become quite obvious to the wife that the husband was lacking in sexual desire and that he was "only doing a job." She found it difficult to maintain her own emotional desire—in spite of her physiological arousal—with someone who was clearly not desiring sex with her any more. This lack of interactional fit would push both partners into a detached role, and their sexual experiences became increasingly negative, resulting in low frequency of intercourse. Therapy was not very successful. The most useful intervention was teaching the wife to maintain an interactional fit with an imaginary partner through fantasy.

An Integrated Model for Dyadic Interactions

As one can see from the clinical example just given, the three levels of interaction described here do not operate in isolation, but are intimately connected to one another. Thus physiological sexual arousal, for instance, clearly influences desire. There is also a reciprocal relationship between the sensate and the symbolic level: One sees what one believes as much as one believes what one sees (Watzlawick, 1984). Futhermore, strong associations develop between and among the levels through learning. For instance, genital odors may lead to reflexive nausea and withdrawal (sensate level) because of associations with feelings of disgust (affective level), based upon cognitive constructs that condemn and repress sexuality (symbolic level). In synthesizing these three levels and their interconnections, we have developed the model presented in Figure 1.

In order to flesh out this model, a few additional points need to be made. The first refers to the structures that are involved in each level's

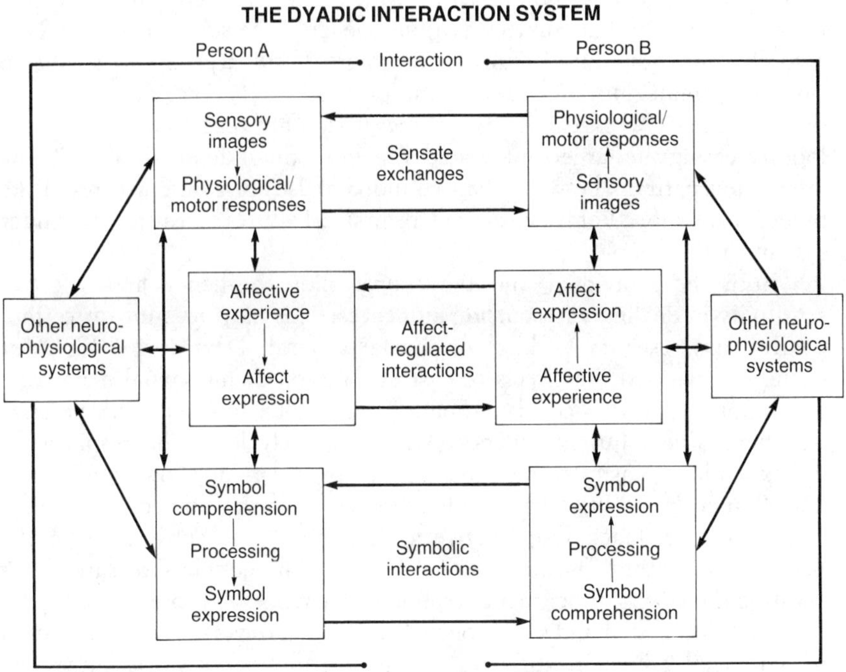

Figure 1. A model for dyadic interactions that integrates the symbolic, affective, and sensate levels.

interactional fit. In the model, they are represented by the boxes that delineate (1) sensory images and the responses to them; (2) affects and their expressions; and (3) symbol comprehension, processing, and expression. These structures should be conceived of as subsystems, with each having some degree of autonomy, based upon internal feedback mechanisms and homeostatic regulation. Therefore, when one subsystem (such as the symbolic structure) interacts with a subsystem at a different level (say, the affective system), one cannot expect a one-to-one response. Cognitive changes influence feelings, but not every new idea changes the emotional equilibrium. The cognitive changes need to reach a certain threshold before the resilience of the emotional system is overcome. Conversely, the emotional system may develop a selective sensitivity to certain symbolic features, and react very strongly to minimal changes in the symbolic structures. Thus, it may take a while for changes in sexual scripts—for instance, a change in attitude from sexual repression to greater acceptance—to take effect at the emotional level. On the other hand, many people have immediate and strong emotional reactions to changes in self-image and self-esteem.

Each of these subsystems belongs to two larger systems: (1) to the totality of the person, by interacting with the other levels; and (2) to the interactional loop that connects (within one level) the subsystems in person A to the corresponding structures in person B. These larger systems have, in turn, self-organizing and homeostatic properties: (1) The intractions between the levels (vertical arrows in the model) are regulated by feedback loops creating the larger, integrated system of the individual; and (2) the interaction patterns between the two individuals (horizontal arrows in the model) also show homeostatic and recursive features, creating the larger system of the couple.

Both the individual and the couple show resiliency and selective sensitivity in dealing with outside influences. This may account for certain clinical and research findings on sexual arousal. Davidson (1972), for example, reviewed the effects of castration upon men's sexual behaviors, and reported a very inconsistent pattern of results: In some cases potency was maintained, but in others it was completely lost. The response of hypogonadal or castrated men to androgen treatment appears equally variable (Bancroft, 1978). One can hypothesize that the homeostatic mechanisms and feedback loops between and among the subsystems of the person, and within the interactional levels of the couple, are capable of resisting the effects of neuroendocrinological changes in those patients who have well-integrated and synchronized sex lives. Conversely, if a subsystem is extremely resilient to influences from other subsystems, the latter may nevertheless be compelled to adapt. A clinical illustration will clarify this point. The patient, the only son of a widow, was raised in a milieu that strongly rejected sexuality. He saw himself as very "pure and idealistic," and he thought of sex as dangerous and disgusting. For him, a "real man" was somebody who could totally control his animalistic sexual instincts. As an adolescent he never masturbated. He claimed that he never had nocturnal ejaculations: "If it is about to happen when I am dreaming, I always wake up in time to stop it." He did well in many areas of life and maintained a job as a bank teller. He married a woman his age and managed to have intercourse, but was never able to ejaculate. The couple consulted a clinic for infertility, as they both wanted children. The results of a physical examination and endocrinological tests were entirely normal. It seemed that the extreme rigidity of the man's symbolic system was shaping his affective system, as well as constraining the sexual response cycle.

Finally, it is important to acknowledge that each subsystem is a psychological as well as a biological structure. Take, for instance, one of the structures with interactional fit—say, an individual's emotional state and its expression. As long as this element is defined as a component of the interaction (i.e., as part of the communication loop that links it to the emotional experience and expression of the partner), there is a tendency to describe this component as a "psychological phenomenon." Indeed, the labels "emotional experience" and "emotional expression" are psychological labels. If, on the other hand, one were to study this same structure in isolation, analyzing its components, one would end up using the language and technology of biology. Thus, each structure with interactional fit can be viewed as both a psychological and a biological structure. As a biological structure, it can be linked to the other neurophysiological systems of the individual organism, as is shown in Figure 1.

The biological factors that have been described as influencing sexual desire operate through the structures with interactional fit. Lack of testosterone, for instance, seems to have a major effect in inhibiting both the emotional state of desire and the physiological response cycle in most people, although "too much" testosterone has not been shown to have much effect upon the frequency and intensity of sexual behavior (Bermant & Davidson, 1974).

Rhythms: Integration and Synchronization

Biological mechanisms that deserve special attention are circadian and other biological rhythms. For example, humans show interindividual differences in circadian rhythms of temperature, cortisol, prolactin, MHPG, and numerous other variables (Suda, Hayaishi, & Nakagawa, 1979). Several of these variables could influence the cyclicity of structures with interactional fit—in particular, those at the sensate and affective levels.[6] Patients some-times report that their lack of sexual synchronicity is caused by "his being a morning person and her being an evening person." This observation should not simply be dismissed out of hand: Though being an "evening" versus a "morning" person may serve as an unconscious way of avoiding sexual intimacy, it may also reflect circadian differences, which may in turn affect each person's cycle of desire.

If the structures with interactional fit may be influenced by biorhythms, some of these structures may also be shown to have their own inherent biological clock. The physiological response system at the sensate level follows a cyclical pattern: There is a refractory period after orgasm, fol-lowed by a gradual increase in sensitivity to stimuli and in physiological responsiveness. After time, the sensitivity can become so extreme that sexual release may be provoked by minimal external cues or by fantasy (e.g., sexual dreams). Conversely, special stimuli—the introduction of a new partner, for instance—can bring early renewal of sexual interest.

The pattern of physiological arousal underlies the rhythm of desire, satisfaction, and renewed desire at the emotional level, but it is only one of the determinants of this rhythm. Emotions and affective states constantly influence the experience of sexual tension and desire. For instance, boys may react to difficult situations that provoke tension and nonspecific arous-al with masturbation. Depression usually inhibits sexual interest, while mania increases it. Furthermore, there is the influence of the symbolic interactions and of the cognitive "scripts" about appropriate frequency of sexual activity. For instance, the expectation of some postmenopausal women that their sexuality belongs to the past may in fact decrease their experienced desire.

The normative rhythm of sexuality at the symbolic level is even further removed from the biorhythms. Personal upbringing, expectations, and so-cial and cultural rules play a major role, as well as the rules of inner consistency of the symbolic system: The sexual scripts need to be integrated into the person's self-concept and map of the world.

For the individual, the task at hand, then, is to coordinate physiological arousal, emotional desire, and cognitive sexual scripts. A person's sexual rhythm is the result of the integration of these three levels. For a couple, the task at hand is the continuous coordination of their individual rhythms, through coordinated activity, affective attunement, and alignment of scripts

6. The influence of biological rhythms on mood states has been the object of recent psychiatric research. Attempts have been made to treat depressive illness by altering the circadian sleep–wake pattern (Wehr, Wirz-Justine, Goodwin, Duncan, & Gillin, 1979). Seasonal depressions have been linked to patients' sensitivity to light as a synchronizing environmental cue, and treated with phototherapy.

and maps of the world. Thus, a patient who complains of low sexual desire may be seen as having difficulty in integrating the rhythm of one level with the other levels, or to have problems in synchronizing his or her sexuality with that of the partner, usually because of incompatibilities in the interactional fit at one or more levels.

Clinical Applications

The model presented here attempts to integrate a number of conceptual and clinical approaches. Neither physiological, social learning, nor psychodynamic theories are necessarily incompatible with the present model, and it can be used to account for the effects of most interventions derived from these theories. Although there is no single or specific therapeutic approach connected with this model, it has significant and far-reaching clinical applications. First, it provides a framework for a broad diagnostic evaluation of low sexual desire, allowing the clinician not only to classify the many factors that play a role, but also to speculate on their interrelationship. Second, it suggests indications for particular psychotherapeutic techniques. Dysfunctional sensate exchanges, for instance, may respond best to psychoeducational review of homework exercises, while problems in affect-regulated interactions require corrective emotional experiences, which can be provided during therapy sessions and/or carefully orchestrated homework exercises. Problems at the symbolic level may require individual psychotherapy, marital therapy, and family-of-origin work.

Indeed, evidence is accumulating that no single form of sex or marital therapy is appropriate for all patients. The therapist who embraces a restricted model of clinical practive runs the risk of behaving in the manner of the legendary Procrustes, who had the rather unsavory habit of making his guests fit his beds by stretching their bodies or mutilating their legs. Conversely, the eclectic therapist who is always ready to adopt different theoretical perspectives and all sorts of clinical interventions runs the risk of behaving in the manner of the guide who tries to lead people out of a complex labyrinth by trial and error only. The following clinical examples show how the systemic model can be used to orient oneself in organizing clinical data and in choosing a therapeutic direction.

First Clinical Example: Ben and Maria

At the intake interview, Ben presented as a dark, somewhat somber-looking, handsome man in his late 30s. He left most of the talking to Maria, who was a few years younger. Maria was dressed in casual but expensive clothes and acted vivacious, with flamboyant gestures. Ben was a successful business-man, and he treated the therapist as he would a business partner, exchang-ing factual information and seeking practical advice. Maria's attitude was more complex: She often would look up to the therapist and smile in a charming and dependent way; yet she could also be assertive and opinionated, and she expressed bitter resentment about Ben's "low sexual desire."

"Ben is a very nice person, and he is always supportive to me and the kids," Maria said, "but he only needs his books and his music . . . that is, when he is not working, which is all the time." She described their sex life as a "disaster." "I am a romantic person. I want to be kissed, and I want to be touched, and I could spend the whole night making love. Ben doesn't need all that. Maybe once every 2 or 3 months we will have sex, and then he tries to touch me and kiss me, but he doesn't know how to touch a woman. He is rough and totally insensitive. He tries hard enough, because he knows that I think that he is a poor lover, but he just does not have the feelings for it."

At this point, Ben shook his shoulders in exasperation: "The problem is that I can't do anything right for her. I have had sex with other women, and I am not saying that I am the world's best lover, but it was very satisfying, and they thought so too. With Maria, nothing is ever good enough. So I have given up. What's the use of trying? I don't look forward to sex. And she is right: I don't need it. I am more interested in cultural things. I know that as long as I have my books and music I'll survive."

It appeared that neither Ben nor Maria ever truly initiated sex. There were no seduction rituals built into their relationship. Yet, with the absence of sex, there was an increasing tension between them, and they periodically drifted into sexual activity about every 2–3 months, usually during a vaca-tion or a long, relaxed weekend. The event was inevitably disappointing. Maria would respond to initial stimulation by becoming passionately aroused and sexually demanding. Ben felt increasingly that his lovemaking was contrived and that his own arousal did not "match" Maria's, either in intensity or in quality. He would finally decide to "get it over with" and would reach orgasm—without pleasure—after a few intense pelvic thrusts. Maria would react with anger: She would not want him to stimulate her again and would push him away.

The physiological sexual rhythm of both partners was not unusual: They both masturbated about once a week. They did not know this about each other until it was discussed in the session. Maria had had an ex-tramarital affair a few years earlier that had lasted about 6 months and that had been "lovely and romantic." Ben had been aware of it and had told her that she needed to make up her mind and either divorce him or quit seeing the man. He did, however, allow her several months to make up her mind, during which time the couple separated; she lived in an apartment for which he paid the rent.

Ben was the oldest child and only son, in a local business family. His upbringing had been almost exclusively achievement-oriented. He was raised to take over the family business, which he eventually did. As a child, his goal in life was to prove that he would be worthy of succeeding his father. Yet his father treated him with sarcasm, constantly ridiculing his efforts. He never felt loved and was rarely touched or cuddled. At the time of intake, in spite of his being fairly successful, his self-esteem was low and he often felt depressed. He reacted to this by seeking strength in isolation—by being rational, friendly, and principled, without ever allowing himself to be emotionally vulnerable. He greatly admired Maria's social skills and emotional responsiveness. He felt proud of her at parties, where she was the center of attention and where other men flocked around her. He also thought that she was "the most warm and caring mother I could have wanted for my children."

Maria grew up in a Catholic family of professionals, with a father who was a distant patriarch and a mother who spent most of her time in social activities. In her family, women only lived for men: "My mother has always needed men. She spent her whole life making men pay attention to her. I have something of that romantic blood in me." The relationship between her father and mother was functional rather than intimate: "They did get along when decisions needed to be made, but they were always quarreling. My father drinks too much and I think that my mother does not really respect him." Toward the children, the father was stern and authoritarian, showing his affection only by being financially generous and spoiling them with expensive toys and clothes.

During the history taking, Maria's attitude alternated between two patterns. Whenever the topic of sex was discussed, she would become active and aggressive, accusing her husband of lack of desire, lack of sensitivity, and poor performance. Ben's response to this would be to withdraw in distant aloofness, often attempting to change the topic. If that did not work, he would react with an angry outburst: "I am the way I am, and if that's not good enough for you, find someone else!" When any other topic was discussed Maria would sit in a submissive posture, carefully listening to what her husband had to say. She admired his rational wisdom and would often seek out his advice or ask him to help her explain things. He would become somewhat of a fatherly teacher, often criticizing her for being "too dramatic and irresponsible."

A first therapeutic issue consisted of determining the strength of their relationship. This couple had been married and unhappy for many years. Was their relationship deteriorating, and was the request for professional help the first step toward a long-overdue divorce decision, or were they still committed to each other? The issue was openly raised by the therapist. Yes, the couple had often considered divorce. Yet they insisted that they really loved each other and wanted to stay together, "not just for the children." They did indeed seem to like and admire each other. The decision to come into therapy was mainly influenced by circumstances—their best friends had received help in our clinic—and by a sense of life change: "The kids are growing up, and we need to do something about this problem before we get old."

Both partners agreed that the underlying problem was Ben's low sexual desire. This label seemed to fit particularly well with the couple's shared ideas about Ben as a rational and controlled human being, and Maria as a person who was longing for sexual passion. The therapist decided to accept the diagnostic label of low sexual desire, but to redefine its meaning as an interactional problem, rather than as Ben's individual issue. It was pointed out to the couple that they had quite comparable biological sexual rhythms (as indicated by their similar masturbation frequency), but that they had problems in communicating sexually. The hypothesis was put forward that they *both* avoided sex, since it seemed only to "happen" to them from time to time without either partner's truly taking the initiative. The couple agreed with this reframing, but Maria insisted nevertheless that she had more basic interest in sex than Ben. Ben concurred. The therapist suggested that perhaps Maria's response to unsatisfactory sex was to maintain interest and to attempt to do something about it by complaining, while Ben's reaction was to withdraw his feelings of desire.

Before proceeding further with the account of the therapy sessions, it is useful to pause and to reflect on the etiology of the problem, using the integrated model. First, the history allows us to rule out major biological factors. Both partners were healthy, and there were no clinical signs of endocrinological disorders. The clients described problems at the sensate level: Maria did not have an adequate physiological response to stimulation by Ben. She never reached orgasm in the context of marital intercourse, even when stimulation persisted for a long time. We can reasonably assume, however, that the issue was not merely a matter of Ben's not possessing the knowledge and skills to provide adequate stimulation. The lack of response was due to interference from other levels. Maria did not accept stimulation from Ben; she perceived it as irritating rather than stimulating. Ben did not express sexual desire when stimulating Maria; his behavior was guided by his own fear of failure and his wish to perform better. Consequently, the pattern of stimulation he provided lacked spontaneity and responsiveness to Maria's state of arousal.

There were also major problems at the level of affect-regulated interactions. Detailed analysis of their behavior and feelings during sexual activity showed that they invariably got sidetracked in ranking–order or dominance interactions. Ben perceived Maria more and more as exerting "quality control" over his performance, as not respecting him, and as treating him like an incompetent boy. Maria saw Ben alternately as cold, superior, and determined not to give her what she wanted, or as clumsy, inadequate, and incapable of giving her what she needed. The focus of their interaction had become power and control, rather than sex, and both partners fought to get sufficient control to be able to change the other's behavior, or at least to avoid being altogether in a one-down, slave-like position. Ben's eventual decision to give up trying to please Maria and to allow himself to ejaculate seemed to be an attempt to focus briefly on pleasure and sex, and to use his high level of general arousal to achieve orgasm quickly. It became clear during the therapy that this decision was also a last escape when he felt that he was losing the ranking–order conflict with Maria.

There were many issues at the symbolic level that interfered with Ben and Maria's sexual communication. Elkaim's (1986) theoretical framework offers a useful way of summarizing these. Maria's "official program" was as follows: "I want Ben to become more sexual and to engage in sex several times per week. I want him to be an equal partner in romantic, loving, and passionate sex." Her "map of the world", however, stated: "All happiness and self-respect has to come from men, but men are superior beings who have no lasting interest in women's needs." As for Ben, his "official program" was clear: "Love me as I am. Don't criticize me. It is unreasonable to ask me to change. I am a normal, mature man and you should be satisfied with me." But his deep seated "map of the world" read differently: "I am not worth being loved. I am incompetent and incapable, and I will never accede to full manhood, just as my father predicted." The conflicts between the couple's official programs and maps of the world were being acted out in their sexual relationship. Maria's aggressive official program confirmed Ben's basic map of the world, and vice versa. The partners were caught in a reciprocal double bind.

The problems at the three levels were clearly interconnected. The symbolic scripts offered justification for the ranking–order interactions at the affective level, while the affect-regulated interactions supported the scripts. Both levels interfered with the couple's patterns of mutual stimulation, as well as with their sensate receptivity. Therapeutic work at all three levels was clearly needed.

The therapist decided to focus first on the symbolic level. Because the model predicts that change at this level may be hindered by continued interactions at the affective and sensate level, Ben and Maria were asked not to allow themselves to attempt intercourse. "We will deal with the sexual communication later, and it is important not to reinforce dissatisfying practices." Seven 1-hour sessions were spent in analyzing each partner's map of the world and its origin. The format chosen was that of "individual psychotherapy in the presence of the partner": The therapist would engage one person in a discussion of his or her family of origin, while the other person listened and might be asked to comment at the end of the session. By being present during empathic interviews, Maria learned to understand how rejected Ben had felt during his childhood and how his isolation and rationality constituted a necessary defense, allowing him to function successfully in a world that he had learned to see as basically hostile. Ben, on the other hand, began to understand how Maria's fear of and love for her authoritarian father, and her ambivalent identification with her mother, had kept her in a dependent position, and how her anger and resentment represented an attempt to become more autonomous. He learned how she used to daydream about a "man without a face," who would be gentle and sensual and meet all her needs, and whose comings and goings she could completely control.

The results of these sessions were mixed. The couple started talking more to each other, and experienced moments of intimacy. They did comply with the no-intercourse rule, but engaged more in kissing, cuddling, and other nonsexual contact. At times, however, they engaged in intense arguments centering around ranking–order issues. Maria was clearly becoming more assertive, and the issues of dominance and dependency were being acted out more openly in their daily interactions, rather than being restricted to the area of sex. The therapist proposed a few more sessions of marital therapy to focus on rules of communication and "fair fighting" techniques. After four sessions, the couple felt that they had more control in discussing conflicts, though the tension in the relationship remained at times explosive. Nevertheless, it was decided to address the communication problems at the sensate and affective levels by introducing classical Masters-and-Johnson-type exercises. The partners (Ben in particular) were instructed to forget about "good" or "bad" stimulation techniques, but to focus on expressing feelings of sexual desire and on exploring each other by touch. In receiving pleasure, the partners (especially Maria) were asked to focus on their individual enjoyment and to express this *actively* by "letting your body and your skin open up to it." Strict rules about initiation, taking turns, and ending the session if the interaction was not pleasurable were given in order to avoid ranking–order conflicts. The couple's response was strikingly positive. At the fourth session they reported that they had broken the rules and had had intercourse, with mutual orgasm. "The best ever," said Maria. In spite of the therapist's warnings, the couple continued having regular intercourse for several weeks. Termination of therapy was considered. At the session that was to be the last session, however, the couple appeared in crisis: Ben had had dinner with a former girlfriend who happened to be in town. This had led to a scene of jealous recrimination and to angry conflict for the rest of the week. Several more sessions of therapy followed, focusing mainly on conflict resolution and on the issues of autonomy and marital equivalence. The couple spontaneously resumed having sex, but at a lower frequency level (once per week to once every 2 weeks). However, both partners expressed satisfaction with their sexual relationship.

In treating this couple, the integrated model proved to be very useful. First, it helped the therapist appreciate the links between and among this couple's unsatisfactory sensate exchanges, their failure to establish and maintain a focus on sexual interaction during intercourse, their bitter rank-ing–order conflicts, and their complementary scripts and maps of the world. Second, the model helped in formulating the therapeutic strategy, with work at the symbolic level being followed by interventions at the affective and sensate levels. It is our hypothesis that, for this couple, progress was made because several levels were addressed sequentially. If the therapist had restricted treatment to an intense focus on one level only, these efforts would have been thwarted by interference from the other levels. For the same reason, the improvement probably has a good chance of being main-tained, because the couple made important progress at all three levels, with changes reinforcing one another.

Second Clinical Example: Andrea and Paul

Although the model has broad applicability, it also has certain limitations. An obvious one is prediction. Therapists and clients may want to know precisely the outcomes of certain systemic interventions. Other therapeutic models might also have a difficult time with this issue, but for different reasons. In a systemic model, the goal is to formulate and enact an interven-tion that will permit the partners to make their own change. The change may be something other than what the couple initially requested, and yet it will in some way resolve their dilemma. Thus the "uncertainty" is based upon the fact that neither therapist nor couple can know all of the couple's unique sensory, emotional, and symbolic interactional patterns. The therap-ist must make an intervention based upon his or her own receptiveness and sensitivity to key interactions as expressed by the couple.

A second therapy example illustrates several complexities and un-predictable aspects of the model. Paul, aged 40, and Andrea, aged 28, a common-law marriage couple, initially came for an evaluation regarding Paul's erection problem. Paul was an adolescent-onset diabetic; the disease had been initially poorly maintained, with vascular and neurological dam-age (including consistently cold and rather numb fingers). Both worked at the same shop, a construction business where she took phone calls and he did woodworking and other physical labor. Both were intelligent, though neither verbal nor self-reflective in discussing their relationship.

The partners first came to therapy in order to explore their options. Paul's urologist was advising a penile implant, but both felt uncertain about this recommendation. The discussion centered on what couples therapy might accomplish, the apparent physical basis for his current erection problem, and the advantages and disadvantages of prostheses. At this stage, their problem appeared to be one of low frequency rather than low desire. They were currently engaging in sex less than once a month, but desired it two to four times per week. He experienced sexual desire once to four times per week, she about once a day. The low frequency was believed to be related to the fact that he could never maintain an erection, felt discouraged, and did not initiate sex.

The couple was very happy; the partners loved each other and were generally pleased about their 7-year relationship, including the affectionate aspects of it. Sex was compartmentalized as the only significant problem, and as such, it did not seem to be endangering their relationship. They were extremely committed to each other and rarely in conflict. The couple decided to think about the options for a while.

In considering the applicability of the present model for this couple's situation, we notice, first of all, the incapacity at the sensate level, with the lack of consistent erectile response as a major focus of disruption in the interaction. Both partners saw this problem as causing their low intercourse frequency. At the symbolic level they both valued erections as essential for adequate sex, and had not experimented extensively with nonintercourse sex. Their subjective experience of desire being quite high, and their relationship being very good, it seemed reasonable to join the couple in the belief that the sensory/physiological incapacity was a primary issue, and that a more satisfying equilibrium could be expected if this problem were solved. The therapist could have obtained more information about their affect-regulated interactions by asking them in detail about specific sexual events; the therapist could also have explored their sexual scripts in detail. Even so, the model would not have predicted what in fact happened.

Two years later the couple reappeared. Paul and Andrea had formally married about 6 months after the last consultation. In addition, they had decided that Paul should have the implant surgery, and he had received a semirigid prosthesis 5 months before returning to see us. Paul stated that the recovery from surgery had been worse than he expected; in fact, he had been in pain for about 6 weeks and sore for 2 weeks after that. He had not been prepared for this, and claimed that his physician had "joked" with him that Paul would never have gone through with it if he had been told how painful the healing was.

"Not finding what one expected" turned out to be the major theme of this couple's postsurgical adjustment. When asked about her feelings concerning his erection, Andrea vacillated, saying that it seemed "kind of unnatural at first" but then she "got used to it," and then it looked strange when he would "walk out of the shower with an erect penis all the time." This erection indeed felt like a new family member to her, a relative that she (and he) did not quite know what to do with and how to relate to.

His perception of the prosthesis was even more revealing. He said that it felt "strange" to have sex with an erect penis without the usual feeling of "getting erect," a feeling that helped him experience a sense of being turned on. He was acting sexual, but felt detached from the experience—as if he had lost part of the code that fit the sexual message. In gaining the permanent erection, he had lost a part of the experience of becoming aroused. The erection did not really feel as if it belonged to him or was a part of his sexuality. Erections had once meant sex; now it was difficult to connect an erection to a sexual experience. The constancy of the erection had desexualized its meaning.

This was not what Paul and Andrea had hoped for. They both appeared rather bewildered and angry at how it had worked out (it did not help that the surgery also cost $8,000, which their insurance did not cover). Both were orgasmic, and Andrea was usually aroused. Neither was as interested in sex as before, however: Andrea was slightly less interested, and Paul's desire for sexual intercourse had declined to less than once a month.

The brief therapeutic intervention was focused on the symbolic and affective interaction levels. The therapist acknowledged that everyone—the professional and the clients alike—had been lulled into believing that functional sex was based on simple and mechanical requirements. This was just not true: Sex was, in fact, a mystery. Paul and Andrea were somehow expecting just to go ahead with their sex life (which had always been problematic), acting as if this erection was the same as any other erection, and pretending that it was not surprising to maintain a constant erection. It was suggested that the partners had not adequately explored the newness and uniqueness of the prosthesis as part of their sexual life. In particular, they had not yet had an opportunity to figure out what sex meant beyond an erecting and erect penis. Daring not to have intercourse was difficult for a couple who had gone into debt to pay for erections. Surprisingly, the couple was interested in the concepts of discovery and mystery. To preserve these themes as the couple's own (and to help reduce the medicalization of their sexuality), the therapist suggested that Paul and Andrea should only return if they were unable to continue changing in a direction they desired. They agreed, and are thus far not in need of further treatment.

If we return to the model, we can still find it useful for understanding and describing what happened to this couple. Though the implant worked well enough, Paul had lost an important feedback mechanism for the affective and symbolic level. Having focused for years on the status of his erection during sex, Paul had learned to be very aware of it and to use it as an indicator of his state of arousal, as well as of his desire. Both were struck by the "strangeness" of this phenomenon, which led to feelings of unfamiliarity and withdrawal. Consequently, one of the therapeutic interventions was to prescribe exploratory interactions. It seems clear that, in its present form, the model does not provide a means of predicting one course of systemic change over another. One can speculate about a range of possible outcomes, but cannot predict a specific one.

Conclusion

The model presented here is based upon an interactional and systemic analysis of the communication between two people. Communication requires an interactional fit between corresponding structures in the participants who are involved in the interaction. On the basis of this observation, three levels of interaction have been distinguished: the levels of sensate exchanges, of affect-regulated interactions, and of symbolic interactions. At each level, some of the problems of "tuning in," of establishing an interactional fit, have been discussed, with special emphasis on sexual communication and its rhythmicity. Finally, the relationships between and among the levels have been examined, and the complex network of interacting structures in a dyadic relationship has been outlined.

The model's usefulness lies in its capacity to show how biological, psychological, and social factors relate to one another. As such, it can be used to interpret isolated research findings in a broader context, as well as to explain data that seem contradictory when viewed from a more narrow perspective. We hope that the model will also inspire researchers to test the many hypotheses that are raised by this network of connections. As for the clinician, the major advantage of this model may be that it imposes a dialectical way of thinking: Clinical findings and statements about one structure or one level immediately call forth questions about other structures and levels. Low sexual desire—like many other conditions that seem to fall outside the classical medical model—is a complaint with different meanings and is the endpoint of a pathway of dysregulations, failed attempts at integration, or the incapacity to reach a consistent interactional fit.

References

Bakker, C., & Bakker-Rabdau, M. (1973). *No trespassing: Explorations in human territoriality.* San Francisco: Chandler & Sharp.

Bancroft, T. (1978). The relationship between hormones and sexual behavior in humans. In J. B. Hutchinson (Ed.), *Biological determinants of sexual behavior.* Chichester, England: Wiley.

Bermant, G., & Davidson, J. M. (1974). *Biological bases of sexual behavior.* New York: Harper & Row.

Bowlby, J. (1969). *Attachment and loss: Vol. 1. Attachment.* New York: Basic Books.

Bowlby, J. (1977). The making and breaking of affectional bonds: I. Aetiology and psychotherapy in light of attachment theory. *British Journal of Psychiatry, 130,* 201–210.

Brody, H. (1973). The systems view of man: Implications for medicine, science, and ethics. *Perspectives in Biology and Medicine, 17*(3), 71–92.

Davidson, T. M. (1972). Hormones and reproductive behavior. In S. Levin (Ed.), *Hormones and behavior.* New York: Academic Press.

Eibl-Eibesfeldt, I. (1970). *Ethology: The biology of behavior.* New York: Holt, Rinehart & Winston.

Elkaim, M. (1986). A systemic approach to couple therapy. *Family Process, 25*(1), 35–42.

Engel, G. L. (1977). The need for a new medical model: A challenge for biomedicine. *Science, 196*, 129–136.

Engel, G. L. (1980). The clinical application of the biopsychosocial model. *American Journal of Psychiatry, 137*, 535–544.

Freeman, W. J. (1983). The physiological basis of mental images. *Biological Psychiatry, 18*, 1107–1125.

Gagnon, J. H., Rosen, R. C., & Leiblum, S. R. (1982). Cognitive and social aspects of sexual dysfunction: Sexual scripts in sex therapy. *Journal of Sex and Marital Therapy, 8*(1), 44–56.

Glenn, M. L. (1984). *On diagnosis: A systemic approach.* New York: Brunner/Mazel.

Hart, B. (1969). Gonadal hormones and sexual reflexes in the female rat. *Hormones and Behavior, 1*, 65–71.

Kandel, E. R. (1979). Small systems of neurons. *Scientific American, 241*, 66–76.

Kandel, E. R. (1983). From metapsychology to molecular biology: Explorations into the nature of anxiety. *American Journal of Psychiatry, 140*, 1277–1293.

Kaplan, H. S. (1979). *Disorders of sexual desire.* New York: Brunner/Mazel.

LoPiccolo, J., & Stock, W. E. (1986). Treatment of sexual dysfunction. *Journal of Consulting and Clinical Psychology, 54*, 158–167.

Masters, W. H., & Johnson, V. E. (1966). *Human sexual response.* Boston: Little, Brown.

Rapoport, A. (1974). *Conflict in man-made environment.* Harmondsworth, England: Penguin.

Reiss, D. (1981). *The family's construction of reality.* Cambridge, MA: Harvard University Press.

Reiss, D. (1982). The working family: A researcher's views of health in the household. *American Journal of Psychiatry, 139*, 1412–1420.

Ross, E. D. (1981). The aprosodias: Functional anatomic organization of the affective components of language in the right hemisphere. *Archives of Neurology, 38*, 561–569.

Sager, C. J. (1976). *Marriage contracts and couple therapy.* New York: Brunner/Mazel.

Sheldon, A., & Baker, F. (Eds.), (1970). *Systems and medical care.* Cambridge, MA: MIT Press.

Stern, D. (1985). *The interpersonal world of the infant: A view from psychoanalysis and developmental psychology.* New York: Basic Books.

Suda, M., Hayaishi, D., & Nakagawa, H. (Eds.). (1979). *Biological rhythms and their central control mechanism.* New York: Elsevier.

Verhulst, J., & Heiman, J. R. (1979). An interactional approach to sexual dysfunctions. *American Journal of Family Therapy, 7*(4), 19–36.

Watzlawick, P. (Ed.), (1984). *The invented reality.* New York: Norton.

Wehr, T. A., Wirz-Justice, A., Goodwin, F. K., Duncan, W., & Gillin, T. C. (1979). Phase advance of circadian sleep–wake cycle as an antidepressant. *Science, 206*, 710–713.

Biological and Medical Perspectives

IV

11

Hormones and Libido

R. Taylor Segraves

Although we realize that biological factors may play a relatively secondary role in the majority of desire problems, we have nevertheless chosen to include three chapters in this section to assess the impact of hormonal, pharmacological, and medical factors. Aside from their obvious importance in certain clinical instances, biological factors need to be included in any comprehensive evaluation of sexual desire. In addition, clinical research has focused increasingly on hormonal correlates of desire disorders, along with a continuing search for new pharmacological treatments. While the chapters in this section review the role of biological factors in considerable detail, both Segraves (in this chapter and the one following) and Bullard (in Chapter 13) emphasize the subtle interplay between physiological and psychological determinants of desire disorders. In fact, a major theme of the section is the need for clinicians to intervene at multiple levels, even in cases of clear-cut organic pathology.

Chapter 11 begins with a succinct overview of the emerging field of behavioral endocrinology. In particular, Segraves, an outstanding psychopharmacologist and psychiatrist, draws our attention to the complex homeostatic mechanisms that regulate the production of sex steroid hormones in males and females. Although sex therapists have traditionally focused on the role of testosterone as the "libido hormone," Segraves notes that other hormones, including prolactin, may be equally as relevant. Furthermore, in considering the role of androgens in male desire, the author points out that the critical levels required to sustain sexual interest have not been firmly established, nor has it been demonstrated that the administration of supraphysiological doses of testosterone can have a libido-enhancing effect. On the other hand, numerous situations of androgen insufficiency have been shown to be associated with diminished desire, and these are reviewed in depth.

Hormonal effects on female sexual desire are reviewed in the next part

271

of the chapter. Beginning with a critical discussion of the role of menstrual cycle effects on female libido, Segraves considers the possible impact of exogenous hormone administration (such as the use of oral contraceptives) on androgen therapy. Although some research in this area has shown promising results for hormonal treatment of low desire in women, the author cautions that more research is needed before these findings can be applied clinically. Regarding the impact of menopause on desire, Segraves suggests that hormone replacement therapy may act indirectly, via an improved sense of general well-being, to stimulate sexual interest in older women.

After providing an incisive review of the key theoretical and research issues in this area, Segraves illustrates by means of a series of intriguing case studies the continual interplay of psychogenic and biogenic factors. These case examples highlight the importance of approaching treatment from a psychological perspective even when hormonal interventions are indicated, if a successful outcome is to be achieved.

R. Taylor Segraves, M.D., Ph.D., is Associate Director of the Department of Psychiatry at Cleveland Metropolitan General Hospital, Cleveland, Ohio, and Professor of Psychiatry at Case Western Reserve University Medical School.

Sexual function is the result of both biological and psychosocial influences. Among the various biological influences on sexual behavior, endocrine function is clearly a major factor. The precise nature and magnitude of the effects of endocrinological function on libido constitute a topic of considerable importance for clinicians involved in the treatment of psychosocial disorders—a topic that has intrigued humans from antiquity to the present (Schiavi & White, 1976). It is clear that normal endocrine function is necessary for human reproduction and that sexual behavior in most mammals is under close endocrinological control. In primates and especially in the human, sexual behavior is more independent of strict hormonal control, and the exact effects of gonadal hormones on the expression of sexual behavior are unclear. The pronounced effects of social learning tend to make it far more difficult to demonstrate the effects of variations in endocrinological function on human libido (Bancroft, 1983). This has led many to propose that humans have transcended their gonads with the development of higher cerebral cortical function, and that hormones play a minor role in controlling human sexual behavior.

Considerable controversy exists in the scientific literature concerning the relative magnitude of endocrinological versus psychosocial influences in the genesis and maintenance of sexual desire and behavior. Nonpsychiatric physicians who have witnessed the devastating effects of low androgen production on sexual function in hypogonadal men, and who have seen dramatic restoration of function with the administration of exogenous androgens, understandably tend to propose that endocrinological factors play the predominant role in human sexual behavior and that psychosocial factors are of minor significance. On the other hand, psychotherapists have observed the crippling effects of interpersonal discord on libido and the restoration of libido after successful psychotherapy. Psychotherapists also tend to see the patients who have received inappropriate endocrinological interventions without benefit, and thus may question the effectiveness of such interventions. Reality rests somewhere between these two viewpoints.

The available literature suggests that humans have not escaped completely from the endocrinological control of sexual behavior and that humans are similar in certain ways to the other mammals. On the other hand, it is also obvious that social learning plays an extremely important role in human sexual behavior. In certain disease states that represent extreme deviations from normality, it is relatively easy to demonstrate the effect of endocrine function on human sexuality. However, these types of patients are rarely seen by psychotherapists. The questions of relevance to practicing therapists are these: (1) What is the role of endocrine variables in determining libido in the typical patient? (2) When should endocrinological evaluations and therapies be considered?

The field of behavioral endocrinology is in its infancy. However, a number of developments, such as the ability to isolate and synthesize the major sex hormones and the development of techniques permitting the accurate measurement of blood levels of most of the significant hormones, permit the study of the relationship between gonadal hormones and behavior. Similarly, the last two decades have witnessed considerable increases in the sophistication and precision of our description and measurement of sexual behavior. These separate developments in differing disciplines permit the contemporary investigator to define the interrelationship of sexual behavior and endocrinological variables more accurately. Unfortunately, much of the information currently available was gathered prior to these recent developments. Thus, the reader is asked to bear with me as we attempt to unravel the connection between gonadal steroids and libido in the human. This unraveling will involve looking for a general pattern across studies of differing levels of methodological sophistication.

Review of Basic Endocrinology

This section is included as a brief review of basic sexual endocrinology for nonphysician readers. It and the one that follows are included to facilitate an understanding of later sections in this chapter. However, readers who find these sections especially tedious may prefer to skip to the clinical sections, which are written to be readable as independent text. For purposes of clarity of presentation, a general outline of endocrinological principles is presented here, and minor exceptions to the major points are not reviewed.

The major endocrine system concerned with sexual behavior is the pituitary–gonadal system, although the adrenal cortex also produces sex hormones. The three principal groups of sex hormones—androgens (e.g., testosterone), estrogens (e.g., estradiol) and progestogens (e.g., progesterone)—have somewhat similar structures, and considerable interconversion occurs. For example, a substantial literature suggests that testosterone is converted to estradiol in the hypothalamus and that it is the intracellular estradiol that virilizes the neuronal pathways (McEven, Davis, & Parsons, 1979). Also, men and women have detectable levels of both androgens and estrogens in the blood. The importance of this information is that one cannot simply conceptualize androgens and estrogens as "male" and "female" hormones in an absolute sense. This point will assume greater significance when the evidence concerning testosterone as the libido hormone for both sexes is reviewed.

Hormones are substances that allow one group of cells to influence the activity of another group of cells, often far removed from the initial cells that produce the hormone. For example, luteinizing hormone (LH) is secreted from the pituitary, travels to the testes, and at the cellular level in the testes stimulates the production of testosterone, another hormone. Most of the sex hormones are bound to plasma proteins in the blood, and only the free or unbound hormone is usually biologically active. The significance of this for the clinician is that measures of free hormone (e.g., free testosterone) may be better indices of effective sex hormone levels at the cellular level than tests that also measure bound hormone levels (e.g., total testosterone). Most of the cells affected by sex hormones have specific receptor sites. Thus, the effective action of a hormone may relate both to receptor sensitivity at the cellular level and to absolute hormone levels in the blood. The importance of this is that absolute measures of circulating free hormones are only an approximation of the magnitude of hormonal effects. There is evidence that the sex hormones alter excitability of cell membranes in the brain (Kang, Singh, & Anand, 1971) and that the hypothalamus has receptors for gonadal steroids (Jones, 1985). Thus, there is a mechanism by which gonadal hormones could influence libido—namely, by their effects on cells in the brain.

Hormonal influences on human sexuality can be grouped into two major effects: organizing and activating. It is well known that adequate levels of androgen are necessary for the fetus, whatever its chromosomal sex, to develop male external genitalia (Money & Ehrhardt, 1972). It is also clear that a variety of reproductive behaviors in mammals are mediated by gonadal steroids and that these behaviors are "imprinted" in the developing brain and elicited in the mature brain. During critical periods of development, androgens are necessary for establishing the male pattern of gonadotropin release. Thus, in lower animals, it is clear that neural patterns are imprinted under the influence of gonadal steriods at certain critical periods of development. This imprinting appears necessary to the elicitation of sexual behavior by gonadal steroids in the adult. The significance of this is that one may be unable to discuss the activating effects of gonadal steroids on adult sexual behavior without also considering the previous organizing effects of the same hormones. The magnitude of the effect of organizing prenatal gonadal steroids in determining sexual behavior in the human adult is unknown; however, several studies (Ehrhardt *et al.*, 1985; Meyer-Bahlburg *et al.*, 1985) have produced suggestive evidence of such an effect.

Another factor complicating the study of the effects of gonadal steroids (hormones) on libido and sexual behavior is the presence of homeostatic mechanisms controlling the release of the sex hormones. Thus, one cannot simply give experimental subjects exogenous sources of such hormones and then measure changes in sexual behavior. Similarly, one cannot administer oral testosterone to a patient without monitoring serum testosterone levels. In many cases, the administration of exogenous hormones will not lead to a sustained increase in the circulating hormone levels in the blood, because the body detects an elevation in the hormone levels and accordingly decreases its endogenous production of such steroids. An understanding of the homeostatic mechanisms requires a brief discussion of the neurophysiology of the anterior pituitary–gonadal system.

Review of Basic Neurophysiology

For the reader's convenience, a schematic representation of the homeostatic control of gonadal hormone secretion is given in Figure 1. Central nervous system effects on the anterior pituitary–gonadal system are mediated through the hypothalamus. The hypothalamus influences the system by means of a controlling hormone, gonadotropin-releasing hormone (GnRH), which it secretes and transports to the anterior pituitary gland via the hypophyseal portal system. GnRH stimulates the basophilic cells of the anterior pituitary to produce LH and follicle-stimulating hormone (FSH). In the male, LH stimulates the interstitial cells of the testes to produce testosterone. The secretion of the gonadal steroids is subject to homeostatic control or negative feedback effects. Thus, the major sex steroids (e.g., testosterone) act primarily at the level of the hypothalamus to decrease the release of GnRH, which in turn decreases the secretion of testosterone.

The neurophysiology of the pituitary–gonadal system in the female is analogous to that in the male, but more complicated because of the existence of both positive and negative effects of estrogen on the hypothalamus

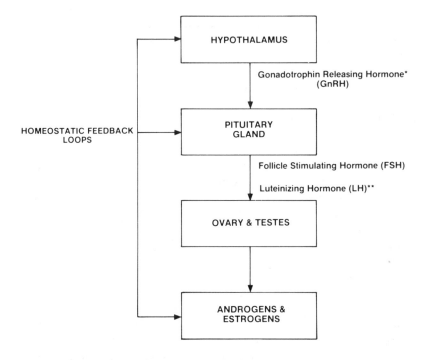

* Also known as Luteinizing Hormone-Releasing Hormone (LHRH)
** Also known as Interstitial Cell Stimulating Hormone (ICSH)

Figure 1. Hypothalamic–pituitary–gonadal axis.

(Sanders & Bancroft, 1982). In the first half of the menstrual cycle, there is a gradual rise in FSH levels, and a new ovarian follicle begins growth. This follicle secretes increasing amounts of estradiol. FSH levels begin to fall because of the negative feedback of estradiol on FSH release. There is a preovulatory surge of LH, provoking ovulation. This surge of LH in the presence of increasing levels of estradiol is referred to as "positive feedback" and is unique to the female. After ovulation, the ovarian follicle (now called the corpus luteum) produces both progesterone and estradiol. When the corpus luteum regresses, menstruation begins (Shaw, 1978). Clearly, in the human female, there is an altered endocrine environment at different points of the menstrual cycle. If there is hormonal control of libido in the female, one might suspect variations in libido during different points of the menstrual cycle. This subject is discussed later in this chapter.

PROLACTIN. There has recently been considerable interest in the pituitary hormone prolactin because of the association between elevated levels of prolactin (hyperprolactinemia) and sexual disorders, including diminished libido (J. N. Carter *et al.*, 1978; Weizman *et al.*, 1983). Prolactin is a hormone capable of initiating and sustaining lactation in the female. Its function in the male is unknown. This hormone is secreted by the pituitary, and the hypothalamic control of pituitary secretion of prolactin appears to be dopaminergic. Drugs that antagonize dopamine appear to facilitate higher levels of dopamine secretion. The evidence concerning the relationship between prolactin and libido is discussed later in this chapter.

Hormones and Libido in the Male

In subprimate mammals, it is quite clear that male sexual behavior is dependent on androgens. With castration (removal of the testes and thus of the major source of testosterone), ejaculation, intromission, and then mounting behavior are lost. However, there is tremendous individual variation in the response to castration even within animal species. This has led some investigators to postulate that the critical factor is the sensitivity of target tissues to small titers of androgen, rather than the absolute levels of androgen (Bancroft, 1983). Since androgen is also produced by the adrenal glands, castration markedly reduces but does not eliminate androgen from the circulation.

In humans, most of the evidence concerning the relationship of androgen levels to libido comes from studies of patients who are hypogonadal (androgen-deficient) as the result of various disease states. These naturalistic studies must be viewed with caution, because variables other than low androgen production may be involved in the various conditions. Another difficulty in interpreting these clinical reports is that many investigators fail to make a clear distinction between libido and performance variables. In spite of these methodological problems, the current evidence clearly indicates a strong relationship between libido and testosterone levels in the human male. In hypogonadal states, the majority of males report a marked decrease of libido, which is restored by the administration of exogenous testosterone. However, the available evidence does not allow one to specify the nature of the relationship between libido and testosterone. For example, it does not appear that the relationship between testosterone and libido is a simple linear function. There is scant evidence that the administration of supraphysiological doses of androgens to men with previously normal levels of libido has a libido-enhancing effect. It is also unclear how low androgen levels need to fall before a detectable change in libido occurs. Clearly, this information is of critical importance to the practicing clinician. At present, it is known that androgen replacement is indicated for men with markedly low testosterone production. Unfortunately, current information does not give clear indications as to when androgen replacement or augmentation should not be included in the treatment regimen. For example, it is not known whether androgen replacement is helpful in men with borderline-low or low-normal testosterone levels.

This section proceeds by first reviewing evidence concerning levels of libido in various hypogonadal states and the effects of replacement testosterone in these conditions; the relationship between libido and variations in testosterone production among men without detectable abnormalities is then discussed. The effects of hyperprolactinemia are also briefly mentioned. The section concludes with a discussion of the clinical ramifications of this information.

Hypogonadal States

Surgical Castration

Castration (orchidectomy) eliminates the testicular sources of androgens and dramatically lowers the level of androgen in the body; thus, the sexual behavior of castrates is a possible source of information concerning the role of androgens in male sexual behavior. Castration is currently used as treatment for sex offenders in countries other than the United States and as a palliative measure for some neoplasms. A fairly extensive literature of varying methodological quality exists on the sexual behavior of castrates (Heim, 1981; Heim & Hursch, 1979). These studies are consistent in reporting that orchidectomy results in a dramatic loss of sexual drive and activity in the majority of patients (Luttge, 1971; Rose, 1972; Sturup, 1979). A typical sequence of events occurs. First, the man notices a dramatic drop in sexual appetite. This is followed in 3–4 weeks by the loss of the ability to ejaculate. Much later, there will be a drop in the level of sexual activity. Also, some men will begin to report erectile problems. It appears that the erectile problems are secondary to a decrease in libido and not due to a specific effect of androgen withdrawal on the erectile mechanism.

Unfortunately, the data concerning the sexual effects of castration do not unequivocally demonstrate that adequate levels of androgens are necessary for human sexual behavior. Castration is a symbolic as well as a physical act, and it is impossible to measure the relative contribution of psychological and endocrinological factors to diminished sexual activity in castrates. The effects of castration are more severe and more difficult to reverse by exogenous androgen therapy if castration occurs prior to puberty. This suggests that adequate androgen levels may be necessary for the acquisition of sexual behavior, but not as necessary for its maintenance once sexual behavior has been established. It is of note that a minority of patients remain sexually active for years past castration (Bremer, 1959). Thus, it is clear that high levels of androgens are not necessary to sustain sexual activity in all men.

These conflicting data can be interpreted in various ways. For example, one could argue that sexual behavior only requires minimal levels of androgen and that the adrenal cortex supplies sufficient androgen to sustain sexual behavior in some castrates. In keeping with this viewpoint, Hamilton (1943) studied two male patients who remained sexually active, although they had been castrated 13 and 18 years previously. Biological assays demonstrated low titers of urinary androgen in both men. From a social learning perspective, one might argue that androgens are necessary for the initial acquisition of sexual behavior, but that social learning can maintain such behavior once it is firmly established, in spite of low testosterone levels. The social learning perspective, however, appears inadequate to explain the devastating effect of orchidectomy on most men and its reversal by exogenous androgens. The explanation I favor is that androgen activation of central nervous system receptors and social learning are both necessary for male sexual behavior, With castration, the biological urge to copulate is lost or dramatically reduced. However, sexual activity may be maintained in certain men by other psychological factors, such as the desire for physical intimacy, the fear of displeasing a life partner, or the need to reaffirm one's manhood.

The available literature is also inconsistent regarding the erectile capacity of castrates. Some studies report that castrated men suffer from impotence, whereas others emphasize the loss of the desire to copulate. It has been suggested that marked reduction of libido is the major observation in hypogonadal men. The reports of impotence may reflect performance anxiety in men who have attempted coitus in the presence of low libido (Bancroft, 1983).

Chemical Castration

Pharmacological sex drive reduction by the antiandrogenic agents (estrogen, medroxyprogesterone, and cyproterone acetate) is an alternative way to manage chronic sexual offenders. Most of these drugs severely depress androgen levels. Thus, studies of the effects of these drugs in sexual offenders offer another situation in which one can observe the effects of androgen withdrawal on sexual behavior. Theoretically, these drugs might antagonize testosterone of both testicular and adrenal origin, and thus might produce a more complete withdrawal of androgen.

Estrogens were originally used to treat male sexual offenders, because of their antiandrogenic and libido-reducing effects (Bancroft, Tennant, Loucas, & Cass, 1974; Golla & Hodge, 1949). These drugs are seldom utilized for that purpose at present because of serious side effects. These agents are mentioned because there have been recent reports of gynecomastia (male breast enlargement) and libido disturbances in men who have been occupationally exposed to estrogenic compounds (Mills, Jeffreys, & Stolley, 1984) or even men who have used hair lotions containing estrogens

(Gottswinger, Korth-Schutz, & Ziegler, 1984). Thus estrogen exposure should be considered in the differential diagnosis of low libido in males.

In the United States, medroxyprogesterone acetate (Depo-Provera) is the principal antiandrogen used for pharmacological sex drive reduction (Freund, 1980). This drug markedly lowers serum testosterone levels and has been found to diminish sexual libido (Blumer & Migeon, 1975; Money, 1970; Money et al., 1975) and recidivism in sexual offenders (Berlin & Meinecke, 1981). In the clinical reports, it appears that this drug markedly diminishes libido without interfering with the capacity to have erections. Its effect against repetition of sexual crimes appears to be related to its effect on libido.

In Europe, cyproterone acetate is the principal antiandrogen utilized to control chronic sexual offenders. This agent appears to work both through competitive blocking of androgen receptors and through antigonadotropic effects on the pituitary (Mugglestone, 1983). It decreases the amount of circulating serum testosterone and has been reported by numerous authors to diminish libido markedly (Boas, 1973; Cooper, Ismail, Phanjoo, & Love, 1972; Jeffcoate, Matthews, Edwards, Field, & Besser, 1980; Laschet & Laschet, 1969) and sexual activity (Herman & Beach, 1980). In a controlled double-blind study, Bancroft et al. (1974) found that cyproterone acetate significantly lowered sexual interest and self-reported sexual activity. However, it has minimal effects on the erectile response to erotic material presented in the laboratory. Like estrogens and medroxyprogesterone, this agent appears to lower libido dramatically without interfering with the capacity to have erections.

Aging

Another situation in which androgen insufficiency occurs is aging. It is well established that androgen levels decline in males after the ages of 40–50 (Pirke & Doerr, 1973; Stearns, MacDonnell, & Kaufman, 1974; Yesawage, Davidson, Widrow, & Berger, 1985). Because plasma gonadotropin levels are frequently elevated in this age group (Rubens, Dhont, & Vermeulen, 1974), the decline in androgens is probably related to testicular failure (Jones, 1985). Sexual function in aging men shows a similar decline (Voerwoerdt, Pfeiffer, & Wang, 1969). These observations have led to the concept of a male "climacteric," with a precipitous decline of testosterone levels accounting for loss of libido in middle-aged and elderly men.

Fortunately, the concept of a male climacteric is not supported by the research data. A gradual, but not precipitous, decline in both sexual activity and testosterone levels occurs with aging. Also, the changes in hormonal function with aging do not appear to explain the change in sexual activity. Davidson, Gray, and Smith (1983) studied the relationship between various endocrinological variables and self-report of libido and sexual behavior in 220 men from the ages of 41 to 93. Although they observed strong relationships between aging and libido, the relationship between libido and androgen activity was low, suggesting that nonendocrinological factors may explain the decline in sexuality with aging. Davidson, Kwan, and Greenleaf (1982) suggested that the decline in sexual activity with aging may be due to a change in receptor sensitivity to androgens, rather than to a decline in circulating androgen levels. Of course, psychosocial variables, such as marital boredom, the decreased attractiveness of the aging partner, and chronic illness may explain some of the decreased sexual activity among aging men.

Hypogonadal States and Androgen Replacement

Disease states associated with hypogonadism also offer an opportunity to study the relationship between androgen levels and sexual function. In endocrinological practice, one encounters patients with hypogonadism that is due either to failure of the gonad or to inappropriate stimulation of the gonad by the pituitary. The usual medical treatment is the administration of exogenous testosterone. Thus, the clinical syndrome of hypogonadism offers a context in which sexual behavior can be observed in the untreated patient, after treatment with exogenous hormone, and during withdrawal of exogenous hormone. The clinical literature is consistent in demonstrating a marked reduction in libido and sexual activity in untreated hypogonadal men (Beumont, Bancroft, Beardwood, & Russell, 1972; Money, 1961). With androgen replacement, libido and sexual activity are restored to normal levels. This effect of androgen replacement has also been demonstrated in controlled studies (Davidson, Camargo, & Smith, 1979; Luisi & Franchi, 1980; Shakkebaek, Bancroft, Davidson, & Warner, 1981). The observation of such a clear relationship between androgen therapy and sexual function is the reason why many contemporary physicians seemingly routinely prescribe androgen for male sexual difficulties, including psychogenic impotence.

In most of the studies of the relationship between androgen replacement and sexual behavior, it is difficult to ascertain whether androgen replacement has had an effect on erectile capacity or libido or both. In other words, dependent measures, such as the frequency of erections or the frequency of problems with erections, have been utilized. In these instances, it is impossible to ascertain whether testosterone influences the capacity to have erections or whether it has a specific effect on libido, independent of the capacity to perform.

Two recent studies suggest that testosterone has a specific effect on libido (presumably mediated by central nervous system receptors) and is not necessary for erectile function. Bancroft and Wu (1983) studied the effect of testosterone undeconoate (oral testosterone, unavailable in the United States) on libido and erectile responsiveness in a double-blind crossover study of eight hypogonadal men and eight normal controls. Patients were requested to self-rate their frequency of sexual acts and thoughts. Also, the magnitude and latency of the erectile response to sexually explicit visual material and personal fantasy were examined. Androgen replacement increased the frequency of sexual acts and thoughts. Untreated hypogonadal men did not differ from normal controls in the magnitude or speed of their erectile response to sexually explicit material, and their erectile response was not augmented by androgen replacement. However, hypogonadal men had decreased responsivity to erotic fantasy as compared to normals, and this response was augmented by androgen replacement. The authors speculated that androgens may facilitate the cognitive processes associated with sexual excitement, and suggested that this may explain the differential effect of androgen on the erectile response to fantasy as compared with visual erotic material. Using a similar design, Kwan, Greenleaf, Mann, Crapo, and Davidson (1983) investigated the effect of testosterone enanthate on self-report of libido and sexual activity, erectile responses to erotic videotapes and fantasy, and nocturnal penile tumescence.. Although self-report data demonstrated a clear effect of testosterone on sexual activity and interest, testosterone did not have an effect on the magnitude or speed of erectile response to erotic videotapes or sexual fantasies. The differential effect of testosterone on the erectile response to fantasy and visual erotic material reported by Bancroft and Wu (1983) was not replicated. Hypogonadal men did demonstrate decreased magnitude and duration of nocturnal erections as compared to normal controls. These erectile parameters were restored to normal with replacement testosterone. The authors concluded that testosterone has a specific effect on libido.

The hypothesis that testosterone has a specific effect on libido and that androgens are not necessary for erectile function is discordant with the clinical impression that impotence frequently occurs with androgen insufficiency and is cured by androgen replacement (Spark, White, & Connolly, 1980; Streem, 1982; Whitehead, 1981). However, Bancroft and Wu (1983) have suggested that the impotence noted in hypogonadism may be related to decreased libido and secondary performance anxiety. In other words, clinicians may be observing psychogenic impotence superimposed upon biogenic desire disorders.

The research on replacement therapy in hypogonadal men has also produced some valuable data concerning the dose–response relationship between androgen levels and sexual activity. In other words, investigators have been able to examine the level at which additional amounts of exogenous testosterone fail to continue to augment sexual activity. This information has relevance to the question of the indications for testosterone therapy in men with complaints of decreased libido. Unfortunately, the data are not clear-cut. On the one hand, investigators have found that there is a linear relationship between circulating androgen levels and sexual activity when testosterone is replaced in hypogonadal men. However, this tends to disappear as one approaches the normal range of blood androgens (Davidson *et al.*, 1982). These data suggest that testosterone therapy in men whose serum levels of testosterone are within the normal range will be ineffective in augmenting sexual responsivity. However, Davidson *et al.* (1982) found that exogenous testosterone therapy improved nocturnal erections in elderly men with diminished sexual activity. These patients had normal serum androgen levels prior to treatment.

Eugonadal States

Endogenous Androgens in the Normal Range and Libido

As reviewed above, it is clear that androgen replacement increases the level of sexual activity in hypogonadal men. However, it remains unclear whether increases of androgen levels within the normal range augment sexual activity or whether there is a certain minimal level necessary for normal function, above which excess androgen has no effect. Another approach to this question is to examine the relationship between endogenous androgen levels and sexual activity of normal men. A number of studies have found minimal evidence of relationship between endogenous androgen levels and self-report of various types of sexual activities (Brown, Monti, & Corriveau, 1978; Kraemer *et al.*, 1976; Raboch & Starka, 1973). However, it is possible that increments of endogenous androgen levels within "normal" ranges may have subtle effects on libido that are not picked up by self-report measures. There is suggestive evidence of a relationship between endogenous androgen levels and the latency and magnitude of the erectile response to erotic stimuli (Lange, Brown, Wincze, & Zwick, 1980; Rubin & Henson, 1979). These data are of theoretical interest, but their clinical significance, if any, is unclear.

Testosterone Therapy in Eugonadal Men

Because of the clear decline of sexual function in men with hypogonadism, a number of clinical investigators have evaluated the effectiveness of various testosterone preparations in the treatment of psychogenic impotence (Cooper, Ismail, Phanjoo, & Love, 1972; Cooper, Smith, Ismail, & Loraine, 1973; Roberts & Sloboda, 1974). These studies have failed to provide evidence that exogenous androgens are of value in the treatment of impotence of psychogenic or undetermined etiology (Schiavi & White, 1976). In a recent study, O'Carroll and Bancroft (1984) investigated the effects of testosterone on sexual interest and activity in two groups of male patients. Patients with normal baseline androgen levels but with a complaint of inhibited sexual desire had a significant increase in the frequency of sexual thoughts when given testosterone. Testosterone was ineffective in changing erectile function in men with inhibited sexual desire and in men with erectile dysfunction.

Comment: Testosterone Effects on Hypogonadal and Eugonadal Men

The studies reviewed appear consistent in finding evidence of diminished sexual activity in various hypogonadal states and in finding restoration of normal sexual function with replacement hormone therapy. The studies whose methodology has allowed the reader to distinguish between effects on libido and effects on erectile capacity also appear to be consistent in suggesting that testosterone has a libido-enhancing effect and that its effect on erectile function (when present) is probably secondary to its libido-enhancing effect. There is no convincing evidence that testosterone influences erectile capacity independently of its effect on libido.

The question of whether there is a certain minimal level of testosterone that is sufficient for normal sexual function and above which excessive testosterone administration is ineffective remains unclear. The available evidence suggests that the effects of testosterone administration to men with normal androgen levels are subtle and of small magnitude if they exist at all. However, a number of studies using different methodology have suggested that testosterone may continue to have a small libido-enhancing effect even within normal physiological ranges.

Hyperprolactinemia

Hyperprolactinemia (excessive blood levels of the pituitary hormone, prolactin) has been reported to be associated with sexual problems in both male (J. N. Carter et al., 1978; Franks, Jacobs, Martin, & Nabarro, 1978) and female (Weizman et al., 1983) patients. It is important that clinicians be aware of this syndrome, as the clinical presentation can appear quite similar to psychogenic problems (Schwartz, Bauman, & Masters, 1982). For example, male patients with hyperprolactinemia may complain of situational impotence. The other reason that clinicians need to be aware of this syndrome is that diminished libido secondary to hyperprolactinemia may be the first sign of a pituitary tumor. The diagnosis is made by determining plasma prolactin levels, using radioimmunoassay techniques that are available in most hospital laboratories. Computerized tomography of the sella turcica is employed when a pituitary tumor is suspected. Referral to a competent endocrinologist is mandatory when one suspects that a patient has hyperprolactinemia.

Although numerous investigators have reported the presence of sexual disorders in patients with hyperprolactinemia, it is difficult to ascertain whether the primary sexual problem is diminished libido, erectile failure, or both. Marrama *et al.* (1984) closely studied ten male patients who received bromocriptine therapy for hyperprolactinemia. All of these patients noted a progressive drop in libido prior to treatment; in a majority of men, this drop led to impotence. It is quite possible that the erectile failure in hyperprolactinemia is secondary to decreased libido, rather than a direct effect on the erectile mechanism.

Indications for Endocrine Evaluation and Treatment

Determination of serum prolactin and testosterone levels should be part of the routine evaluation of every male patient with a primary complaint of low libido. Possible exceptions to this statement would include cases where severe marital discord or a depressive illness has clearly preceded the onset of the libido disturbance. Justifications for the statement that serum prolactin and testosterone assays should be routinely performed include the following: (1) the low cost of such determinations; (2) the difficulty of distinguishing endocrinological from psychological libido disturbances by symptomatology alone; and (3) the possibility of overlooking certain treatable serious illnesses that might present as complaints of low libido.

Routine determination of serum prolactin and testosterone involves negligible risk (i.e., venipuncture) and is relatively inexpensive. The costs for both tests might range from $55 to $200 in various medical centers. Elevated prolactin levels usually occur in conjunction with abnormally low serum testosterone levels (Jones, 1985). However, this relationship is not consistent (Nagulesparem, Ang, & Jenkins, 1978), and attempts to minimize patient costs by utilizing serum testosterone alone are ill advised, because one might miss an occasional patient with hyperprolactinemia. The prevalence of endocrinopathies in patients with sexual disorders may vary considerably with variations in clinical settings and referral networks. One clinical series suggested that the prevalence of endocrinopathies associated with sexual complaints may exceed 30% in a specialized endocrinological practice (Spark *et al.*, 1980). Another study suggested that the incidence of male patients with detectable endocrine abnormalities in a general hospital sexual dysfunction clinic was approximately 15% (Segraves, Schoenberg, & Ivanoff, 1983). This same study found that the incidence of endocrinopathies in men specifically complaining of low libido was higher than in men complaining of erectile problems. Presumably, the prevalence of endocrine disease in the outpatient practice of psychotherapists treating young adults is quite low. However, the low cost and minimal risk associated with prolactin and testosterone determinations warrant the inclusion of these procedures as part of the initial evaluation.

There is no evidence to suggest that the complaint of diminished libido secondary to an endocrinopathy can be distinguished from the same complaint resulting from psychological causes. Sexual problems resulting from endocrinopathies tend to have insidious onsets, and interpersonal discord may result from the diminished libido. Thus, the clinician may not be able to discern from the clinical presentation and history whether the diminished libido is primary or secondary to other interpersonal problems. It is of note in this regard that clinicians at the Masters and Johnson Institute in St. Louis (formerly the Reproductive Biology Research Foundation) have reported moderately successful psychotherapeutic interventions in patients who were later discovered to have hyperprolactinema (Schwartz et al., 1982).

Both hyperprolactinemia and hypogonadism may have relatively benign or more serious etiologies (Streem, 1982). Hyperprolactinemia may result from various causes. The most serious situation to be ruled out is that of a pituitary tumor. Because the optic tracts are located near the pituitary gland, an expanding pituitary tumor can permanently impair vision. Hypogonadism can likewise have serious and more benign causes. The major concern in patients with hypogonadism is to ascertain whether the problem is due to testicular failure (usually benign) or to a central failure in the hypothalamic–pituitary system (possibly a pituitary tumor). A review of Figure 1 demonstrates that hypogonadism may result from an abnormality at either the testes, the hypothalamus, or the pituitary. Thus, a finding of abnormally low testosterone levels should be followed by determination of the levels of pituitary stimulating hormones (FSH and LH). Because of the lack of negative feedback, testicular failure would be associated with increased levels of FSH and LH. The presence of low testosterone in association with normal or low FSH and LH would indicate that the problem is probably at the level of the pituitary or hypothalamus. This information is summarized in Figure 2. Clinically, one would always follow up the finding of low testosterone with the determination of basal LH and FSH levels. If these are high, one can safely conclude that the problem is gonadal failure. If FSH and LH are normal or low, one would administer GnRH to determine whether the problem is pituitary or hypothalamic in origin. Failure to respond to GnRH stimulation would suggest that the problem is pituitary in origin. This information is summarized in Figure 3. If a pituitary origin of the problem is suspected, a pituitary tumor must be carefully excluded. The importance of this information is to reaffirm the necessity of a referral to a competent endocrinologist if there is any evidence of endocrinopathy.

	SERUM TESTOSTERONE	FSH LH
PRIMARY TESTICULAR DISEASE (Hypergonadotrophic Hypogonadism)	LOW	INCREASED
HYPOTHALAMIC OR PITUITARY DISEASE (Hypogonadotrophic Hypogonadism)	LOW	NORMAL OR LOW

Figure 2. Distinguishing primary from secondary hypogonadism.

It is advisable for sex therapists to attempt to establish a close working relationship with a competent endocrinologist who has an interest in human sexuality. Because many sexual difficulties involve a combination of biological and psychological factors, the appropriate intervention will often be a combined intervention. Thus, it is important that the psychotherapist and endocrinologist have a collaborative rather than an antagonistic relationship. As a result of subspecialty rivalries and biases, the development of the optimal alliance may evolve slowly after years of cross-referrals. At this point, each professional may begin to realize that each subspecialist has the patient's interests at heart and that each is attempting to help the patient from a different, but equally valid, conceptual orientation. The most common situation requiring a combined psychotherapeutic–endocrinological intervention involves replacement hormone therapy in men with long-standing desire difficulties. In such situations, it is not uncommon for psychotherapy or endocrine therapy alone to be insufficient. For example, the endocrinological problem may have resulted in decreased libido. This biogenic loss of libido may then lead to marital discord, which also diminishes libido. Endocrine therapy may restore the biological urge to copulate, but psychosocial factors then interfere with its behavioral manifestation. In many situations, the appropriate intervention needs to be a combined one.

Other, less common situations also require a close collaboration between the mental health professional and the clinical endocrinologist. The recommendation to begin testosterone replacement therapy is ambivalently received by many patients. Although the patient should discuss the potential

	RESPONSE TO GnRH
HYPOTHALAMIC HYPOGONADISM	INCREASE OF LH
HYPOPITUITARY HYPOGONADISM	FAILURE TO RESPOND

Figure 3. Distinguishing hypothalamic from pituitary hypogonadism.

risks and medical complications of such an intervention with the endocrinologist, he may need to discuss the emotional significance of such an intervention with his psychotherapist. The therapist's attitude toward the endocrinologist and the concept of endocrinological treatment of desire disorders may influence his or her ability to help the patient. In rare instances, the restoration of libido by testosterone therapy may be contraindicated for psychological reasons. For example, the organogenic loss of libido may help to stabilize a relationship that both members desperately need. There have been reports of the endocrinological restoration of desire precipitating divorce (Tolis, Bertrand, & Pinter, 1979). This type of consideration is alien to the training of most endocrinologists. Thus, the endocrinologist needs to respect the mental health professional's expertise in order even to consider such a recommendation.

The question of whether endocrine therapy is effective or should be employed in men who have desire difficulties but whose serum testosterone levels are within "normal" limits is unanswerable at present. As reviewed previously in this section, there is some evidence that increments of androgens even within normal physiological ranges may have subtle influences on libido. Unfortunately, it is unclear whether these changes are of clinical significance. To conceptualize this problem, one needs to realize that there may be considerable individual variability in the response to exogenous testosterone and that "normal" values are based on statistics derived from studying groups of men. In most cases, physicians do not obtain testosterone levels on patients unless an endocrinopathy is suspected. Thus, one rarely has a baseline value for an individual patient. For example, it is conceivable that a patient complaining of decreased libido might be found to have a testosterone value that is low but within the "normal" range. If that same individual has previously had testosterone levels at the high end of the "normal" range, the low "normal" value may be abnormal for that patient.

In actual practice, physicians vary considerably in their approach to men with borderline testosterone values. Some physicians routinely prescribe exogeneous testosterone to men with sexual complaints without determining baseline values or even monitoring the serum testosterone response to exogenous androgens. There appears to be little justification for such an approach. Other physicians will take a more cautious approach, employing a "trial" of replacement therapy in uncertain situations. The sex therapist can often be an important ally both to the physician and the patient through his or her more sophisticated monitoring of libido. Subtle effects may be missed by the physician who may be monitoring erectile capacity and intercourse frequency.

In conclusion, the complicated interplay of psychosocial and biogenic factors in the treatment of desire disorders mandates a close alliance between the mental health professional and the medical consultant. In most cases, neither professional alone has the necessary knowledge base to offer a comprehensive evaluation and treatment regimen.

Hormones and Libido in the Female

Sexual activity in subprimate animals is strongly associated with the cyclicity of ovarian hormones; however, the situation becomes much more complex with human females. In many subprimates, sexual activity is restricted to the time around ovulation (i.e., estrus) and is clearly related to estrogen and/or progesterone levels (Sanders & Bancroft, 1982). In primates, sexual activity occurs throughout the menstrual cycle, and nonhormonal factors play a much more salient role in influencing sexual behavior. The importance of the subprimate animal research to the sexual therapist is the possibility that similar biological mechanisms may operate in the human but are more difficult to demonstrate because of the tremendous influences of social learning.

Attempts to assess the effects of endocrine function on sexual desire in human females have generally focused on three major lines of investigation: (1) studies of the relationship between libido and endogenous hormone production (e.g., cyclic changes in libido during the menstrual cycle and libido as related to baseline levels of endocrine function); (2) studies of the effects of the use of exogenous hormones in various situations (e.g., disease states, the use of oral contraceptives, and replacement hormone therapy in menopause); and (3) studies of changes in libido after changes in endogenous hormone production (e.g., menopause and surgical menopause).

Relationship of Endogenous Hormone Production to Libido

Because of the animal research indicating an association between sexual activity and cyclic changes in endogenous hormone production, numerous investigations have searched for an association between menstrual phases in the human female and libido. In particular, investigators have searched for evidence of periovulatory increase in sexual activity (e.g., presence of estrus-like behavior). A finding of an association between libido and phases of the menstrual cycle might have clinical significance for the sex therapist. For example, one might recommend that a patient with inhibited sexual desire concentrate her sexual activities around midcycle in order to maximize her biological drive state. Other investigators have examined the possibility of an association between variations in reproductive hormone secretory patterns and libido. If such as association were found, these libido-enhancing hormones might be justifiably used as an adjunctive treatment for desire difficulties. For the reader's convenience in understanding the studies relating to sexual activity to phase of the menstrual cycle, schematic representations of the cyclic variations of reproductive hormones during the menstrual cycle are presented in Figures 4 and 5.

Unfortunately, this area of research has produced minimal evidence of a periovulatory increase in libido or sexual activity (Sanders & Bancroft, 1982; Schreiner-Engel, 1980). Many of the older studies had serious methodological flaws, including imprecise definitions of sexual behaviors (Bancroft, 1983) and inference of hormone secretory pattern from the time in the menstrual cycle rather than determination of the pattern via direct assays (Persky *et al.*, 1978). Only a limited number of studies have investigated the relationship of sexual responsivity to phase of the menstrual cycle, using appropriate sequential hormonal determinations over the menstrual cycle. In one of these, Schreiner-Engel, Schiavi, Smith, and White (1981) investigated sexual responsivity to erotic stimuli (as assessed by vaginal photoplethysmography) in different phases of the menstrual cycle. These phases were confirmed by assays of estradiol, progesterone, and testosterone. They found no evidence of a periovulatory increase in sexual responsivity. In fact, sexual arousability was significantly lower during the ovulatory phase than during the follicular and luteal phases. Variation in plasma estradiol and progesterone did not appear related to sexual arousability; however, average serum testosterone across all phases was related to sexual responsivity. Two subsequent studies by independent investigators (Hoon, Bruce, & Kinchloe, 1982; Morrell, Dixen, Carter, & Davidson,

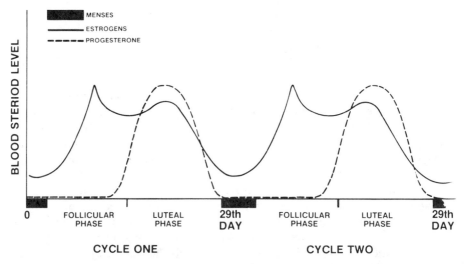

Figure 4. Cyclic variation in progesterone and estrogens over two menstrual cycles.

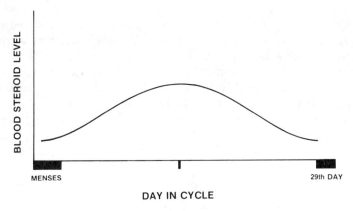

BLOOD STEROID LEVEL

MENSES | 29th DAY

DAY IN CYCLE

Figure 5. Cyclic variation in testosterone.

1984) failed to document a relationship between phase of the menstrual cycle and vaginal response to erotic stimuli.

A number of investigators have attempted to search for associations between cyclic changes in estradiol and progesterone and various indices of female sexuality. Most of the well-conducted studies have failed to document such relationships. A series of studies by Bancroft and his coworkers (Backstrom *et al.,* 1983; Bancroft, Sanders, Davidson, & Warner, 1983; Sanders, Warner, Backstrom, & Bancroft, 1983) investigated the relationship among sexuality, mood, and phase of the menstrual cycle. In their studies, sexual activity was found to be unrelated to plasma estradiol levels. However, the frequency of masturbation was related to midcycle testosterone levels, and sexual interest tended to be highest in the midfollicular phase. The other major group of studies was conducted by Harold Persky and his associates (Persky *et al.,* 1978; Persky, Lief, Strauss, Miller, & O'Brien, 1978; Persky, O'Brien, & Kahn, 1976). They examined the relationship between various aspects of sexual behavior and cyclic variations in reproductive hormones. These studies have been consistent in failing to find an association between estradiol levels and any aspect of sexual behavior. However, there was again suggestive evidence of an association between various measures of sexual activity and testosterone levels.

In summary, current investigation of the relationship (if any) between cyclic changes in estrogens and progesterone during the menstrual cycle and various indices of sexual activity have failed to document any such association. It is possible that such a relationship does exist but that it is difficult to demonstrate because of a number of confounding variables. For example, it is well known that there is a 2- to 3-week time lag between the administration of exogenous testosterone and augmentation of libido in the male. If a similar time lag exists between surges of estradiol or progesterone and libido, an association between variation in these hormones and libido would be very difficult to demonstrate. There is also evidence of an association between sense of well-being and phase of the menstrual cycle. This relationship could complicate the search for a relationship between libido and phase of the menstrual cycle (Sanders *et al.,* 1983). However, a conservative reading of the current data is that there is minimal evidence for the control of human libido by fluctuations in estrogen or progesterone levels. There is suggestive evidence of a relationship between serum testosterone and some aspects of female sexuality. This theme is repeated in later sections of this chapter.

Oral Contraceptive Use

Oral contraceptives remain one of the most frequently used forms of birth control. Early oral contraceptives contained much higher amounts of estrogens and progestogens than steroidal contraceptives in current usage. Oral contraceptives are of two main types: combined (e.g., Enovid, Lo/Ovral) and progesterone alone (e.g., Nor-Q.D., Ovrette). A third type of preparation, known as sequential birth control pills, consists of estrogen for 14–16 days followed by a combination of estrogen and progestin for 5–6 days. Because of reports suggesting increased incidence of endometrial tumors and decreased efficacy, most sequential preparations of this type have been removed from the market. Most of the combined birth control pills contain varying amounts of progestogens (e.g., norgestrel, norethindrone, levonorgestrel, ethynodiol diacetate) combined with either ethinyl estradiol or mestranol (both estrogens). It is clear that exogenous gonadal steroids in oral contraceptives radically alter the normal menstrual cycle, usually inhibiting ovulation and the normal rise in progesterone during the luteal phase. Clearly, if the normal cyclic pattern of endocrine changes were related to libido, one would expect major changes after the administration of oral contraceptives. The question of whether oral contraceptives influence libido is of practical importance to the sexual therapist. For example, one would not wish to begin sex therapy for a complaint that could be more simply remedied by a change in birth control method.

The evidence concerning the effect of oral contraceptives on psychological functioning and sexual activity has been reviewed elsewhere (Bancroft, 1974; Bardwick, 1973; J. Cullberg, 1972; Glick, 1967; Kane, 1976; Sanders & Bancroft, 1982). The available evidence is unclear, but it does not suggest that oral contraceptives have a marked effect on libido apart from other side effects. Some women may experience decreased libido secondary to nausea or mild dysphoria during the first few months on oral contraceptives (Grant & Pryse-Davis, 1968; Kutner & Brown, 1972). A number of controlled studies (e.g., J. Cullberg, 1972; G. Cullberg, 1985; Herzberg, Draper, Johnson, & Nicol, 1971) have failed to demonstrate an effect of oral contraceptives on libido.

Several investigators have produced evidence that oral contraceptive use may be associated with libido disturbances. However, in most cases, the evidence is not totally convincing. For example, Grounds, Davies, and Mowbray (1970) studied side effects of an oral contraceptive (1 mg ethynodiol diacetate plus 0.1 mg mestranol) and reported that there was a significant increase in the complaint of decreased libido during the first month of drug administration. By the end of the second month of use, this complaint was no longer significantly elevated. Other side effects such as nausea also decreased by the second month, suggesting that the decrease of libido may have been secondary to other side effects. Leeton, McMaster, and Worsley (1978) reported that the same oral contraceptive was associated with a decreased sexual response in women in a double-blind crossover study. However, their dependent measure was a composite score taken from five separate questions. The questions included measures of libido, activity, and responsivity. Thus, it is impossible to ascertain what the composite score was really measuring. There are also a number of isolated reports suggesting that oral contraceptives may cause a shift in the phase of the menstrual cycle in which women are more sexually active (e.g., Adams, Gold, & Burt, 1978; Bancroft, Davidson, Warner, & Tyrer, 1980; Udry, Morris & Waller, 1973). These reports have to be evaluated cautiously, because there is minimal evidence of variation in sexual responsivity in different phases of the menstrual cycle in women who are not taking birth control pills.

As reviewed in this section, the evidence concerning a relationship between oral contraceptive use and diminished libido is inconclusive. This does not mean that such an effect does not exist—only that it has not been demonstrated. This state of affairs is obviously not optimal for the practicing clinician who encounters patients with diminished libido while taking oral contraceptives and must make a decision based upon minimal information.

In spite of the absence of conclusive information, certain general guidelines may be offered. If a patient complains of decreased libido in association with other side effects (e.g., nausea and dysphoria) that have persisted beyond the second month of oral contraceptive use, it is possible that the decrease in libido is secondary to these other side effects. In this instance, referral to a gynecologist is clearly indicated. If a patient presents with a solitary complaint of diminished libido that began after oral contraceptive use was initiated, a conservative approach might be a referral to a gynecologist concerning the possibility of a trial period off oral contraceptives. If libido returns with drug discontinuation, another agent might be substituted for the initial drug that was associated with diminished libido. There are no clear guidelines concerning which agents are less likely to interfere with libido.

Androgen Therapy

In the past, androgens were frequently administered to women for a variety of medical conditions, including menstrual irregularities, metastatic cancer, and functional urinary disturbances (A. C. Carter, Cohen, & Shorr, 1947; Greenblatt, 1942). A large number of clinical reports in the older literature document increased libido as a frequent side effect of such treatment (e.g. Abel, 1945; Adair & Hermann, 1946; Greenblatt & Wilcox, 1941). Certain of these case reports are quite striking. Some women requested termination of androgen therapy because they found the increase of libido distressing (Kennedy & Nathanson, 1953; Salmon, 1941). A marked increase in libido was even noted in women receiving androgen therapy for advanced carcinoma (Kennedy & Nathanson, 1953). A number of clinicians were so impressed with the libido-enhancing side effect of androgen therapy that they investigated the effectiveness of androgen therapy for the treatment of hypoactive sexual arousal states and reported beneficial effects (Greenblatt, 1943; Greenblatt, Mortara, & Torpin, 1942; Salmon & Geist, 1943). Loeser (1940) reported that a total dose of 300 mg was necessary to achieve an aphrodisiac effect; however, Groome (1939) reported that testosterone cream applied to the external genitalia had a similar aphrodisiac effect.

The evidence concerning a libido-enhancing effect of exogenous testosterone is impressive. However, these data must be cautiously interpreted. None of the studies reviewed were properly controlled. It is also important to realize that the doses utilized in these studies greatly exceed physiological levels. In other words, it is unclear whether variations in female androgen within the normal physiological range are related to libido. Two separate areas of research suggest that reduction of testosterone below physiological levels reduces libido. Cyproterone acetate, an antiandrogen, adversely affects libido when used for the treatment of hirsutism in women (Appelt & Strauss, 1984). It has also been reported that adrenalectomy following oophorectomy drastically reduces libido. This effect is hypothesized to result from the elimination of adrenal androgens (Waxenberg, Drellich, & Sutherland, 1959). In summary, the web of circumstantial evidence implicating testosterone as the libido hormone in women is intriguing.

Concurrent Use of Androgens and Counseling

Carney, Bancroft, and Mathews (1978) investigated the use of sublingual testosterone (10 mg/day) as an adjunct to sex therapy in women with female sexual unresponsiveness. Blind assessors were utilized. Hormone assays were not employed to ascertain whether plasma testosterone levels were elevated by oral medication. The group receiving androgen had significant improvement on a number of variables, probably related to libido. Unfortunately, Mathews, Whitehead, and Kellett (1983) were unable to replicate this finding. In fact, their data raise questions as to whether this dose of oral testosterone influences plasma testosterone levels. In a different study, Bancroft and associates (Bancroft *et al.*, 1980) evaluated the effectiveness of 20 mg of androstenedione for the treatment of sexually unresponsive women on birth control pills. This dose did significantly elevate plasma testosterone, but was ineffective in alleviating the sexual difficulties.

It should be noted that these studies did not clearly specify the type of complaint being treated. In particular, one might expect supposed libido-enhancing agents such as testosterone to be maximally effective in patients with desire disorders and perhaps ineffective in orgasmic disorders. Because of the hetereogenous populations employed in these studies, one cannot conclude that androgen treatment is ineffective in the treatment of desire problems. Some clinicians (Crenshaw, 1986) have reported that the transient use of testosterone can be helpful in the treatment of women with desire difficulties.

Comment

The use of exogenous androgens to enhance libido in female patients is clearly experimental. If such an approach is utilized, close collaboration with a gynecological endocrinologist is mandatory. Androgen therapy is not without risks. Clitoral enlargement and beard growth are common side effects. Liver damage may be associated with oral androgen, and all androgen treatment involves numerous medical risks, including alteration of salt and water retention, alteration in blood cell production, and hypercalcemia (elevated blood calcium levels). There have been minimal studies of the long-term risks of androgen therapy in females. If androgen therapy can be demonstrated, using good experimental design, to enhance libido, a brief elevation of libido by exogenous androgen might be a useful adjunctive technique in women with inhibited sexual desire who are refractory to conventional sex therapy.

Menopause

Natural Menopause

A complaint of decreased libido attributed by the patient to the "menopause" is not uncommon, and a minority of women report some decline in sexual activity associated with the menopause (Bachmann *et al.*, 1985; Davidson, Gray, & Smith, 1983). With menopause, there is a marked drop in estrogen production, and associated changes take place in the genital tissues. However, it remains unclear whether endocrinological changes associated with the menopause are etiologically related to changes in libido. A wide variety of influences, including aging and decreased sexual ability in the partner (Coop, 1984), may account for decreased sexual activity. A number of nonendocrinological factors, such as sociocultural expectations (Semmens & Semmens, 1984) and psychological distress associated with the symbolic meaning of menopause (Rinehart & Schiff, 1985), may contribute to a report of decreased libido. Similarly, discomfort with menopausal symptoms such as hot flashes (McCoy, Cutler, & Davidson, 1985) may also contribute to a decreased desire for sexual activities.

Two recent psychophysiological studies suggest that many menopausal women experience little or no change in subjective sexual arousal. Morrell *et al.*, (1984) studied the vaginal response (measured by photoplethysmo-graph) to erotic material in premenopausal and postmenopausal women. While a reduced vaginal vasocongestive response to erotic stimuli was found in the postmenopausal women, subjective ratings of arousal did not distinguish premenopausal and postmenopausal women. Even more encouraging results were reported by Myers and Morokoff (1985) in a similar study of premenopausal and postmenopausal women. Premenopausal and post-menopausal women did not differ in their vaginal response (measured by photoplethysmograph) to erotic stimuli. Postmenopausal women who were not on estrogen replacement self-reported decreased vaginal lubrication.

Surgical Menopause

Evidence concerning changes in libido and sexual activity after hysterectomy and bilateral oophorectomy (surgical menopause) is conflicting and difficult to interpret. Although some investigators have reported decreases in libido after hysterectomy (Munday & Cox, 1967; Zussman, Zussman, Sunley, & Bjornson, 1981), others have found no evidence to support the hypothesis of a deleterious effect of surgical menopause on libido (Coppen, Bishop, Beard, Barnard, & Collins, 1981; Patterson & Craig, 1963). Other authors, such as Utian (1972), have noted that decreases in libido occur after hysterectomy whether or not the ovaries are spared, and thus that any libidinal changes observed are unlikely to be related to endocrine factors. In keeping with this observation, other investigators have reported that preoperative expectations constitute the major predictor of postoperative sexual function (Dennerstein, Woods, & Burrows, 1977).

The effects of surgical menopause on libido compose a confusing area of inquiry, with numerous potential confounding variables. In addition to considering the psychological significance of hysterectomy, one also needs to consider the effects of postoperative complications and the time after surgery at which the study was performed. One also needs to ascertain whether the gynecological symptoms mandating hysterectomy were relieved by the surgery, as well as the husband's reaction to the hysterectomy. Most of the published reports do not consider these factors. In fact, many of the studies poorly define the sexual behaviors studied. Others do not clearly specify whether the surgery also included a bilateral oophorectomy or whether replacement hormone therapy was begun.

In summary, the evidence concerning libido changes with menopause (either natural or surgical) is not convincing that endocrinological factors are etiologically involved.

Hormone Replacement Therapy for Menopausal Women

It is clear that estrogen replacement is effective in decreasing transient vasodilation (hot flashes) and atrophic vaginitis associated with menopause (Dennerstein, Burrows, Wood, & Hyman, 1980; Utian, 1972). There is also evidence that estrogen replacement may improve general psychological cognitive function in menopausal women. In a double-blind, placebo-controlled study, Fedor-Freyburgh (1977) found that estrogen replacement decreased measures of neuroticism, depression, and emotional distress, while improving performance in a variety of reaction time and vigilance tasks. However, the effects of estrogen replacement on libido, independent of its effects on general well-being and vaginal lubrication, are less clear. In a double-blind crossover study, Dennerstein and associates (Dennerstein & Burrows, 1982; Dennerstein, Burrows, Senior, & Woods, 1978; Dennerstein et al., 1980) studied the effects of four different hormonal preparations (ethinyl estradiol, levonorgestrel, a combination of ethinyl estradiol and levonorgestrel, and placebo) on sexual responsivity in 49 women who had undergone hysterectomy and bilateral oophorectomy. The estrogen preparation had a significant and positive effect on libido, sexual enjoyment, frequency of orgasm, and vaginal lubrication. The progesterone compound appeared to have a slight inhibitory effect on many of these dimensions of sexuality. No change in coital frequency was noted with these compounds. It is not clear from this report how libido was defined. The study of Fedor-Freybergh (1977) has been cited by others (e.g., Davidson et al., 1983) as indicating a significant effect of estrogen on libido. In this study, an effect of estrogen on libido was found in open trials. However, in the double-blind trial reported by Fedor-Freybergh, the effect of estrogen on libido was not statistically significant. Other studies (e.g., Campbell, 1976; Studd et al., 1977; Utian, 1972) had not found an effect of estrogen replacement on libido. As estrogen replacement is associated with an increase in general well-being, and as libido and general well-being are related (Dennerstein et al., 1980), it is possible that the relationship of estrogen on libido is secondary to its general effect on well-being.

There is suggestive evidence that estrogen–androgen preparations are effective in restoring libido or enhancing libido in postmenopausal women (Burger *et al.*, 1984; Shorr, Papanicolaou, & Stimmel, 1938; Studd *et al.*, 1977). The first double-blind study of the use of androgens in menopausal women was reported from the Medical College of Georgia (Greenblatt, Barfield, Garner, Calk, & Harrod, 1950). Postmenopausal women were given one of four preparations: diethylstilbestral, methyltestosterone, a combination of both, or a placebo. The estrogen preparations were effective in relieving hot flashes, and the androgen preparations were effective in increasing libido. Most women preferred the estrogen–androgen combination preparation. Sherwin and her associates (Sherwin & Gelfand, 1984, 1985; Sherwin, Gelfand, & Brender, 1985) reported similar findings in a recent study. In a prospective, double-blind, crossover study, surgically menopausal women were given either estrogen alone, androgen alone, the combination, or a placebo. Measures of sexual arousal, desire, and fantasy were all elevated in the groups receiving androgens, either alone or in combination. It is important to note that the levels of administered androgens may have exceeded physiological levels, and that other investigators (Dow, Hart, & Forrest, 1983) have not found that estrogen–androgen combination treatment is superior to estrogen alone.

Comment

Natural menopause and surgical menopause are events of considerable psychological significance for most women. From the available evidence, it is impossible to ascertain whether the decrease in libido associated with menopause is endocrinologically based or related to other factors. The studies of estrogen replacement in postmenopausal women are unclear as to whether estrogen replacement has a specific effect on libido apart from its effects on general well-being. The studies suggesting a libido-enhancing effect of preparations containing androgens are fascinating but of uncertain clinical significance at present.

Indications for Endocrine Evaluation and Therapy

Due to the high prevalence of sexual desire problems among women (Ende, Rockwell, & Glasgow, 1984), and the absence of definitive information concerning the endocrinological correlates of libido in the human female (Schiavi, 1985), extensive endocrinological assessment of every case of inhibited sexual desire in females is not indicated. During the evaluation of patients requesting help for desire disorders, one may, of course, discover symptoms such as menstrual abnormalities and pain during coitus, which merit referral for evaluation by a gynecological endocrinologist. However, it is unlikely that the correction of any endocrinological abnormality will have a direct influence on the complaint of impaired sexual desire.

A number of gynecological conditions may impair libido in nonspecific ways. In many instances, correction of the underlying condition may be necessary for the restoration of healthy sexual function and libido. For example, menopausal or perimenopausal women and those recovering from hysterectomy–ovarectomy may have signs of estrogen deficiency, such as vasomotor instability (hot flashes) and atropic vaginitis. Pain associated with osteoporosis in postmenopausal women can also interfere with the desire for sexual interaction. Estrogen replacement therapy may restore libido in nonspecific ways by decreasing dyspareunia secondary to atropic vaginitis and by eliminating vasomotor instability. Postmenopausal women complaining of these symptoms should be referred to a gynecological endocrinologist for consultation. This physician can help the patient weigh the benefits and possible complications of estrogen replacement therapy. If estrogen therapy is contraindicated, other medical interventions may serve to lessen the symptoms of estrogen deprivation (DeFazio, Austin, & Speroff, 1985). A number of other gynecological conditions (e.g., premenstrual tension syndrome, endometriosis) may impair libido in indirect ways by interfering with general well-being or causing pain during intercourse (Kaufman, 1983). For the psychotherapist, a good rule of thumb is always to refer patients with irregular menstrual patterns or complaints of painful coitus to an obstetrician–gynecologist with an interest in sexual medicine.

A number of endocrinopathies, including hypopituitarism, adrenal disease, thyroid disease, and hyperprolactinemia, may be associated with diminished libido in women (Horwith & Imperato-McGinley, 1983). However, in most of these diseases, it is unlikely that a complaint of diminished libido will be the presenting symptom. In most cases, the patient has consulted physicians because of other debilitating effects of these endocrinopathies or because of complaints of infertility or menstrual irregularities. With the possible exception of hyperpituitarism (Schon & Sutherland, 1960) and hyperprolactinemia (Riley, 1984), it is unclear that these diseases have an effect on libido apart from their general effects on decreased well-being. There is evidence that hyperprolactinemia may interfere with female libido as well as male libido (Weizman *et al.*, 1983). This syndrome should be suspected in patients complaining of amenorrhea (absence of menses) and galactorrhea (inappropriate lactation). Hyperprolactinemia may be the result of a variety of causes, including pituitary tumors (Chang, 1978). To date, there is minimal evidence concerning the prevalence of serious pituitary abnormalities in women with the solitary complaint of diminished libido. Therefore, one cannot advise the routine inclusion of serum prolactin determinations in women complaining of inhibited sexual desire.

The use of exogenous androgen for the treatment of decreased libido is still experimental. This is clearly a situation mandating close cooperation between the sex therapist and endocrinologist, as most endocrinologists are not astute observers of subtle changes in subjective states. If future research indicates that exogenous androgen facilitates libido in women, psychotherapists would ideally be part of the treatment team so that the altered level of desire could be successfully integrated into the patient's sexual relationships.

In summary, current information concerning the endocrinological correlates of sexual appetite in the female is minimal. There is little evidence to suggest that an endocrinological consultation will be useful in the evaluation of the solitary symptom of diminished libido. We may hope that this situation will have changed before a revised edition of this text is published.

Clinical Illustrations

It is clear that one rarely encounters purely psychogenic or purely biogenic sexual disorders. Because of the symbolic meaning of sexual activity to patients and their partners, one almost always encounters a mixture of biological, intrapsychic, and interpersonal factors in the clinical practice of sexual medicine. In most cases, one searches for the minimal intervention that will restore functioning.

Combined Psychological and Endocrinological Intervention

The first case is included to illustrate how a combined psychological and endocrinological intervention led to a restoration of function. An additional feature of this case is that it illustrates how a therapeutic alliance formed during the biomedical assessment period facilitated psychotherapeutic interventions with a patient who was highly resistant to the concept of psychotherapy.

Case Description

A 54-year-old construction worker who had been married for 30 years reluctantly accepted a psychiatric referral upon recommendation of his urologist. His presenting complaint was impotence. On further questioning, he revealed a gradual decline in sexual frequency and libido over the past 6 years. For the past 2 years, he had been unable to achieve firm erections in coital activities. He denied extramarital activities or masturbation. Early-morning erections were infrequent. The patient refused to involve his spouse in treatment or to allow me to contact her—"It's my problem; it's got nothing to do with her." He appeared extremely nervous and embarrassed about the consultation. In his words, "I just want to find out what's wrong. If it can be fixed, okay; if not, I can live with it."

Because of the patient's extreme reluctance to discuss interpersonal aspects of his difficulty, and the high probability of his prematurely terminating therapy if the interview continued along interpersonal lines in the face of this reluctance, the patient was informed about the steps in a biological investigation of his complaint. He readily agreed to all physical tests mentioned. Nocturnal penile tumescence recording indicated the presence of firm nocturnal erections, and penile blood pressure was within normal limits. Serum testosterone was mildly depressed (150 ng%; normal range, 376–1490 ng%). Free testosterone was likewise low. Prolactin was within normal limits, and LH was elevated. These results indicated a primary testicular failure, and exogenous testosterone therapy (200 mg i.m. every 2 weeks) was begun.

Monitoring of serum testosterone levels indicated physiological levels after approximately 8 weeks of therapy. However, the patient still complained of impotence. At this point, I began a more thorough assessment of the patient's condition. Apparently, he had experienced a mild increase in libido, as manifested by his having erotic daydreams about a female coworker and his having attempted coitus unsuccessfully with his wife. There was some evidence of discord at home, with his wife being angry about the patient's failure to make sexual overtures. The patient seemed unable to comprehend that his wife might be as concerned about the avoidance of all physical intimacy as about the loss of coital activity. The patient apparently still had considerable fear of failure: "I don't want to start anything that I can't finish."

At this point, my provisional diagnosis was a psychogenic erectile problem superimposed upon a treated biogenic desire difficulty. Lack of effective communication between the patient and spouse appeared to be prolonging the problem, but the patient again refused to involve his spouse in treatment. At this point, I recommended that the patient have frequent foreplay (twice a week) and absolutely make no attempts at penetration. I explained to the patient that such exercises would help to restore libido. The patient was given a note to give to his wife indicating that these instructions came from his physician. The patient was told to return in 1 month. At the next visit, the patient smiled sheepishly, admitting that he had become aroused during the repeated foreplay exercises and had violated the instructions. Follow-up for up to 8 months revealed that this patient's libido and erectile function were restored. Exogenous testosterone therapy was continued at a lower dosage.

Comment

In my experience, working-class males who are highly resistant to the concept of interpersonal contributors to sexual difficulties are not uncommon and require a different psychotherapeutic approach (Segraves, Schoenberg, Goldman, & Ivanoff, 1986). In this case, the patient's insistence that his difficulties were totally biogenic in etiology was not challenged. In fact, the sensate focus exercises were "prescribed" under the rationale that they augment libido. A note from the "doctor" to the patient's wife reinforced the "medical" nature of the intervention.

Clearly, one cannot state with certainty that the endocrinological therapy was a necessary part of the treatment. One could argue that the endocrine part of the therapy sequence merely served to establish a therapeutic alliance and that the prescription of nondemand foreplay was the sole effective therapeutic intervention. In this particular case the answer is unknowable, as the man refused a trial period off replacement testosterone to see whether it was necessary to sustain his renewed sexuality. Serum monitoring indicated that his testosterone levels remained within the normal range for his age.

Prevention of Endocrinological Treatment by Psychological Factors

The second case is included to illustrate how psychological factors may prevent the endocrinological treatment of inhibited sexual desire. This case reiterates the point that it is difficult to conceptualize evaluation and treatment of sexual disorders as either totally biological or psychological.

Case Description

A 62-year-old plumber consulted me because of erectile failure. During the initial interview, it quickly became obvious that the patient suffered from a serious loss of libido. Approximately 5 years earlier, he had become aware of decreased pleasure during sexual activity and decreased interest in sexual activity. He began experiencing transitory erectile problems and had a brief extramarital affair "to see if everything was still working." He was unable to consummate his extramarital affair. At about this time, he discovered that his wife was also having an extramarital affair. A period of marital turmoil ensued. The affairs ended and the marriage continued legally, if not emotionally.

Medical assessment indicated low serum androgen levels, high LH levels, and prolactin within normal range. There was no evidence to indicate the presence of other biological factors interfering with sexual function. The provisional diagnosis was inhibited sexual desire secondary to testicular dysfunction and severe marital discord. The patient was informed of this and was told about testosterone replacement therapy and its probable benefits. The patient replied that he never again desired sex with his wife after what she had done to him, that he was too old to find another woman, and that he would just learn to live with it. "After all, I haven't had sex for over 6 years and it hasn't killed me yet. Sex just isn't worth all of the trouble it brings." Attempts to engage this man in individual therapy and the couple in marital therapy were unsuccessful.

Comment

In my opinion, this man initially suffered from testicular failure, which led to his decreased libido. He became distressed by his loss of libido and withdrew emotionally from his spouse, which contributed to her having an extramarital affair. Because of his inability or unwillingness to forgive his wife, he appeared resigned to spending the rest of his life punishing her for her transgression.

Because of the discovery of a biological "cause" for this man's difficulty, I put on my "biogenic" mind set and pressed for the minimal intervention that would restore function. Clearly, the restoration of libido would have upset this man's role as a quietly suffering martyr. My failure may have been a success for the patient; the patient had an authority figure witness the severity of the pain his wife had caused him. In retrospect, one can envision a way in which both the patient and I could have been successful. A paradoxical intervention might have allowed this man to continue to suffer and yet to enjoy restoration of function. I could have told this man that the stress of discovering that his wife had had an affair (purposely omitting the fact that the patient did also) had influenced his ability to experience sexual desire. However, expensive injections of a drug with possible serious side effects might have partially alleviated his problem.

Persistence of a Psychogenic Problem after Endocrinological Treatment

The third case is included to illustrate that successful treatment of biogenic desire problems does not necessarily influence psychogenic desire problems. In this case, endocrinological restoration of libido did not affect a psychogenic suppression of libido toward a particular sexual partner. In other words, hormones influenced the sexual appetite, but psychological factors predominated in the sexual object choice.

Case Description

A 50-year-old married woman who had had a hysterectomy and bilateral oophorectomy 10 years previously consulted me concerning decreased libido and difficulty in experiencing orgasm. Sexual activity with her spouse had ceased 20 years previously, and she was involved in an extramarital affair of 6 years' duration. She stated that she had no desire to leave her husband, but was concerned with the loss of libido with her lover. She denied any interest in rekindling romance in her marriage: "I never particularly enjoyed sex with him anyway. Other than that, he's a good man."

The patient's history revealed numerous obstetrical–gynecological visits concerning her complaint and trials of a variety of progesterone–estrogen and estrogen preparations. These preparations had relieved symptoms of estrogen deficiency, but were ineffective in relieving her diminished libido. Her only relief had been from an endocrinologist who had given her testosterone injections on a monthly basis. After approximately 3 months of such therapy, her libido had returned. She noted that her libido was maximal for the first $2\frac{1}{2}$ weeks after the injection and waned until her next injection. She had noticed increased facial hair as a result of this therapy, but noted, "This is a small price to pay for the return of one's sexuality." Her endocrinologist had become concerned about the possible medical–legal risks associated with his unconventional therapy and refused further exogenous androgen therapy. She had consulted numerous endocrinologists who refused to prescribe androgen before consulting me: "They all said that the problem was in my head and that I should be content with my husband." Her history seemed compatible with a libido-enhancing effect of androgen, and her symptom did not appear to serve any obvious internal conflict.

A consultation with a gynecological endocrinologist was arranged. All hormone therapy was withdrawn for 3 months for a full endocrinological evaluation. This evaluation was compatible with that of a postmenopausal female of her age. The endocrinologist prescribed testosterone cream to be applied to the labia on a once-a-week basis, plus estrogen replacement. At follow-up, the patient reported a return of libido and orgasmic capacity with her lover. She dispassionately related that she had not noted a return of desire for her husband.

Comment

The therapeutic approach in this case was chosen with some reservation. In addition to my concern over potential medical–legal issues, I was concerned about the effect of libido-enhancing endocrinological treatment on the psychological process involved in the chronic suppression of libido for the spouse but not for an extramarital partner. The prior history of successful treatment without adverse psychological sequelae prompted the decision to seek a referral for endocrinological evaluation and treatment. Once this decision was made, the more difficult task of finding a gynecological endocrinologist willing to take this case seriously was encountered. This required numerous telephone calls to skeptical endocrinologists and gynecologists.

It is of note that the restoration of libido did not influence the patient's sexual attraction to her husband. However, it had a marked effect in the pleasure she experienced in her extramarital affair and in her masturbation frequency. My initial concern that an increase in libido might have adverse psychological sequelae was unfounded.

Testosterone therapy should not be instituted casually. The risk of long-term health consequences in females is uncertain, and the systemic absorption of topical cream is significant. It is imperative that such a therapeutic approach only be undertaken with fully informed consent and long-term follow-up, as was the case with this patient.

Conclusions

Current research indicates that androgens are the major libido hormones of the male and that androgen replacement can greatly facilitate the return of libido in hypogonadal men. Whether exogenous androgens are useful in the treatment of eugonadal men with decreased libido is unclear. The libido hormone in females is unclear. Considerable evidence suggests that supraphysiological levels of exogenous androgens have libido-enhancing effects in many women. The therapeutic implications of this finding await further investigation.

References

Abel, S. (1945). Androgenic therapy in malignant disease of the female genitalia. *American Journal of Obstretrics and Gynecology, 49*, 327–342.

Adair, F. E., & Hermann, J. B. (1946). The use of testosterone propionate in the treatment of advanced carcinoma of the breast. *Annals of Surgery, 123*, 1023–1035.

Adams, D. B., Gold, A. B., & Burt, A. D. (1978). Rise in female sexual activity at ovulation blocked by oral contraceptives. *New England Journal of Medicine, 299*, 1145–1150.

Appelt, H., & Strauss, B. (1984). Effects of antiandrogen treatment on the sexuality of women with hyperandrogenism. *Psychotherapy and Psychosomatics, 42*, 177–181.

Bachman, G. A., Leiblum, S. R., Sandler, B., Ainsley, W., Narcessian, R. Shelden, R., & Hymans, H. N. (1985). Correlates of sexual desire in post-menopausal women. *Maturitas, 7*, 211–216.

Backstrom, T., Sanders, D., Leask, R., Davidson, D., Warner, P., & Bancroft, J. (1983). Mood, sexuality, hormones, and the menstrual cycle. II. Hormone levels and their relationship to the premenstrual syndrome. *Psychosomatic Medicine, 45*, 503–507.

Bancroft, J. (1974). The effects of fertility control on human sexual behavior. In H. B. Parry (Ed.), *Population and its problems*. Edinburgh: Churchill Livingstone.

Bancroft, J. (1983). *Human sexuality and its problems*. Edinburgh: Churchill Livingstone.

Bancroft, J., Davidson, D., Warner, P., & Tyrer, G. (1980). Androgens and sexual behavior in women using oral contraceptives. *Clinical Endocrinology, 12,* 327–340.

Bancroft, J., Sanders, D., Davidson, D., & Warner, P. (1983). Mood, sexuality, hormones, and the menstrual cycle: III. Sexuality and the role of androgens. *Psychosomatic Medicine, 45,* 509–516.

Bancroft, J., Tennent, G., Loucas, K., & Cass, J. (1974). The control of deviant sexual behavior by drugs: 1. Behavioural changes following oestrogens and anti-androgens. *British Journal of Psychiatry, 125,* 310–315.

Bancroft, J., & Wu, F.C.W. (1983). Changes in erectile responsiveness during androgen replacement therapy. *Archives of Sexual Behavior, 12,* 59–66.

Bardwick, J. (1973). Psychological factors in the acceptance and use of oral contraceptives. In J. T. Fawcett (Ed.), *Psychological perspectives on populations*. New York: Basic Books.

Berlin, F. S., & Meinecke, C. F. (1981). Treatment of sex offenders with antiandrogenic medication: Conceptualization, review of treatment modalities, and preliminary findings. *American Journal of Psychiatry, 138,* 601–607.

Beumont, P.J.V., Bancroft, J.H.J., Beardwood, C. J., & Russell, G.F.M. (1972). Behavioral changes after treatment with testosterone: Case report. *Psychological Medicine, 2,* 70–72.

Blumer, D., & Migeon, C. (1975). Hormone and hormonal agents in the treatment of aggression. *Journal of Nervous and Mental Disease, 160,* 127–137.

Boas, C.V.E. (1973). Cyproteronacetate in sexuological outpatient practice. *Psychiatria, Neurologia, Neurochirurgia, 1973, 76,* 151–154.

Bremer, J. (1959). *Asexualization: A follow-up study of 244 cases*. New York: Macmillan.

Brown, W. A., Monti, P. M., & Corriveau, D. P. (1978). Serum testosterone and sexual activity and interest in men. *Archives of Sexual Behavior, 7,* 97–103.

Burger, H. G., Hailes, J., Menelaus, M., Nelson, J., Hudson, B., & Balazs, N. (1984). The management of persistent menopausal symptoms with oestradiol–testosterone implants: Clinical, lipid and hormonal results. *Maturitas, 6,* 351–358.

Campbell, S. (1976). Double-blind psychometric studies on the effects of natural estrogens on post-menopausal women. In S. Campbell (Ed.), *The management of the menopause and post-menopausal years*. Lancaster, PA: MTP Press.

Carney, A., Bancroft, J., & Mathews, A. (1978). Combination of hormonal and psychological treatment for female sexual unresponsiveness: A comparative study. *British Journal of Psychiatry, 133,* 339–346.

Carter, A. C., Cohen, E. J., & Shorr, E. (1947). Androgens in women. *Vitamins and Hormones, 5,* 317–391.

Carter, J. N., Tyson, J. G., Tolis, G., Vliet, S. V., Faiman, C., & Friesen, H. G. (1978). Prolactin-secreting tumors and hypogonadism in 22 men. *New England Journal of Medicine, 299,* 847–852.

Chang, R. J. (1978). Normal and abnormal prolactin metabolism. *Clinical Obstetrics and Gynecology, 21,* 125–137.

Coop, J. (1984). Menopause: Associated problems. *British Medical Journal, 289,* 970.

Cooper, A. J., Ismail, A.A.A., Phanjoo, A. L., & Love, D. L. (1972). Antiandrogen therapy in deviant hypersexuality. *British Journal of Psychiatry, 120,* 59–63.

Cooper, A. J., Smith, C. G., Ismail, A.A.A., & Loraine, J. A. (1973). A controlled trial of potensan (afrodisiac and testosterone combined) in impotence. *Irish Journal of Medical Science, 142,* 155–157.

Coppen, A., Bishop, M., Beard, R. T., Barnard, G.J.R., & Collins, W. P. (1981). Hysterectomy, hormones and behavior. *Lancet, i,* 126–128.

Crenshaw, T. (1986). *Pharmacological enhancement of sexual function*. Paper presented at the annual meeting of the Society for Sex Therapy and Research, Philadelphia.

Cullberg, J. (1985). Pharmacodynamic studies on desogestrel administered alone and in combination with ethinylestradiol. *Acta Obstetrica et Gynecologica Scandinavica, 249,* (Suppl. 133), 1–31.

Cullberg, J. (1972). Mood changes and menstrual symptoms with different gestogen/estrogen combination. *Acta Psychiatrica Scandinavica, 236* (Suppl. 55), 9–86.

Davidson, J. M., Camargo, C. A., & Smith, E. R. (1979). Effects of androgen on sexual behavior in hypogonadal men. *Journal of Clinical Endocrinology and Metabolism, 48,* 955–958.

Davidson, J. M., Gray, G. D., & Smith, E. R. (1983). The sexual psychoendocrinology of aging. In J. Meites (Ed.), *Neuroendocrinology of aging.* New York: Plenum.

Davidson, J. M., Kwan, M., & Greenleaf, W. (1982). Hormonal replacement and sexuality in men. *Clinics in Endocrinology and Metabolism, 11,* 599–623.

DeFazio, J., Austin, C., & Speroff, L. (1985). Pathophysiologic basis for the menopause. In M. B. Rosenthal & D. N. Smith (Eds.), *Psychosomatic obstetrics and gynecology.* Basel: Karger.

Dennerstein, L. & Burrows, G. D. (1982). Hormone replacement therapy and sexuality in women. *Clinics in Endocrinology and Metabolism, 11,* 661–679.

Dennerstein, L., Burrows, G. D., Senior, J., & Woods, C. (1978). Hormone replacement therapy at the menopause: A double-blind controlled study of women's preferences. *Australian and New Zealand Journal of Obstetrics and Gynecology, 18,* 139–143.

Dennerstein, L., Burrows, G. D., Wood, C., & Hyman, G. (1980). Hormones and sexuality: Effect of estrogen and progesterone. *Obstetrics and Gynecology, 36,* 316–322.

Dennerstein, L., Wood, C., & Burrows, G. D. (1977). Sexual response following hysterectomy and oophorectomy. *Obstetrics and Gynecology, 49,* 92–96.

Dow, M.G.T., Hart, D. M., & Forrest, C. A. (1983). Hormonal treatments of sexual unresponsiveness in postmenopausal women: A comparative study. *British Journal of Obstetrics and Gynecology, 90,* 361–366.

Ehrhardt, A. A., Meyer-Bahlburg, H.F.L., Rosen, L. R., Feldman, J. F., Veridiano, N. P., Zimmerman, I., & McEwen, B. S. (1985). Sexual orientation after prenatal exposure to exogenous estrogen. *Archives of Sexual Behavior, 14,* 57–77.

Ende, J., Rockwell, S., & Glasgow, M. (1984). The sexual history in general medical practice. *Archives of Internal Medicine, 144,* 558–561.

Fedor-Freyburgh, P. (1977). The influence of oestrogens on the well being and mental performance in climacteric and postmenopausal women. *Acta Obstretrica et Gynecologica Scandinavica, 47* (Suppl. 64), 1–68.

Franks, S., Jacobs, H.J.S., Martin, N., & Nabarro, J.D.N. (1978). Hyperprolactinemia and impotence. *Clinical Endocrinology, 8,* 277–287.

Freund, K. (1980). Therapeutic sex drive reduction. *Acta Psychiatrica Scandinavica, 62,* (Suppl. 287), 5–38.

Glick, I. D. (1967). Mood and behavioural changes associated with the use of oral contraceptive agents. *Psychopharmacology, 10,* 363–374.

Golla, F. L., & Hodge, R. S. (1949). Hormone treatment of the sexual offender. *Lancet, ii,* 1006–1007.

Gottswinger, J. M., Korth-Schutz, S., & Ziegler, R. (1984). Gynecomastica caused by estrogen containing hair lotion. *Journal of Endocrinological Investigation, 7,* 383–386.

Grant, E.C.G., & Pryse-Davis, J. (1968). Effect of oral contraceptives on depressive mood changes and on endometrial oxidase and phosphatases. *British Medical Journal, iii,* 777–780.

Greenblatt, R. B. (1942). Androgenic therapy in women. *Journal of Clinical Endocrinology, 2,* 665–666.

Greenblatt, R. B. (1943). Testosterone propionate pellet implantation in gynetic disorders. *Journal of the American Medical Association, 121,* 17–24.

Greenblatt, R. B., Barfield, W. E., Garner, J. F., Calk, G. L., & Harrod, J. P. (1950). Evaluation of an estrogen, androgen, estrogen–androgen combination, and a placebo in the treatment of the menopause. *Journal of Clinical Endocrinology, 10*, 1547–1558.

Greenblatt, R. B., Mortara, F., & Torpin, R. (1942). Sexual libido in the female. *American Journal of Obstetrics and Gynecology, 44*, 658–663.

Greenblatt, R. B., & Wilcox, E. A. (1941). Hormonal therapy of fibromyomas of the uterus. *Southern Surgeon, 10*, 339–346.

Groome, J. R. (1939). A local use for testosterone. *Lancet, ii*, 722.

Grounds, D., Davies, B., & Mowbray, R. (1970). The contraceptive pill, side-effects and personality: Report of a controlled double-blind trial. *British Journal of Psychiatry, 116*, 169–172.

Hamilton, J. B. (1943). Demonstrated ability of penile erection in castrate men with markedly low titers of urinary androgens. *Proceedings of the Society for Experimental Biology and Medicine, 504*, 309–312.

Heim, N. (1981). Sex behavior of castrated sex offenders. *Archives of Sexual Behavior, 10*, 11–19.

Heim, N., & Hursch, C. J. (1979). Castration for sex offenders: Treatment or punishment? A review and critique of recent European literature. *Archives of Sexual Behavior, 8*, 281–305.

Herrman, W. M., & Beach, R. C. (1980). Pharmacology for sexual offenders. In T. A. Ban & F. A. Freyhan (Eds.), *Drug treatment of sexual dysfunction.* Basel: Karger.

Herzberg, B., Draper, K. C., Johnson, A. L., & Nicol, G. C. (1971). Oral contraceptives, depression and libido. *British Medical Journal, iii*, 495–500.

Hoon, P. W., Bruce, K., & Kinchloe, B. (1982). Does the menstrual cycle play a role in sexual arousal? *Psychophysiology, 9*, 21–25.

Horwith, M., & Imperato-McGinley, J. (1983). The medical evaluation of disorders of sexual desire in males and females. In H. S. Kaplan (Ed.), *The evaluation of sexual disorders.* New York: Brunner/Mazel.

Jeffcoate, W. J., Matthews, R. W., Edwards, C.R.W., Field, L. H., & Besser, G. M. (1980). The effect of cyproterone acetate on serum testosterone, LH, FSH, and prolactin in male sexual offenders. *Clinical Endocrinology, 13*, 189–195.

Jones, T. M. (1985). Hormonal considerations in the evaluation and treatment of erectile dysfunction. In R. T. Segraves & H. W. Schoenberg (Eds.), *Diagnosis and treatment of erectile disturbances.* New York: Plenum.

Kane, F. J. (1976). Evaluation of emotional reactions to oral contraceptive use. *American Journal of Obstetrics and Gynecology, 126*, 495–500.

Kang, H. K., Singh, B., & Anand, B. K. (1971). Effect of gonadal hormones on electrical activity of brain in adult monkeys. *Journal of Reproductive Fertility, 27*, 298–299.

Kaufman, S. A. (1983). The gynecological evaluation of female dyspareunia and un-consummated marriage. In H. S. Kaplan (Ed.), *The evaluation of sexual disorders.* New York: Brunner/Mazel.

Kennedy, B. J., & Nathanson, I. T. (1953). Effects of intensive sex steroid hormone therapy in advanced breast cancer. *Journal of the American Medical Association, 152*, 1135–1141.

Kraemer, H. C., Becker, H. B., Brodie, H.K.H, Doering, C. H., Moos, R. H., & Hamburg, D. A. (1976). Orgastic frequency and plasma testosterone levels in normal human males. *Archives of Sexual Behavior, 5*, 125–132.

Kutner, S. J., & Brown, S. L. (1972). Types of oral contraceptives, depression and premenstrual problems. *Journal of Nervous and Mental Diseases, 115*, 153–160.

Kwan, M., Greenleaf, W. J., Mann, J., Crapo, L., & Davidson, J. M. (1983). The nature of androgen action on male sexuality: A combined laboratory–self-report study on hypogonadal men. *Journal of Clinical Endocrinology and Metabolism, 57*, 557–562.

Lange, J. D., Brown, W. A., Wincze, J. P., & Zwick, W. (1980). Serum testosterone concentration and penile tumescence changes in men. *Hormones and Behavior, 14*, 267–270.

Laschet, V., & Laschet, L. (1969). Three years' clinical results with cyproterone-acetate in the inhibiting regulation of male sexuality. *Acta Endocrinological, 141* (Suppl. 138), 103.

Leeton, J., McMaster, R., & Worsley, A. (1978). The effects on sexual response and mood after sterilization of women taking long-term oral contraception: Results of a double-blind crossover study. *Australian and New Zealand Journal of Obstetrics and Gynecology, 18,* 194–197.

Loeser, A. A. (1940). Subcutaneous implantation of female and male hormone in tablet form in women. *British Medical Journal, i,* 479–482.

Luisi, M., & Franchi, F. (1980). Double-blind group comparative study of testosterone undeconoate and mesterolone in hypogonadal male patients. *Journal of Endocrinological Investigation, 3,* 305–308.

Luttge, W. B. (1971). The role of gonadal hormones in the sexual behavior of the rhesus monkey and human: A literature survey. *Archives of Sexual Behavior, 1,* 61–68.

Marrama, P., Carani, C., Montamini, V., Baraghini, G. F., Tridenti, A., Pederzini, R. M., Celani, M. F., & Zini, D. (1984). Gonadal function: Sexual behavior in bromocriptine-treated men with prolactinoma. In R. T. Segraves & E. J. Haeberle (Eds.), *Emerging dimensions of sexology.* New York: Praeger.

Mathews, A., Whitehead, A., & Kellet, J. (1983). Psychological and hormonal factors in the treatment of female sexual dysfunction. *Psychological Medicine, 13,* 83–92.

McCoy, N., Cutler, W., & Davidson, J. M. (1985). Relationships among sexual behavior, hot flashes, and hormone levels in premenopausal women. *Archives of Sexual Behavior, 14,* 385–394.

McEven, B. S., Davis, P. G., & Parsons, B. (1979). The brain as a target for steroid hormone action. *Annual Review of Neuroscience, 2,* 65–112.

Meyer-Bahlburg, H.F.L., Ehrhardt, A. A., Feldman, J. F., Rosen, L. R., Veridiano, N. P., & Zimmerman, I. (1985). Sexual activity level amd sexual functioning in women prenatally exposed to diethylstilbestrol. *Psychosomatic Medicine, 47,* 497–511.

Mills, J. L., Jeffreys, J. L., & Stolley, P. D. (1984). Effects of occupational exposure to estrogen and progestogens and how to detect them. *Journal of Occupational Medicine, 26,* 269–272.

Money, J. (1961). Components of eroticism in man: The hormones in relation to sexual morphology and sexual desire. *Journal of Nervous and Mental Disease, 132,* 239–248.

Money, J. (1970). Use of an androgen-depleting hormone in the treatment of male sex offenders. *Journal of Sex Research, 6,* 165–172.

Money, J., & Ehrhardt, A. A. (1972). *Man and woman; Boy and girl.* Baltimore: Johns Hopkins University Press.

Money, J., Wiedeking, C., Walker, P., Migeon, C., Meyer, W., & Borgaonkar, D. (1975). 47-XYY and 46-XY males with antisocial and/or sex offending behavior: Anti-androgen therapy plus counseling. *Psychoendocrinology, 1,* 165–178.

Morrell, M. J., Dixen, J. M., Carter, S. C., & Davidson, J. M. (1984). The influence of age and cycling status on sexual arousability in women. *American Journal of Obstetrics and Gynecology, 148,* 66–71.

Mugglestone, C. J. (1983). Drug treatment of hypersexuality. In D. Wheatley (Ed.), *Psychopharmacology and sexual disorders.* London: Oxford University Press.

Munday, R. N., & Cox, L. W. (1967). Hysterectomy for benign lesions. *Medical Journal of Australia, 2,* 759–763.

Myers, L., & Morokoff, P. (1985). *Physiological and subjective sexual arousal in pre and postmenopausal women.* Poster presented at the meeting of the American Psychological Association, Los Angeles.

Nagulesparem, M., Ang, V., & Jenkins, J. S. (1978). Bromocriptine treatment of males with pituitary tumors, hyperprolactinemia, and hypogonadis. *Clinical Endocrinology, 9,* 73–78.

O'Carroll, R. F., & Bancroft, J. (1984) Testosterone therapy for low sexual interest and erectile dysfunction in men. *British Journal of Psychiatry, 145,* 146–151.

Patterson, R. M., & Craig, J. B. (1963). Misconceptions concerning the psychological effects of hysterectomy. *American Journal of Obstetrics and Gynecology, 85,* 104–111.

Persky, H., Channey, N., Lief, H. I., O'Brien, C. P., Miller, W. R., & Strauss, D. (1978). The relationship of plasma estradiol level to sexual behavior in young women. *Psychosomatic Medicine, 40,* 523 535.

Persky, H., Lief, H. I., Strauss, D., Miller, W. R., & O'Brien, C. P. (1978). Plasma testosterone level and sexual behavior of couples. *Archives of Sexual Behavior, 7,* 157–173.

Persky, H., O'Brien, C. P., & Kahn, M. A. (1976). Reproductive hormone levels, sexual activity and moods during the menstrual cycle. *Psychosomatic Medicine, 38,* 62–63.

Pirke, K. M., & Doerr, P. (1973). Age related changes and interrelationships between plasma testosterone, oestradiol, and testosterone-binding globulin in normal adult males. *Acta Endocrinologica, 74,* 792–800.

Raboch, J., & Starka, L. (1973). Reported coital activity of men and levels of plasma testosterone. *Archives of Sexual Behavior, 2,* 309–315.

Riley, A. J. (1984). Prolactin and female sexual function. *British Journal of Sexual Medicine, 11,* 14–17.

Rinehart, J. S., & Schiff, I. (1985). Sexuality and the menopause. In M. Farber (Ed.), *Human sexuality: Psychosexual effect of disease.* New York: Macmillan.

Roberts, C. D., & Sloboda, W. (1974). Afrodex vs. placebo in the treatment of male impotence: Statistical analysis of two double-blind crossover studies. *Current Therapeutic Research, 16,* 96–99.

Rose, R. M. (1972). The psychological effects of androgens and estrogens: A review. In R. I. Shader (Ed.), *Psychiatric complications of medical drugs.* New York: Raven Press.

Rubens, R., Dhont, M., & Vermeulen, A. (1974). Further studies on Leydig cell function in old age. *Journal of Clinical Endocrinology and Metabolism, 39,* 40–45.

Rubin, H. B., & Henson, D. E. (1979). The relationship between men's endogenous levels of testosterone and their penile responses to erotic stimuli. *Behavior Research and Therapy, 17,* 305–312.

Salmon, V. J. (1941). Rationale for androgen therapy in gynecology. *Journal of Clinical Endocrinology, 1,* 162–179.

Salmon, V. J., & Geist, S. H. (1943). Effects of androgens upon libido in women. *Journal of Clinical Endocrinology, 3,* 235–238.

Sanders, D., & Bancroft, J. (1982). Hormones and the sexuality of women—the menstrual cycle. *Clinics in Endocrinology and Metabolism, 11,* 639–659.

Sanders, D., Warner, P., Backstrom, T., & Bancroft, J. (1983). Mood, sexuality, hormones and the menstrual cycle. 1. Changes in mood and physical state: Description of subjects and method. *Psychosomatic Medicine, 15,* 487–501.

Schiavi, R. C. (1985). Evaluation of impaired sexual desire: biological aspects. In H. S. Kaplan (Ed.), *Comprehensive evaluation of disorders of sexual desire.* Washington, DC: American Psychiatric Press.

Schiavi, R. C., & White, D. (1976). Androgens and male sexual function: A review of human studies. *Journal of Sex and Marital Therapy, 2,* 214–228.

Schon, M., & Sutherland, A. M. (1960). The role of hormones in human behavior: III. Changes in female sexuality after hypophysectomy. *Clinical Endocrinology and Metabolism, 20,* 833–841.

Schreiner-Engel, P. (1980). Female sexual arousability: Its relation to gonadal hormones and the menstrual cycle. *Dissertation Abstracts International, 41.02.* (University Microfilms No. 80-17, 527)

Schreiner-Engel, P., Schiavi, R. C., Smith, H., & White, D. (1981). Sexual arousability and the menstrual cycle. *Psychosomatic Medicine, 43,* 199–214.

Schwartz, M. F., Bauman, J. E., & Masters, W. H. (1982). Hyperprolactinemia and sexual disorders in men. *Biological Psychiatry, 17,* 861–876.

Segraves, R. T., Schoenberg, H. W., Goldman, L., & Ivanoff, J. (1986). Psychiatric treatment of erectile dysfunction in a urology outpatient clinic. *Urology, 27,* 322–327.

Segraves, R. T., Schoenberg, H. W., & Ivanoff, J. (1983). Serum Testosterone and prolactin levels in erectile dysfunction. *Journal of Sex and Marital Therapy, 9,* 19–26.

Semmens, J. P., & Semmens, E. C. (1984). Sexual function and the menopause. *Clinical Obstetrics and Gynecology, 27,* 717–722.

Shakkebaek, N. E., Bancroft, J., Davidson, D. W., & Warner, P. (1981). Androgen replacement with oral testosterone undecanoate in hypogonadal men: A double-blind controlled study. *Clinical Endocrinology, 14,* 49–61.

Shaw, R. W. (1978). Neuroendocrinology of the menstrual cycle in humans. *Clinics in Endocrinology and Metabolism, 7,* 531–559.

Sherwin, B. B., & Gelfand, M. M. (1984). Effects of parental administration of estrogen and androgen on plasma hormone levels and hot flushes in the surgical menopause. *American Journal of Obstetrics and Gynecology, 148,* 552–557.

Sherwin, B. B., & Gelfand, M. M. (1985). Differential symptom response to parental estrogen and/or androgen administration in the surgical menopause. *American Journal of Obstetrics and Gynecology, 151,* 153–160.

Sherwin, B. B., Gelfand, M. M., & Brender, W. (1985). Androgen enhances sexual motivation in females: A prospective, crossover study of sex steroid administration in the surgical menopause. *Psychosomatic Medicine, 47,* 339–351.

Shorr, E., Papanicolaou, G. N., & Stimmel, B. F. (1938). Neutralization of ovarian follicular hormone in women by simultaneous administration of male sex hormone. *Proceedings of the Society for Experimental Biology and Medicine, 38,* 759–767.

Spark, R. F., White, R. A., & Connolly, P. B. (1980). Impotence is not always psychogenic. *Journal of the American Medical Association, 243,* 750–755.

Stearns, E. L., MacDonnell, J. A., & Kaufman, B. J. (1974). Declining testicular function with age. *American Journal of Medicine, 57,* 761–766.

Streem, S. B. (1982). The endocrinology of impotence. In A. H. Bennett (Ed.), *Management of male impotence.* Baltimore: Williams & Wilkins.

Studd, J. W., Collins, W. P., Charkrauarti, S., Newton, J. R., Oram, D., & Parsons, A. (1977). Oestradiol and testosterone implants in the treatment of psychosexual problems in the post-menopausal woman. *British Journal of Obstetrics and Gynaecology, 84,* 314–316.

Sturup, G. K. (1979). Castration: The total treatment. In H.L.P. Resnick & M. E. Wolfgang (Eds.). *Sexual behavior: Social and legal aspects.* Boston: Little, Brown.

Tolis, G., Bertrand, G., & Pinter, E. (1979). Divorce and remarriage in a 65-year-old male following transphenoidal surgery and bromocriptine for hyperprolactinemic impotence: A dilemma. *Psychosomatic Medicine, 41,* 657–659.

Udry, J. R., Morris, N. M., & Waller, L. (1973). Effect of contraceptive pills in sexual activity in the luteal phase of the human menstrual cycle. *Archives of Sexual Behavior, 2,* 205–214.

Utian, W. H. (1972). The true clinical features of postmenopause and oophorectomy, and their response to oestrogen therapy. *South African Medical Journal, 46,* 732–737.

Voerwoerdt, A., Pfeiffer, E., & Wang, H. S. (1969). Sexual behavior in senescence—changes in sexual activity and interest of aging men and women. *Journal of Geriatric Psychiatry, 2,* 165–180.

Waxenberg, S. E., Drellich, M. G., & Sutherland, A. M. (1959). The role of hormones in human behavior: 1. Changes in female sexuality after adrenalectomy. *Journal of Clinical Endocrinology, 19,* 193–202.

Weizman, R., Weizman, A., Levi, J., Gura, V., Zevin, D., Maoz, B., Wijsenbeek, H., & David, M. B. (1983). Sexual dysfunction associated with hyperprolactinemia in males and females undergoing hemodialysis. *Psychosomatic Medicine, 45,* 259–269.

Whitehead, E. D. (1981). Hormonal impotency-diagnostic methodology. *Sexuality and Disability, 4,* 93–97.

Yesawage, J. A., Davidson, J., Widrow, L., & Berger, P. A. (1985). Plasma testosterone levels, depression, sexuality and age. *Biological Psychiatry, 20,* 199–228.

Zussman, L., Zussman, S., Sunley, R., & Bjornson, E. (1981). Sexual response after hysterectomy–oophorectomy: Recent studies and reconsideration of psychogenesis. *American Journal of Obstetrics and Gynecology, 140,* 725–729.

12

Drugs and Desire

R. TAYLOR SEGRAVES

It is a characteristic of Western societies to search for technological solutions to resolve human dilemmas. Noting in this regard that the "search for the perfect aphrodisiac" has been a recurrent theme throughout history, Segraves considers the possible libido-enhancing effects of a wide array of drug substances. He begins this impressive review with the sobering observation that medicine has produced a large array of pharmacological agents that act inadvertently to diminish desire, whereas few if any substances have been reliably found to augment libido. Aside from the obvious significance of these findings for the practitioner, research on drug effects has contributed substantially to our understanding of basic mechanisms in sexual arousal and desire. For example, Segraves notes that studies of this type have focused considerable attention on the role of neurotransmitter systems (e.g., dopamine, serotonin) in the mediation of desire.

Among the many strengths of this chapter are its focus on both hypoactive and hyperactive drive states; on both subjective and physiological dimensions of desire; and on methodological as well as clinical perspectives on the topic. Several classes of drugs are reviewed in depth, including the antihypertensive, psychotropic, and recreational drugs. Regarding pharmacological agents that may enhance libido, such as L-dopa and certain antidepressant drugs, Segraves cautions that the evidence to date is unimpressive and largely anecdotal. Furthermore, apparent changes in sexual interest or activity observed with these drugs may well be confounded by nonspecific effects, such as changes in mood or physical well-being. Nevertheless, Segraves predicts that the search for effective pharmacological enhancement of libido will become a major concern of sex therapy in the next decade.

R. Taylor Segraves M.D., Ph.D, is Associate Director of the Department of Psychiatry at Cleveland Metropolitan General Hospital, Cleveland, Ohio, and Professor of Psychiatry at Case Western Reserve University Medical School.

313

Since the beginning of recorded history, human beings have searched for substances that might augment sexual desire and potency. Folk medicine has long attributed to various substances the ability to influence sexual behavior. Among food substances that have been proposed as aphrodisiacs are mandrake root, roots of orchids, ginseng, olives, oysters, truffles, and potatoes (Benedek, 1971; Segraves, Madsen, Carter, & Davis, 1985). The word "honeymoon" is derived from the European custom of drinking honeyed wine to promote sexual desire during the first moon (month) of marriage, and Arab traders imported rhinoceros horn from Africa to sell to aging Chinese men for its proposed aphrodisiac qualities well before Europeans discovered Africa (R. G. Greenblatt, Verheugen, Chaddha, & Samaras, 1983).

There is little, if any, evidence to suggest that these substances have any pharmacological action on sexual drive. However, the power of suggestion is often grossly underestimated. In the late 19th century, Brown-Sequard (1889) administered an aqueous extract of testicular tissue to himself and reported a marked increase in libido. Sales of "monkey gland" preparations were commercially quite successful in the early 20th century. However, Brown-Sequard's preparation was later shown to be biologically inactive.

Unfortunately, modern science has not confirmed the alleged aphrodisiac qualities of most of the substances proposed by folk medicine. Medicine instead has been far more successful in producing pharmacological agents with unwanted side effects of diminishing libido or interfering with the sexual response cycle. Information concerning pharmacological agents that diminish libido (anaphrodisiacs) is of obvious importance to the clinician treating sexual disorders. The clinician would not wish to begin psychotherapy for inhibited sexual desire that has a pharmacological etiology. Another area of drug–libido interaction of significance for the clinician is the animal research concerning the neuromechanisms (Everitt & Hanson, 1983; MacLean, 1975) and neurotransmitters (Karczmar, 1980; Soulairac & Soulairac, 1975) involved in sexual activity. A considerable body of research demonstrates that pharmacological interventions affecting serotoninergic and dopaminergic neurotransmitter systems can have profound influences on sexual activity in animals (Gessa & Napoli-Farris, 1983; Gessa & Tagliamonte, 1975; Tucker & File, 1983). Many psychoactive medications in current use, such as the antidepressants and antipsychotic drugs, influence these same neurotransmitter systems. There is suggestive evidence that some of the psychoactive drugs may influence basic biological drive states, including libido in humans (Hyyppa, Falck, & Rinne, 1975: Hyyppa, Rinne, & Sonninen, 1970; McLean, Forsythe, & Kapkin, 1983).

The purpose of this chapter is to review the evidence for drug effects on human sexual libido. The chapter is divided into four major sections: (1) definition of libido and libido abnormalities; (2) drug suppression of libido;

(3) drug enhancement of libido; and (4) clinical case examples. Endocrinological agents are not reviewed, as they have been covered in Chapter 11 of this text.

Variations in Sexual Drive

Although the term "libido" is widely used, and various investigations have referred to patients with abnormally low libidinal states as suffering from "sexual apathy" (Kinsey, Pomeroy, & Martin, 1948), "sexual malaise" (Heiman & Morokoff, 1977), and "sexual anorexia" (Kaplan, 1985), its precise definition is seldom clear. Most investigators use the term "libido" as synonomous with the terms "sexual drive," "sexual desire," "sexual appetite," and "the attractive force between beings of reproductive age" (Bancroft, 1983). It refers to a subjective state characterized by a predisposition to seek out sexual stimuli and is analogous to the concept of hunger (Bancroft, 1981). Most investigators would define libido as independent of and distinct from sexual arousability or the capacity to perform sexually. This conceptual distinction between libido and potency may be difficult to operationalize, as desire and the performance variables are often closely interrelated:

> There is reason to postulate a positive feedback mechanism involving sensory afferents which report genital vasocongestive responses to the brain, thereby increasing sexual arousal which in turn augments physiological responses, leading to the rapid buildup of both cognitive sexual excitement and physiological arousal. . . . If this is so, it may be difficult in a normally-functioning individual (i.e., one with intact sensorimotor mechanisms and libido) to distinguish whether a given variable influences sexual function by acting on libido or potency elements. (Davidson, Kwan, & Greenleaf, 1982, p. 615)

Many investigators have operationalized drive as being reflected in the total sexual outlet of an individual (Kinsey *et al.*, 1948; Kinsey, Pomeroy, Martin, & Gebhard, 1953). For example, the Sexual Drive subtest of the Derogatis Sexual Functioning Inventory utilizes a composite score of frequency of coitus, masturbation, kissing and petting, and sexual fantasy as a measure of libido (Derogatis & Melisaratos, 1979). From this perspective, a measure of total sexual outlet would reflect the basic drive state.

Sexual drive has both biological and psychological components (Kaplan, 1985). It is generally assumed that psychological factors are more likely to affect sexual drive in a selective or partner-specific manner (Schiavi, 1985). Drug effects on libido presumably influence the biological component of libido and thus are thought to be manifested by a global loss of sexual interest. This should be reflected in a decrement of erotic activities (both partner-related activities and masturbation), as well as in sexual thoughts and fantasies.

Conditions theoretically capable of being produced and/or treated by pharmacological agents include both hypoactive sexual desire disorders and hyperactive sexual desire disorders. Hypoactive sexual desire disorders have been defined as "persistently or recurrently deficient or absent sexual fantasies and desire for sexual activity" (American Psychiatric Association, 1985, 293). The diagnosis of hyperactive sexual desire is controversial and has not been included in the official nomenclature of the American Psychiatric Association. A number of clinicians in the field of human sexuality have described patients possibly fitting such a diagnostic grouping (Carnes, 1985; Coleman, 1985). High levels of sexual activity have also been observed in patients with paraphilias (e.g., exhibitionsim). In both cases, it is unclear whether such patients are suffering from high libidinal states or whether other intrapsychic and interpersonal needs are being expressed in a sexualized manner (Levine, 1985). There is evidence of genetically determined variability in sexual drive (Eysenck, 1976), and excessive libido had been described in certain medical conditions (Erickson, 1945; R. G. Greenblatt & Karpas, 1983; Shukla, Srivastava, & Katiyar, 1979). Thus, the concept of a hyperactive sexual desire disorder is plausible, in spite of insufficient evidence to date to substantiate the existence of such a disorder.

Drug Suppression of Libido

A large and diverse group of pharmacological agents has been reported to interfere with sexual drive and other aspects of sexual function. Available sources of information are unfortunately mainly limited to case reports or questionnaire studies. Both sources of information are, of course, subject to physician and patient bias. The available evidence is also limited by the fact that one cannot be certain that physicians in nonpsychiatric specialties are using the term "libido" in a manner consistent with that of sex therapists and researchers. The available evidence mainly concerns the influence of drugs on male sexual function, as relatively few investigators have specifically investigated drug effects on female sexuality. It is reasonable to assume that the reported incidence of such side effects is less than the actual incidence, as most investigators only list sexual side effects if patients have volunteered this information (Segraves et al., 1985). In most of the reports, it is difficult to evaluate the effects of drugs on specific phases of the human sexual response, because many authors only report disturbances of one phase without mentioning the other phases (Shen, Sata, & Hofstatter, 1984). For example, it may be unclear from a report of impairment of orgasm whether the orgasmic reflex only was affected or whether other aspects of the sexual response were influenced as well. In other reports, it is difficult to ascertain whether the desire impairment was secondary to the orgasmic impairment or preceded it as an independent effect. This review focuses on drug effects on libido. Drug effects on erectile capacity and female orgasmic capacity have been reviewed elsewhere (Segraves, 1985; Segraves *et al.*, 1985).

Antihypertensive Agents

Among the various classes of pharmacological agents, antihypertensive drugs have been most frequently reported to cause sexual disturbances. These drugs have been found to interfere with erection, ejaculation, orgasm, and libido. Although the majority of these studies have concerned impairment of sexual function in male hypertensives, there is no reason to suspect that female hypertensives are less susceptible to such adverse sequelae to the treatment of arterial hypertensive disease. It is possible that the high frequency of sexual side effects with antihypertensive drugs may be partially responsible for the high rate of noncompliance with treatment. The current evidence suggests that the clinician treating a patient with sexual dysfunction should first review the pharmacological agents that the patient is taking, and that any hypotensive drug should be considered as a possible etiological factor in the pathogenesis of the sexual disturbance until proven otherwise. Table 1 lists the major hypotensive agents reported to decrease libido.

Diuretics are usually the first class of drugs to be used in the treatment of essential hypertension. In mild hypertensive disease, these drugs may be the only hypotensive agents employed. In more severe cases of hypertension, diuretics may be combined with adrenergic-inhibiting agents to obtain

Table 1. Hypotensive Agents Reported to Decrease Libido

Generic name	Trade name
Hydrochlorothiazide	Oretic
Spironolactone	Aldactone
Chlorthalidone	Hygroton
Alpha-methyldopa	Aldomet
Reserpine	Serpasil
Guanethidine	Ismelin
Propranolol	Inderal
Clonidine	Catapres

better control of blood pressure. The diuretics, with the exception of spiro-nolactone, were previously thought to cause sexual disturbance only rarely (Segraves, 1977). However, Yendt, Gray, and Garcia (1970) reported that 3% of male patients on hydrochlorothiazide, a commonly prescribed diuret-ic, complained of decreased libido. Chlorthalidone, a thiazide-like diuretic, has also been found to be associated with decreased libido (Curb *et al.,* 1985). Many researchers have observed that spironolactone frequently causes libido disturbances (Brown, Davies, & Ferris, 1972; Spark & Melby, 1968; Zarren & Black, 1975), but not all investigators agree (Curb *et al.,* 1985). Spironolactone also is associated with gynecomastia (breast enlarge-ment) in males (Clark, 1965; D. J. Greenblatt & Koch-Weser, 1973) and amenorrhea (suppression of menstruation) (Levitt, 1970). Its antilibido effect may be related to its antiandrogenic activity at the receptor site (Loriaux, Menard, Taylor, Pita, & Santer, 1976).

The other major group of antihypertensive drugs suspected to cause libido disturbances are the adrenergic-inhibiting agents (Rosen & Kostis, 1985). These drugs are well known as causing impotence and ejaculatory impairment; however, there is also evidence that these drugs may interfere with libido. Libido disturbances have been noted in patients taking alpha methyldopa, a synthetic phenylalanine derivative related to naturally occur-ring dopa (Horwitz, Pettinger, Orvis, Thomas, & Sjoerdsma, 1967; Laver, 1974; Newman & Salerno, 1974; Pillay, 1976). From these case reports, one can estimate the prevalence of disturbed libido on this agent as being approximately 15%. Reserpine has been used both as an antipsychotic and as an antihypertensive agent. There have been case reports of decreased libido associated with this drug (Boyden, Nugent, Ogihara, & Maeda, 1980; Tuchman & Crumpton, 1955). Curb and associates (1985) found that approximately 2% of patients on reserpine will discontinue this agent because of its adverse effect on libido. Guanethidine is an adrenergic-blocking agent with a selective action on peripheral sympathetic neurons. Although its most common sexual side effect is impairment of ejaculation, several authors have also observed decreased libido with this agent (Adi, Eze, & Anwunah, 1975; Bauer, Hull, Stokes, & Raftos, 1973). Bauer and his associates noted that 28% of men on an average dose of 50 mg/day complained of some disturbance of libido. There is also some evidence that clonidine, a centrally acting antihypertensive with alpha-adrenergic agonist properties, may depress libido (Laver, 1974; Potts, 1976).

Propranolol and other beta-blockers are used primarily for the control of hypertension, angina, and cardiac arrhythmias. Propranolol appears to act peripherally by blocking beta-adrenergic receptors, although it also has central nervous system effects. Several investigators have found decreased libido in male patients taking this drug (Burnett & Chahine, 1979; Holli-field, Sherman, Zwagg, & Shard, 1976; Knarr, 1976). There is not enough research currently available to permit one to evaluate the prevalence of this side effect.

It should be obvious to the reader that the information concerning libido-suppressing effects of antihypertensive agents is far from optimal. Most of the available information is derived from reports by investigators with a primary interest in the pharmacotherapy of hypertensive arterial disease. In most of the studies, sexual side effects were noted only if patients spontaneously reported difficulties. It is reasonable to assume that patients' embarrassment and physicians' lack of interest led to considerable underreporting. It is also possible that many cases of male libido disturbance were erroneously reported as impotence.

The importance of this information to the psychotherapist and sex therapist is the observation that many of the commonly prescribed hypertensive drugs have serious sexual side effects, including diminished libido. Clearly, one would not wish to attempt to treat biogenic desire disorders with psychotherapy on the mistaken assumption that the difficulty is psychological in origin. Unfortunately, in many clinical situations it is difficult to ascertain whether a desire problem is secondary to antihypertensive drugs or to ascertain which antihypertensive agent is the major offender. Many patients with arterial hypertensive disease have long histories of pharmacological treatment with multiple changes of drug regimen and dosage. Combination drug therapy is the usual practice, and the onset of drug-induced desire difficulties tends to be insidious. The patient may not notice a decrement in libido until 3–4 months after a dosage adjustment in the medication. Thus, a careful pharmacological and sexual history may not establish a clear linkage between pharmacotherapy and diminished libido.

As a clinical rule of thumb, it is wise to assume that any of the commonly prescribed hypotensive agents may cause desire difficulties. In patients with mild hypertension and desire problems, it may be possible to have the primary physician temporarily discontinue all medications. If desire returns, antihypertensive medication can be restarted with slow dosage adjustments in order to establish the agent and dosage responsible for the problem. This approach can be used to establish the drug combination that controls hypertension but still permits maximal sexual function. Obviously, if the pharmacologically induced libido disturbance has precipitated marital discord, the interpersonal climate may also require adjustment prior to the restoration of normal libido.

In patients with more severe hypertensive disease, one does not always have the luxury of drug discontinuation as a diagnostic tool. In such cases, a painstaking process of dosage reduction and drug substitution may be required. In patients on combination therapy, each agent needs to be monitored individually for its effect on libido. By history, one might identify the probable offender to be discontinued first. As most of the antihypertensive agents may affect sexual function, and as sexual side effects tend to be idiosyncratic, there are no general rules for drug substitution. On theoretical grounds, one might tend to substitute a drug with primarily peripheral action (e.g., atenolol) for one with more effects on the central nervous system (e.g., propranolol). Such work obviously requires close collaboration between the sex therapist and the prescribing physician. Fortunately, cardiovascular specialists are becoming increasingly aware of the need for careful selection of antihypertensive agents in terms of their side effect profile and acceptability to patients.

In concluding this section, it is worthwhile to emphasize again that there is no reason to suspect that females are less susceptible to drug side effects on libido than are males. The relative absence of such reports probably reflects less physician interest in the study of female sexuality, rather than the absence of such an effect. From the clinician's viewpoint, it is wise to assume comparable effects in the female patient unless future research proves otherwise.

Psychiatric Drugs

Although there are numerous reports of antipsychotic drugs interfering with sexual arousal and orgasm, there are relatively few reports of the effect of these agents on desire. As neuroleptics have the side effects of decreasing plasma testosterone, increasing plasma prolactin, and causing amenorrhea (Beaumont, Corker, et al., 1974; Beaumont, Gelder, et al., 1974), one would expect frequent antilibido effects from such agents. Table 2 lists the major neuroleptics and sedatives reported to decrease libido.

A number of antipsychotic drugs, such as thioridazine, chlorpromazine, thiothixine, fluphenazine, and haloperidol, have been found to be associated with diminished libido. In their study of the effects of thioridazine on ejaculation and erections in the male, Kotin, Wilbert, Verberg, and Soldinger (1976) incidentally reported one female patient who "felt less pleasurably aroused" when taking 200 mg of thioridazine at bedtime.

Table 2. Neuroleptics and Sedatives Reported to Decrease Libido

Generic name	Trade name
Chlorpromazine	Thorazine
Thioridazine	Mellaril
Thiothixine	Navane
Fluphenazine	Prolixin
Haloperidol	Haldol
Diazepam	Valium
Clorazepate	Tranxene
Phenobarbital	—

Greenberg (1971) reported one case of a 38-year-old male teacher who suffered from "greatly diminished libido" while taking 1,000 mg/day of chlorpromazine. In a double-blind comparison of the effectiveness of loxapine with thiothixine, Charalampous, Freemesser, Malou, and Ford (1974) noted that 1 out of a series of 18 patients developed a severe decrease in libido while on thiothixine. Libido disturbances were not noted on loxapine and placebo. Bartholomew (1968) specifically investigated fluphenazine for the treatment of deviant sexual behavior. His research sample consisted of 24 psychiatric patients who were not sexually deviant (predominantly alcoholics) and 26 sexually deviant patients (mixed offenses, mostly court offenses). In each group, 17 patients reported a marked decrease in sexual drive and interest. This change was confirmed by interviews with the spouses. In a controlled double-blind study of haloperidol, chlorpromazine, and placebo on deviant sexual behavior, Tennant, Bancroft, and Cass (1974) reported that haloperidol significantly decreased the frequency of sexual thoughts, although it had no effect on erections elicited by erotic material.

Decreased libido has also been reported with the minor tranquilizers clorazepate (General Practitioner Research Group, 1975; Magnus, Dean, & Curry, 1977) and diazepam (Hughes, 1971; Magnus *et al.*, 1977). Phenobarbital has been used to treat hypersexuality (Chapel & Fahim, 1975). Its presumed mechanism of action is acceleration of the metabolism of androgen.

Many of the tricyclic and heterocyclic antidepressants in current usage have been reported to have sexual side effects, including loss of libido. Table 3 lists some of these drugs. Clomipramine, an antidepressant unavailable in the United States, has been frequently reported to be associated with decreased libido. Most of this information consists of case reports (Yassa,

Table 3. Mood-active Drugs Reported to Decrease Libido

Generic name	Trade name
Clomipramine[a]	Anafranil
Amitriptyline	Elavil
Imipramine	Tofranil
Protriptyline	Vivactyl
Alprazolam	Xanax
Amoxapine	Asendin
Phenelzine	Nardil
Lithium	Eskalith

[a]Not available in the United States.

1982) or poorly documented clinical series (Anath, Pecknold, Steen, & Engels-Mann, 1979; Clarke, 1969; Waxman, 1975a, 1975b; Wooton & Bailey, 1975). Fraser (1984) reported one case of decreased libido in a female patient on 150 mg of clomipramine. This effect occurred after 2 months at this dosage level. Isolated case reports (Baron, Unger, Williams, & Knight, 1976; Hekimian, Friedhoff, & Deever, 1978; Kahn, 1975) suggest that decreased libido may be a side effect of amitriptyline. It is of note that one group of investigators reported success in using this drug to treat patients with compulsive sexual activity (i.e., hyperactive sexual desire disorders). Case reports suggest that both imipramine (Everett, 1975; Ruskin & Goldner, 1959) and protriptyline (Everett, 1975; Simpson, Blair, & Amuso, 1965) may also be associated with decreased libido. One controlled study (Harrison et al., 1986) demonstrated an antilibidinal effect of imipramine. There is one report of decreased libido being associated with alprazolam (Sangal, 1985). However, it appears that the decreased libido may have been secondary to orgasmic inhibition. Hekimian and associates (1978) found decreased libido with amoxapine, although other investigators (Shen, 1982) report that the usual effect observed is normal libido associated with orgasmic inhibition.

The monoamine oxidase inhibitors have been frequently reported to cause both retarded ejaculation in the male (Hollender & Ban, 1980) and anorgasmia in the female (Lesko, Stotland, & Segraves, 1982). Phenelzine appears to be the worst offender among this group of drugs (Rabkin, Quitkin, McGrath, Harrison, & Tricamo, 1985). Friedman, Kantor, Sobel, and Miller (1978) reported that female patients given phenelzine for the treatment of neurodermatitis reported lack of sexual interest and decreased orgasmic capacity. Similarly, Fraser (1984) reported a male patient with both decreased libido and an inability to ejaculate while taking phenelzine. He also reported a female patient on phenelzine who reported orgasmic inhibition but normal libido. Harrison et al. (1986) also demonstrated decreased libido associated with phenelzine.

Blay, Ferraz, and Calil (1982) reported two cases of decreased libido in male patients on therapeutic doses of lithium carbonate. In one patient, substitution of a placebo led to a restoration of sexual function. In the other patient, the sexual symptoms remitted spontaneously after 2 months of pharmacotherapy.

Determining the etiology of inhibited sexual desire in patients taking psychoactive drugs may present considerable diagnostic difficulties. The clinician needs to determine whether the difficulty is secondary to the drug being prescribed or to the psychiatric condition for which the drug was originally prescribed. For example, it may be difficult to ascertain whether diminished libido in a patient taking antidepressant medication (e.g., tricyclic antidepressants or monoamine oxidase inhibitors) is a drug side effect or a manifestation of a partially treated depressive episode. In bipolar illness, increased sexual activity may accompany a manic episode. Thus, if a patient on lithium carbonate complains of decreased libido, this may reflect a drug side effect, or it may simply be a manifestation of successful treatment. Most patients requiring psychoactive medication are acutely aware of their altered affect or mentation. Thus, it is extremely important to diagnose the problem correctly, rather than erroneously attributing the complaint to the patient's psychiatric disturbance. This may further the patient's self-doubt and demoralization.

Given the abysmal lack of hard evidence concerning the effects of psychiatric drugs on libido, it is difficult to make clinically responsible decisions when faced with such complaints by patients. A conservative approach is to take the patient's complaint at face value and to initially assume that the problem is drug-induced. If the clinical situation permits, drug cessation or dose reduction would be the appropriate first step. If the complaint worsens after this action, the clinician has presumptive evidence that the problem is not drug-induced. If libido returns after drug cessation and the clinical situation mandates pharmacotherapy, the clinican may consider substitution by a different agent. Unfortunately, there are no clear guidelines concerning the choice of a substitute drug. If diminished libido occurs while a patient is taking a high-potency neuroleptic (e.g., haloperidol), one might consider switching the patient to a lower-potency neuroleptic such as chlorpromazine. The rationale for such a decision is that considerable animal research indicates that central nervous system dopaminergic pathways are facilitory to sexual behavior (Gessa & Tagliamonte, 1975). It has been suggested that similar mechanisms may operate in the human. Thus one might wish to switch the patient to an agent with less dopaminergic-blocking activity. There is also evidence that serotoninergic (serotonin-enhancing) neurotransmitter pathways may be inhibitory to sexual function. Thus if a patient is on a serotoninergic antidepressant (e.g., imipramine) and complains of decreased libido, one might consider switching the patient to a less serotoninergic antidepressant (e.g., desipramine). Alternatively, one might also consider giving the patient a drug that inhibits serotonin. Such a strategy has been found useful in the treatment of antidepressant-induced anorgasmia (Souner, 1983, 1984). It is unclear whether this principle would also apply to antidepressant-induced libido disturbances. Unfortunately, there are no obvious pharmacological substitutes for lithium carbonate.

Anticonvulsant Drugs

Abnormal increases in libido have been reported to be associated with certain neurological conditions, especially tumors of the paracentral lobule (Erickson, 1945; Ruff, 1980) and seizure foci of the temporal lobes (Remillard *et al.*, 1983). Several case reports document that standard anti-convulsant medications, such as phenytoin and carbamazepine, can correct the state of hypersexuality (Hooshmand, Sepdham, & Vries, 1974; Mohan, Salo, & Nagswami, 1975). There is also some evidence that anticonvulsant medications may also inhibit libido in patients with normal libidinal levels prior to medication. Mattson and Cramer (1985) reported that decreased libido was more commonly reported with phenobarbital and primidone than with phenytoin and carbamazepine. It is difficult to tease out the specific drug effect on libido, as many neurological conditions, especially epilepsy, may be associated with decreased libido independent of drug effects (Fenwick *et al.*, 1985; Saunders & Rawson, 1970).

Anticancer Chemotherapy

The effects of cancer chemotherapy on libido are profound. Most of the cancer chemotherapy agents produce gonadal dysfunction in males and premature gonadal failure in females (Schilsky, Lewis, Sherins, & Young, 1980). Because most of these agents are toxic, and because these drugs are frequently used in combination with other cancer drugs, it is difficult to specify the effects of single agents (Shalet, 1980). It has been reported that 70% of female patients (Chapman, 1982) and from 74% to 85% of male patients (Chapman, 1982; Chapman, Rees, Sutcliffe, Edwards, & Malpas, 1979) have a marked decrease in libido while undergoing cancer chemother-apy. Although some of the decrease in libido may be nonspecific and secondary to the general malaise associated with chemotherapy, the de-crease in libido has been reported to persist long after chemotherapy has terminated (Thachil, Jewett, & Rider, 1981). It is probable that the altered endocrine status of treated patients may be responsible for the persistent loss of libido (Chapman, 1982).

The diagnosis and treatment of cancer have psychological sequelae (e.g., depression, anxiety, change in body image) that may also influence libido. In clinical situations, it is usually impossible to ascertain which proportion of altered libido is due to psychological as opposed to biological factors. The extremity of the physical assault of cancer chemotherapy and its pronounced effects on reproductive endocrinology suggest that biologi-cal factors play a major role in the alteration of libido.

Other Prescribed Drugs

A number of other commonly prescribed drugs have been stated to influence libido in the human. Table 4 lists some of these. Cimetidine, a histamine antagonist at H_2 receptor sites that is widely used in the treatment of

Table 4. Other Drugs Reported to Decrease Libido

Drug	Medical use
Acetazolamide (Diamox)	Glaucoma treatment
Methazolamide (Neptazane)	Glaucoma treatment
Ethoxzolamide	Glaucoma treatment
Dichlorphenamide	Glaucoma treatment
Cimetidine (Tagamet)	Treatment of duodenal ulcers
Fenfluramine (Pondimin)	Appetite suppressant
Digoxin (Lanoxin)	Treatment of heart failure
Clofibrate (Atromid-S)	Antilipid
Primadone (Mysoline)	Anticonvulsant

duodenal ulcers, has been reported to cause diminished libido (Biron, 1979; Gifford, Aeugle, Myerson, & Tannenbaum, 1980; Peden, Cargill, Browning, Saunders, & Wormsley, 1979; Pierce, 1983). Cimetidine also causes gynecomastia (Fave *et al.,* 1977; Hall, 1976) and stimulates prolactin secretion (Carlson & Ippoliti, 1977). This suggests a possible endocrinological mechanism for the deleterious effect of cimetidine on libido. Cimetidine therapy also causes depression (Billings, Tang, & Rakoff, 1981). Thus it is unclear whether the decrease in libido is part of a depressive syndrome or a separate effect of cimetidine therapy.

There is also evidence that digoxin (a drug commonly used to treat cardiac failure) may be associated with libido disturbances. Neri, Aygen, Zukerman, and Bahary (1980) studied sexual function and various endocrine parameters in male cardiac patients receiving chronic digoxin therapy. These results were compared with a control group of similar cardiac functional capacity. The patients on digoxin had significant decreases in sexual desire, sexual excitement, and frequency of sexual relations. The digoxin group also had elevated estradiol levels and depressed testosterone and luteinizing hormone levels, all of which suggest a possible endocrinological mechanism for the effect on libido.

Often less commonly prescribed drugs that may affect libido include clofibrate, fenfluramine, and the carbonic anhydrase inhibitors. Clofibrate, a drug used in the treatment of hyperlipoproteinemia, has been reported to be associated with impotence and decreased libido. In one of the largest series reported to date, patients were randomly allocated to clofibrate, niacin, or placebo. Of the 1,065 patients on clofibrate, 14.1% complained of decreased libido or potency. This was significantly higher than the number of patients experiencing similar problems on niacin or placebo (Coronary Drug Project Research Group, 1975). Fenfluramine, an anorectic drug, has been found to be associated with loss of libido (Hughes, 1971). The study did not specify the frequency of this side effect. The carbonic anyhdrase inhibitors (i.e., acetazolamide, methazolamide, dichlorphenamide, and ethoxzolamide) are used in the treatment of glaucoma and are known to produce side effects of depression, fatigue, and general malaise (Lichter, Newman, Wheeler, & Beall, 1978). Epstein and Grant (1977) noted that more than 50% of patients taking acetazolamide and methazolamide reported a symptom complex of malaise, fatigue, weight loss, depression, anorexia, and loss of libido. Coadministration of sodium bicarbonate alleviated these symptoms in a subgroup of patients. Wallace, Fraunfelder, Petursson, and Epstein (1979) reported a series of 39 patients taking methazolamide, acetazolamide, ethoxzolamide, or dichlorphenamide. All of these patients (including 6 females) reported a decrease in libido. Because of the generalized toxic effects of the carbonic anhydrase inhibitors, it is unlikely that these agents have a specific influence on libido.

Drug Abuse

An area of concern for most clinicians treating patients with inhibited sexual desire is the effect of drug abuse on sexual function. Recreational drug use is quite common in our society and often occurs in a sexual context (Abel, 1985). A number of different methodological problems are involved in the investigation of the relationship between drug abuse and sexual function. Given cultural expectations concerning the libido-enhancing effects of certain pharmacological agents, it is difficult to separate the effects of psychological expectancy from true pharmacological effects. In many investigations, serious discrepancies occur between subjects' subjective report of sexual arousal and objective measures of arousal. These problems are especially problematic when one attempts to measure the effects of drugs on libido. Libido has been defined above as a subjective state or as a potential action—the propensity to seek out sexual stimuli. As such, libido is measurable by self-report and is independent of the capacity to perform. It is far easier to demonstrate that chronic alcohol abuse reduces the *capacity* for both men and women to perform sexually than it is to marshal convincing evidence that such abuse reduces the *desire* to perform.

Alcohol

The study of the effects of alcohol on sexual function has been reviewed elsewhere (Abel, 1985; Buffum, 1982; Leiblum & Rosen, 1984; Wilson, 1981). To comprehend this literature, it is necessary to distinguish between the effects of acute and chronic alcohol ingestion. A number of studies have suggested that acute alcohol ingestion at low doses may be associated with a verbal report of increased sexual desire. However, there is good reason to assume that these libido-enhancing effects of alcohol are due primarily to social expectation rather than to the pharmacological action of alcohol (Farkas & Rosen, 1976). At higher dose levels, sexual arousal to erotic stimuli, as measured by penile tumescence and vaginal photoplethysmography, is clearly diminished by alcohol (Farkas & Rosen, 1976; Wilson & Lawson, 1978). Similarly, alcohol consumption increases the time required to masturbate to orgasm for both sexes (Malatesta, Pollack, Crotty, & Peacock, 1982; Malatesta, Pollack, Wilbanks, & Adams, 1979).

Chronic alcohol abuse is associated with an increased prevalence of sexual dysfunction in both sexes (Abel, 1985). In male alcoholics, there is good reason to assume that the increased prevalence of sexual dysfunction is due, at least in part, to organic factors (Snyder & Karachan, 1981). Libido disturbance in alcoholic males is possibly secondary to advanced alcoholic liver disease, which results in increased reabsorption of estrogens into the blood (feminization). Alcohol abuse also tends to suppress androgen production in the male (Abel, 1985). The effect of chronic alcohol abuse on females is a bit more difficult to assess. There is evidence that alcoholic women are more sexually active when intoxicated than when sober. However, in view of the suppressive effects of alcohol on female sexual responsivity, this probably reflects factors other than a pharmacological effect of increasing libido.

In summary, alcohol consumption has a suppressant effect on most objective measures of sexual function. In some individuals, it may produce an increased willingness to attend sexual stimuli or to engage in sexual activities. It is unclear how much of this "disinhibitory" influence is due to the pharmacological action of alcohol.

Narcotics

The evidence concerning the effect of narcotic drugs on libido is uniform and convincing (Abel, 1985). Anecdotal reports, surveys, and clinical studies in humans and animals are in agreement that these drugs have a marked effect on libido. The prevalence of loss of sex drive has been reported to range from 21% to 100%. This effect has been observed in both sexes, and it appears that heroin has far more deleterious effects than methadone. It also appears that this is indeed a pharmacological effect. Similar changes have been observed in lower animals, and narcotic antagonists have opposite effects. Retrospective studies of sexual drive in the preaddictive phase suggest that the loss of libido coincides with the onset of drug abuse. Similarly, libido has been observed to return in drug-free periods (Segraves *et al.*, 1985).

Marijuana

Evidence concerning the effects of marijuana on libido is ambiguous. Surveys reveal that many individuals feel that marijuana increases sexual desire (Koff, 1974). However, it is unclear whether this effect is due to expectancy or to a pharmacological action (Abel, 1985). It is also possible that the change in perceived sexual desire and pleasure is due to marijuana-related perceptual changes rather than to a specific effect on libido (Traub, 1977). It should be noted that animal studies have consistently failed to demonstrate an aphrodisiac effect of marijuana.

Cocaine

There is considerable anecdotal and survey evidence suggesting that acute cocaine use may have an aphrodisiac-like effect, inducing sexual arousal and spontaneous erections (Abel, 1985). There is also evidence that chronic usage may lead to decreased libido and other sexual dysfunctions (Siegel, 1977). Animal research suggests that this drug may have a biphasic effect, facilitating sexual behavior at lower doses and inhibiting sexual behavior at higher doses (Leavitt, 1969).

Comment

In view of the prevalence of recreational drug use, it is important that a careful drug history be conducted on patients presenting with complaints of inhibited sexual desire. Prolonged alcohol abuse, chronic abuse of cocaine, and narcotic use may decrease sexual desire. In most cases, it will be necessary to reduce the extent of drug abuse significantly before sex therapy will be beneficial.

Drug Enhancement of Libido

While the notion that pharmacological agents may enhance sexual drive in humans is not implausible, there have been no well-documented studies demonstrating such an effect. A considerable body of animal research suggests that sexual behavior may be reciprocally controlled by a central serotoninergic-inhibitory and by a dopaminergic-stimulatory mechanism (Gessa & Tagliamonte, 1975). In particular, drugs that act to deplete brain serotonin tend to augment male sexual behavior (Tucker & Rile, 1983), and drugs that augment central dopaminergic pathways tend to facilitate sexual behavior (Gessa & Napoli-Farris, 1983). The majority of these studies have been carried out in laboratory animals, and the evidence that this model is applicable to humans is scant at present. It is also difficult to ascertain which aspect(s) of animal sexual behavior would be analogous to libido in the human. The importance of that body of research for this chapter is to remind the reader that the concept of pharmacological agents influencing human libido is not implausible. Many of the psychopharmacological agents in current usage influence dopaminergic and serotoninergic pathways. Unfortunately, most of the evidence to date concerning pharmacological enhancement of human libido is anecdotal and impressionistic.

A number of pharmacological agents, such as L-dopa, amphetamines, bromocriptine, and apomorphine, augment central dopaminergic neurotransmission. Similarly, many of the antidepressant agents in current usage influence dopaminergic and/or serotoninergic neurotransmission. Evidence concerning the libido-enhancing effects of these agents (some of which are listed in Table 5) is briefly reviewed here.

L-Dopa

L-dopa, the immediate precursor of the neurotransmitter dopamine, is used in the treatment of Parkinson disease. Many of the early investigators reported that L-dopa had an aphrodisiac effect (Kent, 1981). However, others questioned whether L-dopa truly enhanced sexual interest (Mones, Elizan, & Siegel, 1970), suggesting that the reported increase in sexual interest was due to (1) a nonspecific increase in overall activity as a result of the amelioration of chronic disease (Brogden, Speight, & Avery, 1971; Calne & Sandler, 1970); (2) a decrease in inhibitions secondary to a drug-induced acute brain syndrome (Markham, Treciokas, & Diamond,

Table 5. Drugs Possibly Augmenting Libido

Drug	Medical use
L-dopa (Larodopa)	Treatment of parkinsonism
Amphetamines (Dexedrine)	Appetite suppressant
Parachlorophenylalanine	Experimental
Nomifensine (Merital)	Antidepressant
Clomipramine (Anafranil[a]	Antidepressant
Viloxazine[a]	Antidepressant
Bupropion (Wellbutrin)	Antidepressant
Apomorphine	Experimental
Bromocriptine (Parlodel)	Treatment of hyperprolactinemia

[a]Not available in the United States.

1974); or (3) part of a hypomanic syndrome induced by L-dopa (Goodwin, 1971, 1972; Goodwin, Murphy, Brodie, & Bunney, 1971). As a result of these reports, most of the medical community dismissed the idea that L-dopa might have libido-enhancing effects.

However, numerous clinicians have consistently reported that a small percentage (perhaps 5%) of patients on L-dopa demonstrate a clear-cut elevation in sexual interest (Barbeau, 1969; Hyyppa *et al*, 1970; Jenkins & Groh, 1970; Yaryura-Tobias, Diamond, & Merlis, 1970), and several reports suggest that L-dopa may have a specific libido-enhancing effect independent of other actions of this drug. O'Brian, DiGiancomo, Fahn, and Schwartz (1971) evaluated 20 consecutive patients treated with L-dopa. These patients had an average age of 59. Six patients in this series showed an increase in sexual interest and activity. Of particular interest is the fact that many men of advanced age reported the return of spontaneous erections (i.e., erections not elicited by sexual stimuli). This occurred in one man who had previously been impotent for 10 years. Sathananathan, Angrist, and Gershon (1973) investigated the effect of L-dopa in six nonschizophrenic psychiatric inpatients. One patient reported increasing his masturbatory frequency to four or five times per day, and another 37-year-old patient reported the presence of spontaneous erections while playing ping-pong with the nurse. Bowers, Woert, and Davis (1971) closely interviewed the sexual behavior of 19 patients who were receiving L-dopa for parkinsonism. Seven patients had an activation of sexual behavior. In some patients, the activation appeared to be consistent with the improvement in general well-being. However, in three patients, L-dopa appeared to have a specific sexual effect independent of other changes. For example, one 80-year-old man reported nocturnal emissions and erotic dreams.

Several investigators have studied the usefulness of L-dopa therapy in erectile impotence. Benkert, Crombach, and Kockott (1972) studied the effect of L-dopa on sexual capacity in 10 men suspected to have organogenic impotence. Although L-dopa was ineffective in restoring potency, some of these men reported an increase in degree of penile erections, spontaneous erections, libido, and sexual dreams. Some of these patients were diabetic. Thus, it is possible that L-dopa had a libido-enhancing effect in these men, which was partially obscured by erectile dysfunction due to diabetic peripheral neuropathy. In a single-blind study of diabetics with impotence, Pierini and Nusimovich (1981) reported that 3,000 mg/day of L-dopa had a statistically significant effect on erectile potency. Similar results have also been reported by Leyson (1984).

Other Dopaminergic Drugs

There is suggestive evidence that other drugs that augment dopaminergic activity may have libido-enhancing effects. A number of studies (Lal, Ackman, Thavundayil, Kiely, & Etienne, 1984; Lal & DeLaVega, 1975; Schlatter & Lal, 1972; Strain, Micheler, & Benkert, 1972) have demonstrated that apomorphine, a dopamine receptor agonist, elicits spontaneous penile erections. Unfortunately, it is impossible to discern from these reports whether associated changes in the experience of libido also occur.

Amphetamines release dopamine and are potent dopaminergic agonists (Rees, 1983). Documentation of the effect of amphetamines on sexuality is difficult because of the high incidence of sexual maladjustment and personality disorder in the premorbid personalities of amphetamine users (Angrist & Gershon, 1972, 1976; Gossop, Stern, & Connell, 1974; Greaves, 1972). Although there have been reports of decreased sexual activity after amphetamine abuse, many investigators have reported that amphetamines appear to act as libido enhancers (Angrist & Gershon, 1969, 1976; Bell & Trethowan, 1961). For example, one chronic abuser responded to high-dose amphetamine administration by compulsive masturbation, and one female amphetamine addict reported that she required amphetamines to become orgasmic. Friesen (1976) also reported that approximately 5% of the female patients taking the appetite suppressant mazindol experienced a "passionate desire for sex, even though in some cases they have never before experienced this emotion" (p. 974). Unfortunately, further details were not included in this report.

Bromocriptine is a dopaminergic agonist that has proven effectiveness in restoring sexual function in patients with hyperprolactinemia, presumably by its action of reducing serum prolactin levels (Carter *et al.*, 1978; Franks, Jacobs, Martin, & Nabarro, 1978; Tolis, Bertrand, & Pinter, 1979). This drug has also been helpful in the treatment of sexual impairment in men on renal dialysis (Bommer, Poxo, Ritz, & Bommer, 1979; Weizman *et al.*, 1983). Since dopaminergic activity has been postulated to facilitate sexual activity in lower animals, a number of investigators have studied the effectiveness of bromocriptine in the treatment of impotence (Ambrosi, Bara, & Faglia, 1977; Ambrosi, Bara, Travaglini, *et al.*, 1977; Cooper, 1977; Pierini & Nusimovich, 1981). All of these studies failed to demonstrate an effect of bromocriptine. Cooper (1977) also reported that bromocriptine had no effect on libido. Pierini and Nusimovich (1981) have suggested that the differences between L-dopa and bromocriptine may be due to their stimulation of different dopamine receptors in the brain.

Serotonin Antagonists and Precursors

Parachlorophenylalanine (PCPA), an inhibitor of tissue serotonin biosynthesis, has been shown to induce hypersexual behavior in experimental animals (Sjoerdsma *et al.*, 1970). A number of investigators have failed to demonstrate such an effect in humans. Part of the difficulty of demonstrating such an effect in humans is that high doses of PCPA induce extreme nausea (Cremata & Koe, 1966). In a double-blind placebo controlled study of 1 g/day of PCPA for 4 weeks in 10 patients with impotence, Benkert (1975) failed to find improvement in sexual function associated with this drug. Sicuteri (1974) observed a possible aphrodisiac side effect of PCPA when used to treat patients with headache. He then studied the effects of testosterone (25 mg i.m./day) and PCPA (1 g/day) in 10 patients with decreased sexual activity and headaches. A controlled crossover design was used, and the dependent measure was the number of erections per day. Five different drug conditions were employed: PCPA alone, testosterone alone, testosterone plus PCPA, no drug, and placebo. The average number of daily erections on placebo or no drugs was 6; on testosterone, 15; on PCPA, 12; and on the combined regimen, 36. Only the combined regimen of testosterone plus PCPA produced a statistically significant increase in daily erections. Ambrosi et al. (1979) studied the efficacy of two other anti-serotoninergic agents, methysergide and metergoline, in the treatment of psychogenic impotence. Neither drug was effective. Similarly, methysergide plus bromocriptine, methysergide plus mesterolone, and metergoline plus mesterolone were all ineffective.

Other investigators have studied the effect of tryptophan, a serotonin precursor, on sexual behavior in humans. Again, the evidence is equivocal. Benkert (1975) found minimal evidence for the attenuation of sexual behavior in healthy volunteers and sexual offenders after administration of 5-hyroxytryptophan. There have been several reports of the disinhibition of sexual behavior in psychiatric patients taking tryptophan (Doust & Huszka, 1972; Egan & Hammond, 1976), From the published reports, it appears that the increased sexual activity was part of manic episodes elicited by the drug.

Other Drugs

There have been isolated reports that some of the recently developed antidepressants have libido-enhancing effects. Nomifensine, an isoquinoline antidepressant that inhibits both dopamine and noradrenaline reuptake, has been reported to be associated with increased libido. Freed (1983a) reported two cases of increased libido on this drug. Moore (1983) suggested that the increased sexuality in one of these patients might have been part of an antidepressant-induced hypomania: "I hate to spoil a good story, but fear that the obvious may have been overlooked" (p. 538). However, Freed (1983b) emphasized that the time course and symptomatology did not fit that of a typical manic episode.

McLean and his colleagues (1983) have reported an unusual side effect of clomipramine, an antidepressant marketed in Europe and Canada as Anafranil. It is currently unavailable in the United States. Four patients experienced spontaneous sexual feelings associated with yawning. In one case, irresistible sexual urges occurred. In two cases, orgasm apparently occurred. The dosage used was relatively low—50 to 100 mg per day. To the authors' knowledge, no other group of investigators has reported similar findings. The side effect reported is so unusual that it is difficult to imagine this being a placebo effect. It should be noted that most investigators have noted sexual impairment rather than enhancement with this agent (Segraves *et al.,* 1985).

DeLeo, Magni, and Pavan (1983) investigated the effect of viloxazine, an antidepressant currently unavailable in the United States, on depressive symptoms and libido in 27 depressed outpatients. This agent alleviated depressive symptoms (as measured by the Zung Self-Rating Scale for Depression) and augmented libido. The improvement in libido was significantly greater than that of the depressive symptoms and did not appear directly linked to the improvement in depressive symptoms.

Comments

The evidence concerning pharmacological enhancement of libido in humans is clearly fragmented and largely anecdotal. Although considerable animal research supports the hypothesis of central dopaminergic and serotoninergic control of sexual behavior, the existing evidence concerning this mechanism in humans is suggestive at best. The reports that L-dopa and apomorphine may be associated with increased libido are consistent with the hypothesis that central dopaminergic neurotransmission may be facilitory to sexual behavior. The failure of bromocriptine and serotonin antagonists to influence libido are inconsistent with this hypothesis. The anecdotal reports concerning libido-enhancing effects of nomifensine, clomipramine, and viloxazine are provocative and merit further study.

The purpose of including this section on the possible pharmacological enhancement of libido is to remind the reader that libido disturbances may have biological as well as psychosocial etiologies. It is quite possible that pharmacological enhancement of libido will become a treatment alternative in the next decade. A number of major pharmaceutical companies have recently hired pharmacologists with an interest in the neuropharmacology of sexual behavior. Presumably, this will result in the introduction of new pharmacological agents specifically targeted at changing sexual behavior.

Clinical Illustrations

Sexual functioning is the product of complicated, interactive biological and psychological influences. Thus, libido disturbances can have their etiologies in a myriad of biological and psychological systems. Given the complexity of biological, psychological, and interpersonal influences affecting desire, our abysmal lack of information concerning variations in libido, and the difficulty clinically of separating desire from other sexual problems, diagnosis and treatment planning often constitute a challenging if not an overwhelming task. The purpose of this section is to present some clinical vignettes illustrating the complexity of differential diagnosis and choice of appropriate interventions.

A Biogenic Problem Masked as a Psychogenic Problem

The first case described here was that of a patient with a treatable organic basis for his complaint of decreased libido. This case is included to illustrate three important points: (1) the difficulty of detecting disturbances in libido in patients with other disturbances of sexual functioning; (2) the danger of assuming that other specialists properly evaluate patients with sexual complaints; and (3) the fact that biogenic problems can effectively mimic psychological problems. In this case, I mistakenly assumed that the patient's difficulty was psychogenic in origin.

Case Description

A 45-year-old married businessman was referred to me for sex therapy by his internist. This patient reported an insidious decline in erectile function and libido over the past 1–2 years. Serum androgen levels were in the low-normal range, and exogenous testosterone administered by his internist had been questionably effective. The referring physician was well acquainted with the patient's family and wondered whether the fact that the patient's brother was a homosexual might have contributed to the patient's problem. The patient stated that his decrease in desire was secondary to his erectile problems. In an individual session, the patient reported that during a recent affair with a secretary at work, he had experienced a renewal of desire and had not experienced difficulty with erections. He also reported occasional successes with his wife when they were on vacation. Prior physical examination and routine laboratory studies were unremarkable. With this information, a provisional diagnosis of psychogenic erectile dysfunction was made, and the couple was referred to an experienced sex therapist for counseling.

This therapy focused initially on the emotional distance and monotony in the marriage in sexual and other spheres. Considerable effort was expended on resolving marital conflict and restoring intimacy in the marriage. After approximately 10 weeks, the therapist recontacted me, stating, "They're both more comfortable with sexuality, and their marriage is on solid ground. Something else is wrong. I don't know what it is." The patient continued to experience difficulties both with desire and with erectile function. At this point, the patient's evaluation and treatment was carefully reviewed. It was noted that the referring internist had failed to test for serum prolactin, after which a serum prolactin level was obtained, revealing a value of 1,959 ng/ml (normal range, 0–25 ng/ml). As this value is consistent with a pituitary adenoma, the patient was immediately referred for an endocrinological evaluation. The diagnosis of a pituitary tumor was confirmed, and surgery (transphenoidal adenomectomy) was recommended. Surgery was declined by the patient, and bromocriptine therapy was successful in restoring both function and libido.

Comment

Hyperprolactinemia (elevated serum prolactin level) is frequently associated with erectile problem and decreased libido. Sexual complaints may be the presenting symptoms, and the clinical presentation may be episodic or situational alternation in sexual function (Schwartz, Bauman, & Masters, 1982). Thus, this organic cause of libido disturbance can masquerade as psychogenic impotence. Fortunately, this syndrome is infrequently encountered in the practice of sex therapy (Segraves, Schoenberg, & Ivanoff, 1983) and usually responds to bromocriptine therapy. In this patient, a clinical presentation that appeared psychogenic responded to a pharmacological intervention.

This patient served as a potent reminder to me that sexual functioning is indeed the product of numerous biological and psychological factors. In particular, alterations in biological or in psychological function may result in sexual symptomatology that is indistinguishable. The lesson to be learned from this case is that diagnostic evaluation of sexual complaints should include assessment of both biomedical and psychosexual realms. This, of course, is a strong argument for the use of multidisciplinary evalution teams in the assessment of sexual disorders.

Combined Psychological and Pharmacological Intervention

The second case is included to illustrate the importance of considering the possibility of mixed etiologies of libido problems. In this case, a clear biological factor, diabetes mellitus, interfered with erectile function. Libido problems were secondary to performance anxiety and marital discord. Pharmacological agents may also have contributed to the sexual difficulty. This case documents the need to consider the use of combined psychological–biological interventions. It also illustrates the importance of continuing the search for treatable causes of sexual difficulties when the clinical presentation may initially suggest an untreatable biological difficulty.

Case Description

This patient was a 45-year-old insulin-dependent diabetic male who also took chlorthalidone and hydralazine for arterial hypertensive disease. He requested consultation concerning erectile failure and further questioning revealed decreased sexual desire. A prior trial period off chlorthalidone had failed to relieve his symptoms. Serum testosterone and prolactin were within normal limits, thus eliminating the major endocrinological causes of diminished desire. Penile blood pressure was determined to evaluate vascular integrity of penile arteries and found to be normal. To assess the degree of biogenic erectile capacity, nocturnal penile tumescence recording was conducted. Nocturnal penile tumescence studies revealed clear rapid eye movement episodes associated with 1-cm increases in penile diameter. This was judged by the sleep technician as being 50% of normal erection and incapable of vaginal penetration. The patient also had decreased tactile sensation in his feet, a clinical sign suggestive of peripheral neuropathy. I was unable to locate any evidence in the literature that hydralazine interferes with sexual function. At this point, the presumptive diagnosis was erectile failure secondary to diabetic neuropathy. The etiology of the patient's diminished libido was unclear. The steps in the evaluation are summarized in Table 6.

The patient was extremely concerned about this diagnosis, as his wife was 19 years his junior and, according to him, unsympathetic with his difficulty. He appeared to experience minimal personal desire for sexual

Table 6. Assessment of an Insulin-dependent Diabetic, with Peripheral Neuropathy and on Antihypertensive Medication, Reporting Erectile Failure and Diminished Libido

Rationale	Finding
1. Rule out pharmacological etiology	Trial off chlorthalidone ineffective
2. Rule out endocrine etiology	Serum testosterone and prolactin normal
3. Rule out vascular etiology	Penile blood pressure normal
4. Assess biological erectile capacity	Nocturnal penile tumescence insufficient for penetration
5. Diagnosis	Probable diabetic neuropathy
6. Trial of sex therapy to assess maximal erectile capacity	Increase of erectile function
7. Trial of reduced hydralazine dose	Return of libido and erectile function

activity, yet was extemely concerned with pleasing his wife and morbidly afraid that she would leave him if he could not satisfy her sexually. The patient was informed that there was a remote possibility that psychological interventions might facilitate his sexual performance, in spite of his clear organic deficit. The patient accepted the contract of a trial of behavioral sex therapy.

I then saw the patient and his wife conjointly. The early sessions were focused primarily on a detailed behavioral analysis of their sexual interactions and a close scrutiny of their expectations of each other as spouses. It quickly became obvious that the husband had grossly exaggerated the extent of his wife's sexual displeasure. She experienced displeasure with her spouse in a number of arenas, and her anger about their lack of coitus was much less than he had surmised. He gradually began to realize that his performance anxiety was largely self-induced. As her areas of discontent were addressed, his spouse became more willing to cooperate in helping her husband. At this point, nondemand pleasuring exercises were recommended. The husband began to report erections of increased turgidity during these exercises; however, the erections were still semiflaccid and not sufficient for vaginal penetration. At this point, it was recommended that the patient reduce his dose of hydralazine to 50 mg per day and that he attempt intercourse prior to taking his medication.

The patient reported heightened desire and a return of erectile function with this approach. Although his erections were not fully firm, they achieved enough turgidity to permit penetration on a once every 1–2 weeks basis. He also reported an increase in desire.

Comment

Because of the combined psychological and pharmacological intervention in this case, it is difficult to pinpoint the effective intervention. It is also difficult in this case to separate desire from performance problems. Apparently, demoralization and self-induced pressure after performance failures had contributed to greatly diminished libido. Identification of this phenomenon in combination with nondemand sexual experiences appeared to augment the return of libido. The change in drug regimen preceded the return of satisfactory erectile function and libido. It is, of course, impossible to discern whether the increase in sexual ability was indeed due to the change in pharmacotherapy, to a placebo effect, or to a delayed effect of psychotherapy.

The most important aspect of this case is that a combined psychological and pharmacological approach led to restoration of functioning. This can serve as a reminder that biological and psychological influences are often additive and interactive rather than dichotomous. Considerable education and support were necessary before the spouses could shift their sexual activity to a time of day preceding the drug regimen. In other words, considerable psychotherapy was necessary before a modification of biological factors sufficed to produce symptom remission.

A Treatment Failure

All of us as psychotherapists are aware of the patients who have received appropriate interventions by competent clinicians and still remain treatment failures. Such patients remind us of the limited applicability of our methods and of our lack of omnipotence. The following case is a patient whom numerous clinicians, including myself, failed to help.

Case Description

The patient was a 43-year-old, single male attorney referred by a urologist because of decreased libido and an inabililty to ejaculate. Medical evaluation, including penile blood pressure, nocturnal penile tumescence testing, pudendal nerve latency testing, and a full endocrine evaluation (including serum free testosterone and serum prolactin), were unremarkable. The patient had an extensive psychiatric history, with repeated treatment for decreased desire, inability to ejaculate, fears of intimacy, and depression. Previous therapies included individual behavior therapy, individual psychoanalytically oriented psychotherapy, and various combinations of antidepressants. There was no evidence of a gender identity disorder or of ego-dystonic homosexuality.

The patient had a long-standing relationship with a girlfriend he entertained once every 2–3 weeks in his apartment. He described his girlfriend as sexually aggressive and constantly complaining about his lack of libido and difficulty with ejaculation. A conjoint session was scheduled. In this session, his girlfriend repeated her complaints about him. Attempts to engage the couple in constructive therapy were fruitless, and the girlfriend refused to return for further conjoint meetings. The patient reluctantly returned for another individual session, and stated that he was uninterested in psychotherapy. Previous psychotherapy had been ineffective, although pharmacotherapy had been helpful in alleviating his depression in the past.

Because of the patient's unwillingness to enter psychotherapy, the past failure of psychotherapy to alleviate his symptoms, the presence of signs of a dysthymic disorder, his previous response to antidepressants, and recent reports of increased libido and spontaneous orgasms with clomipramine, a novel approach to the problem was selected. Clomipramine is currently unavailable in the United States but can be obtained by patients from

Canadian pharmacies. The patient corresponded with a Canadian pharmacy and purchased clomipramine. Over a period of weeks, the dose was increased to 400 mg/day without any effect on the patient's libido or ability to ejaculate. Surprisingly, the patient was satisfied with this outcome of therapy and continued the drug at a lower dose, maintaining his increased sense of well-being. His desire problem remained unchanged.

Comment

This patient had extensive problems in interpersonal relationships, and his sexual difficulty was most likely psychologically based. However, previous psychotherapy (of various modalities) had been ineffective, and the patient was adamant in his refusal of more psychotherapy. My fantasy was that a pharmacological agent might be helpful in reversing the sexual symptoms, in spite of the patient's interpersonal difficulties. The rationale for considering a pharmacological approach to his difficulties was clinical experience in depression. Antidepressant drugs are often effective in producing symptomatic relief in patients whose depression appears related to their problems in living. The other rationale for considering the use of an agent with possible libido-enhancing effects was the hope that such an agent might alter this man's ambivalence about sexual intimacy with females. It was hoped that this agent might increase the "approach" side of his approach–avoidance conflict and thus motivate the patient to confront and resolve his difficulties with sexual intimacy. If the patient had continued to be motivated for symptom remission, I would have tried other experimental agents, such as L-dopa or bromocriptine. The patient's statement that he was content with the elevation in mood with clomipramine seemed to indicate that he was unwilling at this time to attempt to overcome his difficulties with sexual intimacy.

Conclusions

Clearly, the research evidence to date concerning drug effects on sexual desire is fragmented and of poor methodological quality. However, there are strong suggestions in the literature that commonly prescribed hypotensive and psychiatric drugs may have side effects of decreasing libido. The syndrome of inhibited sexual desire is poorly understood to date and often refractory to psychological interventions. It is possible that future research will indicate that some of these cases of inhibited sexual desire have biogenic etiologies. Until this syndrome is better understood, and until adequate research is available concerning drug effects on libido, it would appear prudent for the clinician to assume that this syndrome might be iatrogenic and drug-induced until proven otherwise. A temporary cessation or modification of pharmacotherapy may prove to be a relatively inexpensive first step in the diagnostic process. The provision of psychotherapy for a disorder with a treatable biological basis may be a disservice to patients.

The evidence concerning pharmacological enhancement of human sexuality is clearly in its infancy. Because of humans' historic quest for aphrodisiacs and the phenomenal propensity for placebo effects in this area, this evidence has to be treated with caution until replicated by independent investigators using unusually rigorous experimental conditions. A review of medical history reveals that people have been misled in their search for libido enhancers many times in the past. Psychoactive agents influence such basic biological functions as sleep, energy expenditure, appetite, and the capacity for pleasure. It is not unreasonable to suspect that certain drugs may also affect the basic biological urge to copulate. If this area of research comes to fruition, one would expect research in the next decade to focus on ways to differentiate reactive from endogenous desire disorders. It is not overly fanciful to envision this research as being similar in many ways to current research on depression.

References

Abel, E. L. (1985). *Psychoactive drugs and sex.* NY: Plenum.

Adi, F. C., Eze, C. J., & Anwunah, A. (1975). Comparison of debrisoquine and quanethidine in treatment of hypertension. *British Medical Journal, i,* 482–485.

Ambrosi, B., Bara, R., & Faglia, G. (1977). Bromocriptine in impotence. *Lancet, ii,* 987.

Ambrosi, B. Bara, R., Travaglini, P., Weber, G., Peccoz, P. B., Rondena, M., Elli, R., & Faglia, G. (1977). Study of the effects of bromocriptine on sexual impotence. *Clinical Endocrinology, 7,* 417–421.

Ambrosi, B., Travaglini, P., Gaggini, M., Moriondo, P., Elli, R., Bara, R., & Faglia, G. (1979). Effects of serotonin antagonists in sexually impotent men. *Andrologia, 6,* 475–477.

American Psychiatric Association. (1987). *Diagnostic and statistical manual of mental disorders* (3rd ed., rev., draft). Washington, DC: Author.

Anath, J., Pecknold, J. C., Steen, N., & Engels-Mann, F. (1976). Double-blind comparative study of chlorimipramine in obsessive neurosis. *Current Therapeutic Research, 25,* 703–709.

Angrist, B. M., & Gershon, S. (1969). Amphetamine abuse in New York City—1966 to 1968. *Seminars in Psychiatry, 1,* 195–207.

Angrist, B. M., & Gershon, S. (1972). Psychiatric sequelae of amphetamine use. In R. I. Shader (Ed.), *Psychiatric complications of medical drugs.* NY: Raven Press.

Angrist, B. M., & Gershon, S. (1976). Clinical effects of amphetamine and L-dopa on sexuality and agression. *Comprehensive Psychiatry, 17,* 715–722.

Bancroft, J. (1981). Hormones and human sexual behavior. *British Medical Bulletin, 37,* 153–158.

Bancroft, J. (1983). *Human sexuality and its problems.* Edinburgh: Churchill Livingstone.

Barbeau, A. (1969). L-dopa therapy in Parkinson's disease: A critical review of nine years' experience. *Canadian Medical Association Journal, 101,* 59–68.

Baron, D. P., Unger, H. R., Williams, H. E., & Knight, R. G. (1976). A double-blind study of the antidepressants dibenzepin (Noveril) and amitriptyline. *New Zealand Medical Journal, 83,* 273–274.

Bartholomew, A. A. (1968). A long-acting phenothiazine as a possible agent to control deviant sexual behavior. *American Journal of Psychiatry, 124,* 917–922.

Bauer, G. E., Hull, R. D., Stokes, G. S., & Raftos, J. (1973). The reversibility of side-effects of quanethidine therapy. *Medical Journal of Australia, 1,* 930–933.

Bell, D. S., & Trethowan, W. H. (1961). Amphetamine addiction and disturbed sexuality. *Archives of General Psychiatry, 4,* 74–78.

Benedek, T. G. (1971). Aphrodisiacs: Facts and fable. *Medical Aspects of Human Sexuality, 5,* 42–45.

Benkert, O. (1975). Clinical studies on the effects of neurohormones on sexual behavior. In M. Sandler & G. L. Gessa (Eds.), *Sexual behavior: Pharmacology and biochemistry.* New York: Raven Press.

Benkert, O., Crombach, G., & Kockott, G. (1972). Effect of L-dopa on sexually impotent patients. *Psychopharmacology, 23,* 91–95.

Beumont, P.J.V., Corker, C. S., Friesen, H. G., Kolakowska, T., Mandelbrote, B. M., Marshall, J., Murray, M.A.F., & Wiles, D. H. (1974). The effects of phenothiazines on endocrine function: II. Effects in men and post-menopausal women. *British Journal of Psychiatry, 124,* 420–430.

Beumont, P.J.V., Gelder, M. G., Friesen, H. G., Harris, G. W., McKinnon, P.C.B., Mandelbrote, B. M., & Wiles, D. H. (1974). The effects of phenothiazines on endocrine function: I. Patients with inappropriate lactation and amenorrhea. *British Journal of Psychiatry, 124,* 413–419.

Billings, R. F., Tang, S. W., & Rakoff, V. M. (1981). Depression associated with cimetidine. *Canadian Journal of Psychiatry, 26,* 260–261.

Biron, P. (1979). Diminished libido with cimetidine therapy. *Canadian Medical Association Journal, 121,* 404–405.

Blay, S. L., Ferraz, M.P.T., & Calil, H. M. (1982). Lithium-induced male sexual impairment: Two case reports. *Journal of Clinical Psychiatry, 43,* 497–498.

Bommer, J., Pozo, E. D., Ritz, E., & Bommer, G. (1979). Improved sexual function in male hemodialysis patients on bromocriptine. *Lancet, ii,* 496–497.

Bowers, M. B., Woert, M. V., & Davis, L. (1971). Sexual behavior during L-dopa treatment for parkinsonism. *American Journal of Psychiatry, 127,* 1691–1693.

Boyden, T. W., Nugent, C. A., Ogihara, T., & Maeda, T. (1980). Reserpine, hydrochlorothiazide and pituitary–gonadal hormones. *European Journal of Clinical Pharmacology, 17,* 329–332.

Brogden, R. N., Speight, T. M., & Avery, G. S. (1971). Levodopa: A review of its pharmacological properties and therapeutic uses with particular reference to parkinsonism. *Drugs, 2,* 262–400.

Brown, J., Davies, D. L., & Ferris, J. B. (1972). Comparison of surgery and prolonged spironolactone therapy in patients with hypertension, aldosterone excess, and low plasma renin. *British Medical Journal, i,* 729–734.

Brown-Sequard, C. E. (1889). The effects produced on man by subcutaneous injections of a liquid obtained from the testicles of animals. *Lancet, ii,* 105–107.

Buffum, J. (1982). Pharmacosexology: The effect of drugs on sexual function. A review. *Journal of Psychoactive Drugs, 14,* 5–44.

Burnett, W. C., & Chahine, R. A. (1979). Sexual dysfunction as a complication of propranolol therapy in men. *Cardiovascular Medicine, 4,* 811–815.

Calne, D. B., & Sandler, M. (1970). L-dopa and parkinsonism. *Nature, 226,* 21–24.

Carlson, H. E., & Ippoliti, A. F. (1977). Cimetidine, H_2-antihistamine, stimulates prolactin secretion in man. *Journal of Clinical Endocrinology and Metabolism, 45,* 367–370.

Carnes, P. (1985). *Clinical case management of sex addiction.* Paper presented at the annual meeting of the Society for Sex Therapy and Research, Minneapolis.

Carter, J. N., Tyson, J. E., Tolis, G., Uliet, S. V., Faiman, C., & Friesen, H. G. (1978). Prolactin-secreting tumors and hypogonadism in 22 men. *New England Journal of Medicine, 299,* 847–852.

Chapel, J. L., & Fahim, M. (1975). The clinical application of laboratory animal experimental findings: Treatment of hypersexualized behavior in a male. *International Journal of Clinical Pharmacology, 12,* 234–238.

Chapman, R. M. (1982). Effects of cytotoxic therapy on sexuality and gonadal function. *Seminars in Oncology, 9,* 84–94.

Chapman, R. M., Rees, L. H., Sutcliffe, S. B., Edwards, C.R.W., & Malpas, J. S. (1979). Cyclical combination chemotherapy and gonadal function. *Lancet, ii,* 285–289.

Charalampous, K. D., Freemesser, G. F., Maleu, J., & Ford, K. (1974). Loxapine succinate: A controlled double-blind study in schizophrenia. *Current Therapeutic Research, 16,* 829–837.

Clark, E. (1965). Spironolactone therapy and gynecomastia. *Journal of the American Medical Association, 193,* 163–164.

Clarke, F. C. (1969). The treatment of depression in general practice. *South African Medical Journal, 43,* 724–725.

Coleman, E. (1985). *Clinical case management of sex addiction.* Paper presented at the annual meeting of the Society for Sex Therapy and Research, Minneapolis.

Cooper, A. J. (1977). Bromocriptine in impotence. *Lancet, iii,* 567.

Coronary Drug Project Research Group. (1975). Clofibrate and niacin in coronary heart disease. *Journal of the American Medical Association, 231,* 360–381.

Cremata, V. Y., & Koe, B. K. (1966). Clinical–pharmacological evaluation of P-chlorophenylalanine: A new serotonin-depleting agent. *Clinical Pharmacology and Therapeutics, 7,* 768–776.

Curb, J. D., Borhani, N. O., Blaszkowski, T. P., Zimbaldi, N., Fotiv, S., & Williams, W. (1985). Long-term surveillance for adverse effects of antihypertensive drugs. *Journal of the American Medical Association, 253,* 3263–3268.

Davidson, J. M., Kwan, M., & Greenleaf, W. J. (1982). Hormonal replacement and sexuality in men. *Clinics in Endocrinology and Metabolism, 11,* 599–623.

DeLeo, D., Magni, G., & Pavan, L. (1983). Modifications of libido and sex drive during treatment of minor depression with viloxazine. *International Journal of Clinical Pharmacology, Therapy, and Toxicology, 21,* 176–177.

Derogatis, L. R., & Melisaratos, N. (1979). The DSFI: A multidimenstional measure of sexual functioning. *Journal of Sex and Marital Therapy, 5,* 244–281.

Doust, J.W.L., & Huszka, L. (1972). Amines and aphrodisiacs in chronic schizophrenia. *Journal of Nervous and Mental Disease, 155,* 251–264.

Egan, G. P., & Hammond, G.E.M. (1976). Sexual disinhibition with L-tryptophan. *British Medical Journal, ii,* 701.

Epstein, D. L., & Grant, W. M. (1977). Carbonic anhydrase inhibitor side-effects. *Archives of Opthalmology, 95,* 1378–1382.

Erickson, T. C. (1945). Erotomania (nymphomania) as an expression of cortical epileptic discharge. *Archives of Neurology and Psychiatry, 53,* 226–231.

Everett, H. C. (1975). The use of bethanechol chloride with tricyclic antidepressants. *American Journal of Psychiatry, 132,* 1202–1204.

Everitt, B. J., & Hanson, S. (1983). Catecholomines and hypothalmic mechanism. In D. Wheatley (Ed.), *Psychopharmacology and sexual disorders.* London: Oxford University Press.

Eysenck, H. J. (1976). *Sex and personality.* Austin: University of Texas Press.

Farkas, G. M., & Rosen, R. C. (1976). Effect of alcohol on elicited male sexual response. *Journal of Studies on Alcohol, 37,* 265–272.

Fave, G.F.D., Tamburrano, G. Magistris, L. D., Natoli, C., Santoro, M. L., Carratu, R., & Torsoli, A. (1977). Gynaecomastia with cimetidine. *Lancet, i,* 1319.

Fenwick, P.B.C., Toone, B. K., Wheeler, M. J., Nanjee, M. N., Grant, R., & Brown, D. (1985). Sexual behavior in a center for epilepsy. *Acta Neurologica Scandinavica, 71,* 428–435.

Franks, S., Jacobs, H. S., Martin, N., & Nabarro, J.D.N. (1978). Hyperprolactinaemia and impotence. *Clinical Endocrinology, 8,* 277–287.

Fraser, A. R. (1984). Sexual dysfunction following antidepressant drug therapy. *Journal of Clinical Psychopharmacology, 4,* 62–63.

Freed, E. (1983a). Increased sexual function with nomifensine. *Medical Journal of Australia, 1,* 551.

Freed, E. (1983b). In reply. *Medical Journal of Australia, 2,* 538.

Friedman, S., Kantor, I., Sobel, S., & Miller, R. (1978). A follow-up study on the chemotherapy of neurodermatitis with a monoamine oxidase inhibitor. *Journal of Nervous and Mental Disease, 166,* 349–357.

Friesen, L.V. C. (1976). Aphrodisia with mazindol. *Lancet, i,* 974.

General Practitioner Research Group. (1975). A single-dose anti-anxiety drug. *Practitioner, 215,* 98–101.

Gessa, G. L., & Napoli-Farris, L. (1983). Dopamine receptors and premature ejaculation. In D. Wheatley (Ed.), *Psychopharmacology and sexual disorders.* London: Oxford University Press.

Gessa, G. L., & Tagliamonte, A. (1975). Role of brain serotonin and dopamine in male sexual behavior. In M. Sandler & G. L. Gessa (Eds.), *Sexual behavior: Pharmacology and biochemistry.* New York: Raven Press.

Gifford, L. M., Aeugle, M. E., Myerson, R. M., & Tannenbaum, P. J. (1980). Climetidine postmarked outpatient surveillance program. *Journal of the American Medical Association, 243,* 1532–1535.

Goodwin, F. K. (1971). Behavioral effects of l-dopa in man. *Seminars in Psychiatry, 3,* 477–492.

Goodwin, F. K. (1972). Behavioral effects of l-dopa in man. In R. Shader (Ed.), *Psychiatric complications of medical drugs.* New York: Raven Press.

Goodwin, F. K., Murphy, D. L., Brodie, M.K.H., & Bunney, W. E. (1971). Levodopa: Alterations in behavior. *Clinical Pharmacology and Therapeutics, 12,* 383–396.

Gossop, M. R., Stern, R., & Connell, P. H. (1974). Drug dependence and sexual dysfunction: A comparison of intravenous users of narcotics and oral users of amphetamines. *British Journal of Psychiatry, 124,* 431–434.

Greaves, G. (1972). Sexual disturbance among chronic amphetamine users. *Journal of Nervous and Mental Disease, 155,* 363–365.

Greenberg, H. R. (1971). Inhibition of ejaculation by chlorpromazine. *Journal of Nervous and Mental Disease, 152,* 364–366.

Greenblatt, D. J., & Koch-Weser, J. (1973). Gynecomastia and impotence complications of spironolactone therapy. *Journal of the American Medical Association, 233,* 82.

Greenblatt, R. G., & Karpas, A. (1983). Hormone therapy for sexual dysfunction. *Postgraduate Medicine, 74,* 78–89.

Greenblatt, R. G., Verheugen, C., Chaddha, J., & Samaras, C. (1983). Aphrodisiacs in legend and in fact. In D. Wheatley (Ed.), *Psychopharmacology and sexual disorders.* London: Oxford University Press.

Hall, W. H. (1976). Breast changes in males on cimetidine. *New England Journal of Medicine, 295,* 841.

Harrison, W. M., Rabkin, J. G., Ehrhardt, A. A., Stewart, J. W., McGrath, P. J., Ross, D., & Quitkin, F. M. (1986). Effects of antidepressant medication of sexual function: A controlled study. *Journal of Clinical Psychopharmacology, 6,* 144–149.

Hekimian, L. F., Friedhoff, A. J., & Deever, E. (1978). A comparison of the onset of action and therapeutic efficacy of amoxapine and amitriptyline. *Journal of Clinical Psychiatry, 39,* 633–637.

Heiman, J. R., & Morokoff, P. (1977). *Sexual arousal and experience as correlates of sexual malaise*. Paper presented at the meeting of the American Psychological Association, San Francisco.

Hollender, M. H., & Ban, T. A. (1980). Ejaculatio retarda due to phenelzine. *Psychiatric Journal of the University of Ottawa, 4,* 233–234.

Hollifield, J. W., Sherman, K., Zwagg, R. V., & Shard, D. G. (1976). Proposed mechanisms of propranolol's antihypertensive effect in essential hypertension. *New England Journal of Medicine, 295,* 68–73.

Horwitz, D., Pettinger, W. A., Orvis, H., Thomas, R. E., & Sjoerdsma, A. (1967). Effects of methyldopa in fifty hypertensive patients. *Clinical Pharmacology and Therapeutics, 8,* 224–234.

Hooshmand, H., Sepdham, T., & Vries, J. K. (1974). Kluver–Bucy syndrome: Successful treatment with carbamazepine. *Journal of the American Medical Association, 229,* 1782.

Hughes, B. D. (1971). Reports on the use of Ponderax in mentally disturbed patients. *South African Medical Journal, 45,* 37.

Hyyppa, M. T., Falck, S. C., & Rinne, V. K. (1975). Is L-dopa an aphrodisiac in patients with Parkinson's disease? In M. Sandler & G. L. Gessa (Eds.), *Sexual behavior: Pharmacology and biochemistry.* New York: Raven Press.

Hyyppa, M. T., Rinne, V. K., & Sonninen, V. (1970). The activating effect of L-dopa treatment on sexual functions and its experimental background. *Acta Neurologica Scandinavica, 43*(Suppl. 43), 232–234.

Jenkins, R. B., & Groh, R. H. (1970). Mental symptoms in Parkinsonian patients treated with L-dopa. *Lancet, ii,* 177–179.

Kahn, M.A.M. (1975). Side-effects of amitriptyline. *British Medical Journal, iii,* 708.

Kaplan, H. S. (1985). Comprehensive evaluation of disorders of sexual desire: Introduction and review. In H. S. Kaplan (Ed.), *Comprehensive evaluation of disorders of sexual desire.* Washington, DC: American Psychiatric Press.

Karczmar, A. G. (1980). Drugs, transmitters and hormones, and mating behavior. In T. A. Ben & F. A. Freyhan (Eds.), *Drug treatment of sexual dysfunction.* Basel: Karger.

Kent, S. (1981). Drugs to boost sexual potency. *Geriatrics, 36,* 158–166.

Kinsey, A. C., Pomeroy, W. B., & Martin, C. E. (1948). *Sexual behavior in the human male.* Philadelphia: W. B. Saunders.

Kinsey, A. C., Pomeroy, W. B., Martin, C. E., & Gebhard, P. H. (1953). *Sexual behavior in the human female.* Philadelphia: W. B. Saunders.

Knarr, J. W. (1976). Impotence from propranolol? *Annals of Internal Medicine, 85,* 259.

Koff, W. C. (1974). Marihuana and sexual activity. *Journal of Sex Research, 10,* 194.

Kotin, J., Wilbert, D. E., Verburg, D., & Soldinger, S. M. (1976). Thioridazine and sexual dysfunction. *American Journal of Psychiatry, 133,* 82–85.

Lal, S., Ackman, D., Thavundayil, J., Kiely, M., & Etienne, P. (1984). Effect of apomorphine, a dopaminergic receptor agonist, on penile tumescence in normal subjects. *Progress in Neuro-Psychopharmacology and Biological Psychiatry, 8,* 695–699.

Lal, S., & DeLaVega, C. (1975). Apomorphine and psychopathology. *Journal of Neurology, Neurosurgery and Psychiatry, 38,* 722–726.

Laver, M. C. (1974). Sexual behavior patterns in male hypertensives. *Australian and New Zealand Journal of Medicine, 4,* 29–31.

Leavitt, F. I. (1969). Drug induced modification in sexual behavior and open field locomotion of male rats. *Physiology and Behavior, 4,* 677–683.

Leiblum, S. R., & Rosen, R. C. (1984). Alcohol and human sexual response. In D. J. Powell (Ed.), *Alcoholism and sexual dysfunction: Issues in clinical management.* NY: Haworth Press.

Lesko, L. M., Stotland, N. L., & Segraves, R. T. (1982). Three cases of anorgasmia associated with MAOI's. *American Journal of Psychiatry, 139,* 1353–1354.

Levine, S. (1985). *Clinical case management of sex addictions.* Paper presented at the annual meeting of the Society for Sex Therapy and Research, Minneapolis.

Levitt, J. I. (1970). Sprionolactone therapy and amenorrhea. *Journal of the American Medical Association, 211,* 2014–2015.

Leyson, J.F.J. (1984). *Use of dopaminergic drugs in the treatment of impotence.* Paper presented at the annual meeting of the Society for Sex Therapy and Research, New York.

Lichter, P. R., Newman, L. P., Wheeler, N. C., & Beall, O. V. (1978). Patient tolerance to carbonidanhydrase inhibitors. *American Journal of Opthalmology, 85,* 495–502.

Loriaux, D. L., Menard, R., Taylor, A., Pita, J. C., & Santer, R. (1976). Spironolactone and endocrine dysfunction. *Annals of Internal Medicine, 85,* 630–636.

MacLean, P. D. (1975). Brain mechanisms of primal sexual functions and related behavior. In M. Sandler & G. L. Gessa (Eds.), *Sexual Behavior: Pharmacology and biochemistry.* New York: Raven Press.

Magnus, R. V., Dean, B. C., & Curry, S. H. (1977). Clorazepate: Double-blind crossover comparison of a single nightly dose with diazepam thrice daily in anxiety. *Diseases of the Nervous System, 38,* 819–821.

Malatesta, V. J., Pollack, R. H., Crotty, T. D., & Peacock, L. J. (1982). Acute alcohol intoxication and the female orgasmic response. *Journal of Sex Research, 18,* 1–17.

Malatesta, V. J., Pollack, R. H., Wilbanks, W. A., & Adams, H. E. (1979). Alcohol effects on the orgasmic ejaculatory response in human males. *Journal of Sex Research, 15,* 101–107.

Markham, C. H., Treciokas, L. J., & Diamond, S. G. (1974). Parkinson's disease and levodopa. *Western Journal of Medicine, 121,* 188–206.

Mattson, R. H., & Cramer, J. A. (1985). Epilepsy, sex hormones, and antiepileptic drugs. *Epilepsia, 26*(Suppl. 1), 540–551.

McLean, J. D., Forsythe, R. G., & Kapkin, I. A. (1983). Unusual side-effects of clomipramine associated with yawning. *Canadian Journal of Psychiatry, 28,* 569–570.

Mohan, K. J., Salo, M. W., & Nagswami, S. (1975). A case of limbic system dysfunction with hypersexuality and fugue state. *Diseases of the Nervous System, 12,* 621–624.

Mones, R. J., Elizan, T. S., & Siegel, G. J. (1970). Evaluation of L-dopa therapy in Parkinson's disease. *New York State Journal of Medicine, 70,* 2309–2318.

Moore, C. (1983). Increased sexual function with nomifensine. *Medical Journal of Australia, 2,* 538.

Neri, A., Aygen, M., Zukerman, Z., & Bahary, C. (1980). Subjective assessment of sexual dysfunction of patients on long-term administration of digoxin. *Archives of Sexual Behavior, 9,* 343–347.

Newman, R. J., & Salerno, H. R. (1974). Sexual dysfunction due to methyldopa. *British Medical Journal, iv,* 106.

O'Brian, C. P., DiGiancomo, J. N., Fahn, S., & Schwartz, G. A. (1971). Mental effects of high-dosage levodopa. *Archives of General Psychiatry, 24,* 61–64.

Potts, I. (1976). Impotence. *British Journal of Urology, 48,* 150–156.

Peden, N. R., Cargill, J. M., Browning, M.C.K., Saunders, J. H. B., & Wormsley, K. G. (1979). Male sexual dysfunction during treatment with cimetidine. *British Medical Journal, i,* 659.

Pierini, A. A., & Nusimovich, B. (1981). Male diabetic sexual impotence: Effects of dopaminergic agents. *Archives of Andrology, 6,* 347–350.

Pierce, J. R. (1983). Cimetidine associated depression and loss of libido in a woman. *American Journal of the Medical Sciences, 286,* 31–34.

Pillay, V.K.G. (1976). Some side-effects of alpha-methyldopa. *South African Medical Journal, 50,* 625–626.

Rabkin, J. G., Quitkin, F. M., McGrath, P., Harrison, W., & Tricamo, E. (1985). Adverse reactions to monoamine oxidase inhibitors: Part II. *Clinical Psychopharmacology, 5,* 2–9.

Rees, J.M.H. (1983). Sexual dysfunction and prescribed psychotropic drugs. In D. Wheatley (Ed.), *Psychopharmacology and sexual disorders.* London: Oxford University Press.

Remillard, G. M., Andermann, F., Testa, G. F., Gloor, F., Aube, M., Martin, J. B., Feindel, W., Guberman, A., & Simpson, C. (1983). Sexual ictal manifestation predominate in women with temporal lobe epilepsy: A finding suggesting sexual dimorphism in the human brain. *Neurology, 33,* 323–330.

Rosen, R. C., & Kostis, J. B. (1985). Biobehavioral sequellae associated with adrenergic-inhibiting antihypertensive agents: A critical review. *Health Psychology 4,* 579–604.

Ruff, R. L. (1980). Orgasmic epilepsy. *Neurology, 30,* 1252–1253.

Ruskin, D. B., & Goldner, R. D. (1959). Treatment of depressions in private practice with imipramine. *Diseases of the Nervous System, 20,* 391–399.

Sangal, R. (1985). Inhibited female orgasm as a side-effect of alprazolam. *American Journal of Psychiatry, 142,* 1223–1224.

Sathananathan, G., Angrist, B. M., & Gershon, S. (1973). Response threshold to L-dopa in psychiatric patients. *Biological Psychiatry, 7,* 139–146.

Saunders, M., & Rawson, M. (1970). Sexuality in male epileptics. *Journal of Neurological Sciences, 10,* 577–583.

Schiavi, R. C. (1985). Evaluation of impaired sexual desire: Biological aspects. In H. S. Kaplan (Ed.), *Comprehensive evaluation of disorders of sexual desire.* Washington, DC: American Psychiatric Press.

Schilsky, R. L., Lewis, B. J., Sherins, R. J., & Young, R. C. (1980). Gonadal dysfunction in patients receiving chemotherapy for cancer. *Annals of Internal Medicine, 93,* 109–114.

Schlatter, E. K. E., & Lal, S. (1972). Treatment of alcoholism with Dent's oral apomorphine method. *Quarterly Journal of Studies on Alcohol, 33,* 430–436.

Schwartz, M. F., Bauman, J. E., & Masters, W. H. (1982). Hyperprolactinemia and sexual disorders in men. *Biological Psychiatry, 17,* 161–176.

Segraves, R. T. (1977). Pharmacological agents causing sexual dysfunction. *Journal of Sex and Marital Therapy, 3,* 157–176.

Segraves, R. T. (1985). Psychiatric drugs and orgasm in the human female. *Journal of Psychosomatic Obstetrics and Gynecology, 4,* 125–128.

Segraves, R. T., Madsen, R., Carter, S. C., & Davis, J. M. (1985). Erectile dysfunction associated with pharmacological agents. In R. T. Segraves & H. W. Schoenberg (Eds.), *Diagnosis and treatment of erectile disturbances.* New York: Plenum.

Segraves, R. T., Schoenberg, H. W., & Ivanoff, J. (1983). Serum testosterone and prolactin levels in erectile dysfunction. *Journal of Sex and Marital Therapy, 9,* 19–26.

Shalet, S. M. (1980). Effects of cancer chemotherapy of gonadal function of patients. *Cancer Treatment Reviews, 7,* 141–152.

Shen, W. W. (1982). Female orgasmic inhibition by amoxapine. *American Journal of Psychiatry, 139,* 1220–1221.

Shen, W. W., Sata, L., & Hofstatter, L. (1984). Thioridazine and understanding sexual phases in both sexes. *Psychiatric Journal of the University of Ottawa, 9,* 187–190.

Shukla, G. D., Srivastava, O. N., & Katiyar, B. C. (1979). Sexual disturbances in temporal lobe epilepsy: A controlled study. *British Journal of Psychiatry, 134,* 288–292.

Sicuteri, F. (1974). Serotonin and sex in man. *Pharmacological Research Communications, 6,* 403–411.

Siegel, R. K. (1977). Cocaine: Recreational use and intoxication. In R. C. Peterson & R. C. Stillman (Ed.), *Cocaine.* Rockville, MD: National Institute on Drug Abuse.

Simpson, G. M., Blair, H. H., & Amuso, D. (1965). Effects of antidepressants on genito-urinary function. *Diseases of the Nervous System, 26,* 787–789.

Sjoerdsma, A., Lovenberg, W., Engelman, K. Carpenter, W. T., Wyatt, R. J., & Gessa, G. L. (1970). Serotonin now: Clinical implications of inhibiting its synthesis with para-chlorophenylalanine. *Annals of Internal Medicine, 73,* 607–629.

Snyder, S., & Karachan, I. (1981). Effects of chronic alcoholism on nocturnal penile tumescence. *Psychosomatic Medicine, 43,* 423–429.

Soulairac, M. L., & Soulairac, A. (1975) Monoaminergic and cholinergic control of sexual behavior in the male rat. In M. Sandler & G. L. Gessa (Eds.), *Sexual behavior: Pharmacology and biochemistry*. New York: Raven Press.

Souner, R. (1983). Anorgasmia associated with imipramine but not desipramine: A case report. *Journal of Clinical Psychiatry, 44,* 345–346.

Souner, R. (1984). Treatment of tricyclic antidepressant induced orgasmic inhibition with cyproheptadine. *Journal of Clinical Psychopharmacology, 4,* 169.

Spark, R. F., & Melby, J. C. (1968). Aldosternonism in hypertension. *Annals of Internal Medicine, 69,* 685–691.

Strain, F., Micheler, E., & Benkert, O. (1972). Tremor inhibition in Parkinson syndrome after apomorphine administration under L-dopa and decarboxylase-inhibitor basic therapy. *Pharmakopsychiatrie, 5,* 198–205.

Tennant, G., Bancroft, J., & Cass, J. (1974). The control of deviant sexual behavior by drugs: A double-blind controlled study of haloperidol, chlorpromazine, and placebo. *Archives of Sexual Behavior, 3,* 261–271.

Thachil, J. V., Jewett, M.A.S., & Rider, W. D. (1981). The effects of cancer and cancer therapy on male fertility. *Journal of Urology, 126,* 141–145.

Tolis, G., Bertrand, G., & Pinter, E. (1979). Divorce and remarriage in a 65-year-old male following transphenoidal surgery and bromocriptine for hyperprolactinemic impotence: A dilemma. *Psychosomatic Medicine, 41,* 657–659.

Traub, S. H. (1977). Perception of marijuana and its effects: A comparison of users and non-users. *British Journal of Addiction, 72,* 67–71.

Tuchman, H., & Crumpton, C. W. (1955). A comparison of rauwolfia serpentine compounds, crude root, alseroxylon derivative, and single alkaloid in the treatment of hypertension. *American Heart Journal, 49,* 742–750.

Tucker, J. C., & File, S. E. (1983). Serotonin and sexual behavior. In D. Wheatley (Ed.), *Psychopharmacology and sexual disorders*. London: Oxford University Press.

Wallace, T. R., Fraunfelder, F. T., Petursson, G. J., & Epstein, D. L. (1979). Decreased libido—a side-effect of carbonic anhydrase inhibitor. *Annals of Opthalmology, 233,* 1563–1566.

Waxman, D. (1975a). A general practitioner trial of clomipramine (anafranil) in obsessions and phobias. *Journal of International Medical Research, 3*(Suppl. 1), 94–100.

Waxman, D. (1975b). An investigation into the use of anafranil in phobic and obsessional disorders. *Scottish Medical Journal, 20,* 61–65.

Weizman, R., Weizman, A., Levi, J., Gura, V., Zevin, D., Maoz, B., Wijsenbeek, H., & David, M. B. (1983). Sexual dysfunction associated with hyperprolactinemia in males and females undergoing hemodialysis. *Psychosomatic Medicine, 45,* 259–269.

Wilson, G. T. (1981). The effects of alcohol on human sexual behavior. *Advances in Substance Abuse, 2,* 1–40.

Wilson, G. T., & Lawson, D. M. (1978) Expectancies, alcohol and sexual arousal in women. *Journal of Abnormal Psychology, 87,* 358–367.

Wooton, L. W., & Bailey, R. I. (1975). Experiences with chlomipramine (Anafranil) in the treatment of the phobic anxiety states in general practice. *Journal of International Medical Research, 3*(Suppl. 1), 101–107.

Yaryura-Tobias, J. A., Diamond, B., & Merlis, S. (1970). The action of L-dopa on schizophrenic patients. *Current Therapeutic Research, 12,* 528–531.

Yassa, R. (1982). Sexual disorders in the course of clomipramine treatment: A report of three cases. *Canadian Journal of Psychiatry, 27,* 148–149.

Yendt, E. R., Gray, G. F., & Garcia, D. A. (1970). The use of thiazides in the prevention of renal calculi. *Canadian Medical Association Journal, 102,* 614–620.

Zarren, H. S., & Black, P. M. (1975). Unilateral gynecomastia and impotence during low-dose spironolactone adminstration in men. *Military Medicine, 140,* 417–419.

13

The Treatment of Desire Disorders in the Medically Ill and Physically Disabled

DAVID G. BULLARD

Many of us dismiss the notion that physically and medically ill individuals are sexual beings with the same desire for, and difficulties with achieving, sexual gratification as the nondisabled. We tend to desexualize these individuals and, even worse, to discourage their requests for sexual information, permission, and therapy as unrealistic or less important than other aspects of their health care. In his chapter on desire problems in these populations, Bullard reminds us that all *of these individuals are sexual beings and that* many *of them want to explore their potential for sexual pleasure. Furthermore, he urges us to adopt a "wellness" perspective, rather than a sickness model, when working with such individuals and to avoid unnecessarily pessimistic stereotypes of their potential for sexual gratification and growth.*

It is certainly true that medical conditions and the treatments they entail can compromise sexual functioning. However, Bullard reminds us that sophisticated assessment is required to differentiate between the desire difficulties that may result directly from an illness, and the psychological factors that may be responsible for problematic functioning. For instance, anxiety, depression, or anger related to the illness or disability, rather than physiological inhibition may interfere with sexual desire or arousal. When functioning is indeed directly impaired because of a disability, the therapist and client must collaborate creatively to find a path around the difficulty. Experimentation with changes in position, changes in timing of sexual initiation, special devices, and so forth may all prove helpful. At times, a change of medication may be necessary; in other instances, hypnosis or relaxation training can help to counter the side effects of chemotherapy or other pharmacological treatments. The critical issue is keeping the focus on what is possible given the disability, not on what is compromised. For instance, Bullard suggests that vibrators might amplify sensation in individuals who have diminished genital awareness, as can fantasy and guided imagery.

When working with medically ill or disabled individuals, the therapist needs to be sensitive to a host of psychological concerns, as well as realistic concerns about the illness itself. Some individuals may have increased fears about dying or guilt about behaviors they believe may have caused their disease or disability. For example, women with cervical cancer sometimes worry that their coital activities may have caused their cancer, while their partners may wonder whether radiotherapy makes intercourse dangerous for themselves. These issues need to be addressed directly in sex therapy. Like nondisabled individuals, those with physical disabilities or medical illness need to help develop positive attitudes about a wide range of sexual practices in addition to intercourse or genital sex.

Sensitivity is also needed in working with partners of disabled or medically ill persons. Sometimes these individuals fear hurting or damaging their mates. In other instances, they may have negative reactions to the altered body appearance of their partners or the changes in sexual desire, arousal, or response that result from a medical condition or treatment. More problematic is the absence of a viable partner; in these cases, self-help organizations can be a useful resource for developing supportive relationships.

Bullard provides a number of instructive case examples, cogently illustrating how desire problems may be traceable to both physical and psychological factors. His therapy examples demonstrate the importance of utilizing a skillful blend of sensitivity, confrontation, and encouragement when treating the sexual difficulties of the medically and physically ill. In many instances, specific sexual techniques are less important than general psychological savvy. Finally, Bullard reminds us that our helpfulness as therapists is enhanced when we keep the focus on the person rather than the disease.

David G. Bullard, Ph.D., is associated with the Departments of Medicine and Psychiatry at the University of California School of Medicine at San Francisco, and is on the faculty of the Mental Research Institute, Palo Alto, California. For many years, he was involved with several projects funded by the National Institute of Mental Health at the University of California at San Francisco, devoted to exploring sexuality and disability issues.

"I've had 17 operations, hernias and adhesions usually. Every time I brought up the subject of sex, the doctor would tell me I didn't have to worry about that yet. All I wanted to know was *when* should I worry and *what* was I supposed to worry about." (Young, 1984, p. 56)

This quotation highlights two challenges that face people with serious medical conditions who attempt to get information and positive feelings about their sexuality:

1. Health care providers often neglect issues of sexual health or inadequately address them (Unsain, Goodwin, & Schuster, 1982).
2. When these issues are addressed, problems are often emphasized, rather than preventive or corrective interventions that could enhance sexual health (Zilbergeld, 1979).

Persons with a physical disability or chronic illness are susceptible to the same sexual conflicts and disorders as those who are nondisabled. Treatment for arthritis, renal disease, breast cancer, or a spinal cord injury does not provide immunity from relationship struggles, intrapsychic conflicts, or psychogenic sexual disorders. A client may have discussed specific questions or concerns regarding a medical condition and the ways in which it may affect sexuality. But thorny and difficult psychodynamic or relationship issues may remain. The approach to these underlying conflicts may then be the same as that used with a nondisabled client, assuming that the therapist remains sensitive to the client's feelings about his or her illness. There are essentially no special therapeutic "techniques" specific to desire problems in medically disabled clients. Rather, the therapist's attitudes toward and understanding of illness and disability appear to be more important.

Both the clinical and the research literatures suggest many etiological factors that may be implicated in sexual desire disorders among those with serious medical conditions. For the most part, the medical and psychological literatures present the sexuality of the ill and disabled *a priori* as problematic, and rarely focuses attention on enhancement or growth aspects (Anderson & Wolf, 1986; Bullard, 1981; Zilbergeld, 1979). This creates an unnecessarily pessimistic stereotype of the potential for sexual fulfillment, which, if unexamined, can damage a psychotherapist's effectiveness with disabled clients.

The alternative is to approach these issues from an enhancement or "wellness" perspective rather than from a sickness model. Therapists need to know the potential for positive sexual experiences despite serious medical conditions. For example, in contrast to the usual stereotypes, consider the couple who avoided any sexual interaction for several years. Then the woman developed breast cancer and had a mastectomy. As part of their re-evaluation of what was important in life, they sought out a psychotherapist to help them re-establish an active sexual relationship. Or consider a 67-year-old gentleman who, after three transurethral prostatectomies, said that his orgasms felt much *better* now, despite "dry" or retrograde ejaculation. Such experiences of real people illustrate the potential for sexual fulfillment that can exist in the midst of serious illness.

Sexual Desire and Persons with Medical Conditions

How important is sexuality to people with serious illness or disability? Although some literature suggests the survival of sexual interest despite major physical trauma and loss (Anderson & Wolf, 1986; Bullard & Knight, 1981; Chigier, 1972; Cole, 1972; Comfort, 1978; Kolodny, Masters, & Johnson, 1979; Vaeth, 1986; Woods, 1984; Zilbergeld, 1979), health care professionals have not yet successfully integrated sexuality issues into general health care and treatment (Young, 1984).

Despite the applicability of the biopsychosocial model (Engel, 1977) to issues of sexuality and medical conditions, behavioral medicine texts have largely ignored problems of sexual desire and functioning among individuals with medical problems. Similarly, many otherwise useful texts addressing sex therapy in medical practice do not consider desire disorders, or only briefly acknowledge their existence in medical populations. Sexuality texts that discuss, to varying degrees, desire issues with specific medical conditions include Comfort (1978), Kaplan (1985), Kolodny *et al.* (1979), Leiblum and Pervin (1980), Lief (1981), and Woods (1984). The projects described below also explored these issues.

Sex and Disability Unit, Human Sexuality Program, University of California at San Francisco

From 1976 through 1982, the National Institute of Mental Health funded several projects at the University of California School of Medicine in San Francisco to explore sexuality and disability issues. One of these projects trained 100 persons as sex and disability educator/counselors. Of these trainees, 65 were themselves disabled by conditions such as arthritis, cancer, cerebral palsy, hearing impairment, multiple sclerosis, after effects of polio, spinal cord injury, and visual impairment. (Trainee selection criteria, training processes, curricula, and evaluation instruments are detailed in Bullard, Knight, Rodocker, & Wallace, 1980.) These projects also provided sex therapy for people with medical conditions through the Sex and Disability Clinic, directed by Mary Rodocker, R.N., M.S. Clients were seen by staff members, sometimes with trainee cotherapists. Among the 147 clients, there was a wide range of presenting problems, including 20 primary complaints of low sexual desire.

Many clients had been referred by their medical internists or specialists, with a situational desire disorder or with clear psychosocial factors that appeared to contribute to more general sexual inhibition. Of course, selection factors must be kept in mind when reporting on any clinical population. Our experiences have been drawn from a university medical center clinic offering psychotherapeutic and sex therapy services and from private practice. Our conclusions might be significantly different if we had primarily seen patients referred from an endocrine disorders clinic.

Of the 20 clients with a primary complaint of low desire, 6 had erectile dysfunction, 2 reported pain with sexual activities, and 4 had significant relationship problems. Others had loss of ejaculation and/or orgasm; loss of genital sensation; lack of social and sexual skills and experiences; depression; body image and self-image concerns, and chemotherapy-related concerns. Case examples from this group are presented later in this chapter.

Treatment Approach

> Learn your theories as well as you can, but put them aside when you touch the miracle of the living soul. Not theories but your own creative individuality alone must decide. (Jung, 1926/1928, p. 361)

In treating problems of intimacy and sexual desire, I have found my clients to be great teachers. I have also been influenced by my sex therapist colleagues in San Francisco, who run the gamut from A to Z (Apfelbaum, Barbach, Black, Caplan, Knight, Mann, Marlowe, Rodocker, Zilbergeld), and by other friends, therapists and consultants.

Theoretical formulations that have been useful to me have come from a variety of psychotherapeutic theories: behavior and cognitive therapy; the brief therapy models of Milton Erickson and of the Mental Research Institute (Watzlawick, Weakland, & Fisch, 1974); hypnosis; psychodynamic theory (Weiss & Sampson, 1986); systems theory; and traditional sex therapy. Yet a theoretical formulation is like a musical score. Reading it is interesting, but not nearly as rich an experience as hearing the symphony played.

As important as the intellectual framework, *attitudes* held by the therapist can powerfully assist people with medical conditions deal with sexual issues. These include the following:

1. *Each client is completely, totally unique.* A therapist with this attitude can take an empirical approach to each new client or couple situation. This means that the therapist must observe the nuances and avoid putting that person or couple into a box with other "similarly disabled"

clients. The therapist can use what works in the moment with that specific person, and can use the approaches that are helpful in that particular situation. Some people will respond best to very direct suggestions; others deal well with mostly therapeutically posed questions; others get more value from the indirect messages of anecdotes or metaphors; and still others will have a deep need to be understood and listened to without interruptions. Paying attention to what works for a given individual or couple is one of our most basic therapeutic tasks.

2. *Each person is a sexual being, regardless of the amount of past or current sexual activity or level of sexual functioning.* Inherent in everyone, sexuality is not something that people need to prove by being sexually active or functional in particular ways.

3. *It is all right to have problems and to be in therapy.* If you felt disgraced that your yard was a patch of dirt and weeds, while neighbors had lovely, abundant gardens that apparently required no effort, you might be too embarrassed to go out to prepare the soil and plant and water the seeds. If you knew that your neighbors were encouraging you, and that they had to sweat and labor to maintain the beauty and productivity of their gardens, it would be much easier to make the efforts to get what you hope for. Once a person knows it is part of being human to have certain challenges, it becomes easier to address them. Almost everyone has struggled at some time with sexual and relationship problems.

4. *Human adaptability, resourcefulness, and resiliency are great.* The therapist should look for and identify with the strengths and positive qualities of the person who comes to talk to him or her. Of great help to our staff was the opportunity of learning from our trainees and from each other about successful adaptations to chronic illness or disability. Therapists who know people with medical conditions who are comfortable with their sexuality will find it easier to validate the sexuality of their clients.

5. *Therapists can be experts in helping others become more fully themselves and more fully satisfied; they are not experts about their clients or about "sexuality."*

Sexual Desire

Parable: A man met a magician who said, "I will grant you all of your heart's desires. There will be no trickery; your wishes all will come true. You will, however, have to agree to one thing: to get all your heart's desires, you must write them down on a sheet of paper and then forget that you had desired them." (Anonymous)

Human sexual desire is as mysterious as intimacy and love. Welwood (1985) has collected essays from philosophers, poets, and psychotherapists on the nature of human love, and suggests that no one person can fully comprehend its total spectrum. In the sex therapy literature, Zilbergeld and Ellison (1980) clarify the importance of the subjective distinctions between sexual desire and arousal.

There is a wide range of sexual desire issues. Some people enjoy sex but think they should do it more often (this is true of most married couples, according to Frank, Anderson, & Rubenstein, 1978; and possibly of most adults). Some simply do not care about sex; some are inhibited or find sex aversive; and some are clinically phobic (Kaplan, 1987). The problem may reflect a lifelong pattern, or it may be of recent origin. It may pertain to certain sexual practices (aversion to oral sex) and not to others (high desire for intercourse). Some may profess strong sexual desire except for their spouse or an available partner. There may be disagreement as to who has the problem when there is a desire discrepancy. Or there may be subjective agreement on the problem between the individuals; yet an objective third party may disagree with their assessment (when one partner labels himself or herself "abnormal" for not desiring sex as much as the other).

Most couples probably deal with periods of desire discrepancy or of mutually low desire. They either resolve these differences, ignore or accept them, or separate. Some may enact their particular power struggles in the sexual arena, and come to therapists to talk about their sexual problems. For the majority of cases that we have worked with, relationship issues have most often provided the focus for the therapy.

Differential Diagnosis

> Differentiating between organic and psychosocial etiologies of lowered libido is often a difficult process involving a large measure of clinical judgment rather than precise laboratory testing. (Kolodny et al., 1979, p. 565)

Many organic conditions are believed to lower sexual desire *directly* (see Table 1). Virtually any medical condition, however, can *indirectly* affect sexual desire by psychosocial adaptation. For example, fears of anticipated rejection by a sexual partner because of a stoma, mastectomy, or sexual dysfunction may lead to a repression of sexual feelings and avoidance of sexual opportunities.

Psychological manifestations such as depression can either be the *cause* or the *effect* of diminished sexual desire. Both may be present to some degree. In other instances, depression and lack of desire may be the result of a third underlying factor, such as an endocrine disorder (Derogatis & Meyer, 1979, p. 219).

In general, anyone with globally rather than situationally impaired sexual desire should receive a thorough medical examination and testing to

Table 1. Medical Conditions Leading to Loss of Desire

Conditions typically causing loss of/reduction in desire	Conditions sometimes associated with loss of/reduction in desire
Addison disease	Anemia
Alcoholism	Brain tumors
Chronic active hepatitis	Cerebrovascular disease
Chronic renal failure	Chronic obstructive pulmonary disease
Cirrhosis	Collagen diseases
Congestive heart failure	Drug ingestion (see Chapter 12)
Cushing syndrome	General and local infections
Drug addiction	Hyperaldosteronism
Feminizing tumors (in men)	Hypoglycemia
Hemochromatosis	Hypokalemia
Kallman syndrome	Malignancy
Klinefelter syndrome	Multiple sclerosis
Myotonic dystrophy	Nutritional deficiences
Other endocrine disorders (see Chapter 11)	Parasitic infestation
Parkinson disease	Prostatitis
Tuberculosis	Psychomotor epilepsy
	Sarcoidosis

Note. Adapted from *Textbook of Sexual Medicine* by R. C. Kolodny, W. H. Masters, and V. E. Johnson, 1979, Boston: Little, Brown. Used by permission.

rule out organic causes (see Table 1). Kaplan (1985) suggests that even situational losses of desire may reflect a slowly progressing medical disorder; in these cases, she suggests that especially arousing psychic stimulation compensates for decreased sexual desire. She further recommends that *all* patients complaining of sexual problems be asked the following questions:

1. When did you have your last medical examination?
2. Do you have any illness or are you taking any drug at the present time?
3. Have you ever had any serious illnesses or surgical procedures in the past?
4. Do you smoke [or] use alcohol or any other substances?
5. For women: Are your menses normal, regular? Have you had any children? Were any problems associated with pregnancy, delivery, breast-feeding?

6. For men: Do you notice morning or nocturnal erections? Are they
   firm enough for penetration?
7. What sort of birth control methods do you use? (Kaplan, 1983, pp.
   85–86)

In addition, the evaluation of persons with significant medical conditions implicated in desire disorders should include a thorough history
considering psychogenic factors such as response anxiety, panic disorders,
and relationship conflicts. The following section describes factors affecting
sexual desire from the biopsychosocial perspective.

Stressors from Medical Conditions That May Contribute to Decreased Sexual Desire and Treatment Suggestions for Dealing with Them

The biopsychosocial perspective can be useful in considering the factors that
may contribute to lowered sexual desire with chronic physical illness in
general (Anderson & Wolf, 1986), and with specific disorders such as
cancer (Andersen, 1985). The intensity of each stressor, however, varies for
a given individual, and for acute versus chronic conditions. There can also
be as much or more variation among individuals as among medical conditions. Possible stressors and interventions are suggested below.

Biological Stressors

Direct Physiological Effects of the Illness or Disability

One example of a direct effect of an illness is the effect of a medical
condition on testosterone. (The importance of testosterone has been addressed elsewhere in this volume; see Chapter 11.) Testosterone production
is often impaired in men with end-stage renal disease even when they are
undergoing dialysis (Johnson, 1984, p. 320). Chronic alcoholism may also
lower the production of testosterone. Liver damage by alcoholism or other
disease may promote a rapid breakdown of testosterone (Kolodny *et al.*,
1979, p. 240). Medical treatment of some diseases may resolve the desire
problem, such as hormone replacement therapy for a neuroendocrine disorder (see Chapter 11). Brief sex therapy may help people adjust their
expectations and/or find new approaches to lovemaking that accommodate
lowered desire. Focusing on physical arousal may lead them into a satisfying
sexual experience. Some people need permission from a partner to start
sexual caressing despite an apparent lack of desire. Others may need to be
reminded of "nibbling" phenomena (i.e., those occasions when their appe-

tites seemed nil until they had actually begun to taste what was available to them).

Direct Physiological Effects of Medical Treatment and Management

An example of a direct effect of treatment would be corticosteroid administration for arthritis, which may itself decrease sexual desire. The physician may be able to change a dosage or a medication suspected of lessening sexual desire (see Chapter 12). Chemotherapy for cancer may induce nausea and fatigue, or pain and fatigue may follow radiation therapy and surgery. Psychological interventions such as hypnosis and relaxation training may help to counter these side effects. Some surgeries may alter a person's sexual responsiveness, such as decreased lubrication or erectile dysfunction following radical cancer surgery. Some affect capacity for sexual intercourse, such as pelvic exenteration or surgery for penile cancer. Vaginal reconstruction and penile implants may help some people improve their sexual self-image and interest. Psychotherapy or sex therapy may help others to adopt new attitudes about sexuality and expand their ideas of the range of sexual activities that could give them pleasure and satisfaction.

Physical Debilitation

Fatigue and/or pain may be secondary to a disease, a medical treatment, prolonged hospitalization, or impaired mobility. Many people disregard the fact that fatigue may lower their sexual desire, especially those who have acclimated to low levels of energy. They may benefit from validation by the therapist or health care provider that being tired usually hinders sexual interest. They can also be taught to plan for sex at times when they are most rested, rather than following earlier scripts that dictate when and how they *should* attempt to be sexual.

Arthritis is a condition in which sexual desire may be smothered under problems of mobility and pain. Application of moist heat (or cold applications for some individuals) as a preparation to sexual activity may help diminish pain, relax muscles, and increase range of motion. Analgesic or anti-inflammatory medications can be taken from 30 minutes to 1 hour beforehand. Timings of sexual encounters should be suggested that minimize pain, stiffness, and fatigue (Ehrlich, 1978). Experimentation with various sexual positions and with aids such as pillows, water beds, and massage oil may also minimize fatigue and pain. Although some people report hours of pain relief after sexual activity, others find that pain becomes debilitating afterward (Halstead, 1978). A gradual approach of experimentation may enable the person to identify combinations of physical and environmental factors that provide the most pain-free and positive experience.

Bladder or Bowel Incontinence

Techniques and suggestions for bladder and bowel care for people with spinal cord injury, neurological disease, and ostomy stress the importance of preventive management to preclude accidental leakage. Hearing how others have successfully adapted to the possibility of accidents may also be of benefit. When asked gravely by a medical student in a seminar how he dealt with the potential of such an accident, one young man with a spinal cord injury responded, "Well, it helps to have a sense of humor!" The lesson for nondisabled health care practitioners is that their own fears and anxieties about disability may be mistakenly projected onto their clients. The person who has a medical condition is often an expert on coping with these experiences, or is fast becoming one.

Anatomical Difficulty or Inability to Have Intercourse

Anatomical difficulty or inability to have intercourse may result from severe spasticity, introital stenosis, or surgical removal of the penis or vagina for cancer. Most people will find this a difficult loss. Some may be reassured by knowing that many women do not reach orgasm from intercourse alone, and that many men and women enjoy being caressed or orally stimulated. Many people see these activities as enhancements to sexuality and pleasure, rather than as "second-best" alternatives. Under the special stress of a medical condition, many couples communicate more clearly and learn what each other *really* likes, in contrast to the cultural myths and assumptions about what the other is *supposed* to enjoy.

Lack of Genital Sensation

Lack of genital sensation may lead to decreased sexual arousal, physiological readiness, or orgasm. Sensate focusing or hypnosis may assist some people in amplifying any sensation they do have, or may help them unlock dormant sensual and sexual pleasure in nongenital areas. Others may find that the use of vibrators significantly increases their sensation. Fantasy and guided imagery may also enhance the sexual experience. One woman, whose mother had taken diethystilbestrol (DES) during pregnancy, was diagnosed as having cancer of the vagina; the resulting surgery removed one ovary, her uterus, her tubes, the upper two-thirds of her vagina, and the bilateral pelvic lymph nodes. She utilized many of the techniques mentioned here to relearn orgasmic ability and to regain a positive sexual self-image (Burger, 1981).

Psychological Stressors

Adopting the "Patient" Role

Many individuals may feel compelled to adopt the "patient" role and to comply with institutional and societal prescriptions that a person with a serious medical condition is "asexual." A therapist, health care provider, or educator who can validate that sexuality is a part of who we *are*, rather than just a reflection of what we do and how often we do it, can help to counter these negative role "scripts." Children as well as adults with medical conditions can benefit from positive information about their sexuality (Thornton, 1981).

Altered Body Image

Some researchers have questioned the adequacy of current conceptualizations of body image in explaining the sexual problems that occur among people such as those treated for breast cancer (Andersen, 1985; Ray, 1977). Clinically, we cannot deny the powerful effects of radical body changes referred to as "disfigurement." Disturbing self-image issues may surface in an adolescent who is devastated by hair loss from chemotherapy, an adult who is confronted with a colostomy, a woman recovering from a mastectomy, or a man treated surgically for testicular cancer. Grieving for such losses may require substantial time and effort. In addition to an empathic and skilled therapist, peer groups may be of immense benefit in helping the person initially cope with and eventually integrate such changes (Wilbur, 1986).

Anxiety, Depression, and Anger

Anxiety, depression, and/or anger may be related to the illness or disability, or may result from problems with sexual arousal, physiological readiness, orgasm, or satisfaction. A person with a serious medical condition often experiences one or all of these emotions—beginning with the uncertainty of initial physical symptomatology, and continuing through the diagnosis, treatment, and uncertainty of cure, improvement, or relapse. From 17% to 25% of persons hospitalized for cancer could be diagnosed as clinically depressed (Petty & Noyes, 1981). Depression is also commonly associated with uremia and fluid overload in renal disease, as well as with people who are mourning the loss of functioning as a result of diseases such as arthritis, cancer, cardiac problems, renal failure, spinal cord injury, and stroke (Levay, Sharpe, & Kagle, 1981). Diminished sexual desire may be secondary to these psychological states. Direct treatment of a depression by psychotherapy and/or antidepressant medication without any sexual therapy per se may be of benefit in restoring sexual interest in some of these people. Preoperative counseling may prevent sexual problems in people facing surgery for a variety of medical problems (Levay et al., 1981).

Fears of Death, Rejection by a Partner, or Loss of Control

Supportive psychotherapy and couples therapy directed at fears of death, rejection, or loss of control may help the person re-experience sexual feelings and desire. Fears of death resulting from sexual behavior may be especially prominent with cardiac disease, hypertension, and stroke. For example, the most common factor in the decline of sexual activity among 113 persons after a cerebrovascular accident was concern that sexual behavior would increase blood pressure and cause another stroke (Monga, Lawson, & Inglis, 1986). These authors cautioned that a theoretical risk *is* greater in persons with intracerebral hemorrhage. Woods (1984) believes that the most important intervention to promote sexual health for those with cardiac disease is sharing information about when and under what conditions it would be safe to resume intercourse and other sexual behaviors. She suggests a specific "sexual activity program" for patients with uncomplicated myocardial infarction (Woods, 1984, pp. 306–307).

Guilt Regarding Behavior Imagined to Be the Cause of a Disease or Disability

Weiss and Sampson (1986) discuss the power of unconscious beliefs, which may irrationally blame a medical condition on some self-perceived "crime" committed by thought or deed. Conscious fears may also be present. Women treated for cervical cancer often wonder whether coitus in some way has *caused* their cancer, while their partners wonder whether radiotherapy may make intercourse dangerous for them. These questions are usually not addressed unless the primary caregivers initiate a conversation about the effects of the illness and its treatment upon their sexual relationship and intimacy (Vincent, Vincent, Greiss, & Linton, 1975). Obviously, great relief may result from such discussions. The availability of information about "safer" sexual practices will be especially important to people with concerns about acquired immune deficiency syndrome (AIDS).

Lack of Information about and Positive Attitudes toward the Wide Range of Satisfying Sexual Practices

Attitudes of health care providers can be especially powerful in conveying either hopelessness or encouragement about the attainment of a positive sexual life after disability or major illness. In evaluating a human sexuality course for second-year preclinical medical students, Wallace (1980) found that the segment rated most valuable by the students was a panel discussion of personal sexual issues by individuals who themselves were physically disabled. This was rated more valuable than either the modified Sexual Attitude Reassessment (SAR) component or the presentations by practicing physicians on the medical panel. The students' preconceptions gave way to increased awareness of and appreciation for the enjoyment of sexuality by many people with medical conditions.

Lack of Role Models and Overly Narrow Cultural Definitions of Sexuality

In a study of men and women over 50 years of age, Brecher and the Editors of Consumer Reports Books (1984) concluded that the gradual decline in sexual activity, decade by decade, was related more to aging than to health status. Many people in this study indicated continuing interest and activity in sex despite significant medical conditions. As more data are collected and disseminated, there will be more challenges to the stereotypes of the aged and disabled as asexual. The presence of health care providers who themselves are physically disabled can further provide positive role models for staff and patients in medical facilities (Bullard & Wallace, 1978).

Psychological Demands of Coping with a Chronic Disease or Disability

Many people treated for serious medical conditions such as cancer and end-stage kidney disease prefer to discuss their sexuality with their primary health care providers rather than with specialists in sex therapy (Bullard *et al.*, 1986; Levy, 1977). They may have a limited amount of energy after consultations and examinations with several health care professionals. The idea of going to yet another office and meeting yet another "helping" person may be depleting. They may also be using denial to avoid being over-whelmed by problems. This places greater responsibility on every member of the health care team to be comfortable and confident in addressing sexual issues, or to be able to refer the client to a staff member who is.

Reassignment of Priorities

Especially in life-threatening and other serious illnesses, decisions may be made by an individual or couple that may place lower or higher value on sexual behavior. Studies indicate that while the frequency of sexual in-tercourse may decrease in the face of serious medical conditions for some people, others report that physical intimacy, including sex, becomes more important (Bullard *et al.*, 1986; Capone, Westie, & Good, 1986). One couple found that the staff on an inpatient unit at a large hospital dis-approved of their requests for privacy. The man, aged 35, was dying of an inoperable brain tumor. He and his wife found that sexual intimacy was very important to them in his final weeks. In contrast, the medical chart indicated that some staff members felt that the couple's focus on sexuality was a pathological "denial of death." When the couple asked for an opinion as to the "normality" or propriety of their being sexual in their private hospital room, a sympathetic nurse determined that they were quite aware of the man's prognosis. She was able to validate their right to be sexually intimate, and used this situation to do some education with the rest of the staff.

Self-Monitoring

Hyperawareness of body sensations and functioning may diminish a per-son's awareness of sexual feelings. A man who has had a prostatectomy may be more vigilant about monitoring his erection than about perceiving pleasurable sensations. Another person may be self-conscious about an ostomy and avoid sexual situations. Exploring these issues with a therapist or self-help group (such as the United Ostomy Association) may encourage that person over time to take the risk of being vulnerable in a sexual situation. It may take years for some people who have undergone especially traumatic medical experiences to recover a sense of themselves as sexual beings.

Social Skills Deficits

Social skills deficits may affect persons who have been congenitally disabled and restricted from important social and sexual learning experiences. Therapy using educational exercises, such as role playing of common interpersonal situations and dating behavior, may be useful. Body work with a professional sexual surrogate may be appropriate for some to help unlock sexual feelings. Knight (1986) described the case of a 40-year-old man with moderate cerebral palsy who came for counseling because, in his words, "I think I'm old enough to learn about sex." College-educated and employed, he had lived independently of his parents for 3 years. Despite being intelligent and well-functioning, he claimed to have no knowledge of the sexual responses of men or women, and attributed his occasional ejaculations to his cerebral palsy. As he progressed in therapy, he began meeting for 2-hour sessions with a sexual surrogate. This kind of body work therapy can be very helpful in the sexual development of adults with disabilities who have had limited access to sexual experiences (Knight, 1986, p. 241). Important preventive steps to provide disabled children with accurate and validating sex education have been outlined for the schools (Thornton, 1981) and for rehabilitation centers (Evans & Conine, 1985).

Stress

Medical conditions may lead to job loss, financial worries, and role changes that can themselves detract from interest in sexuality. These issues take precedence over sexual concerns for most people. Basic emotional and financial survival may leave little room for sexual interest. However, one young man with a spinal cord injury recounted that upon awakening in the hospital after his diving accident, he remembered the physician telling him he should just think about getting well. "I thought about that for about 5 minutes, got bored, then began wondering about my future sex life!"

Social and Interpersonal Stressors

Negative Attitudes and Lack of Positive Information

Negative attitudes and lack of positive information about the sexuality of the ill and disabled can be highly restrictive and respressive. The person with a disability is often seen as "asexual" by family, educators, peers, and health care providers (Chigier, 1980; Knight, 1986). For example, Sarah had had polio when she was 3 years old and thereafter used a wheelchair. She did not remember feeling different from others until age 10, when her sisters and girlfriends began to exclude her from their secret discussions about boys and sexuality. She also remembered her parents telling her sisters, "When you grow up and get married and have families . . ." Yet the message to Sarah was more likely to be "When you grow up and have a career . . ." Sarah eventually discovered her sexual self-image in her early 30s, after taking a human sexuality course from an instructor who was knowledgeable about sexuality and disability issues. He was able to validate that sexuality need not be measured by physical abilities.

Communication Difficulties Regarding Feelings or Sexuality

As with the nondisabled, becoming more comfortable in expressing oneself can be a major factor in relationships and sexual satisfaction among the ill and disabled. A nonjudgmental, yet validating place to talk about these issues—with a friend, partner, or health care provider—can greatly enhance a person's self-esteem and comfort with sex.

Difficulty Initiating Sex after a Period of Abstinence

"Breaking the ice" to become sexually active again after a period of abstinence dictated by a medical condition and its treatment is difficult for many people. Making an appointment to talk with a therapist about their sexual relationship stimulates some couples to try making love, however awkward they feel. After becoming more comfortable in discussing their sexual feelings in therapy, they can be encouraged to rewrite their sexual scripts to accommodate physical changes and to focus initially on the behaviors most comfortable to them.

Fear of Physically Damaging an Ill or Disabled Partner

Therapists should encourage discussion of any fears or fantasies about the fragility of a partner with conditions such as cardiac problems or renal transplantation. Either person may also feel guilt for desiring sex (e.g., "It would be selfish of me to want sex with my wife after all that she has been through"). Open communication may solve these conflicts, with each person agreeing to take responsibility for discussing his or her own needs and desires.

Lack of a Partner

Lack of a partner is a difficult issue for many people, disabled or not. A therapist can offer encouragement and hope, and help the person analyze what actions could be taken to increase the likelihood of meeting and making new friends. Self-help organizations such as the United Ostomy

Association and independent living organizations provide needed support from others coping with similar situations.

Lack of Privacy when Institutionalized or Otherwise Dependent upon Caretakers

Increasing attention is being paid to the sexual rights of persons who are confined to institutions or otherwise physically dependent (Comfort, 1974; Downey, 1974; Szasz, 1983; Woods, 1979). It is ironic that we deny sexual opportunities to many of these people, yet often encourage "conjugal visits" for prisoners of state and federal penitentiaries. We may hope that there will be important legal decisions and legislative actions pertaining to this issue in the next several years.

Reactions to Body Alterations or to Other Changes in One's Partner

Some people will be unable to recover their sexual desire for partners who have a major debilitating or disfiguring medical condition. Validation that love can continue without an active sexual relationship may be of relief in some instances. In others, desensitization to the changes may occur over time. Therapists can also give permission for, and instruct such clients in the use of, fantasy for sexual enhancement.

Unresolved Couples Issues after the Immediate Crises of Diagnosis and Treatment Have Passed

One woman came for counseling with her husband, complaining that she had lost all sexual desire for him subsequent to her mastectomy at age 35. Within two sessions, it became evident that she was harboring a great deal of unexpressed anger and hurt because he had "abandoned" her during her hospital convalescence. He felt that he had always been judged negatively by her family, and they seemed almost territorial in their occupation of her bedside at the hospital. Furthermore, he had no previous experience with a major illness, and believed that her sisters and parents were better able to communicate emotionally. The therapist likened their situation to that of a couple whose raft had capsized in a swiftly flowing river. Each person had had to survive the immediate crisis and had been unable to lend any support to the other. Understanding her husband's sense of inadequacy, which she had interpreted as a lack of caring for her, helped the woman realize how they had *each* felt abandoned. This expression of a past, deeply felt hurt enabled her to feel loving and giving to him again, and her desire for him returned as they learned to talk together about their feelings.

A great diversity of etiological factors and treatments can be seen in the preceding examples. The following section describes four cases in more detail.

Case Presentations

Unlike other chapters in this volume, this chapter focuses on a wide population, rather than on a specific theoretical model of treatment. Examples are presented here to indicate the diversity of issues and levels of treatment among this population.

Four cases are discussed. In one, the clients responded to fairly brief, traditional sex therapy. The second case involved the blossoming of an adult's sexuality. The third was a more complex case with a positive outcome involving intrapsychic and interpersonal dimensions. In the fourth case, treatment was not successful.[1]

Case 1: Sexual Avoidance Secondary to Presumedly Organic Erectile Dysfunction

Alex and Betty: Case Description

Alex, aged 50, was referred by his internist because he complained that he had "lost" his sexual desire. He arrived for his first appointment with Betty, aged 48, his lover of the past 6 months. Both preferred that Alex talk alone with the male therapist.

After the therapist and Alex were settled in the office, Alex expressed his relief that the parking and the office truly were physically accessible to him. He used an electric wheelchair, and had been assured many times that a given restaurant, office, or other building was accessible, only to arrive and find his way impeded by stairs. "This place seems OK, but I haven't seen the bathrooms yet!" he said with a smile. He then began describing his reason for coming to therapy.

Married at age 20, he had contracted polio at age 21, which necessitated the use of the electric wheelchair. He described his sexual life as

1. All the clients described here had signed research and general consent forms indicating that data from their treatment could be used for educational purposes. Because of the highly visible factors of chronic illness or disability, and in order to preclude the possibilities and problems of client identification (Wallerstein, 1986), certain data have been altered for the selected case studies presented. As many of the salient points of etiology, treatment, and outcome as possible have been retained.

"normal" for the first 24 years of marriage except for lack of ejaculation since contracting polio. Erection problems and decreased interest in sex had coincided with a growing estrangement from his wife over the last 5 years of the marriage. He was now divorced and in a new relationship with Betty. He said that it was easy for him to avoid sexual opportunities with her, but intellectually he wanted to be more in tune with her sexual interest.

Before meeting Betty, Alex had not been sexually active at all for 4 years. He did not masturbate and was unable to have erections with Betty, but was aware of occasional erections in the middle of the night and early morning "when [he] didn't need them." He discounted the latter erections, which, although firm, were "just because of stimulation from my bladder when it is full." He assumed that the desire and erection problems were organic and part of the long-term effects of having had polio. Interestingly, he described it as "wonderful" on those occasions when he and Betty actually did engage in sex. Although he had no erection or ejaculation, Betty was apparently multiply orgasmic from his manual and oral stimulation. However, he thought that she also wanted to be able to have intercourse. Otherwise, the relationship was going very well and he felt he was in love. His one concern about the relationship was his conflict with himself about often avoiding sex.

A sex history was then taken. Alex was asked to describe his earliest awareness of sexuality, including the nonverbal messages and scripts in his home during his childhood, his early learning about masturbation, and other early experiences. He was also asked to describe any changes that had occurred during and after his illness at age 21. The surprising result of this exploration was that the sexual patterns in his marriage had changed very little after the onset of polio, except for the 6 months after the initial diagnosis, during which they had not had sex. Intercourse had usually resulted from Alex's having a spontaneous erection. He and his wife had never discussed their sexual feelings, and she had been fairly passive during their lovemaking. Nonetheless, Alex said that his marital sex life had been "normal" and satisfactory to both him and his wife, despite his lack of ejaculation after the illness. When asked how he felt about the loss of ejaculation, he claimed that his primary concern had been being able to sustain intercourse. He had enjoyed his wife's pleasure, and he "had never enjoyed ejaculation all that much anyway." At this point, it did not seem necessary or helpful to determine whether this was true or simply a defensive rationalization. The therapist then restated the current situation and goals as perceived by Alex, to which he agreed. The therapist then asked whether he could include Betty in the discussion. Alex thought she might be a bit nervous, but agreed that it would be useful to have her in the session.

Alex went out to get her, and the therapist mentioned that, since Alex had a definite interest in enhancing their sexual relationship, it seemed only right that she be included in the discussion. The therapist also acknowledged that many people find it unusual to start talking with a stranger such as himself about something as personal and intimate as sexuality. She nodded her head, and replied that she felt she could talk about these issues, "as long as we don't have to *do* anything here!" She agreed to proceed, satisfied with the therapist's comment that sometimes strange things are written about therapy in magazines and newspapers. The therapist emphasized that *these* meetings would focus on talking about their feelings only to the extent that she and Alex felt comfortable doing so, and that any sexual activity would be done privately by the two of them at home.

Betty began by saying that she felt they had a great sex life, but that she wanted it to happen more often. She said she was orgasmic, but missed intercourse. It was this statement that prompted her to reveal the worrisome thought that she might be a "demanding woman" who was *causing* the erection problem. She thought of herself as an accomplished lover, and was concerned that being in "sex therapy" would mean that she had problems. The therapist validated that this was a concern for many people, and stated that he didn't consider his talking with them to be "sex" therapy, but rather an opportunity for them to discuss ways in which they might increase their obvious enjoyment of each other. Alex reassured her that his problems with erection and low desire had existed before his divorce. The therapist pointedly mentioned to Betty that she could certainly be part of the solution to a problem without having been part of the problem to begin with.

As the couple became more relaxed in the session, the therapist asked them whether they would describe one of their most recent or usual sexual interactions. In their doing so, it was evident that Betty did not directly stimulate Alex's penis during their lovemaking. She said that she would not mind touching his genitals, but had felt through his body language that *he* did not wish her to do so. Her explanation to herself was that perhaps his penis was more fragile or sensitive because of the disability.

As this was openly discussed, Alex admitted that he had never expected such direct stimulation by a partner, and that he felt he *should* be able to attain an erection merely by being "turned on" by a woman he loved. The therapist congratulated him for having been able to get erections that way in the past, and added that most men needed direct (reflexive) stimulation. He suggested that even men with organic erectile problems sometimes benefit from exercises that would be discussed at the end of the session. He then talked about the distinction between orgasm (a subjective response) and ejaculation (a physiological event). Alex found this most helpful and indicated with relief that he was glad that ejaculation, which he had not experienced in many years, would not be the criterion by which his pleasure would be judged. Betty was interested in the fact that Alex might experience orgasm in varying degrees despite lack of ejaculation.

Near the end of this session, the therapist described standard sensate focus exercises and explained why Alex and Betty might want to decide to temporarily set aside the goal of intercourse. The therapist then questioned them as to whether they would enjoy doing anything similar. Betty liked the idea of having the freedom to explore Alex's whole body, while he thought that he would probably enjoy not having to worry about his lack of erection. They agreed to come back the following week and were both surprised at how positive and motivated they now felt about dealing with the sexual issues, in contrast to the silence and anxiety with which they had driven to the appointment.

At the second meeting 1 week later, they mischievously (and classically) admitted to having broken the rule several times against not having intercourse. They attributed their success to being more relaxed and to an increased ability to talk to each other during sex about their needs. Alex was not distracted by pressure to have an erection, and he was able to ask Betty for more direct touching and genital pleasuring. They also found more comfortable sexual positions through experimentation.

Standard interventions for erectile dysfunction, direct stimulation of his penis by Betty, plus open discussion by Alex about how the polio had and had not affected his body, led to his having more reliable erections and more satisfactory sex. As his erections returned, Alex found that his thoughts about sex with Betty also increased. Following their experimenting with a vibrator, he felt that he was close to experiencing ejaculation. He clearly stated that this was not a priority for him, and that he was not yet interested in having ejaculation as a goal "to have to work at." This did not appear to be a problem for her, as she found that he was communicating his enjoyment more verbally. In fact, he now often described an orgasm-like response, including a sudden relaxation of muscle tension and pleasurable sense of being satisfied, without ejaculation.

In subsequent sessions, Alex and Betty focused on basic listening and communication issues, paying less and less direct attention to their sexual relationship. They learned that communication does not need to have the "win–lose" quality of a debate. Accurate listening does not mean that one necessarily *agrees* with what the other is saying. Knowing that they could *listen* without necessarily having to *do* something to make the other feel better allowed them to talk more openly about both their happy and painful past experiences. Betty was also able to ask Alex more directly about what it was like to have a disability. Their enjoyment of sexuality continued to increase. They agreed it was a new milestone when his erection failed on one occasion and they went on making love without thinking of it as a problem. They both seemed genuinely happy with their overall relationship and decided to stop therapy after eight sessions. They attributed their success in increasing and improving their sexual interactions to their newfound ability to talk openly to each other about their needs and desires.

Comments

The therapist hypothesized that Alex's long-standing problems of erectile dysfunction, his marital discord and divorce, and his difficulty in talking about sex had led to his sexual avoidance. He and Betty had assumed that his physical disability was the cause of his desire and erection problems, when, in fact, sensation and sexual functioning are often left intact after polio. Being in love with a new partner motivated him to seek counseling, although his partner was initially resistant to the idea of being in "sex therapy." Treatment was then reframed so that sexuality was seen as inseparable from issues such as communication, intimacy, and self-image. Their motivation was quite high, once they understood that their therapy did not have to be "problem-focused" and that it was all right to have sexual concerns and still regard themselves as good lovers.

Short-term, directive therapy helped improve Alex's erections and increase his sexual desire, and enabled Betty to be more comfortable and assertive talking with him about sensitive topics. Alex did not achieve ejaculation during the course of their eight sessions of therapy. However, in a 6-month telephone follow-up, he spontaneously mentioned having had several ejaculations with vibrator simulation. Interestingly, he said that they were not quite as enjoyable as his "nonejaculatory" orgasms, and he disliked losing his erection after ejaculation. He felt very satisfied with their relationship, and felt that he and Betty could handle problems better because of their increased communication.

High motivation, as well as the absence of entrenched relationship conflicts, allowed this couple to work in therapy with a focus on enhancement rather than on problems. At the 6-month follow-up, their gains in treatment continued, and they clearly attributed the improvement to their own increased ability to communicate.

Case 2: Low Sexual Desire Secondary to Defensive Denial and Lack of Sexual Socialization and Knowledge

Frank: Case Description

Frank, age 30, called for an appointment, stating that he had had "no sex life—ever." He was quadriplegic and used a wheelchair as a result of an injury at age 10. He had felt isolated from peers during his schooling, but had concentrated on academics and completed college and graduate training in business. With the assistance of male attendants, he had been able to live independently since college. He devoted himself almost totally to his work, and had few close relationships with either men or women, even avoiding casual conversations with his attendants. He reported that he had no genital sensation and could not remember ever having masturbated. Recently, he had met a woman from another state and was attracted to her. They were planning to spend a weekend together, so his stated goal for therapy was to obtain information on how he could be sexual and what kinds of emotional responses he could expect to have.

Frank had recently done sufficient reading on his own to know that intercourse was not the only way to be sexual. He also had read several articles on sexuality and spinal cord injury, and had recently seen the educational film *Active Partners* (Lenz & Silverman, 1979), which shows the relationship of a quadriplegic male and his woman partner. The film had been shown at a university workshop on sexuality and disability; it portrays the couple's communication and humor, as well as explicit nonintercourse lovemaking. In the first session, the therapist suggested that Frank also read *For Yourself* (Barbach, 1975) to get additional understanding of how women pleasure themselves.

After two sessions, Frank contracted the therapist to say proudly that he had had sex for the first time and that he was very pleased. He found his partner to be quite orgasmic from his manual and oral pleasuring, and he enjoyed her licking and kissing his neck and ears. He continued in therapy for 13 more sessions, mostly dealing with the emotional aspects of the relationship. He knew intellectually that focusing on pleasurable sensations might lead to orgasm (as distinct from ejaculation), but he felt no particular pressure to reach that goal for himself.

Specific sexual techniques were no longer of primary concern to him at this point, but he did feel vulnerable to emotions whose intensity were new to him. Being sexual and emotionally involved for the first time with another person meant that he experienced feelings of rejection, jealousy, sadness, and fear of losing her, in addition to joyous and exhilarating feelings of closeness. He was exploring an entirely new emotional landscape, and was relieved to have validation of the "normality" of his feelings. He thought that he would try to remain open to having and fully sensing them, even though at times they were almost overwhelming. During one session, he described crying with his lover, and said that he had not cried for as far back as he could remember. He was very courageous in wanting to stay open to the "negative" as well as the positive feelings. As he finished his therapy, he felt good about himself as a sexual being and excited about the depth of his emotional life. He indicated that he might recontact the therapist for future therapy if he felt the need.

Comments

During the 15 sessions, there was much improvement in Frank's self-image as a sexual being. At the 9-month follow-up, he was no longer in his original relationship, but felt it was just a matter of time before he would get involved with someone again. His social life was a higher priority, and he felt he was making progress in establishing friendships. In a follow-up evaluation questionnaire, he indicated that although important information about sexual behaviors and emotions was given during these meetings, the attitudes of the therapist had helped him the most. "The therapist encouraged my taking the risk of becoming a sexual being, and what was even more important, she *saw* me as *being* sexual."

Case 3: Low Sexual Desire Secondary to Marital Stress, Hemodialysis, and Preorgasmia

Frieda and George: Case Description

Frieda, aged 38, had originally contacted a woman therapist for an appointment to discuss her problem of "no desire for sex." Married 9 years with three children (aged 4, 6, and 8), Frieda had a 3-year history of renal disease and dialysis treatment. Before her illness, sex had been "OK, but never really enjoyable," and she had never had an orgasm. She felt she had lost what little sexual interest she had had prior to the illness. Her husband was expressing displeasure at their lack of sexual contact, and she felt pressure to learn how to overcome her own feelings to please him. When questioned about this, she admitted that she might feel resentful if she were to enter treatment only for his sake. She responded positively to the idea that learning to enjoy sex for herself might be an appropriate goal.

Frieda had had a very strict religious upbringing, in which sex was viewed as acceptable only for procreation. She considered herself ignorant about sex and was uncomfortable thinking about it or discussing it. At the conclusion of the first session, she said she was surprised at how relaxed she felt. She had previously attempted to get help with this problem from her physician. She only told him that she "wasn't enjoying sex the way [she] used to." The physician recommended that she and her husband try oral sex and view pornographic movies to become "turned on." Both suggestions were offensive to her, although she did not tell this to her physician.

She was greatly relieved to hear that *both* she and her husband were responsible for creating a happier and more enjoyable sexual relationship, since she had only considered *herself* as having the problem. She doubted that her husband would agree to come to therapy with her at this time, but felt that she would pursue the issue of counseling with him in the future. She asked for some reading material and was told about *For Yourself* (Barbach, 1975) and *Male Sexuality* (Zilbergeld, 1978).

Frieda telephoned the therapist several days later, indicating that her husband was unwilling to come in for therapy. He continued to label her as having "sexual hang-ups" and felt she should be the one getting treatment.

Despite his lack of cooperation, she was enjoying the reading, and felt reassured that many people have to learn to enjoy their sexuality. She decided to continue to focus on learning about her own sexual responses by herself. She did not feel the need for further individual therapy sessions at this time, but expressed interest in joining a women's preorgasmic group. She was also determined to enter counseling with her husband, but felt that this would take some time.

Eighteen months later, Frieda contacted the therapist by telephone to report that several changes had occurred. She had received a successful kidney transplant 10 months earlier and was feeling much better physically. She had also attended a women's preorgasmic group and had become orgasmic through masturbation. She was calling for a referral to a couples therapist because her relationship with her husband continued to be "platonic." She described the support from the group as very meaningful to her, and was able to persevere in requesting that her husband join her for some couples therapy. He finally agreed, but under the condition that they see a male therapist, perhaps in reaction to his wife's newly found sense of support from other women.

George's stated goal in the couple's first session with a male therapist was enhancement of their sexual relationship. He blamed the lack of sexual contact on his wife's illness, but also stated that sex had become a very loaded issue and that it had been safer to ignore it than to pursue sexual relations. He denied any other problems and felt they had dealt well with Frieda's illness and surgery. She remarked that she was finally feeling much better physically, although she had struggled with depression and discomfort for several months after the transplant. Like many recipients of transplanted kidneys, she had anticipated a positive experience to being freed from the hours of hemodialysis. Instead, she found that she had gone through many months of worry about possible rejection of the new kidney, and some depression that might have been related to her medications. Testing now revealed that her kidney was functioning well, and she was beginning to feel the energy levels that she had had prior to her illness. George and Frieda had not had any genital sexual contact since before her surgery, and she continued to feel a lack of sexual desire despite the overall energy increase. However, she was very motivated to begin the couples therapy. She felt they had been under a lot of stress because of her illness, but that there were many other unresolved issues that kept them from being emotionally close.

Frieda voiced her wish to find new ways to manage the discomfort and fatigue she often felt during their lovemaking. She also articulated that she expected better communication to result from counseling, and felt that an enhanced emotional atmosphere would be an "aphrodisiac" for her. Her husband often praised her new assertiveness at home, and told the therapist that he really wanted her to be strong enough to deal with him. "Sometimes I will think things are going fine, only to have her admit to being angry at me for something that had happened last winter!" She admitted that her personal goal was to be able to speak up more, but countered that he would sometimes "blow up" verbally at her and stay angry for days at a time about what she felt were trivial matters. She felt his perfectionistic nature enabled him to be a successful attorney, but that it contributed to his feeling stressed and tense. He denied that this was really a problem, and she countered that he was often oblivious to the effects of his angry moods upon her and their three children.

The therapist suggested an individual session for each during the following week, in order to explore each's personal history. His goal was to enhance therapeutic rapport, especially with George, who seemed less motivated than Frieda. He also wanted to allow for any "hidden agenda" items to surface safely, such as an affair or lack of commitment to the marriage.

George's Individual Session. In his individual session, George began by saying that it was very difficult for him to come for therapy, and that he thought of it as "admitting to a failure." He needed to impress upon the therapist that he had had several relationships with women before meeting his wife, and that he considered himself quite sexually experienced. In contrast, George described Frieda as sexually naive and inexperienced.

George then gave a brief account of his background as the elder of two boys raised by his mother and father in the toughest part of Los Angeles. He had successfully worked his way through college and law school, and was very proud that he had attained financial success and the respect of his peers in the corporate world. He was close to his mother and brother, but never had much enjoyment from his relationship with his father. He suggested that this may have been because his father had "beat the hell out of me on a regular basis, until I was 15 and big enough to threaten to fight back." This was disclosed with a lack of much feeling, and he added, "Those days are long over, and I hold no grudge against my father." George denied any feelings about his father, and switched to emphasizing his own strengths, such as his reputation among other attorneys as being overpowering. He then described himself as being a positive thinker, loving his life and family, and looking forward to better times now that his wife was free from dialysis. The illness had been difficult for her, but he felt they had managed the problems quite well. During a sexual history, he spoke only of positive experiences and denied any problems. He suggested that he had been tempted to have affairs, but had chosen not to do so out of a feeling of commitment to Frieda and their marriage. He masturbated quite regularly and found it enjoyable, but not as fulfilling as he imagined sex could be with Frieda, if she could learn to enjoy it more and be interested in it. Apart from the sexual aspect of their marriage, George felt that she was usually a loyal wife and devoted mother to their children, and having a happy family was of great importance to him.

Frieda's Individual Session. Frieda came in for her individual appointment the next day, and stated that she was very angry at George for being self-centered, "He was wonderful about anything connected with my illness and was always patient, kind, and helpful. But for anything else, he only thinks of himself." He had recently forgotten her birthday, which she felt was because he was still angry with her for a minor car accident she had had. She disliked the idea of sex with him, because of his frequent angry moods and his unwillingness to let her initiate anything new or to change their pattern of intercourse-focused lovemaking. "This was all right in the beginning of our marriage, but our pattern had gotten so predictable that I was bored, and he seemed to be thinking more about some fantasy than about me." He also was not a sensual lover, and seldom touched her genitally in ways that felt good to her. They had actually had very little sexual contact since the birth of their youngest child 4 years before. "In a funny way, my having the illness gave us both an excuse not to be sexual. He seemed to know that I didn't think he was a good lover." Despite her anger, she was highly motivated to address their problems in therapy and to maintain the marriage. She felt he was a good man in many respects, and thought that many of their acquaintences believed they were the "ideal couple." However, she had confided in her closest woman friend about George's angry outbursts and how she detested his attempts to control her.

Their Goals. During George and Frieda's next joint session, each was feeling distant and irritable toward the other, although neither was willing or able to specify what they were upset about. The therapist suggested that, although they had managed extremely well with Frieda's illness, the dialysis treatment, and the surgery, each of them might have more negative feelings about the situation. They were told that there would be times in couples therapy when hurtful things would need to be said or heard. After they acknowledged their difficulty in resolving anger, the therapist directed each to describe a "personal anger history" to the other at some point during the next week when they were apart from their children. The purpose would be to examine the differences and similarities in how anger was expressed in their families when they were children. They were told that couples therapy might be thought of as "learning how to have a relationship *about* their relationship" (Wile, 1981). Communication and conflict resolution were described as skills that they could develop.

Conflict Resolution. Over the next 10 sessions, therapy was oriented toward understanding and deepening the partners' communication, especially about anger. The therapist suggested that each had emotional "bruises" from the past. Frieda had only recently become aware of her anger at how little respect the women in her family had been accorded. As an adult, she was now very sensitive to being controlled by George and rebelled any time she felt he was being dictatorial or imperious. She admitted that, early in their marriage, she had actually encouraged such behavior in George, and had chosen to marry him partly because he was such a "take-charge type of man." George's "bruise" had to do with the repressed anger and sadness he felt about being beaten and about his father's emotional distance. Sometimes it felt good to him to have Frieda challenge him, but other times he felt she did not care about him. He recognized that in his own family he had much experience in "writing off" the other who had hurt him.

They began talking more about the real impact each had felt from Frieda's illness and dialysis treatment. In many ways they believed themselves more fortunate than other people they had met undergoing dialysis. They were affluent and could affort child care and help with the household chores, and they believed in the "power of positive thinking." Yet each admitted to having feelings that had not been shared with the other. They agreed to listen to each other's feelings without judgment or problem solving (which was usually experienced as being told not to have those feelings).

Their couples sessions often centered on processing the upsets that had occurred during the week, and finding new ways to prevent and resolve conflicts. Frieda noticed that she never felt she could get George to "make up" after an argument when she was ready to do so. "He never seems to be affected when I say I am sorry for my part of the upset, and he never has apologized to me for anything." George had difficulty with the idea of forgiveness: "In my family, my dad would say, 'Sorry isn't good enough.' " In fact, he could not remember ever being forgiven by his father for any mistakes.

As therapy continued, George saw how much like his father he had been in his dealings with his wife and children. As these issues were explored, George became much less explosive at home, and Frieda observed that their children were seeking him out more and being closer to him physically.

Sexual Intimacy. With each new disagreement and conflict, the partners were more quickly able to regain a sense of closeness. Sexual intimacy had not yet begun by the 20th session, when Frieda and George began to talk openly about how they would like their sexual relationship to be. They felt ready to renew their sexual contact, and asked for suggestions as to how they could safely proceed to "break the ice." George agreed to read *Male Sexuality* (Zilbergeld, 1978), since Frieda had previously read this and several books on female sexuality. The therapist outlined some standard principles for sensate focus and asked them to talk with each other at home about what they would like to do. He suggested that they make an agreement with each other to forego intercourse at the present time, in order to keep from falling into old habit patterns. After some token resistance to this idea, while acknowledging that they had not had intercourse in several years anyway, Frieda and George made the agreement and shook hands on it at the end of the session.

When seen again by the therapist, they reported that they had had a wonderful time taking a shower together, and later took turns caressing each other with massage oil. They had abided by their agreement not to have intercourse, although George professed that this had been the most difficult aspect of the experience. Each was surprised at how sexually arousing the caressing exercises had been. George had enjoyed the book on male sexuality very much, and Frieda said he was very sensual in the ways that he touched her. George described that, while reading the book and doing the exercises, he had an almost mystical insight having to do with the importance of "being in the moment" rather than thinking of and evaluating his performance, or of focusing solely on a fantasy.

Frieda became more interested in being sexual with George as the weeks went by. She was especially interested in the idea that she could say "yes" to sex with him at times when she initially might not feel much desire herself. "The amazing thing is that he can sometimes 'get me in the mood' by the new and gentle ways he touches me." They were also finding it easier to talk about options to compromise in their sexual relationship, as therapy focused on these issues in the nonsexual areas of their marriage.

Frieda continued to enjoy good health, with no further signs of rejection of the kidney, which had by now been transplanted almost 2 years before. She enjoyed sometimes being in control of their sexual encounters, and was amazed that George now shared the "choreography" of sex with her. She was less focused on pleasing him, and more on her own responses.

After several more weekly sessions, the partners said they had had intercourse twice over the previous weekend. They reported that it was actually fun, but George wondered if Frieda wanted to focus more on trying to have an orgasm with him. She replied that she would like to pursue that in the future, but that it was not currently a priority for her.

Three months later, Frieda and George returned to therapy for four more weekly sessions to help resolve a specific area of conflict that did not involve sex. They had realized that they were repeating their old power struggle, and they wanted to return briefly to therapy as a preventive measure to make sure it was resolved. George and Frieda demonstrated a greatly improved ability to listen to each other's position, and they soon reached a compromise in which each felt validated, with very little intervention by the therapist. Frieda continued to feel healthy and was able to make a significant reduction in the amounts of medication she had been taking. They reported that they had had two memorable sexual encounters while their children were visiting her parents, and that Frieda had experienced her first orgasms with George. They still had occasional fights and arguments, but she felt much stronger in confronting George, and he felt much more forgiving and trusting of her love for him. They wished that their frequency of sex was a bit higher, but felt that they would continue to improve all areas of their relationship. Without a direct suggestion from the therapist, they had decided to continue spending one night per week just nurturing their marriage. They stopped therapy again at this point, with the understanding that they could come back in the future if it would be helpful to them.

Comments

This couple presented an example of the interplay of serious illness, individual factors, and interpersonal factors in the development, maintenance, and treatment of a sexual desire disorder. In this case, intimacy and communication difficulties had a greater impact on the couple's dynamics than did the woman's medical condition. George was the kind of person who was very resistant to entering individual therapy, but for whom individual issues could be dealt with psychotherapeutically in couples counseling. The therapist's respect for their strengths as individuals and as a couple created a safe place to reveal more intimate feelings, so that communication, conflict resolution, and sex therapy techniques could be most effective. Exploration of family-of-origin issues helped defuse their power struggles and frame behavior in a way that evoked empathy in each spouse. Frieda saw that George's blustering and dictatorial moods had been reflections of the way he had been treated by his own father. The focus in therapy on George's relationship with his father enabled long-repressed feelings to surface, which allowed him to act more positively with Frieda and their children. (This process can be understood with the recent psychodynamic theorizing of Weiss & Sampson, 1986.)

Exploring some of Frieda's individual issues in couples therapy enabled George to understand Frieda's need to be treated respectfully and to be seen as a competent person. Although she had felt loved by her father, the women in her family had been taught to be subservient to men at the cost of diminishing their own sense of self. The initial support that Frieda had obtained from the women in her preorgasmic group had led her to consider and question these beliefs more deeply, and she was able to initiate some very healthy changes in her marriage and in her self-image.

Very little in the way of *direct* focus on the sexual aspects was needed; this allowed the couple to attribute their improving sexual relationship to their own feelings and actions, rather than to the techniques, advice, or teaching of an "expert."

Case 4: Low Sexual Desire Secondary to Sexual Dysfunction, Marital Stress, Alcohol, Depression, and Diabetes—Treatment Failure

Henry: Case Description

The therapist was contacted by a urologist who wanted to refer a 52-year-old male with diabetes for evaluation and possible treatment of his problems of low sexual desire and erectile dysfunction, and for assessment of his suitability for a penile prosthesis. The man had tested in the low-normal range for testosterone, and had been given testosterone shots for 3 months with no increase in either desire or erections. The urologist suggested that the therapist contact the man's endocrinologist, who had been treating him for diabetes for several years.

The endocrinologist reported that for the past 15 years Henry had had Type II (adult-onset) diabetes, which was not always well controlled with insulin because of his moderate drinking of alcohol. She had treated Henry for the past 5 years for his diabetes, and noted that he had originally (3 years earlier) complained of lowered sexual desire. He had denied any functional problems until 1 year ago, when he complained of a sudden onset of erectile dysfunction. When asked about possible organic involvement, the endocrinologist stated that Henry did have mild background retinopathy and signs of peripheral sensory neuropathy (tingling or "crawling" sensations in his toes and feet). However, her tests revealed no signs of autonomic neuropathy, which would be implicated in organic dysfunction with diabetes (Bohannon, Zilbergeld, Bullard, & Stoklosa, 1982). She felt that he was atypical in having first complained of decreased desire, and believed that there could be a significant psychogenic component, since he was depressed and possibly had marital problems. She also thought that his alcohol consumption was implicated, but he denied it as a problem. She warned that he was resistant to seeing a psychotherapist or sex therapist, and had consented to do so only after having been treated by the urologist with no improvement in his desire or erections, and being told that it would be a prerequisite to getting a penile implant.

At the first session with the psychotherapist, Henry stated that he did not think that he had any psychological problems and was not sure what good would come from just talking about these issues. The therapist assured him that he certainly had reasons to assume some organic cause for his problems and that therapy might not be able to help, but that it might be useful to explore the larger picture to see what options Henry might pursue.

Henry then agreed to give some background information. He had been married for 26 years, and had two daughters aged 19 and 20 who lived with him and his wife. He stated that he and his wife were "probably old-fashioned," in that they did not communicate about sex and did not engage in practices he knew other people had tried, such as oral sex. He said his marriage was "as good as can be expected after 26 years," and refused to be more specific.

When asked to describe how the problem had begun, Henry said that he had first noticed a gradual lessening in his desire for sex about the time his diabetes had been diagnosed 15 years earlier. His father had also had diabetes and died of complications when Henry was 15 years old. He denied that having diabetes was a worry to him, and said that he had a pretty fatalistic view of his situation, noting that he had already lived 10 years longer than his father. He appeared uncomfortable as he stated that he and his wife probably did not have sex as often as other married people. He said that they managed to have sex at least a couple of times a month until 3 years ago, when Henry found that several months would go by without his having any inclination to be sexual. He did not miss sex very much, but felt it was somehow wrong to give up on it at such a young age. One year earlier, after not having been sexual for 5 months, he had attempted intercourse and been unable to get an erection. Several later attempts also ended in failure, and he believed it was a reflection of the progressive nature of his disease. He was unable to get even partial erections with his wife, and did not recall having had any nocturnal or early-morning erections for several years. He said that he had masturbated very rarely since his marriage, never having really enjoyed it. He denied any problems with his wife because of the sexual issue, mentioning that she never had been very interested in sex, and that she had refused to accompany him to therapy.

Henry was defensive about giving detailed sex history information, protesting that his upbringing had nothing to do with his problems, since he had been sexually active in a way satisfactory to him for many years earlier in his marriage. He said that he knew that psychologists often tried to get information about early childhood, but that it was not relevant in his case. The therapist then suggested that it seemed difficult for him to talk about these problems. Henry denied this assertion and corrected the therapist by saying that it was more difficult *having* the problems. He was "royally sick of" having to go to more doctors' appointments, and asked the therapist for his assessment of whether or not he could be helped by a "shrink."

The therapist responded that Henry himself obviously did not think he needed psychotherapy, but that he might consider talking further about these issues so that together they could determine whether brief sex therapy would be helpful. Henry responded that "just talking" would be a waste of time, but that he would return if any of the sex therapy homework his urologist had mentioned could be tried. The therapist indicated that they could certainly discuss those kinds of exercises at their next visit 1 week later. Henry agreed to this, and another appointment was made.

On the second visit, the therapist was able to get Henry to be more specific about their sexual patterns when he and his wife had been able to have intercourse. It was apparent from the description, that neither Henry nor his wife was comfortable in touching the other's genitals. Foreplay consisted of kissing and nongenital touching prior to intercourse. Henry said that having an erection would usually be the signal to him that he wanted to have sex. He could not remember initiating lovemaking without first having an erection. The therapist suggested that many people need more direct touching, and mentioned that the book *Male Sexuality* (Zilbergeld, 1978) had descriptions of the kinds of caressing exercises Henry had been interested in. Henry liked the idea of getting this information from a book, and said he would call the therapist after he had a chance to read and try some of the book's ideas.

One month later, Henry called to thank the therapist for recommending the book. He liked the ideas expressed, but had been unable to persuade his wife to try them. He did not feel the need for further therapy, but was now aware of other options that he could pursue.

Comments

There were several problem areas that Henry might have profitably addressed in therapy (his anger, depression, problem drinking, and sexual desire and functioning). Unfortunately, the therapist was unable to establish sufficient rapport with him. Henry was a very independent person who was not comfortable with the idea of psychotherapy or sex therapy. Interestingly, 2 years later, Henry's endocrinologist mentioned to the therapist that Henry had gotten divorced and remarried, and had reported that his sexual desire and functioning were once again satisfactory. Fortunately, this may have been a case where the therapy failed, but the person succeeded. Any number of factors could be hypothesized for the improvement in Henry's sexual functioning: Did he cut down on his alcohol intake? How were his sexual desire and functioning affected by leaving a troubled marriage and beginning a new relationship? Did this reflect the "Coolidge effect" (increased desire and arousal for a new partner) or something deeper? Can we attribute the improvement to changes in Henry's psychological state, physiological status, or interpersonal issues? At this point, it is comforting that people can survive and find more satisfaction, despite our limitations as therapists.

Conclusion

Jung wrote that the difference between intellectual and subjective understanding "amounts roughly to that between a severe illness which one reads about in a textbook and the real illness which one has" (Jung, 1951/1959, p. 33). Our helpfulness as therapists increases as we see the person rather than the disease, and as we get closer to understanding the subjective experiences of the people who come to us for help.

Acknowledgments

My deep thanks to Drs. Jerry Nims, Fran and Hal Sampson, and Nancy Kaltreider, for what they have taught me about psychotherapy; to Dr. Lewis Engel and Brandy Engel, for their astute comments regarding this chapter; to Elizabeth Williamson for her spiritual and editorial wisdom; and to Jean and Anna Bullard, for their love. Finally, my greatest debt is to my co-workers Susan Knight and Mary Rodocker, and to the individuals and couples who revealed their most intimate struggles and triumphs to us.

References

Andersen, B. L. (1985). Sexual functioning morbidity among cancer survivors. *Cancer, 55,* 1835–1842.

Anderson, B. J., & Wolf, F. M. (1986). Chronic physical illness and sexual behavior: Psychological issues. *Journal of Consulting and Clinical Psychology, 54,* 168–175.

Barbach, L. (1975). *For yourself: The fulfillment of female sexuality.* New York: Signet.

Bohannon, N. J., Zilbergeld, B., Bullard, D. G., & Stoklosa, J. M. (1982). Treatable impotence in diabetics. *Western Journal of Medicine, 136,* 6–10.

Brecher, E. M., & the Editors of Consumer Reports Books. (Eds.). (1984). *Love, sex and aging.* Mount Vernon, NY: Consumers Union.

Bullard, D. G. (1981). Sexual enhancement in physical disability and disorders. *International Journal of Mental Health, 10,* 169–180.

Bullard, D. G., Causey, C. G., Newman, A. B., Orloff, R., Schanche, K., & Wallace, D. H. (1986). Sexual health care and cancer: A needs assessment. In J. M. Vaeth (Ed.), *Body image, self-esteem, and sexuality in cancer patients* (2nd ed., rev.). Basel: Karger.

Bullard, D. G., & Knight, S. E. (Eds.). (1981). *Sexuality and physical disability: Personal perspectives,* St. Louis: C. V. Mosby.

Bullard, D. G., Knight, S. E., Rodocker, M. M., & Wallace, D. H. (1980). *Final report: The Sex and Disability Training Project.* San Francisco: University of California. (ERIC Document Reproduction Service No. ED 195 883)

Bullard, D. G., & Wallace, D. H. (1978). Peer educator–counselors in sexuality for the disabled. *Sexuality and Disability, 1,* 147–152.

Burger, E. (1981). Radical hysterectomy and vaginectomy for cancer: The story of a 22-year old woman and her recovery. In D. G. Bullard & S. E. Knight (Eds.), *Sexuality and physical disability: Personal perspectives.* St. Louis: C. V. Mosby.

Capone, M. A., Westie, K. S., & Good, R. S. (1986). Enhancing sexual rehabilitation of the gynecologic cancer patient: A counseling treatment model and outcome. In J. M. Vaeth (Ed.), *Body image, self-esteem, and sexuality in cancer patients* (2nd ed., rev). Basel: Karger.

Chigier, E. (1972). Sexual adjustment of the handicapped. *Proceedings Preview: Twelfth World Congress, Rehabilitation International, 1,* 224–227.

Chigier, E. (1980). Sexuality of physically disabled people. *Clinics in Obstetrics and Gynecology, 7,* 325–343.

Cole, T. (1972, January 17). Sex and the paraplegic. *Medical World News,* p. 35

Comfort, A. (1974). Sexuality in old age. *Journal of the American Geriatrics Society, 22,* 440–442.

Comfort, A. (Ed.). (1978). *Sexual consequences of disability.* Philadelphia: Stickley.

Derogatis, L. R., & Meyer, J. K. (1979). A psychological profile of the sexual dysfunctions. *Archives of Sexual Behavior, 8,* 201–223.

Downey, G. W. (1974). The next patient right: Sex in the nursing home. *Modern Healthcare, 1,* 55–59.

Ehrlich, G. E. (1978). Sexual problems of the arthritic. In A. Comfort (Ed.), *Sexual consequences of disability.* Philadelphia: Stickley.

Engel, G. L. (1977). The need for a new medical model: A challenge for biomedicine. *Science, 196,* 129–136.

Evans, J., & Conine, T. (1985). Sexual habilitation of youngsters with chronic illness or disabling conditions. *Journal of Allied Health, 14,* 79–87.

Frank, E., Anderson, C., & Rubinstein, D. (1978). Frequency of sexual dysfunction in "normal" couples. *New England Journal of Medicine, 299,* 111–115.

Halstead, L. S. (1978). Sexual adjustment for arthritic patients. In A. Comfort (Ed.), *Sexual consequences of disability.* Philadelphia: Stickley.

Johnson, R. (1984). Sexuality and renal disease. In N. F. Woods (Ed.), *Human sexuality in health and illness* (3rd ed.). St. Louis: C. V. Mosby.

Jung, C. G. (1928). Analytical psychology and education. In *Contributions to analytical psychology* (H. G. Baynes & C. F. Baynes, Trans.). London: Bailliere, Tindall & Cox. (Original work published 1926)

Jung, C. G. (1959). Aion. In *Collected works* (Vol. 9, Part 2). New York: Pantheon. (Original work published 1951)

Kaplan, H. S. (Ed.). (1983). *The evaluation of sexual disorders: Psychological and medical aspects.* New York: Brunner/Mazel.

Kaplan, H. S. (Ed.). (1985). *Comprehensive evaluation of disorders of sexual desire.* Washington, DC: American Psychiatric Press.

Kaplan, H. S. (1987). *Sexual aversion, sexual phobias, and panic disorder.* New York: Brunner/Mazel.

Knight, S. E. (1986). The physically disabled. In H. L. Gochros, J. S. Gochros, & J. Fischer (Eds.), *Helping the sexually oppressed.* Englewood Cliffs, NJ: Prentice-Hall.

Kolodny, R. C., Masters, W. H., & Johnson, V. E. (1979). *Textbook of sexual medicine.* Boston: Little, Brown.

Leiblum, S. R., & Pervin, L. A. (Eds.). (1980). *Principles and practice of sex therapy.* New York: Guilford Press.

Lenz, R., & Silverman, M. (1979). *Active partners* [Film]. (Available from Multi-Focus, 1525 Franklin Street, San Francisco, CA 94118.)

Levay, A. N., Sharpe, L., & Kagle, A. (1981). Effects of physical illness on sexual functioning. In H. I. Lief (Ed.), *Sexual problems in medical practice.* Chicago: American Medical Association.

Levy, N. B. (1977). Psychological studies on hemodialysis patients at the Downstate Medical Center. *Medical Clinics of North America, 61,* 759.

Lief, H. (Ed.). (1981). *Sexual problems in medical practice.* Chicago: American Medical Association.

Monga, T. N., Lawson, J. S., & Inglis, J. (1986). Sexual dysfunction in stroke patients. *Archives of Physical Medicine and Rehabilitation, 67,* 19–22.

Petty, F., & Noyes, R. (1981). Depression secondary to cancer. *Biological Psychiatry, 16,* 1203–1220.

Ray, C. (1977). Psychological implications of mastectomy. *British Journal of Social and Clinical Psychology, 16,* 373–377.

Szasz, G. (1983). Sexual incidents in an extended care unit for aged men. *Journal of the American Geriatrics Society, 31,* 407–411.

Thornton, C. E. (1981). Sex education for disabled children and adolescents. In D. G. Bullard & S. E. Knight (Eds.), *Sexuality and physical disability: Personal perspectives.* St. Louis: C. V. Mosby.

Unsain, I. C., Goodwin, M. H., & Schuster, E. (1982). Diabetes and sexual functioning. *Nursing Clinics of North America, 17,* 387–393.

Vaeth, J. M. (Ed.). (1986). *Body image, self-esteem, and sexuality in cancer patients* (2nd ed., rev.). Basel: Karger.

Vincent, C. E., Vincent, B., Greiss, F. C., & Linton, E. B. (1975). Some marital–sexual concomitants of carcinoma of the cervix. *Southern Medical Journal, 68,* 552–558.

Wallace, D. H. (1980). Sexuality and the disabled: Implications for the sex education of medical students. *Sexuality and Disability, 3,* 17–25.

Wallerstein, R. S. (1986). *Forty-two lives in treatment.* New York: Guilford Press.

Watzlawick, P., Weakland, J. H., & Fisch, R. (1974). *Change: Principles of problem formation and problem resolution.* New York: Norton.

Weiss, J., & Sampson, H. (1986). *The psychoanalytic process.* New York: Guilford Press.

Welwood, J. (Ed.). (1985). *Challenge of the heart.* Boston: Shambhala.

Wilbur, J. (1986). Sexual development and body image in the teenager with cancer. In J. M.

Vaeth (Ed.), *Body image, self-esteem, and sexuality in cancer patients* (2nd ed., rev.). Basel: Karger.

Wile, D. B. (1981). *Couples therapy: A nontraditional approach.* New York: Wiley.

Woods, N. F. (1979). Sexuality and aging. In A. M. Reinhardt & M. D. Quinn (Eds.), *Current practice in gerontological nursing.* St. Louis: C. V. Mosby.

Woods, N. F. (Ed.). (1984). *Human sexuality in health and illness* (3rd ed.). St. Louis: C. V. Mosby.

Young, E. W. (1984). Patient's plea: Tell us about our sexuality. *Journal of Sex Education and Therapy, 10,* 53–56.

Zilbergeld, B. (1978). *Male sexuality: A guide to sexual fulfillment.* Boston: Little, Brown.

Zilbergeld, B. (1979). Sex and serious illness. In C. A. Garfield (Ed.), *Stress and survival.* St. Louis: C. V. Mosby.

Zilbergeld, B., & Ellison, C. R. (1980). Desire discrepancies and arousal problems in sex therapy. In S. R. Leiblum & L. A. Pervin (Eds.), *Principles and practice of sex therapy.* New York: Guilford Press.

Homosexuality and
Sexual Desire

V

14

Low Sexual Desire in
Lesbian Couples

MARGARET NICHOLS

Margaret Nichols raises several basic and provocative questions about the nature of female sexuality in her chapter on sexual desire disorders in gay women. She notes that lesbian women report the lowest level of sexual exchange of any pair-bonded relationship, and wonders whether this is a commentary on some quintessential feature of female sexuality. Specifically, she proposes that in the absence of male initiation and orchestration, women are socialized to engage in sexual exchange infrequently, and then only in the context of an intimate relationship. Furthermore, in the case of gay women, the very intimacy that seemingly provides the justification for sexual desire discourages it because of the overly enmeshed nature of lesbian relationships. Nichols suggests that this tendency to fuse with a partner so that differences are ignored, discouraged, or denied prevents sexual desire from being experienced. For it is possible, as Tripp (1975) suggests, that desire is dependent upon "barriers" or "differences" between people that are overcome through sexual connection. As Nichols notes, "one can only desire to have sex with another person when that person in fact exists as a distinct, separate entity." Part of the therapeutic task, then, is to help partners in a lesbian relationship to become emotionally autonomous and comfortable with tolerating distance and difference from each other.

Nichols suggests that several other factors may be significant in understanding the dynamics of low desire in gay women. The sexual acculturation of women as a group encourages them to feel greater sexual conflict than men, apart from any biological differences in sexuality (which Nichols believes do not constitute a critical factor accounting for women's lower levels of sexual interest). Furthermore, women are much more likely than men to have experienced sexual abuse. In a lesbian couple, the probability is twice as high that both partners will have sexual conflicts and/or a past history of coercive sexual contact. Consequently, lesbian partners are less likely to initiate sex in the first place, and more ready to adapt comfortably to a relationship without sex. In addition, feelings of sexual guilt and repression limit each partner's repertoire, so that the sexual script is constricted in terms of the motives for undertaking physical exchange, as well as in the nature of the exchange itself. Nichols indicates that the extent of proscribed activities in gay couples is often considerable, ranging from any hint of polarized roles (i.e., dominant–submissive, passive–active) to any sexual activity that appears "male-identified," such as sex involving penetration. The narrower the acceptable sexual repertoire, the greater the likelihood of future sexual boredom and sexual apathy.

Finally, Nichols wonders whether some instances of inhibited desire in gay women stem from repression, blocking noxious and unacceptable sexual impulses or fantasies. Clinically, it sometimes appears that beneath the sexual repression, libido is strong and forceful, and even frightening to some female clients. Such women deal with anxiety about losing control by clamping down on any sexual interest whatsoever.

These and other issues are explored in this fascinating and well-conceived chapter. The questions raised about female sexuality are provocative and deserve consideration, and the case vignettes provide powerful illustrations of the points Nichols makes.

Margaret Nichols, Ph.D., is Director of the Institute for Personal Growth, Highland Park, New Jersey. She works extensively with lesbian couples and individuals. In addition, she is an articulate and active spokeswoman for the rights of people with acquired immune deficiency syndrome (AIDS) and has established a center that provides psychological support for AIDS victims and their families.

It is fitting that this book should contain a chapter on desire disorders in lesbian couples, as evidence suggests both that lesbian couples are the least sexually active of all types of couples, and that lack of desire is the most common complaint of lesbian couples seeking help for sexual difficulties. The data on normative sexual practices of lesbian couples are informative. Sociologists Blumstein and Schwartz (1983), using a large and carefully selected sample, compared heterosexual married, heterosexual unmarried, gay male, and lesbian couples along a number of dimensions, including sexuality. They found that lesbian couples had sex far less frequently than any other type of couple studied. Only about one-third of lesbians in relationships of 2 years or more had sex once a week or more. Of lesbians in long-term relationships, 47% had sex once a month or less. This is in striking contrast, for example, to heterosexual married couples: Two-thirds of these couples had sex once a week or more, and only 15% of long-term married couples had sex once a month or less. Although no comparable study of different types of couples seeking sex therapy exists, clinicians writing about lesbian sexuality (e.g., Loulan, 1984; Nichols, 1982, in press; Todor, 1978) have remarked on the high prevalence of desire disorders, and reports of therapy with lesbian couples frequently mention low sexual frequency as part of the symptomatology of disturbed relations (Burch, 1982; Decker, 1984; Kaufman, Harrison, & Hyde, 1984; Roth, 1984).

Before discussing diagnostic and therapeutic issues, let us consider the meaning of these observations. It is important to reach some understanding about these facts, not only so that we may provide better treatment for lesbian couples, but also so that we may better understand sexual desire—for that matter, sexuality—in all women, not only lesbian women. For the case can be made that the study of lesbian couples allows us to make inferences about how women behave without the mitigating force of men in relationships, just as the study of gay male relationships gives us valuable information about how men behave together without the countervailing influence of women.

As will be argued later in more detail in the section on etiology, the sexual problems of lesbian couples seem to have more to do with the dynamics of female sexuality and the effects of female–female pairings than with dynamics of homosexuality. The clearest evidence for this comes again, from Blumstein and Schwartz's data on gay male couples. Gay men had somewhat less sex in their primary relationships than did heterosexual couples; on the other hand, gay males had the highest rates of extrarelationship sex. This means that lesbians in couple relationships are less sexual both within and outside the relationship than anyone else, just as other studies have found that uncoupled lesbians have less frequent sex and fewer partners than do gay men (Bell & Weinberg, 1978; Jay & Young, 1979).

If this is true—namely, that the low sexual frequency and high incidence of desire problems among lesbian couples has more to do with lesbians' status as women than with their status as gay people—then what questions are raised by those data about female sexuality in general?

First, the data confirm all other studies, from Kinsey, Pomeroy, Martin, and Gebhard (1953) to Hunt (1974), that show women to be less sexually active than men. This suggests not only that contemporary female sexuality is different from contemporary male sexuality, but that the pressure to be sexually active in heterosexual pairings seems to come from male partners more than from female partners. Indeed, at least one prominent researcher suggests that even among those who define themselves as suffering from problems of low sexual desire, men and women differ markedly, with men reporting situational or secondary desire disorders and women reporting primary problems; half of women report *never* experiencing sexual desire (Schreiner-Engel, 1986). Moreover, Blumstein and Schwartz's findings indicate other differences as well. Their lesbian subjects preferred hugging, cuddling, and other nongenital physical contact to genital sex, reminiscent of reports from heterosexual women in such surveys as *The Hite Report* (Hite, 1976). Similarly, lesbians in the Blumstein and Schwartz (1983) study, like those studied by Jay and Young (1979), seemed more constricted in their range of sexual techniques than other couples. For example, 61% of lesbian couples had oral sex "infrequently or not at all," leaving the repertoire of the majority of couples limited to manual stimulation and tribadism. Lesbians had about the same rates of nonmonogamy as did heterosexuals (28% reported at least one extrarelationship episode), although they had far less "outside" sex than gay men, for whom nonmonogamy was the norm rather than the exception. But lesbians, like heterosexual women and unlike both gay and straight men, were likely to have "affairs" rather than just sexual encounters. The conclusions one draws from these data are that lesbians as a group exhibit comparatively low rates of sexual activity, constricted sexual repertoires, and a nongenital orientation, and they appear to link sexuality, including extrarelationship sex, with romance. In other words, they exhibit stereotypic female sexual behavior.

If female sexuality is different from male sexuality, with lesbians showing a "pure" form of this behavior, how and why is it different? This question is a central issue for sexologists. As I attempt to demonstrate in the next section, one's theoretical position on this issue is an important determinant of the treatment methods one employs for lesbian women; in fact, it has implications for treatment of sexual desire problems for all women.

Let us again consider this issue from the perspective of lesbian sexuality. While it is exceedingly difficult to obtain accurate historical data, some researchers have attempted to describe lesbian behavior and relationships in America over the last century and a half (Bullough & Bullough, 1977; Faderman, 1981, 1983; Roberts, 1977, 1982). Faderman (1981) has directly addressed the question of the role of genital sexuality in lesbian relationships. She has described the widespread existence of "romantic friendships," lifelong romantic relationships between women in the 19th and early 20th centuries that resembled heterosexual marriage but probably involved little or no genital sexuality. Faderman argues for a definition of lesbianism that stresses pair bonding and nongenital affection rather than genital sex; she continues this argument in *Scotch Verdict* (1983), her book about the famous legal case that formed the basis for Lillian Hellman's *The Children's Hour*. Other research on this topic is more tentative. Bullough and Bullough (1977) report moralistic, antisex attitudes among a group of lesbians who lived in the 1930s in Salt Lake City. Jonathan Katz and the San Francisco Lesbian and Gay Historical Society (Katz, 1976) have documented the phenomenon of "passing women"—women who successfully masqueraded as men for their entire lives at about the turn of the century. They report that some of these individuals married and were not known to be women even by their wives! Again, this suggests an absence of genital sexuality in these relationships. Certainly not all lesbian relationships in this or previous time periods have been devoid or genital passion. Nevertheless, on the basis of admittedly scanty evidence, it is possible to hypothesize that genital sexuality may play a less important role in lesbian relationships than other pairings, and that this may have been true, at least in Western culture, for the last century and a half. During this historical time period, lesbian sexuality may well have mirrored an extreme version of heterosexual female sexuality (Shade, 1979).

Lesbianism and Female Sexual Identity

If we accept lesbian sexuality as a prototype for all female sexuality, we conclude that women exhibit less interest in genital sex than do men; that female sexuality is more connected to love or at least limerance (i.e., the passionate intensity of a new romantic relationship); that female sexual repertoires are narrower; and that women care more for the nongenital, physical contact aspects of sex than for genital sexual expression. Why might this be so? Arguing one's position on this issue has implications for treatment. While it is beyond the scope of this chapter to examine this question in depth, it is interesting at least to consider the various subissues raised by this question, which have divided not only sexologists but also feminist theorists.[1]

The most obvious question to be asked about these differences is whether they are somehow "intrinsically" gender-related. That is, do lesbians exhibit this particular form of sexuality because women are somehow "wired" differently from men and, in the absence of male influence, display their "true natures"? A number of investigators of gay and lesbian sexuality, most notably Tripp (1975), have argued for this proposition; many feminists, particularly those involved in the antipornography movement, would agree. According to this viewpoint, male sexuality is *genetically* and *hormonally* different from female sexuality, being more polygamous, more active, more aggressive, less tied to love, and more genital-orgasm-focused, while female sexuality is *genetically* and *hormonally* determined to be more monogamous, less active, more tender and gentle, more tied to love, and more sensual than genital and orgasmic. Moreover, some of those who

---

1. One of the current controversies raging within the women's movement centers around feminist interpretations of female sexuality. Readers desiring to pursue this controversy are referred particularly to two books—*Powers of Desire* (Switow, Stansell, & Thompson, 1983) and *Pleasures and Danger* (Vance, 1984)—and to Vol. 10, No. 1 of the journal *Signs*, which contains a forum entitled "The Feminist Sexuality Debate."

argue that these fundamental differences exist—notably feminists in the antipornography movement—would also maintain that our culture in general and the sexology field specifically is dominated by a male-centered point of view.

If one subscribes to this perspective, one might question the very notion of "low sex drive" as being problematic, and indeed might point to the existence of problems created by high sex drive (e.g., promiscuity or sexual compulsivity). A clinician with this belief might counsel a lesbian couple whose sexual frequency is low that their only "problem" is in viewing low frequency as a problem, much as most sexologists these days would counsel a client who complains that his or her urges to masturbate are problematic. In fact, there are undoubtedly many lesbian couples, possibly more than other types of couples, who exist happily for years with little or no genital contact in their relationships. This phenomenon, of course, calls into question many of our most cherished beliefs about relationships. Many of us believe that sex is part of the "glue" that binds couples together, and some of us would not define two people who do not have genital sex together as "lovers." Nevertheless, many lesbian couples continue to define themselves as "lovers" despite an absence of genital contact, and clinicians would do well to keep this in mind when counseling lesbians. For example, in an initial interview with a lesbian couple, one could probe for the *reasons* why low sexual frequency is perceived as a problem: Are one or both partners genuinely disturbed by the low frequency, or do they merely feel that they "should be" having more sex? One might also frame an issue of low frequency or desire as a *discrepancy* between the desires of the two partners, rather than a "problem" for the one with low desire.

However, while it may be true that many women experience sex as a relatively unimportant or even onerous part of their lives, and while it is also possible that lesbian couples may not always want or need frequent genital contact in order to be satisfied with their relationships, it does not necessarily follow that women and men are somehow "intrinsically" different regarding sexuality. The feminist/social-constructionist perspective holds that sexuality has historically always been a "danger zone" for women. Carole Vance (1984) summarizes this position beautifully:

> Women—socialized by mothers to keep their dresses down, their pants up, and their bodies away from strangers—come to experience their own sexual impulses as dangerous. . . . Self-control and watchfulness become major and necessary female virtues. As a result, female desire is suspect from its first tingle, questionable until proven safe, and frequently too expensive when evaluated within the larger cultural framework which poses the question: is it really worth it? When unwanted pregnancy, street harassment, stigma, unemployment, queer-bashing, rape and arrest are arrayed on the side of caution and inaction, passion often doesn't have a chance. (pp. 232–241)

Thus the story of female sexuality can be seen as primarily a story of unrealized, blighted, or thwarted potential. This chapter is written from that perspective. Interestingly, part of the "evidence" for the view comes again from the lesbian community. In the last decade, there has emerged a lesbian "sex radical" movement that stands in polar opposition to the problem of low desire in lesbian couples. Lesbian sex radicals are producing erotica, forming "sex clubs," engaging in "kinky" sex, and otherwise exhibiting what could be viewed as stereotypically "male" behavior, but often with some particularly female influences. The sex radicals suggest that, at least for some women, low sexual desire is not at all normative. Indeed, in my mind the more interesting questions about female sexuality involve *how* it has been, shall we say, contained and limited in relation to male sexuality. Are we dealing with a process of repression, for example, or is it more relevant to think in terms of undeveloped or underdeveloped sexual interest? Do women have a lower "sex drive" than do men, or is it more productive, say, to imagine that men have learned to use sex to serve a variety of functions (intimate, ego-reinforcing, recreational, etc.), while women have learned only to use sex to achieve intimacy? Is it at all relevant to speak of "sex drive" as a *quantity* within an individual, or are we rather describing an end result of an interaction process between (usually) two human beings?

These questions force us to examine the most basic ways in which we conceptualize sexuality. Do we think of sex as a "drive"—that is, some kind of primary energy force that cannot be expressed, repressed, or converted, but that is somehow hydraulically fixed in quantity? Or do we think rather of sets of behaviors that vary in frequency, type of outlet, and functions served, and that may be conditioned or otherwise environmentally encouraged or discouraged, but that are in no way fixed or predetermined in the individual? Throughout this chapter "sexuality" is referred to in both ways: both as an energy that first exists and can be repressed, and presumably somehow is still "present" despite repression; and simply as a "potential" to be developed or undeveloped as circumstances dictate or as the result of interactive processes.

Patterns of Low Sexual Desire in Lesbian Couples

It is important to note that there is no evidence that lesbians are less sexually responsive than heterosexual women in general. In fact, some data suggest that, overall, lesbians may be more sexually responsive and more satisfied with the sex they do have than heterosexual women are (Masters & Johnson, 1979). Indeed, Masters and Johnson (1979) hypothesize that the sexual techniques of lesbians are generally more suited to the sexual needs of women than is heterosexual sexual activity. It is significant that lesbians do

not have pervasive, across-the-board sexual problems. Rather, their problems seem confined to one specific type: sexual desire/frequency *within
committed relationships.*

Barbara and Sharon were a typical couple I saw for therapy. Lovers for
$8\frac{1}{2}$ years, they had had little or no sex for the last 3 years of their relationship. At the onset of therapy, they had lived apart for over a year in an
attempt to reassess the relationship; they were now considering living
together again, but were concerned about the lack of genital sexuality. Both
reported an initially high rate (two to four times per week) of sexual
encounters during their courtship, but a gradual decline in activity over the
years. Both agreed that Sharon was the less sexually interested of the two,
but that after a prolonged period of being rebuffed, Barbara had "given up"
approaching Sharon for sex and had herself lost desire. Nevertheless, the
couple agreed that the sexual encounters themselves, although infrequent,
had always been satisfactory. It was as though it just became inordinately
difficult to "get started" with sex. Both women reported fairly typical
histories of masturbation and arousal; in other words, neither exhibited a
primary desire disorder. Moreover, both were aware of sexual attractions to
other women. Finally (this may seem unusual to the outside observer, but it
is highly typical for lesbian couples), both women had come to accept this
situation. They clearly did not feel the need for genital sex in order to define
themselves as "lovers." While they were sufficiently concerned to seek
therapy, neither was willing to make sex the cause of ending their relationship. This attitude, so typical for lesbian couples exhibiting desire disorders,
is particularly interesting because lesbian pairings are relationships held
together by no social glue—neither legal marriage bonds, children, financial
dependency, social acceptability, nor any of the other types of pressures that
may hold together a heterosexual marriage even when marital satisfaction
is flagging. Lesbians, by and large, have no reason to stay together other
than personal/emotional reasons, yet even under these circumstances women rarely see lack of genital sexuality as an important enough reason to
separate.

This phenomenon again raises the issue of how to define what is and is
not a sexual problem. If lesbians do not seem overly disturbed by a lack of
genital sexuality, why should sex therapists be concerned? Why did I not
simply tell Barbara and Sharon that their worries over the lack of genital sex
in their relationship were simply the result of their being inculcated with
patriarchal, male-oriented standards of sex? They displayed ample evidence
of nonsexual physical affection and companionship. Why did I not reassure
them and send them home? This approach would indeed, have been a
legitimate alternate approach to the one that was adopted, and one that
might have worked as well. Nevertheless, a therapy contract was established
to help Barbara and Sharon reintegrate genital sexuality into their relationship, for several reasons. First, breakup in lesbian couples often does seem

to be associated with low genital sexual activity within the couple (Blumstein & Schwartz, 1983). Although partners may not complain overtly of the lack of sex, one partner often begins an outside affair after a period of sexual abstinence, falls in love with the new partner with whom she is having sexual contact, and ends the first relationship. In other words, although lesbian couples may not consciously experience the lack of sexuality within their relationship as an acute problem, it does seem related to relationship breakup. One could easily argue that this correlation is not causal—that this simply demonstrates a particular pattern by which lesbians end their relationships. While this may be true, it appears that sex is part of the glue that binds many lovers and spouses. Therefore, although couples who maintain that they do not need genital sex should not be directly challenged, when couples complain of lack of sex, one can reinforce the idea that sexual intimacy will enhance the relationship. Indeed, I often find myself in the position of attempting to increase the level of conflict about sex in lesbian relationships, or at least to reinforce the idea that it is permissible to want sex and to be dissatisfied with none! Frequently, lesbians have such a strong consciousness about the degree of sexual harassment that women experience in the culture at large that they are reluctant to pressure their partners at all for sex, lest they appear too "male-identified."

In summary, then, the characteristic patterns of low sexual desire exhibited by lesbians are as follows: (1) secondary rather than primary desire difficulties—that is, women experience low desire only within the context of ongoing, committed relationships (although it is typical for a given woman to have experienced low desire in all her relationships); (2) general satisfaction with sex when it does occur; (3) relatively low rates of argument or conflict about sex within the relationship; (4) often, harmonious or apparently harmonious interactions in nonsexual areas of the relationship. Indeed, these relationships sometimes appear stable and conflict-free; often partners report little or no overt hostility about anything in the relationship. In many cases, it appears that the low-desire problem is part of the more general manner in which the couple handles conflict: through avoidance, smoothing over, and denial.

Causes of Low Sexual Desire in Lesbian Couples

It is easier to specify the things that do not cause low sexual desire in lesbian couples than to explain why it exists. It is certainly not because of distance or lack of intimacy, a common cause of sexual dysfunction in other types of couples. A substantial body of literature exists to document that lesbian couples, if anything, may suffer from too much closeness in their relationships (Burch, 1982; Decker, 1984; Kaufman *et al.*, 1984; Roth, 1984).

Strategies designed to encourage partner intimacy will probably not be necessary for this population.

Low sexual desire is also infrequently caused by power imbalance or sexist roles and concomitant oppression of the "feminine" partner in lesbian partnerships. Again, a substantial body of literature exists to suggest that lesbian couples are idealistically and to some extent pragmatically more egalitarian than other types of couples, especially heterosexual couples (Caldwell & Peplau, 1984; Cochran, Rook, & Padesky, 1978; Maracek, Finn, & Cardell, 1982). And although the phenomenon of "butch–femme" roles was characteristic of lesbian couples of the 1950s and 1960s and is re-emerging in the 1980s as a sexual dynamic, these roles really resemble male–female roles rather superficially (i.e., in terms of physical appearance and dress) and are fairly irrelevant to the population of lesbians generally discussed in this chapter (Nestle, 1984; Nichols & Leiblum, 1986).

Moreover, low sexual desire in lesbians is probably not primarily due to internalized homophobia. Gay men, after all, have experienced as much societal oppression as have lesbians, and it has not seemed to dampen their sexual desire significantly. Berzon (1979), however, has suggested an interesting way in which internalized homophobia may interact with female socialization to suppress sexuality, and her theory has at least some face credibility. She posits that when gay adolescents attempt to reconcile their emerging sexual impulses with the expectations that they and others have that they will be heterosexual, males and females "manage" these impulses differently. According to Berzon, gay male adolescents tend to engage in sexual behaviors while avoiding personal intimacy, and by so doing rationalize that they are not "really" homosexuals. Gay female adolescents, on the other hand, express their impulses through close and intimate but nongenital relations with other women, thereby avoiding the lesbian self-label. Moreover, argues Berzon, this stylistic difference continues to be exhibited by gay men and women into adulthood even after a homosexual identity has been acknowledged.

If low sexual desire among lesbians is not caused by lack of intimacy within the relationship, unequal power within the relationship, or internalized homophobia, what then are its causes? Three dynamics may be relevant: (1) fusion/merging in the lesbian couple; (2) dynamics of guilt and repression; and (3) dynamics related to the particular way in which sexual desire is "fueled" in women. All three of these causes are tied, not to the fact that lesbians are gay, but to the fact that lesbians are women and to the nature of the interaction of women with women as opposed to women with men.

Fusion

What is fusion, and how is it related to low sexual desire? Almost all authors commenting about lesbian couples have noted a tendency for female–female pairings to be close and intimate, sometimes to pathological excess; this phenomenon has been labeled in family systems terms as "fusion" or "merging." It is interesting to speculate why this tendency seems more marked in female couples than in other types of pairings. In our culture, women are socialized to value closeness and "togetherness" and to strive for this in relationships, as opposed to the male socialization toward autonomy and away from closeness. One would expect, then, that males bring a pressure toward autonomy to relationships and women bring a pressure toward closeness. Indeed, fusion is rarely encountered as a problem in gay male couples and appears to be less frequent in heterosexual couples than in lesbian couples. In a sense, fusion represents the pathological extreme of what Gilligan (1982) portrays as the female orientation toward "connectedness": That is, it is the desire to relate so much to the connections between people that interpersonal boundaries, individuality, and separateness become obliterated.

Kaufman *et al.*, (1984) describe this type of relationship as it typically occurs in lesbian couples:

> [This] relationship distress is characterized by excessive closeness between the women, extreme and intense ambivalence, and a failure to establish emotional, territorial, temporal, and cognitive space for each individual. . . . These lesbian couples . . . appeared to be too closely merged and symbiotic. . . . For these couples the initial merging that occurred with the early stage of falling and being in love would not yield to increasing pressures from the environment. The oneness, a kind of narcissistic failure to allow for separateness or a defense against difference had become the norm or the expected state they would strive to achieve and maintain through more and more closeness. . . . Each ignored her own needs for space as well as those of her partner. . . . (p. 530).

Kaufman *et al.* present a cluster of behaviors typical of such couples: (1) attempts to share all social and recreational activities, with contacts limited to only those that the couple does share; (2) no individual friends, only friends shared by the couple; (3) the sharing of professional services, such as doctors, dentists, or therapists; (4) often, the same employer, or, if not, regular telephone intrusions into the workday so that the partners rarely spend even a few hours without contact with each other; (5) little or no separate physical space or belongings, often extending to clothing and other personal possessions; and (6) communication patterns that indicate assumptions of shared thoughts, values, and ideals (e.g., sentences started by one may be completed by the other). As mentioned earlier, these couples represent an extreme version of the kind of closeness and intimacy in which all women are trained so well. In one sense, lesbians often achieve in their relationships what other women idealize. Or, as Kaufman *et al.* suggest: "We believe that these behaviors are strongly reinforced by cultural descriptions of the idealized romantic relationship of lovers, riding off into the sunset, escaping worldly pressures and reality in their isolation, making promises of lifelong fidelity, and believing that they belong to one another" (1984, p. 531).

Lesbian couples make pulp romantic novels come true; in so doing, they may show us the "down side" of closeness—what the need and desire for intimacy can do when it is unmitigated by the more typically male behaviors aimed toward achieving distance and autonomy. For it is important to recognize that the closeness achieved in fused lesbian relationships is gained only through a sacrifice of individuality. Individual differences, dislikes, likes, and interests are suppressed in favor of the dyad; indeed, closeness comes to be defined as sameness. It is questionable, in fact, whether this type of closeness, paid for with the price of negating individuality, can even be defined as true intimacy. This need to suppress individuality, while comforting to some, often produces tension and ambivalence, which is expressed again in some characteristic ways. One way in which ambivalence can be expressed in these couples is through a pattern of fighting to achieve distance, at least temporarily. Another method is by suppressing sexual contact.

The relationship between fusion and suppression of sexuality is probably complex. On one level, avoidance of genital sexuality can be seen as a way to achieve distance in relationships severely in need of space, much as Kaufman et al. (1984) describe fighting in such couples as attempts to achieve at least temporary separation. On another level, one wonders whether genital sexuality is simply *unnecessary* in such couples. If we speculate that part of the desire for genital sex is the desire to have one's personal boundaries obliterated and to merge temporarily with another person, this desire is irrelevant in a relationship that is fused. In a sense, one can only desire to have sex with another person when that person in fact *exists* as a distinct, separate entity. In a merged relationship, only one entity exists, not two. Finally, these speculations raise questions about the nature of sexual desire and sexual attraction. Is desire, as Tripp (1975) believes, dependent upon "barriers" or "differences" between people that are overcome through the sex act? If this is true, then there are no differences to be temporarily bridged.

In therapy, it is important to diagnose the existence of fusion as a cause of low sexual desire, because the interventions one chooses to use in this case are quite specific. In another type of couple, one might often hypothesize that lack of sexual contact is the result of *too little* closeness; indeed, a great deal of marital therapy with heterosexual couples presumes a need for more or renewed closeness. This is rarely a problem for lesbians. Intervention strategies need to focus upon helping the partners achieve some separation and space from each other. The therapist may encourage the development of separate friendships or independent recreational activities, for example, or the expression of different viewpoints or values (even conflict or arguing) in the relationship. Again, Kaufman *et al.* (1984) summarize the types of interventions that can be used with such couples as (1) promoting assertiveness and independence; and (2) helping the couple achieve separate space in areas such as physical territory, financial accountability, recreational activities, and cognitive and emotional life. The therapist must be prepared, however, to encounter several types of resistance. First, it is likely that the women in such a couple will equate individuality and independence with abandonment, and thus attempts to separate partners may arouse powerful feelings of jealousy, fear, and so on. Second, women in fused pairings are partly attracted to such pairings because they are looking for external validation of themselves through similarity (i.e., "If my partner and I *both* agree on a certain value or perspective, then I/we must be 'right'; if she disagrees with me, I *or* she must be 'wrong'"). Thus *difference* is seen as a threat to personal identity, not just couple relatedness.

This is very much a female issue. Typically, a woman is socialized to expect that her identity is incomplete until she has coupled with a man. A woman is expected, in fact, to retain a greater flexibility in goals, career, and the like than a man does, so that her life direction can remain open to the shaping that is given by her male partner. While lesbians reject having their lives defined by males, they often retain the belief that identity is defined *by the couple*. They frequently have no concept of identity as separate from a love relationship and may never have gone through a process of individuation that allows them to feel comfortable as separate individuals. While they have rejected the heterosexual woman's tendency to define self through husband and children, they may have substituted a tendency to define self through couplehood and/or affiliation with groups (e.g., a lesbian–feminist community). Thus, the clinician who begins dealing with a low-desire problem may, in attempting interventions to achieve distance, tap into deep individual issues—not only fear of abandonment, but fear of identity loss and failure to achieve real individuation.

This raises another issue related to fusion and therapeutic attempts to intervene with a fused couple. Partly because women tend to define self through couplehood, many lesbians have never really been "single" and tend to go directly from one relationship to another. This has two major consequences. One is that lesbians, like many other women, are often terrified to be alone and would rather stay in a bad relationship than be single. Second, it means that lesbians often tend to define their couple interactions as committed relationships after an inappropriately short period of "dating." It is quite common for a lesbian to move from the home of one lover directly to the home of a new lover. It is not at all unusual for lesbians to define themselves as being "in a relationship" after two or three dates. Operationally, this means that two women who are virtual strangers to each other are declaring themselves married for life. After such a declaration of commitment, it would be inconvenient, to say the least, for these women to discover incompatibilities. Thus there is increased pressure to obliterate differences, because to acknowledge the existence of differences might lead to the discovery of incompatibilities that are real, concrete, and irresolvable. Thus the clinician attempting to uncover individual differences in a fused couple may indeed be precipitating the dissolution of the relationship through discovery of basic conflicts that, had the partners not become committed to each other so quickly, might have resulted in their never becoming "married" in the first place.

Dynamics of Guilt and Repression

How are dynamics of guilt and repression related to low sexual desire in lesbian couples? There are three major ways in which such dynamics operate. The first and most obvious relates to the facts that women are culturally socialized to feel more conflict about sex than are men and that they experience more sexual abuse than do men. In a lesbian couple, there is twice as much likelihood that both members of the couple will have sexual conflicts. Thus, for example, if one could somehow measure positive influences toward sex and negative influences away from sex, a lesbian couple, as a unit, are likely to have fewer positives and more negatives. Among other things, this effect makes each member of the couple less likely to initiate sex in the first place, given the probability of a less than enthusiastic response from the partner. It also is partly responsible for the relative ease with which lesbian couples accept a sexless relationship: Even the more sexual partner in a lesbian relationship is likely to have some sex-negative attitudes, and her mate's conflicts complement her own doubts.

Second, guilt and repression tend to limit one's sexual repertoire. That is, sex-negative attitudes tend not only to be general ("Sex is bad") but also to be quite specific ("Fantasies are bad" or "———fantasy is bad"). It is typical for lesbians to feel that the only kind of "acceptable" expression of sexuality is the spontaneous desire to have sex with a partner in a committed relationship, when sex is expressed through manual (and possibly oral) stimulation of equal duration for each partner in a loving, gentle, tender way, and both partners have orgasms (preferably at the same time and certainly of the same number and intensity). The list of "unacceptable" or "bad" sexual activities for lesbians may include the following: sex that is planned in advance; sex with any hint of polarized roles (i.e., dominant–submissive, butch–femme, active–passive); sex toys; fantasies about sex, especially fantasies about men; sex when only one partner has an orgasm; masturbation unless one is single; and sometimes sex that involves penetration (this may be seen as "male-identified"). Having a limited sexual repertoire may not be particularly important in the beginning of a relationship, when limerance fuels sexuality, but it probably becomes increasingly important later in the relationship, when variety can help to break routine.

The third way in which guilt and repression operate is the most difficult to describe, but is related to muted female sexuality. When some women who display low sexual desire engage in fairly intensive individual psychotherapy, they may eventually uncover sexual desires that are ego-dystonic. It appears in these cases that low sexual desire has been the result of a generalized sexual repression meant to block a particular noxious sexual impulse (e.g., sexual fantasies about men, sexual fantasies about the father for a father–daughter incest victim, sadomasochistic impulses). Alternatively, repression may serve to block a sexual force that in fact is quite strong and powerful; sometimes women with low sexual desire discover that beneath the apparent lack of libido is a powerful, varied, and sometimes quite terrifying sexual drive.

Notice that I use terms such as "underneath" and "drive," implying a hydraulic view of sexuality. It could be argued that the women I describe are "uncovering" nothing but rather are *developing* a sexuality where none has been developed before. This may be the case, but these terms have been chosen because often the intuitive sense one has in such cases is a feeling of repression of a powerful urge or impulse. A case example may serve to illustrate this point.

Miriam was a 28-year-old lesbian in a relationship for 2 years who complained of low sexual desire, inability to become aroused, and orgasm difficulties. Miriam came from an Orthodox Jewish background with severe antisex injunctions in her family. During nearly a year of treatment, Miriam repeatedly expressed two specific fears of sexuality. One was a fear that, during sex, she would urinate in bed; the other was that, if she allowed herself to become sexual, she would lose control and become promiscuous and therefore "bad." Eventually, I attempted a novel intervention: I suggested to Miriam and her partner that Miriam deliberately urinate in bed during sex. (The difficult part of this intervention was getting the partner to agree!) Perhaps not surprisingly, Miriam experienced this event as intensely pleasurable, and indeed reached orgasm during the episode. Subsequently, it was as if this event opened a literal Pandora's box of sexuality for Miriam. She became aware of a multitude of quite specific and strong desires that were also ego-dystonic: She felt attracted to large women, to women of different races, to strangers she saw on the subway, and so on. These desires frightened her, as she felt "flooded" by them, and in fact management of her desires did become an issue for her. She came quite close to having an extrarelationship affair, an event that was alarming to her.

Two things are interesting about this case: first, that Miriam's low desire seemed directly related to repression of an impulse that was experienced consciously as a fear (i.e., the fear of urinating); and, second, that Miriam's fear of loss of control of her sexual impulses had a grain of truth to it. In other words, once her sexual repression was lifted, Miriam indeed experienced her sexual desires as strong impulses that needed to be controlled. This is a phenomenological experiencing of sexuality that I think is common for men but rather rare for women. One wonders what would happen if women really should succeed in lifting the weight that repression has placed upon their sexuality. Perhaps we might have to deal with some of the consequences of high sexual desire that men have more typically encountered, as well as concomitant problems such as paraphilias and sexual compulsivity.

The "Fueling" of Sexual Behavior in Women

The final area of influence upon low sexual desire in lesbians relates to the one just discussed, and has to do with the way sexual desire is "fueled" or "driven" in women. Women, by and large, are socialized so that one thing and one thing only triggers sexual desire: limerance. Other things—simple physical attractiveness of a partner, a particular sexual act or technique, a desire to use sex for recreation or for tension release, and so on—either do not trigger desire or are not allowed to register as desire on a conscious level. This phenomenon is rather limiting. The limerance phase of a relationship always ends, and then, if limerance is the primary fuel for desire, the woman is left with these alternatives: becoming less sexual; trying to reactivate the limerance (to "bring back the romance" in a relationship, which is not always easy to accomplish); or becoming limerant with someone new. Many lesbian couples choose to become less sexual—and then eventually choose the third option, to become limerant with another partner.

An alternative to these choices is for women to redefine sexuality for themselves and to attempt to develop mechanisms other than limerance that trigger desire. This is, to some extent, happening in the lesbian community via the lesbian sex radical movement. Lesbian sex radicals are promoting a redefinition of sex for lesbians as, first and foremost, a tool for pleasure rather than as a tool for intimacy within a committed relationship. The sex radical movement, by producing written, auditory, and visual erotica, is attempting to broaden the base of women's desire to include fantasy, physical/visual stimuli, and more complex and sophisticated sexual techniques. In addition, these women are attacking many of the taboos women hold about sex in order to liberate sexual interest.

One final example, not clinical, may serve to illustrate many of the points discussed in this section. For the last year or so, I have conducted a series of sex workshops for lesbian and bisexual women. In these workshops, I show sexually explicit slides and tapes of erotica made by women for women, and incorporate experiential exercises designed to encourage women to express fantasies and desires and to share ideas about sexual techniques with each other. At first, I encountered great difficulty within these workshops. Lesbians were willing to share what they *disliked* about sex rather easily, and they invariably framed their dislikes in judgmental terms often justified with political rhetoric: "The women in that film seemed hard and unfeeling, like men," "The sex was too unequal," "The women didn't really seem to care about each other." Finally, I had to make two rules about the workshops: Women were not allowed to talk about what they did *not* like, only what they did like; and feelings had to be expressed in personal "I" phrases instead of in general terms, and especially without political analysis. These rules entirely changed the tone and content of the workshops. Now women invariably express a broad range of quite varied sexual tastes. Most also say that they have never before been in an atmosphere where all their sexual tastes and interests will be accepted uncritically, and where sexual variety will be encouraged. Many say that they are, quite simply, starved for new ideas about sex.

Therapeutic Interventions with Lesbian Couples Experiencing Low Sexual Desire or Frequency

When confronted with a lesbian couple complaining of low sexual frequency or low desire, one's first task, as in all therapy, is accurate and in-depth assessment. Typically, during assessment in these cases, one might attempt to answer the following questions:

1. Is this more the "problem" of one individual in the partnership, or is it more a relationship issue? In making this assessment, one should probe for, among other things, a history of sexual assault or incest in one or both partners.
2. Is this really a low-desire problem, or only a *discrepancy* problem (i.e., both partners experience desire to some significant extent, but there is a discrepancy between their ideal frequencies for sex)?
3. Is this problem the secondary result of another sexual problem (e.g., an aversion to oral sex—not uncommon among lesbians, and quite troublesome when it occurs)?
4. Is the frequency problem the result of simple boredom and need for sexual enhancement techniques?

Accurate assessment depends upon taking individual sex histories as well as a relationship history. The format of therapy must then be decided (e.g., couple sessions, individual therapy, or a combination of both). In making this decision, one must consider not only the perceived origins and maintenance of the problem, but also the willingness of both partners to cooperate in treatment. At times, conjoint counseling for problems that appear more individual is undertaken in order to use the "nonpathological" partner as a sort of sex surrogate for sensate focus or other exercises.

My approach in treatment tends at the outset to be cognitive–

behavioral and uses many of the standard interventions, such as education or sensate focus exercises; treatment becomes more psychodynamic when these approaches are unsuccessful. Because the overall approach is similar to that described in other chapters, it seems most useful to discuss aspects of treatment that are specific to this population or that may be unusual in my particular approach to treatment.

First, when working with lesbians, one always needs to be sensitive to issues of sexual assault or incest, because such occurrences are twice as likely to occur in a lesbian couple. Therefore, therapists working with this population need to be well versed in methods of ameliorating the damage done by sexual abuse. Second, it is important to realize that there does exist a lesbian community or subculture, and that this community, while diverse, is also distinctive in its values, traditions, and standards. In short, being a lesbian is comparable to being a member of an ethnic minority, and therapists should assess the extent to which their lesbian clients are immersed in this community. While this chapter does not permit an extended discussion of what therapy with lesbians entails, there are a few specific issues a therapist would do well to keep in mind:

1. The lesbian–feminist community considers sex to be a political issue for women (rightly, I believe), and all sexuality is subjected to political analysis. Unfortunately, some of this analysis amounts to a replacement of rigid traditional moralistic values by rigid feminist moralistic values. To the extent that clients "buy into" a lesbian–feminist ethic, the therapist may need to deal with cognitive values that support neurotic or unproductive behaviors.

2. If internalized homophobia is an issue, bibliotherapy may be in order. The therapist should consult the closest gay–lesbian or feminist bookstore and some of the hundreds of gay-affirmation publications available. Two indispensable books by and for lesbians specifically dealing with sexuality are Loulan's *Lesbian Sex* (1984) and Califia's *Sapphistry* (1980).

3. "Nonmonogamy" is still a political issue in some parts of the lesbian community. That is, lesbians rarely practice "adultery"; most extrarelationship sex is "above board" and open, and may be defended with political rhetoric. In any case, lesbians, like gay men, are much more likely than are heterosexuals to be experimenting with nontraditional forms of relationships, and clinicians need to keep an open mind about this.

4. Similarly, the lesbian sex radical movement has caused a substantial stir in the lesbian community, at least in urban areas on both coasts. In particular, issues such as pornography/erotica, sadomasochistic sex, and butch–femme roles—in fact, any form of sexuality in which roles are polarized— are controversial and may affect sex therapy. For example, I have had several cases in the last few years in which one partner of the couple wanted to join a lesbian sex radical group and/or experiment with "kinky" sex, and this became a therapeutic issue.

5. Finally, sex therapy with women often becomes more and more oriented toward uncovering deeper layers of intrapsychic meaning in sexuality. To this end, I use a good deal of trance work, as illustrated in one of the cases described below.

Three Cases: High, Medium, and Low Success

Melinda and Joyce: A High-Success Case

Melinda and Joyce were an ideal couple for therapy. Aged 48 and 53, respectively, they had been coupled for 23 years. Both women were well educated and articulate; both had prior histories of individual therapy, were well adjusted, and were knowledgeable about the therapeutic process. They reported that their reason for choosing to enter sex therapy at this time was that they felt that the rest of their relationship was in good order. In fact, they were correct.

At the time they entered treatment, they had had no genital sexual contact for over 1 year and little physical contact for 4 years before that. The first two sessions were spent on assessment. The partners were seen as a couple for the first session, and each was seen individually during the second session. After that, there were three treatment sessions and telephone follow-up over the next 6 months.

Melinda and Joyce's problem was conceptualized as a "script discrepancy" problem. Each woman had an internalized "script" of what she thought the sex act should be. Melinda considered orgasm to be the pinnacle of sexual expression; Joyce enjoyed arousal and all the hugging and cuddling surrounding sex. Joyce was quite willing to pleasure Melinda in any way desired, but she felt that for herself, orgasm was usually not worth the trouble it took to attain. Melinda felt that sex "wasn't sex" unless both women had orgasms; Joyce felt pressured to live up to Melinda's expectations. Over the years, sex had become an ordeal for both women, and it had become easier just to avoid it. During the second session, I probed for levels of sexual desire by asking each woman separately, "If you had sex exactly the way you wanted it, how often would you want it?" Interestingly, reported levels of desire in response to this question were not that discrepant: Joyce said that she would like sex about once a week; Melinda said that she would like it two or three times a week.

Therapy with this couple was brief and straightforward. During the third session, I explained to them that their problem appeared to be one of differing sexual scripts. I explained this concept and stated what I thought the differences were. Most of the session was spent in validating their different sexual performances—in particular, dealing with Melinda's anxiety, reinforced by her interpretation of lesbian–feminist ethics (i.e., that sex where only one partner had orgasm was "unfair" or "oppressive"). She came to see that it was perhaps more "oppressive" to insist that her partner have orgasms. The couple was asked to attempt to do a sensate focus exercise.

This assignment went well, and sensate focus that included genital touching was assigned during the fourth session. At the fifth session, both women appeared, grinning sheepishly, to report that they had "disobeyed" my instructions and had had genital sex (for the first time in over a year). Shortly after this session, they left on a month-long vacation with plans to call me upon their return. They called to report that the vacation had gone well and that they had had several "successful" sexual encounters. Several months later they reported satisfactory sexual relations, which, while not as frequent as either woman would have wished, was a realistic outcome given their lifestyle.

This case was straightforward because the problem, while of long-standing duration, was a matter of misguided communication and values, with no real psychodynamic roots. However, the relative ease of solution depended upon Melinda's accepting Joyce's view that sex need not include orgasm. Some therapists might see Joyce's attitude as indication of an orgasm dysfunction (and perhaps it was), and would have attempted to help her attain orgasm more quickly or easily. I accepted her at face value, and it was upon this acceptance that my interventions rested.

Betty and Helen: A Case of Mixed Success

Betty and Helen had been lovers for 3 years, living together for 1 year, when first seen as clients. Betty made the initial therapy contact for individual treatment, but in her initial sessions she specified sexual problems with Helen as a high-priority issue. Almost immediately, the couple was seen twice monthly; these sessions alternated with individual sessions with Betty.

Betty was a 37-year-old woman who had been married for 16 years to a physically abusive man who raped her routinely. Helen, who was 28, was Betty's first female lover, but Betty reported that she had always had sexual feelings toward women and that when she began the affair with Helen it felt so "right" that she almost immediately began to identify herself as a lesbian. Helen had identified herself as a lesbian since adolescence and had had several female lovers prior to meeting Betty.

Betty and Helen had become lovers while Betty was still married; she left her husband 1 year later. Both women agreed that their sexual relationship was initially intense, frequent, and satisfying. However, since they had begun living together, the frequency had declined to twice a month. The couple agreed that the decline in sexual frequency was due to Betty's loss of sexual interest.

The first two or three couple sessions were spent attempting to get a clearer picture of the problem; Betty had a good deal of difficulty even talking about her feelings. She reported that she sometimes had "flashback" experiences of rape during sex; she was unable to experience orgasm with Helen; and sexual touching had become painful. Upon considerable probing, she revealed in Helen's presence that she actually experienced no sexual desire and that she had sex with Helen only because she was afraid Helen would leave her if they didn't have sex at all. Helen was crushed by this revelation. Considerable therapy time, at this juncture and throughout treatment, was spent in dealing with Helen's feelings of rejection, demoralization, and finally anger not only that Betty did not want to have sex with her but that she had consented to sex and then afterward revealed that she had not wanted it.

This theme emerged as a crucial one for Betty. She was almost incapable of saying "no" to sex, because she felt she would be abandoned by her partner. A "ban" on genital sex was instituted, which initially produced great anxiety in Betty but eventually was a relief to both women. During any homework exercises, however, Betty invariably completed the assignment and then reported that she had felt uncomfortable during the exercise but felt unable to articulate her desire to stop. It appeared that Betty had come to feel that neither her body nor her sexuality "belonged" to her. Both were simply instruments of her partner's desire, and even though Helen was quite unlike her abusive husband, Betty was so convinced that sexual performance was essential to the maintenance of Helen's love that she manufactured her own pressure. Helen was very clear in asserting that she did not want Betty to "pretend" to be sexually responsive. Betty's sexual desire had become lost in the demand requirements for sex. As Betty explained at one point, "You can't feel free to say 'yes' unless you feel free to say 'no.'"

A secondary theme that emerged was Betty's history of sexual abuse, and a resulting pattern common in women with a background of sexual assault and/or incest. During the "honeymoon period" of her relationship with Helen, Betty's sexuality seemed free, spontaneous, and strong. Once the limerance stage began to pass, older sexual conflicts and issues emerged. This became clearer as I guided the couple at an excruciatingly slow pace through sensate focus exercises. The goal with sensate focus was to use the exercises as a tool for uncovering negative thoughts, feelings, or images that might be blocking Betty's sexual desire. They worked well for this purpose; during homework assignments, Betty became aware of very specific fears, and re-experienced them vividly during sessions. For example, during one session, when Betty was reporting her feelings during an exercise involving breast touching, she burst into tears and asked Helen, "Were you going to pinch my nipples? I thought you were going to hurt me." These fears usually represented actual events that had occurred during her marriage; they were so "alien" for Betty that she lost some ability for reality testing, and feared that Helen would repeat this assaultive behavior despite evidence to the contrary. Besides sensate focus and similar exercises in couple sessions, Betty worked on these fears and images in individual sessions. She proved a good trance subject, and so hypnotherapy was used extensively—both to help her uncover, relive, and resolve her marital experiences, and to help her get in touch with and express rage toward her ex-husband.

Meanwhile, unexpectedly, the couple's sessions began to stimulate Helen to uncover some hidden sexual conflicts. She revealed a history of incest with an older brother, and these memories became increasingly vivid to her as therapy progressed. About 1 year after the conjoint treatment began, Helen sought individual therapy with another therapist and joined a peer support group for incest "survivors." Shortly after this, Betty, in individual therapy, began talking about a childhood sexual episode with an older boy in her neighborhood; she had mentioned this at the beginning of treatment but had dismissed it as unimportant. In working through this early experience, it appeared that in many ways her relationship with her husband, especially the rape episodes, was a repetition of this early childhood relationship, with one exception. She had been a partially consenting participant in the childhood experience, and became aware of feelings of guilt and shame about these childhood contacts. In other words, she did not simply feel like a "victim"; underlying her "victim" feelings were intense feelings of guilt and self-blame—first, for her complicity in the childhood events, and more globally over any sexual feelings she had.

At the time of this writing, Betty and Helen are still in treatment and have been for 18 months. It took over a year for the women to resume genital sexual relations with each other. Their sexual contact now is infrequent, but both report that, when they have sex, they are unambivalent and it is satisfying to both. While Helen is actually experiencing lower desire than Betty at this point, she is intensely involved in dealing with her own incest experiences. It remains to be seen whether continued therapy can help these women to recapture a spontaneous and relatively conflict-free sexual relationship.

Miriam and Diane: A Case of Low Success

Miriam was the 28-year-old lesbian discussed earlier in this chapter, whose low sexual desire issues, when uncovered, yielded to feelings of intense, specific, and ego-dystonic sexual impulses. Ultimately, I consider this case a failure; the reasons constitute an interesting lesson in the systemic function low desire may serve.

Miriam and Diane were seen individually and jointly for $1\frac{1}{2}$ years. Miriam contacted me upon referral from her individual therapist, who continued to see her weekly throughout the time I worked with Miriam. I saw Miriam alone for the first few sessions, in part because Miriam reported her problems to be purely individual. Moreover, I never saw Miriam or the couple together more frequently than once or twice a month; both were in individual therapy with other therapists, and they traveled a substantial distance to see me. The infrequency of meetings undoubtedly affected treatment, but under the circumstances it seemed the only arrangement possble.

Miriam was attractive, always slightly nervous, and moderately over-weight. Both she and Diane considered themselves compulsive overeaters and were members of Overeaters Anonymous; both had the rigidity one sometimes encounters in new members of Twelve-Step programs. Miriam initially reported low sexual desire, an inability to experience orgasm with a lover, and a physical feeling of "numbness" when touching during sexual encounters. Despite her antisexual upbringing, she had begun masturbating at 13, and her first sexual experiences with both men and women had occurred in late adolescence. Her attraction to women was stronger than that to men, however, and her sexual contact with men was incidental after her first affair with a woman at age 19. Miriam stated that shortly after this affair ended, she began to feel "afraid" of sex. This fear expressed itself in difficulty reaching orgasm with a partner; an aversion to masturbating (although orgasm during masturbation was not a problem); and a pattern of high sexual desire in the beginning of a relationship, followed by a sharp decrease in desire and arousal after a few months. Miriam and Diane had been partners for 2 years at the time therapy began. Miriam reported that it was her best relationship so far.

Almost immediately, Miriam reported tremendous fear of loss of control over her sexuality. Initially this was expressed as fear of orgasm, but the fear of urinating in bed was reported in her second session. Much early work was focused on this fear and upon the "numbness" she described. Miriam was asked to masturbate as homework; she was requested to "pretend" orgasms to diminish the fear; she was instructed to use a "stop–start" exercise when she began to feel numb during arousal; she was asked to urinate in bed, but she refused. In the first few months, therapy centered on her antisex injunctions. She generated a list of her internalized "rules" about sex (her "rules" included messages about when to have sex, as well as with whom, how, etc.), and then she was asked to set about breaking them one by one. She read Barbach's book *For Yourself* (1975) and did mirror exercises and genital touching exercises. All this seemed to have some impact. Within the first 2 months she had her first orgasm during sex with Diane, although this rarely occurred afterwards. She began to report more arousal and desire.

Four months after Miriam began individual treatment, Miriam and Diane were seen together. Diane presented herself as well adjusted and sexually robust, and extremely patient and supportive of Miriam. Miriam was Diane's first female lover, but Diane appeared to be experiencing no difficulties with her lesbianism. Diane's family background was bizarre: One sibling was schizophrenic, and Diane's mother had left the children in their adolescence in order to join a convent. Nevertheless, Diane appeared to be much the healthier of the two women. Diane's aid as a quasi-surrogate for sex was enlisted in order to have the couple participate in sensate focus exercises.

The combination of individual and conjoint sessions seemed to work well. Miriam gradually became more sexual; as she did so, she began to be aware of more specific sexual fears. Fantasies of domination and submission began to appear to her in a way that seemed invasive and intrusive, and she also became terrified that she would "commit adultery." In addition, as couple therapy progressed, Diane began to express sexual fears for the first time. She became aware that she was uncomfortable with their increasing sexuality, and traced this to a fear of intimacy and especially of abandonment. Although we discussed these fears, I feel in retrospect that they were probably more important than seemed apparent at the time. The couple was encouraged to introduce sexual enhancement techniques into the relationship, such as the use of vibrators and other sex toys, written and visual erotica, and so on. Miriam was again asked to deal with her fear of urination directly by urinating in bed. As described earlier, this intervention "worked" in that it produced a powerful orgasm followed by a flood of strong sexual feelings, which Miriam then had to learn to control. However, Diane's sexual desire had been gradually lessening, and as Miriam became more sexual Diane became noticeably less so. Moreover, at about the time of Miriam's breakthrough, Diane received a devastating letter from her mother condemning her to "hell" for her lesbianism.

In the next few months, Diane became completely asexual and sank into a depression that required treatment by means of medication. Again, the couple's genital sexuality disappeared, and as this happened, Miriam reported that *her* sexual desire was diminishing. Shortly after this, the couple terminated treatment. In retrospect, it is possible that insufficient attention was directed at the system dynamics that were functioning to keep both partners asexual. In particular, Diane's individual conflicts were underestimated, and in dealing with this problem as an individual therapy problem for Miriam, the relative contribution of the partner was ignored.

Conclusion

This chapter has focused upon low sexual desire in lesbian couples as a prototype for sexual issues in all women. The social-constructionist view has been advanced that female sexuality, while distinct from male sexual behavior, is primarily the result of cultural conditioning rather than fundamental biological differences between men and women. Lesbian sexual desire problems, which are almost entirely problems encountered in relationships of committed couples, are seen as the consequence of female–female pairings and the concomitant exaggeration of traits socialized in women. Various theoretical issues arising from this perspective are discussed, and specific causes and interventions are described.

The approach described in this chapter assumes that female sexuality as conditioned in this culture includes some features that are negative, self-defeating, and inhibitory of full sexual functioning. The perspective taken, therefore, implies that at least some women would benefit from therapy that helps expand or "disinhibit" their sexuality. It could be argued, however (and has been argued by both sexologists and feminists), that female sexuality as it currently manifests itself is "natural" and that therapeutic interventions should therefore focus on redefining "male-identified" cultural norms for sex rather than on changing women's sexual behavior. While this latter viewpoint is not the stance taken here, we would do well to remember that, for some women, redefining their problems as normal behavior may be more efficacious than attempting to change them.

References

Barbach, L. (1975). *For yourself: The fulfillment of female sexuality*. New York: Signet.

Bell, A., & Weinberg, M. (1978). *Homosexualities: A Study of diversity among men and women*. New York: Simon & Schuster.

Berzon, B. (1979). *Positively gay*. Millbrae, CA: Celestial Arts.

Blumstein, P., & Schwartz, P. (1983). *American couples: Money, work, and sex*. New York: Morrow.

Bullough, V., & Bullough, B. (1977). Lesbianism in the 1920's and 1930's: A newfound study. *Signs, 2*, 895–904.

Burch, B. (1982). Psychological merger in lesbian couples: A joint ego psychological and systems approach. *Family Therapy, 9*, 201–208.

Caldwell, M., & Peplau, L. (1984). The balance of power in lesbian relationships. *Sex Roles, 10*, 587–599.

Califia, P. (1980). *Sapphistry: The book of lesbian sexuality*. Tallahassee, FL: Naiad Press.

Decker, B. (1984). Counseling gay and lesbian couples. *Journal of Social Work and Human Sexuality, 2*, 39–52.

Faderman, L. (1981). *Surpassing the love of men: Romantic friendship and love between women from the Renaissance to the present*. New York: Morrow.

Faderman, L. (1983). *Scotch verdict*. New York: Morrow.

Gilligan, C. (1982). *In a different voice: Psychological theory and women's development*. Cambridge, MA: Harvard University Press.

Hite, S. (1976). *The Hite report*. New York: Macmillan.

Hunt, M. (1974). *Sexual behaviors in the 1970's*. Chicago: Playboy Press.

Jay, K., & Young, A. (1979). *The gay report*. New York: Summit Books.

Katz, J. (1976). *Gay American history*. New York: Thomas Crowell.

Kaufman, P., Harrison, E., & Hyde, M. (1984). Distancing for intimacy in lesbian relationships. *American Journal of Psychiatry, 141*, 530–533.

Kinsey, A., Pomeroy, W., Martin, C., & Gebhard, D. (1953). *Sexual behavior in the human female*. Philadelphia: W. B. Saunders.

Loulan, J. (1984). *Lesbian sex*. San Francisco: Spinsters Ink.

Maracek, J., Finn, S., & Cardell, M. (1982). Gender roles in the relationships of lesbians and gay men. *Journal of Homosexuality, 8*.

Masters, W. H., & Johnson, V. E. (1979). *Homosexuality in perspective*. Boston: Little, Brown.

Nestle, J. (1984). The fem question. In C. Vance (Ed.), *Pleasure and danger: Exploring female sexuality*. London: Routledge & Kegan Paul.

Nichols, M. (1982). The treatment of inhibited sexual desire in lesbian couples. *Women and Therapy, 1*(4), 49–66.

Nichols, M. (in press). Doing sex therapy with lesbians: Bending a heterosexual paradigm to fit a gay lifestyle. In *Lesbian psychologies*. Urbana: University of Illinois Press.

Nichols, M., & Leiblum, S. (1986, Spring). Lesbianism as personal identity and social role: A model. *Affilia: Journal of Women and Social Work*, pp. 48–59.

Peplau, L., Cochran, S., Rook, K., & Padesky, C. (1978). Loving women: Attachment and autonomy in lesbian relationships. *Journal of Social Issues, 34*(3), 7–28.

Roberts, J. R. (1977). Lesbian hoboes: Their lives and times. *Dyke: A Quarterly*, No. 5, 37–50.

Roberts, J. R. (1982). Black lesbians before 1970: A bibliographical essay. *Lesbianism: New Research/New Perspectives*, 103–113.

Roth, S. (1984). Psychotherapy with lesbian couples: The interrelationships of individual issues, female socialization, and social contest. In E. Hetrick & T. Stein (Eds.), *Psychotherapy with lesbians and gay men*. Washington, DC: American Psychiatric Press.

Schreiner-Engel, P. (1986, September 20). *Clinical aspects of female sexuality*. Paper presented at the meeting of the International Academy of Sex Research, Amsterdam.

Shade, W. (1979). A mental passion: Female sexuality in Victorian America. *International Journal of Women's Studies, 1*, 13–29.

Switow, A., Stansell, C., & Thompson, S. (1983). *Powers of desire: The politics of sexuality*. New York: Monthly Review Press.

Todor, N. (1978). Sexual problems of lesbians. In G. Vida (Ed.), *Our right to love: A lesbian resource book*. Englewood Cliffs, NJ: Prentice-Hall

Tripp, C. (1975). *The homosexual matrix*. New York: McGraw-Hill.

Vance, C. (Ed.). (1984). *Pleasure and danger: Exploring female sexuality*. London: Routledge & Kegan Paul.

15

Treating Low Sexual Desire among Gay Men

Eli Coleman and Rex Reece

Coleman and Reece effectively challenge the myth that homosexual men are immune to disorders of sexual desire. In fact, they indicate that low sexual desire—particularly sexual desire discrepancy—is the most prevalent sexual problem currently being treated in their respective practices. Like the other contributors to this volume, Coleman and Reece embrace a multicausal and multifaceted approach to the assessment and treatment of desire difficulties. They highlight the importance of assessing alcohol and drug abuse as possible etiological contributors to the problem, noting that gay men are at special risk for developing chemical dependency patterns. A critical issue in assessment is evaluating the impact of acquired immune deficiency syndrome (AIDS) on the subjective feeling of desire; the anxiety associated with fear of exposure to the AIDS virus, as well as that associated with the development of AIDS-related symptoms, must be considered. Obviously, living with a partner who either has AIDS or is concerned about viral transmission is an effective deterrent to the experience and expression of sexual interest.

In addition to the dreadful reality and dire consequences of the AIDS epidemic, Coleman and Reece identify a number of psychological factors that may negatively affect sexual interest in homosexual men. These include failure to achieve a positive sexual identity; fears and conflicts concerning intimacy; internalized homophobia; overly rigid male sex-role stereotyping; failure to resolve early traumas, such as sexual or physical abuse; unresolved hostility and fear of men; unresolved grief; and inadequate coping with aging.

Coleman and Reece point out that some of the etiological factors contributing to low sexual interest may also be significant when considering hypersexuality or sexual compulsivity. They suggest that high sexual activ-

413

ity is sometimes motivated by feelings of loneliness, depression, boredom, and anxiety, rather than by genital sexual release. In fact, they note that occasionally one sees hypersexual men become asexual over time.

In treatment, Coleman and Reece emphasize traditional sex therapy techniques, along with considerable attention to teaching communication skills. Relationship conflicts are discussed, and better solutions to couple dissatisfactions are negotiated. At times, referral is made for individual psychotherapy if intrapsychic conflicts seem primary. In fact, the therapy options used with gay men differ little from those practiced with heterosexual couples, and similar rates of success or failure are obtained.

Eli Coleman, Ph.D., is the Associate Director of the Program in Human Sexuality and Associate Professor of Family Practice and Community Health at the University of Minnesota Medical School. He is the editor of two recent books, Psychotherapy with Homosexual Men and Women *and* Chemical Dependency and Intimacy Dysfunction. *Dr. Coleman is also editor of the* Journal of Psychology and Human Sexuality.

Rex Reece, Ph.D., is a sex therapist in private practice in West Hollywood, California.

The treatment of sexual desire disorders in gay men requires an understanding of the particular dynamics, circumstances, and stressors that surround gay male relationships. A failure by therapists to address the intrapersonal, interpersonal, and sociocultural issues that concern gay men—and that contribute to sexual dysfunction—will thwart or defeat therapy.

George and Behrendt (1987) report that many of their gay male clients who have worked with other therapists have never been given the opportunity to discuss the sexual part of their relationship. These authors speculate that many therapists simply do not understand the nature and existence of these problems among gay men, or are uncomfortable about discussing them. Therapists who work with gay male and lesbian clients and who understand the dymanics of sexual problems acknowledge that many clients are reluctant to announce sexual dysfunction difficulties, even when the difficulties have virtually made them celibate.

Therapists first need to reject the stereotypical, popularly held view that gay men are highly sexual ("sexually free") and thus do not experience low sexual desire. Gay men *do* have more sexual partners over a lifetime than do heterosexual or lesbian couples (Bell & Weinberg, 1978; Blumstein & Schwartz, 1983); however, comfort with one's sexuality, sexual satisfaction, desire for sexual activity, and freedom from sexual dysfunction are not directly related to number of sexual partners or amount of sexual activity.

George and Behrendt (1987) report that low sexual desire is the most common kind of sexual dysfunction among their gay male clients. These findings contradict previous reports on sexual dysfunction among gay men (Masters & Johnson, 1979; McWhirter & Mattison, 1978). To confuse matters further, a couple's sexual desire discrepancies are sometimes diagnosed and treated as low sexual desire in one of the partners (Reece, 1987; Zilbergeld & Ellison, 1980). Even with conflicting frequencies of types of problems and inconsistent definitions among researchers, the current literature and clinical impressions do indicate that low sexual desire is a considerable problem among gay men. Therefore, therapists need to explore the organic, intrapsychic, sociocultural, and interpersonal etiologies of these dysfunctions.

Etiology and Treatment

Kaplan (1979, 1983) has offered a multicausal, multilevel treatment model for sexual problems, including the problem of low sexual desire. We share this multicausal and multilevel treatment approach. In addition, other treatment models for low sexual desire have been presented, and many of these models have applicability to the treatment of gay men. Low sexual desire for gay male couples may range from simple misinformation about some aspect of human sexual response to deep intrapsychic and/or interpersonal conflicts. In this chapter, we describe the common types of etiologies and the treatment methods that we have effective in our clinical practices for addressing the problem of low sexual desire among gay men.

For purposes of discussion, the causes of low sexual desire among gay men can be placed into three broad categories that are admittedly overlapping and inexact. Even organic etiologies, which compose the first category, are often complicated by psychogenic factors. A second significant group of factors in low sexual desire consists of intrapsychic ones, such as a defense against the anxiety experienced when struggling with issues of self-identity and intimacy. Also included in this second broad category are issues of the development of a sexual orientation identity, internalized homophobia, rigid sex roles, childhood abuse and trauma, hostility toward and fear of men, and a high frequency of sexual behavior. Each of these can both reflect and compound issues of identity and intimacy, and each is discussed separately below. Sociocultural issues also figure in this second category. The impact of grief and loss, aging, anxieties about acquired immune deficiency snydrome (AIDS), and alcohol and drug abuse all have special significance for gay men. And, third, the etiology may be of an interpersonal nature, such as issues of relationship stage development or sexual desire discrepancies.

Organic Considerations

Medical illness, injury, and prescription drugs that result in impairments of neurogenic, vasculogenic, or endocrinological functioning can all be specific causes of low sexual desire, and these possible factors need to be investigated thoroughly. This is sometimes a greater challenge with gay men, because of the perceived and actual homophobic sentiment in the medical community that prevents optimal health assessment, care, and treatment. The sex therapist must insure that high-quality medical assessment and treatment will be provided by physicians and health care systems that do not harbor such homophobic sentiment. Too often, clients have lacked a family physician—or, if not, have lacked the opportunity to discuss the full range of their sexual concerns comfortably with a physician.

Alcohol and other drug abuse is one of the most common physical causes of low sexual desire and other sexual dysfunctions, and gay men, for reasons that have been discussed elsewhere (Coleman, 1981/1982; Evans, Schaefer, & Coleman, 1987; Kus, 1987), are at risk for developing these chemical dependency patterns. Therefore, careful attention must be paid to alcohol and drug use patterns in the assessment of gay men with low sexual desire. The psychogenic effects of alcohol and drug abuse are discussed in more detail below.

The other organic factor that must be considered especially today, is the effect on gay men of Human Immunodeficiency Virus (HIV) infection, the development of AIDS-related complex (ARC) symptoms, or the development of opportunistic infections related to exposure to the HIV virus (AIDS). All the relationships between these medical conditions and low sexual desire have not been established. However, HIV exposure may affect many organ and central nervous system functions in various ways. Therefore, with the increase in the incidence of AIDS-related illnesses in gay men, more cases of AIDS-related low sexual desire seem likely. The psychogenic effects of AIDS and related conditions are also discussed below.

Intrapsychic Etiologies

Interruptions in Healthy Development of a Sexual Orientation Identity

Healthy development of a sexual orientation identity is one obvious prerequisite for healthy psychosexual and psychosocial development. This tends to be taken for granted among heterosexual individuals, but the task of developing an integrated and positive sexual orientation is a challenging one for many gay men, given the present social and cultural climate. The stigma of homosexuality interferes with the development of a positive sexual self-concept for many, and totally prohibits this development in others (Coleman, 1981/1982). This task has become even more challenging with the advent of new social issues raised by the AIDS epidemic. The development of an integrated sexual orientation identity involves a stage of sexual exploration and experimentation (which appears to be a normal and important developmental stage for all adolescents), but the fear of AIDS has limited some of the opportunities for sexual exploration. And, perhaps even more devastating, the AIDS crisis has inhibited the ability to feel positive about gay male sexuality, because that has been so closely associated with this deadly illness.

The sex therapist should evaluate the individual's stage of sexual orientation identity development. McWhirter and Mattison (1978) found in their study of sexual dysfunctions among gay male couples that many who presented with sexual desire problems had problems with their sexual orientation identity. A number of models of identity development have been described, and the therapist should be familiar with these (e.g., Cass, 1979; Coleman, 1981/1982). In order to assess an individual's stage of sexual orientation development, it is necessary to make a complete assessment of the orientation identity. The therapist should also be familiar with techniques to assess other components of sexual identity, especially gender and sex-role identity. A comprehensive assessment tool has been developed by one of us and has been found to be a useful clinical device (Coleman, 1987a). Conflicts within or between individuals over their sexual orientation identity must be identified. These conflicts can be the major source of low sexual desire dysfunctions, as well as many other psychosexual disorders and psychopathologies. The importance of an extensive assessment of sexual orientation is most important when the client states confusion or conflict about his sexual orientation. However, the clinician should routinely investigate this dimension of the individual's personality whenever he or she encounters a case of low sexual desire.

Treatment methods to help clients develop a positive and integrated sexual orientation identity have been described elsewhere (e.g., Coleman, 1981/1982, 1987c; Gonsiorek, 1982; Sophie, 1987). An understanding of how integrated and positive identities develop, and a knowledge of methods for assisting this identity development, are prerequisites for a clinician. However, perhaps the most salient therapeutic modality is the therapeutic relationship itself (Sophie, 1987). Sophie argues that a therapist is likely to be seen as a representative of society and as an authority figure whose approval or disapproval can greatly influence the individual's developing self-identity and self-esteem. Obviously, it is important for the therapist to convey acceptance of the gay client as a healthy sexual being. Besides conveying this acceptance, the therapist must provide a positive picture of the possibilities for developing an integrated sexual orientation identity, while not minimizing the real obstacles involved. A therapist who is predominantly homosexual in orientation and who has achieved an integrated and healthy identity can also serve as a role model for the client. Therapists who are not predominantly homosexual can probably help clients by insuring that they are introduced to some healthy role models.

Identity and Intimacy Dysfunctions

Kaplan (1979), McCarthy (1984), and Schmidt (1983) have each noted that the etiology of sexual desire problems is sometimes based in ambivalence about intimacy and fears of dependency. Failure to develop a positive and integrated self-identity results in more basic identity and intimacy dysfunctions. Again, given the current sociocultural climate, gay men find the development of healthy identity and intimacy functioning especially challenging. Colgan (1987) has discussed how many gay men can develop identity disorders. He defines an individual with an identity disorder as "one who lacks adequate formation and development of a positive personal construct or self-worth" (p. 97). Identity disorders inevitably lead to intimacy dysfunctions, since a positive identity is a prerequisite for believing oneself capable of "giving and receiving love, and of making positive contributions to the welfare of others." Colgan says:

> Intimacy dysfunction has been described as a pattern of behaviors which require the identity-disordered male to depend on external agents for a positive sense of self. Examples of external agents, or as Smalley (1982) suggests, addictive agents, include sex, alcohol and other drugs, food, work, gambling, body building, or another person. Dependence on external agents precludes the balance of separation and attachment which appears necessary for emotional health. The imbalance seen in intimacy dysfunction is characterized by interpersonal communication problems, unresolved intrapsychic and interpersonal stress, and behavior patterns designed to cope with unresolved stress. (1987, p. 98)

Intimacy problems can cause a variety of psychological problems and psychosexual dysfunctions and disorders, including low sexual desire. Low sexual desire can develop as an adaptive mechanism for avoiding anxiety related to identity and intimacy dysfunctions.

Gay males do seem at more risk for this type of intrapsychic difficulty. Certainly, they do not have "a corner on the market" of these dysfunctions. However, when gay men are reared in homes in which their self-concepts and self-worth are not nurtured, modeled, or reinforced, they have difficulties in developing a positive identity and an ability to relate intimately. Again, because of the sociocultural climate, an emerging homosexual identity is generally not nurtured, modeled, or reinforced. There appears to be at least an unconscious awareness of the emerging homosexual identity in the homosexual child and in the family that interferes in this healthy identity and intimacy development (Coleman, 1981/1982).

The child who does not conform to gender-related expectations seems to be at particular risk because of the societal association between homosexuality and cross-gender behavior. (This societal association is either entirely mistaken or, at least, misunderstood.) Even so, the issue of gender nonconformity negatively affects the child within the family, and the effects of peer socialization pressures add further to tensions.

Outright rejection, or sometimes a more subtle or covert emotional abandonment, is a common experience for the prehomosexual boy. This rejection or abandonment is not unlike various forms of child abuse and neglect in its dynamics and its ultimate effects. Prehomosexual boys suffer, at the least, a form of cultural (and mostly covert) abuse that is often transmitted through the family (Coleman, 1981/1982). When actual physical or emotional abuse is also present, the risk that identity and intimacy dysfunctions will develop increases.

These dysfunctions do not occur in all families. As Colgan (1987) notes in his discussion of the findings of Block (1973), gender-nonconforming males who are socially well adjusted have usually been reared by parents who are secure in their own identities, who provide nurturing home environments, and who are involved in the socialization of their sons. Furthermore, these parents were found to hold nontraditional sex-role behaviors and values. For those gay men who are not reared in such households, identity and intimacy disorders can lead to adaptive mechanisms of overseparation and overattachment—both of which can be precursors of low sexual desire.

Colgan (1987) has described problems of overseparation as involving "forming and maintaining one's identity at the expense of emotionally satisfying human connections, whereas overattachment involves a pattern of forming human connections at the sacrifice of one's own separate identity" (p. 98). The goal of overseparation is to preserve independence by avoiding emotional involvement, which is associated with negative consequences. By "developing" low sexual desire, a man can better maintain a comfortable emotional distance. Or by developing a belief that sex is primarily a recreational function, a person can avoid establishing an ongoing sexual interest in the same partner.

The goal of overattachment is designed to avoid feelings of separation and abandonment and to feel some sense of identity. In Colgan's words:

> The man who displays over-attachment patterns may find himself "walking on air" in the limerance phase of a relationship. The intense emotional connection may be experienced unconsciously as reestablishing the emotional bond interrupted during infancy or childhood. Consequently, he will do

anything to make the relationship work, though unfortunately this is often done at the expense of his attending to needs for separation. Even if the relationship is emotionally painful, he will remain attached until rejected or until he resumes the process of developing an identity based on positive self-worth. (1987, p. 108)

The pressure from someone displaying overattachment patterns will usually cause the object of his attention to flee. The pressure is simply too much to bear. Colgan (1987) notes that gay men who overseparate and gay men who overattach have an "uncanny ability" to find one another. In fact, it is a perfect combination: Both are therefore able to avoid real intimacy, which would require a balance of separation and attachment and a well-developed, positive self-identity. If this combination of behaviors or other combinations does not result in low sexual desire in one or both of the individuals, it certainly can lead to conflicts about differences in the level of sexual interest in each other—a more common experience among gay couples.

In assessing low sexual desire among gay men, the clinician must take into account these issues of identity and intimacy dysfunctions. One or the other of the partners in a gay relationship often says, "I'm just not attracted to him any more." Although attraction may indeed have waned, the clinician must view this statement as a possible clue that identity and intimacy issues are involved. To complain about a lack of attraction to a partner may be an individual's way of announcing his anxieties and fears about being in an intimate relationship.

Extrarelationship sex and the development of other intimate relationships can be, as McWhirter and Mattison (1978, 1984) have noted, an adaptive balance between separation and attachment. It has been noted by Tripp (1975) and Reece and Segrist (1981) that some extrarelationship sex, whether comfortable or not, seems to be the norm for established male couples. So the clinician needs to understand that this behavior may represent a healthy adaptation for some couples. But these arrangements may also signal separation and attachment difficulties.

Moreover, the clinician should be alert for associated dependencies on external agents (e.g., alcohol, drugs, food, sex, etc.; several of these are discussed in more detail below). Again, the use of these agents can be a clinical clue to the presence of identity and intimacy dysfunctions. For example, chemical dependency and intimacy dysfunctions have been found to be inextricably bound (Coleman, 1987b). Often these dependencies exacerbate (while, in many ways, they maintain) the instability of the relationship that serves the need for imbalanced separateness and attachment. They create crises that often bring a couple into therapy.

Treatment of identity and intimacy dysfunctions can be conducted within the context of sex therapy (Smalley & Coleman, 1987). When dependencies on external agents are present to the extent that they continue to destabilize the relationship, the therapy must focus initially on eliminating or stabilizing the use of the external agent or agents. Attempts at resolving the identity or intimacy issues will be thwarted until the dependence on external agents is treated.

The next step in the therapy is intervention directed toward achieving a solid identity through self-observation and self-valuing (Colgan, 1987; Smalley & Coleman, 1987). Colgan (1987) explains that successful psychotherapy at this juncture requires a balance between individual and couples work: "For the individual, psychotherapy appears to attend to the redevelopment of his independent sense of positive self-worth. Within the couple, this will mean developing new skills for affective self-disclosure and affective responses" (p. 110). One frequently useful technique for those couples who want more sex but cannot tolerate more intimacy is to develop ways of occasionally distancing themselves from each other. For example, some individuals may need to spend more free time alone, away from home, or with friends (Reece, 1987).

Hall (1987) has stated that in treating lesbian couples, "The assignment of touching exercises will be futile unless partners can, on a fairly regular basis, have experiences outside the boundaries of the relationship that are pleasurable, stimulating and engaging, activites which recharge the batteries of partners" (p. 134). This approach can apply to gay male couples as well. A focus on the unique issues of attachment and separation, and on consequences of identity and intimacy dysfunctions, will greatly increase the effectiveness of sex therapy with gay male couples.

Internalized Homophobia

Internalized homophobia is an obstacle to positive and integrated identity development and a contributor to sexual desire disorders among gay men. Homophobia characterizes many heterosexual individuals in our society and often becomes internalized in many gay men. Many therapists assume that a client who presents himself as a "gay man" has achieved a sense of identity integration and has eliminated his own homophobia. This is erroneous. Indeed, with the advent of the AIDS health crisis, internalized homophobia among gay men has been rekindled and reinforced. The internalization of these negative attitudes toward homosexuality contributes to a loss of self-esteem. To be sexual with a man is to confront one's homophobia. To be in a relationship with another man is to confront this irrational fear even more. Many gay men use alcohol or other drugs to escape from their own homophobia and to allow themselves to be sexual or to be in relationships with other men. Anonymity in sexual encounters or avoidance of any intimacy in relationships also helps gay men avoid confronting their own homophobia. Low sexual desire is still another of the many ways gay men avoid the anxiety or fears associated with their homosexuality. The clinician should assess the presence of internalized homophobia. It is important to ask questions related to clients' feelings about being gay (George & Behrendt, 1987), such as the following: "How do you feel about being sexual with other men?" "How do your parents view your sexual orientation [sexual activities and partners]?" "How does your family accept your partner?" "Did anything traumatic happen early in your life to cause you to be anxious about your sexual feelings or desires?"

If homophobic responses are evoked, the goal of therapy is then to reduce and eliminate irrational fear and anxiety. Much of the therapy should involve debunking such myths and stereotypes about being gay as the following: Sex between two men is "unnatural" and "immoral"; homosexual relationships are "unnatural" and "immoral"; homosexual relationships are short-lived, and gay men are incapable of sustaining long-term relationships; and gay men have sex with many different partners. (This list could go on; see Hammersmith, 1987.) The clinician should be familiar with gay-affirmative and integrated-identity approaches toward the treatment of homosexuality (see Coleman, 1987c; Gonsiorek, 1982).

Stereotypical Male Sex Roles

A gay man who adheres to stereotypical male sex roles often experiences difficulties in relationships with other men. These difficulties, which may contribute to low sexual desire, are a way of relieving the anxiety associated with transgressing expected male societal roles. The stereotypical male role calls for the man to be unemotional, competitive, in control, strong, capable, and independent. Sexually, the man should be "on top"; the "inserter" and initiator: "always ready and able"; and an experienced, highly competent performer. Two men who try to be "men" in a relationship at the same time inevitably run into conflict. George and Behrendt (1987) note that many gay men worry about whether their partners perceive them as masculine and as good sexual partners. This anxiety leads to relationship conflicts and sexual dysfunctions.

Many gay men worry about whether certain sexual activities are "masculine" or "feminine" activities. The "inserter" may be perceived as the "masculine" partner and the "insertee" as the "feminine" partner. The same is true for positions involving fellatio or other sexual activities that many gay men enjoy. Gay men who did not experience emotional intimacy with another male while growing up (e.g., a father) or have seen only rigid male sex-role stereotypes often experience difficulty in this area.

Sex therapists sometimes find that challenging rigid sex-role behavior in couples may lead to greater sexual satisfaction. Many heterosexual couples have found these traditional roles to be maladaptive in today's society, but they are especially maladaptive for men who have relationships with other men. If rigid sex roles are found to be a primary factor in inhibiting sexual desire, it would be helpful for the client to consider adoption of a more androgynous sex-role identity.

When the rule against having sex and relationships with other males (the ultimate taboo of traditional sex-role stereotypes) is broken, other rules are easier to break. New roles are easier to learn, especially those related to affective expressiveness. Those gender-nonconforming homosexuals who have successfully transcended the stigma of gender nonconformity and have developed a sense of positive self-worth have an easier time in forming relationships and developing healthy sexual lives. They allow for sexual flexibility and do not assign labels of "masculinity" and "femininity" to various sexual acts (Colgan, 1987). Gender-conforming homosexuals may be more at risk for overcoming the obstacles of traditional, rigid sex-role stereotypes.

Unresolved Childhood Abuse and Trauma

In working with gay men, clinicians need to overcome the misconception that men do not experience abuse as children. Although sexual abuse occurs with greater frequency among young girls than among young boys (Finkelhor, 1979), many gay male clients have histories of childhood abuse and trauma, including sexual, physical, and emotional abuse as well as physical and emotional neglect. This is particularly true among gay men who have been juvenile prostitutes.

Unresolved childhood abuse and trauma often result in disruption of identity and intimacy development. At times, the dynamics of parental transferences are acted out in adult relationships (Levine, 1984). For many gay men, sex with anyone *except* a loved object is acceptable. These individuals still attempt to protect themselves from pain, rejection, abuse, disrespect, torture, or harm they experienced in childhood. Even when their partners can be trusted, these men fear a repetition of their early trauma. Schmidt and Arentewicz (1983) describe how a person who attempts to recreate the early unfulfilling relationship (i.e., to fuse with the parent substitute, his lover) develops a low interest in sex—a tactic that helps him avoid regression to total dependency, and the accompanying fear of loss and abandonment.

There is not room here to describe the treatment strategies for addressing unresolved childhood abuse and trauma. It is most important, however, for the clinician to recognize this dynamic as part of the etiology of low sexual desire in gay men and to treat these problems. Usually, treatment involves individual or group psychotherapy in order to help these clients review the abusive experiences, reach some catharsis of emotion regarding loss, grieve, understand the dynamics of victimization, and see how this process is internalized and perpetuated in adulthood. Finally, the clients must begin the process of recovery from guilt and shame and must stop engaging in behaviors that perpetuate the victimization process. This psychotherapy need not be long and exhaustive; rather, it is time-limited and psychoeducational. We have found that the use of therapy groups composed of other "victims"—both men and women—helps diffuse many of the potential iatrogenic negative effects of therapy.

Unresolved Hostility and Fear toward Men

Some men develop hostility and fear toward other men as a result of early childhood abuse from their fathers or other older men. Such feelings may contribute to distrust and suspicion of men, avoidance of intimacy, and asexuality. Alternatively, some gay men develop sexual styles that place a premium on brief and anonymous sexual encounters rather than extended relationships. Some gay men feel hostile or suspicious of other men as a result of never having had an emotionally satisfying relationship with a father or father figure. Such emotional neglect may lead to feelings of resentment, mistrust, and fear that are experienced during any and all subsequent male relationships.

This dynamic needs to be discussed in order to achieve cognitive understanding. In addition, a therapeutic relationship with an older male can help the client overcome these feelings through positive modeling and regard for the client. When possible, family psychotherapy (or at least sessions with the father) can help resolve past problems and develop a better father–son relationship. Many gay men are afraid of and angry at their fathers. Therapists need to help clients address their relationship with their fathers, especially when identity and intimacy dysfunctions exist. Resolution of these family-of-origin difficulties may pave the way for improved relationships with other adult males and/or help reduce symptomatic coping mechanisms such as low sexual desire.

Unresolved Grief

Unresolved grief resulting from the loss of a significant relationship may contribute to a reduction in sexual interest among both homosexual and heterosexual individuals. For instance, some bisexual men are surprised and unsettled to discover that they are experiencing sexual dysfunction and loss of sexual desire after terminating heterosexual relationships, although they may be confident that they have made the right decision.

Dealing with the loss of a loved one is sometimes especially difficult for homosexual men, because they often adhere to traditional notions that "strong men don't cry"; furthermore, they often lack strong supportive social networks. This issue is particularly poignant and significant at present, as so many gay men are losing their lovers and friends to AIDS.

Clinicians need to be aware of unresolved grief issues that may underlie sexual desire disorders among gay men. Often less societal support exists for the gay man coping with loss, and he may rely on the therapist for greater support, or the therapist may need to provide greater assistance in finding support.

Coping with the Aging Process

Many men—both heterosexual and homosexual—have difficulty adjusting to the inevitable changes accompanying aging. While some men age gracefully, with little despair, others experience feelings of reduced "masculinity," loss of attractiveness, and even loss of potency. Some men attempt to reassure themselves of adequacy by throwing themselves into the pursuit of sexual conquests (preferably with younger persons); others display resignation and sexual apathy. Loss of sexual interest may be used defensively to deal with the anxiety that accompanies aging.

Many homosexual men exhibit more concerns about aging than do their lesbian peers, and they do so earlier in the life cycle. Friend (1987) suggests that gay men may experience "accelerated aging," defined as "the experiencing of oneself as old at a time before one's chronological age peers define themselves as old" (p. 300).

Many older homosexual adults are faced with the double stigma of old age and an unpopular sexual orientation (Friend, 1987). As gay men age, they develop a fear of the consequences of illness, as well as a fear of facing the health care system, which is perceived as homophobic. The fear of institutionalization in nursing homes or other rehabilitation centers is great. Many gay men joke about these anxieties and speak of "gay nursing homes," which they know are more a fantasy than a coming reality. Again, the AIDS health crisis and the number of gay men who are dying at very early ages have forced gay men to acknowledge the reality of death much earlier than heterosexual men or lesbians.

The clinician should be aware of the special problems faced by gay men in coping with the aging process. (Treatment of these issues can be facilitated by the knowledge that the potential problems of growing older can prompt the development of coping mechanisms that can serve the client well throughout the rest of his life.) The research clearly indicates that being homosexual can facilitate successful aging (Friend, 1987). Friend states, "In counseling it is useful to capitalize on these resources and remind the older

homosexual client of these strengths and how to make best use of them"
(p. 302).

Reactions to AIDS

The cold, hard realities of AIDS are fueling panic and anxiety among the
homosexual and bisexual populations—and, increasingly, among the heterosexual population as well. Hardest hit have been gay and bisexual men,
intravenous drug users, hemophiliacs, and their families. Fear of AIDS
among gay men is enormous and contributes to a variety of psychological
reactions, including disturbances in sexual desire. The typical reactions have
been described by Morin, Charles, and Maylon (1984), Forstein (1984), and
Harowski (1987). They include initial denial responses followed by panic
attacks, somatic preoccupations, depression, and obsessive worrying. Initial
denial is seen more frequently where fewer people are actually ill and dying.
The primitive defense of denial usually breaks down when AIDS is diagnosed in an acquaintance, friend, or lover.

The "worried well" are burdened both by the fear of the disease and
the way in which society uses the illness as a metaphor (Harowski, 1987) to
link homosexuality with death and illness. As one client put it, "I look at my
semen and I see death." The AIDS epidemic is creating depression, anxiety,
and mourning; for some gay men, these emotions revive negative attitudes
toward themselves and other homosexual men, and toward sexuality in
general (Quadland & Shattls, 1987).

One of the potentially serious inhibiting factors for gay couples is the
anxiety about whether one has been or will be exposed to the AIDS virus.
Each partner often recalls his own or his partner's earlier unsafe sex acts.
Some individuals have become so obsessed with the fear of getting the virus
or of giving it to their partners that sex is next to impossible, even with
current educational guidelines for safer sex practices. Certainly, the anxiety
promotes poorer sexual response, and consequently possible insecurities
about oneself, one's sex role, and the durability of the relationship. Even if
the anxiety is not severe, it may still be great enough to inhibit or prohibit
two individuals from discussing what they feel comfortable doing within the
guidelines for safe sex. Certain sexual practices then begin to drop out of
their repertoire, or the frequency or desire for sex may decrease. This
anxiety may contribute to hurt, retaliation, and more conflict. Certainly,
having AIDS or ARC, having tested positive for the HIV antibody, or even
being with a lover or partner who is faced with either of these conditions
may negatively affect one's interest in sex. Some single gay men have
decided that the way to protect themselves from AIDS is to "find a relationship." This pressure creates its own set of anxieties. Individuals searching
for this kind of relationship deal with a number of fears: Has my partner

been exposed to the AIDS virus? Should we be tested for the HIV antibodies before being sexual? What sexual activities are really safe? How long must we have safe sex if we can be monogamous? How can I be sure that my partner is remaining monogamous? These questions can stultify freedom of sexual expression and the development of intimacy, in which sexuality plays such an important part.

So, for a variety of AIDS-related reasons, some gay men have withdrawn from sex. Some of these changes in sexual behavior patterns can be seen as positive if one considers a reduction in the number of sexual partners and high-risk sexual activities as ways of reducing the chances of exposure to the AIDS virus. On the other hand, this response has a negative impact on many gay men. One disturbing pattern that we and others (Quadland & Shattls, 1987) have noted is a reduction in sexual drive accompanied by occasional lapses into high-risk sexual behavior (periodic "fits" of frustration). A number of these clients feel that this pattern is "better" because they are reducing their exposure rate. They are not taking into account the increased risk of exposure that exists because of the greater number of individuals who have been exposed over the years.

In treating the "worried well" or those with anxieties related to AIDS, the clinician should keep in mind that many gay men have made changes in their sexual activities and have found satisfying alternatives to "unsafe" sexual practices. The clinician can provide accurate information and can make specific suggestions on how to reduce risk (and thus to relieve anxiety) by altering sexual activities.

Clients can be encouraged to participate in healthy sex education programs that can enable gay men, and ultimately others, to enjoy satisfying and healthy sexual lives without jeopardizing their health and the health of their partners. Quadland and Shattls (1987) believe these programs should go beyond attempts to influence individuals to reduce high-risk behavior. Clients should be offered alternatives to unsafe behaviors that are not only healthy, but also attractive and appealing.

It is essential to help clients keep focused on the facts and not just on the purely emotional responses to this crisis. Clients need to be continually reminded that germs and viruses, not sexuality or sexual orientation, cause the disease. And although a cure is not presently available, prevention is possible (Quadland & Shattls, 1987).

Encouraging community involvement is another useful therapeutic approach. As Harowski (1987) points out, "Besides decreasing isolation and withdrawal, community participation decreases the sense of powerlessness often experienced by the worried well (and AIDS or ARC patients), provides the access to accurate information and allows them to perceive themselves as effective, in-control people" (p. 297). Professionals should use resources that communities have developed, without "passing these clients off." Professionals who are not gay can be of great assistance to gay clients and professionals who are coping with anxiety about AIDS; professionals who are gay or bisexual may already be overstressed with their own anxieties and fears.

Hypnosis and guided imagery can also be useful in reducing anxiety and heightening sexual arousal for gay men who are concerned about their level of sexual desire. The hypnotic sex therapy approaches described by Araoz (1982), especially his "becoming alive" exercise (pp. 143–144), can be extremely effective. This technique, which calls for clients to imagine all of their body parts (including their genitals) as alive and joyful, is very effective in countering the connection between same-sex activity and death. To remove the emotional and political overlay and the metaphorical associations is a challenging task in the current social climate, but a vital step in helping gay men cope with anxieties and fears about AIDS (Harowski, 1987).

High Sexual Activity as a Response to Low Sexual Desire and Other Factors

Many of the etiological factors of low sexual desire apply also to high sexual activity, or what has been variously termed "sexual compulsivity," "hyperactive sexual desire disorders," "sexual addiction," "sexaholism," and "problems with sexual control." (The debate over terminology, etiology, and treatment is enormous on this issue; see Colman, 1986.) In addition, we and others (Quadland, 1985) have noted that some gay men who are sexually compulsive are frequently experiencing low sexual desire even when seeking sexual activity. Their sexual activity is commonly prompted by loneliness, depression, boredom, anxiety, or other feelings of psychological pain (Coleman, 1987d). As Quadland and Shattls (1987) have noted,

> While the sexual experiences reported were genital, the primary motivation and satisfaction seemed often not to be purely sexual. For many, the sexual behavior functioned to reduce anxiety, and this anxiety often having to deal with low self esteem, loneliness, and isolation, and in some cases internalized homophobia and fears of an intimate relationship with another man. (p. 280)

Gay men are at high risk for developing sexual compulsions and other types of dependencies. This is especially true for those men who have had histories of abuse or disruptions in their psychosocial and psychosexual development. Consequently, the clinician should be alert to these disorders in general when treating gay men with low sexual desire. We have treated a number of individuals who had been compulsive in their sexual behavior and then suddenly, or over time, simply became asexual.

A full discussion of all the controversies surrounding the definition of compulsive sexual activity, or of the methods of assessment or treatment, is not possible here. The reader is directed to articles by Quadland (1985), Coleman (1986), Carnes (1986), and Quadland and Shattls (1987), and to Patrick Carnes's book *Out of the Shadows: Understanding Sexual Addiction* (1983). These authors have offered some new hypotheses and theoretical formulations for understanding and treating these sexual problems. Since no consensus exists regarding this disorder, the reader should be cautious in accepting any existing "truths" and should continue to seek new information on this subject in the future.

Alcohol and Drug Abuse

Alcohol and drug abuse problems commonly contribute to desire disorders. These problems seem to be prevalent among the gay male population (Fifield, Latham, & Philips, 1978). Many gay men have learned to be sexual beings in association with the use of drugs or alcohol. Repeated association of alcohol and other drugs with a developing sexuality can inhibit the development of an integrated identity, including the development of intimacy skills. Some gay men can be sexual only when under the influence of some substance. Others, who stop using alcohol or drugs because of former abuse patterns, must face their fears, anxieties, and homophobic attitudes without the "crutch." Such fears and anxieties can inhibit one's sexual participation and can contribute to a low interest or a narrow repertoire that fails to satisfy a partner's preferences.

Many gay men who stop using alcohol or other drugs and enter treatment centers, or who become involved in self-help organizations, become "frozen" in their homophobia and may need to go through another "coming-out" process (Evans *et al.*, 1987). Those who identified themselves as "gay and proud" before sobriety usually possess a pseudopositive identity. Some react with low sexual desire, while others replace the alcohol with some other external agent to make them feel good (e.g., food, sex, work, etc.). Stripped of their familiar coping mechanisms, they need to avoid the dependence upon external agents for relieving pain and anxiety and to begin developing a truly integrated positive identity (see also Kus, 1987).

The impact of these changes on a relationship is enormous for anyone who lives in a relationship with someone who is chemically dependent. This problem is aggravated for the gay man or gay couple, because of the homophobic sentiment that exists in so many traditional chemical dependency treatment centers and Alcoholics Anonymous (AA) groups. This is why specialized treatment centers have been set up for gay alcoholics, and why gay AA and Al-Anon groups are widespread.

Besides these psychosocial aspects of alcoholism and drug abuse, the clinician must also be alert to the possible physical damage that may have occurred and that may relate directly to complaints of low sexual desire, as noted earlier.

Interpersonal Etiologies and Treatment

Stage Discrepancy Conflicts

To understand gay relationships and interpersonal etiologies of low sexual desire, the clinician should first become familiar with the six stages of relationship development outlined by McWhirter and Mattison (1984). An understanding of these stages is important, because many clinicians and clients see relationship conflicts arising out of underlying individual psychopathology or personality disorders, when in fact they often arise naturally at various stages of a relationship or in what McWhirter and Mattison (1987) describe as "stage discrepancy."

Therefore, low sexual desire may be viewed as symptomatic of conflict in a particular developmental stage of a relationship. For example, after the loss of limerance or the stage of blending, there is a decline in sexual interest. This can be overinterpreted by the gay man as "the beginning of the end," or more accurately understood as a natural step in the evolution of the relationship. Some clients, feeling a decline in their sexual drive, develop an irrational fear of losing the relationship; in some cases, this leads to a total loss of sexual desire.

In other cases, the problem may have its source in stage discrepancy. McWhirter and Mattison (1987) define "stage discrepancy" as the situation that exists "[w]hen one partner experiences characteristics of a stage sooner than the other" (p. 89). Stage discrepancies may manifest themselves in a variety of ways. Usually the conflicts that are seen in psychotherapy are (1) developing or maintaining intimacy; (2) power, competition, or control issues; (3) jealousy; and (4) differences in dealing with expressions of anger or tenderness (including sexual interest or desire).

McWhirter and Mattison's approach to working with gay couples emphasizes helping them to "normalize" the disturbances. Lessened sexual interest can be understood as a normal part of a particular relationship stage or a result of inevitable stage discrepancy difficulties. Often, the presenting or identified problem is reframed for a couple: The partners hear their problem described in terms of stage-related difficulties. As McWhirter and Mattison (1987) point out, "Providing a cognitive framework for looking at their relationship and the problems that they are experiencing removes some of the emotional pain that each is experiencing, and reduces the blame or the guilt that each may feel and interpret as failure in the relationship" (pp. 91–92). The cognitive realignment or reframing becomes the focus for subsequent therapeutic interactions. Once clients understand their struggle in terms of this different frame of reference, the clinician can help avoid the vicious cycle downward toward loss of sexual desire and/or termination of the relationship.

Furthermore, the therapist is able to help the couple to learn ways of finding compatability, to make compromises, and to adjust to undesirable habits and personality differences. Ultimately, the partners need to develop skills that allow them to be more accepting of each other and to view the differences in their relationship as assets rather than flaws. This model is extremely helpful in treating couples with problems of low sexual desire or discrepant levels of sexual desire.

Sexual Desire Discrepancies

As noted earlier, there may be more cases of sexual desire discrepancies in gay men than actual cases of low sexual desire. Levine (1984) recognizes that desire discrepancies constitute one type of desire problem that does not necessarily reflect a deficiency. He observes that desire levels range from absent or infrequent through frequent or strong and on to relentless. We define "desire discrepancies" as differences in the desired frequency of sex, or differences in preferences for time, place, style, role, or activities. In their discussion of desire discrepancies, Zilbergeld and Ellison (1980) suggest that the focus of therapists on low desire reflects a professional bias toward "more sex is better sex." Their treatment methods focus on desire discrepancies, rather than on high or low desire, as *the* problem to be treated. Individual pathology can cause low sexual desire or sexual compulsivity, but many typical cases can be understood from this systemic point of view.

The high-interest partner may learn through therapy that a desire for sex may really be a need for closeness or reassurance, or a need to diffuse exciting, uncomfortable, or anxious feelings. Such a client can learn to differentiate these feelings from sexual interest, or to relabel them and diffuse or express them in a nonsexual way. Conversely, the low-interest partner may be taught to relabel internal feelings such as excitement, restlessness, or even anxiety as sexual desire and then move from some appropriate "getting in the mood" activity to sex. Kaplan (1979) notes that the low-interest partner may have learned to associate negative thoughts and feelings with anticipation. Kaplan (1983) also points out that the low-interest partner may participate in sex not because he is interested, but perhaps to reassure himself of his own potency or to avoid hurting or losing his partner. Under such circumstances, he may comply with his partner's request reluctantly, with an attitude of "let's get it over with." He may be able to respond with an erection and orgasm if properly stimulated, but it may require intense use of fantasy, and he may experience little pleasure. He may be compelled to "tidy up" immediately after an orgasm and turn his attention quickly to other activities. Some low-interest partners enjoy physical affection, such as kissing, touching, and cuddling; others have developed an aversion even to affectionate touching, expecially if such activities usually lead either to unwanted sex or to yet another sexual rejection of the partner, both of which outcomes result in discomfort. The low-interest partner may avoid sex by bringing home work, by becoming busy or tired or depressed, or by starting an argument during the times at which sex could occur. Schmidt and Arentewicz (1983) observe that the low-interest partner's responses to his partner's interest in sex may vary among resigned patience, passive resistance, an impulse to escape, or a fear of failure.

In the assessment of sexual desire discrepancies, it is important to distinguish between low-interest partners who simply have a low interest in sex from those whose sexual desire is inhibited because of intrapsychic or interpersonal conflicts. It is equally important to understand the difference between high-interest partners who have a naturally high interest in sex and those whose sexual desire is hyperactive as a result of their own intrapsychic or interpersonal conflicts.

In most of the gay male couples we see, the partners do not have an equal sexual interest in each other. Zilbergeld and Ellison (1980) have stated that compatibility is an issue for every couple (regardless of sexual orientation) and is not insoluble. In attempting to resolve conflicts arising out of discrepancies in sexual interests, we seek to "normalize" the problem. It is helpful to explain to the partners that they did not decide to commit themselves to each other because of equal levels of interest in sex. There were many other dimensions of each other's personalities that drew them together.

Beyond normalizing their experience, it is helpful for couples to learn how to adjust to these desire discrepancies and how to keep them from interfering with their own individual psychological functioning or the functioning of the relationship (see Kaplan, 1979). The skills that are needed to help resolve these issues in work with gay couples are no different from the skills sex therapists need in work with similarly troubled hetero-sexual couples.

In preparing a couple for therapy, it is helpful to keep in mind the partners' level of commitment, extrarelational activities, power and control issues, individual motivations for sex, sexual repertoire, and communica-tion skills.

Commitment

The level of commitment must be evaluated and somehow judged "deep enough" before one proceeds with therapy. McWhirter and Mattison

(1978) have suggested that lack of commitment may be due to a lack of institutional supports (religious, family, or legal) for gay men in relationships. Consequently, many gay male couples see the stress of sexual desire discrepancies as a sign that the relationship is over, rather than as a problem to be solved. Perhaps because sex has been so easily available for most urban gay males, the immediate response to a sexual problem in a committed relationship is often to compensate by going outside the relationship for sexual satisfaction, or to end the relationship and to try to find someone more "sexually compatible." As McWhirter and Mattison (1984) note, some of this outside sexual activity has been psychologically functional for many couples. However, with the high degree of current concern over AIDS, more gay couples are looking for ways to solve these problems within the relationship rather than risk exposure to the AIDS virus.

Extrarelational Activity

If extrarelational sexual activities are taking place, the therapist needs to be careful not to impose values of monogamy or sexual exclusivity. Certainly, couples need to be educated about the risk of AIDS and about risk reduction measures. And they need to consider complications in the ways in which outside emotional or sexual relationships may interfere with the treatment of sexual and intimacy problems. If the therapist believes that outside relationships are the source of distancing or sexual desire problems, the couple should be given that information. The therapist may decide not to initiate therapy until these outside interferences are resolved in one way or another. The therapist needs to keep in mind that, in general, heterosexual and lesbian couples seem to have more difficulties in handling outside relationships than gay male couples. But, of course, each situation must be viewed individually.

Power Differences and Conflicts

Sexual desire discrepancies may have their roots in power differences and conflicts. Felt differences in power in a relationship can certainly contribute to less frequent sex. Seeing one's partner as having more prestige—whether because of age, attractiveness, material assets, education, or social status—may cause the "less powerful" partner to withhold sex, control it in some way, or make sexual demands in order to maintain the balance. A partner who feels less emotionally secure or has greater dependency needs (attachment or separation fears) sometimes attempts to manipulate the sexual relationship, usually unconsciously, to reassure himself. While the partner who feels less powerful may withhold sex or limit his participation in certain ways, the partner who feels more insecure or dependent is more likely to contribute to conflicts in his attempts to get reassurance through sex. The less powerful partner is more likely to decline sexual overtures, while the more dependent partner is more likely to want or demand more sex.

These power differences and conflicts are sometimes felt more acutely among gay male couples because of the competitive nature of two males in a relationship. Both typically have been socially conditioned or scripted to be in the position of control or power. Either the struggle for power or the perceived inequality of power can cause difficulties. For example, gay men are particularly overburdened with sociocultural expectations that push them toward becoming sexually "masculine" and using sex to deal with feelings. Tension states created by "being gay" or being in a gay male relationship can push one to acquire either a low interest or an excessive interest in sex.

Individual Motivations for Sex

Therapists can help couples learn to distinguish between "having sex," which includes tension relief, and "making love," which includes mutual pleasuring and assurances of love and appreciation. Both motivations can be alien to one or both of the individuals in a couple because of intrapsychic issues such as separation and attachment fears and anxieties, or because of sex-role stereotype conditioning and scripting.

For example, a number of gay men, especially those with rigid sex-role expectations, have difficulty seeing sex as an expression of love because they fear gender inappropriateness. Therefore, they avoid tender, devotional surrender, with which they associate passivity and femininity, and for which they compensate with genital-centered, explosive sexuality. Also, gay men who have had extensive experience with anonymous sexual encounters in sexually oriented settings (bath houses, adult book stores) may internalize negative or stereotypical attitudes about homosexuality. Consequently, these men have difficulties with intimacy once they find themselves in an intimate relationship in intimate surroundings. They are often quite uncomfortable with other than genitally oriented sex. Conversely, without some effort, a relatively emotionally insecure, dependent partner whose sexual needs include reassurances of attractiveness and permanence—and who is guilty and sexually inhibited—may not be able to enjoy a sexual relationship that is frequently genitally focused.

Knowing their own sexual preferences and appreciating the meanings of their lovers' individual preferences can help individuals ask for sexual activities that fit their needs or moods of the moment and that motivate them to develop a wider repertoire for themselves.

Sexual Repertoire

The etiology of decreased frequency of sex, or the immediate cause of sexual conflicts for some male couples, may relate to limits in sexual activities imposed by one of the partners. Or one of the lovers may not enjoy or may even dislike a specific activity that his partner feels is important. McWhirter and Mattison (1980), in their work with desire-phase disorders in male couples, noted that an aversion to specific acts was a greater issue than was a generalized lack of sexual desire. Preferences for anal or oral sex, a genitally focused orgasm versus more general sensuality, an imagination-based (emphasizing fantasy or role playing) versus a partner-focused sexual interaction, or an "earthy" attitude toward bodily secretions and smells versus a "hygienic" approach to sex are areas of conflict that are frequently mentioned. If some specific acts are issues, some education about compromise in these areas can alleviate many of these differences. Assistance in helping couples expand their sexual repertoires can be appropriate.

Communication Patterns

As indicated, many issues need to be considered in the treatment of sexual desire discrepancies. Effectively addressing these issues requires good communication. Problematic communication styles and patterns not only may be the cause of a problem, but can exacerbate any problem. Problems with initiating and refusing sex are frequently observed areas of conflict that may be related only to inadequate communication skills. McWhirter and Mattison (1980) found that problems with initiating sex were a greater issue among the couples they saw than a lack of sexual interest was. Poor communication skills add to almost any other issue or problem, whether it is a difference in preferred ways of having sex or a problem of parental transferences from childhood. Couples can become frustrated to the point of defeat.

The therapy of desire-phase disorders, including desire discrepancies, involves basic communication skills. Each individual needs to discover or rediscover his own sexual desires and anxieties, and to communicate these appropriately to his partner; the partners can then accommodate themselves in some degree to each other's particular sexual preferences. All this increases their mutual satisfaction, and, as Levine (1984) observes, helps resolve problems through negotiation rather than through desire.

Case Illustrations

To illustrate some of the etiological and treatment considerations discussed above, we present the following two cases. The first case represents a more successful outcome; the second case illustrates more complexity and a poorer outcome.

Case 1: Alan and Bill

Description and Background

Alan was referred for sex therapy because of his dissatisfaction with the frequency of sex in his relationship with Bill. Both men were in individual psychotherapy with separate therapists, were in their late 20s, and were involved in successful careers.

In their first session, Alan and Bill complained of having had sex together only a few times during the course of their 18-month relationship. Alan was angry and blamed Bill for not providing him with a fully satisfying sex life; Bill blamed Alan and criticized his inhibitions about sex and his lack of effort in their attempts to increase the frequency of sex with each other.

Alan had grown up in an upper-class, highly educated, New England Protestant family in which emotional expression was inhibited and references to sex were rare. Alan remembered that when he was a young child his mother had discovered him masturbating and had reacted with embarrassment and anger. Alan's therapist thought that Alan's mother had attempted in some way to use Alan as a replacement for his father because of the frustrations in her marriage. Alan had become aware of his anger about being used that way, his feelings of inadequacy about not being able to satisfy his mother's needs, and his guilt about his attempt to replace his father. Bill had grown up in a middle-class, urban, second-generation Irish–Catholic family in which he was the "good" child. Both his older and his younger brothers were more defiant, rebellious, and antisocial.

Alan's and Bill's attainment of a positive gay identity had been successful. They had struggled against negative internalized parental messages and injurious contemporary cultural attitudes and had "come out" to most of their family members, friends, and coworkers; they had developed an integrated and balanced view about themselves, their associates, and their work.

Bill had been involved once before in a committed, loving relationship with another man, but this was the first time Alan had become seriously involved. Sex in Bill's previous relationship had been satisfying and nonproblematic. Each had experienced one-time encounters with many different partners, and each had also experienced short periods of sexual and social involvement with one person.

Bill tended to use frequent sex to manage anxiety, and his sexual activity bordered on sexual compulsivity or addiction. His early sexual experiences had primarily consisted of encounters with strangers in public restrooms. He referred frequently to his feelings of emptiness and to his attempts to fill that void with sex—more so in the past, but occasionally in his more recent history. He recognized that he still used masturbation as a way of reducing anxiety. He said that he consistently felt "bad" after sex, both in the past with new partners and currently with Alan. He felt guilty about imposing his needs on Alan, and felt fearful that Alan might not agree to some of what he wanted.

Even though Alan's history of sexual experiences was less varied than Bill's, he had always been sexually comfortable with new partners whom he never expected to see again. Only when he liked someone well enough to see him again did his need to please, his feelings of inadequacy, and his discomfort about sexual contact with more emotionally intimate partners surface and create difficulty. At the time that Alan and Bill entered sex therapy, neither was having sex outside the relationship. That had occurred rarely since they had become involved, and only early in their relationship.

Course of Treatment

Initial screening revealed that both partners had a commitment to the relationship and a motivation to work on their issues. For the first several weeks, they participated in a series of highly structured sensate focus activities.

Several resistances or blocks emerged and were addressed during the early phase of the process. Alan had always thoroughly enjoyed frequent masturbation alone and had developed rather imaginative fantasies in association with this activity. Because it is often helpful to expand on and integrate into the relationship ways in which a person already enjoys sex, attempts were made to help the partners develop role-playing sessions together using some of Alan's fantasies. However, Alan was too embarrassed to describe his sexual fantasies to Bill or to stimulate his genitals directly in Bill's presence. The therapist helped Alan become comfortable both with using erotic language and with masturbating in front of Bill. With desensitization to touching his body and describing both the physical sensations and emotional discomforts he was experiencing, Alan was able to become comfortable with touching himself genitally in Bill's presence. This sequence of exercises increased Alan's ability to communicate specific desires, and they relieved the anger he felt at Bill's not being able to somehow perceive his (Alan's) sexual needs and to meet them (without Alan's having to confront his own inhibitions and anxieties).

Both partners were oriented toward focusing on the other person's pleasure and felt trapped by performance pressure and guilt. Bill wanted to indulge himself sometimes in his own pleasure and preferences, yet he saw this as selfish. He was also fearful of Alan's revulsion toward some of his desires, such as wanting Alan to stimulate his genitals orally. Therefore, he held himself back; he tried to distance himself and respond to Alan's preferences. At the beginning of therapy, Alan was so oriented toward Bill's needs and responses that he was unaware of his own needs. He felt that he was unable to satisfy Bill's sexual preferences.

A series of exercises was designed to help the partners learn how to express their own pleasurable sensations. Both experienced some anxiety during these exercises, but they learned to verbalize the fear and to continue the structured activity. Out of these experiences, Alan learned the extent to which he resented the pressure to please Bill.

Alan returned to individual therapy for a few sessions to explore some feelings he was having about his mother's expected visit. He quickly associated his attempts to satisfy Bill with his lifelong attempts to please his mother in order to gain her love and acceptance; concurrently, he rebelled against the therapist's structure and control of the therapy process. He frequently became angry at Bill when it was time for them to work together, and their jobs or social plans often interfered with their assigned activities. Alan took more and more responsibility for setting the time for their activities together and designed the specifics of these activities. They were encouraged to talk out their angry feelings to help keep them from interfering with their structured activities.

Other issues arose as the weeks went on. Work, expecially out-ot-town trips for one or both of them, frequently interrupted the therapy process; social obligations also interfered. The partners were repeatedly encouraged to make the therapy process a high priority, and they began making appointments with each other to do the exercises before they left the therapist's office.

One session was spent clarifying their understandings about safer sex practices and defining the sexual activities about which they felt comfortable. Therapy goals were altered accordingly. For example, neither felt completely safe engaging in anal sex even with the use of condoms, so achieving a degree of comfort about that specific act no longer remained a goal. Alan had an aversion to natural body fluids associated with sex; when Bill was sexually aroused, his body produced large amounts of pre-ejaculatory fluid. Alan was so put off by this that he was even unable to stimulate Bill's genitals manually, and they had agreed that oral sex (without ejaculation) was within their acceptable range of safer sex practices. Since Alan had already learned to focus on his own sensations while stimulating Bill, that principle was incorporated into his step-by-step process of manual stimulation of Bill's genitals. He also practiced that activity while he was otherwise sexually excited, and became somewhat desensitized through the use of large amounts of various lubricants.

As the process of therapy entered its third and last phase, the frequency of their structured activities decreased while the frequency of sex increased, often at Alan's initiation. Each had long felt unappreciated by the other (for the effort extended and the sacrifice endured). Bill had learned during the middle phase of the therapy that to demand sex, complain about skipping exercises, or to act otherwise in a way that increased Alan's performance pressures, guilt, or feelings of inadequacy was detrimental to their progress. Yet he needed acknowledgment of his patience. They explored ways in which Bill could initiate sex and could experience and verbalize his inhibitions and pressure anxieties, yet could take the necessary actions in spite of his discomfort. They learned the value of reinforcing each other and of stating their appreciation of each other.

As the process entered the closing sessions, they continued to do fewer of the structured activities, yet they reported more frequent spontaneous sex, which Alan often initiated. At the close of therapy they both agreed that they had learned how to talk better about their feelings and conflicts and to be supportive and appreciative; they had also significantly increased the frequency and variety of sex together. Alan had not become comfortable with fellating Bill.

During a 3-month telephone follow-up, the partners indicated that they were continuing to use their newfound communication skills to advantage and were having sex one to two times a week with more variety. Alan was still aversive to performing oral sex, and they were beginning to talk of including anal sex in their repertoire.

Commentary

In this case, the inhibited sexual desire was specifically related to the context of the relationship. Organicity was ruled out in the assessment, as were physical or functional effects of alcohol or drug abuse. Assessment for intrapsychic factors did not reveal anything specific, except that the effects of AIDS fears in both individuals were recognized as important to address in therapy.

While there was a strong commitment to the relationship, and no stage discrepancy problems were evident, Alan and Bill never experienced much of a blending or limerance stage as described by McWhirter and Mattison (1984). Communication problems were evident, and the etiology of the dysfunction was mostly interpersonal.

Treating this case was relatively simple, and the results were positive.

Case 2: Cid and Dave

Cid initiated sex therapy because he was concerned about the growing distance between himself and his lover of 6 years, Dave. Cid felt that Dave was a workaholic and, furthermore, was too sexually demanding. He felt confused, frustrated, angry, anxious, and depressed. When asked whether Dave was available for therapy, Cid indicated that it was unlikely Dave would cooperate. Over the next few weeks, Cid extended the invitation to Dave several times, and Dave eventually came to a session. He entered therapy cautiously, but stated his willingness to work on the relationship, since he was committed to Cid and loved him very much. Individual therapy continued with Cid between couples sessions.

Early Course of Treatment

During those first few weeks, Cid worked to identify and express his hurt feelings about Dave's general unavailability and lack of emotional support. Cid was feeling left out of the relationship and was beginning to question his own worth. In conjoint sessions, attempts to get Dave to explore his feelings about the relationship were largely unproductive. In many of the sessions, Cid worked to develop his ability to communicate his vulnerabilities to Dave, and Dave worked on acquiring an understanding of Cid's feelings and learning to provide more attention, support, and nurturing.

At one conjoint session Dave, who had become consistently cooperative and supportive of Cid, became angry. He expressed his resentment about being treated as the "bad guy" in the relationship, the only one who had to change. He resented Cid's lesser workload and his propensity to spend his (Dave's) money freely (their incomes were at quite different levels), which contributed to Dave's felt need to work harder. He also stated his desire for more frequent and more varied sex, and his incomprehension of and impatience about Cid's resistance. Dave also indicated that he wanted to explore some of his feelings about work; he began individual sessions as well.

In couples therapy, both quickly learned some new communication skills and implemented them into their relationship, which allowed them to air resentments and hurts and to cooperate on resolving problems. Cid, who had become more content, talked about leaving therapy, but with Dave's urging, he agreed to stay in conjoint therapy to work on sexual issues. Dave wanted to explore more fully ways of coping better with job pressures, so he stayed in individual therapy.

Description and Background

Although pieces of their histories relevant to their sexual relationship had emerged, more specific and detailed information now began to come out. Except for the first few months of their relationship, sex had occurred only once every 2–3 weeks, usually at Dave's insistence, and was limited to genital self-stimulation in each other's presence. Cid was quite satisfied with this, but Dave wanted more frequency and more variety. He had tried strategies to steer Cid in these directions—everything from wooing Cid romantically to role-playing "heavier" sex scenes. But nothing seemed to make a difference, and Dave had almost stopped trying to effect change, feeling that he could no longer suffer the repeated rejections. Cid complained that he usually felt alone in sex with Dave; it seemed to him that when Dave became aroused he went away, into his head, and left Cid out.

Both had been involved in earlier committed relationships that had lasted from a few months to several years. Between periods of being with a lover, Cid was virtually sexually abstinent. Between serious involvements, Dave typically dated one person for short periods and had occasional one-night stands.

At the time they met, Cid was a part of a bawdy, outrageous nightclub act that included many explicit references to exotic sexual acts and libertine lifestyles. Dave had expected that Cid would be an uninhibited partner, and he was puzzled about the sexual incompatibility in their relationship.

Cid's family history seemed conventional, as did his sexual history, except for two elements. He began sexual explorations with partners in his early 20s, which is rather late, but not an unusual experience for a young gay man who is ambivalent about his sexual orientation or ambivalent about acting on his desires. Even after his initial experiences, his sexual contacts were sporadic and infrequent. However, during one of those encounters, he was sexually forced and anally raped. During sexual history taking and in subsequent sessions, he had little to say about his past sexual feelings and attitudes, insisting that the subject was not important to him. He was also reluctant to discuss the rape, but acknowledged that it had been traumatic and that he had avoided sex for a long time after the rape. He insisted, however, that he had recovered and that the rape no longer caused problems. He also agreed to explore the subject further but did not feel as if there was much to say.

Dave had grown up in a family in which his father's business, of a public service nature, claimed first priority. As a child, he had to be ready to respond to customers 24 hours a day, 7 days a week. Family members' schedules, needs, and problems were second in importance to the business. His parents had separated for about a year when he was 3, and he had lived with his mother. He remembered how hard he worked to please his father, who was always involved with some project related to either the home or the business. Vacations were nonexistent.

Dave's sexual history was unremarkable. Although he had explored the "bar scene," his shyness and fear of rejection kept him from feeling comfortable about it. He had always met his sexual partners and past lovers primarily through friends. In past relationships, the sexual aspects had not been problematic.

During the course of their relationship, outside sexual contacts were rare to nonexistent, although Dave feared that Cid might be draining off sexual energy with outside partners. In private sessions, Cid never indicated anything of that nature, and it seemed that Dave's doubts were based more on his own fear of inadequacy and abandonment.

Later Course of Treatment

Since the partners seemed committed and otherwise very happy with their relationship, especially after the earlier conjoint sessions, they began a series of sensate focus exercises that did not include sex. The purpose was to sharpen their ability to focus on their independent sensatons, to learn how to communicate their wishes and desires more comfortably and clearly to each other, and to learn how to complement each other sexually.

All went smoothly the first few sessions, but then Cid started resisting by postponing the exercises. When confronted about that behavior, he renewed commitments to follow through. Yet his resistance persisted. The structure was changed to provide him more opportunity to explore his desires at his own pace. Dave remained cooperative, only occasionally showing his hurt and impatience. In the sessions, Cid recognized his lack of follow-through, but insisted he simply had a low sex drive. Attempts were then made to find ways for Cid to respond to Dave's sexual needs more often without going through a full sexual response cycle, by simply being available and affectionate. That worked for a while, but soon they were locked in the old patterns: Dave would suggest sex, Cid would put it off, and Dave would feel frustrated and hurt.

Dave became increasingly depressed. Work pressures intensified, and he began to question his competency more, working harder and longer as a result. His depression caused him to become more interested in Cid's emotional support than in sex; thus sexual issues were postponed. Cid stopped sex therapy, and Dave continued in individual therapy for another year, during which time he sometimes achieved a satisfactory level of sex but often encountered the usual frustrations. As his depression lifted and his interest in sex re-emerged, he made some effort to persuade Cid to return to therapy to work on those issues; however, Cid seemed even more resistant. Dave left therapy, relieved of his depression and happier with the relationship than ever before, even though the sexual aspects had not changed. Over the past year, Cid and Dave have indicated that their relationship continues to be a devoted and happy one, although no change has occurred in the sexual area.

Commentary

In this second case, Cid was experiencing inhibited sexual desire in general. Organicity was ruled out, and assessment for intrapsychic and interpersonal problems was completed. While some interpersonal problems were noted (communication difficulties), most of the problems seemed to be intrapsychic in nature—for Cid. There was a strong commitment to the relationship.

In the assessment, all of the intrapsychic problems were not revealed. In retrospect, several factors seemed to be relevant. While Cid described no overt problems with sexual identity development or homophobia, these were probably deep-seated and disguised problems for him.

Treatment in this second case was not as successful as in the first. In retrospect, Cid had many more feelings in regard to being raped than he ever discussed in the assessment or treatment. Nor was he ever able to talk deeply about his family of origin and the way sex was dealt with as he was growing up. In fact, he was never able to talk comfortably about sex at all, in spite of the fact that he was involved in a nightclub act that was highly sexual. He was, underneath the surface, extremely inhibited about sex. These factors were given too little attention in therapy and contributed to a less successful outcome in this case. More time should have been spent in exploring the sexual trauma; more psychotherapy for Cid along with the conjoint psychotherapy could have helped.

Conclusion

The treatment of low sexual desire among gay men presents some unique problems and circumstances. This chapter has attempted to summarize these unique dynamics. While many methods of treating inhibited sexual desire are applicable to treating gay male couples, understanding these unique dynamics will improve the outcome of treatment. We hope that this information will be helpful to many sex therapists by furthering their understanding of potential etiological factors—intrapsychic, interpersonal, and cultural. Furthermore, we hope that the treatment strategies outlined in this chapter will increase treatment effectiveness.

References

Araoz, D. (1982). *Hypnosis and sex therapy.* New York: Brunner/Mazel.

Arentewicz, G., Schmidt, G. (Eds.). (1983). *The treatment of sexual disorders.* New York: Basic Books.

Bell, A. P., & Weinberg, M. S. (1978). *Homosexualities: A study of diversity among men and women.* New York: Simon & Schuster.

Block, J. H. (1973). Conceptions of sex role: Some cross cultural and longitudinal perspectives. *American Psychologist, 28,* 512–526.

Blumstein, P., & Schwartz, P. (1983). *American couples: Money, work, and sex.* New York: Morrow.

Carnes, P. (1983). *Out of the shadows: Understanding sexual addiction.* Minneapolis: Comp-Care.

Carnes, P. (1986). Progress in sexual addiction: An addiction perspective. *SIECUS Report, 14*(6), 4–6.

Cass, V. (1979). Homosexual identity formation: A theoretical model. *Journal of Homosexuality, 4,* 219–235.

Coleman, E. (1981/1982). Developmental stages of the coming out process. *Journal of Homosexuality, 7*(2/3), 31–43.

Coleman, E. (1986). Sexual compulsion vs. sexual addiction: The debate contines. *SIECUS Report, 14*(6), 7–11.

Coleman, E. (1987a). Assessment of sexual orientation. *Journal of Homosexuality, 14*(1/2), 13–22.

Coleman, E. (Ed.) (1987b). *Chemical dependency and intimacy dysfunction.* New York: Haworth Press.

Coleman, E. (Ed.) (1987c). *Psychotherapy with homosexual men and women: Integrated identity approaches for clinical practice.* New York: Haworth Press.

Coleman, E. (1987d). Sexual compulsivity: Definition, etiology and treatment. *Journal of Chemical Dependency Treatment, 1*(1).

Colgan, P. (1987). Treatment of identity and intimacy issues in gay males. *Journal of Homosexuality, 14*(1/2), 97–118.

Evans, S., Schaefer, S., & Coleman, E. (1987). Sexual orientation concerns among chemically dependent individuals. *Journal of Chemical Dependency Treatment, 1*(1).

Fifield, L., Latham, T. D., & Philips, C. (1978). *Alcoholism in the gay community: The price of alienation, isolation and oppression.* Sacramento: California Division of Substance Abuse.

Finkelhor, D. (1979). *Sexually victimized children.* New York: Free Press.

Forstein, M. (1984). AIDS anxiety in the "worried well." In S. Nichols & D. Ostrow (Eds.), *Psychiatric implications of acquired immune deficiency syndrome.* Washington, DC: American Psychiatric Press.

Friend, R. (1987). The individual and social psychology of aging: Clinical implications for lesbians and gay men. *Journal of Homosexuality, 14*(1.2), 299–323.

George, K. D., & Behrendt, A. E. (1987). Therapy for male couples experiencing relationship problems and sexual problems. *Journal of Homosexuality, 14*(1/2), 75–86.

Gonsiorek, J. (Ed.). (1982). *Homosexuality and psychotherapy.* New York: Haworth Press.

Hall, M. (1987). Sex therapy with lesbian couples. A four stage approach. *Journal of Homosexuality, 14*(1/2), 131–150.

Hammersmith, S. K. (1987). A sociological approach to counseling homosexual clients and their families. *Journal of Homosexuality, 14*(1/2). 151–168.

Harowski, K. (1987). The worried well: Maximizing coping in the face of AIDS. *Journal of Homosexuality, 14*(1/2), 291–298.

Kaplan, H. S. (1979). *Disorders of sexual desire.* New York: Brunner/Mazel.

Kaplan, H. S. (1983). *The evaluation of sexual disorders.* New York: Brunner/Mazel.

Kus, R. J. (1987). Alcoholics Anonymous and gay American men. *Journal of Homosexuality, 14*(1/2), 245–267.

Levine, S. B. (1984). An essay on the nature of sexual desire. *Journal of Sex and Marital Therapy, 10,* 84–96.

Masters, W. H., & Johnson, V. E. (1979). *Homosexuality in perspective.* Boston: Little, Brown.

McCarthy, W. B. (1984). Strategies and techniques for the treatment of inhibited sexual desire. *Journal of Sex and Marital Therapy, 10,* 97–105.

McWhirter, D. P., & Mattison, A. M. (1978). The treatment of sexual dysfunction in gay male couples. *Journal of Sex and Marital Therapy, 4,* 213–218.

McWhirter, D. P., & Mattison, A. M. (1980). Treatment of sexual dysfunction in homosexual male couples. In S. R. Leiblum & L. A. Pervin (Eds.), *Principles and practice of sex therapy.* New York: Guilford Press.

McWhirter, D. P., & Mattison, A. M. (1984). *The male couple: How relationships develop.* Englewood Cliffs, NJ: Prentice-Hall.

McWhirter, D. P., & Mattison, A. M. (1987). Stage discrepancy in male couples. *Journal of Homosexuality, 14*(1/2), 87–96.

Morin, S., Charles, K., & Maylon, A. (1984). The psychological impact of AIDS on gay men. *American Psychologist, 39,* 1288–1293.

Quadland, M. (1985). Compulsive sexual behavior: Definition of a problem and an approach to treatment. *Journal of Sex and Marital Therapy, 1*(2).

Quadland, M. C., & Shattls, W. D. (1987). AIDS, sexuality and sexual control. *Journal of Homosexuality, 14*(1/2), 269–290.

Reece, R. (1987). Causes and treatments of sexual desire discrepancies in male couples. *Journal of Homosexuality, 14*(1/2), 169–184.

Reece, R., & Segrist, A. E. (1981). The association of selected "masculine" sex-role variables with length of relationship in gay male couples. *Journal of Homosexuality, 7*(1), 33–47.

Schmidt, G. (1983). Introduction: Sexuality and relationships. In G. Arentewicz & G. Schmidt (Eds.), *The treatment of sexual disorders.* New York: Basic Books.

Smalley, S. (1982). *Co-dependency: An introduction.* Brighton, MN: SBS.

Smalley, S., & Coleman, E. (1987). Treatment of intimacy dysfunction in dyadic relationships among chemically dependent and codependent clients. *Journal of Chemical Dependency Treatment, 1*(1).

Sophie, J. (1987). Internalized homophobia and lesbian identity. *Journal of Homosexuality, 14*(1/2), 51–63.

Tripp, C. A. (1975). *The homosexual matrix.* New York: McGraw-Hill.

Zilbergeld, B., & Ellison, C. R. (1980). Desire discrepancies and arousal problems in sex therapy. In S. R. Leiblum & L. A. Pervin (Eds.), *Principles and practice of sex therapy.* New York: Guilford Press.

16

Conclusion: Conceptual and Clinical Overview

SANDRA R. LEIBLUM AND RAYMOND C. ROSEN

As evidenced by the preceding chapters, disorders of desire have clearly come to occupy a central position in current sex therapy theory and practice. In addition to being among the most prevalent and perplexing sexual complaints facing practitioners nowadays, desire problems present a theoretically challenging "new frontier" for the field. Our overall goal in the present book has been to explore current models of sexual desire, in addition to capturing the prevailing clinical climate regarding assessment and treatment of desire disorders. Contributors have been selected as outstanding innovators in the practice sex therapy generally, as well as representing the current spectrum of treatment approaches to desire problems in particular. Finally, a kaleidoscopic array of clinical approaches has been presented, yielding a many-faceted and diverse perspective on the topic.

In reviewing the chapters in the present book, it is clear that there is considerable disagreement among our contributors with respect to both theory and practice. In fact, there are few generalizations that can safely be made about a topic as broad as this. Nonetheless, we would suggest that at least five central issues or concerns presently stand out as paramount: the diversity of conceptual and theoretical models for desire disorders; the diversity of causes proposed for problems of desire; the role of organic factors, psychiatric illness, and drug effects; the role of relationship factors; and factors associated with treatment success or failure.

Diversity of Conceptual and Theoretical Models

Treatment methods for desire problems are evolving rapidly in response to growing clinical needs, and appear to be proliferating despite the lack of basic research and theory on sexual desire. It is noteworthy that much of the conceptual and theoretical framework for our present discussion of desire disorders has been developed on the basis of clinical observations and practice, rather than from laboratory or field research. This is in marked contrast to the historical development of other aspects of our discipline. For example, before publishing *Human Sexual Inadequacy* in 1970, Masters and Johnson had completed a decade of laboratory physiological studies on sexual response, the results of which formed the foundation of their diagnostic and classification system and subsequent sex therapy treatment model. Similarly, Wolpe's (1958) densensitization method for the clinical treatment of anxiety-based sexual dysfunctions was derived from his theory of "reciprocal inhibition" and from earlier studies of conditioned avoidance behavior in cats.

Conceptual models of sexual desire have also tended to focus on specific, and at times rather narrow, views of libido. Some of the chapters in this book have been specifically written to reflect the importance of a particular contributing factor (e.g., drugs, hormones) or technique (e.g., hypnosis, script modification), rather than presenting a broader theory of sexual desire. The value of discussing specific issues and techniques should not be minimized, however, in view of the variety of patients and problems discussed. Nevertheless, no single theoretical approach has achieved ascendancy, and a lack of consensus exists at present concerning both etiology and treatment.

At a theoretical level, the conceptual formulations of desire offered run the gamut from the global and comprehensive (e.g., Levine, Chapter 2; Verhulst and Heiman, Chapter 10) to the detailed and specific. In Chapter 15, for example, Coleman and Reece address the particular sexual desire issues in the gay male population, and the impact of the acquired immune deficiency syndrom (AIDS) epidemic on the experience and expression of desire in this group. AIDS can affect the experience of desire directly (e.g., by creating anxiety that inhibits the subjective experience) or indirectly (i.e., by leading to the suppression of sexual activity because of the threat of possible fatal long-term consequences). As Coleman and Reece note, many gay men who would have been likely to seek anonymous sexual contacts are attempting to develop and maintain monogamous sexual lifestyles. Similarly, heterosexual men and women are more likely to think twice before engaging in casual sex. Masturbation frequency and sexual fantasy may come to be more reliable indices of sexual interest than dyadic sexual behavior in future years. Certainly, the omnipresent reality of sexually transmitted diseases generally has been a major factor in influencing sexual interactions for both homosexual and heterosexual individuals in recent years.

Diversity of Proposed Causes

Desire difficulties are evident across a diversity of individuals, couples, and lifestyles. In reviewing the present chapters, we are struck by the multiplicity of causal factors and patient characteristics presented. LoPiccolo and Friedman (Chapter 5), for example, identify 12 specific individual causes and 7 relationship factors often operative in these cases. Similarly, Verhulst and Heiman (Chapter 10) have discussed numerous systemic and interactional effects that determine desire. Writing from a multimodal framework, Lazarus (Chapter 6) encourages the evaluation of seven separate modalities that may underlie or be associated with these difficulties. Finally, the chapters by Segraves (Chapters 11 and 12) and Bullard (Chapter 13) attest further to the plethora of physical and hormonal antecedents that are potentially contributors to these problems.

Given this striking diversity of patient and problem types, some authors have argued that the diagnosis of inhibited sexual desire (ISD) reflects a premature labeling and possible pathologizing of purely symptomatic behavior (Clearing-Sky & Thornton, 1987). According to this viewpoint, the label of "ISD" represents nothing more than a catch-all descriptor for a relatively heterogenous set of underlying individual or relationship problems. In addition, while most of our contributors have emphasized the role of intrapsychic determinants of low desire, empirical evidence for this association has been equivocal at best. For example, one recent study investigating psychological characteristics of female patients with low desire (Stuart, Hammond, & Pett, 1986) found no statistically significant differences between women with ISD and married controls on any of the 10 primary clinical scales of the Minnesota Multiphasic Personality Inventory (MMPI). In fact, the two groups differed only in their level of sexual interest in their mates. These authors caution: "Until our knowledge is more complete, it may be judicious for clinicians to refrain from assuming that intrapsychic symptomatology is associated with ISD" (1986, p. 114).

Nevertheless, several of our contributors include assessment of character type and ego defenses in their etiological and treatment formulations. In particular, Levine (Chapter 2), Scharff (Chapter 3), and Apfelbaum (Chapter 4) make frequent reference to personality style and transferential issues. Furthermore, Scharff suggests that the working out of the transference relationship is a critical component in successful outcome for long-standing desire problems.

Even those chapters written from a cognitive–behavioral perspective seem to include personality traits as etiologically significant. LoPiccolo and Friedman (Chapter 5), for example, identify the anhedonic or obsessive–compulsive personality as particularly vulnerable to these problems. Such individuals may not only lack the capacity to "play," but may find the expression of any strong emotion to be conflict-laden. Furthermore, these authors suggest that obsessive–compulsive individuals may experience close bodily contact and sticky fluid emissions as unpleasant or even aversive. Clinically, it is not uncommon to find some obsessive–compulsive individuals presenting with long-term lack of sexual interest. It is not at all clear, however, why many other obsessive–compulsive individuals are sexually competent and desirous!

Male–female differences in desire are similarly controversial. LoPiccolo and Friedman, for example, observe that while problems of ISD initially were more obvious in women than in men, the sex ratio seems to have changed markedly over the last decade. In fact, statistics from their center suggest that more males than females currently present with this problem. Data from our own recent large-scale follow-up study of 500 patients (Rosen & Leiblum, 1987) indicate that approximately equal numbers of men and women have been treated for desire disorders in the past 5 years. On the other hand, our statistics indicate that the mean age of women presenting with ISD is in the early 30s, while for men it is in the early 40s. Also, women in our sample more frequently presented with *situational* desire problems, whereas men were more often diagnosed as experiencing *global* low desire. In accounting for this difference, we have found that female partners are both more aware of and less willing to tolerate relationship distress, and consequently that desire in women is more readily disrupted by relationship factors.

The Role of Organic Factors, Psychiatric Illness, and Drug Effects

Recognizing that biological factors may be implicated in some instances of global low desire, we have found little evidence for a more general role of organic etiology in desire disorders. Our contributors also seem to differ widely in the degree of emphasis placed on these factors. According to Levine (Chapter 2), for example, "biological drive" represents a core dimension of sexual desire, but he nevertheless views it as a less important cause of low desire than psychological motivation. Certainly any medical condition that affects endocrine function can be associated with diminished desire, as discussed in detail by Segraves (Chapter 11) and Bullard (Chapter 13). Both of these authors caution, however, that psychological factors can frequently augment or override the effects of any particular medical condition. Furthermore, Apfelbaum (Chapter 4) suggests that clinicians may tend to invoke a biological explanation for these problems in response to an inadequate understanding of the relevant intrapsychic or interpersonal determinants. Biological factors, according to Apfelbaum, account for an insignificant number of desire problems; he presents these problems as essentially due to "response anxiety."

In addition to organic factors, several authors have commented on the role of psychiatric illness as etiologically important. Perhaps the best evidence of this to date comes from a recent study by Schreiner-Engel and Schiavi (1986), showing that a history of affective disorder (namely, major or intermittent episodes of depression) is significantly associated with the diagnosis of global ISD. Specifically, these authors compared 46 married subjects with low desire to 26 matched controls on a variety of psychological and endocrine measures. Although few of the low-desire subjects were found to have symptoms of overt psychiatric illness at the time of assessment, most had a significantly elevated lifetime prevalence of affective disorder, particularly severe depression. Moreover, the first depressive episode nearly always preceded or occurred concomitantly with the onset of low desire. In addition, more women with the diagnosis of ISD had symptoms indicative of severe premenstrual syndrome. These researchers suggest that abnormalities in central monaminergic processes may be involved in the etiology of both affective disorders and sexual desire disorders.

In general, attempts to enhance desire pharmacologically or hormonally have generally met with disappointing results. On the basis of his comprehensive review of drug effects on desire, Segraves (Chapter 12) concludes that the perennial "search for libido enhancers" has all too often led to erroneous and misleading results. The evidence is much stronger, according to Segraves, for drug-induced supression of desire in individuals being treated with antihypertensive or psychotropic medications. It should be noted, however, that several controlled clinical trials are currently evaluating the effects of antidepressant and antianxiety drugs as direct or indirect treatment for low desire (e.g., Crenshaw, Goldberg, & Stern, 1987; Klein, Mendels, Lief, & Phillips, 1987). Certainly it has been shown that tricyclic antidepressants can have a positive effect on desire in clinically depressed individuals (Thase *et al.,* 1986). It is not clear, however, to what extent these enhancing effects are mediated by the nonspecific impact of the drugs on overall physical or psychological health.

Although they have met with little success to date, specific pharmacological interventions for sexual dysfunctions generally continue to capture the interest and imagination of professionals and patients alike. Furthermore, given that the search for a perfect aphrodisiac has been a continuing theme throughout the history of our society, it is likely that pharmacological solutions will continue to be sought in the future. Certainly, there is mounting evidence that suppression of desire in sexually compulsive males is readily accomplished via the use of antiandrogenic agents (e.g., Berlin, 1983), and these drugs are currently the treatment of choice for many of these individuals. Overall, it seems that pharmacological interventions are of more value in cases of hyperactive desire than of ISD.

The Role of Relationship Factors

At the present time, a majority of therapists (and their clients) tend to subscribe to the belief that sexual exchange belongs solely in the context of a loving, intimate, and committed relationship. It is not surprising, therefore, that relationship factors and couples dynamics have featured prominently in most clinical accounts of desire disorders. However, we have been reminded recently by Gagnon (1987) and others that this association is entirely a product of the values and expectations of our present-day society. Thus, in other places or times, the presence of an intimate relationship might be regarded as irrelevant to or even incompatible with sexual interest.

Furthermore, while several contributors have emphasized the role of emotional distance or conflict in a relationship as contributing to low desire, Nichols (Chapter 14) aptly observes that excessive closeness can be as deleterious to desire as insufficient intimacy. For example, when a couple begins to "fuse" psychologically, or fails to establish sufficient interpersonal distance, the relationship may become filial rather than sexual. Similarly, Schwartz and Masters (Chapter 9) have described the role of "enmeshment" in suppressing sexual desire. It is noteworthy, however, that in many of our cases involving severe marital discord, we have found that relationship improvement may occur following treatment, without a concomitant change in sexual desire. This is especially apparent in our treatment "failure" cases, where couples frequently report enhanced feelings of closeness and intimacy at treatment termination, without displaying any significant change in the quantity or quality of sexual initiation. We have little basis at present for predicting when relationship improvement is likely to lead to enhanced desire.

In addition, we would encourage greater attention by researchers and clinicians alike to those factors that might stimulate or suppress libido over the course of long-term relationships. The waxing and waning of desire, which clearly characterize many of these relationships (cf. Blumstein & Schwartz, 1983), should be assumed to be normative rather than exceptional. Certainly, the arrival of children, the demands and stresses of dual-career relationships, and the daily "wear and tear" of contemporary family life are obvious examples of factors that may adversely affect sexual interest. While long-lasting sexual monogamy need not become monotonous, couples must be cautioned that the flames of desire will not burn continuously without stoking and refueling!

Given the multiplicity of causes that can suppress desire, we have also found it valuable to invite couples to identify those situations, contexts, or scripts that elicit sexual interest. The oft-repeated refrain in this regard is about lusting after a mate until one "catches" him or her. Thus, clients typically recall experiencing a high level of desire in the courtship stages of a relationship, when idealization of the partner is common and a state of "limerance" prevails. During this early stage, compliments may flow like champagne, and a partner's virtues rather than flaws are lovingly extolled. Ambiguity and uncertainty about the future may further stimulate sexual interest. Resistance or obstacles to the relationship can similarly function as lust enhancers, as does the disapproval of significant others.

During the later stages in the relationship, when access to the partner becomes reliably available and sexual exchange is expected rather than sought after, the defects or limitations of the partner may become the focus of attention. Over time, repetition and routine come to replace novelty and spontaneity; desire flounders, and occasionally may disappear altogether. In Chapter 7, we emphasize the importance of assessing the current viability of the sexual script, and the usual necessity of negotiating script alternations if desire is to be maintained over the entire course of a long-term relationship.

Overall, relationship conflicts are viewed by the majority of our contributors as the single most common cause of desire difficulties. Commenting on the importance of these factors, Schwartz and Masters (Chapter 9) state emphatically that "frequency of sexual desire and behavior becomes both a mirror and a manifestation of intimacy in the relationship." Among the specific problems that various authors identify in this regard are unexpressed hostilities, power and dependency conflicts, anxious attachments, distrust, and inadequate boundary separation. Verhulst and Heiman (Chapter 10) have additionally emphasized the role of territorial interactions, ranking–order conflicts, and seduction rituals. These authors further suggest that desire problems be "reframed" wherever possible to reflect the underlying relationship concern, thereby assisting the therapist and couple in identifying and dealing with the relevant issues.

Factors Associated with Treatment Success or Failure

Notwithstanding the expectation that many desire problems are complex and difficult to treat, successful outcomes are reported by most of our contributors. Even in those cases involving global or long-standing sexual inhibition, we have found that considerable gains can be made (in either the sexual or nonsexual aspects of the relationship) through sex therapy or psychotherapy. In unsuccessful cases, however, it is not always possible to identify, except in the most speculative or post hoc fashion, the cause of the difficulty or the factors responsible for treatment failure.

How successful is the treatment of desire disorders? Clearly, there is considerable variability in outcome from one sex therapy center to another. In a recent random survey of sex therapists and counselors, for example, Kilmann, Boland, Norton, Davidson, and Caid (1986) reported that problems of desire required the greatest number of treatment sessions, and that fewer than 50% of clients reported a successful treatment outcome for their desire difficulty. On the other hand, Schover and LoPiccolo (1982) had earlier reported outcome data comparable to those for other sexual dysfunctions, such as premature ejaculation and anorgasmia. It should be noted, however, that the 1982 study included only a very brief (i.e., 3-month) follow-up period, and that only modest gains were achieved at the conclusion of treatment. Rather than a "life of sexual ecstasy," most couples reported some limited increase in initiation and greater responsivity to partners' sexual advances.

In contrast, LoPiccolo and Friedman (Chapter 5) indicate that positive outcome is generally achieved with their present treatment model, which involves the four elements of experiential/sensory awareness, insight, cognitive restructuring, and behavior therapy. Masters and Schwartz (Chapter 9) also report that desire problems are as likely to be successfully treated as are the other sexual dysfunctions. Apfelbaum (Chapter 4) writes, "We find cases of low sexual desire among the easiest to treat, and have not had a failure case of this type in which treatment was pursued to its conclusion." However, he goes on to qualify this statement by indicating that he has noted a sizeable number of treatment dropouts. Also, Apfelbaum indicates more equivocal outcome when it is the female partner who has the higher drive level.

Two separate aspects of treatment outcome need to be addressed. First, the number of treatment sessions required for therapy (i.e., treatment duration) must be differentiated from the ultimate success or failure achieved (i.e., treatment outcome). Most therapists would acknowledge that desire problems require a greater number of treatment sessions than other dysfunctions. Even in our own center, where a short-term cognitive–behavioral treatment approach is encouraged, most cases involving desire problems require longer treatment (Rosen & Leiblum, 1987). Similar results were obtained in the Kilmann *et al.* (1986) study. It should not be assumed, however, that the number of sessions is positively correlated with treatment success.

Second, given the variability in reported outcome rates with this problem, it is important to consider what factors are associated with treatment success or failure. For example, in reviewing the cases presented in this book, it is interesting to note that among the successfully treated cases, about two-thirds of the identified patient were males; that approximately equal numbers were in their 30s, 40s, and 50s; and that more than half reported concomitant sexual dysfunctions, most notably erectile dysfunction. Clearly, then, the presence of specific performance difficulties in addition to ISD does not constitute, in and of itself, a significant impediment to successful outcome.

It is interesting to note that at least one-third of the successfully treated cases involved couples with fairly serious degrees of marital distress. In several of these cases, however, the authors have emphasized the degree of *commitment* to the marriage, despite areas of conflict or disagreement. Successfully treated patients are also referred to more frequently as committed to the therapy process, although this is true for most areas of psychotherapy or couples therapy.

An interesting question in this regard is the possible value of traditional sex therapy techniques in the treatment of desire disorders. Overall, it is noteworthy that sensate focus or other nondemand pleasuring techniques were used in roughly half of the cases presented, with no clear difference in this regard between cases with successful or unsuccessful outcomes. In Chapter 9 (which unfortunately does not include specific case examples), Schwartz and Masters claim that these techniques are applicable in *all* cases of ISD. Other therapists seem to recommend these techniques only when other performance difficulties are involved.

On the other hand, to prescribe sexual exercises for an individual who complains of sexual apathy or aversion may exacerbate the already existing subjective experience of sexual pressure. Apfelbaum (Chapter 4) has identified "response anxiety," or the pressure to engage in and enjoy sexual exchange, as constituting the primary cause of all desire disorders. Accordingly, he would find the prescription of sensate focus exercises for these individuals to be countertherapeutic.

What factors contribute to unsuccessful outcomes? Some of the salient issues identified in the failure cases in this book are the presence of secrets in the marital relationship (Levine, Chapter 2); a history of chronic alcoholism (Scharff, Chapter 3); religious orthodoxy (Lazarus, Chapter 6; Rosen & Leiblum, Chapter 7); a history of depression (Segraves, Chapter 12), organogenic erectile dysfunction (Bullard, Chapter 13); and major body image problems (Rosen & Leiblum, Chapter 7). Some authors (e.g., Apfelbaum, Chapter 4) claim to have had few, if any, unsuccessfully treated cases of ISD, whereas Schwartz and Masters (Chapter 9) and others emphasize the skill of the therapist as the major determinant of therapy outcome.

It is worth noting how many of our contributors are perplexed and disarmingly honest about not fully understanding the causes of treatment failure. While it is sometimes possible to play the role of "Monday-morning quarterback" at the conclusion of an unsuccessful case, Zilbergeld and Hammond (Chapter 8) and Lazarus (Chapter 6), among others, admit that even after consultation and discussion with respected colleagues, they are unable to identify the causes of some treatment failures. Clearly, more research is needed before we can specify which factors are likely to predict outcome in these cases.

Other Issues of Interest

Sexual Aversion

Little has been said in this volume about the topic of sexual aversion. In fact, a review of the cases presented indicates that symptoms of sexual aversion were relatively rare among the individuals discussed. Other authors, however, identify this problem as being quite prevalent. For example, Crenshaw (1985) states that the sexual aversion syndrome is among the most common sexual dysfunctions presenting to her clinic, and Kaplan and Klein (1987) report a high incidence of sexually phobic patients in their practices. The diagnosis of "sexual aversion" refers to major physical distress and high levels of anxiety when one is thinking about or confronted with sexual situations. Typically, individuals displaying sexual aversion have other sexual dysfunctions as well. For example, primary sexual aversion may be found in conjunction with vaginismus in women or with primary impotence in males.

Kaplan views sexual aversion (or the "sexual panic disorder") as constituting a distinct clinical entity, separate from hypoactive desire or ISD. While the latter refers to an absence or loss of the subjective experience of desire, sexual aversion implies a significant phobic response to sexuality. Over the last 10 years, Kaplan reports seeing several hundred individuals with symptoms of sexual aversion or avoidance. These patients are differentiated into two categories: "quiet avoiders" (i.e., those who display no appetite or interest in sexual exchange), and "phobic avoiders" (i.e., those who show the full-blown clinical symptomatology of panic disorder).

According to Kaplan, accurate diagnosis of panic disorders is essential in assessing sexual aversion. In particular, she suggests that the following diagnostic features are especially noteworthy: Recurrent panic attacks that occur unpredictably in sexual situations; multiple phobias; severe separation anxiety; an overreaction to partner rejection; and oversensitivity to criticism. Physiologically, Kaplan believes that panic disorders are associated with a defect in brain-regulatory neurotransmitter systems, creating a low threshold for panic. Sexually phobic individuals may be constitutionally prone to autonomic overreactivity.

According to Kaplan's model, the immediate cause of sexual panic is the irrational fear of sex, which is maintained by avoidance behavior. Kaplan suggests that while some instances of sexual aversion may reflect deeper underlying intimacy and intrapsychic conflicts, others may not. Consequently, she recommends initial behavioral intervention in these cases—that is, systematic desensitization combined with sensate focus. When resistances arise, they may be dealt with directly or bypassed. However, if the underlying disorder involves conflict concerning intimacy, long-term psychotherapy is generally the treatment of choice. In those cases where the individual displays a true panic reaction to sexual exchange, complete with nausea, palpitations, and other physical evidence of high anxiety, Kaplan believes that antipanic or antianxiety medications may be indicated, at least initially. These patients tend not to be responsive to sex therapy, but may react positively to pharmacological intervention for at least 3–4 months, after which they may be withdrawn from medication without remission.

Triggers for Desire

The tendency in discussing desire disorders is to focus on instances of desire inhibition or aversion. Little attention is generally directed to individuals displaying hypersexual interest, or even to the antecedents of desire in otherwise "normal" individuals. Only in those cases of extreme hypersexuality are hypotheses advanced as to the alternative motivations that may be expressed via intense or compulsive sexual motivation. Such factors as low self-esteem, the early conditioning of paraphilic arousal, anxiety-reducing properties of sexual release, and the use of sex for affirming gender role and self-efficacy may all serve at times as catalysts for sexual expressiveness. While the diagnosis of sexual addiction continues to be controversial, there is no doubt that clinical instances of sexual compulsivity exist; in these cases, treatment is often similar to that employed with other addictive disorders, such as alcoholism or gambling (Carnes, 1983). In cases of paraphilic compulsivity, pharmacological treatment with antiandrogens is often employed.

Determining the individualistic wellsprings of sexual interest provides a constant challenge in the treatment of desire disorders. For example, one patient noted that although she experienced minimal sexual interest with her loving and devoted husband, throughout her life she had been very "turned on" to men who mistreated or neglected her. When she was required to "beg for sex," or was put in a submissive role, she reported intense feelings of desire. Similarly, there are other familiar scenarios that stimulate desire. A common one is a situation in which an individual, typically the male, experiences high desire prior to securing the affections (or commitment) of the sought-after partner, whereupon all sexual interest evaporates.

Often, less obvious situational determinants may whet sexual appetite, such as the subtle resemblance between a present partner and a figure from the past that has been sexually encoded; the opportunity to play out hostile, forbidden, or masochistic wishes; the need to repeat sexual abuse experiences; and the like. While these sources of sexual interest have received little research attention, they are nonetheless significant and deserve closer scrutiny in our future investigations of this topic.

Finally, judging by the endless propaganda and marketing "hype" of the cosmetic industry, it is conceivable that visual and olfactory stimuli (perhaps subliminal at times) may serve as important triggers for desire. In other animals, there is no doubt that olfaction is a critical antecedent of sexual receptivity or initiation. Pheromones, in particulary have received much discussion as the specific olfactory cues for sexual motivation. Despite enthusiasm among researchers and the lay public alike for finding the "ultimate scent," the likelihood of identifying a particular substance or releaser of this type in humans appears slim. At present, "musk" is not a sexual "must"!

Looking Ahead

Throughout this chapter, we have alluded to several areas of unfinished business in the evaluation and treatment of desire problems. Now, finally, we would like to take stock of specific avenues of future emphasis for research and clinical practice. It is clear that desire problems will be the focus of considerable controversy and debate in the decades to come, and like most editors, we cannot resist the urge to gaze into our crystal ball.

First, in the area of research, it is clear that the search for hormone–behavior relationships will continue to dominate laboratory investigation. The role of androgens, in particular, as the putative wellspring of desire needs clarification in carefully designed human studies. Even though we remain skeptical about the clinical importance of endocrine insufficiency as a determinant of lack of sexual interest in most cases, biologically oriented sex researchers are actively pursuing this link. Similarly, as indicated earlier, the search for pharmacological agents to stimulate desire is likely to increase, as the trend continues to seek medical solutions for sexual problems generally.

As noted in Chapter 1, present research on sexual desire is handicapped by the lack of operational and standardized laboratory measures. There is a pressing need for the development of both physiological and subjective measures of sexual interest. Unlike measures of erection, where numerous parameters can be specified and quantitatively assessed, the measurement of desire is wholly undeveloped. However, since an acceptable instrument or measure is so essential to future outcome research, we anticipate that several investigators (including ourselves) will be devoting time and effort to this undertaking.

Clinically, desire disorders are clearly among the most intriguing of sexual problems. As the chapters in this book aptly illustrate, special skill is required for comprehensive assessment of the multitude of factors potentially contributing to this problem. Moreover, treatment will rarely proceed in a linear fashion, since so many intrapsychic and intrapersonal determinants are operative. Consequently, greater skill and psychological sophistication are required of therapists working with individuals and couples presenting with desire problems. Furthermore, it is clear that familiarity and comfort with systemic approaches may be every bit as important as traditional sex therapy and psychodynamic therapy skills.

From a training perspective, we need to alert our trainees, as well as to be aware ourselves, of the inevitable biases and personal beliefs that influence our conduct of these cases. For example, it is all too easy for a naive or insensitive therapist to join forces with the high-desire partner in pressuring the apathetic partner to become sexually enthusiastic. Not only is this unfortunate for the outcome of treatment, but it is disrespectful to the individual. Similarly, the current imbroglio over the diagnosis of ISD or excessive desire highlights the difficulties in training therapists to recognize or classify these problems. Issues of values are thus critical in the training of future therapists to deal with these problems.

It is clear that problems of sexual desire continue to occupy a provocative and challenging position in the field of sex therapy. The pressure on individuals to be sexually interested, responsive, and enthusiastic within a committed relationship is at an all-time high in our society. This cultural pressure is derived, in part, from a growing concern with the consequences of nonmonogamous sexual relationships. Also, as alternative lifestyles are portrayed less positively in the media, and "traditional family values" are touted once again, the emphasis on the linkage between love and sex is reaffirmed.

References

Berlin, F. S. (1983). Sex offenders: A biomedical perspective and status report on biomedical treatment. In J. G. Greer & I. R. Stuart (Eds.), *The sexual aggressor: Current perspectives on treatment*. New York: Van Nostrand Reinhold.

Blumstein, P., & Schwartz, P. (1983). *American couples: Money, work, and sex*. New York: Morrow.

Carnes, P. (1983). *Out of the shadows: Understanding sexual addiction*. Minneapolis: Comp-Care.

Clearing-Sky, M., & Thornton, D. W. (1987). *Inhibited sexual desire: A diagnostic dilemma*. Unpublished manuscript.

Crenshaw, T. L. (1985). The sexual aversion syndrome. *Journal of Sex and Marital Therapy, 11*, 285–292.

Crenshaw, T. L., Goldberg, J. P., & Stern, W. L. (1987). *Pharmacologic modification of psychosexual dysfunction*. Unpublished manuscript.

Gagnon, J. H. (1987, March). *A sociological perspective on intimacy*. Paper presented at the annual meeting of the Society for Sex Therapy and Research, New Orleans.

Kaplan, H. S., & Kline, D. (1987). *Sexual phobias and aversion*. New York: Brunner/Mazel.

Kilmann, P. R., Boland, J. P., Norton, S. P., Davidson, E., & Caid, C. (1986). Perspectives on sex therapy outcome: A survey of AASECT providers. *Journal of Sex and Marital Therapy, 12*, 116–138.

Klein, K., Mendels, J., Lief, H., & Phillips, J. (1987, March). *Drug treatment of inhibited sexual desire: A controlled clinical trial*. Paper presented at the annual meeting of the Society for Sex Therapy and Research, New Orleans.

Masters, W. H., & Johnson, V. E. (1970). *Human sexual inadequacy*. Boston: Little, Brown.

Rosen, R. C., Leiblum, S. R., & Hall, K. (1987, March). *Etiological and predictive factors in sex therapy*. Paper presented at the annual meeting of the Society for Sex Therapy and Research, New Orleans.

Schover, L., & LoPiccolo, J. (1982). Effectiveness of treatment for dysfunction of sexual desire. *Journal of Sex and Marital Therapy, 8*, 179–197.

Schreiner-Engel, P., & Schiavi, R. (1986). Life-time psychopathology in individuals with low sexual desire. *Journal of Nervous and Mental Disease, 174*, 646–651.

Stuart, F. M., Hammond, C., & Pett, M. A. (1986). Psychological characteristics of women with inhibited sexual desire. *Journal of Sex and Marital Therapy, 12*, 108–116.

Thase, M. E., Reynolds, J. R., Jennings, D. E., Sewitch, L. M., Glanz, E., Frank, E., & Kupfer, D. J. (1986, June). *Alterations of nocturnal penile tumescence in depressed men*. Paper presented at the annual meeting of the Sleep Research Society, Columbus, OH.

Wolpe, J. (1958). *Psychotherapy by reciprocal inhibition*. Stanford, CA: Stanford University Press.

Index

459